Oregon

Oregon

Mark Highberger

FIRST EDITION

The Countryman Press ✱ Woodstock, Vermont

We welcome your comments and suggestions. Please contact Explorer's Guide Editor, The Countryman Press, P.O. Box 748, Woodstock, VT 05091, or e-mail www.countrymanpress.com.

First Edition

ISBN: 0-88150-561-7
ISSN: 1544-4120

Maps by Moore Creative Designs, © 2003 The Countryman Press
Cover and text design by Bodenweber Design
Front cover photograph © Dennis Frates, www.fratesphoto.com
Back cover photograph by Mark Highberger
Interior photographs by Mark Highberger
Text composition by Melinda Belter

Published by The Countryman Press,
P.O. Box 748, Woodstock, Vermont 05091

Distributed by W. W. Norton & Company, Inc., 500 Fifth Avenue, New York, NY 10110

Printed in the United States of America

10 9 8 7 6 5 4 3 2 1

DEDICATION

To Oregon: her borders embrace my home,
her beauty and spirit hold my heart.

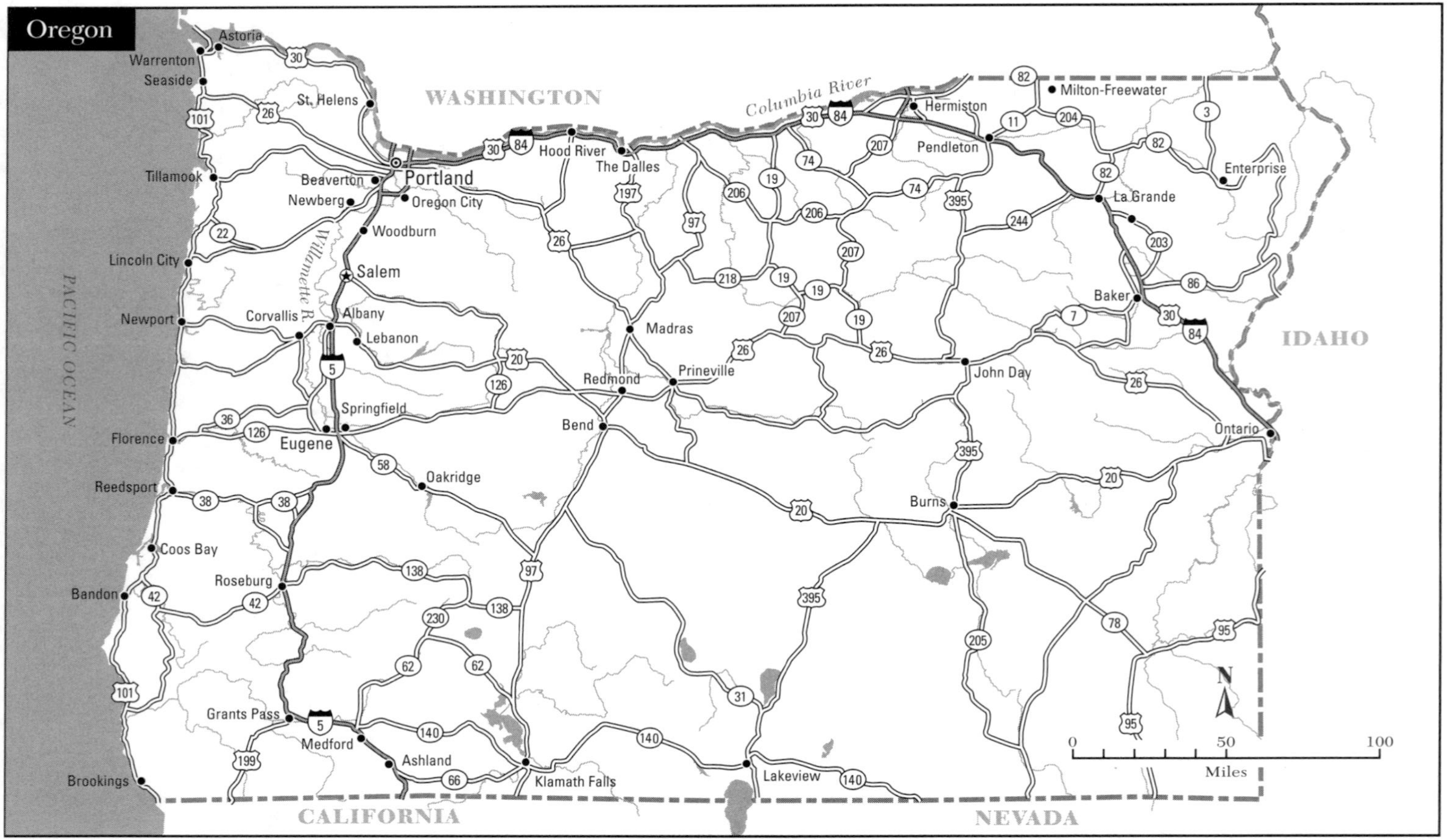

Oregon

WASHINGTON
IDAHO
CALIFORNIA
NEVADA
PACIFIC OCEAN
Columbia River
Willamette R.
Astoria
Warrenton
Seaside
St. Helens
Tillamook
Portland
Beaverton
Newberg
Oregon City
Woodburn
Salem
Lincoln City
Newport
Corvallis
Albany
Lebanon
Springfield
Eugene
Florence
Reedsport
Coos Bay
Bandon
Roseburg
Grants Pass
Medford
Ashland
Brookings
Hood River
The Dalles
Madras
Redmond
Prineville
Bend
Oakridge
Klamath Falls
Lakeview
Hermiston
Pendleton
Milton-Freewater
La Grande
Enterprise
Baker
John Day
Burns
Ontario
N
0 50 100
Miles

EXPLORE WITH US!

Welcome to the first edition of *Oregon: An Explorer's Guide.* All attractions, activities, lodgings, and restaurants in this guide have been selected on the basis of merit, not paid advertising. The organization of the book is simple, but the following points will help to get you started on your way.

WHAT'S WHERE

In the beginning of the book is an alphabetical listing with thumbnail sketches of special highlights and important information for travelers.

LODGING

Lodging establishments are selected for mention in this book on the basis of merit; no innkeeper or business owner was charged for inclusion. When making reservations, ask about the establishment's policy on children, pets, smoking, and credit cards.

Rates: Please don't hold us or the respective innkeepers responsible for the rates listed as of press time in 2003. Some changes are inevitable. Oregon has no meals tax; room taxes vary by city or county and can be anywhere from 0 to 9 percent. Therefore room taxes are not included in the prices listed unless specifically noted.

RESTAURANTS

In most sections please note a distinction between *Dining Out* and *Eating Out.* By their nature, restaurants listed in the *Eating Out* group are generally inexpensive.

KEY TO SYMBOLS

- **Child-friendly.** The crayon symbol appears next to lodgings, restaurants, and activities of special interest to families with children.
- ♿ **Handicapped access.** The wheelchair symbol appears next to lodgings, restaurants, and attractions that are partially or completely handicapped accessible.
- **Pet-friendly.** The dog paw symbol appears next to lodgings that accept pets, almost always only by prior approval.

We would appreciate any comments or corrections. Please write to Explorer's Guide Editor, The Countryman Press, P.O. Box 748, Woodstock, Vermont 05091, or e-mail countrymanpress@wwnorton.com.

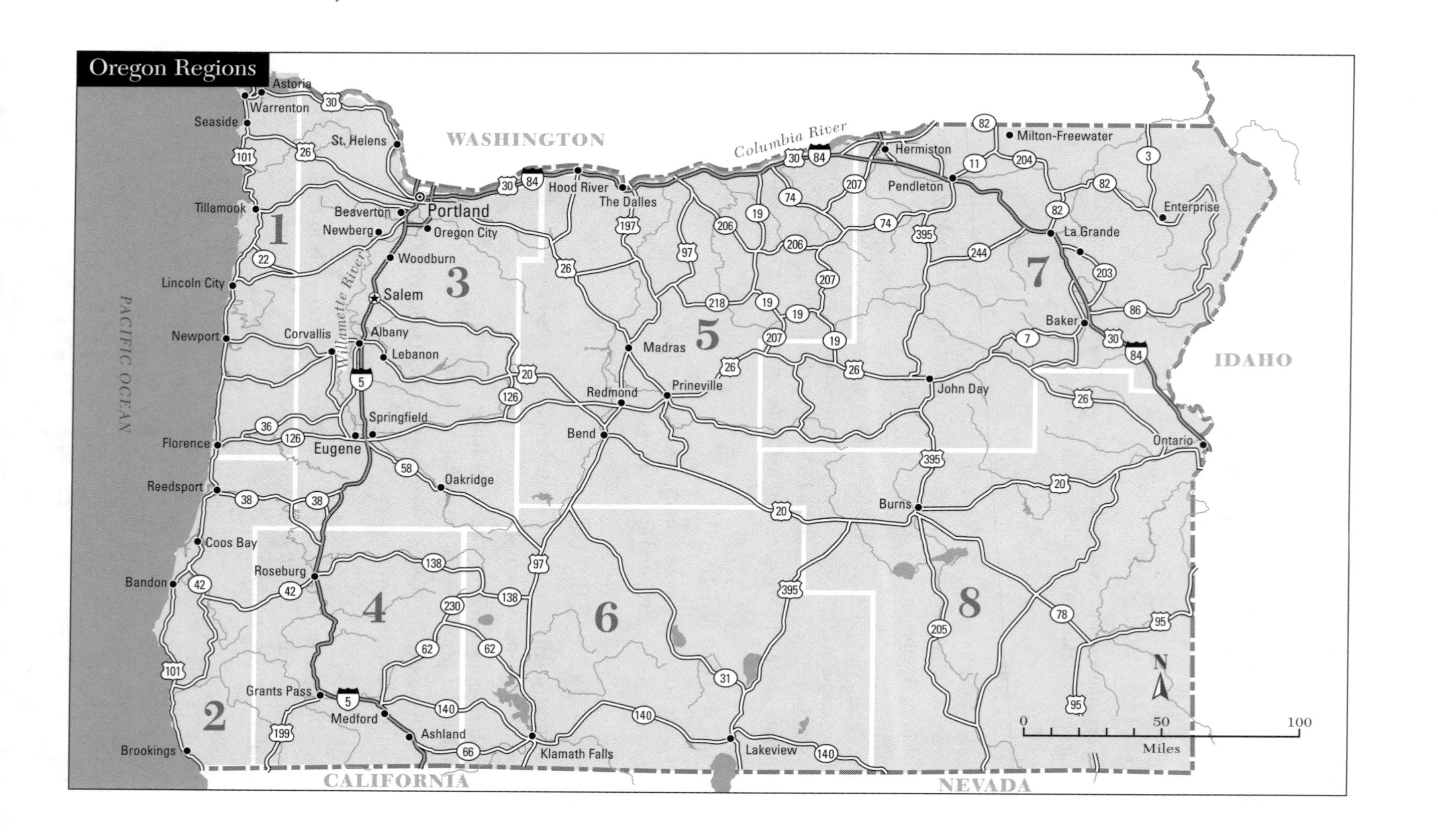
Oregon Regions
WASHINGTON
IDAHO
CALIFORNIA
NEVADA
PACIFIC OCEAN
Columbia River
Willamette River
1
2
3
4
5
6
7
8
Astoria
Warrenton
Seaside
St. Helens
Tillamook
Beaverton
Portland
Newberg
Oregon City
Woodburn
Lincoln City
Salem
Newport
Corvallis
Albany
Lebanon
Springfield
Florence
Eugene
Reedsport
Oakridge
Coos Bay
Roseburg
Bandon
Grants Pass
Medford
Ashland
Brookings
Hood River
The Dalles
Madras
Redmond
Prineville
Bend
Klamath Falls
Lakeview
Hermiston
Pendleton
Milton-Freewater
La Grande
Enterprise
Baker
John Day
Ontario
Burns
N
0
50
100
Miles

CONTENTS

11 INTRODUCTION
13 WHAT'S WHERE

1 North Coast
35 ASTORIA–WARRENTON–SEASIDE AREA
50 CANNON BEACH–TILLAMOOK–PACIFIC CITY AREA
65 LINCOLN CITY–DEPOE BAY–NEWPORT AREA
77 WALDPORT–YACHATS–FLORENCE AREA

2 South Coast
91 REEDSPORT–COOS BAY AREA
102 BANDON–PORT ORFORD AREA
112 GOLD BEACH–BROOKINGS AREA

3 Northwest
123 LOWER COLUMBIA RIVER AREA
129 PORTLAND–METROPOLITAN AREA
153 MOUNT HOOD–COLUMBIA GORGE AREA
175 NORTH WILLAMETTE VALLEY
210 SOUTH WILLAMETTE VALLEY

4 Southwest
231 OAKLAND–ROSEBURG–MYRTLE CREEK AREA
242 GRANTS PASS–ROGUE RIVER AREA
250 ILLINOIS VALLEY AREA
254 MEDFORD–ASHLAND–APPLEGATE VALLEY AREA

5 North Central
281 MID–COLUMBIA RIVER
292 COLUMBIA PLATEAU
312 REDMOND–PRINEVILLE–MADRAS AREA
319 BEND–SISTERS–LA PINE AREA

6 South Central

340 KLAMATH BASIN–CRATER LAKE AREA
354 LAKEVIEW–PAISLEY–BLY AREA
365 SILVER LAKE–CHRISTMAS VALLEY–FORT ROCK AREA

7 Northeast

375 PENDLETON–HERMISTON–MILTON-FREEWATER AREA
384 LA GRANDE–UNION–ELGIN AREA
396 WALLOWA VALLEY–SNAKE RIVER AREA
411 POWDER RIVER–SUMPTER VALLEY–UKIAH AREA
430 JOHN DAY RIVER AREA

8 Southeast

445 ONTARIO–NYSSA–VALE AREA
452 JORDAN VALLEY AREA
457 HARPER–JUNTURA–DREWSEY AREA
461 BURNS AREA
468 MALHEUR REFUGE–STEENS MOUNTAIN AREA

480 INDEX

INTRODUCTION

"Through all our trials, I cannot say that I have ever regretted that we have undertaken this journey."

—Asahel Munger, Oregon Trail emigrant, 1849

When you come right down to it, the road trip might represent what life in America is all about. After all, we're a people of sailing ships and pack trains, of freight wagons and stern-wheelers; a people of Saturday-night cruises and Sunday-morning drives, of Boeing flights and sleepless nights of planning the next excursion away from home. Oregon in particular is a place that seems to resonate with what Walt Whitman called the "Song of the Open Road":

Afoot and light-hearted I take to the open road,
Healthy, free, the world before me,
The long brown path before me leading wherever I choose.

Hearing such a song in the 19th century, thousands of folks loaded their prairie schooners, hitched up their oxen, and headed out on the long brown path of the Oregon Trail, geeing and hawing their way across rivers and over mountains to reach the edge of an ocean and the middle of a wilderness. To this day, it's as though Whitman knew we'd come running whenever the echo of his voice calls to us, "Whoever you are come travel with me! Traveling with me you find what never tires."

"You bet, Walt!" we seem always to be telling him, like Border collies begging for the chance to leap into the back of a pickup. For what never tires in Oregon might be a roll of ocean surf or a span of desert sand; might shine white with alpine snow or blue with basin sky, carry the scent of pine or sage or the sounds of waterfowl wings or waterfalls. And finding it can be as simple as packing the cooler, grabbing the kids, and hitting the road. So if travelers in Oregon have a motto, it might come from Benjamin Franklin's observation that "Wherever you go, there you are."

Nevertheless, where you are within the state's almost 100,000 square miles might include any of its 13 national forests, 40 wilderness areas, 46 wildlife refuges, 57 designated Wild and Scenic rivers (or segments of rivers), 228 state parks, more than 2,500 waterfalls (with heights of 10 or more feet), almost 6,000 campsites, and more than 6,000 lakes. As a result, this book steers you toward specific points along the state's ocean shores and mountain peaks, sagebrush deserts and wildflower valleys before you once again turn yourself gently toward home.

The structure of the book follows an age-old routine of explorers well illustrated by Lewis and Clark, for when the Corps of Discovery made their legendary journey into the Oregon Country two centuries ago, their days revolved around three activities—eating, sleeping, and exploring. Unlike the corps, however, your shelter will consist of more than an open sky or a leaky roof, and your meals will include fare other than dried salmon, young dog, and "pore elke." But the exploring will remain essentially the same as you venture onto the open road to discover new worlds.

To begin those discoveries as well as to smooth parts of the journey, it might help to remember that bouts of trial and error seem to be necessary ingredients in any adventure. In fact, if you tread far enough along the paths of Oregon, you may come to believe, as 18th-century English novelist Laurence Sterne did, that "The true value of travel is not in strenuous sightseeing. It is in opening one's heart to feeling."

With that in mind, may you always hear the song of the open road, and may all your journeys lead you safely back home again.

WHAT'S WHERE IN OREGON

AGRICULTURE Since the first settler turned the first furrow of earth and planted the first seed, Oregon has been an agricultural state. Even in these days of big cities and high tech, Oregon produces more agricultural commodities than any other state, some 230 in all, ranging from potatoes and pears to cattle and Christmas trees, and raising more than 3 billion dollars from 3 million acres. Usually, the top county in agricultural receipts is Marion in the Willamette Valley, and lately the highest-earning crop is nursery products.

AIR SERVICE **Portland International Airport (PDX)** (1-877-739-4636) is the state's major airport. Airlines serving PDX include the following: Air Canada Jazz (1-888-247-2262), Alaska (1-800-426-0333), America West (1-800-235-9292), American (1-800-433-7300), Continental (1-800-525-0280), Delta (1-800-221-1212), Frontier (1-800-432-1359), Hawaiian (1-800-367-5320), Horizon (1-800-547-9308), Northwest (1-800-225-2525), Skywest (1-800-241-6522), Southwest (1-800-435-9792), Sun Country (1-866-797-2537), United (1-800-241-6522), and United Express (1-800-241-6522).

AMTRAK AMTRAK, the train that still thinks it can, offers three runs in Oregon: the Coast Starlight, from Los Angeles and San Francisco to Seattle, with Oregon stops between Klamath Falls and Portland; the Empire Builder, from Chicago to Portland; and the Mt. Adams, from Seattle to Eugene. For information, contact AMTRAK at 1-800-872-7245, or visit their web sites: AMTRAK Cascades (www.wsdot.wa.gov/amtrak) and Coast Starlight (www.trainweb.com/coast-starlight/index.html).

ANTIQUES If part of your traveling adventure involves searching for antiques, the on-line Oregon Directory of antiques shops (www.antiqueshopsa2z.com/oregon.htm) lists more than 500 shops, malls, and dealers in more than 160 Oregon cities.

AREA CODES Oregon telephone numbers are divided into two primary area codes: 503 for the north coast and northern Willamette Valley, including most of the Portland–Metropolitan area, and 541 for the rest of the state. In addition, a few 971 prefixes are floating around out there in the Portland–Metropolitan area, though they seem to be scattered so randomly that even the telephone company appears to be confused by how the number fits into the system. The result is that some people living in the metropolitan area must dial a 10-digit phone number, beginning with the 971 area code, to call their next-door neighbors.

BACK ROADS AND BYWAYS If you're looking to escape the metallic whine of cars along grids of asphalt, it may help to know that Oregon has more designated scenic byways than any other state, including three All-American Roads (one-fifth the national total) and five National Scenic Byways (one-third the national total). "These roads are the best America has to offer," says Rodney Slater, former Secretary of Transportation. "They are jewels." But wait—more jewels wait up ahead, because now throw in Oregon's six Tour Routes, four State Scenic Byways, and bushels and baskets of routes designated as "backcountry" or "scenic" or "historic" by the Bureau of Land Management, U.S. Forest Service, or chambers of commerce, and you'll see that Oregon takes its sight-seeing seriously. Yet be warned: All byways are not created equal, except in the brochures. While some will make you shake your head in wonder, others will make you scratch your head as you wonder why you ever took the detour. Nevertheless, the adventure will most likely be worth it. So to help in your planning, order *Off the Beaten Freeway: A Guide to Oregon's Scenic Byways*—it's free—from the Oregon Travel Commission (1-800-547-7842; info.oregontourism@state.or.us; www.traveloregon.com).

BICYCLING It's true—some people aren't happy unless they're straddling a mountain bike and huffing up a hillside that would give a mountain goat vertigo. For gung ho commandos such as these, the bike routes in this book are for sissies—pleasant pedals, as flat as possible, along forest roads, mountain streams, quiet parks, maybe just enough to show you a smattering of what the poet e. e. cummings describes as "the leaping greenly spirits of trees / and a blue true dream of sky." On the other hand, for those who want a more complete road biking adventure, the *Oregon Bicycling Guide*, a map that illustrates highways and roads as well as prevailing winds and basic topography, is available from I B CYCLIST, 43500 Marshall Drive S. E., Bend, OR 97701 (503-986-3556; charlotte.l.king@state.or.us; www.odot.state.or.us/techserv/bikewalk/maporder.htm). Available through the same contacts are the *Oregon Coast Bike Route Map* and the *Oregon Bicyclist Manual*. All publications are free.

BIRD-WATCHING Approximately 100 billion birds live on this planet of ours, which means our feathered friends outnumber us humans by a ratio of about 20 to 1. Good thing we're above them in the food chain. At any rate, this leaves plenty of birds to watch, especially when you consider that about one-third of them migrate, leaving the other two-thirds to stay put through much of the year. If you want to find your share in Oregon, the web site "Where Do You Want to Go Birding in Oregon Today?" (http://www.camacdonald.com/birding/usoregon.htm) lists local events, tours and guides, rare-bird alerts, birding checklists, and other items sure to please birders everywhere. (Also see *Wildlife Areas* and *Wildlife Refuges* in this section.)

BOATING With 2,383 square miles of Oregon covered by water, it's no wonder that Oregonians sometimes seem to own as many boats as they do cars. The folks in charge of most things that float in the state is the **Oregon State Marine Board** (503-378-8587; www.marinebd.osmb.state.or.us), who'll send you a free copy of the *Oregon Marina Guide.* In addition, a good on-line source for information about campgrounds, marinas, and waterways is **BoatEscape.com** (www.boatescape.com). (See also *Canoeing* in this section.)

BUREAU OF LAND MANAGEMENT (BLM) LANDS Even though the lands now administered by the Bureau of Land Management have been called "the largest patchwork of public lands on Earth," once upon a time you couldn't give the land away. That happened near the turn of the 20th century, when the federal government tried to encourage settlement in the West by opening its lands to homesteading. But after homesteaders by the thousands poured into this new Eden, it didn't take long for them to discover that a desert won't grow crops. Consequently, most of them packed up and left the sagebrush behind, the old homesteads reverted to public ownership, and the Bureau of Land Management eventually became the managers of almost 16 million acres—25,000 square miles—of Oregon land, approximately one-fourth of the state's total area. That's more than enough room for the buffalo to roam and for the deer and the antelope (and you) to play.

BUS SERVICE Greyhound Bus Lines (1-800-231-2222; www.tripcheck.com/About/busrail.htm) provides Oregon's only intercity bus service. Contact Greyhound for information about fares, routes, and schedules.

CAMPGROUNDS Even though this book lists numerous campgrounds across the state, one publication that puts many of them all together at a glance is *The Official Guide to Oregon Campgrounds,* available free from the **Oregon Tourism Commission** (1-800-547-7842; info.oregontourism@state.or.us; www.traveloregon.com).

CANOEING The primary requirement in this book for naming any pond, lake, or reservoir as deserving of a visit by canoe, raft, or kayak is that motors on boats are either prohibited or restricted. Quiet waters, they call these places—and for good reason. (See also *Boating* in this section.)

CITIES Oregon has 240 incorporated cities. The largest is Portland with a population of approximately 529,000; the smallest is Greenhorn with a population of exactly 3. Alphabetically, this list begins with Adams and ends with Zig Zag (in case you ever find yourself on a quiz show where this information comes in handy).

CLIMATE Even though Oregon has nine climatic zones that range from rain forest to high desert, the common climate fable goes something like this: Oregon is wet, it rains all the time, its people have webbed feet or moss growing between their toes. Actually, the webbed-footed among us live only along the coast or in the Willamette Valley, where it really *does* seem to rain one heckuva lot of the time. This is because the major weather systems arise over the Pacific and move inland, losing moisture first to the Coast Range and then to the Cascades. But because most of the state lies east of the Cascades, Oregon has more sagebrush than fir trees, more sun than clouds. (The rain shadow cast by the Cascades is so significant that a 20-mile stretch between the Santiam Pass on the west slope and Sisters on the east slope has a difference of 60 inches of annual precipitation, one of the biggest extremes in the world.)

CONSERVATION GROUPS So many conservation groups are at work in Oregon that the **Oregon Conservation Network** (ocn@olcv.org; www.olcv.org/ocn) unifies some 100 of them into a master guide. A list of 75 of these citizen-led groups, as well as links to some of their web sites, are available on-line (www.olcv.org/ocn/members.html).

COUNTIES Oregon is divided into 36 counties. **Harney** in the southeast is the largest with 10,228 square miles, and **Multnomah** in the northwest is the smallest with 465 square miles. Multnomah, however, has the most people with 650,000 (1,500 per square mile), while **Wheeler** in north-central Oregon has the fewest with 1,500 (less than 1 person per square mile, a density shared by Lake and Harney Counties out yonder on the high lonesome). The largest county seat is Multnomah's **Portland** with 500,000, and the smallest is Sherman's **Moro** with 290.

COVERED BRIDGES With more than 50 covered bridges still standing in the state, Oregon is home to more such bridges than any other place in the West. Even though the book lists most of these by region, you can find lists, photos, and directions at http://coveredbridges.stateoforegon.com.

EMERGENCIES Oregon uses a **911** system statewide. In addition, each chapter of this book contains the phone numbers and addresses of regional hospitals.

EVENTS A list of all events sponsored by Oregon communities throughout the year would reach the size of a big-city phone book. The beginnings of the oldest of these reach back to local celebrations and traditional festivals, whether the purpose was to commemorate the wheat harvest or to shed the winter blues. But because the intent of many special events these days is to attract visitors, the book's listings focus on those that can offer an unusual experience or that are integral parts of the state's culture—rodeos or Oktoberfests, timber carnivals or sand castle contests, or whatever else seems to celebrate the joy of living in Oregon.

FARMER'S MARKETS A summertime mainstay of the lifestyle in many Oregon communities is the farmer's market, where the stuff of gardens and fields is sold by the people who grow it. So widespread are these gatherings that the **Oregon Farmers' Markets Association** (503-233-8425; www.oregonfarmersmarkets.org) labors to keep it all organized. Farmer's markets are listed in several chapters.

FISHING Because Oregon streams travel through widely diverse landscapes ranging from coastal bays to desert basins, the state's fishing waters are divided into eight zones. For each of these, the species and opportunities as well as the regulations and techniques can be as varied as the countryside you're fishing. So before starting out it's wise to check with the **Oregon Department of Fish and Wildlife** (503-872-5268; odfw.info@state.or.us; www.dfw.state.or.us) for information about fishing the regions you're visiting. As far as the fishing itself is concerned, perhaps the most comprehensive guide is *Fishing in Oregon* by Dan Casali and Madelynne Diness. If there's water with fish in it, this book probably covers it.

But to give you a head start, the folks at the Fish and Wildlife Department have chosen two dozen fishing spots that they consider among the best in each zone. You can download this introductory guide—"24 Great Places to Fish in Oregon: Let's Go Fishing!" (at www.dfw.state.or.us/ODFWhtml/InfoCntrFish/InfoCntrFish.html.

GARDENS Some parts of Oregon, especially the wet, fertile Willamette Valley, can grow almost anything that sprouts from the ground, almost anything at all from apples to zucchini with the possible exception of baobab trees. As a result, gardens for some folks—whether growing them or visiting them—are more passion than hobby. Although this book describes many of these gardens, you might also want to find a copy of Amy Houchen's *Green Afternoon: Oregon Gardens to Visit.*

GEOGRAPHY Geographers divide Oregon into at least six and as many as nine distinct regions, including the following: the **Coast Range,** which runs north–south along the Pacific Coast, its mountains low (less than 2,000 feet elevation) and heavily forested with spruce, fir, and hemlock; the **Klamath Mountains,** a rugged, heavily forested range that forms the divide for the streams in the southwest corner of the state; the **Willamette Valley,** a narrow valley of mild temperatures and deep soil, formed by the Willamette River, which runs between the Coast Range and the Cascades and empties into the Columbia River; the **Cascade Mountains,** the high volcanic peaks that form the north–south spine of the state and that create the rain shadow for the deserts of eastern Oregon; the **Columbia Plateau** (sometimes called the Deschutes-Columbia Plateau), formed by ancient lava flows that now cover most of eastern Oregon, including the state's sprawling wheat belt; the **Blue Mountains,** which rise from the edge of the Columbia Plateau in the northeast corner, forming some of the state's most impressive ranges and valleys; and the **Basin and Range** in the southeast corner, where uplifted mountains, characterized by their steep escarpments, rise above high-desert basins that have no outlets to the sea.

GEOLOGY A few hundred million years ago, the land that would one day be Oregon lay beneath the sea, and Idaho basked in the sun as the western shore of the continent. But the plate of the continent was shifting westward, the floor of the Pacific Ocean moving eastward, and wouldn't you know that eventually—maybe 200 million years ago—they began nudging each other, playfully at first, and then more seriously, until push came to shove and something had to give. The continent gave an inch, and so did the ocean floor, and inch by inch the land buckled and rose, until Oregon began to emerge from the sea. Her mountains towered toward the clouds, her valleys spread along the foothills, and Oregon at last stood above the sea at the edge of a new world. If you want to know the rest of the story, the best source for learning about geology from your car is probably *Roadside Geology of Oregon* by David D. Alt and Donald W. Hyndman, while those who explore by foot might want to check *Hiking Oregon's Geology* by Ellen Morris Bishop and John Eliot Allen.

GOLF COURSES Oregon's attitude toward golf courses seems to be, "If you build it, they will come." And sure enough, that's pretty much what happens. As a result, you can find golf courses in far-flung areas as well as in large cities. Good sources of information include the *Official Guide to Golf in Oregon* (it's free) from the **Oregon Travel Commission** (1-800-547-7842; info.oregontourism@state.or.us; www.traveloregon.com) as well as these web sites: www.orgolf.org/ course_list.html; www.oregongolf.com; www.mygolf.com/golf/courses/ OR; and www.netcaddie.com/or/oregon.htm.

GUIDES AND OUTFITTERS If you face an adventure where an experienced hand is welcome, one source of professional help is the **Oregon Guides and Packers Association** (1-800-747-9552; dennis@suncountrytours.com; www.ogpa.org), a nonprofit organization that advocate a code of ethics for its members. Other sources include the following regional associations: **Eastern Oregon Guide Association** (541-432-6545), **McKenzie River Guides Association** (541-896-3480), **Rogue River Guides Association** (1-800-219-9644), and **Tillamook Guides Association** (503-656-1777).

HIGHWAYS The primary north–south routes through Oregon include **Highway 101,** which runs the entire length of the Oregon coast; **Interstate 5,** the major link from California to Washington through the Rogue River and Willamette Valleys; **Highway 97,** the major north–south highway through central Oregon; and **Highway 395,** the major north–south highway in eastern Oregon. The major east–west highways crossing the state include **Interstate 84,** which runs from Ontario to Portland; **Highway 26,** from Ontario to the coast; **Highway 20,** from Ontario to the mid–Willamette Valley; and **Highways 140** and **66,** through southern Oregon from the Nevada border to Interstate 5 near Ashland.

HIKING Enough hiking books about Oregon are printed each year to make ballast for an oceangoing ship, so this book focuses only on short walks or special trails that people of almost any age can undertake. Trails and hiking opportunities are mentioned under *To Do—Camping* and under *Wilder Places—Wilderness Areas,* as well as in the *Hiking* sections. For more serious treks, perhaps the most informative and accurate guides available are the books written by William Sullivan and published by Navillus Press (1958 Onyx Street, Eugene, OR 97403). But don't let mileage determine whether you'll take that walk, thinking you have to reach the end of the trail. "The beauty lies in the walking," said Irish writer Gwynn Thomas. "We are betrayed by destinations."

HISTORICAL MARKERS Standing along highway shoulders all across Oregon are almost 100 historical markers that commemorate significant events in the history of the state. To help locate them, you can contact the **Travel Information Council** (1-800-574-9397) for a free brochure, or you can view the same brochure on-line (http://rutnut.com/tic/markers.html).

HISTORICAL MUSEUMS Regional museums are receptacles of the collective memories of the communities in which they reside. Gathered here are the remnants that tell the story of how we lived in the past and how we got to where we are today. Thankfully, almost every community in the state is located relatively close to a museum that holds the stuff of our lives and that reminds us of the way we were not so long ago. (See *To See—Museums* in individual chapters for listings.)

HISTORIC SITES Although historic sites in Oregon are almost as numerous as the state's pine trees, sometimes you'll find not much left at a site other than its history, a sense that tells you that this place is important for what happened here, even though the reminders of it are long gone. Most of the Oregon Trail, for example, has been plowed or paved, and many of the places Lewis and Clark saw are drowned behind dams. Nevertheless, it's worth your time and effort to find what's left and to fill in the blanks with your imagination. (See *To See—Historic Sites* in individual chapters for listings; also see *Historical Markers*, above.)

HISTORY The history of Oregon is the story of travelers finding their way to our shores and forests, mountains and deserts. The first arrived at least 10,000—and perhaps as long as 30,000—years ago. Since then, a rousing blend of sinners and saints, ruffians, reformers, and just regular folks have written some of the most important and interesting chapters in Oregon's history. By ship or by horse, by wagon or by foot, for patriotic purpose or for personal profit these wanderers came searching for water passages or overland routes, to find fur or save souls, to claim land, cut timber, or dig gold. As a result, we have our share of great names and heroic quests. It was here, after all, that Sir Francis Drake came for the Northwest Passage, Lewis and Clark for Manifest Destiny, Jedidiah Smith for the beaver, David Douglas for the trees, and Thomas Condon for the bones. The list, of course, goes on. But perhaps the most notable quest of all was the six-month, 2,000-mile journey along the **Oregon Trail** that brought more than 50,000 pioneers to new homes in a faraway land they knew only by its name—Oregon. It's all in the books if you want to look it up. What's not there, however, is the sense of the way that history shapes the attitudes of people living here today. Some call it pioneer spirit; some say it's fierce independence or cussed orneriness. Whatever you call it, it's usually a compliment for an Oregonian to be branded a "maverick." In this land sweeping enough to include both ocean shores and alpine peaks, alluring enough to have compelled thousands of families to walk across a continent and begin new lives in a wilderness, "it" just seems to come with the territory.

HOT SPRINGS Because Oregon has more than 100 hot springs, the result in part of its volcanic past, the opportunities for a heated soak are numerous, especially in rural pockets of the central and southeastern portions of the state, some of which seem to hold the mother lode of geothermal energy. To locate a hot springs open to the public during your journey, visit www.hotsprings-enthusiast.com/OR.htm for a list and locations.

HUNTING If it's furred or feathered and fits in a game pouch or hangs from a meat pole, then the **Oregon Department of Fish and Wildlife** probably regulates the hunting of it within the state's boundaries. To find out more, contact the department's **headquarters** (503-872-5268; odfw.info@state.or.us; www.dfw.state.or.us) or one of its regional offices: **Northwest Region,** Clackamas (503-657-2000); **Southwest Region,** Roseburg (541-440-3353); **High Desert Region,** Bend (541-388-6363); **Northeast Region,** La Grande (541-963-2138).

INDIAN RESERVATIONS The **Affiliated Tribes of Northwest Indians**

(1-877-987-4237) offers a gracious invitation to visitors. "We invite you," the tribes say, "to leave your native soil by exploring ours." This visit can include the casinos, resorts, museums, powwows, waterways, and golf courses of the tribes' reservation lands. Those tribes opening their doors include the **Confederated Tribes of the Umatilla** near Pendleton in northeast Oregon (1-800-654-9453; www.umatilla.nsn.us), the **Cow Creek Band of the Umpqua** near Roseburg in southwest Oregon (1-800-548-8461, ext. 1334; www.cowcreek.com), the **Confederated Tribes of Siletz Indians** near Lincoln City on the north coast (1-800-922-1399; www.ctsi.nsn.us), the **Confederated Tribes of Warm Springs** near Madras in north-central Oregon (541-553-1112; www.kah-nee-taresort.com; www.tmaws.org), and the **Confederated Tribes of Grande Ronde** in the western Willamette Valley near the town of Grand Ronde (1-800-760-7977; www.spirit-mountain.com).

In addition, Oregon is home to 10 recognized tribes: members of **Celilo Village,** near milepost 97 off Interstate 84, near the site of Celilo Falls, now drowned beneath the backwaters of The Dalles Dam; **Burns-Paiute Tribe** at Burns; the **Confederated Tribes of Coos, Lower Umpqua and Siuslaw Indians** near Coos Bay; the **Klamath Reservation** near Chiloquin; the **Confederated Tribes of Grande Ronde** at Grand Ronde; the **Confederated Tribes of Warm Springs** at Warm Springs; the **Cow Creek Band of Umpqua Indians** near Roseburg; the **Confederated Tribes of the Umatilla** at Pendleton; and the **Confederated Tribes of Siletz Indians** at Siletz (503-444-2532). Oregon is also home to members of six unrecognized tribes: **Celilio-Wyam Indian Community, Tolowa-Tututni Tribe, Tchinouk Indians, NW Cherokee Wolf Band of SE Cherokee Confederacy, Chinook Indian Tribe,** and **Chetco Tribe.**

LEWIS AND CLARK TRAIL Because Oregon was the homestretch and the winter quarters of Lewis and Clark's journey to the sea, the trail they blazed still runs deep in the memory of the state. This book describes that trail as it enters the state in the north-central region and then follows the Columbia River to the Pacific. Although you can pick the trail up at any point along that route, the descriptions have a more complete context if read in sequence from east to west. (See *To See—Historic Sites* in individual chapters for listings.)

LIBRARIES A state of 240 incorporated cities, Oregon is home to 127 public libraries. A good portion of these, as well as a number of the state's academic libraries, have web sites linked to the **Oregon Library Association** at "Oregon Libraries on the Web" (www.olaweb.org/oregon-libraries.html).

LODGING Lodges, inns, and, especially, bed & breakfasts are the focus of the book's *Lodging* listings because, after all, even if Motel 6 didn't leave the light on for you, it's no surprise what you'll find once you get there. This certainty, of course, is one of the comforts of staying in a motel, where the unexpected often involves what you find left under the bed or in the shower drain. Besides, staying at an old-fashioned B&B is participating in a tradition of hospitality that reaches back to the days when our ancestors first invited wayfaring strangers to share their campfires. You may be surprised at how many new friends you can make that way.

You will, however, find some motels listed, especially when they offer the only lodging for miles around. The southeast corner of Oregon, for instance, is so vast that it's larger than some states and so remote that its accommodations average one B&B every 2,900 square miles and one motel every 750 square miles. So it's important to know where you can stop for the night. "When people come here to stay," says one of the region's B&B owners, "they say, 'We don't want to drive anymore!'" The same is true of the few motels scattered through the region: Knowing where to find one can save you from having miles to go before you sleep. (For a comprehensive list of motels, order *Where to Stay in Oregon*—it's free—from the **Oregon Travel Commission** (1-800-547-7842; info.oregontourism@state.or.us; www.traveloregon.com).

But no matter where you plan to stay, keep in mind that the world of the open road is an ever-changing one, that what's true one day can alter significantly the next, especially when it comes to lodging rates, restrictions, policies, practices, and even owners. (One Ashland inn, for example, changes its rates almost *monthly*, depending on the theater schedule for the city's Oregon Shakespeare Festival.)

MAPS No matter where you head in Oregon, your journey (as well as your peace of mind) depends to some degree on the quality and thoroughness of your map. Well, the state maps they give away at the Texaco station might show you the major thoroughfares and a few blue highways, but if you really want to find what you're looking for, the **best Oregon maps** on the planet are in *Oregon Road & Recreation Atlas*, published by Benchmark Maps (34 N. Central Avenue, Medford, Oregon 97501; 541-772-3989; atlas@benchmarkmaps.com), which, by the way, paid nothing for this endorsement. Neither did the respectable second-place finisher, *State of Oregon Topographic Map and Travel Guide* by Imus Geographics (P.O. Box 161, Eugene, Oregon 97440). After these two, however, you're left holding the gas station maps.

MICROBREWERIES With more than 70 microbreweries and almost as many brewpubs, more per capita than in any other state, Oregon is often regarded as the microbrew capital of America. So if you find malt and hops and mugs of amber ale whispering your name, it might interest you to know that each year the state produces more than 1 million kegs and more than 1,000 varieties of beer. To find out about the state's beer scene, contact the **Oregon Brewers Guild** (32 S. E. Oak Street #108, Portland 97214; 503-295-18622; info@oregonbeer.org; www.oregonbeer.org). In addition, a list of 126 of the state's microbreweries and brewpubs is available on-line (http:// brewpubzone.com/States/Oregon.html).

MILEAGE Before you put too much faith in mileage figures as you're plotting your course and figuring the miles, please remember they're all approximate if not downright rough, depending on the precision of the odometer, the reliability of the source, or the accuracy of the navigator (and accurate navigators are tough to find these days). As a result, the distance from here to there seems to be one of those things on which people just cannot agree. On the other hand, if you find it taking longer to reach a destination than any mileage discrepancy can account for, then please consider the fact that you may be lost. Then recite to yourself or a loved one those memorable words from the movie *Star Trek V:* Chekhov: "Admit it—we're lost." Sulu: "Okay, we're lost—but we're making good time."

MUSIC To learn about many things musical in Oregon, visit the **Music in Oregon** web sites (http://libweb.uoregon.edu/music/musor.html). Radio stations, music stores, publishing companies, record labels, music venues—you'll find links to these and a whole lot more here.

MUSIC FESTIVALS Summertime is music time in many Oregon communities. The following are a few of the festivals that either include or highlight a wide range of musical performances, from classical to country (for dates and details, visit http://libweb.uoregon.edu/music/musor.html): **Ashland,** Ashland Smooth Jazz and Blues Festival; **Coos Bay,** Oregon Coast Festival; **Corvallis,** Da Vinci Days; **Eugene,** Oregon Bach Festival, Oregon Country Fair, Oregon Festival of American Music; **Jacksonville,** Britt Music Festival; **Mount Angel,** Mount Angel Oktoberfest; **Portland,** Portland Rose Festival, Portland Waterfront Blues Festival; **Sisters,** High Mountains Dixieland Jazz Festival; **Sunriver,** Sunriver Festival; **Sweet Home,** Oregon Jamboree.

For those interested specifically in folk music, the following communities play host to musicians playing bluegrass, Irish, Cajun, blues, swing, country, and a bunch more (for dates and details visit www.folkfests.com/or-fest.htm): **Burns,** June (541-573-1323; burgess@orednet.org), Country Music Jamboree; **Corvallis,** June (541-758-3243; mmeyer@proaxis.com), Oregon Folk Life Festival; **Eugene,** May, Willamette Valley Folk Festival; **Odell,** August, Oregon Bluegrass and Cowboy Music Festival; **Portland,** September, Pickathon; **Salem,** July (503-399-1130; jlkelly@teleport.com), Oregon State Bluegrass Festival; **Sisters,** September, Sisters Folk Festival.

MUST-SEE SIGHTS The **Oregon Travel Commission** has "officially" named the following 14 scenic and natural wonders as "Must-See Sights" for Oregon travelers: the **Oregon coast,** an almost indescribable stretch of sea, surf, and sand that is open to the public along virtually its entire length; the Oregon Dunes National Recreation Area, which humps up in waves and crests, stretching its sandy self for more than 40 miles along the central coast; **Portland,** the state's largest and most vibrant city; Portland's **International Rose Test Garden,** which contains some 500 varieties of roses, but why this is on the list instead of other places is anyone's guess; **Mount Hood,** the tallest mountain in Oregon, a volcanic member of the Cascade Range that serves as a snowcapped beacon to northwest and north-central Oregon; the **Historic Columbia River Highway Scenic Byway,** an engineering marvel and an artistic creation that uses asphalt as its medium; **Silver Falls State Park,** where at least 10 waterfalls spill their foamy, white waters into a quiet, forested creek; the **McKenzie River Valley,** which bends its green way into the foothills of the Cascades, all the while following one of the loveliest streams in America; **Crater Lake,** our one national park, which comes from a past of geological upheaval and mythological wonder and retains a sense of timeless beauty and majesty in its land as well as in its deep, blue waters; the **Oregon Caves National Monument,**

which shows us that some of the beauty of the world lies beneath the surface of our planet; **Mount Bachelor,** another curiosity on the list because it's not nearly as imposing as its Cascade brothers and sisters, though that's one reason so many skiers flock here in the winter; **Smith Rock State Park,** a sure sign that the loveliness of our Earth is present even in its rocks, especially those shaped by the ages; **John Day Fossil Beds National Monument,** a testament to endurance, change, and the powers that have shaped our world; **Hells Canyon National Recreation Area,** the deepest gorge on the continent, the home to some of the wildest whitewater in the Northwest, and a receptacle for the history of this corner of the West, from the Nez Perce to the homesteaders.

Unbelievably, the commission overlooked some of the most awe-inspiring wonders the state has to offer, including **Steens Mountain** and the **Malheur National Wildlife Refuge** near Frenchglen in southeast Oregon, **Leslie Gulch** near Jordan Valley in southeast Oregon, **Fort Rock** near the town of Fort Rock in south-central Oregon, **Klamath Lake** near Klamath Falls in south-central Oregon, and the **Wallowa Valley** between Wallowa and Joseph in northeast Oregon, and . . . well, the list goes on.

NATIONAL FORESTS Almost half of Oregon's total area is forested (holding about one-tenth of all the nation's timber) and almost half of the forests are contained within the state's 13 national forests. This means that 30 million acres—almost 47,000 square miles—of trees and their shade and streams are open as public playgrounds. These include the **Siuslaw** along the north coast; the **Siskiyou** on the south coast; the **Willamette** and **Mount Hood** in the northwest; the **Umpqua** and **Rogue River** in the southwest; the **Winema** and **Fremont** in south-central region; the **Deschutes** in north–central region; the **Umatilla, Wallowa-Whitman,** and **Ochoco** in the northeast; and the **Malheur** in the southeast.

NEWSPAPERS If you want the news of the state, of almost any community within the state, Oregon is home to more than 90 newspapers, 19 of them published daily. The largest is Portland's ***Oregonian*** with more than 400,000 subscribers, and the smallest is the ***Dayton Tribune*** with just over 400. In between are weeklies and multiweeklies that together cover what's newsworthy across almost every mile of Oregon.

OREGON TRAIL If a single historic episode can define the character of any state, then the migration along the Oregon Trail comes close to doing that for Oregon. After all, this was the new Eden waiting for thousands of pioneers as they left their homes behind and trudged their weary way across the continent to make new lives for themselves in a land of promise. Within the state's boundaries, the trail those pioneers followed begins near the **Snake River,** crosses the **Blue Mountains** and the high grasslands, then makes its way either down the **Columbia River** or around **Mount Hood** before finally reaching the **Willamette Valley** (note: all Oregon Trail listings are under *To See—Historic Sites*).

PUBLIC LANDS See *Bureau of Land Management (BLM) Lands* and *National Forests* in this section.

REST AREAS On your drive across the state, one thing you won't have to look very hard for is a rest area. More than 70 such facilities that stand along Oregon's highways and byways offer travelers not only rest rooms but also picnic tables, drinking fountains, area information, historical markers, pet exercise areas, and RV dump stations. You can find a map and details online (www.tripcheck.com/General/restareas.htm), or you can call the **Oregon Department of Transportation** (from within Oregon: 1-800-977-6368; outside Oregon: 503-588-2941).

RESTAURANTS Throughout this land of greasy spoons, golden arches, and mom-and-pop cafés, some extremes seem often to prevail. On one hand, you have the gentility of those establishments that offer "fine dining," such as one in Portland where, when you arrive, white-jacketed valets cluster out front like moths around a Coleman lantern; in the end, diners examine the evening's tab with deer-in-the headlights stares; and in between, waiters who resemble Richard Simmons stand at casual attention, their hands clasped behind their backs, as they recite the special: "This evening's special is brisket of Saskatchewan mousse braised in a succulent Klingon fusillade and accompanied by an existential nebulousness of tartar, all blended together in an ensemble of Sousaesque brassiness."

On the other hand, a more earthy atmosphere exists at such eateries as the one in Pilot Rock, where the waitress used to slap down the menus with the warning, "This ain't no Burger King—you get it *my* way." Or the one in Christmas Valley—located near the kitty-litter plant and now under new management—whose menu once offered a "soup of the day," accompanied by the owner-manager-cook-waiter-custodian's assurance that you could have "any kind of soup you want." He would then tip his head toward the corner, where a pine shelf held a row of Campbell's soup cans.

Yet it's somewhere between these two extremes—in what *Oregonian* columnist John Foyston calls "the antithesis of the foodie scene and all its preciousness of the past few decades"—that most of us seek to fill our plates. As a result, that's where most of the book's restaurant listings lie, somewhere between the world of pastel pastries on one hand, and Wonder bread on the other. The intent is to steer you toward those places that offer a unique or quality dining experience, whether it's a café around the corner or the fanciest place in town. See *Dining Out* for more elegant offerings, *Eating Out* listings for more casual fare.

ROAD REPORTS If you want to see how the road ahead looks before you get there, visit the **"TripCheck"** web site of the **Oregon Department of Transportation** (www.tripcheck.com). Here you'll find information about weather and travel delays, mileage calculations, and road reports. It even has more than a hundred cameras scattered across the state, so you can see the road and the weather *live* before you even start the car. You can also call the Oregon Department of Transportation (from within Oregon: 1-800-977-6368; outside Oregon: 503-588-2941).

ROCKHOUNDING If you dig rocks, really dig them in the lapidary sense, then you're not alone. Parts of Oregon, especially the central and southeastern regions, lure rockhounds from far, far away. To learn about some of the best sites, visit **"Oregon Rockhounds Online"** (http://orerockon.com/ore_rock.htm). (With the web site comes a great version of the theme from *Mission Impossible.*)

RODEOS Some folks in Oregon call it Rock 'n' Roll—the pummeling ride of a cowboy straddling the back of a bronc or a bull. But when it comes time to rodeo in these parts, more than just a snort and sinew come roaring out of the chute, for the arm-flailing, hoof-kicking dance of man and beast is part of a history whose influence endures in the region today. In short, the Old West is alive and kicking in different parts of the state—even if it's just for a weekend. **Baker City, Canby, Elgin, Eugene, Haines, Heppner, Hillsboro, Jordan Valley, Joseph, Molalla, Nyssa, Pendleton, Prineville**—whew!—**Roseburg, Salem, Sisters, St. Paul, Stayton, Sublimity, The Dalles, Union, Vale**—these are just some of the communities across the state east or west, north or south that play host to cowboys and cowgirls at one time or another during the year. The best way to get schedules and locations is to check the regional visitors centers listed under *Guidance* at the beginning of each chapter in this book.

RV PARKS If you pack your home along with you when you travel, **The Oregon Tourism Commission** (1-800-547-7842; info.oregontourism@state.or.us; www.traveloregon.com) maintains a web site (www.traveloregon.com/search/lodginggateway.cfm?lodgingtype=1) that lets you search for the state's RV parks by either region or city.

SNOW SPORTS Whether you travel by skis, snowshoes, or snowboard during the white time of the year, Oregon has enough high-mountain playgrounds to make it a destination for many snow worshippers. For an introduction to what the state has to offer, either order the free *Official Oregon Snowsports Directory* from the **Oregon Travel Commission** (1-800-547-7842; info.oregontourism@state.or.us; www.traveloregon.com), or visit "Oregon Ski/Snow Information Links" at http://web.pdx.edu/~cyjh/orresorts.html. This site includes everything from resort information to weather reports.

STATE FORESTS Besides Oregon's wealth of national forests, the state also has more than 1,200 square miles of land managed by the **Oregon State Department of Forestry** (503-945-7200; www.dfw.state.or.us). These forests are **Clatsop** and **Tillamook** on the north coast, **Santiam** in the northwest, **Elliott** on the south coast, and **Sun Pass** in south-central Oregon. (Also see *National Forests* in this section.)

STATE PARKS Oregon might have 228 state parks, though it's hard to tell, what with campgrounds, picnic areas, viewpoints, and waysides scattered hither and yon across the state, often showing up in the most unexpected places. To even begin keeping track of these gems, contact the **Oregon Parks and Recreation Department** (1-800-735-2900) for a free copy of the *Oregon State Parks Guide,* or buy Jan Bannan's *Oregon State Parks,* probably the most complete guide currently published.

STATE THIS AND THAT For the curious, the following are some of Oregon's official state symbols: state flower, Oregon grape; state bird, western meadowlark; state animal, beaver; state tree, Douglas fir; state colors, navy blue and gold; state motto, "She Flies with her Own Wings" (voted by the state legislature in 1987 to replace the old motto, "The Union"); state song, "Oregon, My Oregon"; state gemstone, Oregon sunstone; state fish, chinook salmon; state rock, thunderegg; state insect, Oregon swallowtail butterfly; state dance, square dance; state nut, hazelnut; state shell, Oregon triton.

STATISTICS For those who need a few numbers to help put the state in perspective, the following might help—area: 97,949 square miles (10th largest in the nation and bigger than all of the United Kingdom); population: approximately 3.5 million (ranks 30th nationally); population density: approximately 37 people per square mile (the national average is 75 per square mile); highest point: Mount Hood, 11,235 feet; lowest point: sea level; northernmost point: Point Adams near the mouth of the Columbia River; southernmost point: 42nd parallel; westernmost point: Cape Blanco on the south coast; easternmost point: Hat Point near the Snake River.

TOURIST RAILROADS If you find yourself with a hankering to ride the rails, to sway in time to the *clackety-clack* of steel wheels rolling over steel tracks, then you should know that the following four railroads still operate excursions for Oregon tourists: **City of Prineville Railway** (541-447-6251; www.cityofprinevillerailway.com), **Mount Hood Railroad** (1-800-872-4661; mthoodrr@gorge.net; www.mthoodrr.com), **Port of Tillamook Bay** (503-842-2413; info@potb.org; http://www.potb.org), **Sumpter Valley Railroad Restoration** (541-894-2268; www.svry.com).

TRAVEL INFORMATION For an overview of the state or to receive travel publications and maps, contact the **Oregon Travel Commission** (1-800-547-7842; info.oregontourism@state.or.us; www.traveloregon.com). In addition to the local **Visitors Centers and Regional Tourism Associations,** all of which are listed within the book in their appropriate regions (under *Guidance*), Oregon has a series of **State Welcome Centers** along its borders that provide information to out-of-state travelers. The basic hours of operation for these are 8 AM–6 PM, Monday through Saturday; and 9 AM–5 PM on Sunday. (The 5 PM closing hour also applies to the months of April and October.)

UNIVERSITIES The state's university system includes seven public schools: Oregon State University, **Corvallis;** University of Oregon, **Eugene**; Portland State University, **Portland;** Western Oregon University, **Monmouth;** Southern Oregon University, **Ashland,** Eastern Oregon University, **La Grande;** and Oregon Institute of Technology, **Klamath Falls.** Private universities in the state include Concordia University, **Portland;** George Fox University, **Newberg**; Lewis and Clark College, **Portland;** Linfield College, **McMinnville;** Marylhurst University, **Marylhurst;** Pacific University, **Forest Grove;** Reed College, **Portland;** University of Portland, **Portland;** Warner Pacific College, **Portland;** Willamette University, **Salem,** founded in 1842, making it the oldest institution of higher learning in the West.

WEATHER You can find current weather reports for areas throughout the state by contacting the **National Weather Service** at the following locations: for northwest Oregon, **Portland** Weather Forecast Office (5241 N. E. 122nd Avenue, Portland; 503-261-9246; www.wrh.noaa.gov/Portland); for southwest Oregon, **Medford** Weather Forecast Office, (4003 Cirrus Drive, Medford; 541-776-4303; www.wrh.noaa.gov/Medford); for eastern Oregon, **Pendleton**

Weather Forecast Office (2001 N. W. 56th Drive, Pendleton; 541-276-7832; www.wrh.noaa.gov/pendleton/index.shml). You can also visit the **Interactive Weather Information Network**'s web site (http://iwin.nws.noaa.gov/iwin/or/or.html). (For the curious, the highest temperature ever recorded in Oregon was 119 degrees at Pendleton on August 10, 1938; the lowest temperature was 54 degrees below zero at Seneca on February 10, 1933.)

WILDLIFE Oregon is something of a Northwest ark when it comes to the critters that live within her borders, for it is home to more than 640 species, which is more than 40 percent of all the amphibians, reptiles, birds, and mammal species found in the United States and Canada. One of the reasons for the great number and variety of the state's wildlife is that Oregon has at least 31 distinct wildlife habitats, ranging from wet meadow to salt-desert shrub to coastal dunes. Consequently, you're bound to spot wildlife wherever you go, even in the downtown areas of the larger cities. (Portlanders have seen peregrine falcons nesting in downtown buildings and beneath bridges.)

WILDLIFE AREAS (STATE) Across Oregon, **the Oregon Department of Fish and Wildlife** manages almost 200,000 acres—more than 300 square miles—for fish, wildlife, and public recreation. Even though the book describes these areas in appropriate sections (most often under *Wilder Places*), the following is an overview of the areas and their locations: Bridge Creek in northeast Oregon near **Ukiah,** Coyote Springs (541-276-2344) in north-central Oregon near **Boardman,** Denman (541-826-8774) in southwest Oregon near **Medford,** E. E. Wilson (541-745-5334) in northwest Oregon near **Corvallis,** Elkhorn (541-898-2826) in northeast Oregon near **Baker City,** Enterprise (541-426-3279) in northeast Oregon near the town of **Enterprise,** Fern Ridge (541-935-2591) in northwest Oregon near **Eugene,** Irrigon (541-276-2344) in northeast Oregon near **Irrigon,** Jewell Meadows (503-755-2264) in northwest Oregon near **Jewell,** Klamath (541-883-5734) in south-central Oregon near **Klamath Falls,** Ladd Marsh (541-963-4954) in northeast Oregon near **La Grande,** Lower Deschutes (541-388-6363) in north-central Oregon near **Biggs,** Phillip W. Schneider (541-987-2843) in northeast Oregon near **Dayville,** Power City (541-922-3232) in northeast Oregon near **Hermiston,** Riverside (541-573-6582) in southeast Oregon near **Juntura,** Sauvie Island (503-621-3488) in northwest Oregon near **Portland,** Summer Lake (541-943-3152) in south-central Oregon near **Summer Lake,** Wenaha (541-828-7721) in northeast Oregon near **Troy,** White River (541-544-2126) in north-central Oregon near **Tygh Valley,** and Willow Creek (541-676-5230) in north-central Oregon near **Boardman**.

WILDLIFE REFUGES (FEDERAL) In every region of Oregon, federal refuges provide homes for hundreds of species of wildlife. The book describes most of these (under *Wilder Places*), but the following is a summary of their locations: Ankeny National Wildlife Refuge (541-757-7236) in northwest Oregon near **Salem**, Bandon Marsh National Wildlife Refuge (541-867-4550) on the south coast near **Bandon,** Baskett Slough National Wildlife Refuge (541-757-7236) in northwest Oregon near **Dallas,** Bear Valley National Wildlife Refuge (530-667-2231) in south-central

Oregon near **Klamath Falls,** Cape Meares National Wildlife Refuge (503-842-4981) on the north coast near **Tillamook,** Cold Springs National Wildlife Refuge (509-545-8588) in northeast Oregon near **Pendleton,** Hart Mountain National Wildlife Refuge (541-947-2731) in south-central Oregon near **Plush,** Klamath Marsh National Wildlife Refuge in south-central Oregon near **Chiloquin** (530-667-2231), Lewis and Clark National Wildlife Refuge (360-795-3915) on the north coast near **Astoria,** Malheur National Wildlife Refuge (541-493-2612) in southeast Oregon near **Frenchglen,** McKay Creek National Wildlife Refuge (509-545-8588) in northeast Oregon near **Pendleton,** Nestucca Bay National Wildlife Refuge on the north coast near **Pacific City,** Siletz Bay National Wildlife Refuge on the north coast near **Lincoln City,** Three Arch Rocks National Wildlife Refuge on the north coast near **Netarts,** Tualatin National Wildlife Refuge in northwest Oregon near **Sherwood,** Umatilla National Wildlife Refuge (509-545-8588) in northeast Oregon near **Umatilla,** Upper Klamath National Wildlife Refuge (530-667-2231) in south-central Oregon near **Klamath Falls,** Warm Springs National Wildlife Refuge in north-central Oregon near **Warm Springs,** and William L, Finley National Wildlife Refuge in northwest Oregon near **Corvallis.**

WILDERNESS AREAS Not surprisingly, designated Wilderness Areas are, indeed, wild. You can swing by for a look-see, break out the picnic basket, hoof it up the trail a ways—but you're asking for trouble if you venture into its depths without the right gear. If you do it anyway and make a mistake, you can expect to be the next morning's topic of conversation at the local café. To avoid this, pack along at least the **"Ten Essentials"** recommended by the U.S. Forest Service—whistle for signaling, map, compass, flashlight, food, clothing, fire starter, first-aid kit, pocket knife, sunscreen, waterproof matches—and be sure to register either at the Forest Service office or at the trailhead, whichever is appropriate at your location. (The book includes descriptions of all 40 of these locations; see *Wilder Places* in individual chapters.)

WILD AND SCENIC RIVERS Oregon can claim 48 of its streams as part of the federal Wild and Scenic River designation. Some of these streams are gentle enough that they invite you to cast a fishing line into their waters or take a snooze along their banks. Others are so wild that their whitewater swallows rafts and then spits them out again. All of them, however, are worth a visit, even if you just want to glance at them as you drive past.

WINE If your idea of a good time sometimes involves wine—where they grow it, how they make it, and how it tastes—then you should know that Oregon is a gathering force in the growing of grapes and the world of wine. Each year its almost 200 wineries (second largest in the nation) produce more than 1 million cases of wine that sell for almost $200 million (fourth in the nation). A few wine country tours are described in the book, but if you want to know more, contact the **Oregon Travel Commission** (1-800-547-7842; info.oregontourism@state.or.us; www.traveloregon.com) for the free publication *Official Oregon Wine Guide,* and visit the web site of the **Oregon Wine Advisory Board** (www.oregonwine.org).

ZIP CODES All Oregon zip codes, from Adams to Zig Zag, begin with 97. Not that anyone would want to know that, but it helps balance out the Z section.

ZOOS The Oregon Zoo in **Portland** (4001 S. W. Canyon Road; 503-226-1561), one of the foremost in the nation, is the state's only traditional zoo. Two other facilities, however, give visitors a chance to view wildlife not behind bars: West Coast Game Park (on the south coast 7 miles south of **Bandon** off Highway 101; 541-347-3106), with more than 20 acres that holds 450 animals representing 75 different species; and southwest Oregon's Wildlife Safari (6 miles south of **Winston** off Interstate 5—take exit 119—and Highway 42; 1-800-355-4848; www.wildlifesafari.org), almost a square mile where lions and tigers and bears wander freely as you drive through their home. In addition, some Oregonians insist that our fourth zoo is the State Capitol in **Salem** (900 Court Street N. E.; 503-986-1388) when the legislature is in session.

North Coast

ASTORIA–WARRENTON–SEASIDE AREA

CANNON BEACH–TILLAMOOK–PACIFIC CITY AREA

LINCOLN CITY–DEPOE BAY–NEWPORT AREA

WALDPORT–YACHATS–FLORENCE AREA

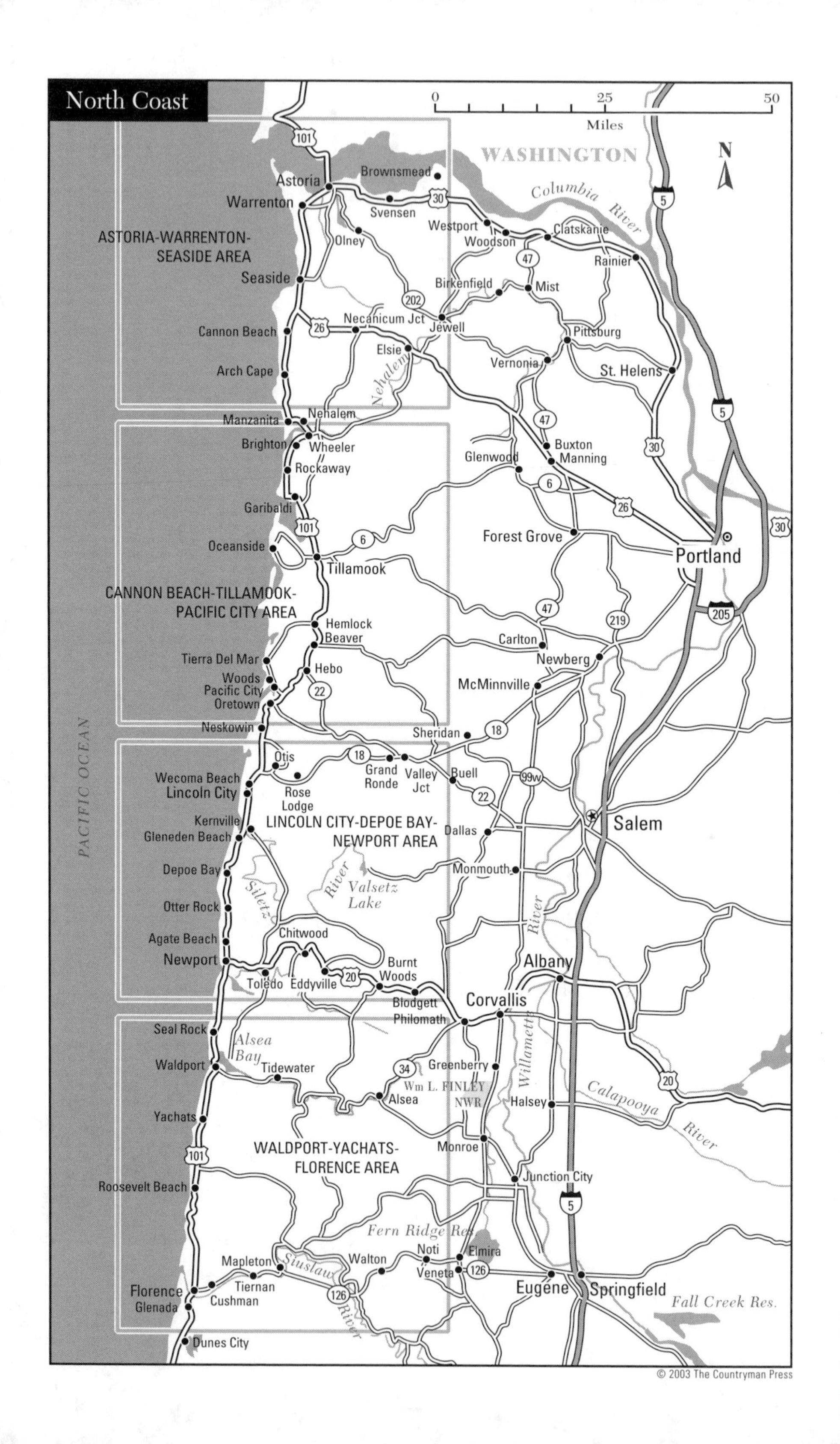

North Coast
0
25
50
Miles
WASHINGTON
N
PACIFIC OCEAN
Columbia River
ASTORIA-WARRENTON-SEASIDE AREA
CANNON BEACH-TILLAMOOK-PACIFIC CITY AREA
LINCOLN CITY-DEPOE BAY-NEWPORT AREA
WALDPORT-YACHATS-FLORENCE AREA
Astoria
Warrenton
Brownsmead
Svensen
Westport
Woodson
Clatskanie
Rainier
Olney
Seaside
Birkenfield
Mist
Necanicum Jct
Jewell
Cannon Beach
Elsie
Pittsburg
Vernonia
St. Helens
Arch Cape
Nehalem
Manzanita
Brighton
Wheeler
Rockaway
Garibaldi
Buxton
Manning
Glenwood
Forest Grove
Portland
Oceanside
Tillamook
Hemlock
Beaver
Carlton
Newberg
Tierra Del Mar
Woods
Pacific City
Oretown
Hebo
McMinnville
Neskowin
Sheridan
Otis
Grand Ronde
Valley Jct
Buell
Wecoma Beach
Lincoln City
Rose Lodge
Salem
Kernville
Gleneden Beach
Dallas
Depoe Bay
Monmouth
Siletz
River
Valsetz Lake
Otter Rock
Agate Beach
Chitwood
Newport
Toledo
Eddyville
Burnt Woods
Blodgett
Philomath
Albany
Corvallis
Willamette
Seal Rock
Alsea Bay
Waldport
Tidewater
Greenberry
Wm L. FINLEY NWR
Alsea
Halsey
Calapooya River
Yachats
Monroe
Junction City
Roosevelt Beach
Fern Ridge Res
Mapleton
Siuslaw
Walton
Noti
Elmira
Veneta
Florence
Glenada
Tiernan
Cushman
Eugene
Springfield
Fall Creek Res.
Dunes City
101
30
26
202
47
6
5
219
205
22
18
99W
20
34
126

INTRODUCTION

I pointed out that thus we would come into miles and miles

of highway without cost to the taxpayer.

The legislature took the bait—hook, line, and sinker.

—Governor Oswald West, explaining how he persuaded the 1913 Oregon Legislature to make Oregon's beaches public property

Along the Oregon coast, some things are forever: the migration of whales, the rise and fall of tides, the swell of weekend and summertime tourists, and the fact that nobody—*nobody*—can keep you from walking on the beach. The entire beach. From Washington to California. No fences and no gates. With the exception of coves lying back from the oceanfront and of cliffs plunging straight to sea, virtually all of Oregon's 362-mile shoreline belongs to the public.

"Only 5 percent of the recreational shoreland in the United States is open and available to the public," says Brian Booth of the Oregon Parks and Recreation Commission. "In California, only 90 miles out of 1,072 miles of coastline are publicly owned. That will give you some idea of how unique Oregon is."

So if in this region you want to examine the shipwreck near Warrenton or wade the mouth of the Necanicum, photograph the sea stacks at Cannon Beach or stroll the beach at Manzanita, explore the spit at Netarts Bay or fish the surf at Cape Kiwanda, dig for clams at Lincoln City or have a picnic near the waves at Otter Rock, visit the lighthouse at Yaquina Head or see the tide pools at Cape Perpetua, watch for whales at Seal Rock or wander the South Jetty at Florence —then go right on ahead. Kick off your shoes, roll up your cuffs, and hit the beach.

There you'll find this gift of the sea opening doors to a world of surf, sand, and driftwood piles carrying a scent of salt and kelp, a world with enough room for the wavering shrieks of gulls and the skinny-legged skitters of shorebirds, for the careening romp of dogs and kids and the lazy float of a Frisbee or kite. Yet it's also a gift that many are working to protect so it does last forever.

"You think of this thing having so much space it will never be gone, but it [can] be gone in short order," says Fran Recht of the Oregon Shores Conservation Coalition, which every day keeps a protective watch over Oregon's coastline. "One of the reasons I fight so hard is I realize how much there is to lose."

ASTORIA–WARRENTON–SEASIDE AREA

GUIDANCE **Astoria–Warrenton Area Chamber of Commerce** (1-800-875-6807), 111 W. Marine Drive, Astoria 97103.

Astoria–Warrenton Highway 101 Visitor Center (503-861-1031; www.oldoregon.com), 143 S. Highway 101, Warrenton 97146.

Oregon State Parks: Headquarters (503-378-6305), State Parks and Recreation Department, 525 Trade Street S. E., Salem 97301.

Seaside Visitors Bureau (1-888-306-2326; www.seasideor.com), 7 N. Roosevelt Street, Seaside 97138.

Siuslaw National Forest: Headquarters (541-750-7000), 4077 S. W. Research Way, Corvallis 97330.

GETTING THERE Astoria, Warrenton, Seaside, and nearby communities are reached from the east by Highways 30, 202, and 26 and are linked by Highway 101, which runs the entire length of the Oregon coast.

MEDICAL EMERGENCY **Columbia Memorial Hospital** (503-325-4321), 2111 Exchange Street, Astoria.

Providence Seaside Hospital (503-717-7000), 725 S. Wahanna Road, Seaside.

* To See

MUSEUMS **Columbia River Maritime Museum** (503-325-2323), 1792 Marine Drive, Astoria. The memory of the Columbia River and Oregon ships for the past 200 years, from explorers' routes to naval battles, is stored in the seven galleries of the Columbia River Maritime Museum, a gray-shingled building with a wave-sloped roof located on Astoria's waterfront. With 37,000 square feet devoted to the world of water, the museum may be as close as many landlubbers get to an understanding of how it feels to go to sea. In addition, recent developments at the museum, seemingly an attempt to satisfy the modern craving for a blitzkrieg of sound and images, include a series of "interactive family exhibits" that enable visitors to "participate" in experiences such as rescuing a boat at sea or steering a towboat along the river. "Our goal," says museum director Jerry Ostermiller, "has been to break out of the box of a traditional museum." The best parts of the museum, however, probably still remain with the stuff in the box.

Heritage Museum (503-325-2203), 16th and Exchange Streets, Astoria. Housed in Astoria's 1904 City Hall, the Heritage Museum traces the area's human history from Native Americans (Chinook, Clatsop, Wahkiakum, Kathlamet, Shoalwater) to explorers (mariners, trappers, traders) to pioneers (emigrants, farmers, loggers, fishermen). Perhaps the most interesting slice of area history, however, is the "Vice and Virtue Exhibit" upstairs, which tells the more tame parts of some of the stories connected to Astoria's past, when bars and brothels and shanghaied sailors were a way of life. In 1888, for example, businesses along the city's infamous Astor Street included one shoemaker, two boatbuilders, three laundries, and 21 saloons. "Astor Street was famous along with the Barbary Coast," reported the local newspaper, "as one of the worst seaport hell-holes in the world."

Uppertown Firefighters Museum (503-325-2203), 30th and Marine Drive, Astoria. Astoria is a city that knows something about fires—it almost burned to the ground in 1922. But once the smoke settled, the town went to work rebuilding the downtown and waterfront. "In the blackest hour of the destruction," the local newspaper said, "there was no wailing voice of defeat." That fire may be why the city has long paid attention to its firefighters. This museum, for instance, is a tribute to them, its collection of fire-fighting equipment covering more than 80 years, from 1879 to 1963. The primary feature housed in this 1896 building—a brewery before it was a fire station—is the display of hand-pulled, horse-drawn, and motor-driven fire engines.

Fort Stevens Historic Area and Military Museum (503-861-200), 1 mile south of Hammond off Highway 101. From the Civil War through World War II, Fort Stevens guarded the mouth of the Columbia River. Through the years the fort has earned for itself a handful of *onlys:* the only enclosed Civil War earthworks site on the West Coast, the only mainland military post to receive enemy fire since the War of 1812 (from a Japanese submarine in World War II), and the only artillery battery open to the public in the United States. Today most of its guns are gone but its batteries remain, and a museum tells the story of the old post while either guided or do-it-yourself tours show you the fort itself.

Seaside Museum (503-738-7065), 570 Necanicum Drive, Seaside. The history of Seaside, Oregon's first coastal resort, begins with the Chinooks and Clatsops, moves through Lewis and Clark, and eventually reaches the townspeople who turned the community into a home and built it into such a major tourist attraction that it was hailed as "the Atlantic City of the West Coast." A tour through this museum joins those pieces of area history, showing you the town as it has changed through the years.

Camp 18 Logging Museum (503-755-1818), 2 miles west of Elsie off Highway 26, milepost 18. Clustered around the log building that serves as a restaurant is a collection of logging equipment gathered from the old camps and mills of the area. Chances are, if it has anything to do with steel, cable, gears, or steam in cutting down trees or sawing up boards, it's standing somewhere here on the grounds.

HISTORIC HOMES **Lindgren Cabin** (503-654-0448), 7 miles north of Seaside in Cullaby Lake County Park off Highway 101, Cullaby Lake Road, and Hawkins Road. While in his late sixties, Finnish immigrant Erik Lindgren built this homestead cabin for his family, who lived at the end of a mile-long dirt trail in the wilderness along Soapstone Creek, a tributary of the North Fork Nehalem River. Built of hand-hewn cedar planks that Mr. Lindgren and his neighbor William Merila pegged together with dowels and joined at the corners with dovetailed notches—you'll find nary a nail in these boards—the cabin became part of a homestead operation that eventually included a barn as well as a sauna, which was a Saturday-night gathering spot for Finnish neighbors. The Lindgren family lived in the cabin for 10 years before moving—soon after, Mr. Lindgren died in Astoria—and the family home became a victim of weather and vandals until it was rescued and moved to this park in the 1970s.

Astoria Walking Tour of Homes. With more historic homes per capita than any other city in Oregon, and with many of those homes perched on the steep hillsides overlooking the Columbia River, Astoria is sometimes compared to a "Little San Francisco." You can find a good selection of the city's older homes—especially of the elegant Queen Anne Victorians built by the owners of the area's moneymaking industries involving logs and ships and fish—by simply traveling uphill from the waterfront's **Marine Drive** and taking a stroll through the neighborhoods, especially along **Franklin and Grand Avenues.**

Flavel House (503-325-2563), 441 Eighth Street, Astoria. Before he died in 1893 at age 70, George Flavel led an adventurous life: sailed around Cape Horn, worked as a Columbia River bar pilot, invested in tugboats and real estate, served as a community leader, and, at age 30, married a 14-year-old girl named Mary who, not surprisingly, outlived her husband by 35 years. Captain Flavel also built this home, an 1885 Victorian with all the necessary towers and porches and balconies, gabled dormers and bay windows and winding staircases. So grand was the home even in an age of grand homes that its two-story carriage house, reported the local newspaper, "looks more stylish outside than any ordinary dwelling house."

THE HISTORIC BUTTERFIELD COTTAGE ON THE GROUNDS OF THE SEASIDE MUSEUM

Butterfield Cottage (503-738-7065), 570 Necanicum Drive, Seaside. Unlike the heavy ornamentation that adorns so many historic buildings, the simplicity of this 1893 cottage is a reflection of Seaside's early years as a tourist destination, a playground for the wealthier

families from Portland who built their beachside getaways along the shore. With its furnishings and decor restored to depict such a home in 1912, the cottage gives visitors a glimpse of what a Seaside stay would have been like in the early part of the last century.

HISTORIC SITES **Lewis and Clark Trail** (Mouth of the Columbia River to Cannon Beach). "Ocian in view!" Captain Clark wrote in his journal on November 7, 1805. "O! the joy." Yet what he believed to be "this great Pacific Octean which we been so long anxious to See" was actually the ever-widening Columbia River, and the sea still lay 20 miles and more than a week's travel downriver. As they continued their journey, the Corps of Discovery found the days growing wetter, the river wilder, and the traffic of Indian canoes heavier. Camping on what is today the Washington bank of the Columbia, the corps stopped at native villages to trade fishhooks for salmon, dogs, and pelts and to hire guides who steered them around the numerous islands. Battling biting fleas and rising tides, as well as drenching rains and wind-tossed waves that made "every man as wet as water could make them," the corps paddled westward.

Mouth of the Columbia River, November 15, 1805 (north end of the Clatsop Spit and the Columbia River South Jetty). For six days the Corps of Discovery hunkered down against the wind and rain. "We have no tents, or covering to defend us," Sergeant Patrick Gass wrote, "except our blankets and some mats we got from the Indians." When the rain paused on the morning of November 15, the corps packed their camp, loaded their canoes, and paddled downriver to the mouth of the Columbia. "Here we halted on a sand beach," Sergeant Gass wrote, "formed a comfortable camp, and remained in full view of the ocean, at this time more raging than pacific." Their camp at the river's mouth they named Cape Disappointment, though the seemingly ever-optimistic Sergeant Gass saw it in a different light. "We are now at the end of our voyage," he wrote, "which has been completely accomplished according to the intention of the expedition." Yet they still faced the task of building winter quarters.

Fort Clatsop, December 7, 1805–March 22, 1806 (3 miles southwest of Astoria off Highway 101). In early December, with their clothes rotting and their diets reduced to dried salmon and arrowhead-root flour, Lewis and Clark followed the advice of the Clatsop people and abandoned Cape Disappointment and moved to the southern bank of the river, where elk and timber were plentiful. "We put our canoes into the water," Sergeant Gass wrote, "loaded them, and started for our intended wintering place." That place eventually became Fort Clatsop, a compound built of logs on the bank of what is today the Lewis and Clark River. The location, Captain Clark wrote, was "certainly the most eligable Situation for our purposes of any in its neighbourhood." And by Christmas Eve, the Corps of Discovery had moved into its new home.

Seaside Saltworks, began December 27, 1805 (near the junction of Lewis and Clark Way and the South Promenade, Seaside). Soon after their Christmas celebration—which included a dinner of elk, fish, and roots "without salt to season"—the captains dispatched a crew of five men to the ocean's shore, where they boiled seawater to extract salt. "The means we have of boiling the salt

THE REPLICA OF HISTORIC FORT CLATSOP

water we find it a very tedious operation, that of making salt," Captain Lewis wrote, "notwithstanding we keep the kettles boiling day and night."

Tillamook Head, January 7, 1806 (between Seaside and Cannon Beach off Highway 101). "In the evening of [December] 27th," Sergeant Gass wrote, "we were informed that a large fish, answering to the description of a whale, was driven upon the shore." So Captain Clark, accompanied by 14 of his men, hired a "young Indian to pilot me to the whale," and their journey took them around the point of Tillamook Head. "I hesitated a moment & view this emence mountain the top of which was obscured in the clouds," the captain wrote, "and the assent appeared to be almost perpindecular." Once on the trail, Captain Clark found the going even worse than expected; he sometimes grabbed bushes and roots to pull himself up the slope. Nevertheless, near the top he found Indian men and women packing home the oil and blubber of the whale and a view he described as "the grandest and most pleasing . . . my eyes ever surveyed."

Ecola Creek, January 8, 1806 (Les Shirley Park, north of downtown Cannon Beach off Highway 101). When Captain Clark and his party reached the beached whale, whose length measured 105 feet, they found it stripped to its skeleton and local villagers boiling the blubber and extracting the oil, using the whale's bladder and intestines as storage containers. He was, however, able to trade a "Small Stock of merchandize" for approximately 300 pounds of blubber and a few gallons of oil. This was the southernmost point reached by the Lewis and Clark Expedition.

Youngs River Falls, noted March 1, 1806 (7 miles south of Astoria off Highway 101 Business Loop and Youngs River Loop). As the winter wore on, the hunters found themselves wandering farther from the fort to find the elk that were the mainstay of their diet. On one such hunt, they discovered this waterfall. "Our hunters discovered falls," wrote Sergeant Patrick Gass, "which had about 60 feet of a perpendicular pitch." Today the falls, located approximately 6 miles from Fort Clatsop (see above), draws picnickers to its beach and swimmers to its pool.

The Corps of Discovery spent the winter hunting elk, making moccasins, exploring the country, and healing themselves of various afflictions probably caused by their poor diet. In the spring of the year, on March 22, the corps began the long journey home, leaving Fort Clatsop behind forever. "Altho' we have not fared sumptuously this winter and spring at Fort Clatsop," Captain Lewis wrote, "we have lived quite as comfortably as we had any reason to expect we should."

Clatsop County Courthouse, 749 Commercial Street, Astoria. This is a courthouse that almost didn't get built—at least not when it was supposed to. After deciding in 1891 that the county's wooden courthouse, built in 1855, was "a disgrace to the city" of Astoria—then the third largest in the state—county commissioners took 10 years to make a decision to replace it, a couple more years to approve an architect's plans and begin construction, a couple *more* years to fight state laws and local lawsuits aimed at making the county keep within a given limit of debt, and a couple more years after *that* to pass a levy and finish construction. In the winter of 1908, however, the waiting finally came to an end, and the doors opened on this American Renaissance brick building that stands symmetrical and solid as a badge of Astoria's past.

Fort Astoria, corner of 15th and Exchange Streets, Astoria. This hilltop park with its replica blockhouse marks one corner of old Fort Astoria, built in 1811 by the 33 men who arrived on the *Tonquin,* the ship sent by John Jacob Astor to establish a fur trade in the Northwest. "We imagined ourselves in the Garden of Eden," wrote one of the men. "Buildings were of boards tightly covered and roofed with cedar bark." Providing the oldest American settlement in the Oregon Country and the predecessor to the city of Astoria, the fort became a British possession during the War of 1812 (and renamed Fort George), reverted back to the United States in 1818, and was finally abandoned in 1825.

THE ASTORIA COLUMN PRESENTS A PICTORIAL HISTORY OF OREGON

Astoria Column (1-800-875-6807), Coxcomb Hill, Astoria (from downtown drive uphill on 16th Street and follow the signs). Outside this 125-foot columnar hilltop monument, 14 painted panels portraying 22 scenes from Oregon history twirl their way skyward along the stucco walls; inside, 164 steps of a spiral staircase lead to far-reaching views of the city, the mountains, and the river. Built in 1926 to commemorate Northwest history, the column has become a landmark of history itself, something a local group of supporters calls "the only monument of its kind." And it's worth the 164-step climb to see what they mean.

Astoria Waterfront. On the city's waterfront, the Astoria Riverwalk, a mile-long

THE ASTORIA RIVERWALK BLENDS TOURISM AND INDUSTRY ALONG A STRETCH OF THE COLUMBIA RIVER

pathway along the bank of the Columbia River, takes you along what was once one of the toughest ports on the West Coast.

***Peter Iredale* Shipwreck,** 1 mile southwest of Hammond off Highway 101, at Clatsop Beach near Fort Stevens State Park. On an October day in 1906, the 287-foot, four-masted, steel-hulled British sailing ship *Peter Iredale* ran aground on this beach. It has lain here ever since, gathering rust and barnacles and sliding slowly and silently back into seawater.

Seaside Promenade and Old Town. Known locally as *the Prom,* this 8,000-foot walkway and seawall along Seaside's beachfront has been the resort town's favorite place to take a stroll since 1920. In addition, the Prom bypasses the **salt-works** site of the Lewis and Clark Expedition, and edges past the front yards of at least two dozen **early-20th-century homes,** many of which were built as vacation cottages in the days when a boardwalk lined this same route. Farther away from the water, on the banks of the Necanicum River, the **Broadway Bridge** leads to Seaside's **Old Town,** which holds a collection of early-20th-century buildings that replaced those lost in the devastating 1912 fire.

FOR FAMILIES ✐ **Trolley Tours** (541-861-1031), Astoria Riverfront Trolley, Columbia Riverfront, Astoria. Built in 1913 to join the fleet of trolleys that coursed along the streets of San Antonio, Texas, the trolley known as Old 300, all 44 feet and 40 tons of her, today carries passengers along the Astoria riverfront.

✐ **Seaside Aquarium** (503-738-6211), 200 N. Promenade, Seaside. The Seaside Aquarium, one of the oldest on the entire Pacific Coast, started out in 1924 as a natatorium, an indoor swimming pool. But when the pool fell on hard times during the Great Depression and was converted to an aquarium, it soon became what the local newspaper called "one of the most popular, and one of the most prosperous, entertainment features on the Oregon coast." It still is. In fact, if you take a stroll along the town's shoreline promenade (see **Seaside Promenade and Old Town** under *Historic Sites*), the echoing barks of the aquarium's harbor seals are almost guaranteed to lure you inside. Once there, and once you've tossed the seals the fishy morsels they chortle and clap for, the aquarium sells itself. "It has a lot of luxuries that bigger aquariums don't have," says longtime general manager and lifelong Seaside resident Keith Chandler, who began working here soon after graduating from high school. "People from [aquariums in] Seattle and other large cities who have seen it are envious of what we have here."

SCENIC DRIVES **Pacific Coast Scenic Byway—northern segment,** 185 paved miles from Astoria to Florence along Highway 101. From the Columbia River at **Astoria to the Siuslaw River at Florence,** this road skirts the shoreline of the Pacific, winding past headlands and beaches, crossing over estuaries and bays, and climbing through foothills and toward ocean views along a route that is one of the most beautiful and famous drives in America. In addition, numerous viewpoints, pullouts, and state parks along the way provide dozens of entries for anyone wanting to wade the surf, comb the beach, or watch a sunset.

NATURAL WONDERS **Mouth of the Columbia River,** 4 miles northwest of Hammond off Jetty Road, at South Jetty Overlook in Fort Stevens State Park. So notorious and deadly is the mouth of the Columbia River that for more than a century mariners called it "the Graveyard of the Pacific." Shifting sandbars and weather, strong tides and currents, heavy fog and rain, and towering breakers reaching 30 feet have grounded, capsized, and broken ships through the years, claiming more than 2,000 craft—including more than 200 major vessels—and 700 lives, making the Columbia River bar one of the most dangerous crossings in the maritime world. No wonder the unofficial motto of the U.S. Life-Saving Service (the predecessor of today's Coast Guard) stationed near the river's mouth was "You have to go out . . . You don't have to come back."

Klootchy Creek Spruce, Klootchy Creek County Park, 6 miles southeast of Seaside off Highway 26. When Columbus reached America, this Sitka spruce tree was more than 250 years old; when Oregon began its Heritage Tree program to honor trees that signify Oregon's natural or human history, this spruce was the first to be listed. "People come from all over the world to see this tree," says Maynard Drawson, a retired barber who is the state's expert on historical trees. "It's Oregon's ambassador to the world." With a height of 216 feet, a circumference of 56 feet, and a diameter of 17 feet—enough wood to build six two-bedroom houses—the spruce named the Klootchy Creek Giant is said to be the biggest Sitka spruce in the nation and the largest tree in circumference in the state. And for a tree, it must also draw some of the state's largest crowds, with as many as 1,000 visitors per day in the summer and 100,000 throughout the year stopping to gawk at the old giant.

* To Do

BICYCLING **Astoria Loops.** Paved loops beginning and ending in Astoria, located at the junction of Highways 101 and 30. Three paved, connected routes that begin and end at Oregon's oldest city carry bikers through a quiet green countryside to a historic site, a waterfall, and a coastal river. Two of these start by heading south from the city on the Highway 101 Business Loop. From there the 20-mile **Fort Clatsop Loop** follows

Lewis & Clark Road to the Fort Clatsop National Memorial, and the 18-mile **Youngs River Loop** leads to a 65-foot waterfall once visited by members of the Lewis and Clark Expedition. The third ride follows Highway 202 southeast from Astoria to the 15-mile **Walluski Loop** along the Walluski River. This route connects with the Youngs River Loop by continuing southeast through Olney and then on to Youngs River Falls.

Fort Stevens State Park, 1 mile south of Hammond off Highway 101. Almost 9 miles of paved bike paths lead pedalers on a tour of the park's lakes, forests, and wildlife and historic areas. (See also *Wilder Places—Parks.*)

CAMPING **Spruce Run Park,** 6 miles south of Elsie off Highway 26 and Foss Road. Twenty campsites along the forested Nehalem River.

HIKING **Column Trail,** 28th and Irving Streets, Astoria. Two highlights of this forested city trail—besides its green, its quiet, and its smells of needles and duff—are its encounter with the **Cathedral Tree,** a giant spruce, and its emergence at the crest of Coxcomb Hill and the hilltop **Astoria Column** (see *To See—Historic Sites*).

Warrenton Waterfront Trail, starting at Second Street Park in Warrenton, located on Highway 101. Edging its way through thickets, near wetlands, and along riverbanks, this 4-mile trail, an abandoned railway, follows the Columbia River and its backwaters, taking hikers through a cross section of waterfront, with neighbors ranging from wetlands to lumber mills, packing houses to cargo ships, seabirds to gillnetters.

Peter Iredale Loop, near Fort Stevens State Park, 1 mile south of Hammond off Highway 101. For 4 miles along pavement, across sand, and over dunes this trail runs, beginning near Fort Stevens State Park (see *Wilder Places—Parks*) and eventually leading to the 1906 wreck of the ***Peter Iredale*** (see *To See—Historic Sites*).

Tillamook Head, between Seaside and Cannon Beach off Highway 101. When William Clark and some of his men left Fort Clatsop to investigate a beached whale at Ecola Creek (see **Lewis and Clark Trail** under *To See—Historic Sites*), this is the 6-mile route they followed from what is today Seaside. It's also the setting where Captain Clark—standing near the trail's highest point, some 1,200 feet above the sea—proclaimed the view to be "the grandest and most pleasing prospects which my eyes ever surveyed."

Saddle Mountain, 14 miles east of Seaside off Highway 26. Don't climb Saddle Mountain because it's there—climb it because it takes you to the top of the northwest corner of the state, where each shift of your eyes or turn of your head reveals a different piece of the water or mountains or forests of an Oregon mosaic: the Pacific, the Columbia, the Cascades, the Coast Range. Although the trail is steep (1,600-foot elevation gain), it's length is manageable (less than 3 miles). To keep your mind off complaining legs and lungs, you'll probably have lots of entertaining company along the way, people who drift in off Highway 26 or 101 to see what all the fuss is about. Most of those who reach the summit seem to find what they're looking for.

THE VIEW FROM SADDLE MOUNTAIN STRETCHES FROM THE PACIFIC OCEAN TO THE CASCADE MOUNTAINS

See also **Saddle Mountain State Park** under *Wilder Places—Parks*.

✷ Wilder Places

PARKS **Shively Park,** Williamsport Road just off Niagara Avenue, Astoria. More than a century old, this forested city park welcomes visitors to its paved walking paths with an entrance arch that came from Astoria's old Weinhard Hotel, which burned down in 1922.

Lighthouse Park, corner of Main Street and Fort Stevens Highway, Warrenton. Unlike typical parks with their playgrounds and picnic tables, Lighthouse Park contains the only memorial to the area's men and women who have lost their lives at sea, and a 35-foot replica lighthouse that serves as an interpretive center and small museum for the fishing industry. In addition, the money and labor that built this park came from local fishermen and Warrenton residents.

E. H. Carruthers Park, N. W. Warrenton Drive, Warrenton. Located along the **Warrenton Waterfront Trail** (see *To Do— Hiking*), this park contains a riverside segment of that trail as well as a viewing platform that overlooks the Columbia River. From here you can catch glimpses not only of the river's **waterfowl, seabirds, and raptors** winging past, but also its seagoing vessels chugging along the main navigation channel between Astoria and the sea.

Necanicum Estuary Park, north end of Holladay Drive, Seaside. A doorway to the estuary at the mouth of the Necanicum River, this park has an observation deck that overlooks the area, while a boardwalk and shoreline trail lead to nearby marshes and mudflats.

Fort Stevens State Park, 1 mile south of Hammond off Highway 101, day use and overnight. Located near the mouth of the Columbia River, this park of almost 4,000 acres includes more than 600 campsites—making it the largest state park campground in the nation—as well as almost 20 miles of walking and biking trails that lead around lakes, through forests, across dunes, along beaches, and to a military museum (see **Fort Stevens His-**

toric Area and Military Museum under *To See—Museums*), an army fort, wildlife areas, and the remains of an early-20th-century shipwreck that's slowly settling into the sea (see ***Peter Iredale*** **Shipwreck** under *To See—Historic Sites*).

Hug Point State Park, 5 miles south of Cannon Beach off Highway 101, day use only. In the days when Oregon's beaches were also the main coastal highways, motorists waited for low tide, then "hugged" this point tightly to get around it. Today, sightseers and hikers still must keep an eye on the tide when exploring this headland, though the reward for doing so is a fine stretch of beach with a waterfall and sandstone caves.

Saddle Mountain State Park, 14 miles east of Seaside off Highway 26 to park entrance, then 7 more miles to campground and trailhead, day use and overnight. Even though this park consists of almost 5 square miles of untamed second-growth forest, most of its visitors come seeking only a few of its lofty, rocky acres, climbing the zigzag path toward the summit of the mountain that stands tall enough to gather clouds (see *To Do—Hiking*).

WILDLIFE REFUGES **Twilight Creek Eagle Sanctuary,** 7 miles east of Astoria off Highway 30. Near the shore of the Columbia River's Cathlamet Bay lies this 34-acre habitat protected for **bald eagles,** one of the few such areas along the lower Columbia. An observation platform gives you an elevated view into the eagle's sanctuary, with some winter birders reporting as many as 50 sightings from this point.

Neawanna Creek, off South Wahanna Road between Spruce Drive and Providence Hospital, Seaside. Above ground, these wetlands lying so close to Highway 101 are the home of **waterfowl** and **hawks, elk** and **deer;** below ground, they hold critters even more rare. "The extensive tidal marshes along Neawanna Creek," says the Nature Conservancy, which is restoring the area, "represent a side of Seaside most tourists never see: a relatively healthy coastal wetland system that supports one of the strongest remaining runs of **native coho salmon** on the north coast."

Jewell Meadows Wildlife Area, 2 miles west of Jewell off Highway 202. More than 1,100 acres of forests and streams support as many as 200 **Roosevelt elk** that graze and loaf in the meadows lying beside the area's two creeks. (A question some elk-viewing visitors have asked the local chamber of commerce is, "When do the elk become deer?" If you should have the urge to ask the same question, the answer is, they don't.)

* Lodging

INN **Astor Haus** (1-888-505-8925; Uniqhorn@Pacifier.com; www.skybusiness.com/astorhausbandb), 1370 Madison Avenue, Astoria 97103. From the deck of the Astor Haus the views stretch across the Columbia River and into Washington. Its three guest rooms come with either private or shared bathrooms as well as a family room that contains a fully equipped kitchen ($70–135).

BED & BREAKFASTS

Astoria

Astoria Inn (1-800-718-8153; www.astoriainnbb.com), 3391 Irving Avenue, Astoria 97103. Standing in a quiet neighborhood on a hill overlooking the Columbia River, this 1890 three-story Victorian farmhouse is within earshot of sea lions and foghorns down on the water, while raccoons and deer make a habit of visiting the yard. The inn's four guest rooms come with a private bath ($70–85), and the full breakfast, prepared by hostess Mickey Cox, can include such house specialties as crab quiche, Dutch babies, or Grand Marnier French toast.

Benjamin Young Inn (1-800-201-1286; benjamin@benjaminyounginn.com; www.BenjaminYoungInn.com), 3652 Duane Street, Astoria 97103. This 1888 Queen Anne Victorian still has its original carriage house on this three-quarter-acre lot above the Columbia River. Its five guest rooms all have private baths, and the Fireplace Room has a double Jacuzzi ($85–145). The full breakfast is served either family style in a dining room with a river view or privately in the guest rooms. Specialties include fresh local fruits and fresh-baked breads.

Clementine's Bed & Breakfast (1-800-521-6801; jttaylor@clementinesbb.com; www.clementines-bb.com), 847 Exchange Street, Astoria 97103. Standing across the street from the **Flavel House** (see *To See—Historic Homes*), Clementine's is an 1888 Italianate Victorian that takes in views of the river and mountains. Its gardens provide herbs for the kitchen and flowers for the seven guest rooms, all of which have private baths while some have private balconies and sitting rooms ($70–135). Breakfast, says owner Judith Taylor, is "a multicourse event" that includes specialties from around the Pacific Northwest. Children and pets are welcome.

Columbia River Inn (1-800-953-5044; www.columbiariverbb.com), 681 Franklin Street, Astoria 97103. Owner Karen Nelson says that visiting her 19th-century Victorian home, one of the oldest B&Bs in the city, is like "going home to Grandmother's house." Its four guest rooms all come with private baths and a full breakfast, and most have views of the Columbia River ($75–125). Perhaps the most important aspect of a stay here, Karen says, is that "you'll discover memories which really do last forever."

Franklin Street Station (1-800-448-1098; innkeeper@franklin-st-station-bb.com; www.franklin-st-station-bb.com), 1140 Franklin Street, Astoria 97103. Its 1986 opening makes this 1900 Victorian home Astoria's first B&B. It has six guest rooms with queen beds, private baths, and a full breakfast ($75–135). "Some rooms have wonderful views of the Columbia River and historical downtown Astoria," says owner Sharon Middleton. "Others have balconies or fireplaces." One room, the Starlight Suite, even has a telescope to help you take in the view above the Columbia River.

Grandview (1-800-488-3250; grandview@grandviewbedandbreakfat.com; www.moriah.com/grandview), 1574 Grand Avenue, Astoria 97103. A four-story Victorian with a . . . er . . . grand view of the Columbia River, the Grandview offers six rooms, three of them suites, all with private baths and some with canopy beds ($49–100). A full breakfast is included, and **winter rates** are almost unheard of these days: after the first night, only $22 for each consecutive following night.

Rosebriar Hotel (1-800-487-0224; rbhotel@pacifier.com; www.astoria-usa.com /rosebriar), 636 14th Street, Astoria 97103. One of Astoria's historic landmarks and a former convent, this 1902 neoclassic Georgian hotel has been restored to period architecture and traditional furnishings. All 11 of its guest rooms have private baths ($85–125). Gourmet breakfasts are served restaurant style, and the menu changes daily.

Rose River Inn (1-888-876-0028; roseriver@moriah.com; www.moriah.com/roseriver), 1510 Franklin Street, Astoria 97103. Here in the Rose River Inn, a 1912 home located just a few blocks from Astoria's waterfront, reside parts of Finland: the sauna, the art and antiques, even the owners, Kati and Jaakko Tuominen. "It's an outstanding way," says Kati, who grew up in Helsinki, "to enjoy Astoria's Scandinavian heritage." The inn's four guest rooms include private baths ($85–125) and a gourmet breakfast in a dining room that overlooks the Columbia River. (One unusual offering of a stay here is the opportunity for a massage by Kati, a licensed massage therapist.)

Hammond

Officer's Inn (1-800-377-2524; www.officersinn.net), 540 Russell Place, Hammond 97121. Officer's Inn really was an officer's inn, built in 1905 to house U.S. Army officers and their families stationed at nearby Fort Stevens. Today the covered front porch of the 8,000-square-foot historic building still overlooks the old parade grounds. Its eight guest rooms each come with a king or queen bed as well as a private bath and a full breakfast ($79–99).

Seaside

The Guest House (1-800-340-8150; guest-house@moriah.com; www.moriah.com/guest-house), 486 Necanicum Drive, Seaside 97138. "Far enough away to be quiet and

THE HAMMOND TOWN HALL RETAINS A SENSE OF SMALL-TOWN LIFE ALONG THE COLUMBIA RIVER

close enough to be handy." That's how owner Nancy Bailey describes the Guest House's location in the city of Seaside—less than three blocks from the beach but still within walking distance of everything downtown has to offer, including its museums, shops, and restaurants. "We are like a casual country lodge," Nancy says, "with friendly hosts, nice views of the river and mountains, delicious and generous breakfasts, and comfortable beds." Those beds are stationed in the B&B's four guest rooms, which all have private baths ($60–95). Children and pets are welcome.

10th Avenue Inn (1-800-745-2378; summerhs@seasurf.com; www.10avei nn.com), 125 10th Avenue, Seaside 97138. At this 1908 historic inn by the sea, hospitality seems to be part of the furnishings. "We like to consider our home a true B&B," says owner Lesle Palmeri. "We've been innkeepers since 1994, and our son has grown up while we've been welcoming people from all over the world into our living room." Guest accommodations include three rooms with king beds, private baths, and a full breakfast as well as panoramic views of the mountains, the sea, and Seaside itself ($89.99–129). During their stay, guests might also have the opportunity to join Lesle and her family at a beach bonfire, part of what she describes as "a wonderful life."

* Where to Eat

EATING OUT

Astoria

Cannery Café (503-325-8642), 218 W. Marine Drive, Astoria. Yes, this café set on pilings along the edge of the Columbia River really *was* an old cannery. Its location gives diners a close-up view of the river along with ships and wildlife, while its kitchen specializes in steaks and seafoods.

Columbian Café (503-325-8642), 1114 Marine Drive, Astoria. Its vegetarian dishes and fresh seafood are two reasons this café is popular with locals and visitors alike, but another reason is the talent and personality of chef Uriah Hulsey, whose interaction with the café's customers provides the informal entertainment.

Home Spirit Bakery Café (503-325-6846), 1585 Exchange Street, Astoria. Mornings at this restored 1892 Victorian are characterized by the scent of fresh-baked bread and pastry, while lunches feature thick sandwiches and homemade soups, and dinners offer menus that change often but that always include international cuisine.

Rio Café (503-324-2409), 125 Ninth Street, Astoria. Offering authentic Mexican food in an area that can't seem to get enough seafood, the Rio Café grills and stews its dishes with enough jalapeños and garlic, tomatoes and onions to make diners believe they just dropped into a south-of-the-border cantina.

Gearhart

Pacific Way Bakery and Café (503-738-0245), 601 Pacific Way, Gearhart. Labeled "a must" by some locals, this bakery and café serves up soups, sandwiches, and special desserts that draw big crowds to its turn-of-the-20th-century building. A husband-and-wife team—she does all the baking—handles the chores, including making the breads for their locally famous sandwiches. If you want to sample the baked goods here, arrive early because they sell out fast.

✱ Special Events

February: **Chocolate and Coffee Lovers Festival** (1-800-444-6740), Seaside.

April: **Astoria–Warrenton Crab and Seafood Festival** (503-325-6311), Astoria.

June: **Scandinavian Midsummer Festival** (503-325-3099), Astoria. The community's pride in its Scandinavian ancestry—Danish, Finnish, Icelandic, Norwegian, and Swedish—comes shining through in this annual festival that celebrates the cultures of the north countries through food, crafts, music, and dances. It's also a chance for visitors to say, *"Hyvaa paiva. Mita Kuuluu"* to the Finns they meet.

September: **Lewis and Clark Kite Festival** (503-717-0138), Seaside. Events at this competition can involve sky divers, kite ballet, and choreographed and precision kite flying.

Sandcastle Contest (1-800-738-6391), Seaside. What began as a way to keep the kids busy on the beach has grown through the years into this community celebration that uses sand as an artistic medium. *Labor Day Weekend:* **Civil War Encampment and Reenactment,** Fort Stevens State Park, 1 mile southwest of Hammond off Highway 101. This event may put you as close as you'll ever get to the most tragic of American events. "The reenactment," says Gale Hemmen, Fort Stevens historian, "is an opportunity for visitors to experience what life must have been like for people during the Civil War." As many as 1,000 participants don authentic uniforms and costumes, assume roles as soldiers or civilians, and turn the clock back to the days of the 1860s and the battlefields and encampments of the Civil War.

CANNON BEACH–TILLAMOOK–PACIFIC CITY AREA

GUIDANCE **Cannon Beach Chamber of Commerce** (503-436-2623; www.cannonbeach.org), 207 N. Spruce Street, Cannon Beach 97110.

Garibaldi Chamber of Commerce (503-322-0301; www.garibaldioregon.com), 605 Garibaldi Avenue, Garibaldi 97118.

Nehalem Bay Area Visitor Center (1-877-368-5100; www.nehalembaychamber.com), Eighth and Tohl Streets, Nehalem Street.

Oregon State Parks: Headquarters (503-378-6305), State Parks and Recreation Department, 525 Trade Street S. E., Salem 97301; **Tillamook office** (503-842-5501).

Pacific City Chamber of Commerce (503-965-6161; www.pacificcity.net), Pacific City 97135.

Rockaway Beach Chamber of Commerce (503-355-8108; www.rockawaybeach.net), 103 S. First Street, Rockaway Beach 97136.

Siuslaw National Forest: Headquarters (541-750-7000), 4077 S. W. Research Way, Corvallis 97330; **Hebo Ranger District** (503-392-3161).

Tillamook Chamber of Commerce (503-842-7525; www.tillamookchamber.org), 3705 Highway 101 North, Tillamook 97141.

GETTING THERE Cannon Beach, Tillamook, Pacific City, and nearby communities are reached from the east by Highways 26, 6, and 22 and are linked by Highway 101, which runs the entire length of the Oregon coast.

MEDICAL EMERGENCY **Tillamook County General Hospital** (503-842-4444), 1000 Third Street, Tillamook.

✱ To See

MUSEUMS **Tillamook Air Museum** (503-842-1130), 2 miles south of Tillamook off Highway 101. Inside this 1,000-foot-long building, a former navy blimp hangar built during World War II, stands a collection of more than two dozen vintage aircraft that played significant roles in aviation history. As a result, the museum can claim two prestigious titles: the biggest wooden building in the world—the roof alone covers 11 acres—and the largest collection of war planes in the Pacific Northwest. A large number of the visitors here seem to be veterans of World War II, men who flew or knew the planes in days when their lives could depend upon the power harnessed between silver wings. Consequently, if you'll shadow one of these fellows, and if you're courteous in your eavesdropping, you're likely to learn far more than what you would from the interpretive signs.

Tillamook County Pioneer Museum (503-842-4553; www.oregoncoast.com/pionrmus), 2106 Second Street (the junction of Highways 101 and 6), Tillamook. With more than 35,000 artifacts stored in this 1905 former courthouse, the Pioneer Museum has been a storehouse for the area's natural and human history since 1935. In fact, the second-floor Alex Walker Natural History Room, named for the self-taught naturalist who became the museum's first curator, may contain one of the state's finest exhibits of life on earth, the displays ranging from hummingbird eggs to Cape buffalo heads, all of it collected by Mr. Walker. "A humble man small of stature, yet resolute, and in certain fields, a giant among men," a journalist once wrote of Mr. Walker. "His devotion to duty, his lifelong love of natural things, especially birds . . . is worthy of the highest praise."

HISTORIC SITES **Tillamook Rock Lighthouse,** 2 miles north of Cannon Beach and offshore from Ecola State Park, off Highway 101 and Park Road. Standing a mile offshore, 100-foot tall Tillamook Rock—a three-quarter-acre chunk of basalt known affectionately as "Terrible Tilly"—is home to an 1881 lighthouse that has given up its light to spend its retirement years as a columbarium, where urns of cremated ashes are stored. In its ship-saving days, however, Oregon's northernmost lighthouse endured in spite of its location, considered one of the

ECOLA STATE PARK

BAYOCEAN, ONCE THE SITE OF NUMEROUS HOMES AND AN OCEAN RESORT

most exposed stations in the world. An 1896 storm, for instance, tossed 135-pound rocks through the roof and into the kitchen. Such violent outbursts meant that lightkeepers staffed their posts alone; no families were permitted at the station. The light was finally turned off in 1957.

Morning Star, 2 miles north of Tillamook off Highway 101. In the early days of its settlement, Tillamook was home to people who rarely saw the world beyond the coast. With the Coast Range cutting them off from the Willamette Valley, they found the sea to be their only route to the outside. That's why in the summer of 1854 (following the wreck of a sloop carrying the settlement's salmon, potatoes, and butter that were to be traded for the valley's flour, sugar, coffee, and other staples) the people of Tillamook decided to build their own ship. They cut and hewed the lumber from the nearby forests and salvaged the metal, rigging, and sails from a wrecked ship. When they were done, the *Morning Star,* a two-masted schooner, sailed out of Tillamook Bay on a January day in 1855. Though its history was short—it served the community for less than two years before being sold and later lost at sea—the ship emerged again during the state's 100th birthday in 1959 when the *Morning Star II,* a three-quarter-sized replica, sailed out of Tillamook Bay with a load of local dairy products and anchored at Oregon's Centennial Exposition in Portland. This, then, is a second replica, a third *Morning Star,* dedicated in 1992 and adopted as the logo for Tillamook dairy products.

Bayocean, 8 miles northwest of **Tillamook** off Three Capes Scenic Loop (see *Scenic Drives*). A peninsula of sand that clings to the mainland with one slender finger of dike, Bayocean is the result of an entrepreneur's dream and an ocean's waves. The dream belonged to Kansas City developer Thomas Potter, whose plan in 1906 was to convert this 4 miles of sand, which separates Tillamook Bay from the Pacific Ocean, into a resort that would become what he called "the Atlantic City of the West." And by 1912, Mr. Potter—probably no relation to the Mr. Potter of *It's a Wonderful Life* infamy—was celebrating the grand opening of Bayocean, which had been subdivided into building lots, crisscrossed with paved roads, strung with electric lights and telephone wires, and furnished with a general store and post office, bowling alley and swimming pool, even a three-story hotel. For a while, Mr. Potter was to call his resort "Oregon's $1,000,000 Summer Playground." But then in 1917 the Army Corps of Engineers built a jetty on the north side of the bay's mouth, the jetty redirected the force of the ocean's waves, the waves began to eat away at Bayocean, and Bayocean began sliding away into the sea. Today on the peninsula, all that's left of the resort is its memory.

Cape Meares Lighthouse, 9 miles northwest of Tillamook off Three Capes Scenic Loop (see *Scenic Drives*). Built in 1890 atop a 200-foot cliff, this lighthouse flashed its red-and-white light—its 1-ton crystal lens hand ground in France and shipped around Cape Horn—toward sea for 73 years before an automated halogen light took its place.

FOR FAMILIES ✐ **Train Excursions** (503-842-2768), Oregon Coastline Express, Tillamook. This outfit offers two rides: the **Caboose Run,** in which a switcher engine pulls three cabooses along a 5-mile route from the city of Tillamook to the Port of Tillamook Bay Industrial Park, and the **Coastline Express,** a 25-mile ride from Tillamook to Wheeler.

Whale-Watching (1-800-551-6949; www.whalespoken.org), Oregon Parks and Recreation Department. Bigger than Greyhound buses and grayed from the barnacles growing on their skin, gray whales are wanderers that follow a schedule. During the peak of the spring season, which extends from mid-March through early June, 27 prime observation points marked by WHALE WATCHING SPOKEN HERE signs stretch along the coastline. At each site, volunteers answer visitors' questions as they help them spot whales. Whale-watching sites along this segment of the north coast include **Ecola State Park** near Cannon Beach, the historic marker at the **Neahkahnie Mountain** turnout near Manzanita, and the **Cape Meares State Scenic Viewpoint** and the tip of the cape at **Cape Lookout State Park** outside Tillamook.

SCENIC DRIVES **Mount Hebo,** 8 paved miles along Forest Road 14 from Hebo to Mount Hebo. The destination of this short, climbing drive is a 3,000-foot summit, where the view on a clear day can reach from the Cascade Mountains to the Pacific Ocean. It's a country so rugged and a mountain so buckled that the name *Hebo* supposedly comes from the reaction of an early-day survey party that climbed the mountain while searching for a route to the Willamette Valley and while at the summit named it "Heave Ho," which was subsequently misspelled "Hevo." The road to the top of old Heave Ho comes courtesy of the U.S. Air Force,

CAPE MEARES LIGHTHOUSE

which built a radar station here during the Cold War of the 1950s and operated it until 1980.

Nestucca River Back Country Byway, 54 paved and graveled miles along Blaine Road and the Nestucca River from Carlton to Beaver. Along this winding, slow-going route you'll follow one of the region's premier salmon and steelhead rivers as it passes through old-growth Douglas firs. (Some are claimed to be 200 feet tall and 400 years old, though that might be a stretch when it comes to this heavily logged area.) Along the way five recreation sites give you chances to camp, fish, swim, or explore near the river's riffles and pools.

Three Capes Scenic Loop, 32 paved miles from Tillamook to Pacific City. This byway that runs roughly parallel to Highway 101 hugs the ocean as its asphalt strings a connection among three bays (Tillamook, Netarts, and Nestucca), three capes (Meares, Lookout, and Kiwanda), and a passel of beaches, parks, and dunes before merging with the highway south of Pacific City.

NATURAL WONDERS **Haystack Rocks** (Cannon Beach and Pacific City). The Oregon coast has *two* rocks named Haystack because . . . well, because both rocks look like haystacks. One of the two landmarks stands offshore at Cannon Beach, a designated Marine Garden of such high sensitivity that all living things are protected for 300 meters in all directions. At 235 feet tall, it's listed by some sources as the third largest freestanding monolith in the world, a fact that has some folks in Pacific City scratching their heads in wonder, for *their* Haystack Rock, which looms offshore near Cape Kiwanda, stands more than 100 feet higher. Go figure.

✷ To Do

CAMPING **Wilson River Road,** northeast of Tillamook along Highway 6 and the Wilson River. Campgrounds from east to west include **Gales Creek,** with a trailhead leading up the slopes of the Coast Range; **Camp Brown,** popular with off-road vehicle enthusiasts; **Stagecoach,** designed as an equestrian camp; **Elk Creek,** the starting point for the Wilson River Wagon Route Trail for mountain bikers; **Diamond Mill,** popular with off-road vehicle enthusiasts; **Jones Creek,** near the Diamond Mill staging area for off-highway vehicles (OHVs); and **Keenig Creek,** near the confluence of Jordan Creek and the Wilson River.

Nehalem Falls, 7 miles east of Wheeler off Highway 101 and Foss Road, 18 campsites, including 4 walk-in sites among old-growth cedars and firs, along the Nehalem River and near Nehalem Falls, with nearby hiking trails.

Tillamook Area, north or east of Tillamook, located at the junction of Highways 6 and 101. In this land of rivers connecting the mountains to the sea, the waterways are famous for their runs of steelhead and salmon, and the campgrounds are often full with the anglers chasing them. In the off-season, however, both the fish and the camps are far less harried and more restful: **Barview County Park,** 2 miles north of Garibaldi off Highway 101, 260 shoreline campsites near the mouth of Tillamook Bay with nearby fishing from the jetty and hik-

TILLAMOOK BAY

ing along a segment of the Oregon Coast Trail that from here stretches north 64 miles to Fort Stevens; **Kilchis River Park,** 8 miles northeast of Tillamook off Highway 101 and the Kilchis River Road, 40 campsites along a lovely stretch of salmon stream that can show some wear and tear from eager anglers; **Trask River Park,** 12 miles east of Tillamook off Highway 101 and the Trask River Road, 60 campsites used heavily by steelheaders during the season.

Nestucca River, east of Blaine along Blaine Road and the Nestucca River, 5 primitive riverside campgrounds along the Nestucca River and just off a road designated a Back County Byway: **Rocky Bend, Alder Glen, Elks Bend, Fan Creek,** and **Dovre.**

Pacific City Area, north of Pacific City along Three Capes Scenic Loop (see *To See—Scenic Drives*) and near Sand Lake. A series of campgrounds for people drawn to the nearby ocean shore, sand dunes—and dune buggies—and Cape Kiwanda: **East Dunes, Island Park, Sandbeach, Webb County Park, Whalen Island,** and **West Winds.**

Hebo Area, south or east of Hebo, located at the junction of Highways 101 and 22: **Castle Rock,** 5 miles southeast of Hebo off Highway 22, 4 primitive campsites located near the highway and Three Rivers in the Siuslaw National Forest; **Hebo Lake,** 5 miles east of Hebo off Forest Road 14, 16 lakeside campsites near trailheads to the Pioneer Indian Trail and the Plantation Trail; **Mount Hebo,** 8 miles east of Hebo off Forest Road 14; **South Lake,** 10 miles east of Hebo off Forest Road 14.

See also *Wilder Places—Parks.*

HIKING **Ecola Point,** 2 miles north of Cannon Beach off Highway 101 and Park Road. This state park and **Lewis and Clark historic site** provides trailheads for two coastline hikes: **Indian Point,** a 3-mile round trip through meadows and forests;

and **Crescent Beach,** a 2.5-mile round trip that takes you down a forested slope to the beach.

Arch Cape, 4 miles south of Cannon Beach off Highway 101 and Arch Cape Mill Road. Less than 2 miles long, this trail begins at a suspension bridge, crosses a creek, cuts through a forest, and ends at the highway.

Neahkahnie Mountain, 11 miles south of Cannon Beach off Highway 101. A mile-long trail leads you not only to the top of this 1,631-foot mountain and its panoramic ocean views but also to a legend. When an 18th-century Spanish ship wrecked near here, the legend says, the survivors buried their treasure chests on this mountain, and treasure hunters have been searching for it ever since.

Netarts Spit, beginning at Cape Lookout State Park, 12 miles southwest of Tillamook off Highway 101 and Three Capes Scenic Loop (see *Scenic Drives*). This 5-mile stretch of surf-washed sand holds a slice of beach notable for its nothingness: no shops, no houses, no cars, no crowds—only driftwood and kelp, seabirds and harbor seals, and an occasional wanderer who finds pleasure in the long rumbles of breaking waves.

NETARTS SPIT

Niagara Falls, 8 miles southeast of Blaine off Blaine Road and Forest Road 1400. Everywhere in this forest lies the layered softness of quiet—until you near the trail's end and hear water plunging down a mountainside. Follow the sound, and a series of switchbacks, the only grade on the trail with any steepness to it, leads you down into a box canyon and two waterfalls: 100-foot **Pheasant Falls,** a cascade splashing its way down the cliff, and 130-foot **Niagara,** which pours in a tumbling free fall past a basalt rock wall.

Cape Lookout, 12 miles southwest of Tillamook off Highway 101 and Three Capes Scenic Loop (see *To See—Scenic Drives*). Formed by lava and cooled by the sea, Cape Lookout is a 2-mile finger of basalt that points to the sea. The 2.5-mile trail that traces this finger along its 800-foot top wanders through a forest that soaks up 100 inches of rain per year, ending at a cliff-top meadow that overlooks the passing of whales. "Cape Lookout," said Sam Boardman, the father of Oregon's park system, "[is] an ocean observatory with a seaward view unexcelled from any point of the coastal universe."

♿ **Hebo Area,** east of Hebo off Forest Road 14. On the way to Hebo Mountain, you can explore swatches of countryside by following any of four trails: **Plantation Trail,** 4 miles east of Hebo, a half-mile path through stands of Douglas fir planted in 1910 to replace the old-growth trees lost in an 1890 fire, one of the country's oldest reforestation projects; **Hebo Lake,** 5 miles east of Hebo, a half-mile, **wheel-**

chair-accessible shoreline trail with fishing platforms along the way; **Pioneer Indian Trail,** 5 miles east of Hebo, an 1854 road converted to an 8-mile trail lying between Hebo Lake and South Lake—its trailhead is at Hebo Lake—though you can shorten the hike to 3 miles by arranging a pickup near Mount Hebo on Forest Road 14; **Mount Hebo,** 8 miles east of Hebo, a short but steep climb to a view at the summit, though you can also drive to the top.

Cascade Head, 5 miles northwest of Otis off Highway 101 and Three Rocks Road. From the 1,200-foot highlands of Cascade Head, the views encompass sea and river and estuary, forests and mountains and sky, all of it connected with climbing and winding trails that total 6 miles in length. But please tread softly here. "It's a place that's in danger of being loved to death," says an official with the Nature Conservancy, which owns a portion of Cascade Head. The problem results when large numbers of visitors (more than 10,000 per year) come into contact with a fragile environment (the site of some of the state's last remaining prairie lands of native grasses and wildflowers as well as some rare species of plants and threatened species of butterflies). As a result, you're asked to stay on the trails and leave your dogs behind.

See also *Camping* and *Wilder Places—Parks.*

✷ Wilder Places

PARKS **Hug Point State Park,** 5 miles south of Cannon Beach off Highway 101, day use only. In the days when Oregon's beaches were also the main coastal highways, motorists waited for low tide, then "hugged" this point tightly to get around it. Today, sightseers and hikers still must keep an eye on the tide when exploring this headland, though the reward for doing so is a fine stretch of beach with a waterfall and sandstone caves.

Oswald West State Park, 11 miles south of Cannon Beach off Highway 101, day use and overnight. Named for the governor who gave Oregon's beaches to its people, this park lies at the end of a short walk into a new world, a quarter-mile stroll that leaves behind the rumble of traffic along Highway 101 and leads to the shoreline and headlands of what has been called "the scenic window of our coastline." Providing a front-row seat at the window—whose views include two rocky capes, one quiet cove, and a partridge in . . . er, a mountain with a cloud-swirled summit—is a primitive, walk-in campground nestled beneath the towering limbs of an old-growth forest. This park also provides trailheads for hikes to **Cape Falcon** and **Neahkahnie Mountain.**

Nehalem Bay State Park, 3 miles southwest of Nehalem off Highway 101, day use and overnight. Through the millennia, the outgoing flow of the Nehalem River has shoved back at the incoming waves and tide of the Pacific, forming a sand spit that protects this bay from the sea. And along this spit today, hundreds of campsites and miles of trails lie within walking distance of the ocean, the estuary, and the bay, opening the door to exploring the area by foot or horse, bike or boat.

Memorial Lumberman's Park, Third and American Streets, Garibaldi. A combination of picnic area and history display, Memorial Lumberman's Park exhibits logging and railroad equipment from the area's timber cutting and milling days.

Munson Creek Falls State Park, 7 miles south of Tillamook off Highway 101 and Munson Creek Road, day use only. This is Oregon's newest state park, number 228 on the list, a 61-acre tract of century-old forest that is home to the state's second-highest waterfall. With 266 feet of vertical plunge—some say the height of the falls is 300 feet—Munson Creek roars its splashy way down over toppled logs, dripping ferns, and mossy rocks. If you cross a rocky sidestream, duck beneath a fallen trunk, and step down the bank, you'll find at the foot of the falls a picnic table, where nearby springs dribble off basalt hillsides smothered in green. (Oregon's highest waterfall is 620-foot Multnomah Falls in the Columbia River Gorge east of Portland.)

Cape Meares State Park, 9 miles northwest of Tillamook off Three Capes Scenic Loop (see *To See—Scenic Drives*), day use only. Gathered here at this 233-acre day-use park are an offshore wildlife refuge, a historic lighthouse, a picnic area, a system of nature trails, and the **Octopus Tree**—a Sitka spruce whose gigantic, contorted limbs have become the object of wonder and the subject of a legend, which says local tribes shaped the tree to hold the canoes of the dead.

Cape Lookout State Park, 12 miles southwest of Tillamook off Highway 101 and Three Capes Scenic Loop (see *To See—Scenic Drives*), day use and overnight. When the original park was established in 1935, plans called for it to remain mostly in a primitive state. "If there were ever the need of a bird sanctuary," said park superintendent Sam Boardman, "it is here." Mr. Boardman had in mind the 154 species of birds found here, their presence creating what he called "a recreational wonderland unequaled in the nation." Yet that's exactly what made the cape an increasingly popular place, until today the park consists of more than 2,000 acres and a very busy campground.

Cape Kiwanda State Park, 1 mile north of Pacific City off Three Capes Scenic Loop (see *To See—Scenic Drives*), day use only. The sculpted cliffs of Cape Kiwanda and the craggy sides of **Haystack Rock** (see *To See—Natural Wonders*) are the landmarks of this beach where dories launch into the waves and hang gliders from the dunes.

Bob Straub State Park, end of Sunset Drive in Pacific City off Highway 101, day use only. If you want to take a shoreline stroll that leaves behind most of the crowd, follow the surf through pathless Bob Straub Park. "Very few people use the park, which is good," says the park's namesake, Bob Straub, who spent a noteworthy career in state politics, including serving as governor from 1975 to 1979. "You can always be by yourself hiking up and down the beach." That flat, sandy hike will lead you 2.5 miles to the mouth of Nestucca Bay, an estuary edged by shore pines and mudflats and the wriggling slide and snort of seals.

WILDLIFE REFUGES **Tide Pools.** The tide rolls in and then rolls out, and in the hollows of the rocks and the sand, it leaves behind a watery world of animals and plant forms. And if you step carefully and patiently into this world during a calm low tide, you may meet the citizens of the tide pool: **sea urchins** and **starfish, mussels** and

barnacles and **crabs. Ecola State Park,** 2 miles north of Cannon Beach off Highway 101; **Haystack Rock,** offshore of Cannon Beach off Highway 101, access at Gower and Second; **Cape Meares,** 10 miles northwest of Tillamook off Three Capes Scenic Loop (see *To See—Scenic Drives*), access at Short Beach, 1 mile north of Oceanside; **Maxwell Point,** 9 miles northwest of Tillamook off Three Capes Scenic Loop and near Oceanside; **Cape Lookout,** 18 southwest of Tillamook off Three Capes Scenic Loop and on the south side of the cape; **Cape Kiwanda State Natural Area,** 2 miles north of Pacific City off Three Capes Scenic Loop.

Oregon Islands National Wildlife Refuge. Scattered along the Oregon coast are more than 1,400 reefs, rocks, and islands that provide a total of 762 acres of habitat for wildlife. These offshore refuges provide nesting sites for more than a million **seabirds**—a population greater than that found along the combined coastlines of Washington and California—and resting, pupping, and molting sites for thousands of **seals** and **seal lions.** Even though these areas are closed to the public, many are visible from shoreline viewpoints in this region, including at the following state parks off Highway 101 or the Three Capes Scenic Loop (see *To See—Scenic Drives*): **Ecola,** 2 miles north of Cannon Beach; **Oswald West,** 11 miles south of Cannon Beach; **Cape Meares,** 9 miles northwest of Tillamook; **Oceanside,** 11 miles northwest of Tillamook; and **Cape Lookout,** 12 miles southwest of Tillamook.

OSWALD WEST STATE PARK

Three Arch Rocks, 11 miles west of Tillamook off Three Capes Scenic Loop (see *To See—Scenic Drives*). This was the nation's first wildlife refuge established west of the Mississippi River, and each year from April through August a quarter-million seabirds nest on the 15 acres here, making it the home of Oregon's largest seabird colonies. **Tufted puffins, storm petrels, pigeon guillemots, cormorants,** and **gulls** all nest here, with **common murres** especially numerous, reaching numbers of 75,000. In addition, harbor seals and sea lions haul out here near the base of the rocks. Even though the area is off-limits to human visitors, good observation points exist nearby; one of them is at **Oceanside State Park.**

✷ Lodging

INNS

Cannon Beach

Cannon Beach Hotel (1-800-238-4107; cbh@oregoncoastlodgings.com; www.cannonbeachhotel.com), 116 S.

Hemlock, Cannon Beach 97110. Built in 1900 and remodeled in 1992, this hotel has kept its guest-gathering lobby and fireplace while offering nine guest rooms ($69–159). Four of the rooms have spas, four have fireplaces, and all have private baths. In addition, guests can gather in front of the fireplace in the lobby. Each morning, a continental breakfast and the morning paper are delivered to your room.

Inn at Haystack Rock (1-877-507-2714; haystack@innathaystackrock.com; www.innathaystackrock.com), 487 S. Hemlock, Cannon Beach 97110. If when you first see Inn at Haystack Rock you find it to be a small, quaint inn, you'd be right. "Ours is a small, quaint inn," says owner Marsha La Farge. But it's also clean and bright with baskets and pots and beds of flowers growing as only the coast can grow them. The inn has seven guest rooms, each with a deck so you can watch those flowers, and most have skylights, vaulted ceilings, queen beds, fireplaces, and a "snack kitchen" containing microwaves and refrigerators ($67–126).

Wheeler

Old Wheeler Hotel (1-877-653-4683; winston@oldwheelerhotel.com; www.oldwheelerhotel.com), 495 Highway 101, Wheeler 97147. In an earlier life, this historic hotel on the edge of Nehalem Bay served time as the Rhinehart Clinic, where people came to be cured of arthritis. "The history of the place includes many stories of healing, of people coming in on crutches and leaving by dancing out the door!" says owner Winston Laszlo. "We believe that this spirit of healing and transformation still inhabits the building, and have often felt it guiding us throughout the restoration project." That restoration, which required more than three years, has brought new life to the old building. "It was a labor of love," Winston says, "to turn what was a neglected—almost abandoned—structure into a retreat that we like to think of as having old-world comfort and charm." The hotel's five guest rooms come with private baths, bay views, king or queen beds, a newspaper delivered to your door, and a continental breakfast served in the "common room" ($55–110). Perhaps more important, however, is that the hotel can be the beginning of a larger experience with the area itself. "It offers a relaxing stay in a curious old building," Winston says, "in a sweet little historic town with a panoramic view of Nehalem Bay."

BED & BREAKFASTS

Arch Cape

St. Bernards, a Bed & Breakfast (1-800-436-2848; bernards@pacifier.com; www.pacifier.com/~bernards), 3 E. Ocean Road, Arch Cape 97102. The French influence carries beyond the name of this B&B, for this 1995 home with an ocean view is built in the style of a two-story French chateau and furnished with European antiques. Its seven rooms all come with private baths, and guests have access to a workout room and sauna ($129–189). Children older than 12 are welcome.

Shaw's Oceanfront Bed & Breakfast (1-888-269-4483; innkeeper@shawsoceanfrontbb.com; www.shawsoceanfrontbb.com), 79924 Cannon Road, Arch Cape 97102. With a garden in front and the ocean in back, the home of Barbara and Jim Shaw can carry the scent of flowers and surf. "We have direct access to a clean beach," Jim says, "and all its good activities—kite flying, sand castles, beach fires, and games." The inn's ocean-view suite includes two bathrooms, a full kitchen, and a fireplace ($135–195).

Bay City

Miami River Inn (503-322-0291; miamiriverinn@wcn.net; www.wcn.net/miamiriverinn), 13555 Ekroth Road, Bay City 97107. Settled on 37 wooded hillside acres that include a blueberry farm, this inn shares its large yard with wildlife. "We have about a half mile of Miami River frontage," says owner Janna Crabb, "where salmon runs still flourish and wildlife abounds." Nearby lies the beach as well as trails running along the river and through the forest. Three of the inn's rooms come with shared baths ($75–90) and one room with a private bath ($110). All are situated near a view of Tillamook Bay at Garibaldi, and the full breakfast Janna says, "always begins with dessert. Cobbler and biscotti are specialties." In addition, the entire inn is wheelchair and handicapped accessible. "We honor diversity," Jan says, "and enjoy serving families at affordable rates."

Cannon Beach

Littell's Bed & Breakfast (503-436-1306; littell@seasurf.com; www.visitcb.com/littell), 3623 S. Hemlock, Cannon Beach 97110. Built in the traditional design of a 19th-century farmhouse, Littell's offers three rooms, each with a queen bed and private bath ($150–175). Breakfast features fresh baking and homemade jelly, jam, and syrup.

Tern Inn Bed & Breakfast (503-436-1528; innkeeper@terninn.com; www.terninn.com), 3663 S. Hemlock Street, Cannon Beach 97110. Standing high enough on a rise in Cannon Beach to look over the rooftops and out to the Pacific, this small inn has two big rooms. Both have queen beds as well as private baths, entrances, and decks ($125–170). A full breakfast is served in the dining room, which has a view of Haystack Rock.

Cloverdale

Hudson House Bed & Breakfast (1-888-835-3533; mharris@worldpost.com; www.hudsonhouse.com), 37700 Highway 101 S. Cloverdale 97112. A Victorian home that overlooks the Nestucca River Valley and the Coast Range, Hudson House gives guests space and calm. "It's an escape to slower, quieter times," says owner Irma Scroggins, "a relaxing getaway from the stresses of everyday life." Of its four rooms, three have queen beds and all come with private baths and a full breakfast ($90–110) in a place that Irma calls "a home away from home."

Sandlake Country Inn (503-965-6745; rondiane@pacifier.com; www.sandlakecountryinn.com), 8505 Galloway Road, Cloverdale 97112. Some of the material that makes up this inn came from bridge timbers that were the cargo of an 1894 ship that wrecked along the coast, yet its four guest rooms ($100–145) are completely modern. "I believe the thing that sets us apart from other B&Bs is the pampering we offer our guests along with privacy and romance," says owner Diane Emineth. "We deliver breakfast to each spacious room, there are no shared walls, and the rooms have Jacuzzi tubs for two people and fireplaces." In addition, the inn is settled in an area of creeks, forests, and wildlife just a mile from the ocean.

Garibaldi

✐ **Pelican's Perch Lodge** (503-322-3633; thomas@pelicansperchlodge.com; www.pelicansperchlodge.com), 112 E. Cypress Ave., Garibaldi 97118. This shingled home began its life in 1913 as a boardinghouse in a fishing village. Today the views from here of Tillamook Bay and the Coast Range remain much the same, though the house has changed to include four antiques-decorated guest rooms ($108–128), Jacuzzi tubs, a koi pond, and gardens. In addition, each morning's breakfast is prepared by a resident chef. Children older than 12 are welcome.

Manzanita

The Arbors Bed & Breakfast (1-888-664-9587; arbors@doormat.com), 78 Idaho Avenue, Manzanita 97130. Bordered by a white picket fence and surrounded by flower gardens, this 1922 English cottage offers a beach just 200 feet away, three guest rooms with private baths ($105–115), a full breakfast served family style, and friendly hospitality. "We offer our inn as *your* place at the beach," say owners Judd and Lee Burrows. "Many of our guests, even those from across the world, comment on how much 'at home' they feel here."

Oceanside

SeaRose Bed & Breakfast (503-842-6126; www.searosebandb.com), 1685 Maxwell Mountain Road, Oceanside 97134. The drive to this B&B by the sea is part of the adventure, for it lies along **Three Capes Scenic Loop** (see *To See—Scenic Drives*), one of the loveliest stretches of road anywhere. Yet it was one stop along the way that made SeaRose owner Judy Gregoire fall in love. "When I discovered tiny Oceanside clinging to the side of Maxwell Mountain," she says, "it felt as though time reversed suddenly and we were back in the '50s, before high-rise, strip, and discount malls and a revved up pace that didn't allow for leisure walks on a secluded beach." So Judy settled into life at Oceanside, which she calls "my favorite place on earth," and opened the SeaRose, which is far from the strip malls yet just a hop from **Oceanside State Park,** a skip from **Three Arch Rocks National Wildlife Refuge** and the **Cape Meares Lighthouse,** and a jump from **Bayocean Peninsula** and **Netarts Bay.** "Here in Oceanside," Judy says "we are proud that our only attractions are natural beauty, wildlife, miles of sandy beach, and a return to the 'stuff' that matters." The B&B's two guest room each come with a queen bed, private bath, and full breakfast ($95–115) as well as a warm welcome. "My mission at SeaRose," Judy says, "is to open the door wide for the unmet friend and offer hospitality second to none."

Pacific City

Eagle's View Bed & Breakfast (1-888-846-3292; innkeeper@eaglesviewbb.com; www.eaglesviewbb.com), 37975 Brooten Road, Pacific City 97135. With a high hilltop view of the Little Nestucca River and Nestucca Bay, this 1995 two-story home is lined with porches and decks while its 4 acres of grounds are crossed with walking paths. "Eagle's View is a unique experience for visitors because of our private setting," says owner Steve Westmoreland. "We offer a hot-tub spa under the stars, nature trails, a fish pond, a bird sanctuary, and a wraparound deck for relaxation." The inn's five guest rooms all have private baths (three of them have Jacuzzi tubs) and come with a full breakfast served in either the great room or your guest room ($99–125).

COTTAGES **McBee Motel Cottages** (866-262-2336; info@sandtrapinn.com; www.mcbeecottages.com), 888 S. Hemlock Street, Cannon Beach 97110. If you're old enough to remember VJ Day, the "I Like Ike" presidential campaign, and Joe DiMaggio, then this motel might seem strangely familiar—probably because it has changed little since it opened for business in 1941. Sure, the paint is fresh and the rooms clean, but these small cottages have escaped glitzy development. Located less than a block from the ocean, the motel offers 12 units, some with fireplaces and kitchens, and outside lies a lawn and picnic tables ($45–145).

* Where to Eat

DINING OUT

Cannon Beach

The Bistro (503-436-2661), 263 N. Hemlock Street, Cannon Beach. Short on space but big on quality, the Bistro opened in the mid-1980s as one of the first restaurants in Cannon Beach to earn a reputation for quality dining. Today that reputation draws folks eager to sample the restaurant's seafood and steaks.

Kalypso (503-436-1586), 140 N. Hemlock Street, Cannon Beach. Even though seafood is a staple along the Oregon coast, the Kalypso, named for the Siren in Homer's *Odyssey*, manages to make its offerings stand out above those of many other restaurants in the area.

Manzanita

Jarboe's (503-368-5113), 137 Laneda Avenue, Manzanita. With only eight linen-covered tables gathered in its soft light, Jarboe's provides a romantic atmosphere for diners as well as the mesquite-grilled steaks or fish.

Oceanside

Roseanna's Café (503-842-7351), 1490 Pacific Avenue N. W., Oceanside. The decor, the view, the service, the conviviality, the food, the presentation—all go into making Roseanna's one of the finest restaurants on the Oregon coast. The menu features fresh seafood prepared in many variations, several pastas served with chicken, as well as baked or grilled oysters and much more. Recommended starters with intriguing names include Angels on Horseback and Saints on a Wire; desserts are all made in-house from family recipes; and the view of the sun setting behind Three Arch Rocks National Wildlife Refuge is memorable.

EATING OUT

Cannon Beach

Midtown Café (503-436-1016), 1235 S. Hemlock, Cannon Beach. A local favorite, the Midtown serves some of the best breakfasts and lunches around. From banana waffles to salami and eggs, and from lentil burgers to pork burritos, almost everything offered on the menu is homemade.

Manzanita

Blue Sky Café (503-368-5712), 154 Laneda Avenue, Manzanita. Perhaps the genius of some chefs lies in their talent to concoct delicious dishes from seemingly . . . er . . . weird combinations. A meal at the Blue Sky Café, for instance, can include fare such as crab and coconut soup, or salmon with squash polenta. Unusual, sure, but also good enough that if you don't have reservations you may not find a seat.

Cassandra's (503-368-5593), 60 Laneda Avenue, Manzanita. With a seashore and surfboard motif decorating its interior, Cassandra's doesn't look like what it does—makes some of the best pizza on the coast. The stuff that goes on the crust is fresh, organic, and compelling enough to make you return again, as many people do.

Oceanside

Anchor Tavern (503-842-2041), 1495 Pacific Avenue, Oceanside. A local hangout and tourist attraction, the Anchor Tavern offers pub food such as hamburgers, smoked ribs, fish-and-chips, and pizza good enough that it borders on legendary status in the area.

Pacific City

Grateful Bread (503-965-7337), 34805 Brooten Road, Pacific City. The name of this bakery is an indication of its relaxed, fun atmosphere, a place where locals gather over coffee and where anyone can find some of the best breakfasts and lunches in the area.

Pelican Pub (503-965-7007), 33180 Cape Kiwanda Drive, Pacific City. Award-winning beer, excellent food, ocean views, and a friendly atmosphere make this a good place to stop when you're in the Cape Kiwanda area.

Riverhouse (503-965-6722), 34450 Brooten Road, Pacific City. This is a funky, homey, 40-seat restaurant where they offer at least three fresh soups daily and make their own salad dressings. In addition, when they tell you the seafood on the menu is fresh, they mean *really* fresh. The same sense of quality characterizes the restaurant's steak dinners. And if that's not enough, sometimes you can catch live music in the form of a couple of guitar players and singers.

✷ Special Events

May: **Spring Kite Festival** (503-355-8108), Rockaway. A strong breeze, a long string, and an agile kite can seem to lift you to the kind of heights John Gillespie Magee describes in his poem "High Flight": Sunward I've climbed, and joined the tumbling mirth / Of sun-split clouds—and done a hundred things / You have not dreamed of—wheeled and soared and swung / High in the sunlit silence.

June: **Tillamook Dairy Festival and Parade** (503-842-7525), Tillamook. **Sand Castle Contest** (503-436-2623), Cannon Beach. Open to all comers, this contest is for both serious and playful artists who don't mind a day's work being erased by an incoming tide.

July: **Dory Festival** (503-965-6162), Pacific City. To appreciate this festival you must first understand its guest of honor, the dory, which is a flat-bottomed, double-ended fishing boat whose pointed bow and stern let it slide over the waves. Though most of today's dories use outboard motors, the traditional power source consisted of two fishermen rowing with long spruce oars. Since the early 1920s, local fishermen have launched their dories from the beach at the base of Cape Kiwanda and near Haystack Rock, perhaps the only such site on the Pacific Coast. Highlights of this summertime tribute to the boat and its fishermen include a lineup of dories in the town's parade, as well as a dory race that begins and ends at the traditional launch site near Haystack Rock.

September: **Sand Castle Contest** (503-355-8108), Rockaway. Everyone's welcome at this sand-sculpting contest where sand assumes the shapes of contestants' imagination.

LINCOLN CITY–DEPOE BAY–NEWPORT AREA

GUIDANCE **Depoe Bay Chamber of Commerce** (541-765-2889; www.stateof-oregon.com/depoe_bay/chamber), 70 N. E. Highway 101, Depoe Bay 97341.

Greater Newport Chamber of Commerce (1-800-262-7844; www.newportchamber.org), 555 S. W. Coast Highway, Newport 97365.

Lincoln City Visitors and Convention Bureau (1-800-452-2151; www.oregoncoast.org), 801 S. W. Highway 101, Lincoln City 97367.

Oregon State Parks: **Headquarters** (503-378-6305), State Parks and Recreation Department, 525 Trade Street S. E., Salem 97301.

Toledo Chamber of Commerce (541-336-3183), 311 N. E. First Street, Toledo 97391.

GETTING THERE Lincoln City, Depoe Bay, Newport, and nearby communities are reached from the east by Highways 18 and 20 and are linked by Highway 101, which runs the entire length of the Oregon coast.

MEDICAL EMERGENCY **Samaritan North Lincoln Hospital** (541-994-3661), 3043 N. E. 28th Street, Lincoln City.
Samaritan Pacific Communities Hospital (541-265-2244), 930 S. W. Abbey, Newport.

✷ To See

MUSEUMS **North Lincoln County Historical Museum** (541-996-6614), 4907 S. W. Highway 101, Lincoln City. Housed in a former fire station, this museum contains artifacts of the Siletz tribe, memorabilia from the area's homesteading era, tools used in regional logging operations, and replicas of a 1920s store and a 1930s home. One of the museum's most curious artifacts is a deactivated Japanese horned mine that washed ashore at nearby Gleneden Beach in 1949. And one of its most interesting stories concerns Jane Baxter, a Tillamook woman whose fishing technique involved wading the mudflats of Salmon River and pinning flounder beneath her feet. She would then "thrust a spear held between her toes into the fish, pick it up and put it in her sack." When she died in 1935, this aspect of the angler's art most likely died with her.

Oregon Coast History Center (541-265-7509), 545 S. W. Ninth Street, Newport. With almost 40,000 artifacts collected since 1948, and with its displays dating back to the mid-1800s and ranging in subject matter from native tribes to modern tourism, this center is a storehouse of local history divided into two museums, one housed in a log cabin and the other in an 1895 Victorian house.

Toledo History Museum (541-265-7509), 206 N. Main Street, Toledo. Because this city was built on a tradition of logging and sawmills, its museum does the same, featuring memorabilia gathered from forests, mills, and railroads.

Yaquina Pacific Railroad Society (541-336-5256), next to the post office in Toledo. Take a do-it-yourself tour of the rolling stock and other artifacts collected here to preserve the area's railroad and logging history.

HISTORIC SITES **Jason Lee Campsite,** 1333 N. W. 17th Street, Lincoln City. This site helps answer a daunting question: If you get married on the edge of a wilderness more than 2,000 miles by horseback from home, where do you go for a honeymoon? Well, if you're Jason Lee or Cyrus Shepard, two early-day missionaries in the Oregon Country, you do in 1837 what many people do today—you head for the coast. And so they hired a guide, packed up their horses, and brought their brides over the mountains and through the brush to this campsite, where they stayed for a week. As a result, the Lees and the Shepards have earned the title of First [White] Honeymooners on the Oregon coast. (No word about what guide Joe Gervais did to make himself scarce during the honeymoon week.)

Yaquina Head Lighthouse, 3 miles north of Newport off Highway 101. This is the lighthouse that replaced the one at Yaquina Bay—but it didn't come easily. First, workers built stairs to the construction site, cutting the steps out of rock; then they used a windlass and derrick to pull lumber and cement up the stone staircase to build the lighthouse. But the work paid off in a still-active lighthouse whose years of service are exceeded in Oregon only by the Cape Blanco Light Station on the southern coast.

Newport Waterfront. Built in the late 19th or early 20th century, the buildings lining Yaquina Bay Road are still in use as shops, restaurants, or fish-packing houses. The fishing boats and sea lions along the waterfront, however, make it easy to imagine the days when men would return from the sea to swagger their way into taverns such as the Sea Hag.

Yaquina Bay Lighthouse, 1 mile south of Newport at Yaquina Bay State Park off Highway 101. Soon after this lighthouse was constructed in 1870, its major flaw became apparent: Yaquina Head, jutting out from the mainland several miles to the north, blocked its light. Oops. So after serving only a few years, this lighthouse was replaced in 1873 by a new, more visible one standing on Yaquina Head. Today the combination lighthouse/lighthouse keeper's quarters—the only one like it in the state—retains a sense of the 1870s in its furnishings as well as in the persistence of the stories that claim the place has long been haunted by a ghost named Muriel.

COVERED BRIDGES Before bridges carried people and freight over the rivers, ferries did the job. But once folks balancing the books figured out that bridges cost less to build and maintain than ferries did to operate, the state legislature began encouraging the private construction of toll bridges. And covering those bridges, especially along the coast, was a good way to shed the wet and so ensure a long-term investment. **Drift Creek,** 5 miles southeast of Lincoln City off Highway 101 and Drift Creek Road, built in 1914 (the state's oldest surviving covered bridge), 66 feet long. **Chitwood,** 10 miles northeast of Toledo off Highway 20 near Chitwood, built in 1926 (rebuilt 1983–1984), 96 feet long.

FOR FAMILIES **Garden Tour** (541-994-6338), Connie Hansen Garden, 1931 N. W. 33rd Street, Lincoln City. For 20 years, from the time she moved to Lincoln City in 1973 until she died in 1993, Constance P. Hansen worked to turn the 1-acre plot of land surrounding her home into a garden. The result is a showcase of azaleas, primroses, irises, geraniums, and more than 300 species of rare rhododendrons. "Today," says the Lincoln City *News Guard,* "the Connie Hansen Garden is a wonder to behold." And it's open all year to visitors.

✐ **Hatfield Marine Science Center** (541-867-0271), Marine Science Drive, Newport, on the south shore of Yaquina Bay off Highway 101. Think of this center as an apartment house for fish, the walls lined with aquarium glass and filled with seawater, the inhabitants within going about the routine of their lives with undulating fins and gills and occasionally returning the stares of those taking peeks into their fishy world. Yet the center appeals to more than just the eyes, for here you'll find a miniature tide pool in a tub, where kids of all ages are invited to plunge their hands and touch the critters, as well as an octopus tank, whose resident appears willing to shake tentacles with you.

✐ **Oregon Coast Aquarium** (541-867-3474; www.aquarium.org), 2820 S. E. Ferry Slip Road, Newport. On 29 acres of the south shore of Yaquina Bay stands one of Oregon's major tourist attractions: a 40,000-square-foot aquarium that is home to 90 species of coastal or marine animals. Inside, the accommodations include replications of water, shore, and wetlands habitats; outside, the animals live in a tide pool, trout stream, otter pool, octopus cave, or seabird aviary.

Whale-Watching (1-800-551-6949; www.whalespoken.org), Oregon Parks and Recreation Department. In November, gray whales leave their summer home in the Bering Sea, and by December they begin reaching the sunny lagoons of Mexico's Baja Peninsula, where they breed and calve. Once the calves are able to travel—most are born in January and February—the whales begin heading north again to the Bering Sea. During that spring migration, you have a good chance of spotting whales near **Depoe Bay** at **Boiler Bay, Rocky Creek,** and **Otter Crest State Scenic Viewpoints** off Highway 101 and near **Newport** at **Devils Punch Bowl State Natural Area, Yaquina Head Lighthouse and Outstanding Natural Area, Don A. Davis City Kiosk,** and **Yaquina Bay State Recreation Site.**

SCENIC DRIVES **Pacific Coast Scenic Byway—northern segment** (185 paved miles from Astoria to Florence along Highway 101). From the Columbia River at Astoria to the Siuslaw River at Florence, this road skirts the shoreline of the Pacific, winding past headlands and beaches, crossing over estuaries and bays, and climbing through foothills and toward ocean views along a route that is one of the most beautiful and famous drives in America. In addition, numerous viewpoints, pullouts, and state parks along the way provide dozens of entries for anyone wanting to wade the surf, comb the beach, or watch a sunset.

NATURAL WONDERS **D River,** flows beneath Highway 101 in Lincoln City. Starting at its headwaters in Devils Lake, D River flows 120 feet to the sea, making it the shortest river in the world. Even if you pause with every step to peer into the water or beneath the rocks, you'll still be able to walk its length in short order, then go home and tell your friends how you followed a stream from its source to the sea.

Valley of the Giants, 18 miles northeast of Siletz off County Road 410 and the North Siletz River Road. The home of some of Oregon's largest trees, this 47-acre preserve of old-growth forest was first protected in 1976 as an "outstanding natural area." Here some of the **Douglas firs** and **western hemlocks** date back as far as 500 years, with a dozen or more reaching circumferences of more than 20 feet—the combined arm span of four people—and a 2-mile loop steers you to them. (Access to the area is through land owned by timber companies, open only on weekends during daylight hours.)

Spouting Horns, off Highway 101 at **Depoe Bay**. When high tides or surging storms—or, preferably, both—push the ocean toward the shore and into a collision with the mainland, the result can be a spouting horn, a towering spray of water shooting into the air. One of the best and most accessible places along the coast to find spouting horns is at the roadside seawall overlooking Depoe Bay.

* To Do

CAMPING **Elk City,** 6 miles east of Toledo off Highway 20, 7 campsites along the bank of the Yaquina River. See also *Wilder Places—Parks.*

GOLF **Salishan Golf Links** (1-800-890-0387), 7760 N. Highway 101, Gleneden Beach, 18 holes.

Sandpines Golf Links (1-800-917-4653), 1201 35th Street, Florence, 18 holes.

HIKING **Drift Creek Falls,** 13 miles southeast of Lincoln City off Highway 101, Drift Creek Road, and Forest Road 17. This 1.5-mile path—it's steep going in, just as steep coming out—leads to a waterfall that plunges 75 feet into a pool and a suspension bridge that spans 240 feet, holding you loftily above the creek's chasm, the waters flowing 100 feet below.

* Wilder Places

PARKS **Devils Lake State Park,** 1 mile north of Lincoln City off Highway 101, day use and overnight. Local tribes may have believed a devilish spirit inhabited this lake's waters, and Jason Lee, one of the Oregon Country's first missionaries, may have honeymooned near here in 1837 (see

Jason Lee Campsite under *To See—Historic Sites*), yet today this 678-acre park with its 3-mile long freshwater lake is a welcome retreat for visitors who come to use its campgrounds, picnic areas, boat launch, and wildlife viewing.

Taft Waterfront Park, 51st Street off Highway 101 at the mouth of the Siletz River, Lincoln City. Not many parks can offer visitors what this one does: the chance to go clamming at low tide while listening to the barks of sea lions.

Siletz River Parks, northwest and northeast of Siletz along Highway 219, County Road 410, and the Siletz River. Follow the Siletz River into the Coast Range, and you'll find the river changing from tidal slack to mountain stream. You'll also find a few streamside parks that give you a chance to try out the waters: **Jack Morgan Park,** 7 free campsites along the riverbank and a boat ramp; **Twin Bridges Memorial Park,** a swimming hole popular with area residents; **Moonshine County Park,** 18 acres of campsites, picnic areas, playgrounds, and a boat launch.

Fogarty Creek State Park, 2 miles north of Depoe Bay off Highway 101, day use only. The creek itself shapes this park: Trees shade it, trails trace it, bridges cross it, and a cove finally drains it to the sea. For many people, this is enough to make the park a favorite stop.

State Scenic Viewpoints, from north of Depoe Bay to north of Florence along Highway 101. If you just want to slip quietly off the road for a moment and leave the traffic behind as you watch waves, birds, or whales, this stretch of highway offers some exceptional wayside viewpoints, including the following from north to south: **Boiler Bay, Rocky Creek, Otter Crest, Yachats Ocean Road, Muriel O. Ponsler,** and **Sea Lion Point.**

Devils Punch Bowl State Park, 8 miles north of Newport off Highway 101 and Otter Crest Loop, day use only. The punch bowl that serves as the centerpiece of this 4-acre park is a rock cavern where in-rushing waves churn themselves into a high-splashing froth.

Beverly Beach State Park, 7 miles north of Newport off Highway 101, day use and overnight. Its beach is what makes this park one of the most used in the state, with its long stretch of sand appealing to kite flyers, surfboard riders, and sand castle builders. Its campground, which lies on the opposite side of the highway, includes a nature trail and playground, and a walkway leads beneath the highway to the beach.

Yaquina Bay State Park, on the western edge of Newport and near the mouth of Yaquina Bay, day use only. Standing on a bluff 100 feet above the mouth of Yaquina Bay stands one of the most popular parks in the state with almost 2 million visitors per year. One of the main attractions here—besides the nearby bay, beach, and sea—is the **historic 1871 lighthouse,** now serving as a museum.

South Beach State Park, 2 miles south of Newport off Highway 101, day use and overnight. This park offers a doorway to all things Yaquina: Yaquina Bay, Yaquina Bay Bridge, Yaquina Bay jetty, **Yaquina Bay Lighthouse, Yaquina Head Lighthouse.** Mixed in with the Yaquinas are campgrounds, picnic areas, and nature trails.

Lost Creek State Park, 7 miles south of Newport off Highway 101, day use only. This park's 34 acres consists mostly of shoreline spotted with a few picnic tables that overlook the rolling surf, a stretch of the Oregon Coast Trail, and the flights of gulls and pelicans.

Ona Beach State Park, 8 miles south of Newport off Highway 101, day use only. Here where the flow of Beaver Creek meets the tidewater of the Pacific, the banks bend and the waters deepen and folks can settle down with their picnic baskets and watch the slow drift of this coastal stream and its wildlife.

Ellmaker State Park, 31 miles east of Newport off Highway 20, day use only. This 77-acre rest area contains little in the way of development (a few picnic tables and a rest room) but lots in the way of quiet among its trees and meadow and stream. The land's donor, Harlan D. Ellmaker, called it "My Garden of Eden."

WILDLIFE REFUGES **Tide Pools.** The ebb and flow of tides, and the life the tidal change supports in the hollows and crevices of rocks and sand, can introduce you to a whole new universe spread out beneath your feet. Along this segment of the north coast, some of the best tide pools can be found at **Otter Rock,** 9 miles north of Newport at **Devils Punch Bowl State Natural Area** (see *Wilder Places—Parks*) off Highway 101, and at **Yaquina Head,** 3 miles north of Newport off Highway 101.

Yaquina Head, 3 miles north of Newport. Part of the **Oregon Islands National Wildlife Refuge,** this area is part of a complex containing more than 1,400 offshore reefs, rocks, and islands where more than a million **seabirds** nest.

Yaquina Head Natural Area, 3 miles north of Newport off Highway 101. Built from basalt that 14 million years ago flowed some 300 miles before finding the sea, Yaquina Head juts into the Pacific, takes a pounding from wind and waves, yet stands relatively rock solid against the erosion eating away the nearby beach. As a result, the headland and its tide pools have long provided a home to critters ranging from **seals** and **seabirds** to **sea stars** and **anemones.** Providing a thorough view of the area is a series of five short trails that lead along the head's hills, coves, tide pools (one of the only **handicapped-accessible tide pools** in the world), and beach.

* Lodging

INNS **Inn at Arch Rock** (1-800-767-1835; innkeeper@innatarchrock.com; www.innatarchrock.com), 70 N. W. Sunset Street, Depoe Bay 97341. Don't expect a quaint beach cottage here, for this is a modern complex with multiple units, tucked away near the edge of the sea. "Inn at Arch Rock is a one-of-a-kind getaway," says innkeeper Terry McGrath, "with sweeping views and its own private cove." Accommodations include 13 rooms ranging in size from small to suite ($69–259). Coffee and a continental breakfast is included.

Sweetwater Inn (541-994-4708; info@sweetwaterinn.biz; www.sweetwaterinn.biz), 4006 W. Devils Lake Road, Lincoln City 97367. This inn doesn't just overlook the lake, it sidles right up next to it so close the water is almost right outside the window. Its eight rooms all have queen beds and some have kitchenettes ($60–70).

House of Rogue (541-265-3188; www.rogue.com), 748 S. W. Bay Boulevard, Newport 97365. Think of this inn as a B&B, a Bed and Beer, for it's located above **Rogue Ales Public House** (see *Eating Out*) on Newport's historic waterfront, and its amenities include a six-pack of Rogue and two pint glasses for each guest. The inn's three rooms all come with private baths, and kids are welcome.

BED & BREAKFASTS

Depoe Bay

Channel House (1-800-447-2140; cfinseth@channelhouse.com; www.channelhouse.com), 35 Ellingson Street, Depoe Bay 97341. Overlooking the entry to the harbor at Depoe Bay, the Channel House stands on a bluff sloping down to the surf. Of its 15 guest rooms, many come with ocean views, and all come with a buffet continental breakfast that features home-baked pastries ($90–270).

Gracie's Landing (1-800-228-0448; enjoytheview@gracieslanding.com; www.gracieslanding.com), 235 S. E. Bay View Avenue, Depoe Bay 97341. The smallest harbor in the world is one view from Gracie's Landing, located within sight of the boats huddled at dockside. Each of the inn's 12 guest rooms has a balcony, patio, view, and private bath; some have fireplaces, king beds, and jetted tubs ($90–135). All come with a full breakfast.

The Homestead Bed & Breakfast (1-877-321-3363; innkeeper@thehomesteadbb.com; www.thehomesteadbb.com), 614 N. E. Highway 101, Depot Bay 97341. The Homestead deserves its name. Built in 1911, this historic farmhouse was the home of Depoe Bay's first white settlers, and in some ways a stay here is reminiscent of older days. "Guests have the run of the house," says owner Dorothy Shafer, "and that reminds one of a visit to Grandma and Grandpa's house." Its eight guest rooms come with either shared or private bathrooms ($60–110), and some rooms can be combined into suites ($130–150). The four- to six-course breakfast—the menu changes daily—is served in a dining room that, Dorothy says, "offers a full ocean view, clear to the horizon." Children who "do not disrupt other guests" are welcome, and some dogs are accepted on a limited basis and for an extra charge.

Lincoln Beach

Pana-Sea-Ah (541-764-3368; innkeeper@panaseah.com; www.panaseah.com), 4028 Lincoln Avenue, Lincoln Beach 97388. Can't get much closer to the beach than this without getting your feet wet. "We're just steps from beach access," says owner Nancy Buchanan, "and we have miles of beach to walk." As a result, almost every room has a far-reaching view of the sea, including the two second-floor guest rooms ($130). These come with queen or king beds, private baths, and a full breakfast.

Linclon City

An Exceptional Place to Bed & Breakfast Inn (1-888-723-3862; EKuntz7171@aol.com; www.anexceptionalbandb.com), 1213 S. W. 52nd Court, Lincoln City 97367. Much of the "exceptional" in this B&B's name comes from its location on the north end of Siletz Bay along with its panoramic views and beach access. Its three guest rooms all have king beds and private baths, and some have either a hot tub, a fireplace, a kitchen, or scenic views ($99–149).

Brey House Bed & Breakfast (541-994-7123; unclemiltcookn@webtv.net; www.moriah.com/breyhouse), 3725 N. W. Keel Street, Lincoln City 97367. Since 1941 this three-story Cape Cod–style house has been keeping an eye on the ocean across the street. It's a view that guests at this B&B can enjoy from their rooms or the sundecks. Its four guest rooms all come with private baths and a full breakfast. Year-round rates are $75–160, which includes a full breakfast.

🐾 ✐ **Coast Inn** (1-888-994-7932; coastinn@oregoncoastinn.com; www.oregoncoastinn.com), 4507 S. W. Coast Avenue, Lincoln City 97367. Built in 1939 and completely remodeled in 2001, this 4,000-square-foot Craftsman-style home stands a short walk away from Siletz Bay and Lincoln City beaches. "It's a haven for readers and writers," says innkeeper Rosie Huntemann, "with stimulating conversation about our life experiences and how they relate to our writing a frequent topic." The inn's four guest rooms all come with private baths, queen beds, lots of coastal air and sunlight, and a full breakfast ($95–125). "We pamper our guests with great breakfasts," Rosie says, "featuring Oregon-grown fruits and berries." Children older than 5 are welcome, and small pets are permitted in one of the guest rooms.

Pacific Rest Bed & Breakfast (1-888-405-7378; jwaetjen@wcn.net; pacificrestbb.hypermart.net), 611 N. E. 11th Street, Lincoln City 97367. Located on a landscaped hillside above Highway 101 and close to the beach, Pacific Rest has a special appeal to lovers of the language looking for a home away from home. "What makes our B and B special?" asks owner Judy Waetjen. "I think it's the peaceful atmosphere where books abound. There's something for everyone. There's a feeling of coming home." She even uses a poem to describe this atmosphere: "Home is where the heart is, / The soul's bright guiding star. / Home means someone waiting / To give a welcome smile. / Home means peace / And joy and rest / And everything worthwhile." Judy's inn offers two kinds of accommodations: a pair of guest rooms with private baths and a full breakfast ($110), and multibedroom cottages that come with sundecks, ocean views, and equipped kitchens, but breakfast is not included ($125–190). Either way, guests can expect to receive a warm welcome because, as Judy says, "We're a family of readers and writers."

Salmonberry Inn (541-994-0411; innkeeper@salmonberryinn.com; www.salmonberryinn.com), 843 S. W. 50th Street, Lincoln City 97367. Named for the woodland plants that surround it, the Salmonberry Inn is located near ocean waters and Siletz Bay. Its three guest rooms all come with private baths and entrances, a full breakfast, and access to a sauna, Jacuzzi, and indoor swimming pool ($150–175).

Newport

Green Gables Bed & Breakfast (1-800-515-9065; gables@greengablesbb.com; www.greengablesbb.com), 156 S. W. Coast Street, Newport 97365. Combine historic architecture with modern construction and one result is this 1981 Queen Anne Victorian that offers guests two rooms with private baths, views from the decks, soaks in a whirlpool, and coffee in your room ($85–125). Toss in a full breakfast, an on-site bookstore, and access to 4 miles of beaches, and you'll understand why the Victorians never had it so good.

Newport Belle Bed & Breakfast (541-265-6940; SPorter@NewportBelle.com; www.newportbelle.com), South Beach Marina, Newport 97365. You'll have to search a long time before you find anything else like this B&B: a new **three-deck sternwheeler riverboat** almost 100 feet long and containing more than 3,000 square feet of living space divided into five staterooms. "What sets the Belle apart from the other B&Bs," says hostess Sherry Porter, "is that it's a real 'boat' in the Newport Marina with a spectacular view of the Yaquina Bay Bridge." The boat's accommodations includes private baths with showers, king or queen beds, and a gourmet breakfast. "The one comment that I hear over and over again from my guests," Sherry says, "is that it's so relaxing here that they instantly feel at home."

Oar House (1-800-252-2358; oarhouse@newportnet.com; www.oarhouse-bed-breakfast.com), 520 S. W. Second Street, Newport 97365. Located on historic Nye Beach, the Oar House was built originally as a boardinghouse and in the 1920s served as a bordello. "Oar House is the only historic bed and breakfast inn in Newport," says innkeeper Jan LeBrun. "The house was built in 1900 and has been completely renovated in the last few years. Guests now enjoy all the modern amenities—whirlpool tubs, soaking tubs, oversized showers—along with the character inherent in a historical site." Of the five guest rooms ($120–140), two have Jacuzzi tubs, four have an ocean view, and all have private baths and queen beds. In addition, guests are welcome to share a living room, sitting room with fireplace, and bar area with refrigerator.

Ocean House (1-800-562-2632; garrard@oceanhouse.com; www.oceanhouse.com), 4920 N. W. Woody Way, Newport 97365. Because spectacular views demand numerous windows, this oceanfront house has its share, the glass everywhere seeming to gather scenery stretching all the way from Yaquina Head to Cape Perpetua. Besides the views, the inn—doing business since 1984, a remarkable record of longevity—offers seven rooms ($95–225) with private baths, fireplaces, nearby decks, and access to gardens, walking trails, and miles of beach. In addition, a guest cottage suite contains a fireplace and kitchenette, loft bedroom with king bed, and private bath with spa.

Sea Cliff Bed & Breakfast (1-888-858-6660; aprils@newportnet.com; www.seacliffbb.com), 749 N. W. Third Street, Newport 97365. On the bluffs above Nye Beach near Newport stands this 1910 Craftsman home that has seemingly been renovated into a B&B with enough glass that you couldn't escape the ocean views if you wanted to. Its two guest rooms both come with private baths and, of course, ocean views ($95–105). A full breakfast is served each morning in a dining room with, yes, ocean views that reach along the shoreline all the way to Yaquina Head and its lighthouse.

Sylvia Beach Hotel (541-265-5428;

goods2@aol.com; www.sylviabeachhotel.com), 267 N. W. Cliff Street, Newport 97365. The Sylvia Beach is fast becoming an Oregon icon, a place that people know about even if they have yet to see it much less stay there. The reason for the hotel's fame is its approach to hospitality, for it's definitely a place for readers. Each of its 20 rooms ($63–173) has been named and decorated for a well-known author, from Emily Dickinson to Dr. Seuss; volumes of guest journals lie in each room, but you'll find no TVs, radios, or phones; a library and reading room, along with its overstuffed chairs and fireplace, is a main attraction, especially during coast storms. Even the breakfasts—served family style in, of course, the Tables of Contents room—seem to be accompanied by the atmosphere created by thoughtful readers. "My favorite part of the experience is the shared meals," says owner Goody Cable. "The food and company are both delightful. Our guests are from all over the country, and sometimes out of the country, and they're thoughtful, curious, and high spirited."

Tyee Lodge Oceanfront Bed & Breakfast (1-888-553-8933; mcconn @teleport.com; www.newportnet.com/tyee), 4925 N. W. Woody Way, Newport 97365. Standing just a short walk from seashore and tide pools but still only five minutes from Newport, Tyee Lodge offers five oceanfront guest rooms ($125–145; full breakfast included), all with private baths, gas fireplaces, queen beds with down comforters, and spacious windows that connect you to a view of the sea. In addition, guests are invited to share the lodge's great room, which has a lounge with fireplace and bar.

Otis

Lake House Bed & Breakfast (1-888-996-8938; innkeeper@lakehousebb.com; www.lakehousebb.com), 2165 N. E. East Devils Lake Road, Otis 97368. Perched on a hillside above Devils Lake, the Lake House consists of a 1915 lakeside home and adjacent guest cabin located just 2 miles from the Pacific and downtown Lincoln City. Its two housetop guest rooms have lake views, king or queen beds, and a private entrance and bath ($125), while the cottage includes a gas fireplace, equipped kitchen, and front porch that overlooks the lake and the home's private dock ($105). A full breakfast is included, and children are welcome.

South Beach

Oregon Bed and Beach (541-867-6830; oregonbednbeach@aol.com; www.hometown.aol.com/oregonbednbeach), South Beach 97366. The first floor of this oceanfront home belongs to the guests who stay here. "The thing that makes our B and B special is the intimate privacy we provide," says owner George Ulrich. "We've been told it's like staying in a private corner of nowhere." This privacy includes the entrance and bath, the living room and kitchen—even the beach. "Our secluded spot," George says, "offers five miles of beach with no houses or motels peering down." He also mentions that this is "a bed and breakfast with no breakfast." Instead, the room is stocked with snacks, and guests can fix their own meals in a kitchen furnished with "classic 1939 appliances that really work." Rates, too, seem to hearken back to older days: $75 for the first night, $65 for each additional night.

✷ Where to Eat

DINING OUT **Tidal Raves** (541-765-2995), 279 N. W. Highway 101, Depoe Bay. It's a good bet that virtually everyone who's tried this restaurant recommends it to their friends. Perched on an oceanside cliff and looking out toward the sea, Tidal Raves offers a remarkable view as well as an extensive menu that specializes, of course, in fresh seafood.

Chez Jeanette (541-764-3434), 7150 Old Highway 101, Gleneden Beach. If it once swam in the sea or scuttled along the shore, grazed in a pasture or flew through the sky, then they probably serve it with a swirl of elegance at Chez Jeanette. You can also expect to find elaborate desserts and an extensive wine list.

Bay House (541-996-3222), 5911 S. W. Highway 101, Lincoln City. Some people claim it's the view of Siletz Bay that's the Bay House's finest quality, while others argue it's the gourmet cooking. Either way, many consider this to be one of the best restaurants on the Oregon coast.

Canyon Way Bookstore and Restaurant (541-265-8319), 1216 S. W. Canyon Way, Newport. You might get sidetracked in the bookstore or the gift shop, but you'll know you've found the restaurant at Canyon Way by the room's candlelit quiet. Here fine dining—including some of the freshest seafood in the area—meets romantic getaway.

EATING OUT

Gleneden Beach

Side Door Café (541-764-3825), 6675 Gleneden Beach Loop, Gleneden Beach. This café's small, well-designed menu features fresh seafood, local fruits, vegetarian dishes, and highly regarded desserts, all offered in an airy building with ceiling fans, lush plants, and a friendly atmosphere.

Lincoln City

Blackfish Café (541-996-1007), 2733 N. W. Highway 101, Lincoln City. By offering a changing menu and using local ingredients, chef-owner Rob Pounding has earned a reputation for serving up some of the best lunches and dinners on this part of the coast. How local is the food? Well, the pork comes from the Willamette Valley, the cheese from Tillamook, the oysters from Newport, the sea bass from Neskowin—and the homemade chocolate ding-dongs are made right in the kitchen.

Chameleon Café (541-994-8422), 2145 N. W. Highway 101, Lincoln City. This café that shows different sides to the world: While its eclectic menu offers international fare—South American, Asian, Indonesian—its storefront design retains a Northwest casualness. (Maybe the multiple impressions are the reason for its name.) At any rate, the result is a restaurant worth a stop.

Wildflower Grill (541-994-9663), 4250 N. Highway 101, Lincoln City. A new restaurant located close to a golf course, the Wildflower Grill offers huge portions, nice presentations, and lush landscaping and outdoor seating in summer.

Newport

April's at Nye Beach (541-265-6855), 749 N. W. Third Street, Newport. The dozen tables in this sidewalk café are often full, a tribute to the inviting atmosphere and notable food—fish, shellfish, pasta, and chicken, among other offerings on a varied menu.

Chowder Bowl Newport (541-265-7477), 728 N. W. Beach Drive, Newport. For many years, the Chowder Bowl has been doing business here in the historic Nye Beach area. Naturally, its specialty is clam chowder, though its menu includes many other items.

Georgie's Beachside Grill (541-265-9800), 744 S. W. Elizabeth Street, Newport. If oceanfront dining is what you're looking for, then come to Georgie's, a newer restaurant with a bit of polish to its feel, as well as great views, good food, and reasonable prices.

Mo's (541-265-2979), 622 S. W. Bay Boulevard, Newport. Mo's is a tradition on the coast, and even though outlets are located in many oceanfront towns, Mo's was started right here in Newport, years ago, by Mo Neimi, a local woman who achieved wide fame for her clam chowder. Even though her family now runs the business, the restaurants still follow Mo's recipe—and still pack in the crowds.

Rogue Ales Public House (541-265-3188), 748 S. W. Bay Boulevard, Newport. Rogue Ales is something of a secret in Newport, a brewery that serves great food and beer in a *very* relaxed environment. "A good mixture of salty natives and tourists" is how one local describes the mix of people here. (See also **House of Rogue** under *Lodging—Inns.*)

Shirley's at Agate Beach (541-265-3090), 5188 N. E. Lucky Gap Street, Newport. Original recipes, scratch cooking, good food, large servings, and friendly service characterize Shirley's. And a woman named Shirley actually owns and operates the place.

Whale's Tale (541-265-8660), 452 S. W. Bay Boulevard, Newport. Known for its unique dishes, comfortable atmosphere, and mouthwatering desserts, the Whale's Tale has been a fixture on the Newport waterfront for decades.

✷ Special Events

February: **Newport Seafood and Wine Festival** (1-800-262-7844), Newport.

May: **Sand Castle Contests** (1-800-452-2151), Lincoln City. **Spring Kite Festival** (1-800-452-2151), Lincoln City. If you want to experience flight while keeping your feet planted on the ground, then watch the kites soar at this festival.

September: **Indian-Style Salmon Bake** (1-877-485-8348), Depoe Bay.

October: **International Kite Festival** (1-800-452-2151), D River Wayside off Highway 101, Lincoln City. Unlike the informal, come-as-you-are, everybody's-welcome kite festivals held in some communities along the Oregon coast, the activities at this event brings together competitive kite flyers. **Glass Galore Art Fair** (1-800-452-2151), Lincoln City.

WALDPORT–YACHATS–FLORENCE AREA

GUIDANCE **Florence Area Chamber of Commerce** (1-800-524-4864; www.florencechamber.com), 270 Highway 101, Florence 97439.

Oregon State Parks: Headquarters (503-378-6305), State Parks and Recreation Department, 525 Trade Street S. E., Salem 97301.

Siuslaw National Forest: Headquarters (541-750-7000), 4077 S. W. Research Way, Corvallis 97330; **Mapleton Ranger District** (541-902-8526); **Waldport Ranger District** (541-563-3211).

Waldport Visitors Center (541-563-2133), 620 N. W. Spring Street, Waldport 97394.

Yachats Area Visitors Center (1-800-929-0477; www.yachats.org), 241 Highway 101, Yachats 97498.

GETTING THERE Waldport, Yachats, and Florence are reached from the east by Highways 34 and 126 and are linked by Highway 101, which runs the entire length of the Oregon coast.

MEDICAL EMERGENCY **Samaritan North Lincoln Hospital** (541-994-3661), 3043 N. E. 28th Street, Lincoln City.

Samaritan Pacific Communities Hospital (541-265-2244), 930 S. W. Abbey, Newport.

Peace Harbor Hospital (541-997-8412), 400 Ninth Street, Florence.

✱ To See

MUSEUMS **Waldport Heritage Museum** (541-563-7092), 320 N. E. Grant Street, Waldport. Now standing in Waldport's Old Town, the Heritage Museum was first a barracks, built some 4 miles south of here by the Civilian Conservation Corps (CCC) and used by the government to house conscientious objectors during World War II. Eventually, however, it was moved into town and now houses the community's collection of historical exhibits, which include Indian artifacts, logging equipment, fishing gear, and school memorabilia.

Little Log Church and Museum (541-547-3976), Third and Pontiac Streets, Yachats. This 1930 log church contains many of its original furnishings as well as displays of local art and historical artifacts, including the trappings and tools of pioneer life, and a few things just downright rare, such as a molar from a woolly mammoth.

Siuslaw Pioneer Museum (541-997-7884), 85294 Highway 101 South (near milepost 192), Florence. From the time the area opened to homesteading in 1876 until the day the first road connected the area to the outside world, the Siuslaw River was the main highway in and out of this part of the coast, where farming, fishing, and logging were the mainstays of the economy. Today this museum preserves those pioneer days, displaying a collection of artifacts that Louis Campbell describes in verse as "The books they read / The tales they told / The things they said / The goods they sold."

HISTORIC SITES **Heceta Head Lighthouse,** 13 miles north of Florence off Highway 101. Named for Spanish mariner Bruno Heceta—who in 1775 took soundings near here during his search for the Strait of Anian, the Spanish version of the Northwest Passage—Heceta Head is home to a still-active 1894 lighthouse—its light shines 21 miles to sea—as well as an 1893 Queen Anne Victorian house that serves as the keeper's residence.

Florence Old Town. Along Bay Street in Florence, located near the mouth of the Siuslaw River, stand more than 60 historic buildings that have been converted to modern shops that sell food and clothes, antiques and art. Yet it's the 19th-century architectural styles blending with the scents of sea and rain that may be the street's major attraction.

COVERED BRIDGES In the days when covered bridges crossed many an Oregon stream, one way to preserve the bridge was to control the flow of traffic. "No veahcle drawn by moar than one animile," said the message hanging on the entry to one bridge, "is aloud to cros this Bridg in opposite direxions at the sam Time." **Fisher School** (also called Fiver Rivers), 21 miles east of Waldport off Highway 34 and Fisher–Fiver Rivers Road, built in 1919, 72 feet long. **North Fork of the Yachats,** 9 miles east of Yachats off Yachats River Road, built in 1938, 42 feet long. **Deadwood Bridge,** 5 miles north of Deadwood off Highway 36 and Lower Deadwood Road, built in 1932, 105 feet long. **Hayden Bridge,** 2 miles west of Alsea off Highway 34 and Hayden Road, built in 1918, 91 feet long. **Nelson Mountain Bridge**—also known as the **Lake Creek Bridge**—6 miles east of Deadwood off Highway 36 and Nelson Mountain Road, built in 1928, 105 feet long. **Wildcat Bridge,** 14 miles east of Mapleton off Highway 126, built in 1925, 75 feetlong.

FOR FAMILIES **Stern-Wheeler Cruises** (541-997-9691), *Westward HO!* Stern-wheeler, Bay Street, Florence. Four times a day this 65-foot stern-wheeler chugs along the Siuslaw River, carrying passengers on either half-hour or one-hour tours. Hop aboard, and you'll get to see the river the way they did in the days when steam-powered stern-wheelers were one of the few connections people on the coast had to the outside world.

✐ **Whale-Watching** (1-800-551-6949; www.whalespoken.org), Oregon Parks and Recreation Department. Because gray whales swim near the shoreline in their migrations both south to Mexico and north to Alaska, whale-watching has become a popular spectator sport along the Oregon coast. Prime whale-watching sites along this stretch of the coast, especially in the spring, include **Seal Rock State Park** near **Waldport; Yachats State Park, Cape Perpetua Interpretive Center, Cape Perpetua Overlook,** and **Devils Churn Viewpoint** near **Yachats;** and the **Sea Lion Caves** turnout near **Florence.**

SCENIC DRIVES **Pacific Coast Scenic Byway—northern segment** (185 paved miles from Astoria to Florence along Highway 101). From the Columbia River at Astoria to the Siuslaw River at Florence, this road skirts the shoreline of the Pacific, winding past headlands and beaches, crossing over estuaries and bays, and climbing through foothills and toward ocean views along a route that is one of the most beautiful and famous drives in America. In addition, numerous viewpoints, pullouts, and state parks along the way provide dozens of entries for anyone wanting to wade the surf, comb the beach, or watch a sunset.

NATURAL WONDERS **Spouting Horns,** off Highway 101 near Yachats. When waves collide with the mainland, spouting horns are often the result. One of the best places to see these spraying splashes of seawater is near the shoreline rocks at Yachats.

✷ To Do

CAMPING **Waldport Area,** east or south of Waldport, located on Highway 101: **Blackberry,** 18 miles east of Waldport off Highway 34, 35 campsites along the bank of the Alsea River with amenities that include a boat ramp and flush toilets; **Tillicum Beach,** 7 miles south of Waldport off Highway 101, 60 campsites near the beach. **Salmonberry County Park,** 7 miles west of Alsea off Highway 34. Twenty campsites along the bank of the Alsea River, with nearby hiking and fishing.

Cape Perpetua, 3 miles south of Yachats off Highway 101: 38 campsites near the Cape Perpetua Scenic Area, with nearby tide pools, visitors center, and hiking trails.

Florence Area, north or south of Florence, located on Highway 101: **Alder Dune,** 5 miles north of Florence off Highway 101, 39 campsites; **Baker Beach,** 6 miles north of Florence off Highway 101 and Baker Beach Road, 5 primitive campsites with nearby hiking trails to Lilly Lake and Wet Sand Area near the Pacific shoreline; **North Fork Siuslaw,** 14 miles northeast of Florence off Highway 126 and Forest Road 5070, 5 riverside campsites; **Siuslaw Harbor,** 3 miles north of Florence off Highway 101 and North Jetty Road, 38 campgrounds with beach access, playgrounds, even showers—one of few Oregon coast campgrounds with an ocean view; **Siltcoos Lake,** 6 miles south of Florence off Highway 101, more than 160 campsites divided among three developed camps—**Driftwood, Lagoon,** and **Waxmyr-**

tle; Sutton Creek, 5 miles north of Florence off Highway 101, 81 campsites near a small lake and the beach; **Tyee,** 6 miles south of Florence off Highway 101, 8 campsites and a boat ramp adjacent to the Siltcoos River.

Yachats Area, north or south of Yachats, located on Highway 101: **Lanham,** 10 miles south of Yachats off Highway 101, 8 hiker/biker campsites located a half mile from the beach; **Rock Creek,** 10 miles south of Yachats off Highway 101, 11 creekside campsites near the beach; **Sharps Creek,** 13 miles south of Yachats off Highway 101, 10 campsites on the bank of the creek; **Tenmile Creek,** 13 miles southeast of Yachats off Highway 101 and Forest Road 56, 4 campsites along the creek.

HIKING **Siuslaw River Drainage,** south of Mapleton off Highway 26 and Forest Road 48. A series of trailheads along this route lead to a number of waterfalls, including **Sweet Creek Falls, Beaver Creek Falls, North Fork Falls,** and **Kentucky Falls.**

Florence Area, north and south of Florence, located on Highway 101. A myriad hiking trails crisscross through this coastal playground, including the following: **Carter Dunes** and **Taylor Dunes Trails** at Carter Lake Campground, 8 miles south of Florence off Highway 101, both leading to views of dunes and ocean as they near the beach; **Mapleton Hill Pioneer Trail,** 16 miles northeast of Florence off Highway 126 and North Fork Siuslaw Road, an easy hike along an interpretive trail; **Overlook Beach Trail,** 10 miles south of Florence off Highway 101, a 1-mile trail to the beach; **Pawn Old Growth,** 18 miles northeast of Florence off Highway 126 and North Fork Siuslaw Road, less than a 1-mile loop through an old-growth forest; **Siltcoos Beach,** 7 miles south of Florence off Highway 101 and Siltcoos Bay Road, three short trails—**Chief Tsiltcoos, Lagoon,** and **Waxmyrtle**—leading toward or along the beach; **Siltcoos Lake,** 7 miles south of Florence off Highway 101, a 2-mile pathway through a second-growth forest at the lakeshore; **Sutton Creek,** 5 miles north of Florence off Highway 101, 5 miles of relatively flat trails; **Tahkenitch Creek,** 11 miles south of Florence off Highway 101, 2 to 4 miles that wander through forests, over dunes, and past marshes and meadows; **Tahkenitch Dunes,** 13 miles south of Florence off Highway 101, a 2-mile trail through forests and across dunes to a creek's mouth at shoreline; **Threemile Lake,** 14 miles south of Florence off Highway 101, one of the longer trails at 7 miles round trip; **Valley/China Creek Trail,** 14 miles north of Florence off Highway 101, 4 miles through relatively flat terrain and a picnic area located a mile from the trailhead at the site of an old homestead.

Cape Perpetua, 3 miles south of Yachats off Highway 101. This forested headland has 17 miles of walking paths, including paved trails for the most popular hikes. Shorter routes include less than a mile to both **Devils Churn** and **Captain Cook Point,** a 1-mile nature trail and the 1-mile **Cummins Creek Trail,** and a 3-mile round trip to a viewpoint at the top of the cape. (See also *Wilder Places—Wildlife Refuges.*)

Yachats 804 Trail, 1 mile northwest of Yachats off Highway 101 at Smelt

Sands Wayside. Back in the days when the beaches were public highways, this shoreline path was a road right-of-way. Today, however, it's part of the **Oregon Coast Trail,** a 0.75-mile route that leads past rocks and surf and shore pines on its way to the beach.

See also *Wilder Places—Parks.*

✷ Wilder Places

PARKS **Clemens Park** ((503-378-6305, 2 miles east of Alsea off Highway 34). The star attraction of Clemens Park is its half mile of river frontage, which comes with walking trails and picnic areas.

Governor Patterson State Park, 1 mile north of Waldport off Highway 101, day use only. With this site's sandy beaches and forested bluffs, walking trails and ocean views, it's a good bet that Oregon governor Isaac Lee Patterson—a parks supporter who died in office in 1929, the same year he appointed the state's first Park Commission—would have loved this site named for him. (Two years after the governor's death, the state bought this land from Patterson's widow and other owners.)

♿ **Yachats State Park,** on the western edge of Yachats on the north bank of the Yachats River, day use only. More than 90 acres is preserved here, where the Yachats River enters the sea and where salmon and steelhead enter the river to begin their upstream migration to spawn. A **wheelchair-accessible trail** that stretches for three quarters of a mile along a rocky beach provides an explorer's path for wave-watchers.

Neptune State Park, 4 miles south of Yachats off Highway 101, day use only. Bordered on the east by the **Cummins Creek Wilderness Area** (see *Wilderness Areas*) and on the north by the Cape Perpetua Scenic Area, this park features a series of trails that wanders through a mosaic of land and sea: roaring surf and craggy rocks, coastal forest and shoreline tide pools.

Carl G. Washburne State Park, 14 miles north of Florence off Highway 101, day use and overnight. Beneath a ragged, rolling carpet of spruce and pine and huckleberry that makes up parts of this more than 1,000-acre park lie the remains of old sand dunes, their contours still rippling their way toward one of Oregon's longest uninterrupted beaches—5 miles of sand and tide pools. Two trails that start at the campground and that are connected by that beach steer hikers through most of it.

Devils Elbow State Park, 13 miles north of Florence off Highway 101, day use only. Jutting into the sea and bordered to the north by **Heceta Head** (with its **lighthouse**) and to the south by Sea Lion Point (with its **Sea Lion Caves;** see *Wildlife Refuges*), this park offers stunning views of surf and sand to picnickers and sightseers.

State Scenic Viewpoints, from north of Florence to north of Depoe Bay along Highway 101. If you just want to slip quietly off the road for a moment and leave the traffic behind as you watch waves, birds, or whales, this stretch of highway offers some exceptional wayside viewpoints, including the following from south to north: **Sea Lion Point, Muriel O. Ponsler, Yachats Ocean Road, Otter Crest, Rocky Creek,** and **Boiler Bay.**

Jessie M. Honeyman State Park, 3 miles south of Florence off Highway

101, day use and overnight. Back in the days when Dwight Eisenhower was president, *Life Magazine* named this site one of the nation's outstanding state parks. The reasons for that honor are still here: quiet campgrounds, freshwater lakes, sand dunes, hiking trails, picnic areas, boat ramps, swimming and fishing areas.

WILDERNESS AREAS **Drift Creek**, 12 miles east of Waldport off Highway 34, Forest Road 3446 and connecting spurs, 9 square miles. Here stand some of the largest stands of old-growth **rain forest** left in the Coast Range, the trunks of the area's fir, spruce, and hemlock sometimes reaching diameters of 7 feet. Along the edge of this forest's long, steep slopes, two trails converge on Drift Creek: the **Horse Creek** and the southern segment of the Harris Ranch trails, 2 miles each, with the northern segment of the Horse Creek Trail extending 3 more miles into old-growth forest.

Cummins Creek, 4 miles south of Yachats off Highway 101, 15 square miles. The Cummins Creek Wilderness stretches from coastal rain forest and old-growth timber toward sandy beaches and rocky headlands, and ranges in elevation from 100 to 2,400 feet. Its campgrounds lie off Highway 101, and its trails run east (one climbs **Cummins Ridge** and another follows Cummins Creek) with some of them beginning or connecting at **Neptune State Park** (see *Parks*) and **Cape Perpetua** (see *Wildlife Refuges* and *To Do—Hiking*).

Rock Creek, 8 miles south of Yachats off Highway 101, 12 square miles. Beginning near the edge of Highway 101, where its two major campgrounds are located, the Rock Creek Wilderness extends eastward into the wet thickness of forest and stream, its major hiking trail a makeshift path that follows Rock Creek, home to **salmon, steelhead,** and **cutthroat trout.**

WILDLIFE REFUGES **Tide Pools. Seal Rock State Recreation Site,** 5 miles north of Waldport off Highway 101; **Yachats State Recreation Area,** near Yachats off Highway 101, access at Second Street or Ocean Drive; **Cape Perpetua,** 2 miles south of Yachats off Highway 101; **Neptune State Park,** 13 miles south of Waldport off Highway 101; **Bob Creek to Bray Point,** southern boundary of Neptune State Park, access is south of Bob Creek.

Cape Perpetua, 3 miles south of Yachats off Highway 101. Named on Saint Perpetua's Day in 1778 by British sea explorer Captain James Cook, Cape Perpetua consists of more than 4 square miles of oceanside wonderland. So rich is the life of its rain forest, for example, that it supports 400 tons of plant life per acre, more than twice the botanical mass of the tropical Amazon River region. Just a short walk from the visitor center perching on the cape's 800-foot-high headland takes you either to these mountainside forests or to surfside tide pools, where you can see or touch—but *not* collect—**sea stars, anemones, barnacles, hermit crabs,** and **sea urchins.**

Strawberry Hill, 4 miles south of Yachats off Highway 101. Close to the shore here lies a year-round rock-basking site for **harbor seals,** the largest concentrations occurring in summer.

Sea Lion Caves (541-547-3111), 12 miles north of Florence off Highway

101. During fall and winter, as many as 200 **Steller's sea lions**—perhaps 20 percent of Oregon's wild population—gather here at the world's largest sea cave, a 25-million-year-old amphitheater that reaches the height of a 12-story building and the length of a football field. To reach the sea lion sanctuary, you'll take a 208-foot elevator trip down to a viewing area set off with a block wall and a chain-link fence. "We cage the people rather than the animals," says Tim Henson, assistant manager of the caves. Once you see one of the sea lion bulls, which can weigh as much as a ton, you'll probably agree this is a wise decision.

South Jetty, 6 miles southwest of Florence off Highway 101 and South Jetty Road. What this sprawl of sand hides from those who won't leave the pavement is a series of shallow ponds where **waterfowl** and **shorebirds** gather. Granted, these waters are far more populated in the winter, when hundreds of **tundra swans** arrive to spend the winter, joining company with **mallards** and **bluebills** and **pintails,** but it's still an adventure to head out across the dunes and through the beach grass just to see what you might find on the other side of the next rise.

✷ Lodging

INNS **Ocean Haven** (541-547-3583; office@oceanhaven.com; www.oceanhaven.com), 94770 Highway 101, Yachats 97498. Standing on a bluff just beyond the reach of high tide, Ocean Haven is closer to tide pools than it is to TVs. "This is a good place for folks who are interested in just counting the waves, watching the whales, and exploring the old-growth forest," says owner Christie DeMoll. Because so many people come here to do just those things, you won't find a TV or a telephone in any of Ocean Haven's six guest rooms ($65–100). You will, however, find big beds, small kitchens, and lots of glass to let in views of the sea. Nevertheless, what's most important still lies beyond that glass. "We specialize in providing information on marine and wildlife viewing, planning hikes and marine explorations," Christie says. "And we notify guests when the whales, eagles, otters, and elk are wandering by."

BED & BREAKFASTS

Florence

Blue Heron Inn (1-800-997-7780; www.blue-heroninn.com), 6563 Highway 126, Florence 97439. Yes, blue herons really are part of the Blue Heron Inn—at least, they're part of the view on the nearby Siuslaw River. Built in the 1940s, this ranch-style home offers five guest rooms with private baths ($65–140). Two of the rooms have jetted tubs and all come with a gourmet breakfast that can feature such entrées as homemade yeast waffles with strawberries or smoked-salmon quiche. Children older than 10 are welcome.

Edwin K Bed & Breakfast (1-800-833-9465; edwink@pressys.com; www.edwink.com), 1155 Bay Street, Florence 97439. A restored 1914 Craftsman home with antique furniture and fine woodworking, this B&B offers six rooms with private baths ($125–175). Specialties served at the five-course breakfast can include marionberry compote with cream, fresh-made biscuits, a fruit plate, an egg or cheese soufflé, and ham or sausage entrées. Children older than 12 are welcome.

The English Rose (1-877-997-8162; deni@englishroseflorence.com; www.englishroseflorence.com), 85574 Glenada Road, Florence 97439. Sitting atop a hillside acre filled with flowers, The English Rose offers guests views of the ocean as well as shelter from its storms. "We are the only B and B here in Florence with an acre of gardens and a view of the historic Siuslaw Bridge out to the ocean," says owner Deni Harris. "Another uniqueness of ours is that we have very little wind here on our property when it's blowing others sideways on the coast." Guests can choose one of two rooms that have queen beds, gas fireplaces, and private bathrooms and balconies ($95–99), or a separate cottage with a full kitchen ($135). Accommodations include a continental breakfast. "Many of our guests have a long agenda of places to go when they arrive," Deni says, "but after an hour here they cut it in half because they find the place so beautiful and relaxing."

Hallquist Hollow Bed & Breakfast (866-046-3922; lodging@hallquisthollowbb.com; www.hallquisthollowbb.com), Florence 97439. Standing on the rolling hillside of a peninsula jutting into Mercer Lake, this 1945 cabin has been recently remodeled into a lodge that opens onto a world of water and trees. "Fish off the dock or take a bike ride," says owner Ron Hallquist. "Fishing poles and bikes are here for your use." The lodge's two suites come with queen beds, private baths, and a full breakfast ($185–275). "No minimum stay is required," Ron says, "but you'll want to stay more than a night after experiencing what true relaxation is all about."

Waldport

Cliff House (541-563-2506; innkeeper@cliffhouseoregon.com), 1450 S. W. Adahi Avenue, Waldport 97394. "If location, location, location is important," says owner Sharon Robinson, "then the Cliff House is a ten." Located where the Alsea River flows into the Pacific, this inn has a window on a world of wildlife—and the window fronts a 65-foot oceanfront deck. "There is drama in each tide change," Sharon says. "Eagles soar, osprey fish, and seals put on a show that seems meant for those of us looking over the 78-foot cliff to the waters below." Three of the four guest rooms also have world-class views as well as private decks ($110–225). A stay here includes a full breakfast, a chance to have a massage in the gazebo, and an opportunity to explore miles of beach.

Yachats

Ambrosia Gardens (541-547-3013; Mary@ambrosia-gardens.com; www.ambrosia-gardens.com), 95435 Highway 101, Yachats 97498. Forests and beaches, gardens and ponds—these are what surround or border this 3-acre homesite on the edge of the Siuslaw National Forest and Sea Rose Beach. "I fell in love with this stretch of the Oregon coast many years ago while vacationing," says owner Mary Coello, who moved here from Indiana. "I truly enjoy providing guests with a beautiful room in a stunning home surrounded by fantastic garden, forest, and ocean views, topped with a heaping helping of good old midwestern hospitality." To sample that hospitality, guests here can stay in either a room or a carriage-house suite, both with private bathrooms and those lovely views Mary mentions, and decorated with antiques, artwork, and handmade quilts ($100–115). "This," Mary says of her home, "has truly been a dream come true."

Kittiwake Bed & Breakfast (541-547-4470; holidays@kittiwakebandb.com; www.kittiwakebandb.com), 95368 Highway 101 S., Yachats 97498. Within this 4,000-square-foot home that stands by the ocean's edge, three rooms offer guests private baths, jetted tubs, queen beds, private entrances, and ocean views ($150).

New England House (541-547-4799; nehouse@newenglandhouse.com; www.newenglandhouse.com), 95354 Highway 101, Yachats 97498. If you stay here, you and yours will be the only guests at this contemporary home that overlooks ocean and gardens. Amenities include a featherbed and goose-down comforter, both in king size, and a fireplace and sundeck; a five-course breakfast often includes ingredients fresh from the garden ($139–149). Children older than 12 welcome at an extra charge.

Sea Quest (1-800-341-4878; seaquest@newportnet.com; www.seaq.com), 95354 Highway 101, Yachats 97498. Standing on 2 acres just 100 feet from sand and surf, the Sea Quest is a remodeled, cedar-shingled, 6,000-square-foot inn originally built in 1900. "A perfect combination of a coastal retreat and elegance" is how owner George Rozsa describes his B&B. Its five guest rooms ($150) all have private baths, entrances, and decks, while the world outside can seem as wild as the inn is comfortable. "The Sea Quest," Rozsa says, "is surrounded by the brilliance of forests, agate beaches, and tide pools teeming with life." Rooms come with a full breakfast that features a breakfast bar, and children older than 14 are welcome.

Serenity Bed & Breakfast (541-547-3813; serenitybnb@casco.net; www.casco.net/~serenitybnb/serenity.htm), 5985 Yachats River Road, Yachats 97498. Located on 10 landscaped, countryside acres that blend into the Siuslaw National Forest, this B&B offers three guest rooms that have borrowed parts of Europe in their decorating scheme as well as in their names—Europa, Bavaria, and La Italia. In fact, owners Sam and Baerbel Morgan call the style of their home, "a commitment to European comfort and entertainment." This carries through even to the German breakfast that includes specialties such as *Strammer Max* and *Reibekartoffel* or *Kaiserschmarren* and *Kartoffelpuffer.* Even if you can't pronounce the names, chances are you won't forget the meal.

Wayside Lodge (541-547-3450; wayside@casco.net; www.casco.net/~wayside), 5773 Highway 101 N., Yachats 97498. Sitting on a bluff 14 feet above the beach, these seven cottages stare with glassy eyes toward the sea. "We have one unit with four six-foot by five-foot windows facing the Pacific, and when people walk in, they usually exclaim, 'Wow!'" says owner Frank Walter. "So I introduce it as the 'Wow!' room." Even the windows vary in different units, and all the fully equipped cottages have ocean views, a sense of seclusion, and a front door that opens to the beach ($45–125). "Our real secret to success rests with our attitude toward the nicest people in the world, our guests," says Frank, a retired teacher. "They resemble family more than paying customers. We have the best of two worlds: to be surrounded by people we like, and to let them pay us for the privilege."

* Where to Eat

DINING OUT **La Serre Restaurant** (541-547-3420), 160 W. Second Street, Yachats. *La Serre,* French for "the greenhouse," is an appropriate name for this restaurant whose plant collection provides a green backdrop to the opened-beamed, skylighted dining room. The menu also has its share of French influences, though the local seafood is largely responsible for the restaurant's reputation for fine dining.

EATING OUT

Florence

Benny's International Café (541-997-4549), 1517 Highway 101. In spite of its "International" label, Benny's is known locally for cooking up the best omelets and hamburgers and serving the healthiest fresh food in town.

The Blue Hen (541-997-3907), 1675 Highway 101, Florence. As its name implies, but as it's almost always too much to expect, the Blue Hen serves fried chicken and real mashed potatoes and gravy and biscuits . . . and gravy.

Bridgewater (541-997-9405), 1297 Bay Street, Florence. With a casual atmosphere in a historic building, Bridgewater serves simple but delicious food: stacks of pancakes for breakfast, hamburgers and sandwiches for lunch, seafood and pasta for dinner. The list goes on and the quality is always first-rate.

Lovejoy's (541-902-0502), 85625 Highway 10, Florence. Imposing a taste of old England—what, what—on the Oregon coast, the London- and Dutch Indonesian–born owners of Lovejoy's fly British flags, serve high tea and English brews, and offer such fare as chops, steaks, and seafood. In addition, the Siuslaw River provides the view, and piano music the weekend entertainment.

* Special Events

March: **Yachats Original Arts and Crafts Fair** (1-800-929-0477), Yachats.

May: **Rhododendron Festival** (1-800-524-4864), Florence. If you visit Florence in May, you'll see how this coastal town known as the "City of Rhododendrons" came by its nickname: The rhodies are everywhere—looming along roadsides, in yards, and across parks, blooming with such dazzling colors and robust health from the spring rains that you can't beat them back with a stick (not that you'd want to). This annual festival, then, is a celebration of this evergreen shrub with the clustered flowers.

South Coast

REEDSPORT–COOS BAY AREA

BANDON–PORT ORFORD AREA

GOLD BEACH–BROOKINGS AREA

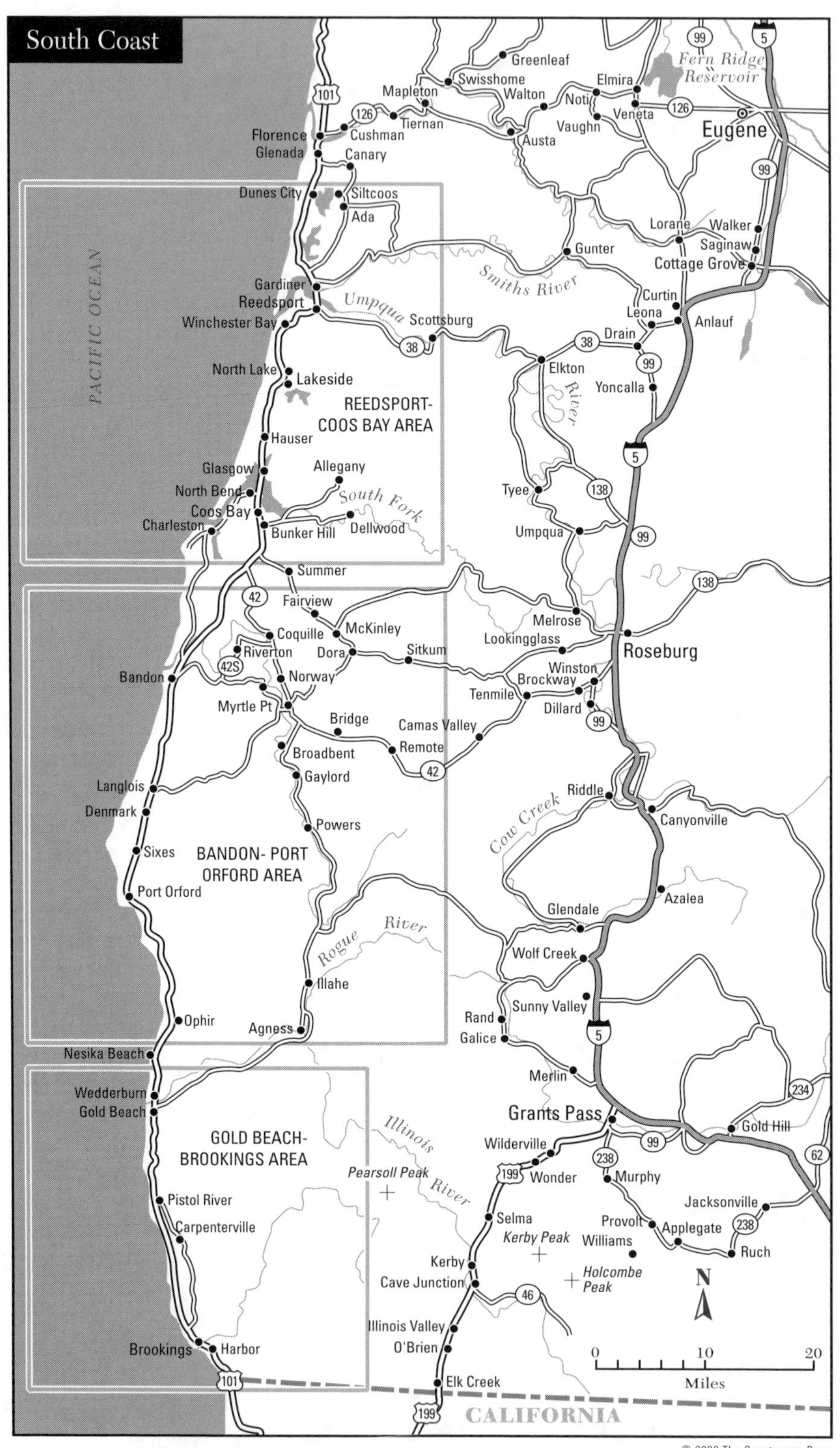
South Coast
PACIFIC OCEAN
Greenleaf
Swisshome
Mapleton
Walton
Elmira
Noti
Veneta
Fern Ridge Reservoir
Eugene
Tiernan
Cushman
Florence
Glenada
Canary
Austa
Vaughn
Dunes City
Siltcoos
Ada
Lorane
Walker
Saginaw
Cottage Grove
Gunter
Smiths River
Gardiner
Reedsport
Winchester Bay
Umpqua
Scottsburg
Curtin
Leona
Anlauf
Drain
Elkton
Yoncalla
North Lake
Lakeside
REEDSPORT-COOS BAY AREA
Hauser
Glasgow
Allegany
North Bend
Coos Bay
Charleston
Bunker Hill
Dellwood
South Fork
Tyee
Umpqua
Summer
Fairview
McKinley
Coquille
Riverton
Dora
Sitkum
Melrose
Lookingglass
Roseburg
Bandon
Norway
Winston
Brockway
Tenmile
Dillard
Myrtle Pt
Bridge
Camas Valley
Broadbent
Remote
Gaylord
Langlois
Denmark
Riddle
Canyonville
Cow Creek
Powers
Sixes
BANDON- PORT ORFORD AREA
Port Orford
Azalea
Glendale
Rogue River
Wolf Creek
Illahe
Sunny Valley
Rand
Galice
Ophir
Agness
Nesika Beach
Merlin
Wedderburn
Gold Beach
Grants Pass
Gold Hill
GOLD BEACH-BROOKINGS AREA
Illinois River
Wilderville
Pearsoll Peak
Wonder
Murphy
Pistol River
Jacksonville
Selma
Provolt
Applegate
Carpenterville
Kerby Peak
Williams
Ruch
Kerby
Cave Junction
Holcombe Peak
N
Illinois Valley
O'Brien
Brookings
Harbor
Elk Creek
CALIFORNIA
0
10
20
Miles
101
126
99
5
38
138
42
42S
234
238
62
199
46

INTRODUCTION

"All through the long winter they toiled . . . cutting, rolling, burning and grubbing [the trees they had cut], day in and day out and often till ten o'clock at night, so that when the June roses blushed and nodded in the sun, ten acres were raising as fine a crop of grain and grass as ever grew."

—Reuben Mast, describing his family's arrival from North Carolina to start a homestead on the south Oregon coast, 1872

The early history of Oregon's south coast is filled with conflict—the mariners fighting its storms, the trappers its Indians, and the homesteaders its trees and isolation. Yet once beyond these skirmishes, the old battleground settled down as a sunlit shoreline that seems to serve as the front for a magic show.

The show opens, of course, with the surf-washed beaches, where sea stacks and headlands jut their craggy way above the sea, the adjoining sand and stones catching enough daylong light to eventually kindle the sky into an orange-tinted, smoldering dusk. Roll some blue water and white waves beneath this, and it's no wonder the place seems ripe with romance. Beyond the breakers, however, less-noticed players perform their own magic.

Hunkering inland, for example, are the Coast Range and Klamath Mountains, the birthplace for rivers such as the Coos, Coquille, and Chetco, which drain the slopes and forests on their run to the sea. Along the way they carry salmon, water valleys, and fill lakes, and once they reach the shore they feed coves, shape dunes, and form sloughs, bays, and estuaries. The result is a landscape as intricately webbed as a fisherman's net—and most of it is open to those wanting to explore it.

Containing parts of the Siskiyou National Forest (more than 1,800 square miles), the Elliott State Forest (more than 140 square miles), and the Oregon Dunes National Recreation Area (almost 50 miles of coastline) as well as more than a dozen major Oregon state parks, the south coast has plenty of room to roam in. Perhaps most important, however, is the fact that the entire beach is open to the public.

"This sand is your sand; This sand is my sand." This headline appeared in an Oregon newspaper in 1967 when some state legislators and real estate developers were trying to wrestle the beaches away from Oregonians, challenging a 1913 law that gave the beaches to the public. The problem began when a motel owner kicked a woman off the beach in front of his property.

"They had fenced off part of the beach for their guests [and] told her she couldn't walk through there," says Larry Bitte, who first raised the alarm. "Being a native Oregonian, I said, 'They can't do that.'"

He was right. The resulting "Beach Bill" passed by the 1967 legislature keeps virtually the entire 362 miles of Oregon's coast open to the public. (In comparison, only 92 miles of California's 1,072 miles are open; in Massachusetts, only 10 miles of 1,300.)

Turns out it really *is* our sand. And that's the best magic of all.

REEDSPORT–COOS BAY AREA

GUIDANCE **Bay Area Chamber of Commerce** (1-800-824-8486; www.ucinet.com/~bacc), 50 E. Central, Coos Bay 97420.

Bureau of Land Management: Coos Bay District (541-756-0100), 1300 Airport Lane, North Bend 97459.

Charleston Information Center (541-888-2311), Boat Basin Drive and Cape Arago Highway, Charleston 97420.

Coos Bay–North Bend Promotions and Convention Bureau (541-269-8921), 500 Central, Room 10, Coos Bay 97420.

Lakeside Chamber of Commerce (541-759-3981), 72327 Highway 101, Lakeside 97449.

North Bend Visitor Center (541-756-4613; www.coos.or.us/~nbend), 1380 Sherman Avenue, North Bend 97459.

Oregon Dunes National Recreation Area (541-271-3611), 855 Highway Avenue, Reedsport 97467.

Oregon State Parks: Headquarters (503-378-6305), State Parks and Recreation Department, 525 Trade Street S. E., Salem 97301; **Coos Bay office** (503-269-9410).

Reedsport/Winchester Bay Chamber of Commerce (1-800-247-2155; www.reedsportcc.org), corner of Highways 101 and 38, Reedsport 97467.

Siskiyou National Forest: Headquarters (541-471-6500), 200 N. E. Greenfield Road, Grants Pass 97526.

GETTING THERE Reedsport, Coos Bay, and nearby communities are reached from the east by Highways 38 and 42 and are linked by Highway 101, which runs the entire length of the Oregon coast.

MEDICAL EMERGENCY **Bay Area Hospital** (541-269-8111), 1775 Thompson Road, Coos Bay.

Lower Umpqua Hospital (541-271-2171), 600 Ranch Road, Reedsport.

✷ To See

MUSEUMS **Coos County Historical Museum** (541-756-6320), 1220 Sherman Avenue, North Bend. With Locomotive #104 from the Coos Bay Lumber company enjoying its retirement outside the museum's doors, this museum preserves the heritage of the region, from Native American cultures to pioneer, logging, and mining lifestyles.

HISTORIC SITES **Gardiner Walking Tour,** Front Street and its cross streets on the banks of the Umpqua River. The community of Gardiner—named for Captain Gardiner, whose ship, the *Bostonian,* wrecked nearby in 1850—was once known as "the White City by the Sea" for the color of its buildings. Today more than 50 of these historical buildings still stand along the town's waterfront hillside, their styles of architecture ranging from the simple bungalows of fishermen to the ornate Queen Anne Victorian of mill owner Wilson Jewett.

Steam Donkey, Third and Water Streets in downtown Reedsport. When it arrived in Reedsport in 1915, this Smith & Watson Steam Donkey was a marvel of a machine, the most advanced and sophisticated source of power any logging operation could have. With its steel cables stretched through the woods and fastened to felled trees, with the belly of its boiler filled with fire and its engine turning with steam, the donkey's drums and winches wound tight, reeling in the logs. Yarding logs this way year after year, this steam donkey eventually worked its way through the woods outside Reedsport, all the way to a canyon of Winchester Creek. There it was abandoned in the 1930s, and there it stayed for six decades, its only visitors the hunters who used it as a shelter, until volunteers rescued it, restored it, and moved the old machine to its current downtown location.

UMPQUA RIVER LIGHTHOUSE

Brandy Bar, 9 miles east of Reedsport off Highway 38. If you're cruising down Highway 38, take a look at the bar in the Umpqua River, near the Umpqua State Wayside. This is Brandy Bar, whose name dates back to August 1850 when the schooner *Samuel Roberts,* the first ship to cross the bar on the Umpqua River, ran aground here. And while the crew waited for the tide to rise and free the ship, reported the captain in his journal, "the bounds of sobriety were exceeded by not a few."

Umpqua River Lighthouse, 2 miles southwest of Winchester Bay off Highway 101 and Discovery Drive. Ignoring the proverbial lesson of the man who built his house upon the sand, the builders of the original Umpqua Lighthouse in 1857—the first lighthouse on the Oregon coast—placed it at the mouth of the Umpqua River. On the sand. It lasted four years. Four decades later they tried again, but this time they built the tower some 100 feet above the river, and since 1894 the Umpqua Lighthouse has stood its ground, the red-and-white beam of its light reaching 20 miles out to sea.

Marshfield Sun Printing Museum, 1049 N. Front, Coos Bay. Before it folded in 1944, the *Sun* was the oldest newspaper in Oregon continuously published by one editor: 54 years, beginning in 1891. Today the paper may be gone, but its building remains, including all its printing equipment and type cases. Adding to the significance of this collection are exhibits of historical photographs of Coos Bay, once known as Marshfield.

Cape Arago Lighthouse, 2 miles southwest of Charleston off Cape Arago Highway near Sunset Bay State Park. Standing offshore from Sunset Bay on Gregory Point islet, the Cape Arago Lighthouse was built in 1934 as the third lighthouse since 1866 to occupy this site—the Pacific pummeled the first two into early retirement—and to protect the shipping lanes leading to and from the timber centers of North Bend and Coos Bay.

FOR FAMILIES **Umpqua Discovery Center** (541-271-4816), 409 Riverfront Way, Reedsport. This interpretive center and museum, which stands on the bank of the Umpqua River, provides lessons in how land, water, and people are the forces that shape the coastal environment in general and the town of Reedsport in particular. Outside the center, however, the lessons range farther afield, for anchored in the river is the ***Hero,*** a research vessel that spent 16 years exploring the Antarctic and that is now open for tours.

CAPE ARAGO LIGHTHOUSE

Whale-Watching (1-800-551-6949; www.whalespoken.org), Oregon Parks and Recreation Department. From the blue lagoons of Mexico to the Bering Sea they swim each spring, these leviathans of the deep that can measure 45 feet and weigh 45 tons, these barnacle-encrusted gray whales whose 10,000-mile round trip is the longest known migration of any animal in the world. But the journey is an uneven one, with the whales heading south in the winter at speeds of about 5 miles per hour and passing the coast in groups of 30 whales per hour, then heading north in the spring at about half the speed and in more scattered groups, the females with calves bringing up the rear. As a result, spring on the Oregon coast signals the beginning of a new whale-watching season, and from mid-March through early June you'll find more than two dozen shoreline sites where volunteers help introduce visitors to these far-ranging whales. In this area, look for the WHALE WATCHING SPOKEN HERE signs at **Umpqua Lighthouse** near Winchester Bay and **Shore Acres State Park** near Charleston.

Agate Hunting, Whiskey Run Beach, access at Seven Devils State Wayside, 8 miles south of Charleston off Seven Devils Road. With every rise and fall of the tide, the beach changes, the waves shifting sand and raising or burying stones. Yet it's the outgoing tide that reveals the agates, the gems of the beach, in newly washed banks and agitated gravel. And so it is along **Whiskey Run Beach,** one of the region's prime agate-bearing areas, where beachcombers can find several varieties of these sea-washed gemstones that have been cut, polished, and prized for at least 6,000 years. The true value of such discoveries, however, may lie beyond the agate itself. "If we knew everything there is to know about even one rock," says beachcomber and agate hunter Sharon Ramirez, "we would know the whole universe, wouldn't we?"

SCENIC DRIVES **Pacific Coast Scenic Byway—southern segment,** 160 paved miles from Florence to the California border along Highway 101. This must be one of the world's great auto tours, miles of highway that hug the coastline, miles of sandy beaches and rolling surf stretching toward that thin blue line where the sea meets the sky. Along the way are scattered enough viewpoints, waysides, and state parks to give visitors a chance to stop whenever the urge strikes to explore a quiet cove or a stretch of shore.

Coos Bay Wagon Road, 78 paved miles in a loop beginning and ending in Coos Bay, or 69 paved and graveled miles from Coos Bay to Roseburg. Because the Coast Range was a mountainous blockade between the early coast settlers and the outside world, it wasn't until 1872 that a road finally crossed the mountains to link Coos Bay with Roseburg and points in between. Even though most of the Coos Bay Wagon Road is paved today, it still bends its way through some tough but beautiful stretches of countryside. To experience it for yourself, you have two choices, both of which begin at the Sumner turnoff on Highway 101, just south of Coos Bay: a 78-mile drive (all paved) that follows the old road for 31 miles to a junction near **Dora** before turning south to **Myrtle Point** and the return trip through **Coquille** to **Coos Bay;** or a 69-mile drive (all but a dozen or so miles paved) that follows the Wagon Road all the way to **Roseburg** and **Interstate 5.**

OREGON DUNES, A 50-MILE-LONG SPAN OF SAND ALONG THE COAST

NATURAL WONDERS **Oregon Dunes National Recreation Area,** along Highway 101 between Florence and North Bend, headquarters at the junction of Highways 101 and 38 in Reedsport. The name of this area describes it well, for the *dunes* consist of 32,000 acres stretching along 47 miles of coastline and protruding as far inland as 3 miles; and the *recreation area* includes—take a breath here—30 lakes, 14 hiking trails, 13 campgrounds, 11 beach parking areas, 9 day-use areas, 3 off-highway vehicle areas, and 1 dunes overlook. This playground with its giant sandbox—along with its beaches, wetlands, forests, and rivers—is the result of wind- and waved-pushed sand forming dunes, damming streams, and shaping one of the largest coastal dunes in the world. (See also *To Do—Camping.*)

Myrtlewood Groves. Because the coasts of California and southwest Oregon are the only places where myrtlewood trees grow, and because the wood is so commercially valuable, the old-growth groves at these locations are rare: **Myrtle Grove Park,** Reedsport city park located at the junction of Highways 101 and 38; **Umpqua Myrtlewood Corridor,** 16 miles east of Reedsport off Highway 38 and near Scottsburg County Park; **Millicoma Myrtlewood Corridor,** 21 miles northeast of Coos Bay off Highway 101, Coos River Highway, and adjacent roads along the East Fork Millicoma River between Nesika County Park and Golden and Silver Falls State Park.

South Slough, 5 miles south of Coos Bay off Seven Devils Road. The nation's first designated Estuarine Sanctuary and the southwest arm of Coos Bay, South Slough is one of the few estuaries in the nation to have escaped development. Consequently, it offers visitors one of the best and closest looks possible at an estuary in its natural state—a combination of tideflats, salt marshes, open waters, and upland forests that involve a chain of life covering 7 square miles. (See also *To Do—Canoeing* and *Hiking.*)

✷ To Do

CAMPING **Lost Lake,** 12 miles north of **Reedsport** off Highway 101, 4 campsites near the shore of a small lake.

Smith River, northeast of Reedsport along the Smith River, its roads or tributaries, 4 campgrounds near **Smith River, Smith River Falls, Vincent Creek,** and **Twin Sisters.**

Loon Lake, 20 miles east of Reedsport off Highway 38, more than 60 lakeside campsites at two camps that lie near nature trails: **Loon Lake** and **East Shore.**

Oregon Dunes National Recreation Area, off Highway 101 between Florence and North Bend, 7 campgrounds near the edge of one of the nation's largest sandboxes as well as near hiking trails and coastal lakes: **Eel Creek** and **North Eel,** 9 miles south of Reedsport off Highway 101; **Windy Cove,** 1 mile southwest of Winchester Bay off Discovery Drive; **Spinreel**, 8 miles south of Winchester Bay off Highway 101; **Blue Bill Lake, Horsefall, Horsefall Beach,** and **Wild Mare,** all 4 miles north of North Bend off Beach Access Road and along the shorelines of Bluebill or Horsefall Lakes. (See also *To See—Natural Wonders.*)

See also *Wilder Places—Parks.*

CANOEING **Empire Lakes Park** (541-2698-1181), off Newmark Avenue, Coos Bay. Within the city limits of Coos Bay lies this 120 acres that consists of areas left to their natural state as well as a lake that prohibits motors.

Sunset Bay, 2 miles southwest of Charleston off Cape Arago Highway. The quiet, lovely cove that protects Sunset Bay from the temperament of the sea also serves to make it an ideal place to scoot a raft or canoe across the water. Even if you're not a paddler yourself, watching kayak paddles flash and drip across the bay can be an intriguing spectacle, a memorable experience.

South Slough, 5 miles south of Charleston off Seven Devils Road (launch areas off Cape Arago Highway and Hinch Road). Ride the tide at South Slough, one of the only undeveloped estuaries in America, and the ebb and flow will move you between worlds—from historical sites of old fish traps, logging camps, railroad pilings, and cattle ranches to wildlife habitats ranging from otter slides to oyster beds. (See also *To See—Natural Wonders.*)

HIKING **Millicoma Marsh,** Blossom Gulch near Blossom Gulch School, Coos Bay. A mile-long nature trail leads to an estuary and adjacent marshes.

Pack Trail, 4 miles southwest of Charleston off the Cape Arago Highway. The ends of this 2-mile trail and former wagon road lie near two state parks, **Shore Acres** and **Cape Arago** (see *Wilder Places—Parks*), and the journey between them—almost all of it accompanied by the raucous, wheezing barks of the coastline's seals—takes you to a World War II bunker, a picnic site and viewpoint, spruce forests and clear-cuts, and scattered stumps of logged cedars.

South Slough, 5 miles south of Charleston off Seven Devils Road. Edging its way through the pieces of the landscape puzzle that comprise South Slough, one of the only estuaries in the country retaining a relatively primitive state, is a system of trails that shows off the countryside while it teaches lessons about watersheds, wildlife, and the workings of tides and rivers. These trails vary in length and character from a quarter-mile overlook of the slough to a 3-mile loop that wanders along a boardwalk and through knee-high skunk cabbage on its way to the estuary itself. (See also *Canoeing* and *To See—Natural Wonders.*)

See also *Wilder Places—Parks.*

✷ Wilder Places

PARKS **Umpqua Lighthouse State Park,** 2 miles southwest of Winchester Bay off Highway 101 and Discovery Drive, day use only. This dune-bordered park located along the shore of **Lake Marie** contains a campground and a shoreline trail and is a short stroll away from the beach as well the historic **Umpqua Lighthouse.** Yet that's just part of it. This park "is featured with unexcelled natural scenic and recreational attributes second to none," wrote Sam Boardman, Oregon's first state park superintendent. "A sea with its various whims. The beautiful **Umpqua River.** Two lovely lakes. An ocean frontage of four miles frescoed with a series of mountainous sand dunes."

William M. Tugman State Park, 5 miles south of Winchester Bay off Highway 101, day use and overnight. Located on the wriggly curved shoreline of freshwater **Eel Lake,** this park melds with coastal forest, sand dunes **(Umpqua Dunes Scenic Area),** and shoreline via the **Umpqua Dunes Trail.**

Golden and Silver Falls State Park, 24 miles northeast of Coos Bay off Highway 101, Coos River Highway, and adjacent roads, day use only. It's to the end of the road you go to find this park, a site sitting along a route that starts out paved and then grows graveled and so narrow that a single logging truck almost fills it from edge to edge. Yet if you make it this far, following two rivers—the **Coos** and the **Millicoma**—to a picnic site spread out beside two creeks and three trails, your reward will be the shade and silence of ancient trees and the spill of water along stone-smooth canyon walls.

Mingus Park, 10th and Commercial Streets, Coos Bay. Every sunny afternoon at Mingus Park takes on the appearance of an old-timey Sunday, where visitors can feed the ducks at the pond, picnic near the gazebo, or wander through the Japanese and rhododendron gardens.

Bastendorff Beach County Park, 2 miles southwest of Charleston off the Cape Arago Highway. Some area residents consider this their favorite place to play on the

THE BOARDWALK AT SOUTH SLOUGH LEADS TO ONE OF THE MOST PRIMITIVE ESTUARIES IN AMERICA

SHORE ACRES, THE FORMER ESTATE OF LUMBER BARON LOUIS SIMPSON, NOW A STATE PARK

beach. Special attractions include a picnic area with covered shelters; campgrounds with showers; and a playground with a fort and **lighthouse,** swings and slides, horseshoe pits and basketball court. But the park's best feature is probably its panoramic view of the ocean and the sunsets.

Cape Arago State Park, 2 to 5 miles southwest of Charleston off the Cape Arago Highway. This may be the most remarkable 5 miles anywhere in Oregon, a dead-end road that stops at the sea and that leads to a historic lighthouse, a hiking trail, a wildlife area, and three state parks that are jewels among parks: **Sunset Bay,** with its sheltered cove of quiet water, its walking trail and ocean overlook, and its view of the **Cape Arago lighthouse; Shore Acres,** site of the manicured grounds and flower beds that were once part of the estate of lumber baron Louis Simpson and that are now the envy of many a gardener's world; and **Cape Arago,** the end of the road and the edge of the sea, where **sea lions** and **seals** outnumber the people.

WILDLIFE REFUGES **Dean Creek,** 3 miles east of Reedsport off Highway 38. Highway turnouts lining this 1,000-acre tract bordering the Umpqua River give visitors a glimpse at the area's herd of as many as 120 **Roosevelt elk,** which wander the wetlands and woodlands and streamside meadows year-round. These elk, which can weigh as much as 1,100 pounds and stand 5 feet at the shoulder, are Oregon's largest land mammal. But the elk aren't the only show at the refuge, for here also gather **waterfowl, ospreys, bald eagles,** and **great blue herons.** Interpretive displays and spotting scopes at the site help visitors sort out the critters.

Estuaries. Some of the most fertile areas on the planet are found in estuaries, where outgoing streams meet incoming tides. Here the blending of waters brews a potent concoction that grows a great variety and number of plant-life and wildlife species. Along Oregon's coast, these can be some of best places to see the food chain in action, from **plankton** and **salmon** to **sea lions** and **elk.** In this area, you can find estuaries at the mouth of the **Umpqua River** west of Winchester Bay, and at **Coos Bay** near the city of Coos Bay.

Tide Pools. The heartbeat of a fragile world pulses beneath the briny water of the beach's rocky shores—the waver of tentacles, the scudding of legs, the glitter of kaleidoscopic greens and reds, oranges and yellows in things algaed and kelped, periwinkled and barnacled that change with the ebb and flow of tides. So if you would look into a universe of life, look here, in the tide pools of the sea. Along the south coast, some of the best tide pools can be found at **Sunset Bay State Park,** 2 miles southwest of Charleston off the Cape Arago Highway and a half mile south of the lighthouse; **Cape Arago State Park,** 5 miles southwest of Charleston off the Cape Arago Highway, consists of three separate intertidal areas; and **Five-Mile Point,** 13 miles south of Coos Bay off Seven Devils Road, with access at Whiskey Run Beach.

Simpson Reef, 5 miles southwest of Charleston off Cape Arago Highway. Considered one of the best viewing areas for pinnipeds—sea mammals with flippers, such as sea lions and seals—on the entire Pacific coast, Simpson Reef can become a tumultuous place during mating, breeding, and pupping seasons. **Northern elephant seals, Steller's** and **California sea lions,** and **harbor seals** all use the area at one time or another, making it the largest haul-out site on the Oregon coast—and a pair of binoculars from a roadside vantage point will take you to the edge of this shoreline sanctuary.

SIMPSON REEF, A REFUGE FOR SEA LIONS AND SEALS

✷ Lodging

BED & BREAKFASTS

Coos Bay

Coos Bay Manor (1-800-269-1224; cbmanor@charter.net; www.virtualcities.com/ons/or/c/orc3601.htm), 955 S. Fifth Street, Coos Bay 97420. "I think our best feature is the uniqueness of the building in a mill town," says Coos Bay Manor owner Patricia Williams. "It is neo-Colonial of all things." Built in 1912 by two Finnish brothers who developed a new—and unprofitable—method of using salt water in making pulp, the home today retains its high ceilings, large rooms, fine woodworking, and second-floor balcony, but it also offers three guest rooms with private baths ($100) and two rooms that share a bath ($80). In addition, a full breakfast is served each morning in the dining room. "I make blueberry Belgian waffles almost daily," Patricia says. She also welcomes well-behaved children older than 4 and, at an extra charge, pets of any age.

The Old Tower House (541-888-6058; donspan1@gte.net, www.virtualcities.com/ons/or/c/orc3602.htm), 476 Newmark, Coos Bay 97420. In 1872 this was the brand-new bayside home of Dr. C. W. Tower, and today guests will find its interior clinging to parts of its past, brass and four-poster beds, Oriental and Persian rugs, wicker rocking chairs and handmade quilts, pedestal sinks and claw-foot tubs, and an upstairs view that includes century-old trees. The home's accommodations include the Carriage House suite, the Ivy Cottage, and five rooms—two with private baths and three with shared bathrooms ($70–100). Children older than 10 are welcome.

This Olde House (541-267-5224; thisoldehouse@harborside.com; www.bnbweb.com/thisoldehouse.html), 202 Alder Street, Coos Bay 97420. From top to bottom the "olde" parts of this 1893 Victorian may also be its best parts: crystal chandeliers, antique furniture, handcrafted woodwork, and inlaid floors. Toss in its second-floor balcony, picket fence, and hillside location that overlooks Coos Bay and you've got a house to reckon with. Its four rooms come with private baths, king or queen beds, and a full breakfast ($85–155). In addition, owner Sally White, a gourmet cook who specializes in Japanese cuisine, will prepare a free dinner for guests staying at least three nights.

COTTAGES

Winchester Bay House (1-800-395-8765; winchesterbayhouse@usa.net; www.winchesterbayhouse.com), corner of Eighth and Beach Streets, Winchester Bay 97467. Located just two blocks off Highway 101 and on the edge of the bay fed by the Umpqua River, this house offers guests the use of a furnished two-bedroom cottage ($65).

✷ Where to Eat

EATING OUT

Charleston

Portside (541-888-5544), 8001 Kingfisher Road, Charleston. Not surprisingly, this restaurant that stands on the edge of Charleston's marina specializes in fresh seafood. With the bustle of fishing boats scooting their way out to sea and back again and with fishermen on the dock tending to their tackle and gear, you'll have a good sense of what's involved in getting that salmon or shrimp or crab you ordered to your table. Helping out with this seafaring atmosphere are the crabs and lobsters living in the Portside's aquariums; they're among the first to greet visitors through the door.

Coos Bay

Blue Heron Bistro (541-267-3933), 100 Commercial Avenue, Coos Bay. A big menu, varied selections, and decent prices are distinguishing characteristics of the Blue Heron, which offers unique dishes ranging from omelets to lasagnas and cooking styles from German to Mexican, Deep South to Northwest.

Cedar Grill (541-267-7100), 274 S. Broadway, Coos Bay. This relatively new restaurant in an old bank building is a gathering spot for a spectrum of people living in or passing through Coos Bay. Wearing blue collars, white collars, or no collars at all, diners come for the stick-to-your-ribs offerings of steak, seafood, ribs, and other fare grilled, fried, or breaded.

Kum-Yon's (541-269-2662), 835 S. Broadway, Coos Bay. Here under one roof are gathered cuisines from around the Asian world, which makes the dishes difficult to pronounce but exotic to experience.

North Bend

Pancake Mill (541-756-2751), Highway 101, North Bend. As the name implies, the Pancake Mill, a local favorite, specializes in breakfasts—and oh, what breakfasts. Pancakes layered and omelets filled and French toast dripping with all the right stuff and served by friendly folks in an inviting, wood-paneled atmosphere.

✷ Special Events

July: **Oregon Coast Music Festival** (1-800-824-8486), Shore Acres State Park, 4 miles southwest of Charleston off Cape Arago Highway. These concerts feature almost every style of music available, from folk to rock and classical to jazz. This is a good excuse to visit this most extraordinary of state parks (see **Cape Arago State Park** under *Wilder Places—Parks*).

August: **Charleston Seafood Festival** (1-800-824-8486), Charleston.

Smith River Country Fair (1-800-247-2155), Smith River Grange, northeast of Reedsport at milepost 9 on Smith River Road. Toss a half ton of beef into a pit barbecue, rustle up a crowd of 500 people, and turn the kids loose for some three-legged races, a chicken scramble, and a greased pig chase, and you've got yourself the annual Smith River Country Fair, a one-day celebration of summertime food and games whose roots run deep into farming's past.

BANDON–PORT ORFORD AREA

GUIDANCE **Bandon by the Sea Chamber of Commerce** (541-347-9616; www.bandon.com), 300 Second Street, Bandon 97411.

Coquille Chamber of Commerce (541-396-3414; www.harborside.com/~chamber2000), 119 N. Birch, Coquille 97423.

Myrtle Point Chamber of Commerce (541-572-2002), 424 Fifth Street, Myrtle Point 97458.

Oregon State Parks: Headquarters (503-378-6305), State Parks and Recreation Department, 525 Trade Street S. E., Salem 97301.

Port Orford Chamber of Commerce (541-332-8055; www.portorfordoregon.com), 520 Jefferson and Highway 101, Port Orford 97465.

Siskiyou National Forest: Headquarters (541-471-6500), 200 N. E. Greenfield Road, Grants Pass 97526; **Powers Ranger District** (541-439-3011).

GETTING THERE Bandon, Port Orford, and nearby communities are reached from the east by Highway 42 and are linked by Highway 101, which runs the entire length of the Oregon coast.

MEDICAL EMERGENCY **Coquille Valley Hospital** (541-396-3101), 940 E. Fifth Street, Coquille.

Southern Coos Hospital (541-347-2426), 900 11th Street S. E., Bandon.

✷ To See

MUSEUMS **Coquille River Museum** (541-347-2164), 270 Fillmore Street and Highway 101, Bandon. Gold strikes, Indian wars, coal mines, steamships, downtown fires—these are chapters in the region's story that are preserved and explained at the Coquille River Museum in Bandon. Also within the walls of this former City Hall and bar—though not at the same time—visitors can learn what it takes for a small coastal town to carve out a name for itself, from growing cranberries and making cheese to promoting tourism through the congenial-looking group of young men known in the 1920s as the "Sons of the Beaches."

BANDON BEACH

Coos County Logging Museum (541-572-3153), corner of Seventh and Maple Streets, Myrtle Point. Logging has shaped not only Oregon's forests but also its people, especially along the coast, where generations of men have gone to the woods in answer to the only calling they ever heard. As a result, logging has become not just a job, but a way of life, complete with its own language and tools. So if you want to know about bindle stiffs or butt riggings, nose bags or donkey doctors, pickaroons or peter hooks, stop by this museum, which preserves and honors the logging industry, its people, and its history. In fact, the museum building—with its rooflines rounded or pointed or arched, built in 1910 in the style of the Mormon Temple in Salt Lake City—is worth a stop in itself.

HISTORIC HOMES **Wagner House,** along the main road in Powers. Hand-hewn and log-slabbed, this 1872 house is the oldest in the area, built by David Wagner and his family, who moved from North Carolina to settle here near the South Fork of the Coquille River.

HISTORIC SITES **Coquille River Lighthouse,** 2 miles north of Bandon off Highway 101 in Bullard State Park. Built in 1891 near the north jetty at the mouth of the Coquille River—the last lighthouse built on the Oregon coast—the Coquille River Light protected steamships crossing the treacherous bar on their way upriver to the logging camps and sawmills. After its abandonment in 1939, it became the target of vandals and neglect until it was rescued, restored, and placed on the National Park Service's Register of Historic Places during America's bicentennial. Today it serves as a museum to visitors and as a beloved landmark to the residents of nearby Bandon, who decorate it with lights every Christmas.

Bandon Old Town, Bandon waterfront off Highway 101. You can't keep a good town down. Take Bandon, for example, which has been destroyed twice by fire. "Bandon, the beautiful city by the sea, lies stricken," reported the *Coos Bay Times* in June 1914, "smoke-stained, fire-scarred, in a heap of ashes today." But when the fire was over, the people of Bandon rebuilt their town. Then in 1936, fire struck again, burning to the ground all but 16 of the town's 500 buildings. "You could hear it coming with a roar," says Mary Capps, who survived the fire. "But the mills didn't burn. Seventy-five to eighty percent of the people lost houses and the stores burned, but people still had jobs." And once again, the people of Bandon rebuilt their town. Although Bandon's Old Town today holds a collection of crafts and retail shops, it also holds the memories of a fiery past.

Cape Blanco Lighthouse, 9 miles northwest of Port Orford off Highway 101 and Cape Blanco Highway. In operation since 1870, longer than any other lighthouse on the Oregon coast, this light stands 245 feet tall on the westernmost point in Oregon. Even though winds can blast it at over 100 miles per hour, its light continues to flash every 20 seconds, warning nearby ships of offshore reefs.

Battle Rock, south shoreline of Port Orford off Highway 101. One of the first attempts to settle the south coast ended in disaster, when Captain William Tichenor of the steamer *Sea Gull,* which operated between Portland and San Francisco, dropped off nine men just offshore of today's Port Orford, near a rock islet that was soon to earn the name Battle Rock. "On the morning of the ninth of June, 1851, we were landed on the beach just below Battle Rock," wrote J. M. Kirkpatrick, who was in charge of the group. "There were a few Indians in sight who appeared to be friendly but I could see that they did not like to have us there." Kirkpatrick and his men moved their camp to Battle Rock, loaded their cannon, and waited. The next day, when a group of Indians approached the camp, Kirkpatrick lit the cannon's fuse. "At least twelve or thirteen men were killed outright," Kirkpatrick wrote, "and such a tumbling of scared Indians I never saw before or since." After a subsequent battle 15 days later, the men abandoned their camp and fled northward, eventually reaching help on the Umpqua River. Captain Tichenor later returned to the Battle Rock area, filed a homestead claim, and platted the town of Port Orford.

FOR FAMILIES ✐ **West Coast Game Park** (541-347-3106), 7 miles south of Bandon off Highway 101. This must be the nation's largest petting zoo: more than 450 animals representing 75 different species wandering about the 21-acre grounds, mingling with the visitors and looking to be rubbed, stroked, or cuddled. This includes some creatures—including lions and tigers and bears, oh my!—that in the wild might consider you to be merely a snack before dinner. (Granted, most of the affection comes from the young of the species, before they realize they have claws and fangs.) The reason for the docile behavior on this dryland Noah's ark is that the animals are raised by hand and accustomed to people, a practice that has been going on for more than 30 years at the park. The result is an encounter that seems almost mythological. After all, how often do you get the chance to pet a snow leopard?

Whale-Watching (1-800-551-6949; www.whalespoken.org), Oregon Parks and Recreation Department. **Face Rock State Scenic Viewpoint** near Bandon, and **Cape Blanco Lighthouse** and **Battle Rock City Park** near Port Orford.

SCENIC DRIVES **Pacific Coast Scenic Byway—southern segment,** 160 paved miles from Florence to the California border along Highway 101. This must be one of the world's great auto tours, miles of highway that hug the coastline, miles of sandy beaches and rolling surf stretching toward that thin blue line where the sea meets the sky. Along the way are scattered enough viewpoints, waysides, and state parks to give visitors a chance to stop whenever the urge strikes to explore a quiet cove or a stretch of shore.

Coquille River Drive, 18 paved miles from Bandon to Coquille along the Coquille River and Highway 42S. This is the paved version of the 19th-century river route followed by stern-wheelers as they hauled passengers and freight in to Coquille and shipments of coal out to San Francisco. Along the way you'll pass through the historical communities of **Prosper, Parkersburg,** and **Riverton,** whose once thriving mills, canneries, and shipyards went the way of the steamships that made them all possible.

Powers Route, 100 paved and graveled miles along Highways 42S, 42, and 242; and Powers South Road, Forest Road 33, and Rogue River Road from Bandon to Gold Beach. An inland bypass of the coast highway, this route carries travelers into coastal valleys, onto mountain slopes, and along three major **rivers**—the **Coquille,** the **Rogue,** and the **Illinois**—before breaking out again near the shoreline.

NATURAL WONDERS **Doerner Fir,** 41 miles east of Coquille off the Fairview–Coquille, Coos Bay Wagon, Middle Creek, and Burnt Mountain Roads. If you're willing to drive 40 miles of back roads for the chance to take a half-mile hike, you'll come face-to-face with the 500-year-old Doerner Fir, the **National Champion Coast Douglas Fir Tree,** which measures 329 feet tall and almost 12 feet thick and contains enough wood to build five houses.

Myrtlewood Groves. As bending as an old myrtlewood's limbs, this route leads to some of the largest remaining groves of myrtlewood trees, which grow only along the coast of California and in southwestern Oregon. And because the myrtlewood grows oh, so slowly but produces wood that's oh, so lovely and commercially valuable, groves such as these are treasures. **Laverne County Park,** 15 miles northeast of Coquille off Coquille–Fairview Road; **Cherry Creek County Park,** 10 miles east of Coquille off Coquille–Fairview and Lee– McKinley Roads; **Wallace Dement Myrtlewood Grove,** 5 miles south of Coquille off Highway 42 and Fishtrap Road and near Coos County Park; **Myrtle Point,** on Highway 42, walking tour of the city's myrtlewood trees; **Bennett County Park,**

8 miles northeast of Myrtle Point off North Fork Road and across the Gravelford Bridge; **Maria C. Jackson State Park,** 22 miles northeast of Myrtle Point off the Myrtle Point–Sitkum Road; **Hoffman Memorial Myrtle Grove,** 3 miles east of Myrtle Point off Highway 42; **Albert Powers Memorial State Park,** 7 miles south of Myrtle Point off Highways 42 and 242; **Coquille Myrtle Grove State Park,** 14 miles south of Myrtle Point off Highways 42 and 242; **Orchard Park,** 2 miles south of Powers off Powers South Road; **Myrtle Grove Campground,** 8 miles south of Powers off Powers South Road and Forest Road 33; **Rogue River Myrtle Groves,** 10 to 12 miles northeast of Gold Beach off Jerry's Flat Road and along the Rogue River, sites include the **world's largest myrtlewood tree** (88 feet tall and almost 42 feet in circumference) as well as groves near Quosatana and Lobster Creek Campgrounds; **Alfred A. Loeb State Park,** 10 miles northeast of Brookings off North Bank Chetco River Road; **Humbug Myrtle Grove,** 6 miles south of Port Orford off Highway 101; **Edson County Park,** 4 miles east of Sixes off Sixes River Road; **Sweet Myrtle Preserve,** 8 miles east of Bandon off the Coquille–Bandon Highway.

✷ To Do

CAMPING **Burnt Mountain,** 28 miles northeast of Coquille off the Coquille–Fairview, Coos Bay Wagon, Middle Creek, and Burnt Mountain Roads, 95 campsites, including a horse camp and yurts.

Frona County Park, 18 miles northeast of Myrtle Point off the North Fork Road, 17 campsites on the bank of the East Fork Coquille River.

South Fork Coquille River, south of Powers off Highway 242, South Powers Road, or Forest Road 33 or its spur roads, 12 campgrounds stretching out along the South Fork of the Coquille River: **Powers County Park, Orchard City Park, Myrtle Grove, Daphne Grove, Island, Rock Creek, Squaw Lake, Peacock, Lockhart, Buck Creek, Pioneer,** and **Eden Valley.**

Elk River, southeast of Port Orford along Elk River Road (access is north of Port Orford off Highway 101), 4 campgrounds near Grassy Knob Wilderness and along Elk River or its tributaries: **Sunshine Bar, Butler Bar,** and **Laird Lake.**

See also *Wilder Places—Parks.*

GOLF **Bandon Dunes** (1-888-345-6008), Round Lake Drive, Bandon, 18 holes.

HIKING **New River,** 10 miles south of Bandon off Highway 101 and Croft Road. Wandering along the borders and banks of Oregon's newest river is a 3-mile system of trails divided into seven linking pathways. These range in length from a quarter mile to 1 mile and lead to pieces of the area's landscape mosaic, including lakeshores, riverbanks, sand dunes, mudflats, and meadowlands.

See also *Wilder Places—Wilderness Areas.*

✷ Wilder Places

PARKS **Laverne County Park,** 18 miles northeast of Coquille off the Coquille–Fairview Road. With the North Fork Coquille River running along its edge, this park invites visitors to take a dip or cast a line in the stream, take a stroll through the old-growth **Douglas firs** or **myrtlewood groves,** maybe put down overnight roots at its campground—its rest rooms include showers—or give the kids a push on the swings on the playground.

Bullards Beach State Park, 2 miles north of Bandon off Highway 101 and at the mouth of the Coquille River, day use and overnight. Flowing west, as any well-behaved stream on the Pacific coast should, the Coquille River nears its joining with the sea—and then seems to change its mind. It turns away, bends to the south, runs sideways to the surf until it seems to change its mind again, then, the tease over, veers west and this time finds its way to the sea. And in that strip of beach the south-flowing segment carves lies this park, named for pioneer settlers who once operated a store, a ferry, and a post office near the river's mouth. Within the park are a campground with almost 200 campsites (including 13 yurts), 7 miles of trails, and almost 5 miles of beach, while nearby stands a **historic lighthouse** and a **wildlife refuge.**

Bandon State Park, 1 to 5 miles south of Bandon off Beach Loop Road, day use only. Seabirds and sea stacks and sandy stretches of beach have folks peering through their cameras at this 900-acre day-use park. One of the most popular places for photographers is **Face Rock** near downtown Bandon. According to an ancient legend, the "face" in the rock belongs to that of Ewauna, an Indian woman who one day went swimming in the sea and was caught by the evil spirit Seatka. In spite of the valiant efforts of Ewauna's dog, Komax, to save her, Seatka kept a tight hold on Ewauna, trying to get her to look into his eyes, the source of his power. Yet Ewauna kept her face turned to the sky, gazing at the moon so steadily and for so long that she eventually

NEW RIVER AND SOME OF ITS WETLANDSS

turned to stone. But today if you stare long enough at the face in the rock, especially as the sun is setting and the tide turning and the light dimming toward a star-spangled night along the beach, you might swear you see Ewauna shift her gaze just long enough to stare back.

Floras Lake State Park, 12 miles northwest of Port Orford off Highway 101 and Airport Road, day use only. If you're searching for a spot of wild along the coast, a place where the roads remain rutted and the tangles ungroomed, where the sounds come naturally from the roar of surf and the throats of seabirds, then look here at the more than 1,300 acres that makes up one of the few undeveloped parks on the coast. Even the few times that civilization poked its way in here, including during the digging of a sandstone quarry in the 1880s and the building of a navy airstrip in the 1940s, the land remains relatively untouched by machines, though windsurfers have discovered the shallow lake, and developers have staked out parts of the lakeshore.

Cape Blanco State Park, 9 miles northwest of Port Orford off Highway 101 and Cape Blanco Highway, day use and overnight. This 3-square-mile park located on Cape Blanco, the westernmost point in Oregon, was once the ranchland of Irish immigrants Patrick Hughes and Jane O'Neil Hughes, who arrived here in 1860 and before long made their fortune by raising meat, milk, and butter and selling it as far away as San Francisco. The historic **Hughes House**—an Eastlake Victorian built in 1898, just three years before Patrick's death—is all that's left of the family that for 111 years lived here on the cape, near where the Sixes River flows into the sea. Today the park contains an extensive system of campgrounds and trails as well as a **historic lighthouse.**

Battle Rock City Park, south shoreline of Port Orford off Highway 101. Located near historic Battle Rock, this city park offers a shoreline picnic area and a nearby hiking trail.

Humbug Mountain State Park, 6 miles south of Port Orford off Highway 101, day use and overnight. Prime attractions of this park and campground are its 4 miles of beach and its 3-mile, Civilian Conservation Corps (CCC)–built hiking trail that leads to the summit of Humbug Mountain, the highest point on the coastline at 1,748 feet.

WILDERNESS AREAS **Grassy Knob,** 9 miles east of Port Orford off Highway 101 and Grassy Knob Road, 27 square miles. This steep, brushy wilderness in the northern portion of the **Siskiyou National Forest** receives 11 feet of annual rainfall, grows some of the biggest **Port Orford cedars** left in the world, and was the target of an incendiary bomb dropped in 1942 from a seaplane transported to the Oregon coast by a Japanese submarine. (The pilot, Nubuo Fujita, and his submarine escaped, though he returned after the war to apologize; the unexploded bomb has never been found.) Few trails cut this forested region, though the **Grassy Knob Trail,** part of which is a gravel road, penetrates less than a mile and a half from the wilderness boundary near the end of Grassy Knob Road. From here it leads to the top of Grassy Knob and its panoramic views of the Pacific.

WILDLIFE REFUGES **Bandon Marsh National Wildlife Refuge,** 2 miles north of Bandon off Highway 101 near Bullards Beach State Park. For at least four centuries this estuary at the mouth of the Coquille River was the site of native tribes' fishing camps and summer villages, until a massive earthquake forced them to abandon it some 300 years ago. Then when the first settlers arrived on the coast and decided such places were better suited for fields and pastures, the filling and draining began, and Oregon lost three-fourths of all its salt marshes. Yet somehow the Bandon Marsh survived, and today it provides more than 300 acres of habitat for more than 100 species of migrating **waterfowl** and **shorebirds** and 45 species of **fish,** as well as for **resident raptors** such as **bald eagles** and **ospreys.** Plus, plans call for the addition of 570 acres of adjacent uplands and pastures, which will be restored to their original wetlands condition. The best viewing of the area is probably at nearby **Bullards Beach State Park** (see *Parks*).

Estuaries. Coquille River, near Bandon; **Sixes River** and **Elk River,** north of Port Orford.

New River, 10 miles south of Bandon off Highway 101 and Croft Road. Pindar, the great lyric poet of ancient Greece, called water "the noblest of the elements." Along this stretch of south coast, it's also one of the *newest* of the elements—at least as far as this freshwater stream is concerned. Created in the 1890s either by settlers digging a marsh-draining channel or by floods carving a new bed for Floras Creek—it depends on the story you believe—New River is a 9-mile stream separated from the sea by a spit of sand, and its adjacent wetlands, mudflats, and lakes provide habitat for resident **raptors, spawning salmon,** and **migrating waterfowl** and **shorebirds.**

Tide Pools. Coquille Point, west of Bandon, access at either the south bank of the Coquille River or the trailhead at 11th Street; **Cape Blanco State Park,** 9 miles northwest of **Port Orford** off Highway 101 and Cape Blanco Highway; **Port Orford,** north of the boat dock off Ninth Street; Rocky Point, 3 miles south of Port Orford off Highway 101; **Arizona Ranch Beach,** 12 miles south of Port Orford, access through private, fee-charging Arizona Ranch Campground.

Oregon Islands National Wildlife Refuge. Even though this refuge consists of just over a square mile, and even though that area is spread across 1,477 offshore rocks and islands, this is one of the most important wildlife refuges in the state, a seasonal home to more than a million **seabirds** as well as thousands of **sea lions** and **seals.** These areas are off-limits to human visitors, but good viewing sites along Highway 101 or its spur roads include **Cape Blanco,** 9 miles northwest of Port Orford, and **Battle Rock** on the south shoreline of Port Orford.

* Lodging

BED & BREAKFASTS

Bandon

Beach Street Bed & Breakfast (1-888-335-1076; sharon@beach-street.com; www.beach-street.com), 200 Beach Street, Bandon 97411. The guest rooms and private decks of this B&B, which sits atop an 80,000-year-old sand dune just 100 yards from shoreline, have views of the ocean and access to the beach. All six rooms ($125–180) have private baths and include a gourmet breakfast, and guests are invited to use the skylight-lit great room with fireplace.

🐾 ✐ **Dunshee House at Face Rock** (1-888-347-5030; dnd@dunshee.com; www.dunshee.com), 1860 Beach Loop Drive, Bandon 97411. This home is close enough to Bandon's beachfront that the sea rocks seem to loom just outside the windows. It offers two suites, each with a furnished kitchen, a path to the beach, and a deck with an ocean view ($75–140). Children and pets are welcome in the Sunset suite.

Lighthouse Bed & Breakfast (541-347-9316; shirley@lighthouselodging.com; www.moriah.com/lighthouse), 650 Jetty Road, Bandon 97411. The river, the ocean, and the lighthouse—these are your views from this inn that's located on the beach across from the **Coquille River Lighthouse** but still within walking distance of town. The five guest rooms in this 1980 home come with private baths, whirlpool tubs, and fireplaces ($110–185). A full breakfast is served in the dining room, and wine is available in the evening.

The River House (1-888-221-6936; info@riverhousebandon.com; www.riverhousebandon.com), Bandon 97411. Located near the beach as well as the **Coquille River and its lighthouse,** this 1905 two-story Colonial Revival building, which once did business as Boots, Shoes and Gents' Furnishings, survived the fires of 1914 and 1936, each of which almost destroyed Bandon, to stand today as the city's oldest commercial building. Its four guest rooms include two master suites. Rates $175-–195.

Langlois

Floras Lake House by the Sea (541-348-2573; floraslk@harborside.com; www.floraslake.com), 92870 Boice Cope Road, Langlois 97450. A sprawling 1990s home framed by flowers and trees, this B&B nuzzles up to the shoreline of Flora Lake. It is, says owners Liz and Will Brady, "The only B and B on the coast that offers lake and ocean views from all rooms." Those four, second-floor guest rooms come with private baths, vaulted ceilings, deck entrances, and a buffet breakfast ($110–135). In addition, nearby hiking trails lead to lake or beach.

Port Orford

Home by the Sea Bed & Breakfast (541-332-2855; b2b@homebythesea.com; www.homebythesea.com), 444 Jackson Street, Port Orford 97465. It took two decades for owners Alan and Brenda Mitchell to design and build their home by the sea, and in 1988 they opened it as a B&B. "We have direct beach access and are located on a bit of a peninsula looking southeasterly over miles of unspoiled beach," Alan says. "It's a short walk to restaurants, public beaches, historic **Battle Rock Park,** and the town's harbor—the home port of Oregon's only crane-launched commercial fishing fleet." The two guest rooms come with queen beds, private baths, and a full breakfast ($95–105). In addition, because the beach lies just outside the back door, the hosts also provide a **shuttle service** for those who want to hike the beach in one direction, then pick up their cars for the return trip.

✱ Where to Eat

DINING OUT **Harp's** (541-347-9057), 480 I Street S. W., Bandon. Harp's resides in one of the toughest buildings in Bandon, a survivor of two major fires that burned down most of the town, as well as floods that tried to carry it away. Now it sits quietly on the bank of the Coquille River, minding its own business as it watches the nearby lighthouse. Yet retirement must be far from its mind, for it still serves some of the best seafood and offers one of the most extensive wine lists on this part of the coast.

EATING OUT

Bandon

Keefer's Old Town Café (541-347-1133), 160 Baltimore Avenue, Bandon. Weekend breakfasts, especially Sunday brunch, can send the waiting line at Keefer's out the door, while lunches (sandwiches and soups) and dinners (beef, chicken, seafood, and daily specials) attract crowds of their own. The wooden floors and booths and the antique furnishings promote a sense of casual, comfortable dining.

Lord Bennett's (541-347-3163), 1695 Beach Loop Drive, Bandon. With one of the best views going in a view-happy town, Lord Bennett's could probably rest on its scenery and scrimp on the food—but it doesn't. The chicken and fish and shellfish here are grilled, marinated, or stuffed with enough flavor that the restaurant would probably do just fine without the ocean looming just beyond the windows.

Port Orford

Crazy Norwegians (541-332-8601), 259 Highway 101, Port Orford. Sure, it's a fish-and-chips restaurant, but the meals and the service here win loyal customers.

Paradise Café (541-332-8104), 1825 Highway 101, Port Orford. The Paradise Café features the home-style cooking of Cathy Ross, which many locals believe is *far* better than what Mom used to make.

Paula's Bistro (541-332-9378), 236 Highway 101, Port Orford. Even though this is a casual, come-as-you-are restaurant, it offers fine dining prepared by Paula herself, who has cooked in fine restaurants in Sausalito, San Francisco, Lake Tahoe, and Ashland, among other places. She also furnishes most of the paintings that hang in the bistro, which sometimes features professional musicians to serenade diners. (Other forms of entertainment include pool tables, dartboards, and pinball machines.) The menu changes almost daily to ensure freshness and, one locals says, "to prevent boredom."

Salsa Rita's (541-332-748), 2812 Highway 101, Port Orford. This is the best Mexican restaurant in town, some say in the region.

✷ Special Events

May: **Food and Wine Festival** (541-347-9616), Bandon. **Sand Castle and Sand Sculpture Contest** (541-347-9616), Bandon. Every spring along the lovely beach of Bandon there gather individuals, families, and teams of builders who spend the day converting sand in to castles or ships, fish or birds, mermaids or dragons, or any other shape that fits their imaginations.

GOLD BEACH–BROOKINGS AREA

GUIDANCE **Brookings-Harbor Chamber of Commerce** (1-800-535-9469; www.brookingsor.com), 16330 Lower Harbor Road, Brookings 97415.

Gold Beach Visitors Center (1-800-525-2334; www.goldbeach.org), 29279 Ellensburg #3, Gold Beach 97444.

Oregon State Parks: Headquarters (503-378-6305), State Parks and Recreation Department, 525 Trade Street S. E., Salem 97301.

Siskiyou National Forest: Headquarters (541-471-6500), 200 N. E. Greenfield Road, Grants Pass 97526; **Chetco Ranger District** (541-469-2196); **Gold Beach Ranger District** (541-247-3600).

GETTING THERE Gold Beach, Brookings, and nearby communities are reached from the east by Highways 42 and 199 and are linked by Highway 101, which runs the entire length of the Oregon coast.

MEDICAL EMERGENCY **Curry General Hospital** (541-247-6621), 94220 E. Fourth Street, Gold Beach.

✷ To See

MUSEUMS **Curry County Historical Museum** (541-247-6113), 920 S. Ellensburg Avenue, Curry County Fairgrounds, Gold Beach. Within this rustic building lies the stuff of the history of this part of the south coast: Native American artifacts, baskets, arrowheads, and petroglyphs; photographic collections devoted to pioneer settlements, logging equipment, commercial fishing, and natural disasters; maritime displays depicting ships and their wrecks; and, perhaps the star of the show, Herman the Miner, a mannequin rather than a man, but a nice fellow all the same, spending his days in his one-room cabin, surrounded by the gear and gadgets that make a miner's life much as it was almost 150 years ago.

Chetco Valley Historical Museum (541-469-6651), 15461 Museum Road, Brookings. Big chunks of the Chetco Valley's history might fall under these headings: Chetco Indians (the area's first inhabitants; some 500 surviving members are seeking tribal status), lumber and boxes (the town's namesake, Robert Brookings, owned the local company that started the town), incendiary bombs (the only Japanese bombs dropped by a World War II plane to hit the mainland United States; they landed east of town), and Easter lilies (the area raises 90 percent of the country's supply). And the Chetco Valley Museum fills in many of the gaps. (It also grows the nation's **largest Monterey cypress** tree on its grounds.)

FOR FAMILIES **Jet Boat Rides.** The only machines that can tackle the wild **Rogue River** on an upstream ride, jet boats haul passengers through rapids and splashes for an adventure along one of the most famous whitewater rivers in the Northwest. **Jerry's Jet Boats** (1-800-451-3645; www.roguejets.com), Gold Beach.**Mail Boat Hydro Jets** (1-800-458-3511; www.mailboat.com), Gold Beach.

Whale-Watching (1-800-551-6949; www.whalespoken.org), Oregon Parks and Recreation Department. **Cape Sebastian State Scenic Corridor** near Gold Beach and **Harris Beach State Park** near Brookings.

Fire Lookout Rentals (541-471-6516), Siskiyou National Forest, 200 N. E. Greenfield Road, Grants Pass. If you find the thought of camping at the tops of towers on the summits of mountains in some of the state's most remote areas an appealing adventure, then consider renting a fire lookout in the **Siskiyou National Forest.** As with any camping trip, you'll need to pack along your own food and water, but waiting for you in these 12- to 15-foot-square perches is a bunk for the night and a view you can find nowhere else: **Lake of the Woods,** 21 miles northeast of Brookings, a 90-minute drive from Gold Beach along narrow roads; **Snow Camp** (in 1990, the first lookout in the Northwest offered for rental), 36 miles northeast of Brookings and 4,200 feet in elevation, with views that reach from the Pacific Ocean to the Kalmiopsis Wilderness; **Quail Prairie,** 26 miles east of Brookings, a 52-foot tower located near the western edge of the Kalmiopsis Wilderness.

SCENIC DRIVES **Pacific Coast Scenic Byway—southern segment,** 160 paved miles from Florence to the California border along Highway 101. This must be one of the world's great auto tours, miles of highway that hug the coastline, miles of sandy beaches and rolling surf stretching toward that thin blue line where the sea meets the sky. Along the way are scattered enough viewpoints, waysides, and state parks to give visitors a chance to stop whenever the urge strikes to explore a quiet cove or a stretch of shore.

Gold Beach to Grants Pass, 98 paved miles along Jerrys Flat and Agness Roads, Forest Road 23, and the Galice Access, Galice-Merlin, Upper River, and Lower River Roads. One way to see some of the wild stretches of the lower Rogue River and the countryside it drains is to follow it along this route, which traces the river's canyon and highlands upstream.

Carpenterville Road, 21 paved miles from south of Pistol River to north of Brookings. Before the completion in 1961 of the Thomas Creek Bridge—located approximately halfway between Pistol River and Brookings, and at 345 feet the highest bridge on the entire Pacific coast north of San Francisco—the coast highway veered away from the shoreline and headed inland, where it climbed and bent its way along this road that cuts through the foothills of the **Siskiyou Mountains.** Today most of the traffic along the southern coast follows the beaches and misses this road, leaving it as a scenic byway for those seeking a less hurried pace. To the north, its beginning lies just south of Pistol River Scenic Viewpoint; to the south, near Harris Beach State Park.

NATURAL WONDERS **Siskiyou Coast,** off Highway 101 from New River to the California border. To the north, nature may have whittled away at the coast and loggers at the hills, but along the last 85 miles of Oregon's southern coastline stretches a beach that is the way the entire Pacific Coast used to be—its offshore lined with craggy sea stacks, its mountain slopes dark with ancient forests.

✷ To Do

CAMPING **Sixes River,** east of Sixes off Sixes River Road, 2 campgrounds along the river's bank: **Edson County Park** and **Sixes River.**

Rogue River, off Jerrys Flat and Agness Roads and along the Rogue River northwest of Gold Beach, 5 campgrounds for those who want to experience a segment of one of the Northwest's wildest rivers: **Lobster Creek, Quosatana Creek, Oak Flat, Illahe,** and **Foster Bar.**

North Chetco River, northeast of Brookings along North Bank Chetco River Road, 4 camps located along the bank of the North Chetco River: **Little Redwood, South Fork, Miller Bar,** and **Nook Bar.**

Winchuck River, southeast of Brookings off Highway 101, Winchuck River Road, and Forest Roads 1107 or 1108, 2 campgrounds located near the river: **Winchuck** and **Ludlum House.**

See also *Wilder Places—Parks.*

GOLF **Salmon Run Golf Course** (1-877-423-1234), 99040 S. Bank Chetco River Road, Brookings, 18 holes.

HIKING **Shrader Old Growth Trail,** 12 miles northeast of Gold Beach off Highway 101, Jerrys Flat Road, and Forest Road 100. This 1-mile loop trail passes through the shade of some of the region's largest old-growth Douglas fir and hardwood groves.

Redwood Grove Nature Trail, 9 miles northeast of Brookings off the North Bank Chetco River Road. Along this trail you'll find a sanctuary for the region's northernmost stands of **coastal redwoods.**

See also *Wilder Places—Parks.*

✷ Wilder Places

PARKS **Cape Sebastian State Park,** 7 miles south of Gold Beach off Highway 101, day use only. On a clear day you can see almost 100 miles of coastline from the viewpoints along this day-use park, 100 miles of sand and sea and sky stretching south into California and north to Cape Blanco. Two miles away, along a trail that cuts through meadows and forests, lies the beach, sighted in 1603 by the Spaniard Sebastian Vizcaino from the deck of his ship, and visited in 1942 by a Japanese submarine that had stopped to recharge its batteries.

Pistol River State Park, 11 miles south of Gold Beach off Highway 101, day use only. The lure this park uses to catch visitors coming down the hill toward it is a view of sandy beaches and sea stacks and the curved banks of the Pistol River sweeping toward the sea. Although the area contains no campgrounds, walks along the beach and birdwatching near the estuary are reason enough to spend time here.

Alfred A. Loeb State Park, 10 miles northeast of Brookings off North Bank Chetco River Road, day use and overnight. One reason for this park along the Chetco River is to protect its grove of old-growth myrtlewood trees, whose wood has been in such high commercial demand for so long that it's the West's most expensive hardwood. As a result, trees such as these are a rare find. Many of this park's campsites, both traditional and hiker/biker camps, lie in the shade of that grove as well as adjacent to a hiking trail that leads along the riverbank and through a redwood forest, some of its trees dating back more than 800 years.

Samuel H. Boardman State Park, 4 miles north of Brookings off Highway 101, day use only. For those who want to know the coast's tangled forests and jutting headlands, its rolling surf and craggy rocks, this park contains one of its finest stretches—12 miles of sand, tide, and woods.

Harris Beach State Park, 2 miles north of Brookings off Highway 101, day use and overnight. You can't camp much closer to the beach than this without getting your feet wet. Although few overnight sites at the park offer ocean views, you're only a short stroll from sand, surf, and several trails that lead throughout the area.

WILDLIFE REFUGES **Estuaries. Rogue River,** north of Gold Beach; **Pistol River,** west of Pistol River; and **Chetco River** and **Winchuck River,** south of Brookings.

Tide Pools. Lone Ranch Beach, 5 miles north of Brooking off Highway 101; **Harris Beach State Park,** 2 miles north of Brookings and west of campground, access south of main parking lot and along beach; **Winchuck Beach,** 5 miles south of Brookings off Highway 101 and north side of Winchuck River.

Oregon Islands National Wildlife Refuge. Part of the more than 1,400 offshore rocks that make up this refuge are found at **Cape Sebastian,** 7 miles south of Gold Beach; **Samuel H. Boardman,** 4 miles north of Brookings; and **Harris Beach,** 2 miles north of Brookings.

✱ Lodging

See also **Fire Lookout Rentals** under *To Do—For Families.*

BED & BREAKFASTS

Brookings

Brookings South Coast Inn (1-800-525-9273; innkeeper@southcoastinn.com; www.southcoastinn.com), 516 Redwood Street, Brookings 97415. This 1917 two-story Craftsman with a wraparound porch and antique furnishings is set up with a hot tub and sauna, a stone fireplace and grand piano, and panoramic ocean views. Its four guest rooms each come with a private bath and a full breakfast ($89–129). Children older than 12 are welcome.

✐ **Chetco River Inn** (541-670-1645; chetcoriverinn@chetcoriverinn.com; www.chetcoriverinn.com), 21202 High Prairie Road, Brookings 97415. Described by owner Sandra Brugger as an "environmentally sensitive lodge," this 1987 inn has marble floors and Oriental rugs inside, a garden and woods outside, all of it seemingly wrapped in 40 private, quiet acres of land. All five of its guest rooms come with private baths, river views, and a full breakfast ($115–135). Kids "old enough to stay in their own room" are welcome.

Pacific View Bed & Breakfast (1-800-461-4830; ursula@pacificview-bb.com; wwwpacificviewbb.com), 18814 Montbretia Lane, Brookings 97415. The name of this B&B explains one of its outstanding features. "At the Pacific View we have a suite of rooms overlooking the Pacific," says owner Ursula Mackey, "and we have some of the best sunsets in the entire U.S." And if you stay here, you won't have to fight to get a front-row seat at one of these sunsets, either. "Being very small we only take two guests at a time," Ursula says. "Therefore, it's very quiet." One of the two suites comes with a private bathroom and entrance as well as a fireplace and stove ($80–85). In addition, a full breakfast is served in an enclosed sunroom, where you can also watch storms and migrating whales. "We are very proud of our area," Ursula says. "It is much different from other parts of Oregon."

Sea Dreamer Inn (1-800-408-4367; innkeeper@seadreamerinn.com), 15167 McVay Lane, Brookings 97415. Once a hospital and then a doctor's residence, this 1912 Victorian has views of both the seashore and lily fields. Of its four guest rooms, one comes with a private bath ($60–70), and the other three share two baths ($50–80). The inn's breakfasts can include scrapple biscuits with sausage gravy, eggs divan, eggs Florentine, or quiche.

Gold Beach

Inn at Nesika Beach (541-247-6463; leminn@harborside.com; www.moriah.com/nesikazzz), 33026 Nesika Road, Gold Beach 97444. Even though it looks like a century-old Victorian standing on a shoreline bluff above the Pacific, this home is a newcomer to the area. "Ann built this spacious inn as a B and B and opened in May 1992," says Larry Minnich, husband of Ann and co-host at the inn. Its four guest rooms have featherbeds and private bathrooms; three of them have Jacuzzis and fireplaces, and two of *those* have decks facing the ocean ($130–165). "Ann offers sumptuous breakfasts and warm hospitality," Larry says, "and the featherbeds and the sound of the ocean give you the best sleep you've ever had."

Rogue Reef Inn (1-877-234-7333; innkeepers@roguereef.com; www.roguereef.com), 30530 Old Coast Road, Gold Beach 97444. Seals, sea lions, and whales are often not-too-distant neighbors to this oceanfront contemporary home, and a trail leading from its door to the beach can put guests even closer to the wildlife of the sea. All four of its rooms come with private baths and a full breakfast, and three of them have king beds and private balconies ($85–95).

✷ Where to Eat

DINING OUT **Chives** (541-247-4121), 21292 Highway 101, Gold Beach. Move a chef from San Francisco to Gold Beach, have him set up a restaurant with an ocean view and design a menu with gourmet entrées, and you're likely to end up with something like Chives, considered one of the premier restaurants on the south coast.

EATING OUT

Gold Beach

The Captain's Table (541-247-6308), 1295 S. Ellensburg Avenue, Gold Beach. As far as seafood is concerned, just about the only thing you can't get at the Captain's Table is a meal deep-fried. The rest of it—rustic building, antique furnishings, efficient service, good food—comes with the dinner.

Nor'Wester (541-247-2333), Port of Gold Beach, Gold Beach. Since 1980 Nor'Wester has stood on the waterfront near the mouth of the Rogue River, overlooked Gold Beach's boat harbor, and offered diners a quality of steaks, seafood, and pasta—as well as salads and chowder—that makes them come back again and again.

Port Hole Café (541-247-7411), 29975 Harbor Way, Gold Beach. Located on the waterfront in a historic cannery that stands near the Rogue River Bridge, the Port Hole is where the locals go for home-cooked meals, including pies and desserts. Fish (fresh)-and-chips, clam chowder, and salads are specialties, and everything you order will be both tasty and abundant.

Spinners (541-247-5160), 29430 Ellensburg Avenue, Gold Beach. The view at Spinners is panoramic, the menu long, the service excellent, and the offerings varied, ranging from grilled prawns and pan-roasted halibut to charbroiled steak and half-pound hamburgers.

✷ Special Events

May: **Azalea Festival** (1-800-535-9469), Brookings.

Northwest

LOWER COLUMBIA RIVER AREA

PORTLAND–METROPOLITAN AREA

MOUNT HOOD–COLUMBIA GORGE AREA

NORTH WILLAMETTE VALLEY

SOUTH WILLAMETTE VALLEY

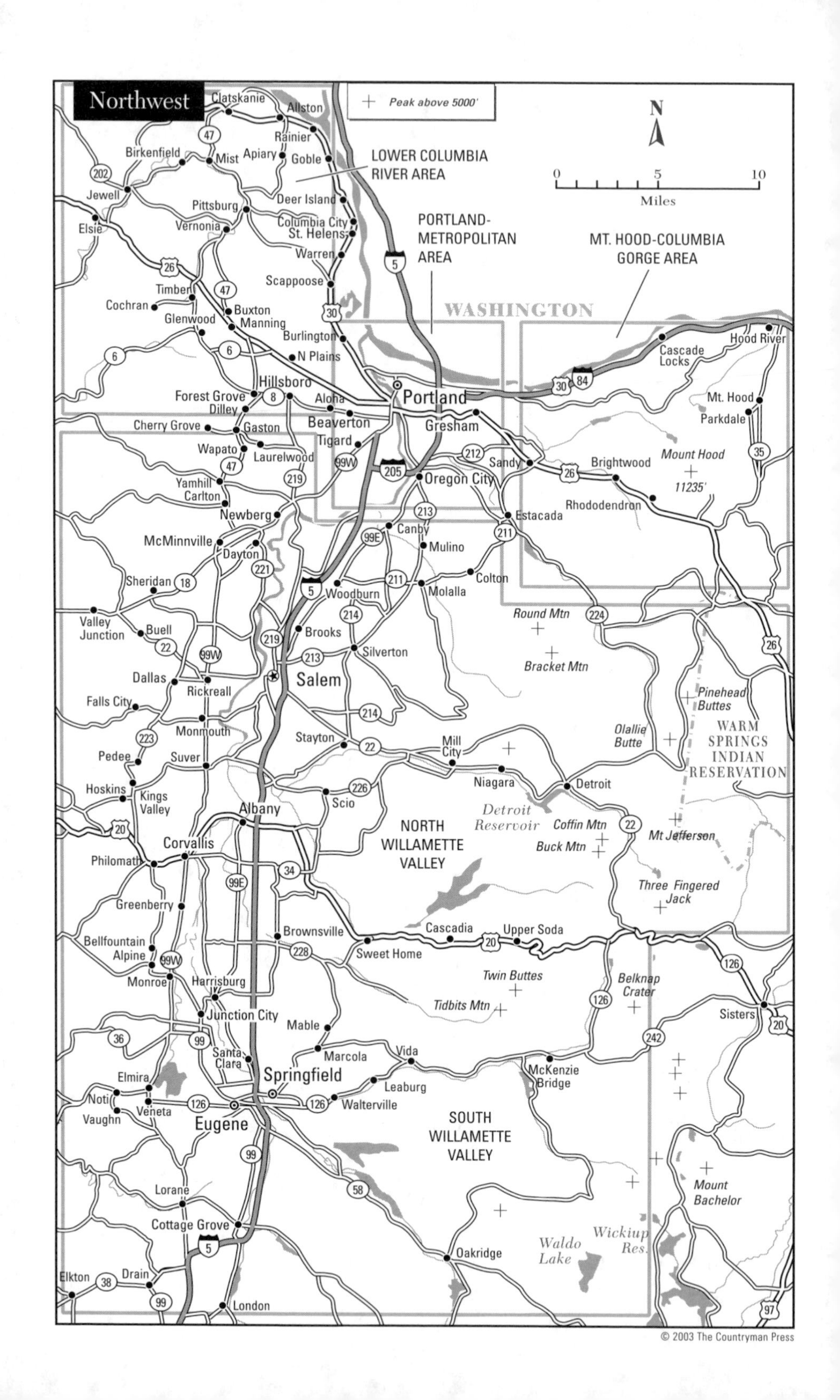
Northwest
Peak above 5000'
N
0 5 10
Miles
LOWER COLUMBIA RIVER AREA
PORTLAND-METROPOLITAN AREA
MT. HOOD-COLUMBIA GORGE AREA
WASHINGTON
NORTH WILLAMETTE VALLEY
SOUTH WILLAMETTE VALLEY
WARM SPRINGS INDIAN RESERVATION
Clatskanie
Allston
Rainier
Goble
Apiary
Mist
Birkenfield
Jewell
Elsie
Pittsburg
Vernonia
Deer Island
Columbia City
St. Helens
Warren
Scappoose
Timber
Cochran
Glenwood
Buxton
Manning
Burlington
N Plains
Hillsboro
Forest Grove
Dilley
Aloha
Portland
Beaverton
Gresham
Tigard
Cherry Grove
Gaston
Wapato
Laurelwood
Sandy
Oregon City
Yamhill
Carlton
Newberg
McMinnville
Dayton
Canby
Mulino
Estacada
Sheridan
Woodburn
Molalla
Colton
Valley Junction
Buell
Brooks
Silverton
Dallas
Rickreall
Salem
Falls City
Monmouth
Stayton
Mill City
Pedee
Suver
Niagara
Detroit
Hoskins
Kings Valley
Scio
Albany
Corvallis
Philomath
Greenberry
Brownsville
Bellfountain
Alpine
Monroe
Sweet Home
Cascadia
Upper Soda
Harrisburg
Junction City
Mable
Marcola
Vida
Santa Clara
Springfield
Elmira
Leaburg
Noti
Veneta
Vaughn
Eugene
Walterville
McKenzie Bridge
Lorane
Cottage Grove
Oakridge
Elkton
Drain
London
Cascade Locks
Hood River
Mt. Hood
Parkdale
Brightwood
Rhododendron
Mount Hood
11235'
Round Mtn
Bracket Mtn
Pinehead Buttes
Olallie Butte
Detroit Reservoir
Coffin Mtn
Buck Mtn
Mt Jefferson
Three Fingered Jack
Twin Buttes
Tidbits Mtn
Belknap Crater
Sisters
Mount Bachelor
Waldo Lake
Wickiup Res.
202
47
26
6
8
99W
219
205
213
99E
211
221
18
22
214
224
35
84
30
5
223
226
20
34
228
126
36
99
242
58
38
97

INTRODUCTION

"In a school geography I saw . . . a half page description of Oregon, about its heavy forests towards the North and its open country towards the South, abounding in game and wild horses . . . that page was thumbed until it was very dark. I would take it up as I came out of the coal mine, and look at that old book."

—John Minto, explaining why he tackled the Oregon Trail in 1844

The eyes of the pioneers were set on this corner of old Oregon, their gazes measuring the dusty distance to the Willamette Valley as their oxen clopped out the miles, mile after mile, one hoofbeat at a time along the trail leading to the far, lonely edge of the continent. And on that edge, the emigrants imagined, awaited the welcoming embrace of a promised land. "There'll be apples on each branch in Oregon; there'll be valleys filled with golden grain" go the words to an old song. "There'll be plenty of sun and rain."

Sure enough, at trail's end the newly arrived settlers found a land of plenty (not to mention of rain), but they also found it rooted so deeply in the region's soil and forests that it wouldn't let go without a fight. And so with axes and plows they began grappling with their surroundings, building their homes while shaping the beginnings of a new state. The struggle often resulted in a fierce measure of frontier independence that could border on the cantankerous, though circumstances ensured it was accompanied by a portion of virtue.

"I never saw so fine a population as in Oregon," an early settler wrote. "They were honest because there was nothing to steal; sober because there was no liquor; there were no misers because there was no money; they were industrious because it was work or starve."

With increasing numbers of wagon trains arriving each fall, this population was also expanding, and it wasn't long before farms lined the Willamette River's valley, logging camps spread through its foothills, and towns grew in between. Part of the resulting pattern exists to this day, though travelers who stick close to the interstates are likely to form the impression that most of the region consists of congested roads and cities. But as one of the old-time settlers might have said, "Fiddlesticks!"

Steer your way onto the side roads and back roads of this broad, green swale whose edges sidle up to the foothills of the Cascades and the Coast Range, and you'll find the lush fields and thick forests that made the pioneers pack their belongings and take a journey to the farthest reaches of their world. And you may even find, as they did, a promised land waiting for you at the end of your journey.

LOWER COLUMBIA RIVER AREA

GUIDANCE **Clatskanie Chamber of Commerce** (503-728-2502), 155 W. Highway 30, Clatskanie 97016.

Oregon State Parks (503-378-6305), State Parks and Recreation Department, 525 Trade Street S. E., Salem 97301.

St. Helens–Scappoose Chamber of Commerce (503-397-0685), 2194 Columbia Boulevard, St. Helens 97051.

Vernonia Area Chamber of Commerce (503-429-6081; www.vernoniachamber.org), 1001 Bridge Street, Vernonia 97064.

GETTING THERE The lower Columbia River area can be reached by Highway 30, which runs between Portland and Astoria; by Highway 101, which stretches north and south along the entire Oregon coast; or by Highways 202 and 47 from the south.

MEDICAL EMERGENCY **Eastmoreland Hospital** (503-234-0411), 2900 S. E. Steele Street, Portland.

Legacy Emanuel Hospital (503-413-4008), 2801 N. Gantenbein Street, Portland.

Legacy Good Samaritan Hospital and Medical Center (503-413-7711), 1015 N. W. 22nd Avenue, Portland.

Providence Portland Medical Center (503-215-1111), 4805 N. E. Glisan Street, Portland.

Providence Street Vincent Medical Center (503-216-1234), 9205 S. W. Barnes Road, Portland.

Woodland Park Hospital (503-257-5500), 10300 N. E. Hancock Street, Portland.

✷ To See

HISTORIC HOMES Caples House (503-397-5390), 1915 First Street, Columbia City. This simple, two-story home with a gable roof was the home of Dr. Charles Caples and his family from 1870 until 1959. The last resident of the house was Charles's daughter Dell, who lived to age 99. Living all but the last 10 years of her life in the home, Dell continued using most of its earliest "conveniences," including a wood-burning stove for cooking and a single outside spigot for water. As a result, the house remains relatively unchanged from its earliest years.

Flippin Castle (503-728-3608), 620 S. W. Tichenor Street, Clatskanie. Although not a castle in the Arthurian sense of the term, this Queen Anne Victorian with its twin turrets is an imposing home, built by sawmill owner Thomas Flippin at the turn of the 20th century. Before moving into their new home in 1900, 35-year-old Thomas and his wife, Florence, had lived in the cookhouse of their West Oregon Lumber Company logging camp. For Thomas, the move marked a giant leap in his life. "From my father's viewpoint," Thomas Flippin Jr. once said, "progressing from a skidgreaser on a bull-team skidroad at the age of 17 to a home like this . . . was a tremendous accomplishment." But alas, Florence seemed to have detested the change from logging camp hubbub to citified hostess, and soon after moving in, the Flippins moved out and went their separate ways.

HISTORIC SITES Lewis and Clark Trail (Kelley Point to Puget Island). **Kelley Point,** November 4, 1805, and March 30, 1806 (11 miles northwest of Portland near the intersection of Marine Drive and Lombard Street; from Interstate 5, take exit 307). On their way downriver to the sea, Lewis and Clark passed near the confluence of the Willamette River and the Columbia, but an island blocked their view of the Willamette. "We presumed there was a channel on that side of the river," Captain Lewis wrote, "but we were anxious to press forward, and therefore did not stop to examine more minutely." On their return trip in the spring, they had almost reached the Sandy River before deciding to turn back

KELLEY POINT, WHERE THE WILLAMETTE AND COLUMBIA RIVERS MEET

and look for the river they now believed drained the western slope of the Cascade Mountains. "In order to verify this information," Lewis wrote, "Captain Clark . . . immediately set out with a canoe and seven of our men." The next day, William Clark found the mouth of the Willamette and explored upriver to the approximate site of today's north Portland.

Sauvie Island, November 4, 1805, and March 29, 1806 (12 miles northwest of Portland off Highway 30). While camped on the north bank of the river across from Sauvie Island, the Corps of Discovery found this stretch of the Columbia to be, as Sergeant Gass described it, "a beautiful part of the river," where flights of waterfowl filled the sky. "I slept but very little last night for the noise kept during the whole of the night by the swans, geese, white and gray brant ducks," Captain Clark wrote, "they were immensely numerous and their noise horrid." The captains estimated that 2,400 people of the Multnomah tribe lived on the island, and another 1,800 lived across the channel.

Prescott Beach, November 5, 1805, and March 27, 1806 (4 miles south of Rainier off Highway 30). Want a historical perspective? Then consider this: Near this county park—where the Corps of Discovery camped in the rain and the woods, where "a great many Indian camps" stood, and where flocks of a "great many swans, geese, ducks, cranes, and gulls" filled the air—now stands the remnants of the Trojan Nuclear Power Plant. Camping in the rain, the corps saw "Canoes of Indians" moving along the river, yet none stopped to visit. "This is the first night which we have been entirely clear of Indians," Captain Clark wrote, "since our arrival on the waters of the Columbia River."

Puget Island, November 6, 1805, and March 25, 1806 (across the river from Wauna off Highway 30). The expedition found the islands too "thick with under groth" to hunt and insufficiently "large and leavil for our camp." By nightfall, however, they at last found a campsite above tidewater on the Washington side of the river, though the rain still hindered them. "We are all wet and disagreeable," Captain Clark wrote, "had large fires made . . . and dried our bedding and kill the flees which collected in our blankets . . ." Yet they also knew they were drawing ever closer to the sea.

Howell Territorial Park (503-222-1741), on Sauvie Island, 12 miles northwest of Portland off Highway 30, Sauvie Island Road, and Howell Park Road. Even though picnickers and bird-watchers come here to enjoy the solitude and see the wildlife, the centerpiece of this 93-acre park concerns its history, for here stands the 1850s **James F. Bybee House** and orchard, with an adjacent barn serving as an **Agriculture Museum** of farm implements used in the Northwest from 1890 to 1920.

Columbia County Courthouse, Plaza Square, St. Helens. The story goes that in 1903 when the towns of St. Helens and Rainier were competing for the county seat, Rainier tried to "borrow" voters from Portland by bringing them in on a steamship. But folks from St. Helens intercepted the steamship, persuaded the Portlanders to vote for St. Helens, and then kept them in town until the polls closed. After winning the county seat, St. Helens needed a courthouse to replace what its newspaper called a "miserable old shack." Before long the same newspaper could point proudly to the "noble structure rising on the river's bank," and in 1907 county officials moved into a finished courthouse constructed of locally quarried basalt. Standing in a downtown plaza as the centerpiece of the city, the courthouse through the years has achieved at least two distinctions among Oregon's historic buildings, both related to the building's rest rooms: the view of the Columbia River from the window in the women's and the giant porcelain urinals in the men's. (The view, reputedly, is still there, though the urinals have been removed.)

✷ To Do

BICYCLING **Banks–Vernonia Linear State Park** (503-324-0606), 21 paved and graveled miles off Highway 47 from Banks to Vernonia. A former logging railway during the days of steam locomotives as well as Oregon's first Rails-to-Trails conversion, this "linear park" rolls with the terrain, climbing and dipping over the foothills of the Coast Range. Between the towns on either end, trailheads are located at **Manning, Pongratz, Buxton, Tophill,** and **Beaver Creek,** so you can hike or bike the trail in segments. In addition, camping is available at Anderson City Park in Vernonia.

CAMPING **Hudson-Parcher Campground,** 2 miles northwest of Rainier off Highway 30 and Larson Road, 34 campsites near the Columbia River, with nearby hiking, fishing, and boating.

Big Eddy, 7 miles north of Vernonia off Highway 47, 34 riverside campsites, along with a playground and boat launch, on the bank of the Nehalem River and near the big eddy that's its namesake.

See also *Wilder Places—Parks* and *Wildlife Refuges.*

CANOEING **Lewis and Clark Heritage Canoe Trail** (503-728-2502), Clatskanie City Park, Clatskanie, at the intersection of Highways 30 and 47. This trail follows the Clatskanie River downstream to the Columbia, working its way through a network of sloughs.

Lewis and Clark National Wildlife Refuge, 15 miles northwest of Westport off Highway 30. Stretching for 15 miles along the Columbia River, this refuge is the largest natural marsh in western Oregon and an important wintering grounds for **migrating ducks** and **geese.** With 55 square miles of sandbars and mudflats and islands, and with numerous channels separating its 20 islands, the refuge is best explored by canoe (you'll find a boat ramp at Aldrich Point, north of Brownsmead). Be aware of shifting tides and cautious of large ships in the main channel.

HIKING **Sauvie Island Trails** (541-621-3488), 13 to 18 miles northwest of Portland off Highway 30 and Sauvie Island Road. Lying near the confluence of the Willamette and Columbia Rivers, Sauvie Island is one of the largest river islands in North America. Along its 15-mile length, two trails introduce you to relatively untamed parts of the island: **Oak Island,** a 3-mile loop that crosses through part of a peninsula of Sturgeon Lake; and **Virginia Lake,** a 2-mile loop with one segment stretching along the bank of Multnomah Channel.

Four County Point Trail, 40 miles west of Portland off Highway 26, near milepost 35. Take the plunge off this busy highway's shoulder, and you almost immediately enter a world of fir forests and dappled sunlight, where a half-hour stroll lets you stand in four Oregon counties at once. That's right—*four* counties. That's because near the end of this shaded trail lies a granite slab and a surveyor's stake that mark the only intersection in Oregon where four counties meet.

See also **Banks–Vernonia Linear State Park** under *Bicycling*.

✷ Wilder Places

PARKS **Clatskanie City Park,** downtown Clatskanie. What sets this park apart is its location on the bank of the Clatskanie River, giving visitors a chance to fish, boat, swim, and even feed the ducks and geese that seem to spend more time mooching than swimming.

Scaponia Park, 13 miles northwest of Scappoose off the Scappoose–Vernonia Road. Surrounded by a forest of fir and alder and bordered by the East Fork Nehalem River, this park offers visitors woodland trails, primitive campsites, and a 7-acre nature park.

Vernonia Lake, Vernonia. The former millpond of the Oregon-American Lumber Company, which in 1922 built the "biggest electric sawmill in the world" near Vernonia, is the centerpiece for this park popular with fishermen and bird-watchers. In addition, a paved path for walkers and bikers circles the lake.

Camp Wilkerson, 16 miles south of Rainier off Apiary Road. Even though camping in this 280-acre forested park is by reservation only, its day lodge with cooking facilities is open to visitors who drop by for a picnic.

WILDLIFE REFUGES **Sauvie Island Wildlife Area,** 11 miles northwest of Portland off Highway 30 and Sauvie Island Road. Spread across the 45 square miles of this island are 12,000 acres of Columbia River floodplain devoted to wildlife. With its shallow lakes, extensive uplands, and cottonwood groves the island is a major stop on the **Pacific Flyway** for migrating ducks and geese. In fact, half of the wintering waterfowl in the Willamette Valley—more than 150,000 ducks and geese—stay here. It is also either a permanent or seasonal home for some 220 species of birds, including **sandhill cranes, bald eagles,** and **great blue herons.** Some areas contain hiking trails, viewing platforms, and interpretive areas, though entry is restricted from October through April to help protect wildlife.

J. J. Collins Marine Park (503-397-2353), in the Multnomah Channel near Scappoose. One of Oregon's two marine parks—accessible by boat only, as is nearby Sand Island Park (see next listing)—this 23-acre island in the Multnomah Channel serves as a wildlife preserve, especially for the area's **waterfowl,** as well as a campground, picnic area, nature trail, and bird-watching site for boaters.

Sand Island Park (503-397-6272), across from the St. Helens Marina, St. Helens. Accessible by boat only, this Columbia River island was created when the Corps of Engineers deepened the channel to Portland and dumped the dredgings in front of St. Helens' harbor. Now a wildlife preserve and one of only two marine parks in the state—the other is nearby J. J. Collins Marine Park (see previous listing)—Sand Island provides picnic sites and campgrounds for people, and habitat for both **resident and migrating waterfowl.**

Jewell Meadows Wildlife Refuge, 2 miles west of Jewell off Highway 202. This 1,200-acre wildlife area is a haven for **Roosevelt elk** as well as for the folks who come here to see them. During winter, from 75 to 200 elk gather within range of the viewpoints scattered along the highway. The closest view is usually from the second entrance, near park headquarters.

✷ Lodging

BED & BREAKFASTS

Sauvie Island

Sauvie Island Bed & Breakfast (503-621-3216; www.moriah.com/sauvie), Reeder Road, Sauvie Island. Even though you might be able to see the lights of Portland casting a dim glow skyward from here, Sauvie Island still seems to belong to an older world of starlit nights and waterfowl flights—and this inn stands near the edge of it. Guest rooms come with either a shared ($70) or private ($85) bath, views of the river, access to a beach, and a full breakfast.

Westlund's River's Edge Bed & Breakfast (503-621-9856; westlund@riversedge-bb.com; www.riversedge-bb.com), Gillihan Road, Portland 97231. On the edge of Sauvie Island and the bank of the Columbia River, sunrise sheds its red glow on stream water and mountain flanks, and guests at this inn can watch it happen. They can also stroll the nearby beach, visit a wildlife area, barbecue at the picnic area, or just sit on the deck and watch the river flow past. The B&B's guest area, say hosts Wes and Beverley Westlund, is a "home away from home" that includes two guest rooms with a shared bath, a kitchenette and common room, and beach access ($85 for a room to $140 for the entire space). Children are welcome.

PORTLAND–METROPOLITAN AREA

GUIDANCE **Beaverton Area Chamber of Commerce** (503-644-0123; www.beaverton.org), 4800 S. W. Griffith Drive #100, Beaverton 97005.

Clackamas County Regional Visitor Information Center (1-877-682-3314; www.wils-chamber.org), 29600 S. W. Park Place, Wilsonville 97070.

Cornelius Visitors Center (503-359-4037), 120 N. 13th Street, Cornelius 97113.

Forest Grove Chamber of Commerce (503-357-3006; www.fgchamber.com), 2417 Pacific Avenue, Forest Grove 97116.

Gresham Area Visitor Center (503-665-1131; www.greshamchamber.org), 150 W. Powell Street, Gresham 97030.

Greater Hillsboro Chamber of Commerce (503-648-1102; www.hilchamber.org), 334 S. E. Fifth Avenue, Hillsboro 97123.

Hood National Forest (503-668-1771), 16400 Champion Way, Sandy 970955; **Clackamas River Ranger District** (503-630-8700); **Zigzag Ranger District** (503-622-3191); **Mount Hood Information Center** (503-622-7674).

Lake Oswego Chamber of Commerce (503-636-3634; www.lake-oswego.com), 242 B Avenue, Lake Oswego 97034.

North Clackamas County Chamber of Commerce (503-654-7777; www.yourchamber.com), 7740 S. E. Harmony Road, Milwaukie 97222.

Oregon City Chamber of Commerce (1-800-424-3002; www.oregoncity.org), 1810 Washington Street, Oregon City 97045.

Oregon State Parks (503-378-6305), State Parks and Recreation Department, 525 Trade Street S. E., Salem 97301; **Portland office** (503-731-3293).

Portland Oregon Visitors Association (1-877-678-5263; www.travelportland.com), 26 S. W. Salmon Street, Portland 97201.

Tigard Area Chamber of Commerce (503-639-1656; www.tigardchamber.com), 12345 S. W. Main Street, Tigard 97223.

Tualatin Chamber of Commerce (503-692-0780; www.tualatinchamber.com), 19358 S. W. Boones Ferry Road, Tualatin 97062.

Washington County Convention and Visitors Bureau (1-800-537-3149; www.wcva.org), 5075 S. W. Griffith Drive #120, Beaverton 97005.

Wilsonville Chamber of Commerce (503-682-0411; www.wils-chamber.org), 29600 S. W. Park Place, Wilsonville 97070.

GETTING THERE The Portland–Metropolitan area can be reached from the east by Interstate 84 or Highway 26, from the south by Interstate 5 or Highways 99E and 99W, from the west by Highway 26, and from the north by Highway 30. In addition, Interstates 205 and 405 connect numerous cities within the metropolitan area.

GETTING AROUND ✐ **MAX Rides** (503-238-7433; www.tri-met.org), Portland and the metropolitan area. If you want to explore the Portland area but want to leave behind the traffic, take MAX (Metropolitan Area eXpress), Portland's public light-rail system. The rails lead throughout the metropolitan area, carrying riders to parks, gardens, trails, shops, libraries, and museums. You can travel on MAX all day for less than the cost of a deli sandwich, and rides through a large portion of downtown are free. If you're not sure where to get on or off, call the folks at MAX, tell them where you are and where you want to go, and they'll take care of the rest. This is fun—no kidding.

MEDICAL EMERGENCY **Eastmoreland Hospital** (503-234-0411), 2900 S. E. Steele Street, Portland.

Legacy Emanuel Hospital (503-413-4008), 2801 N. Gantenbein Street, Portland.

Legacy Good Samaritan Hospital and Medical Center (503-413-7711), 1015 N. W. 22nd Avenue, Portland.

Providence Portland Medical Center (503-215-1111), 4805 N. E. Glisan Street, Portland.

Providence Street Vincent Medical Center (503-216-1234), 9205 S. W. Barnes Road, Portland.

Woodland Park Hospital (503-257-5500), 10300 N. E. Hancock Street, Portland.

Kaiser Sunnyside Medical Center (503-652-2880), 10180 S. E. Sunnyside Drive, Clackamas.

Tualitin Community Hospital (503-681-1111), 335 S. E. 8th Avenue, Hillsboro.

Legacy Meridian Park Hospital (503-692-12121), 9300 S. W. 65th Avenue, Tualatin.

Legacy Mount Hood Medical Center (503-674-1191), 24800 S. E. Stark Street, Gresham.

Providence Milwaukie Hospital (503-513-8300), 10150 S. E. 32nd Street, Milwaukie.

Willamette Falls Hospital (503-656-1631), 1500 Division Street, Oregon City.

✷ To See

BOAT TOURS **Willamette River Jetboat Tours** (1-888-538-2628; www.willamette-jet.com), Portland. Get a view from the river of the bridges, shipyards, and waterfront of Oregon's largest city. Boarding location is at OMSI (Oregon Museum of Science and Industry), 1945 S. E. Water Avenue, Portland.

TROLLEY TOURS Ever since trolleys departed our city streets to make way for those newfangled automobiles, they seem to have left behind a shadow of their sleek-metal presence, an echo of their clacking wheels, of their bells and whistles that seemed to signal simpler times in American life. As a result, some folks have worked to make trolleys once again part of the urban experience.

Willamette Shore Trolley (503-222-2226), Portland and Lake Oswego. For 7 miles between Portland and Lake Oswego this trolley runs along the west bank of the Willamette River, following the old right-of-way of the Willamette Valley Railroad, which began operating in 1887. The line was electrified in 1914 and reached its peak of traffic in 1920, when 64 trolleys made daily runs. Even though passenger service ended in 1929, freight service continued until 1983, and today the 1902 trolley hauls sightseers through a mixed world of shipyards and warehouses, condominiums and mansions.

WILLAMETTE SHORE TROLLEY

Oregon City Trolley (503-657-9336), Oregon City. In 1893 the nation's first and longest electric trolley line stretched 16 miles from Portland to Oregon City. But after seven decades of service, the trolleys stopped running in 1958, and their tracks soon followed them to the scrap yard. Today, however, the Oregon City Trolley, a motor-driven replica of an old car, makes a run from the End of the Oregon Trail Interpretive Center (see *Museums*) and through Oregon City's two National Historic Districts (see *Historic Sites*).

MUSEUMS **American Advertising Museum** (503-226-0000; www.admuseum.org), 5025 S. E. 24th Avenue, Portland. This is the nation's first museum devoted to advertising, its exhibits displaying the memorabilia, recalling the commercials, and tracing the history of advertising through the ages. Gathered here are the slogans that sold us coffee good to the last drop; cereal shot from guns; cigarettes we'd walk a mile for; bread that would build our bodies 12 ways; candy that would melt in our mouths, not in our hands; and toothpaste that would make us exclaim, "Look, Ma—no cavities!" Also collected here are some familiar faces: Buster Brown, Aunt Jemimah, Mr. Peanut, Speedy Alka-Seltzer, the Jolly Green Giant, and the Pillsbury Doughboy. Together, these slogans and images have been our longtime companions as they helped shape our buying habits.

Oregon History Center (503-222-1741; www.ohs.org), 1200 S. W. Park Avenue, Portland. This is the face the Oregon Historical Society shows the world, its nine galleries filled with ever-changing displays of images and artifacts from Oregon history. To find it near Portland's South Park Blocks, look for the murals covering two walls of the nine-story Sovereign Hotel—a total of almost 7,000 square feet—that depict historical scenes featuring Native Americans, Lewis and Clark, trappers, and pioneers.

Oregon Museum of Science and Industry (503-797-4000; www.omsi.org), 1945 S. E. Water Avenue, Portland. Where can you explore galaxies far, far away or take a journey beneath the sea, yet never wander far from a parking lot or rest room? The Oregon Museum of Science and Industry (OMSI). Whether the space is outer or inner or the subject is the cosmos or microbes—one of the museum's recent advertisements boasted of "more flagellums than any other exhibit in town!"—OMSI can transport you there through its six major exhibit halls, its five-story domed screen, or its 200-seat planetarium. And if you watch kids' faces as they scurry about the place, trying out all the techno-widgets and sci-fi gadgets set out as lures to teach visitors a thing or two about the world, you'll see that OMSI, more than anything else, makes learning fun.

World Forestry Center (503-228-1367), 4033 S. W. Canyon Road ("Zoo-Forestry Center" exit), Portland. Walk through the door here and you'll find yourself staring up at a 70-foot talking tree. Push a button, and it tells you all about itself, about its roots and bark and leaves, how it eats and breathes and grows. It's a fitting introduction to a place devoted to trees, to their role in natural and human history, and their contributions to our world, from the creation of oxygen to two-by-fours.

Washington County Museum (503-645-5353), 17677 N. W. Springville Road (on Portland Community College's Rock Creek campus), Portland. For this county, the second most populated in the state, much of history is about change—in the people, the landscapes, and the communities that stretch through the years from the days of Atfalatis Indians to pioneer farmers to high-tech workers. And to record those changes, this museum offers a series of ever-changing exhibits.

End of the Oregon Trail Interpretive Center (503-657-9336), 1726 Washington Street (exit 10 on Interstate 205), Oregon City. Three 50-foot covered wagons provide the housing for this interpretive center, which attempts to give visitors a sense of pioneer life along the Oregon Trail. Although it contains some displays and artifacts, the emphasis is on the "living-history" element of the story, for here you can pack a wagon, make candles, or grind sugar; you can also listen to storytellers, watch actors, and visit theaters and galleries.

Museum of the Oregon Territory (503-655-5574), 211 Tumwater Drive, Oregon City. Standing on the bluffs above Willamette Falls, this museum attempts to capture the story of the people and events that have shaped the region. From prehistoric tribes to Oregon Trail emigrants and their descendants, this story encompasses the area's natural and human history through the centuries.

Oregon Military Museum (503-557-5359), 10101 S. E. Clackamas Road (exit 12 or 12A on Interstate 205), Clackamas. Founded in 1974 and located at the Oregon National Guard's Camp Withycombe, this museum preserves the military heritage of Oregon from its years as a territory to its contributions in Afghanistan. Its collection of artifacts ranges from helmets to Howitzers, torpedoes to tanks, Civil War cannons to Japanese artillery. Its research library is equally diverse, containing military texts, field manuals, and war histories.

HISTORIC HOMES **Pittock Mansion** (503-823-3624), 3229 N. W. Pittock Drive, Portland. Take a tour of this 22-room, 16,000-square-foot mansion built in 1914 by Henry Pittock, former publisher of the *Oregonian* newspaper, and you may wonder at the world of the wealthy as well as who dusted this house.

McLoughlin House (503-656-5146), 713 Center Street, Oregon City. Dr. John McLoughlin was a man big enough to match the country he ruled. Chief factor of the Hudson's Bay Company's Fort Vancouver, a Columbia River fur-trading post whose power stretched from the Rockies to the Pacific and from Alaska to California, Dr. John dispensed authority, justice, wheat, tools, and most of the other trappings of civilization throughout the Oregon Country for 20 years. And here, in this house high above the Willamette River, is where Dr. McLoughlin, the Father of Oregon, spent the last dozen years of his life, dying in 1857. "He was one of the towering personalities of the Far West," poet Edwin Markham wrote 75 years after the doctor's death. "He was a lover of man, a lover of justice, a lover of the common people."

Stevens-Crawford House (503-655-2866), 603 Sixth Street, Oregon City. A step into this 1908 house is a step back to the era of its construction: wallpaper and drapes, furniture and appliances, photographs and decorations, and everything else that makes a house a home is original, as though the owners stepped out very recently. Which is what happened in a way. After living here for 60 years before dying in 1968 at the age of 95, Mertie Stevens, daughter of the Oregon Trail emigrants who built the house, left her home and its furnishings to the Clackamas County Historical Society.

Ermatinger House (503-656-1619), 619 Sixth Street, Oregon City. This 1845 frame building with the white clapboards, the oldest house in Oregon City and the third oldest in the state, was the home of Frances Ermatinger, former trader with the Hudson's Bay Company. But the single event that distinguishes the home is that its front room was the site of an 1843 coin flip between Asa Lovejoy and Francis Pettygrove to determine the name of the city they'd just platted on their joint 640-acre site. Lovejoy, from Boston, and Pettygrove, from Portland, Maine, each wanted to name the city after his home town. Pettygrove won.

Rose Farm (503-245-0488), corner of Holmes Street and Rilance Lane, Oregon City. Built in 1848, the same year that Oregon became a territory, this home was the site of the first meeting of the territorial legislature. It was also where Joseph Lane, in March 1849, took his vows as Oregon's first territorial governor, then delivered his inaugural address from the home's balcony.

Sweek House (503-692-4006), 18815 S. W. Boones Ferry Road, Tualatin. This fully restored 1858 Southern Plantation house is one of the oldest homes in the state.

Baker Cabin (503-631-8274), corner of Hattan and Gronlund Road (off Highway 224), Carver. Built in 1856 by Horace and Jane Baker, who were part of the first wagon train to use the Barlow Road, this cantilevered log cabin is the only one of its kind west of the Mississippi River. Next door stands an 1896 church.

HISTORIC SITES **Portland Walking Tour**, from Interstate 5 or Interstate 205 take "Downtown Portland" exits. In Oregon, Portland is to historic districts what Barry Bonds is to home-run hitting: Nobody else comes even close. The state's largest city boasts of 10 historic districts that contain more than 1,000 historic buildings, and more than 400 of those are listed on the **National Register of Historic Places.** "You don't have to pay close attention when you walk through the city," says an editorial in the *Oregonian,* the city's major newspaper. "You can just glide along, eavesdropping on what amounts to an architectural conversation between different eras." For those who'd like more structure, however, a good start is a guided walking tour of downtown (503-736-3248; www.portlandwalkingtours.com). This walkabout provides a casual but enlightening introduction to the city's art, architecture, parks, and history.

Japanese American Historical Plaza, Tom McCall Waterfront Park (off S. W. Naito Avenue and near the Burnside Bridge), Portland. Here on the bank of the Willamette River, poetry-carved stones speak from the past, in voices that capture the memories of the Japanese internment during World War II. One recalls arriving at the kind of camp where some 112,000 Japanese Americans were imprisoned after Pearl Harbor: "Rounded up / In the sweltering yard / Unable to endure any longer / Standing in line / Some collapse." Others speak of humiliation, pride, or shame. And at least one remembers coming back home again: "Through the car window / A glimpse of pines, / Oregon mountains. / My heart beats faster. / Returning home."

JAPANESE AMERICAN HISTORICAL PLAZA, A TRIBUTE TO JAPANESE AMERICANS IMPRISONED IN INTERNMENT CAMPS DURING WORLD WAR II

Willamette Stone, 4 miles west of Portland off Skyline Boulevard. The stake gripped in concrete in this 1.6-acre park marks the intersection of the **Willamette Meridian** and the **Willamette Baseline,** the point from which all lands in Oregon and Washington were surveyed and sectioned after Congress opened the door wider to homesteading in the Northwest by passing the Donation Land Claim Act in 1850. (The first Surveyor General of Oregon, John B. Preston, established this point in 1851.) Therefore, if you live in one of these two states, this stake has determined the location of the fence standing between your house and your neighbor's.

Willamette Falls Locks (503-656-3381), at the foot of Mill Street (take exit 8 on Interstate 205), West Linn. Built in the early 1870s to move barges and boats around the Willamette River's 40-foot falls near Oregon City, these locks—the oldest multilift locks in the nation—still have their original watertight walls constructed of locally quarried stone. Other changes, however, have taken place: the locks deepened, their wooden gates replaced with steel, the opening and closing of those gates evolving from manual operation to a hydraulic system, and the bulk of the river traffic moving from commercial and industrial to recreational. The locks earned a place on the **National Register of Historic Places** in 1974.

Hillsboro Walking Tour, downtown Hillsboro, near the junction of Highways 8 and 219. Along the city's **Walnut Street, Main Street,** and **Second Avenue**—a total area of approximately 23 blocks—stand a number of historic homes and buildings built in a variety of architectural styles ranging from Baroque to bungalow.

Courthouse Square Giant Sequoias, Washington County Courthouse, First Avenue and Main Street, Hillsboro. On his way to Oregon from the California gold rush, John R. Porter gathered the seeds of cones dropped by giant sequoias, and from these he planted this tree in 1880. For more information contact **Heritage Trees** (1-800-574-9397).

Aurora Walking Tour, from Interstate 5 take exit 278. This small city, a former Christian communal colony established in 1856 and now a **National Historic District,** calls itself "Oregon's Antique Capital" for good reason: Its 22-store shopping district not only contains numerous original buildings but also houses more than 200 **antiques** dealers that draw people from all over the country.

Oregon City Municipal Elevator, Railroad Avenue and Seventh Street, Oregon City. As Oregon City outgrew its riverbank beginnings, as its citizens began building their homes and businesses along the hillside to the east, the town became a vertical community that had folks climbing up and down the city's streets. The first solution to the problem came in 1867, when the city built a stairway system that was used until 1912. Then a public elevator took over the climbing chores. Powered by water—it used 200,000 gallons a day—the elevator provided a three-minute ride up or down the 90-foot hill. In 1924, electricity reduced that time to 30 seconds. Today the elevator—the only municipal elevator in North America and one of only four in the world—averages one passenger per minute during its hours of operation.

Oregon City Walking Tour (503-657-0891), from Interstate 205 take exit 10. Because this city, the first one incorporated west of the Mississippi River, grew in two directions—first along the river and then up the hill—it has two **National Historic Districts:** the **Canemah District,** located just above Willamette Falls, where there survive some of the homes built by 19th-century steamboat captains; and the **McLoughlin District** on the hilltop, where some of the city's oldest homes were moved from the original riverbank location.

Butteville General Store, Butteville Road south of Wilsonville, take exit 282 off Interstate 5. During Oregon's early years, when French-Canadians were settling down and turning their attention from beaver trapping to wheat farming along the Willamette River, a series of towns sprung up as river landings and supply centers. One of these was Butteville. "There were but a few cabins there when I left," settler Joel Palmer wrote after his visit to the town in 1845. "The proprietor had erected a warehouse to store wheat they might purchase of the settlers, who should find it convenient to sell their crops at this point." This general store, built in 1863 but still in use, is a remnant of those days.

NATURAL WONDERS **Dawn Redwood,** Hoyt Arboretum, 4000 S. W. Fairview Boulevard, Portland. Fossils show that this species grew in the Willamette Valley more than 38 million years ago, yet eventually it became extinct in North America. Then in 1948, seeds of the tree were discovered in China and planted in the United States. This Heritage Tree became the first Dawn Redwood in the hemisphere to produce cones in millions of years. For more information contact **Heritage Trees** (1-800-574-9397).

Willamette Falls, viewpoints off Highway 99E near Oregon City and off Interstate 205 near West Linn. Here where the Willamette River takes a 40-foot plunge over a horseshoe-shaped ledge of basalt, native people fished for thousands of years, fur trappers came exploring, and businessmen built trading posts, sawmills, paper mills, and power plants.

FOR FAMILIES **Oaks Amusement Park** (503-233-5777; www.oakspark.com), along the Willamette River just east of the Sellwood Bridge, Portland. With its beginnings going back to 1904, this is America's oldest running amusement park. Today it offers visitors a roller-skating rink with a 1923 Wurlitzer organ, an antique carousel, roller coasters, toddler swings, and a picnic area with a sandy beach.

Oregon Zoo (503-226-1561), 4001 S. W. Canyon Road, Portland. In the zoo's early days, an advertising jingle coaxed people to visit with the promise that "All the animals in the zoo / are jumping up and down for you / hoping you'll be sure to plan / to visit the zoo as soon as you can." Even though visitors found more animals sleeping than jumping, a day at the zoo was always a memorable experience, and today it's better than ever with more than 1,000 furred, feathered, or scaled animals representing 200 species that range from penguins to polar bears, mandrills to musk oxen, snow leopards to naked mole rats.

GARDEN TOURS In the foothills of Oregon's Wallowa Mountains—where rocky soil, summer frosts, and hungry deer seem to conspire against anything cultivated—a man compares his garden to life. "It doesn't last long," he says. "But it's lovely while it does." So if taking the time to stop and smell the roses is more than a cliché to you, consider taking a peek at one of the following.

Portland Classical Chinese Garden (503-228-8131), downtown Portland in the block bordered on the east and west by N. W. Second and Third, and on the north and south by N. W. Flanders and Everett. Covering an entire block of downtown Portland, this is the largest classical Chinese garden to be found outside China. In fact, part of the garden came from *inside* China. The garden's buildings, for instance, were built by craftsmen in Suzhou—Portland's sister city—and then shipped here in 100 40-foot containers. Meanwhile, on this side of the Pacific, numerous volunteers and more than 50 nurseries donated the plants. The result within the walled garden is a balance of the Chinese concepts of yin (the feminine element of the universe: passive, fluid, private, emotional) and yang (the masculine element: aggressive, rigid, open, rational) that join together in the heart of the city.

Berry Botanic Garden (503-636-4112; www.berrybot.org), 11505 S. W. Summerville Avenue, Portland. Since 1938, when Rae Selling Berry first moved to this 6-acre site and then planted and nurtured its garden until her death at the age of 96, the Berry Botanic Garden has been growing and changing, until today it features an herb lawn, a rhododendron forest, a native-plant trail, a collection of endangered plants and their seeds, and various sections devoted to ferns, rocks, and water. Its appeal is strong enough to draw visitors who don't fit the gardener stereotype. "I remember this one big, burly guy, a logger," says Jack Poff, who has volunteered at the garden since 1968. "He'd get down on his knees [in front of the cold frames] and say, 'Look at that little darlin.'"

Bishop's Close (503-636-5613), 11800 S. W. Military Lane, Portland. In 1905 Peter Kerr, a Scottish grain exporter, bought 3 acres on a bluff above the Willamette River and soon created an estate notable for its stately English gardens. Today Kerr's Elk Rock estate is the Episcopal Diocese of Oregon—Kerr left it to the church after his death in 1957 at the age of 95—as well as a public garden that features forests of redwoods and oaks, waterfalls and pools, and panoramic views of the river.

HOYT ARBORETUM

Crystal Springs Rhododendron Garden (503-771-8386), S. E. 28th and Woodstock Streets, Portland. Across this 7-acre garden from March through June bloom more than 2,000 rhododendrons and azaleas. It's also a good place to feed ducks and geese, which live at the garden's spring-fed lake.

Hoyt Arboretum (503-823-3655), 400 S. W. Fairview Boulevard, Portland. Ten miles of trails crisscross through this 200-acre site, leading walkers to more than 800 species of shrubs and trees from six continents. (Can you guess which continent is *not* represented? Hint: Penguins don't need shade.)

Japanese Gardens (503-223-1321), 611 S. W. Kingston Avenue, Portland. Since their beginning in 1963, these gardens have been considered to be some of the best in the world. (The Japanese ambassador himself said as much when he toured the gardens in 1988.) Walking paths lead to five traditional forms of the Japanese garden, a teahouse, and a pavilion that looks toward Mount Hood.

Leach Botanical Garden (503-761-9503), 6704 S. E. 122nd Street, Portland. When it opened in 1983, this was Portland's first public botanical garden, yet its beginnings actually date back to 1931, when John and Lilla Leach planted hundreds of species of trees and other plants around the grounds surrounding their home in southeast Portland. The Leaches' botanical adventures, however, extended far beyond their home, reaching into some of the wildest areas of Oregon in search of new plants. Those excursions afield resulted in Lilla's discovery of five species new to science, as well as to the establishment of two botanical areas and the Kalmiopsis Wilderness Area in southwest Oregon (see *Wilder Places—Wilderness Areas* in "Illinois Valley Area"). Yet their most generous contribution to lovers of plants is probably this home and garden left open to thousands of visitors each year.

FARMER'S MARKETS One of the quirks of metropolitan living seems to be that the freshest farm-grown food in the area is available downtown—not at grocery stores but at farmer's markets. Starting each spring, the crops of countryside fields and gardens—as well as the creations of bakers, artists, and musicians—make their way to these gathering places to spend their Saturdays in the city. Unless otherwise noted, the following markets are open Saturday mornings and early afternoons from spring through fall, though specific times and dates vary: **Beaverton** (www.beavertonfarmersmarket.com), S. W. Hall Boulevard between Third and Fifth Streets; **Canby**, First Avenue between Grant and Holly Streets; **Gresham**, Northwest Miller Avenue between Second and Third Streets; **Hillsboro**, Courthouse Square, Second Avenue and E. Main Street; **Hillsdale** (503-475-6555), parking lot at Mucho Grande, 6319 S. W. Capitol Highway; **Hollywood** (Portland), N. E. Hancock Street between 44th and 45th Avenues, one block south of Sandy Boulevard; **Lake Oswego**, Millennium Plaza Park, First and Evergreen Streets; **Milwaukie**, across from City Hall on S. E. Main Street between S. E. Harrison and Jackson Streets; **Portland**, Saturdays in the South Park Blocks between S. W. Montgomery and Harrison Streets, Wednesdays in the South Park Blocks at S. W. Salmon Street and Park Avenue, and Wednesday 2–7 PM at 3029 S. E. 21st Avenue, one block north of Powell Boulevard; **Tigard** (503-244-2479), S. W. Hall Boulevard at the intersection of Greenburg and Oleson Roads.

SPECIAL SHOPS ✐ **Portland Saturday Market** (503-222-6072; www.saturdaymarket.org), 108 W. Burnside (beneath the west end of the Burnside Bridge between S. W. Naito Parkway and First Avenue), Portland. Established in 1973 and open every Saturday and Sunday from March through Christmas, this open-air market of approximately 450 food and crafts booths advertises itself as "the largest outdoor arts and crafts market in continuous operation in the United States." It features international food, live music, and locally made crafts sold by the people who created them. And even if you're not in the market for buying, this is a great place for people watching.

Powell's City of Books (www.powells.com), 1005 W. Burnside Street, Portland. For bibliophiles of all ages and tastes, this is reputedly the largest bookstore in the world, filling one whole city block and containing more than a half-million new and used volumes in 43,000 square feet.

✱ To Do

BICYCLING **Marine Drive,** exit 307 off Interstate 5, Portland. Running along the top of a 40-foot-high levee that keeps the Columbia River inside its banks is a paved path 4 miles long that lifts bicyclists above the roar of the traffic. A good starting point for a west-to-east ride is the James Gleason Boat Ramp, N. E. 43rd Avenue and Marine Drive.

♿ **Springwater Corridor,** 17 paved miles from southeast Portland to Boring. For more than 80 years the Springwater Line was the railway that served the communities along Johnson Creek in this area. But when its trains stopped hauling passengers in the 1950s and freight in the 1980s, the city of Portland bought the right-of-way and converted it to a pathway for walkers and bicyclists. Its mostly paved, relatively flat (less than 2 percent) grade also makes it suitable for skates, strollers, and wheelchairs. In addition, the fact that it not only bypasses wetlands and woodlands but also connects to more than 100 miles of other trails makes this a rare entryway for the adventures of urban explorers.

See also *Parks.*

CAMPING See **Oxbow Regional Park** under *Wilder Places—Parks.*

CANOEING **Smith and Bybee Lakes,** 8 miles northwest of Portland off Interstate 5 (take exit 307) and Marine Drive. You'd never guess to see such a thing here—near interstate traffic, chain-link fences, and steel-walled warehouses—but there it is, anyway: a 2,000-acre sprawl of water and woods, where hikers and paddlers are welcome but motorboats are verboten.

GOLF **Charbonneau Golf Club** (503-694-1246), 32020 S. W. Charbonneau Drive, Wilsonville, 27-hole executive course.

Eastmoreland (503-775-2900), 2425 S. E. Bybee Boulevard, Portland, 18 holes.

Forest Hills Golf Course (503-357-3347) 36260 S. W. Tongue Lane, Cornelius, 18 holes.

Greenlea Golf Course (503-663-3934), 26736 S. E. Kelso Road, Boring, 9 holes.

Heron Lakes (503-289-1818), 3500 N. Victory Boulevard, Portland, 18 holes.

Lake Oswego Golf Course (503-636-8228), 17525 S. W. Stafford Road, Lake Oswego, 18 holes.

Pumpkin Ridge Golf Course and Ghost Creek Golf Course (503-647-

9977), 12930 Old Pumpkin Ridge Road, North Plains, 18 holes.

Quail Valley Golf Course (503-324-4444), 12565 N. W. Aerts Road, Banks: 18 holes.

Oregon City Golf Club (503-656-2846), 20214 Beavercreek Road, Oregon City, 18 holes.

Red Tail (503-646-5166), 8200 S. W. Scholls Ferry Road, Beaverton, 18 holes.

Rose City (503-253-4744), 2200 N. E. 71st Avenue, Portland, 18 holes.

Sandelie Golf Course (503-655-1461), 28333 S. W. Mountain Road, West Linn.

The Reserve Vineyards and Golf Club (503-649-2345), 4747 S. W. 229th Avenue, Aloha. Cupp Course, 18 holes; Fought Course, 18 holes.

HIKING See **Oxbow Regional Park** under *Wilder Places—Parks.*

✷ Wilder Places

PARKS **Oxbow Regional Park,** 8 miles east of Gresham off Division Street. Because it's located in the Sandy River Gorge, this 1,200-acre park includes old-growth trees and spawning salmon as well as picnic areas, playgrounds, hiking trails (more than 15 miles), and campgrounds (45 year-round sites).

Blue Lake Regional Park, 4 miles northwest of Troutdale off Interstate 84 and Marine Drive. Its location just 20 minutes from downtown Portland tells you this park will be busy, with people coming here to play softball, pitch horseshoes, paddle boats, pedal bikes, or explore trails in the 185 acres that surrounds the 64-acre, spring-fed lake.

Portland City Parks (503-823-7529; www.parks.ci.portland.or.us). Oregon's largest city has more than 200 parks, including the nation's largest (**Forest Park,** more than 5,000 acres) and smallest (**Mills End Park,** less than 4 square feet) urban parks. The following handful, then, is only a sample of what the city has to offer.

Fernhill Park, N. E. 37th Avenue and Ainsworth Street. Sure, this park might look like others, might offer similar playground rides, tennis courts, and horseshoe pits—but this park's specialty has to do with **kite flying,** for here lies a wide-open field that catches the wind from the Columbia River Gorge.

Forest Park, northwest of Portland between Highway 30 and Skyline Boulevard. With almost 8 square miles of deep forests and more than 70 miles of shaded trails, this park is worthy of modern-day Daniel Boones, whether they want to hike or bike, watch birds or just loll in the shade.

Laurelhurst Park, S. E. 39th and Stark. Big firs, thick rhododendrons, busy playgrounds, and bold ducks begging for bread crumbs along the shore of **Laurelhurst Lake** make this one of the city's favorite parks.

🐾 **Luscher Farm Dog Park,** Stafford Road near Rosemont Road. Rare, rare, rare—that's what a park is where you can let your dog scurry and romp hither and yon. Perhaps even more rare, however, are dog owners who scoop up after their pets, so this would be a good place to get into the practice.

Mills End Park, corner of S. W. Taylor Street and Naito Parkway. Only 2 feet in diameter, this circular park perches on a median on Naito Parkway, just a step away from the whiz and rumble of traffic. The park had its start in 1961 when Dick Fagan, a writer for the now-defunct *Oregon Journal,* planted some flowers on the median, which he could see from his office window. "I decided it would be much better if there were flowers instead of weeds," Fagan wrote in his column, "and thus Mills End Park was born." Ten years after the planting of the first flowers, the *Guinness Book of World Records* listed Mill Ends as the world's smallest park. Today, pansies and a miniature Cyprus tree help distinguish the park from the rest of the median.

Mount Tabor Park, corner of S. E. 60th Avenue and Salmon Street. Spread across 200 acres of an ancient volcano, Mount Tabor Park is a place that offers something for almost everybody: gravel trails and dirt paths, shady woods and picnic areas, playgrounds and courts, and hilltop benches with **skyline views of the city.**

South Park Blocks, Ninth and Park Streets. This 25-block area was created n 1852 as a community gathering area, and today it's still one of the city's great places for people watching. In addition, its proximity to downtown, the Portland Art Museum, the Oregon History Center, and numerous shops and restaurants makes the park a cosmopolitan crossroads.

Tom McCall Waterfront Park, on the west bank of the Willamette River along S. W. Naito Avenue. Through 36 acres and along 22 blocks this greenway edges along the Willamette River, its paved walkways carrying strollers and joggers past flower beds and lawns.

Washington Park, 200 S. W. Kingston Street. Perched in the hills west of the city, Washington Park is a place of winding trails and sprawling lawn that connect to the **Oregon Zoo** (see *To See—For Families*) as well as the city's **Rose Garden, Japanese Gardens,** and **Hoyt Arboretum** (see Garden Tours under *To See—For Families*).

The Grotto (503-254-7371), 85th Street and N. E. Sandy Boulevard.

TOM McCALL WATERFRONT PARK

Fountains and pools, forests and gardens give this **62-acre sanctuary** its solitude as well as its beauty. Flower-lined paths show you the way. Pay a small fee to ride an elevator to an upper level, and you'll be rewarded with one of the **best views** from anywhere in area: the **Columbia River, the Cascade Range,** and the **city of Portland.**

Mary S. Young State Park, 9 miles south of Portland and north of West Linn off Highway 43 (take exit 8 on Interstate 205) along the banks of the **Willamette River,** day use only. This 133 acres of woods, marshes, and meadows was a gift from Mary S. Young, who lived nearby for more than a half century. Today the old homesite offers visitors 2 miles of unpaved trails and a mile of paved bike path—as well as various connections to other trails—that bend through a forest of firs and cedars and oaks before heading toward the bank of the Willamette River.

Tryon Creek State Park, 11321 S. W. Terwilliger Boulevard, 6 miles south of downtown Portland (take exit 297 on Interstate 5), day use only. First homesteaded, then logged, and finally eyed for development, this square mile of land spread across Portland's suburbs was at last rescued by its neighbors, who had grown to love this sprawl of wild in their backyards. "We have almost the entire history of Oregon in this park," says M. G. Devereux of the Oregon Parks and Recreation Department. "We had a pioneer seeking a new life here, then we had logging and urban development, then the environmental movement of the 1960s and 1970s that saw the need for green spaces." As a result, today the park is a place of forest and streams and trails that carry the whispers of voices and the thudding of feet as families, couples, and solitary walkers wander their way through it all.

George Rogers Park, in Lake Oswego off Highway 43 (Macadam Avenue) and along the bank of the **Willamette River.** Located near the confluence of Oswego Creek and the Willamette River, this park offers walking paths, river views, and a **waterfall** as well as chunks of the area's industrial history, including the remnants of Oregon's first iron furnace and a steam-powered log hoist.

AUDUBON SOCIETY OF PORTLAND WILDLIFE SANCTUARY

Blaylock Rest Area, 2 miles south of Wilsonville off Interstate 5, between mileposts 281 and 282. Beyond its rest rooms and vending machines, this rest area holds a small but beautiful secret: a short cinder trail leading through the **Grove of the States,** where 47 trees from different parts of the country are planted.

WILDLIFE REFUGES **Audubon Society of Portland** (503-292-6855), 5151 N. W. Cornell Road (drive west on N. W. Lovejoy to N. W. Cornell Road), Portland. Less than 2 miles from downtown Portland lies this 160-acre wildlife sanctuary whose quiet woods and clean water seem to be remnants of the city's horse-and-buggy days. A series of loop trails will show you the refuge's forests, ponds, and streams, and when you're done you might want to visit its **Wildlife Care Center,** the state's largest wildlife rehabilitation facility that each year takes care of more than 3,500 injured animals before returning them to the wild.

Beggars-Tick Wildlife Refuge, S. E. 111th Avenue, just north of Foster Road, Portland. Settled down in the midst of asphalt and chain link, this 21-acre refuge wears two different cloaks through the year: a marsh in winter, a meadow in summer. The change from mud and flood to grass and flowers also signals a shift in wildlife residents, with the rainy season luring **ducks** and **herons** to the area's cattailed wetlands, and the summer sun bringing out **songbirds** and **dragonflies.** A walking path with a footbridge and several viewpoints wanders through the area. In addition, its location near the **Springwater Corridor** (see *To Do—Bicycling*) makes the refuge—named for a species of native sunflower, *not* for the blood-sucking insect—accessible by foot and bicycle.

♿ **Smith and Bybee Lakes,** 8 miles northwest of Portland off Interstate 5 (take exit 307) and Marine Drive. Living within minutes of downtown Portland in these 2,000 acres comprising the largest wetlands in Portland—in fact, the largest wetlands within any American city—are a menagerie of wildlife that include **beavers** and **otters, deer** and **eagles, turtles** and **ospreys.** A mile-long trail is wheelchair- and stroller-accessible, and two platforms provide excellent views of the area.

Jackson Bottom, in Hillsboro off Highway 219, approximately seven blocks south of Baseline Road. A man in a quilted blue jacket leans against the railing of the viewing platform, peers through his binoculars, and says, "The **eagles** are back." For a moment he lifts the binoculars in an arc, following the eagles' flight, then settles again. "The hawks are out there, too," he says "Up in that snag. They've been hunting for 15 or 20 minutes." The man and the birds are sharing a square mile of wildlife habitat, of sloughs and marshes and ponds, that lies within a modern city. Jackson Bottom they call it, part of a 3,000-acre floodplain carved from the Columbia River's Missoula Floods more than 10,000 years ago. First dredged and drained and diked for farming, the area is now a wildlife preserve, its wetlands filled in winter by flooding of the Tualatin River, and in summer by wastewater from the nearby sewage treatment plant. People use the interpretive trails and viewing platforms; multitudes of birds and mammals use the rest. "**Red-tailed hawks,**" the man says, again lifting his binoculars in an arc. "They winter here, raise their chicks."

♿ **Tualatin Hills Nature Park** (503-645-6433), 15655 S. W. Millikan Boulevard, Beaverton. Near the heart of the city of Beaverton lies this wildlife haven, 219 acres of trees and water that supports a wide variety of animals and habitats. "We have five miles of trails, ponds, **Beaverton Creek, Cedar Mill Creek,** forested areas, wetlands, and a mile and a half of paved wheelchair and stroller trail," says park manager Joan Andersen-Wells. "We have **mammals, birds,** and **amphibians.**"

Camassia Nature Reserve, at the end of Walnut Street in West Linn, near the high school. Named for the camas lily that blooms here in the spring, Camassia was Oregon's first preserve of the Nature Conservancy. Growing on its 26 acres of rocky plateau and wetland meadows are woodlands of **oak, madrone,** and **aspen,** as well as more than 300 plant species that visitors can see as they walk along a system of interpretive trails.

✷ Lodging

BED & BREAKFASTS

Beaverton

Aloha Junction Inn and Gardens (1-888-832-5251; aloha@moriah.com), 5085 S. W. 170th Avenue, Beaverton 97007. Settled on 2 acres of fields and gardens like the farmhouse it once was, this 1920s-era two-story home has one room with a private bath, three rooms that share two baths, and a suite ($59–110). Amenities include a gazebo and hot tub, and the full breakfast includes foods grown in the inn's organic garden. In addition, owner

Sandra Eimers supplies brown bag picnic lunches by request.

The Yankee Tinker Bed & Breakfast (1-800-846-5372; yankeetb7b@aol.com), 5480 S. W. 183rd Avenue, Beaverton 97007. Within this 1970 ranch-style house are three guest rooms: one with a private bath and two with a shared bathroom ($50–75). In addition, guest refrigerators are stocked with pop, beer, and wine. The full breakfast includes coffee fresh-ground, orange juice fresh-squeezed, and specialties such as peaches and cream and French toast.

Forest Grove

Oak Tree Bed & Breakfast (503-357-6939; oaktreeBnB@aol.com; www.moriah.com/oaktree), 2300 N. W. Thatcher Road, Forest Grove 97116. In one way, Oak Tree doesn't quite fit the mold of what some people expect in a B&B. "We are a bit unique," says owner Donna McIntosh, "in that we do not have a historical home but just a comfortable, large, and very clean ranch-style home." Many who take advantage of Donna's hospitality, however, find exactly what they're looking for: a countryside setting, comfortable rooms with private baths ($60), a full breakfast, and nearby opportunities for adventure. "We are located on the outskirts of Forest Grove, one mile from Pacific University," Donna says. "Attractions in this quiet town include the numerous wineries and the excellent golf courses in the area."

Milwaukie

Historic Broetje House (503-659-8860), 3101 S. E. Courtney Road, Milwaukie 97222. The world around it may have changed, but this 1889 Queen Anne retains the historic elegance of quieter times. (The house still has its four-story, 50-foot-high water tower built in 1909.) Set in a residential neighborhood and shaded by redwoods, the home offers one guest room with a private bath ($95) and two rooms that share a bath ($55–70). Both come with a full breakfast served in the dining room as well as the chance to wander the home's gardens and sit in the gazebo.

Oregon City

Captain Ainsworth House (1-888-655-3055; www.ainsworthhouse.com), 19139 Lot Whitcomb Drive, Oregon City 97045. As you might guess, this house once belonged to Captain John C. Ainsworth, a steamboat captain first on the Mississippi and then on the Willamette and Columbia, a path that eventually led to his Oregon Steam Navigation Company commanding the river traffic of the state. In 1851 the captain built this Greek Revival mansion on 18 acres he received as a wedding gift when he married Nancy Jane White, and their home soon became a social center in what was then one of the most important cities in the Northwest. Today the restored mansion still has the tall windows, open staircases, and multiple chimneys popular in its day, but it also has four guest rooms that come with private baths and a full breakfast ($85–100). In addition, guests can use a swimming pool and tennis court across the street.

Portland

Brickrose Cottage (1-800-780-6830; brickrosecottage@yahoo.com; www.portland-bedandbreakfast.com), Piedmont neighborhood, Portland 97217. Both inside and out, this 1930s English Tudor reflects old-world details: climbing roses, lead-glass windows, mahogany woodwork, and heirloom antiques that hold special meaning to owners Tiffany and Sean Scott. "How can we provide old-world charm and true character if we don't have the items out that we love and cherish?" Tiffany says. "We have a crocheted tablecloth that my great-grandmother Angelina embroidered while she was still in Italy, and a camelback chair my husband's Grandfather Scott brought over from England." This personal touch, however, extends beyond the furnishings. "We go out of our way," Tiffany says, "to make our guests' stays as comfortable and pleasant as possible." One of the cottage's guest rooms has a private bath ($135), while the other shares a bathroom ($95). Both come with a breakfast that features such house favorites as (take a breath here) "Amaretto French toast made with a sour cream batter and finished with shaved almonds; crêpes filled with fresh strawberries and whipped cream or nectarines warmed with Grand Marnier; or our savory omelet filled with avocado, sun-dried tomatoes and bleu cheese, accompanied by roasted red potatoes and garlic."

Century Garden Bed & Breakfast (503-235-6846; www.centurygarden.com), 1960 S. E. Larch Avenue, Portland 97214. On the grounds of this 1909 American Four Square home, which is located in one of Portland's historic districts, lie **five gardens** that invite a quiet stroll and a sniff or two of the roses. The two guest rooms come with private baths and a full breakfast ($99).

Clinkerbrick House (503-281-2533), 2311 N. E. Schuyler Street, Portland 97212. A 1908 Dutch Colonial, the Clinkerbrick House is located just 10 minutes from downtown Portland and even closer to area theaters, shops, and restaurants. Of its three antiques-decorated and quilt-furnished guest rooms, one comes with a private bath, and all include a full breakfast ($60–78).

Gedney Gardens (503-226-6514; www.gedneygardens.com), 2651 N. W. Cornell Road, Portland 97210. Standing high in Portland's West Hills, this 1908 Edwardian overlooks downtown, while **Forest Park** (see *Wilder Places—Parks*) and the **Japanese Gardens** (see Garden Tours under *To See—For Families*) lie just minutes away. The three guest rooms have fireplaces or balconies as well as views of Mount Hood or Mount St. Helens. A full breakfast is included ($55–75).

✐ **General Hooker's Bed & Breakfast** (1-800-745-4135; lori@generalhookers.com), 125 S. W. Hooker Street, Portland 97201. Since 1888 this two-story Queen Anne Victorian has stood along Portland's Lair Hill, watching the changes in the city below. (For guests, the best view comes from the home's roof deck.) Two of the guest rooms share a bath ($85–95), while two others come with private bathrooms ($95–125). The "heart-healthy" full breakfast revolves around juices, seasonal fruits, and various cereals. Children older than 10 are welcome.

Georgian House (1-888-282-2250; rlcanning@juno.com; www.thegeorgianhouse.com), 1828 N. E. Siskiyou Street, Portland 97212. This centrally located 1922 red-brick Georgian Colonial brings a piece of the Old Country to the Northwest: French doors and windows, English wardrobes and rose garden, Victorian beds, stained glass, winding staircase, and wrought-iron gate. In addition, owner Willie Canning issues a most gracious invitation to guests. "Come relax on the back deck or in the charming gazebo with a glass of wine after a busy day," she says. "Or stroll along the brick paths, through the colorful English rose garden, and past the berry patch, whose fruit you'll enjoy at breakfast." Two of its four guest rooms come with private baths, while one other has a fireplace ($65–115). And the full breakfast includes those berries picked fresh from the garden.

Heron Haus (503-274-1846; www.heronhaus.com), 2545 N. W. Westover Road, Portland 97210. Settled in a quiet and historic residential neighborhood in Portland's northwest hills, this 10,000-square-foot 1904 Tudor home looks over the city and toward the Cascades. Its six guest rooms come with private baths, king or queen beds, and a continental breakfast ($135–350).

✐ **Hostess House** (503-282-7892; hostess@hostesshouse.com; www.hostesshouse.com), 5758 N. E. Emerson Street, Portland 97218. Nothing fancy about the Hostess House, which is a simple home in a modest neighborhood, yet the fact that it has been operating as a B&B since 1988 tells you that hostess Milli Laughlin must be doing something right. Gracious hospitality and darn good cooking probably have much to do with it, as does a reasonable price. "Hostess House is an economy inn where guests are pampered, coddled, and well fed—gourmet style," says Milli. "Our place is not for the conspicuous consumer but for the low-maintenance person who is looking for quality accommodations with a smile." As a result, here you can expect a friendly welcome, a generous breakfast, and an inviting room ($55–65). Quiet, supervised children are welcome.

Irvington Inn (503-280-2299; irvingtoninn@msn.com; www.irvingtoninn.com), 2727 N. E. 21st Street, Portland 97212. Set in a neighborhood of tree-lined streets, historic homes, and private gardens, its interior graced with arched doorways and cove ceilings, antique furniture and Oriental carpets, this 1934 home built in the style of a Tudor cottage seems to encompass different parts of the globe. "It's an English country-style bed and breakfast, but each room is furnished in a different cultural style," says innkeeper Vicki Pflaumer, "from the Asian sitting room, to the African room to the American heritage room and South American hallway filled with folk art." It's an international theme with a specific intent in mind, especially when it comes to the inn's guest rooms ($65–105). "Comfort is the key emphasis here," Vicki says. "Comfortable beds, comfortable casual sitting chairs, colorful cottage garden borders, and a full gourmet breakfast, too."

Knott Street Inn (503-249-1855; www.knottstreetinn.com), 2331 N. E. Knot Street, Portland 97211. Restored and furnished so it seems still to be standing in 1910, the year of its construction, this historic Craftsman home offers three antiques-furnished guest rooms, all with private baths containing claw-foot tubs ($85–100). A full breakfast is included.

The Lion and the Rose Victorian (1-800-955-1647; lionrose@ix.netcom.com; www.lionrose.com), 1810 N. E. 15th Street, Portland 97212. Built for a brewery owner in 1906, this historic home blends beauty and space in a Queen Anne design. "The Lion and The Rose prides itself in a clean, comfortable environment of beautiful furnishings," says owner Kay Peffer. "We have set out to create a beautiful space for our guests to enjoy." That space, approximately 10,000 square feet of it, is furnished with turn-of-the-20th-century carpets, drapes, and antiques, while the landscaped grounds are a blend of English gardens, brick pathways, birdbaths, fountains, and statues. Five of its guest rooms come with private baths, and one shares a bathroom ($120–140). In addition, the inn's gourmet breakfast has been featured in several cookbooks.

Macmaster House (1-800-774-9523; innkeeper@macmaster.com; www.macmaster.com), 1041 S. W. Vista Avenue, Portland 97205. Neighbors to this 1895 Colonial mansion include the lawns, woods, and gardens of **Washington Park** (see *Wilder Places—Parks*), yet downtown Portland lies only a short drive away. Guest rooms with shared baths ($95–110) and suites with private baths ($140) occupy the home's second and third floors. Amenities can include fireplaces, balconies, city views, and in-room libraries.

Mt. Scott Hideaway (503-777-6170; network8@netzero.com; www.mtscotthideaway.com), 9350 S. E. 92nd Avenue, Portland 97266. From this B&B's wraparound deck, the night view of Portland comes as a spangled glow of city lights. The scenery from the Rainbows and Magical Lights Room, one of the inn's two guest rooms, is almost as good because it opens to the world beyond through 15 vertical feet of windows running from floor to ceiling. Both rooms come with private baths and a full breakfast ($75–135). In addition, a spa and an indoor swimming pool are available to guests. Adult-supervised children are welcome.

Portland Guest House (503-282-1402; pgh@teleport.com; www.teleport.com/~pgh), 1720 N. E. 15th Avenue, Portland 97212. Built in 1890 and later restored to serve exclusively as a guest house, this Victorian located just 10 minutes from downtown Portland offers a number of guest rooms with either private ($85–95) or shared ($65–75) bathrooms, all of which include a full breakfast that can feature blueberries or strawberries picked fresh from the garden.

Portland's White House (1-800-272-7131; pdxwhi@aol.com; www.portlandswhitehouse.com), 1914 N. E. 22nd Avenue, Portland 97212. This B&B isn't just a white house, it's a *White House,* built along the same lines as the one in Washington, D.C., though without the presidential pomp. Located in a historic residential neighborhood but still close to downtown Portland, the White House began in 1911 as a lumber baron's home, complete with Greek columns, circular driveway, and fountains outside; and mahogany doors, hand-painted murals, and inlaid oak floors inside. Six second-floor guest rooms come with private baths, antique furnishings, and featherbeds ($98–169), and breakfast is served on crystal in the formal dining room.

Riverview Guesthouse (503-287-3937; gilmores@riverviewguesthousebb.com; www.riverview guesthousebb.com), 3909 N. Overlook Terrace, Portland 97227. Even though it's located in a residential neighborhood, this B&B has a piece of some of **Portland's best views**—including the Willamette River and the West Hills—as well as of neighborhood gardens. "We're located on the northern bluff of the Willamette River," says owner Rozell Gilmore. "This allow guests to have a view of the city, but our house is still less than ten minutes by auto to the heart of Portland." Two of its guest rooms share a bath ($55–60), while one has a private bathroom ($70). All rooms include either a full or continental breakfast. "The unique thing about Riverview

Guest House," Rozell says, "is that we offer a variety of breakfasts, including a southern-style one."

🐾 **Sullivan's Gulch Bed & Breakfast** (503-331-1104; thegulch@sullivangulch.com; www.sullivansgulch.com), 1744 N. E. Clackamas Street, Portland 97232. This B&B, which fits quietly into a tree-lined neighborhood, has managed to pull together two distinct styles. "Too many B&Bs are littered with 'cute' family photographs, dried flowers, straw hats nailed to the wall, and jammed with old furniture that the owners consider 'antiques,'" says owner Skip Rognlien. "But Sullivan's Gulch has been carefully designed without clutter, reflecting the aesthetic of Frank Lloyd Wright, combined with Western art and Native American arts and crafts—Frank Lloyd Wright meets Buffalo Bill." Within this decorating scheme, four guest rooms are available: two suites with private baths ($90) and two rooms that share a bath ($75). Well-behaved pets are welcome.

Terwilliger Vista Bed & Breakfast (1-888-244-0602; www.terwilligervista.com), 515 S. W. Westwood Drive, Portland 97201. Even though this 1940 inn is located just minutes from downtown Portland, it's the site of a half acre of countryside growing lawns and gardens, camellias and rhododendrons, shade and fruit trees. All five of its guest rooms ($85–145) have private baths, and some come with bay windows that overlook the gardens or the Willamette River. A full breakfast is included, and children older than 10 are welcome.

Tudor House (503-287-9476; milan@tudor-house.com; www.tudor-house.com), 2321 N. E. 28th Avenue, Portland 97212. Standing on a green, shaded yard in a historic neighborhood of fine old homes, this Tudor manor is in its third decade of offering accommodations to travelers. Its five guest rooms have king or queen beds, and three have private baths ($90–125). A full breakfast is served, and children are welcome.

Tigard

The Woven Glass Inn (1-800-484-2192; wovenglass@wovenglassinn.com; www.wovenglassinn.com), 14645 Beef Bend Road, Tigard 97224. Standing along a scenic driving loop and surrounded by wine country, this 1938 farmhouse offers guests sitting rooms, fireplaces, decks, and gardens as well as two guest rooms with private baths and a full breakfast ($75–85). "The Woven Glass Inn is a 3,000-square-foot, elegantly furnished historic house in a rural setting," says owner Renee Giroux. "Stained-glass windows are featured in every room of the house, along with four common areas and a large perennial garden."

West Linn

Rose Cottage (503-650-6053; innkeeper@rosecottagebb.com; www.rosecottagebb.com), 2248 Fifth Avenue, West Linn 97068. Built and landscaped in the style of an English thatched-roof cottage, this bed & breakfast is a quiet retreat within a residential neighborhood. Its accommodations include two guest rooms with private baths, king beds, and a refrigerator ($95–125), as well as a sitting room with a fireplace. "We place a big emphasis on the comfort of our rooms and the excellence of our breakfasts," says owner Sally Palmer. "Our rooms are spacious and inviting, and we choose the ingredients for our breakfasts with both the health and satisfaction of our guests in mind." Those breakfasts can feature foods so varied and numerous—the menu changes daily—that Sally says they're certain "to please a gourmand."

* Where to Eat

DINING OUT

Portland

Café Azul (503-525-4422), 112 N. W. Ninth Avenue, Portland. Its style of cooking is Mexican; its reputation for quality is unsurpassed; and the ingredients in its recipes are local and organic. As a result, the chances of finding a throng of diners eager to find a seat at the Café Azul are excellent.

Café Des Amis (503-295-6487), 1987 N. W. Kearney Street, Portland. Standing cozy and quiet in a residential neighborhood, the Café Des Amis is so consistent that for years it has drawn diners who know exactly what to expect once they walk through the door—including the menu selections, which often feature beef, duck, or salmon in port, blackberry, or sorrel sauce. That same consistency carries over to the restaurant's quality in its food and preparation, ranging from its cobblers to its soups.

Genoa (503-238-1464), 2832 S. E. Belmont Street, Portland. Famous for its food and service, Genoa has been serving elegant, seven-course meals to guests for more than 30 years. For many diners in the area, this is *the* place to go to celebrate a special occasion—even if that occasion involves seeing what's new on the menu, which changes every two weeks.

The Heathman (503-241-4100), 1009 S. W. Broadway, Portland. One of the city's most famous fine-dining restaurants, the Heathman is known for the elegance of its dining room, the privacy of its seating, and the quality of its French and Northwest cuisine.

Higgins (503-222-9070), 1239 S. W. Broadway, Portland. The owner's involvement with organic foods and local producers is evident in a menu that features dishes homegrown, expertly prepared, and beautifully presented.

Laslow's Northwest (503-241-8092), 2327 N. W. Kearney Street, Portland. Laslow's is a restaurant with split personalities: casual bistro serving Cuban burgers downstairs, elegant eatery featuring duck confit upstairs. Friendly service and good wine are almost guaranteed on both levels.

McCormick and Schmick's Seafood Restaurant (503-224-7522), 235 S. W. First Avenue, Portland. One of Portland's landmark restaurant's, one that's frequently crowded, McCormick and Schmick's changes its menu daily but not its seafood specialties, including bouillabaisse, crabcakes, and grilled alder-smoked salmon.

West Linn

Bugatti's Ristorante (503-636-9555), 18740 Willamette Drive, West Linn. An Italian restaurant that understands how to be comfortable and elegant at the same time, Bugatti's offers daily specials that feature seasonal food, fresh ingredients, and unique desserts.

EATING OUT

Forest Grove

El Torero (503-359-8471), 2009 Main Street, Forest Grove. Some of the best authentic Mexican food can be found here at El Torero, where fajitas and frijoles are specialties as well as favorites, but where almost everything on the menu is almost certain to be a winner.

Hillsboro

Helvetia Tavern (503-647-5286), 10275 N. W. Helvetia Road, Hillsboro. Once a country store and now a burger and beer joint, this tavern packs 'em in from all around, some coming for the food, others for the escape from nearby cities, swapping hot asphalt for green farms. The tavern's specialty is its Jumbo Hamburger, the star of the annual fund-raising Jumbo Hamburger Eating Contest.

Portland

3 Doors Down Café (503-236-6886), 1429 S. E. 37th Avenue, Portland. Casual, friendly, and personal are three traits of this Italian café, but so are good food, big servings, and homemade ravioli.

Alexis (503-224-8577), 215 W. Burnside Street, Portland. Owned and operated by the same family for more than 20 years, Alexis has long been a destination for those who love authentic Greek food and appreciate a warm, friendly atmosphere. After all, where else in the Northwest can you find lamb souvlaki *and* weekend belly dancers?

Basta's Trattoria and Bar (503-274-1572), 40 N. W. 21st Avenue, Portland. Good food, decent prices, unique specials, and an extensive wine list are distinguishing traits of this Italian restaurant.

Bernie's Southern Bistro (503-282-9864), 2904 N. E. Alberta Street, Portland. With a taste of Southern cooking and hospitality transplanted to the Northwest, Bernie's offers what's labeled "Southern comfort food," which includes blackened catfish, crawfish cakes, and bourbon that's probably best sipped while sitting on a plantation's veranda.

Bluehour (503-226-3394), 250 N. W. 13th Avenue, Portland. A restaurant so swank that valet parking is provided free of charge, the Bluehour is a place of wide-open spaces: tall ceilings, expansive windows, and shimmering light. The range of its menu is equally impressive, featuring both Mediterranean and Northwest dishes, though seafood and desserts are specialties.

Blue Nile Café (503-284-4653), 2225 N. E. Broadway, Portland. The owner of this Ethiopian diner greets you at your table, takes your order, and cooks and serves your food in a remarkable one-woman operation.

Bread and Ink Café (503-239-4756), 3610 S. E. Hawthorne Boulevard, Portland. Located in the midst of the trendy Hawthorne district, this café offers a window to a bustling world, while its menu includes big sandwiches, baked desserts, and almost legendary blintzes.

Byways Café (503-221-0011), 1212 N. W. Glisan Street, Portland. Decorated as a roadhouse, Byways is the place to go for *real* breakfast food, from its pancake syrup to its corned beef hash.

Café Castagna (503-231-9959), 1758 S. E. Hawthorne, Portland. This is café food with substance, including hamburgers, roast chicken, and some of Portland's best pizza.

Caffé Mingo (503-226-4646), 807 N. W. 21st Avenue, Portland. An Italian restaurant where diners often line up to wait for the next open table, the Caffé Mingo specializes in pasta, but also offers risotto and pizza, all of it prepared and served by a friendly staff.

Delta Café (503-771-3101), 4607 S. E. Woodstock Boulevard, Portland. Even though fried chicken is just one specialty of this café that specializes in Deep South cooking, it's reason enough to make a stop here.

Doris Café (503-287-9249), 325 N. E. Russell Street, Portland. One of Portland's "soul food" eateries, Doris serves up chicken and ribs and most anything else you can barbecue on a grill, as well as sweet-potato pie and an everyone-is-welcome atmosphere.

Esparza's Tex-Mex Café (503-234-7909), 2725 S. E. Ankeny Street, Portland. From its tequila to its Cowboy Tacos, this café seems to belong in the Lone Star State, yet satisfied diners have made it a destination restaurant in Portland.

Fat Albert's Breakfast Café (503-873-9822), 6668 S. E. Milwaukie Avenue, Portland. If you want something for breakfast, you can probably find it here. Specialties include *big* omelets, plate-sized pancakes, home fries, and a "bottomless" bowl of oatmeal.

Fratelli (503-241-8800), 1230 N. W. Hoyt Street, Portland. Specializing in regional Italian food, Fratelli cooks up some of the most unusual dishes in town, changes its menu often, and provides a casual but lively atmosphere for its guests.

Gustav's Bier Stube (503-288-5503), 5035 N. E. Sandy Boulevard, Portland. At Gustav's you can find German food in a comfortable atmosphere, one without the Lederhosen costumes and affected accents that plague some German restaurants. *Bratwurst* or *Weisswurst,* fondue or *Schnitzel*—it's all here without the Alp horns.

John St. Café (503-247-1066), 8338 N. Lombard Street, Portland. Daily breakfast specials—including hash, pancakes, and omelets—and wonderful sandwiches make this café a morning and noon destination drive for numerous Portlanders.

Justa Pasta (503-243-2249), 21326 N. W. 19th Avenue, Portland. Even if you don't love Justa Pasta's name, you'll adore what this storefront restaurant serves—made-from-scratch pastas created with fresh ingredients—along with its big helpings and low prices.

Ken's Artisan Bakery (503-248-2202), 338 N. W. 21st Avenue, Portland. Modest prices and exceptional pastries and breads distinguish this bakery, which has built a devoted following among those who appreciate genuine craftsmanship in their baked goods.

Kornblatt's (503-242-0055), 628 N. W. 23rd Avenue, Portland. This deli and bakery guarantees that it offers the finest "delicatessen-style food west of the Hudson"—and many diners agree. "It has terrific food, great service, and wonderful ambiance," says a Portland woman who makes Kornblatt's a regular destination. "It reminds me of my Jewish mother's kitchen."

Milo's City Café (503-288-6456), 1325 N. E. Broadway, Portland. One of downtown's most popular breakfast destinations, Milo's has built its reputation by taking its omelets, hash, and French toast far beyond the traditional.

The Original Pancake House (503-246-9007), 8600 S. W. Barbur Boulevard, Portland. Since the day it opened in 1955, this landmark restaurant has served made-from-scratch pancakes and six-egg omelets to crowds of people who believe The Original Pancake House serves the best breakfast on the planet.

Pearl Bakery (503-827-0910), 102 N. W. Ninth Avenue, Portland. Limited seating and excellent breads and sandwiches almost guarantee you'll find plenty of company at this storefront bakery.

Pho Van Bistro (503-248-2172), 1012 N. W. Glisan Street, Portland. This Vietnamese restaurant has found a winning combination in its fast service, fresh food, good prices, and a unique atmosphere that somehow manages to blend a casual setting with elegant dining.

Queen of Sheba (503-287-6302), 2413 N. E. MLK Jr. Boulevard, Portland. Specializing in "Fiery Ethiopian" food and friendly service, the Queen of Sheba offers some of the city's best African food.

Rose's Deli and Bakery (503-222-5292), 838 N. W. 23rd Avenue, Portland. If you've ever wanted to order a cinnamon roll bigger-around than a saucer and thicker than a bricklayer's fist, this is the place to do it. For more than a half century, this deli and bakery has specialized in such a behemoth bun, yet it also offers locally famous sandwiches and desserts.

Southpark (503-326-1300), 901 S. W. Salmon Street, Portland. From the South Park Blocks in Portland, this restaurant is easy to spot—just look for the salmon swimming through the corner of the building. Inside you'll find high ceilings and big windows bordering a dining room that bustles with conversation and laughter and the scurry of tray-toting waiters and waitresses. The food is good and the selections are unique.

The Yummy Garden (503-239-8551), 4729 S. E. Milwaukie Avenue, Portland. Fresh food, excellent cooking, and friendly service make The Yummy Garden one of the best Chinese restaurants in the area.

Zell's: An American Café (503-239-0196), 1300 S. E. Morrison Street, Portland. Before you stop here for breakfast, you might not realize how many ingredients can fit quite nicely into eggs. Chorizo and peppers, for instance. Or brie and tomatoes. Or smoked salmon and green onions. Zell's, however, also serves its share of waffles and pancakes, and come lunch time it hauls out its specialty sandwiches and soups.

✷ Special Events

May: **Cinco de Mayo** (503-222-9807), Portland. **Indian Art Northwest** (503-224-8650), Portland.

June: **Tigard Festival of Balloons** (503-590-1828), Tigard. **Lake Oswego Festival of the Arts** (503-636-1060), Lake Oswego.

July: **Waterfront Blues Festival** (503-282-0555), Portland.

August: **Mount Hood Jazz Festival** (503-219-9833), Gresham. **Tualatin Crawfish Festival** (503-692-0780), Tualatin. **Homowo Festival** (503-288-33025), Portland. **Oregon City Antique Fair** (503-656-1619), Oregon City. **The Bite: A Taste of Portland** (503-248-0600), Portland. Widely imitated, this annual festival held in the city's Tom McCall Waterfront Park features food from area restaurants, beer from local microbreweries, and bands from the Northwest.

October: **Portland Greek Festival** (503-234-0468), Portland.

November–December: **Festival of Lights at the Grotto** (503-261-2400), Portland. (See also Garden Tours under *To See—For Families.*) **Zoolights Festival Oregon Zoo** (503-226-1561), Portland. (See also *To See—For Families.*)

MOUNT HOOD–COLUMBIA GORGE AREA

GUIDANCE **Clackamas River Ranger District** (503-630-8700); **Zigzag Ranger District**, (503-622-3191); **Mount Hood Information Center** (503-622-7674).

Columbia River Gorge National Scenic Area: Headquarters (541-386-2333), 902 Wasco Avenue, Suite 200, Hood River 97031.

Estacada–Clackamas River Area Visitors Information Center (503-630-3483), 595 N. W. Industrial Way, Estacada 97023.

Hood River County Chamber of Commerce (1-800-366-3530; www.hoodriver.org), 405 Portway Avenue, Hood River 97031.

Mount Hood Area Chamber of Commerce (1-888-622-4822; www.mthood.org), 65000 E. Highway 26, Welches 97067.

Mount Hood National Forest: Headquarters (503-668-1771), 16400 Champion Way, Sandy 97055; **Barlow Ranger District** (541-467-2291).

Oregon State Parks (503-378-6305), State Parks and Recreation Department, 525 Trade Street S. E., Salem 97301.

Port of Cascade Locks Visitors Center (541-374-8619), 355 Wanapa Street at Marine Park, Cascade Locks 97014.

Sandy Area Chamber of Commerce (503-668-4006; www.sandyoregonchamber.org), 39260 Pioneer Boulevard, Sandy 97055.

Troutdale Area Chamber of Commerce (503-669-7473; www.oregonstate.net/troutdale/tacc), 338 E. Historic Columbia River Highway, Troutdale 97060.

GETTING THERE The Mount Hood area can be reached from the east and west by Highway 26 and from the north and south by Highway 35. The Columbia Gorge area is connected by Interstate 84 and the Historic Columbia River Highway, both of which run east–west.

MEDICAL EMERGENCY **Kaiser Sunnyside Medical Center** (503-652-2880), 10180 S. E. Sunnyside Drive, Clackamas.

Legacy Mount Hood Medical Center (503-674-1191), 24800 S. E. Stark, Gresham.

Providence Hood River Memorial Hospital (541-386-3911), 811 13th Street, Hood River.

Willamette Falls Hospital (503-656-1631), 1500 Division, Oregon City.

✷ Towns

Hood River. Miles of blossoms, slopes of snow, and gusts of wind—these are the distinguishing elements of this city perched above the Columbia River. "Throngs of visitors come to the city and its environs," says a 1940 travel guide, "and make it their headquarters while exploring the clear streams, green hills, and clean orchard land." Even after more than six decades of change, Hood River is still clear, green, and clean.

Mount Hood. This is the community, not the mountain, and the arrival here of the first homesteader in 1859 makes this the oldest settlement in the upper Hood River Valley. Before that it served as a campsite and a root- and berry-gathering place for Wasco and Klickitat Indians and then as a crossroads for comings and goings first of trappers and freighters and now of tourists and skiers.

Parkdale. Located in the upper Hood River Valley, Parkdale first . . . er . . . blossomed as the result of its thriving orchards. Then when the timbered slopes of the mountain caught the eye of the Oregon Lumber Company, Parkdale became the southern terminus of the timber company's railroad, a role the community still plays today.

✷ To See

MUSEUMS **Troutdale Rail Museum** (503-669-7473), 473 E. Historic Columbia River Highway, Troutdale. This depot, one of the earliest train stations along the Columbia River, stands in Troutdale because of Captain John Harlow, the town's founder and a man with an attitude. It started in 1882 when the railroad refused to build a depot in town, even though it planned on building a trestle across the Sandy River, which flows next to Troutdale. So the captain waited for a spring high water, sailed his boat up the Sandy River, declared the water navigable, and demanded that instead of a trestle a far more expensive drawbridge be built to handle river traffic. Stuck by the laws governing the state's navigable waters, the railroad agreed to swap the depot for the drawbridge. As a result, Troutdale thrived, and even though the original depot burned down in 1907, this building took its place the same year.

Cascade Locks Historical Museum (541-374-8535), Marine Park in Cascade Locks off Interstate 84, exit 44. The artifacts and photographs in this museum trace the community's history through the changes in the Columbia River—starting from the days of the river's wild rapids and native fishermen and then moving through the years to paddlewheelers chugging through its current, fishwheels scooping up its fish, and engineers building the locks and canals that opened

Oregon's interior to boats and trains. Remnants of the river's first lock—which opened here in 1896, permitting ships to bypass the furious Cascade Rapids—are visible near the museum at Marine Park.

Hood River County Museum (541-386-6772), Port Marina Park, exit 64 on Interstate 84, Hood River. When members of the Pioneer Historical Society began collecting clippings to preserve local history, their collection eventually grew into the Hood River County Museum, which now displays the story of this community's growth alongside what was once the wildest river in the Northwest.

Hutson Museum (541-352-6808), off Highway 281 in Parkdale. Located on a 2-acre complex in the foothills of Mount Hood and at the end of the Mount Hood Railroad line, the Hutson Museum displays an impressive private collection of native and pioneer artifacts.

Reptile Man's Living Museum (503-824-6423), 31265-A S. E. Highway 26 (Ashley's Swiss Village, near the intersection of Highways 26 and 212), Boring. The purpose of this museum, says owner and self-taught herpetologist Richard Ritchey, is "to teach the importance of reptiles and the balance of nature." The collection housed in this 2,000-square-foot museum includes rattlesnakes, alligators, king cobras, and Julius Squeezer, a 20-foot python, the largest in Oregon.

Sandy Pioneer Museum (503-668-4006), at City Hall, 39250 Pioneer Boulevard (Highway 26), Sandy. Since 1926 this museum has collected and displayed the artifacts and photographs that tell the story of Sandy, a town that grew up as a wagon stop alongside the Oregon Trail's Barlow Road. Yet so vast is its collection and so small its space—just 1,200 square feet of the City Hall's main floor—that the Pioneer Museum will soon have its own building.

Stage Stop Road Interpretive Center (503-622-4798), 24525 E. Welches Road (off Highway 26), Welches. The Cascade Geographic Society established this center to tell the story of Mount Hood, both its human and natural history and the role it played on the Oregon Trail. Its collection of artifacts stems from wagon trains, native cultures, and area wildlife.

HISTORIC SITES **Columbia Gorge Hotel** (541-386-5566), 2 miles west of Hood River off Interstate 84, exit 62. Standing on an ancient gathering site for native tribes, this elegant building has come full circle through the years. When it began in 1904 as the Waw Gwin Gwin Hotel—a Native American word (meaning "rushing water") for the nearby 208-foot waterfall—it served the passengers of Columbia River steamships. But when the Columbia River Highway reached the area in 1920, timber baron Simon Benson bought the hotel, invested a half-million dollars in it, and turned it into an elegant destination that earned an international reputation. Soon it was drawing presidents (Franklin Roosevelt and Calvin Coolidge) and movie stars (Myrna Loy, Jane Powell, Rudolph Valentino, and Clara Bow) to its doors. Through the years, however, the hotel began fading, until it was transformed in 1952 to a retirement and nursing home for lumber-industry workers belonging to the Neighbors of Woodcraft fraternal order, and then underwent restoration in the late 1970s to stand once again as one of the premier hotels in the region.

Bridge of the Gods, near Cascade Locks, exit 44 on Interstate 84. The history of this bridge concerns not what's there, but what *isn't.* According to geologists, a massive landslide, known as the Bonneville Landslide, occurred here as recently as 300 years ago. Tumbling from the slopes of Washington's Table Mountain, the slide covered more than 5 square miles, created a 200-foot dam across more than 3 miles of the Columbia River, drowned 35 miles of riverside forest, and formed a lake that sprawled all the way to what is now Idaho. When the lake waters finally broke through—perhaps as soon as two years after the dam's creation—the ensuing flood eroded the slide and filled parts of the Willamette Valley with 100 feet of water. The destruction seemed so recent to Lewis and Clark when they saw it in 1805 that they calculated the slide as having occurred perhaps two decades before. The large rocks obstructing the Columbia, they noted, "seem to have fallen promiscuously from the mountains into the bed of the river," and all that was left of the drowned forest were "stumps of pine trees scattered for some distance." The great dam, which may have served as a bridge, also played a role in the legend of the area's native peoples, who believed it was a gift from the Great Spirit—*The Great Cross Over,* they called it—and its destruction the result of a quarrel between his sons, Klickitat and Wy'East, who loved the same woman. When the brothers began a volcanic brawl, they hurled fire and tossed stones and made the earth tremble until the bridge collapsed. Today the feuding brothers still face each other across the Columbia, with Wy'East (Mount Hood) on the south bank and Klickitat (Mount Adams) on the north. The current Bridge of the Gods was built in 1926 and raised 44 feet in 1938 to make room for the backwaters of Bonneville Dam (see next listing).

Bonneville Dam (503-374-8820), 37 miles east of Portland off Interstate 84, exit 40. This 1,100-foot length of concrete is the result of doing what everyone knew could never be done—dam the Columbia, the River of the West. Today the dam creates a 48-mile pool that stretches upstream as far as The Dalles. Construction began in 1933 and concluded four years later; in 1986 the dam was placed on the **National Register of Historic Places.**

Eagle Creek Campground, 6 miles west of Cascade Locks off Interstate 84, exit 41. Standing beside the old Columbia River Highway, this was the first U.S. Forest Service campground in the nation. To meet the demands of a motoring public in the 1930s, the Civilian Conservation Corps (CCC) added some modern conveniences, many of them built of native stone, including fireplaces, water fountains, picnic shelters, overlooks, and rest rooms—which contained the first flush toilet in a Forest Service facility. Many of these structures, as well as remnants of the old highway, remain intact.

Vista House (503-695-2246), 10 miles east of Troutdale on the Historic Columbia River Highway. Perched on Crown Point more than 700 feet above the Columbia River, this memorial to Oregon Trail pioneers was designed by Samuel Lancaster, the chief engineer of the Columbia River Highway, to be "an observatory from which the vista both up and down the Columbia could be viewed in silent communication with the infinite." In the decades following its opening in 1918, the Vista House has performed that job admirably for tens of thousands of visitors who have stopped here for breathless stares at the river.

Multnomah Falls Lodge (503-695-2376), 28 miles east of Portland off Interstate 84, exit 31. Located at the foot of Multnomah Falls, Oregon's most popular tourist attraction with 2.5 million visitors per year, the lodge was built in 1925 as a way station for travelers along the old Columbia River Highway. "There are higher waterfalls and falls of greater volume," said the highway's engineer, Samuel Lancaster, "but there are none more beautiful than Multnomah."

Harlow House (503-661-2164), 726 E. Historic Columbia River Highway, Troutdale. Built by Fred Harlow, the son of Troutdale founder Captain John Harlow (see Troutdale Rail Museum under *Museums*), this 1900 farmhouse is almost as interesting as Fred himself. Fred, you see, joined his brother Lou in opening Troutdale's first bank, but it failed because Fred was embezzling from it. So Fred and his wife, Minnie, left town, leaving Lou to pay off the debts. Before long, however, Fred divorced Minnie and married another woman, who in later years took care of Fred when he became ill. Meanwhile, Minnie, Fred's ex-wife, also became ill, so she moved in with Fred and his new wife, who also played nurse to Minnie. And remember—those were the good old days.

Lewis and Clark Trail (Cascade Locks to Sandy River). Once past the rapids of the Cascades, the Lewis and Clark Expedition found the going smoother, their world changing. "At the end of eight miles [past the Cascades], the river opens to the breadth of a mile, with a gentle current," Sergeant Patrick Gass wrote. "The country here becomes level, and the river broader."

The Cascades, October 31 to November 2, 1805 (Cascade Locks Marine Park off Interstate 84, exit 44). These are the rapids that Captain Clark called the "Great Shute," describing them as a half-mile long with "the great river compressed within the space of 150 paces." The result was "water passing in great velocity foaming and boiling in a most horrible manner." According to Sergeant Gass, the portage around these rapids involved a struggle "over rocks 8 or 10 feet in height." The men worked all day to travel a mile. "It was," the sergeant wrote, "the most fatiguing business we have been engaged in for a long time."

Beacon Rock, November 2, 1805, and April 9, 1806 (7 miles west of Cascade Locks on the Washington side of the river). Described by Captain Clark as a "remarkable high detached rock . . . about 800 feet high and 400 paces around," Beacon Rock—sometimes spelled in the journals as "Beaten Rock"—was "the commencement of tide-water" in the Columbia River, so they knew they were close to their destination. Today, the rock is a Washington state park with a trail leading to its top.

Rooster Rock, November 2, 1805, and April 6–8, 1806 (22 miles east of Portland off Interstate 84, exit 25). According to a legend of the river's native Wishram people, Rooster Rock and Beacon Rock (see previous listing) were once brothers, sons of the trickster-hero Coyote, who turned them to stone and set them down on opposite banks of the river to prevent them from fighting over a woman. Lewis and Clark camped here on both their westward and eastward journeys. On their return trip in April 1806, Captain Lewis noted that in this area "the wind blew with great violence, and we were obliged to unload our boats, which were soon after filled with water."

ROOSTER ROCK (LEFT), A 200-FOOT SPIRE CREATED BY A LANDSLIDE THAT SEPARATED IT FROM CROWN POINT (RIGHT) WAS A CAMPSITE OF LEWIS AND CLARK.

Sandy River: November 3, 1805, and April 5, 1806 (15 miles east of Portland off Interstate 84, exit 18). The morning they broke camp near Rooster Rock (see above) was so foggy, Captain Clark wrote, "that we could not see a man 50 steps off." When the weather cleared about noon, they spotted the Sandy River, which Sergeant Gass describes as "a quarter of a mile broad, but not more than six or eight inches deep, running over a bar of quicksand. At this place we dined on venison and goose." It was this river, the captains mistakenly believed at the time, that drained the western slope of the Cascades.

Oregon Trail (Mount Hood to Oregon City). "I herby report that I have viewed and marked by blasing and cuting away bushes and logs a rout or line for a road begining at the dalls Mission thence South . . ." With this beginning to a single sentence consisting of more than 250 words, Oregon Trail emigrant Samuel K. Barlow introduced the 1845 Oregon Provisional Legislature to one of the most rugged wagon roads in the American West, a route that left the overland trail at The Dalles and cut south around Mount Hood before finally reaching Oregon City. Even though most of the route has been altered by logging or buried beneath the pavement of Highway 26, a few places still retain a sense not only of the trail itself but also of the people who tackled it. "The Barlow Road . . . seems to be a symbol for the pioneer people who came to Oregon," writes historian Evelyn L. Greenstreet, "brave, foolhardy, but magnificent in their obsession."

Laurel Hill, 3 miles east of Government Camp off Highway 26. For many pioneers, these cliffs made up one of the most dreaded stretches of countryside along the entire 2,000-mile journey: a broken ridge with slopes tilted at 60 degrees and containing a series of rock-strewn chutes through which the wagons had to be lowered. Even though emigrants tried to slow the descent of their wagons by snubbing them to trees or dragging logs behind, these efforts didn't always work. "Like shot off a shovel," William Barlow said in describing how some of the wagons rolled down the hill. Nevertheless, through the years so many wagons made the 4-mile descent that they eventually carved a narrow trench into the hill. "The road on this hill is something terrible," W. W. Conyers wrote in 1852. "It is worn down into the soil from five to seven feet, leaving steep banks on both sides, and so narrow that it is almost impossible to walk alongside of the cattle for any distance without leaning against the oxen."

Last Tollgate, 1 mile east of Rhododendron off Highway 26. After Sam Barlow blazed his trail around Mount Hood to Oregon City, Oregon's Provisional Legislature granted him a franchise to operate the route as Oregon's first toll road. Now this replica tollgate, standing in the shade of maple trees planted by the tollgate's last keeper, marks one of five sites where, beginning in 1846, travelers paid fees for their stock and themselves to use the road. That first year, almost 1,000 emigrants paid fares of 5 dollars per wagon and 10 cents per head of livestock. In later years those costs ranged from 3 cents per sheep or hog, to 2 dollars for each vehicle drawn by a span of horses or a yoke of oxen. This segment of the Oregon Trail operated as a toll road for the next 73 years.

Foster Farm (503-637-6324), 29912 S. E. Oregon 211 (near the intersection of Highways 224 and 211), Eagle Creek. With more than 2,000 miles behind them, the Oregon Trail emigrants traveling the Barlow Road descended their last hill and made their final stop at this farm before reaching their new homes in the Willamette Valley. "We started on again," Esther Belle Hanna wrote in 1852, "having now but ten miles to go until we could reach Mr. Philip Foster's, which is the first settlement in the valley." Philip Foster, who arrived in Oregon from Maine by sailing around Cape Horn with his wife and children in 1843, ran a general store, helped build and operate the Barlow Road, and provided services, provisions, and hospitality to an estimated 10,000 emigrants during Oregon's early years. And today his farm—as well as the lilac that Charlotte, Philip's wife, brought to Oregon from Maine—survives from those days.

Pioneer Woman's Grave, 38 miles south of Hood River on the old Barlow Road, near the junction of Highway 35 and Forest Road 3550. While crossing Sam Barlow's Road in 1847, a woman died and was buried on the trail near here. Even though time and weather erased her grave, workers discovered it in 1924 while building the Mount Hood Loop Highway (see *Scenic Drives*). Today the stone and plaque marking the site symbolize the loss of life among those who traveled the Oregon Trail, and schoolchildren visiting on field trips occasionally decorate the woman's grave with ribbons and flowers or small wooden crosses they make from the limbs of the cedars and firs that shade it.

Timberline Lodge (503-295-1828), 6 miles north of Government Camp off Highway 26 and at the end of Timberline Road. Built in 1937 during the Great Depression, Timberline Lodge provided jobs for more than 500 people, many of them expert craftsmen employed in the federal Works Project Administration (WPA) program. The result of their labor is a building that's a work of art, a **National Historic Landmark** constructed of native wood and rock collected from the local area, and distinguished by its handcrafted furniture, metals, woodwork, and fabrics.

Clackamas Lake Ranger Station, 18 miles southeast of Government Camp off Highway 26 and Forest Road 42. The result of the handcrafted labors of the Civilian Conservation Corps (CCC), this ranger station complex was built during the years of the Great Depression and has changed little, if any, since then. With its structures built of native stone and timber, the ranger station still functions as part of the Mount Hood National Forest.

FOR FAMILIES **Stern-Wheeler Cruises** (541-374-8619), Marine Park in Cascade Locks, exit 44 on Interstate 84. Three times a day though the summer, the 300-ton stern-wheeler *Columbia Gorge* paddles its way along the Columbia River on two-hour excursions that give visitors a chance to learn about the mythology, the history, and the geology connected to the River of the West.

Mount Hood Railroad (1-800-872-4661; www.mthoodrr.com), 110 Railroad Avenue, exit 63 on Interstate 84, Hood River. Established in 1906 as a way to transport the valley's fruit and timber to market, the Mount Hood Railroad still chugs the 22-mile grade every day between Hood River and Parkdale—but now it hauls people instead of lumber and apples. Twice a day the excursion train loads up its passengers—who sit in restored Pullman coaches, an open-air touring car, an antique concession car, or even a red caboose—for the four-hour round trip that includes a one-hour layover at Parkdale, located just 5 miles from the base of Mount Hood.

Farmer's Market (1-800-366-3530), parking lot between Fifth and Seventh, Cascade and Columbia Streets, Hood River. Saturdays from spring till fall, local growers sell the stuff of their orchards and gardens in this open-air market.

SCENIC DRIVES **Historic Columbia River Highway—western segment,** 22 paved miles from Troutdale to Ainsworth, exits 18 to 35 on Interstate 84. Before the construction of this highway began in 1913—a year in which Oregonians owned only 12,000 cars—the only means of connecting towns in the Columbia Gorge with those in the Willamette Valley were by raft through wild river rapids or by wagon along rocky, rutted trails. When the road finally reached The Dalles nine years later, Oregon had its first paved thoroughfare, America its first scenic highway, and the world an achievement of engineering so remarkable that some have compared it to a work of art. "The highway possesses the best of all the great highways in the world, glorified!" reported the *Illustrated London News*. "It is the king of the roads." It still may be. This portion of the old highway gives you a sense of what it was like to travel in the days of the Model T Ford, rolling across forested hillsides, over elegant bridges, past thundering waterfalls, and through a countryside of water, wind, and wildflowers.

Columbia Gorge Waterfalls Tour, along the Historic Columbia River Highway from Troutdale to Ainsworth, exits 18 to 35 on Interstate 84. When the Missoula Floods tore down the Columbia River during the last Ice Age, they ripped the ground out from beneath the creeks and streams that fed the river, leaving them hanging high in the air. The result is the greatest concentration of waterfalls on the continent—11 falls are found along this 12-mile stretch of highway—

many of which tumble their way to roadside pools and streams. **Latourell Falls** (249 feet), located near the former town of Latourell, an early-20th-century destination for tourists who came for the band, the billiards, or the brothel; **Shepherd's Dell Falls** (upper tier 50 feet and lower tier 60 feet), a tiered falls with a paved trail leading to its top; **Bridal Veil Falls** (upper portion 100 feet and lower portion 60 feet), a tiered waterfall with two drops, a trail leading to the lower falls, and a popular wedding site at the nearby community of Bridal Veil; **Wahkeena Falls** (242 feet), whose name comes from the Yakama word for "most beautiful"; **Multnomah Falls** (620 feet), the second-highest waterfall in the country with a system of trails to show you around; **Oneonta Gorge**, home to more than 50 species of plants that favor this cool, wet site as well as 100-foot **Oneonta Falls,** which lies 1,000 feet from the highway at the end of a wade through the stream; and **Horsetail Falls** (176 feet), whose water plummets into a roadside pool, and whose spray often drifts across the highway.

Fruit Loop, 45 paved miles around the Hood River Valley along Highways 35 and 281. This is a warm-weather, pink-blossomed tour of the orchards, farmlands, and forests in one of Oregon's most beautiful valleys. Spotted with orchards and vineyards and fruit stands, the route probably offers as many opportunities for food as it does for views, for along the way you can buy freshly harvested vegetables, gathered fruit, picked flowers, baked pies. Although you can take the tour anytime, spring is when the blossoms seem to make the blue skies shimmer.

Mount Hood Loop, 40 paved miles along Highway 35, from Hood River to Mount Hood. After decades of struggles to build a road through the Hood River Valley between the Columbia River and Mount Hood, after years of clearing brush and smoothing ruts and leveling grades, this highway finally opened in 1925. "At its dedication," journalist and mountaineer Fred McNeil wrote in 1937, "the Mount Hood Loop was called the necklace about the old volcano [Mount Hood] with Portland as the pendant." Even though two parts of the

THE PEAK OF MOUNT HOOD, OREGON'S HIGHEST MOUNTAIN, ENCLOSED IN CLOUDS

loop—Highway 26 between Mount Hood and Portland, and Highway 84 between Portland and Hood River—long ago surrendered to the whiz and rumble of four-lane traffic, this third leg of the route is still maintained as a pristine byway. Through green valleys and past white streams the road runs, climbing ever higher and closer toward the sloped shoulders and cragged face of Mount Hood.

NATURAL WONDERS **Columbia River Gorge,** along the Historic Columbia River Highway or Interstate 84 from Troutdale to The Dalles. The people who calculate such things figure that the last Missoula Flood—which some 12,000 years ago broke free from its giant lake near the Rockies to wallop the Columbia River's valley, blasting its slopes into cliffs and leaving its creeks to tumble over the rims—carried 10 times the combined flow of all the rivers in the world then. The looming basalt and cascading waterfalls in today's gorge are reminders of that age when the lands of the Northwest crumbled beneath this surge of water.

Foster Lilac, Foster Farm, 29912 S. E. Oregon 211, Eagle Creek. When Mary Charlotte Foster boarded a ship on the coast of Maine in 1843, she packed along with her the start from a lilac tree. Then after arriving in Oregon and settling with her husband and children on this Willamette Valley farm and Oregon Trail wagon stop, she planted the lilac, which has been growing ever since. For more information contact **Heritage Trees** (1-800-574-9397).

* To Do

BICYCLING **Historic Columbia River Highway,** 5 paved miles from Bonneville Dam to Cascade Locks, exits 40 to 44 on Interstate 84. Starting at the Toothrock Trailhead near Bonneville Dam, this hiking and biking trail follows curved viaducts and stone bridges, shady forests and mountain streams along a section of the old highway that retains a sense of its 1920s quiet because it's now closed to cars. (See also *To See—Scenic Drives.*)

CAMPING **Cascade Locks Area: Herman Creek**, 3 miles east of Cascade Locks off Interstate 84, 7 campsites, horse facilities, and trails for hiking or riding; **Wyeth,** 7 miles east of Cascade Locks off Interstate 84 (exit 51), 17 campsites near the Columbia River, nearby hiking trails.

Zigzag Area, near the community of Zigzag off Highway 26 and connecting county and forest roads. **Camp Creek,** 4 miles southeast of Zigzag, 37 campsites; **Green Canyon,** 9 miles south of Zigzag off Forest Road 2618, 15 campsites; **Lost Creek,** 7 miles north of Zigzag off County Road 18 and Forest Road 1825, 16 campsites near the headwaters of the Sandy River; **McNeil,** 6 miles north of Zigzag off County Road 18, 34 campsites near the headwaters of the Sandy River.

Mount Hood—north slope, south of Hood River between Highways 35 and 218. **Cloud Cap Saddle** and **Tilly Jane,** 20 miles south of Hood River off Highway 35 and Forest Road 3512, 17 tent sites near mountain trails; **Gibson Prairie,** 15 miles south of Hood River off Highway 35 and Forest Road 17, 4 campsites and horse facilities; **Kingsley Reservoir,**

12 miles southwest of Hood River off Kingsley Road, 20 tent sites near the reservoir; **Kinnikinnick,** 10 miles south of Parkdale off Highway 281 and Forest Road 2840, 8 campsites near Laurance Lake; **Lost Lake**, 15 miles southwest of Dee off Highway 281 and Forest Road 13, 91 lakeside campsites with boat and cabin rentals and a general store; **Rainy Lake**, 24 miles southwest of Hood River off Highway 281 and Forest Road 2820, 4 tent sites a quarter mile from the lake; **Robinhood,** 25 miles south of Hood River off Highway 35, 24 campsites along the bank of Hood River and near Elk Meadows Trail and the Badger Creek Wilderness; **Routson Park,** 20 miles south of Hood River, 20 campsites along the bank of the Hood River off Highway 35; **Sherwood,** 21 miles south of Hood River off Highway 35, 14 campsites along the bank of the Hood River and close to Tamawanas Falls Trail; **Toll Bridge Park,** 17 miles south of Hood River off Highway 35, 80 streamside campsites along with showers and rest rooms; **Tucker Park,** 5 miles south of Hood River off Highway 281, 18 campsites in a 36-acre park located on the south bank of the Hood River.

Mount Hood—south slope, south of Government Camp off Highways 26 or 35 and connecting forest roads. **Barlow Creek,** southeast of Government Camp off Highway 35 and Forest Service Road 3530, a total of 19 campsites divided among **Barlow Creek, Devil's Half Acre, Grindstone, Barlow Crossing,** and **White River,** all near fishing at Barlow Creek or White River; **Clackamas Lake,** 18 miles southeast of Government Camp off Highway 26 and Forest Road 42, 42 campsites near a small lake; **Clear Lake,** 12 miles southeast of Government Camp off Highway 26, 28 campsites along Clear Lake with fishing and nearby hiking; **Frog Lake,** 26 miles southeast of Government Camp off Highway 26, 33 campsites along Frog Lake with fishing and nearby hiking; **Little Crater Lake,** 20 miles southeast of Government Camp off Highway 26 and Forest Service Roads 42 and 58, 16 campsites near an artesian spring-fed lake surrounded by a wet meadow that attracts deer, elk, and numerous birds; **Still Creek,** 2 miles southeast of Government Camp off Highway 26, 27 campsites; **Summit Lake,** 29 miles southeast of Government Camp off Highway 26 and Forest Road 42, 5 campsites near the lake; **Timothy Lake,** 7 miles south of Government Camp off Highway 26 and Forest Roads 42 and 57, 165 campsites divided among seven areas, all near the lakeshore; **Tollgate,** 1 mile east of Rhododendron off Highway 26, 15 campsites; **Trillium Lake,** 3 miles southeast of Government Camp off Highway 26 and Forest Road 2650, 57 campsites near the lakeshore.

♿ **Mount Hood—east slope,** south of the Dalles between Highways 35 and 26 to the west and Highway 197 to the west. **Bonney Meadows,** 32 miles west of Tygh Valley off Highway 197 and Forest Roads 48 and 4891, 6 campsites near Boulder Lake; **Eightmile Creek,** 17 miles west of Dufur off Highway 197 and Forest Road 44, 27 campsites divided among **Eightmile Crossing, Lower Crossing,** and **Pebble Ford,** all located near Eightmile Creek; **Fifteen Mile,** 23 miles west of Dufur off Highway 197 and Forest Roads 44, 4420, and 2730, 3 campsites near Fifteenmile Creek;

Forest Creek, 26 miles southwest of Tygh Valley off Highway 197 and Forest Road 48, 5 campsites along Frog Lake; **Knebel Springs,** 24 miles west of Dufur off Highway 197 and Forest Road 1720, 8 campsites; **McCubbins Gulch,** 25 miles west of Maupin off Highway 216, 5 campsites; **Rock Creek Reservoir,** 19 miles west of Tygh Valley off Highway 197 and Forest Road 48, 33 campsites along the reservoir with **handicapped-accessible fishing; Underhill Site,** 17 miles west of Dufur off Highway 197 and Forest Road 44, 2 campsites near Rainy Creek.

Clackamas River Area, southeast of Estacada along the Clackamas River and its tributaries, and off Highway 224, Forest Road 46, and connecting forest roads. More campsites than you can shake a stick at in the foothills and along the slopes of the Cascades: **Promontory, Lockaby, Memaloose, Lazy Bend, Carter Bridge; Armstrong, Fish Creek, Roaring River, Sunstrip, Indian Henry, Alder Flat, Rainbow, Ripplebrook, Riverside, River Ford, Raab, Kingfisher, Harriet Lake, Shellrock Creek, Hideaway Lake,** and **Highrock Springs.**

Olallie Lake Scenic Area, northeast of Detroit off Forest Roads 46 and 4220, or south of Government Camp off Highway 26 and Forest Roads 42 and 4220, 5 campgrounds on or near the shoreline of Olallie Lake: **Camp Ten, Peninsula, Paul Dennis, Lower Lake, Olallie Meadows,** and **Olallie Lake;** in addition, to the south at Breitenbush Lake stand another 2 camps: **Horseshoe Lake** and **Breitenbush Lake.**

See also *Wilder Places—Parks.*

CANOEING **Olallie Lake Scenic Area,** northeast of Detroit off Forest Roads 46 and 4220, or south of Government Camp off Highway 26 and Forest Roads 42 and 4220. Located near the crest of the Cascades, this area contains more than 200 lakes and ponds scattered across more than 10,000 acres. Ranging in size from 3 to 238 acres, these waters prohibit motors while furnishing campgrounds, hiking trails, mountain views, stocked fisheries, and sometimes even cabin and boat rentals.

Mount Hood—north slope lakes, south of Hood River off Highways 35 and 218. Three lakes in the foothills of Mount Hood place restrictions on the use of motors: **Laurance Lake,** 10 miles south of Parkdale off Highway 281 and Forest Road 2840, permits electric motors only; and both **Lost Lake,** 15 miles southwest of Dee off Highway 281 and Forest Road 13, and **Wahtum Lake,** 15 miles southwest of Dee off Highway 281 and Forest Roads 13 and 1310, prohibit all motors.

GOLF **Eagle Creek Golf Course** (503-630-4676), 25805 S. E. Dowty Street, Eagle Creek. 18 holes.

Indian Creek Golf Course (541-386-7770), 3605 Brookside Drive, Hood River, 18 holes.

The Resort at the Mountain (1-800-669-4653), 68010 E. Fairway Avenue, Welches, 27 holes.

HIKING **Columbia Gorge Waterfalls,** east of Troutdale along the Historic Columbia River Highway or Interstate 84. **Latourell Falls** (Interstate 84 exit 28) offers two connected trails: a 1-mile loop that leads hikers across two footbridges and along a green hillside to a viewpoint above the falls, and a 2-mile loop that continues on from the viewpoint, climbing to a footbridge at the base of **Upper Latourell Falls** before turning back to the trailhead. Up the road, the fern-lined trail at **Horsetail Falls** (Interstate 84 exit 35) climbs a half mile before passing behind **Upper Horsetail Falls,** then continues for another mile to a view of **Oneonta Gorge,** and finally crosses Oneonta Creek above **Lower Oneonta Falls** before making its way back toward the highway, a total hike of less than 3 miles. Another trail involves a 2-mile, up-and-back hike to **Wahclella Falls** (Interstate 84 exit 40), a two-tier cataract that plunges first onto a ledge, then into a pool. The longest hike in this group is a 4-mile round trip along Eagle Creek and its canyon walls to **Punchbowl Falls** (Interstate 84 exit 41), a low falls that drops into a wide pool. Along the way, you can also take a side trail to a view of **Metlako Falls.**

Salmon River Trail, 3 miles south of Zigzag off Highway 26 and the Salmon River Road. A level trail, a riffling stream, and towering firs and cedars make this stretch something of a forest wonderland. The pathway squeezes between the Salmon River and the Salmon River Road for about 2.5 miles before veering off into the Salmon-Huckleberry Wilderness (see *Wilder Places—Wilderness Areas*). Along the way numerous access points connect the road to the trail.

Little Zigzag Falls, 7 miles northeast of Zigzag off Highway 26 and Forest Road 2639. A half-mile stroll along the stream and through the canyon of Little Zigzag Creek ends at Little Zigzag Falls, which slides and plunges and sprays its way over mossy rocks.

Canyon Overlooks, starting from Timberline Lodge, 6 miles north of Government Camp off Highway 26 and at the end of Timberline Road. Two trails from Timberline Lodge lead to viewpoints of nearby canyons: **White River Canyon Overlook,** a half mile to the east, and **Zigzag Canyon Overlook,** 2 miles to the west.

Mirror Lake, 2 miles west of Government Camp off Highway 26. Its length and the view make this one of the most frequently used trails in the Mount Hood area. A 1.5-mile hike takes you up to Mirror Lake and around its shoreline, while Mount Hood looms high in the sky to the north.

Tamawanas Falls, 25 miles south of Hood River off Highway 35—use East Fork Trailhead. After leaving behind the highway at about the half-mile mark, this trail follows Cold Spring Creek upstream for a couple of miles—including some steep switchbacks—to 100-foot Tamawanas Falls.

Sahalie Falls and Umbrella Falls, 33 miles south of Hood River off Highway 35 and Forest Road 3545. A 4-mile loop crosses Meadows Creek and East Fork Hood River—as well as the ski runs of Mount Hood Meadows—as it leads through forests, meadows, and huckleberry bushes to Sahalie Falls and Umbrella Falls, located about 1.5 miles from each other.

Barlow Road, 37 miles south of Hood River near the junction of Highway 35 and Forest Road 48.

Follow this trail to get a feel for the Barlow Road, one of the most heartbreaking routes of the **Oregon Trail.** Starting from a parking lot near the junction of the old road and Highway 35, the trail slants downhill over the duff and through the shade and silence of hemlocks and cedar, the path unfolding in switchbacks littered with rocks, clogged with logs, and cut by washes and gullies. And remember—they used to drive *wagons* along this terrain.

See also *Wilder Places—Parks* and *Wilderness Areas.*

✷ Wilder Places

PARKS **Panorama Point,** 2 miles southeast of Hood River off Highway 35 and East Side Road. From this county park's hilltop overlook you can see several hundred square miles of the Hood River Valley's rivers and ridges and orchards sprawling south toward Mount Hood.

Interstate 84 Parks, from east of Troutdale to west of Hood River off Interstate 84. **Lewis and Clark State Recreation Site,** 1 mile east of Troutdale, beach area, boat ramp, and nature trail near the Sandy River, a popular steelheading stream named by Lewis and Clark in 1805; **Rooster Rock State Park,** 7 miles east of Troutdale, heavily used, lots of lawn along the Columbia River, boat basin, nature trail, and even a clothing-optional beach; **Benson State Recreation Area,** 13 miles east of Troutdale, lakeside picnic area, fishing and boating; **John B. Yeon State Scenic Corridor,** 20 miles east of Troutdale, short trail to **Elowah Falls** and a longer one to **Upper McCord Creek Falls; Starvation Creek State Park,** 10 miles west of Hood River, no water or rest rooms, but access to hiking trails leading to waterfalls as well as to a stretch of the old Columbia River Highway that passes beneath a ceiling of maples and firs, its asphalt sprouting grass and ferns; **Viento State Park,** 8 miles west of Hood River, 75 campsites along both sides of the freeway, several nearby trailheads; **Wygant, Vinzenz Lausmann,** and **Seneca Fouts State Natural Areas,** 5 to 7 miles west of Hood River, access via Mitchell Point, three sites connected by one hiking trail—trailhead at Seneca Fouts—that leads to views of the Columbia River.

Columbia Gorge Parks, along the Historic Columbia River Highway from east of Troutdale to west of Cascade Locks. **Dabney State Recreation Area,** 4 miles east of Troutdale, picnicking, swimming, and hiking on 135 acres along the bank and near the wetlands of the Sandy River; **Portland Women's Forum State Scenic Viewpoint,** 9 miles east of Troutdale, probably the best- as well as the most-photographed view of Crown Point and the Vista House (see *To See—Historic Sites*); **Crown Point,** 10 miles east of Troutdale, take your pick of views from this 720-foot perch and decide which is more grand—the Vista House or the Columbia Gorge; **Guy W. Talbot State Park,** 12 miles east of Troutdale, shady picnic area and a short trail to **Latourell Falls; Shepherd's Dell State Natural Area,** 14 miles east of Troutdale, a short trail to **Young's Creek waterfalls; Bridal Veil Falls State Scenic Viewpoint,** 15 miles east of Troutdale, picnic grounds and two trails, one to Bridal Veil Falls and one to Columbia River viewpoints;

Ainsworth State Park, 22 miles east of Troutdale, more than 48 campsites, a hiker/biker camp, and a hiking trail that connects to other trails in the area.

Columbia River Parks, off Highway 30 and along the Columbia River, from south of Rainier to north of Clatskanie. A series of parks strung along the bank of the Columbia River offers opportunities for picnicking, fishing, swimming, boating, bird-watching, and sometimes even wind-surfing: **Walton Beach,** 10 miles north of Wildlife Headquarters on Sauvie Island; **Prescott Beach,** 4 miles south of Rainier; **Laurel Beach,** 1 mile south of Rainier; **Mayger Beach,** 8 miles northeast of Clatskanie; **Jones Beach,** 9 miles northwest of Clatskanie.

Bonnie Lure State Park, 6 miles north of Estacada off Highway 224 and Burdett Road, day use only. The location of this 94-acre day-use park is its main attraction: near the confluence of Eagle Creek and the Clackamas River. Riverside woodlands and a sparkling, shallow creek make this a memorable place to play on a sunlit day.

Milo McIver State Park, 5 miles west of Estacada off Highway 211 and Springwater Road, day use and overnight. With enough lawn to hold as many as 1,000 people—a good thing because it's only 20 miles from Portland—Milo McIver State Park spreads across more than 900 acres on the bank of the Clackamas River. It's space enough for birders and bikers, hikers and horses to share its trails; rafters and boaters, swimmers and anglers its waters. The park also counts among its features a model airplane strip and a **fish hatchery,** which every year raises and releases as many as a million **chinook salmon.**

Estacada Area, near Estacada off Highway 211. **Barton County Park,** 9 miles northwest of Estacada off Highway 211 and Bakers Ferry Road, 100 acres on the bank of the Clackamas River, offerings ranging from campgrounds with flush toilets to horseshoes and volleyball; **Metzler County Park,** 6 miles southeast of Estacada off Highway 211 and Metzler Park Road, nature trails, picnic shelters, and campgrounds with hot showers; **North Fork Eagle Creek,** 8 miles northeast of Estacada off Highway 211, camping and fishing on a tributary of Eagle Creek.

WILDERNESS AREAS **Columbia,** 24 miles east of Portland off Interstate 84, 61 square miles. The face this wilderness shows travelers zipping along Interstate 84 is made up of the towering cliffs and plunging waterfalls of the Columbia Gorge. Behind that face, however, stretches a land rugged and steep and crisscrossed by 200 miles of trails that serve as winding, climbing sanctuaries to city dwellers from nearby Portland.

Salmon-Huckleberry, 16 miles southeast of Sandy off Highway 26 and East Wildcat Creek Road, 70 square miles. With salmon swimming in its river and huckleberries growing along its ridges, this wilderness—a combination of **rain forest, canyon lands, and subalpine lakes**—has earned its name. For those visitors willing to take longer hikes, the main attraction is the Salmon River's series of **waterfalls.**

Bull of the Woods, 42 miles southeast of Estacada off Highway 224 and

Forest Roads 46, 63, and 70, 54 square miles. Often called the "hidden wilderness" because of its seclusion deep and high in the rainy foothills of the **Cascade Mountains,** Bull of the Woods holds the headwaters of numerous streams, including the Collawash, Breitenbush, and Little North Santiam. In addition, a dozen **trout lakes** speckle the wilderness, separated from one another by high, steep ridges and by forests old enough—it contains one of the last old-growth stands of **western hemlock** in the region—to provide homes to six species of owls, including the endangered **northern spotted owl.** Almost 70 miles of trails cross the area, and two of the most manageable day hikes take off to **Pansy lake Trail,** 1.2 miles to the lake before climbing to **lookout tower;** and **Hog Springs Trail,** 1.5 miles to **Bagby Hot Springs.**

WILDLIFE REFUGES ✐ **Bonneville Fish Hatchery** (541-374-8393), 37 miles east of Portland off Interstate 84, exit 40. For many people, the best parts of a visit to this hatchery involve feeding the brooder **rainbow trout,** which thrash the water in their fluid scurry for fish food, and seeing Herman the Sturgeon, a 9-foot member of the fish family whose ancestry on this continent goes back 200 million years.

Wildwood Recreation Site, 1 mile west of Wemme off Highway 26. This 480-acre site is all about **salmon** and **steelhead**—their lives, their habitat, and their future as told from viewpoints ranging from poetry to science. Located along a channel of the **Salmon River**—the only stream in the Lower 48 states to earn Wild and Scenic protection along its entire length, 33 miles—the site offers a 5-mile trail system that leads visitors to forests and marshes, ponds and streams, and even to windows that give you a watery peek deep into the fish's world.

✷ Lodging

INNS

Government Camp

Falcon's Crest Inn (1-800-624-7384; www.falconscrest.com), 87287 Government Camp Loop Highway, Government Camp 97028. This glass-fronted chalet is located within the **Mount Hood National Forest,** which brings a number of recreational opportunities almost as close as the doorstep. Each of the five guest room at this inn comes with a private bath and a full breakfast ($95–179, with discounts for stays of more than two nights), with six-course dinners available at the on-premise **restaurant.**

Hood River

Columbia Gorge Hotel (1-800-345-1921; chhotel@gorge.net; www.columbiagorgehotel.com), Westcliff Drive, 2 miles west of Hood River off Interstate 84, exit 62. This historic hotel stands on 11 landscaped acres, contains 40 guest rooms, and features meals that draw people from miles around. The rates, which range from $189–319, include champagne, caviar, and a five-course breakfast for two. And for that much money, they'll even give you a newspaper and put a rose on your pillow.

Hood River Hotel and Pasquale's Ristorante (1-800-386-1859; HRHotel@gorge.net; www.HoodRiverHotel.com), 102 Oak Avenue, Hood River 97031. Built in 1913 as the annex to the Victorian Mt. Hood Hotel, which appeared in Hood River at the same time as the region's first trains, the Hood River Hotel survived years of neglect and eventual abandonment, until Pasquale and Jacquie Barone of Vancouver, British Columbia, finally rescued it in 1988. Now fully restored and listed as a **National Historic Landmark,** the hotel contains 41 rooms, each of which comes with a private bathroom as well as a continental breakfast ($59–145). In addition, a Jacuzzi, sauna, and exercise facility are available to guests.

Oak Street Hotel (541-386-3845; reservations@oakstreethotel.com; www.oakstreethotel.com), 610 Oak Avenue, Hood River 97031. Built 1910 and renovated in 1994, the Oak Street Hotel stands just two blocks from downtown Hood River but still has views of the Columbia River and Mount Adams. Its nine guest rooms all come with queen beds, private baths, and refrigerators, while some have river views or deck access ($55–120).

BED & BREAKFASTS

Bridal Veil

Bridal Veil Lodge (503-695-2333; bridalveil@moriah.com; www.bridalveillodge.com), 46650 E. Historic Columbia River Highway, Bridal Veil 97010. Surrounded by the river and forest and waterfalls of the Columbia Gorge, this 1920s lodge offers two guest rooms that come with a full breakfast ($80–85).

Brightwood

Maple River Bed & Breakfast (503-622-6273), 20525 E. Mount Country Lane, Brightwood 97011. Both guest rooms in this B&B come with queen beds, fireplaces, a private bath, and patios with hot tubs that overlook the Salmon River ($90–120).

Salmon River Retreat (503-622-5706; info@salmonriverretreat.com; www.SalmonRiverRetreat.com), 20550 E. Country Club Road, Brightwood 97011. One distinguishing feature of this lodge is evident in its subtitle: "A Bed and Breakfast for Body and Soul." Hiking, biking, or fishing; spas, massages, and yoga—these help take care of the "body" part, while breathing mountain air, listening to river water, feeling the breeze in the trees, and sitting in front of a fire assist in the "soul" department. Three guest rooms ($110–130) are available with private baths and a full breakfast, and women traveling alone are especially welcome. For the people who stay in these rooms, the place seems to impart a sense of magic that begins early. "The river makes rippling sounds that can be heard all about the property," says owner Ann Yuhas. "People love gathering on the back deck over the river to have morning coffee and scones or muffins." Sometimes, however, the experience goes even deeper. One guest, for instance, explained how her boyfriend proposed to her during their visit. "We arrived here very much in love," she wrote, "and we will leave here very much in love and with the promise of forever."

Government Camp

Mt. Hood Manor (1-800-514-3440), 88900 Government Camp Loop Highway, Government Camp 97028. Built in 1993 in a Tudor style, Mt. Hood Manor offers four guest rooms with private baths as well as an adjoining sitting room containing a fireplace and wet bar (BYOB). Rates range from $90–140, which includes a family-style breakfast. Two guest rooms accommodate children.

Hood River

Avalon Bed & Breakfast (1-888-386-3941), 3444 Avalon Drive, Hood River 97031. Located in a quiet neighborhood, this 1906 two-story farmhouse with its flowers and gardens offers three guest rooms that share one bath, a deck with a hot tub, and a view of Mount Adams, and include a full country breakfast ($50–65).

Bella Vista Bed & Breakfast (541-386-1545), 3000 Reed Road, Hood River 97031. This 1920 home is still a functioning farmhouse located near the end of a forested country road and on the edge of pear and cherry orchards. A stay in either of its two guest rooms includes a traditional farm breakfast ($85).

Beryl House (541-386-5567; beryl@moriah.com; www.berylhouse.com), 4079 Barrett Drive, Hood River 97031. With a wraparound porch that offers views of a working pear orchard as well as the mountains Hood and Adams, this 1910 home has four guest rooms that share two baths and come with a full breakfast that features locally grown foods ($75–85).

Brown's Bed & Breakfast (541-386-1545), 3000 Reed Road, Hood River 97031. From this restored 1930 two-story farmhouse with a hillside orchard and a nearby forest, you probably won't hear traffic but certainly will see Mount Hood and the Hood River Valley. Its two guest rooms contain king-sized beds, share one bathroom, and come with a full gourmet breakfast ($50–70).

✐ **Gorge View Bed & Breakfast** (541-386-5770; gorgeview@gorge.net; http://business.gorge.net/gorgeview), 1009 Columbia Street, Hood River 97031. Located within walking distance of downtown Hood River, this 1917 two-story Victorian bungalow comes with a wraparound porch, a panoramic view of the Columbia River and Mount Adams, and four guest rooms, one with a private bath ($75–85) and three others that share two bathrooms ($69–79). All rooms come with a full breakfast that can include specialties such as huevos Gorge View and blueberry cakes, French toast and homemade muffins, omelets and fresh fruit. In addition, a hot tub, outdoor shower, refrigerator, and barbecue are available to guests. Children are welcome.

Inn at the Gorge (541-386-4429; inn @gorge.net; www.innatthegorge.com), 1113 Eugene Street, Hood River 97031. This 1908 Victorian home with a wraparound porch, sweeping rooflines, and backyard terrace has been operated as a B&B since 1987. Its five guest rooms—three are suites—come with private baths and entrances as well as a full breakfast ($85–135).

Lakecliff Estates (541-386-7000; lakecliff@hotmail.com), 3820 Westcliff Drive, Hood River 97031. Standing on 11 acres that overlook the Columbia River, this historic lodge retains the architecture and decor of its 1908 beginnings, from its shingled siding and beamed ceilings to its five native-stone fireplaces. Two of its guest rooms come with private bathrooms ($110), two others share a bath ($90), and all come with a fireplace as well as a full breakfast.

Panorama Lodge (1-888-403-2687; info@panoramalodge.com; www.panoramalodge.com), 2290 Old Dalles Drive, Hood River 97031. Even though it's a short stroll to downtown Hood River from this log lodge, the home gets its name from the mountain and river views that seem to surround it. "It sits on a ridge peacefully surrounded by fir and pine forest," says owner Linda Kremin, "with a breathtaking view of Mount Hood and the Hood River Valley." The lodge has four guest rooms ($65–90) and a suite ($195), and all stays include a full breakfast.

Pheasant Valley Orchards B&B (541-386-2803; sgopear@gorge.net; www.pheasantvalleyorchards.com), 3890 Acree Drive, Hood River 97031. Situated in the foothills of Mount Hood and alongside organic pear and apple orchards, this inn looks out at a world that changes colors with the blossoms and snowfall of the season. Its three guest rooms—two are suites—come with king or queen beds, private baths, and a full breakfast ($95–135).

Mount Hood

Mt. Hood Hamlet (1-800-407-0570; hoodhamlet@gorge.net; www.mthoodhamlet.com, 6741 Highway 35, Mount Hood 97041. Probably never before has a New England home seen the likes of Mount Hood, nor Mount Hood a New England home—but there they are anyway, standing just miles apart, staring at each other. "What makes our B&B special," says Paul Romans, "is the blending of our family's historical past in New England with the spirit of eastern Oregon pioneers and the modern representation of Colonial architecture." That result is this Colonial home in the foothills of Oregon's tallest mountain. Its three guest rooms ($105–145) all come with king or queen beds, private bathrooms, a full breakfast, and, of course, views of the mountain. "Guests often comment on the ever-changing mood of Mount Hood," Paul says, "a mere thirteen miles from our rooftop."

Parkdale

Mount Hood Bed & Breakfast
(1-800-557-8885; mthoodbnb@linkport.com; www.mthoodbnb.com), 8885 Cooper Spur Road, Parkdale 97041. Standing on the sloped shoulders of Mount Hood—*low* on its shoulders, to be sure—this B&B offers three guest rooms (beginning at $110) that seem to have the mountains Hood, Adams, and Rainier peeking in through their windows.

The Old Parkdale Inn (541-352-5551; parkdaleinn@hoodriverlodging.com; www.hoodriverlodging.com), 4932 Baseline Road, Parkdale 97041. Located near downtown Parkdale and at the foot of Mount Hood, this 1912 two-story Craftsman inn features fireplaces, balconies, and views of Oregon's highest mountain. Its three guest rooms—two are suites—all come with private baths and a full breakfast ($125–145).

Sandy

Brookside Bed & Breakfast (503-668-4766; sandy@brooksidebandb.com; www.brooksidebandb.com), 45232 S. E. Paha Loop, Sandy 97055. From its deck, this B&B offers views of Mount Hood in the distance and of a woodlands creek and pond nearby. And if you take a stroll about the yard and garden, keeping you company might be a menagerie of chickens, ducks, geese, and even peacocks. Its five guest rooms share bathrooms and come with a full breakfast ($55–70). "The best thing people say about us is that they feel at home here," says owner Barbara Brooks. "That's the highest compliment, as far as I am concerned—in addition to what a great breakfast we serve."

Troutdale

Cedarplace Inn (1-800-267-4744; www.cedarplaceinn.com; innkeeper@cedarplaceinn.com), 2611 S. Troutdale Road, Troutdale 97060. Shaded by old-growth firs and set off with a wraparound porch, this 1907 historic home is furnished and decorated to reflect its early-20th-century birth. The four guest rooms come with fireplaces, private baths, featherbeds, down comforters, and a five-course breakfast ($95–135). Children older than 12 are welcome.

Welches

Old Welches Inn Bed & Breakfast (503-622-3754; info@mthoodlodging.com; www.lodging-mthood.com), 26401 E. Welches Road, Welches 97067. The Salmon River runs through the backyard of this old inn, which was built in 1890 as the Welches Hotel, one of the first resorts on Mount Hood. Guests can stay in either the main house's four guest rooms or in a private cottage that has a stone fireplace, a full kitchen, and two bedrooms. Views of the Welches Valley's mountains and meadows, as well as a breakfast featuring old family recipes, comes as part of the package ($106.50–162.50).

GUEST HOUSES **Brightwood Guest House** (1-888-503-5783; brightwoodbnb@hotmail.com; www.MountHoodBnB.com), 64725 E. Barlow Trail Road, Brightwoood 97011. Because it's separated from the main house, the cedar-paneled guest cottage at this B&B provides privacy in a forested setting. "Peaceful, private, romantic" is how owner Jan Estep describes Brightwood. Special attractions of the cottage ($125) include a stocked kitchenette and Oriental furnishings inside, and a stream with a waterfall and a koi pond outside. But perhaps one of its strongest appeals comes from the Brightwood Guest House Commandments. "Guests will do *no* dishes," Jan recites. "Neither shall they make beds nor fold towels. They will be as the little children from whom they flee." If you want to flee farther still and explore the area, Jan will even lend you bicycles and helmets. A stay here includes a full breakfast served at your convenience, featuring such specialties as homemade cream waffles, berries and whipped cream, roasted potato and onion omelet, or truffle muffins. Children younger than 6 months and older than 13 years are welcome.

LODGES **The Cabins, Creekside at Welches** (503-622-4275; info@mthoodcabins.com; www.mthood cabins.com), 25086 E. Welches Road, Welches 97067. Owners Margaret and Bob Thurman approached the building of their inn, one of the newest in the Mount Hood area, with a goal in mind. "We designed it," Margaret says, "to evoke a strong, nostalgic feeling for early Welches resorts." To accomplish this, the Thurmans brought the outdoors into the guest cabins, using knotty pine for the vaulted ceilings as well as for the kitchen cabinets, and furnishing them with log furniture. The five cabins contain a total of nine living units with complete kitchens for guests ($79–119). In addition, all units have access to a laundry facility as well as to a seasonal creek that runs through the center of the property. "It's the lowest-priced, best-value overnight accommodations on Welches Road," Margaret says.

✷ Where to Eat

DINING OUT For more dining options also see **Falcon's Crest Inn, Columbia Gorge Hotel,** and **Hood River Hotel and Pasquale's Restaurant** under *Lodging.*

Government Camp

Cascade Dining Room (503-622-0700), Timberline Lodge, 6 miles north of Government Camp. Tucked away upstairs in the historic Timberline Lodge, whose rustic beauty is a monument to Depression-era craftsmanship, the Cascade Dining Room offers award-winning cuisine that features Northwest foods served in a memorable setting.

Hood River

Columbia Gorge Hotel (1-800-345-1921), 4000 Westcliff Drive, Hood River, exit 62 off Interstate 84. This elegant hotel perched on a cliff overlooking the Columbia River home of the "World Famous Farm Breakfast," which is more than just a fancy title. After all, this morning meal includes five courses that range from apple fritters to mountain trout, with servings of oatmeal and eggs and biscuits, potatoes and pancakes and pork chops making their way to the table at one time or another during this belt-bulging food fest. Oh yes, the hotel also serves à la carte lunches and dinners, but if you come for breakfast you probably won't want to tackle another meal for quite some time.

Stonehedge Gardens (541-386-3940), 3405 Cascade Street, Hood River. Even though this historic estate is the site of a house built in 1908, it's the garden that attracts most of the attention. Here spread across five levels of landscaping lies an outdoor dining area probably unrivaled in the Columbia River Gorge. The food, as well as the service and prices, can also be a pleasant surprise.

EATING OUT

Bridal Veil

Multnomah Falls Lodge (503-695-2376), 53000 Historic Columbia River Highway, Bridal Veil. Built of stone near one of Oregon's premier waterfalls and one of its most scenic byways, this lodge is known more for its architecture and view than it is for its food. Nevertheless, it offers decent meals in a historic and beautiful setting.

Government Camp

The Brew Pub at Mount Hood Brewing Company (503-272-3724), 87304 E. Government Camp Loop Highway, Government Camp. Known for its stout and unique beers and ales, the Brew Pub also serves up memorable pizza and offers an extensive menu for kids.

Hood River

Abruzzo (541-386-7779), 1810 W. Cascade Street, Hood River. Through its simple design and modest appearance, Abruzzo announces itself as a casual, friendly place to find great Italian food—and plenty of it—at inexpensive prices.

The Big Easy Cajun Barbeque (541-386-1970), 1302 B Street, Hood River. Far away from any backwoods bayou stands this Cajun restaurant, its atmosphere as well as its food coming with a zing. For even more Cajun flavor, dash some hot sauce on your crawfish or oysters, your jambalaya or bisque.

Sixth Street Bistro and Loft (541-386-5737), 509 Cascade Street, Hood River. The upstairs "loft" of this restaurant is a casual place of pool tables and microbrews where you can grab a sandwich or some pasta for lunch. The downstairs "bistro," however, shows another personality, one of linen-covered tables, a varied wine list, and well-prepared dinners of steak or seafood and fresh-baked bread.

Sandy

The Elusive Trout Pub (503-668-7884), 39333 Proctor Boulevard, Sandy. The Elusive Trout is an all-Northwest pub, decorated with canoes and wagon wheels and serving almost 20 regional microbrew beers. Meals, however, can stray south toward Mexican fare, though hamburgers and vegetarian dishes are also mainstays of the menu.

Troutdale

Tad's Chicken 'n' Dumplins (503-666-5337), 1325 E. Historic Columbia River Highway, Troutdale. Tad's is a restaurant that tells you straight out what it cooks best, what the crowds come for—chicken and dumplings. Nothing fancy about it, which is one of the best things about it. As a bonus, along with the chicken comes a view of the Sandy River.

Welches

The Rendezvous Grill and Tap Room (503-622-6837), 67149 E. Highway 26, Welches. Locals and visitors alike consider this one of the best places to eat on the mountain. It serves consistently good food at reasonable prices—house specialties feature locally grown ingredients ranging from huckleberries to salmon—and any slowness in the service is generally attributed to the staff's being on "mountain time." Especially high culinary marks go to the fish, the steaks, and the garlic mashed potatoes.

✷ Special Events

April: **Hood River Blossom Festival** (1-800-366-3530), Hood River. This festival celebrates the spring and what it does to the local orchards of apple and pear trees, speckling this green river valley with sunlit blossoms of white and pink.

May: **Song Bird Celebration** (503-622-4011, ext. 215), Welches.

June: **Stern-Wheeler Days** (541-374-8619), Cascade Locks.

July: **Sandy Mountain Festival** (503-668-5900), Sandy.

August: **Gravenstein Apple Days** (541-386-2000), Hood River.

October: **Salmon Festival** (503-797-1850), Troutdale. **Hood River Valley Fest** (541-386-2000), Hood River.

November: **The Resort at the Mountain Wine and Art Festival** (503-622-3101), Welches.

December: **Christmas Tree Trains** (1-800-87246-61), Hood River. **Christmas Along the Barlow Trail** (503-622-4011), Welches. **New Year's Eve Festival of Lights** (503-287-5438), Mount Hood.

NORTH WILLAMETTE VALLEY

GUIDANCE **Albany Convention and Visitors Association** (1-800-526-2256; www.albanyvisitors.com), 300 Second Avenue, Albany 97321.

Bureau of Land Management: Salem District (503-375-5646), 1717 Fabry Road S. E., Salem 97301.

Canby Area Chamber of Commerce (503-266-4600; www.canby.com/chamber), 140 N. E. Second Avenue, Canby 97013.

Corvallis Convention and Visitors Bureau (1-800-334-8118; www.visitcorvallis.com), 420 N. W. Second Street, Corvallis 97330.

Dallas Area Chamber of Commerce (503-623-2564; www.open.org/dallascc), 580 Main, Suite C, Dallas 97338.

Greater Sheridan Chamber of Commerce (503-843-4964; www.sheridancofc.locality.com), 144 E. Main Street, Sheridan 97378.

Keizer Visitors Center (503-393-9111; www.keizerchamber.com), 980 Chemawa Road N. E., Keizer 97303.

Lebanon Area Chamber of Commerce (541-258-7164; www.lebanonoregon.com), 1040 Park Street, Lebanon 97355.

McMinnville Chamber of Commerce (503-472-6196; www.mcminnville.org), 417 N. W. Adams Street, McMinnville 97128.

Molalla Area Chamber of Commerce (503-829-6941; www.molalla.net/community/chamber), 103 S. Molalla Avenue, Molalla 97038.

Monmouth-Independence Chamber of Commerce (1-800-772-2806; www.open.org/micc), 148 Monmouth Street, Independence 97351.

Mount Angel Chamber of Commerce (503-845-9440; www.oktoberfest.org), 5 N. Garfield Street, Mount Angel 97362.

Newberg Area Visitors Center (503-538-2014; www.newberg.org), 115 N. Washington, Newberg 97132.

North Santiam Visitors Information Center (503-897-2865), 115 Wall Street, Mill City 97360.

Oregon State Parks (503-378-6305), State Parks and Recreation Department, 525 Trade Street S. E., Salem 97301.

Philomath Area Chamber of Commerce (541-929-2454; www.philomath-chamber.org), 2935 Main Street, Philomath 97370.

Salem Convention and Visitors Association (1-800-874-7012; www.scva.org), 1313 Mill Street S. E., Salem 97301.

Silverton Area Chamber of Commerce (503-873-5615), 208 S. Water Street, Silverton 97381.

Siuslaw National Forest (541-750-7000), 4077 S. W. Research Way, Corvallis 97330.

Stayton-Sublimity Chamber of Commerce (503-769-3464; www.staytonsub-limitychamber.org), 266 N. Third Avenue, Stayton 97383.

Sweet Home Chamber of Commerce (541-367-6186), 1575 Main Street, Sweet Home 97386.

Willamette National Forest (541-465-6521), 211 E. Seventh Avenue, Eugene 97401; **Detroit Ranger District** (503-854-3366); **Sweet Home Ranger District** (541-367-5168).

Woodburn Area Chamber of Commerce (503-982-8221; www.woodburn-chamber.org), 2233 Country Club Road, Woodburn 97071.

GETTING THERE The North Willamette Valley can be reached from the east and west by Highways 22 and 20 and from the north and south by Interstate 5 and Highways 99W and 99E. Other major roads connecting this area include Highways 18, 34, 221, and 223 in the west and Highways 34, 226, 228, and 213 in the east.

MEDICAL EMERGENCY **Albany General Hospital** (541-812-4000), 1046 W. Sixth Street, Albany.

Good Samaritan Regional Medical Center (541-768-5009), 3600 N. W. Samaritan Drive, Corvallis.

Lebanon Community Hospital (541-451-7107), 525 North Santiam Highway, Lebanon.

Providence Newberg Hospital (503-537-1555), 501 Villa Road, Newberg.

Salem Hospital (503-561-5200), 665 Winter Street S. E., Salem.

Silverton Hospital (503-873-1500), 342 Fairview, Silverton.

Stayton Memorial Hospital (503-769-217), 1401 N. 10th Avenue, Stayton.

West Valley Hospital (503-623-8301), 525 S. E. Washington, Dallas.

Willamette Valley Medical Center (503-472-6131), 2700 Three Mile Lane, McMinnville.

* To See

MUSEUMS **Old Aurora Colony Museum** (503-678-5754), 15008 Second Street (exit 278 on Interstate 5), Aurora. The Aurora Colony was a communal Christian society that thrived here for 27 years, beginning with its founding in 1856 by Dr. William Keil. Sharing both labor and property, the colony's 400 members supported themselves through logging, farming, and manufacturing such products as furniture, baskets, and textiles. With the death of Dr. Keil in 1883, the colony folded, though some of its descendants still live nearby. Today this five-building complex preserves remnants of the old colony, displaying original artifacts, furniture, tools, and even houses.

Canby Depot Museum (503-266-9421), 888 N. E. Fourth Street, Canby. The star of this museum's collection is the 1873 building itself, thought to be Oregon's oldest remaining railroad station. Owned by the Southern Pacific from 1887 until it donated the building to the city of Canby in 1978, the old depot includes in its displays some of the square nails used in its construction, a cedar block that served as part of the foundation, and a framed linen copy of an 1870 townsite map.

Antique Powerland Museum (503-393-2424; www.antiquepowerland.com), 3995 Brooklake Road N. E. (exit 263 on Interstate 5), Brooks. Dedicated to the preservation of antique machinery, this complex consists of museums for tractors, trucks, trolleys, and other machines and equipment whose horsepower was generated by steam, kerosene, electricity, and, yes, even horses. Also on the grounds is the **Pacific Northwest Truck Museum,** which contains a collection of restored trucks from the first half of the 20th century. Want to see a 1917 Packard with a crank start, a 1920 Doane that could haul 6 tons but that was limited by its warranty to a maximum speed of 20 miles per hour, or a 1923 Mack log truck whose ride must have been as stiff as its load? Then this is the place for you.

A. C. Gilbert's Discovery Village (503-371-3631), 116 Marion Street N. E., Salem. Housed in two historic 1880s Victorian homes on the bank of the Willamette River and named for the man who gave the world Erector Sets, this museum is devoted to giving children the opportunity to explore elements of science, art, music, and drama.

Marion County Historical Society Museum (503-364-2128), 260 12th Street (on the northwest corner of Mission Mill Village), Salem. From the culture of the Kalapuya people to the homes, businesses, and schools of the pioneers, this museum stores the memories of the county in general and of the capital city of Salem in particular.

Mission Mill Village (1-800-874-7012), 1313 Mill Street S. E., Salem. Gathered near this 1889 woolen mill that once turned fleece to fabric is a collection of 14 historic structures, including frame houses dating as far back as 1841—the oldest in the Northwest—as well as a woolen-mill museum, the old millrace and turbine, a picnic area, and the usual supply of gift shops. Sometimes they even crank up some of the mill's

MISSION MILL VILLAGE IS HOME TO SOME OF THE OLDEST HOUSES IN THE NORTHWEST

machinery. "We don't run it on a day-to-day basis," says museum official Maureen Thomas, "but it works if we hold our breath right."

Macleay Village (503-362-4225), 8362 Macleay Road S. E., Salem. This historic village on the edge of Oregon's capital city includes an 1848 cemetery, an 1889 schoolhouse, and a 1900 grange hall as well as restored homes and businesses.

Evergreen Aviation Museum (503-434-4180; www.sprucegoose.org), 2685 N. E. Three Mile Lane (off Highway 18), McMinnville. Even though this museum displays at least 40 vintage aircraft as part of a collection devoted to the history and science of aviation, it's the ***Spruce Goose*** people come to see. "Unless you see it," says a woman visiting from New Mexico, "you can't believe it." The **Howard Hughes–built plane** has a wingspan of 320 feet, longer than a football field, and flew just once in its career, a 70-second flight in 1947. The size and the mystique surrounding the *Spruce Goose,* which is actually built of birch, is enough to draw more than 200,000 people a year through the museum's doors. "I want this to be a living museum, a learning institute," says museum owner Del Smith, "not some dusty old warehouse."

Polk County Museum (503-623-6251), Polk County Fairgrounds off Highway 99W, Rickreall. Displays at this two-story museum include Native American cultures, pioneer settlers, military campaigns, homestead life, and logging industry. "One theme in the museum is 'They Came to Polk County,'" says museum spokesman Arlie Holt. "The goal is that the visitor knows when leaving that he has been in Polk County."

Jensen Arctic Museum (503-838-8468), 590 W. Church Street, Monmouth. Located in a corner of the **Western Oregon University campus,** this is the only museum on the West Coast devoted entirely to the Arctic culture and environment. Much of its story, which was assembled as a result of the travels and labors of former WOU professor Paul Jensen, concerns survival in the Arctic region, where people are *not* at the top of the food chain. During his travels to Arctic Alaska, the late professor collected some 2,500 native artifacts, a collection that has since grown to more than 4,000, though the museum's space permits the display of only 10 to 20 percent of that total. "The museum's preservation of facts," says curator Keni Sturgeon, "shows a way of life that doesn't exist anymore."

Heritage Museum (503-838-4989), 112 S. Third Street, Independence. To experience the parade of history that has come marching through Independence, visit this 1888 former Baptist Church that houses the city's museum. From Kalapuya bows to cowboy saddles, replica schoolrooms to blacksmith shops, the museum depicts the growth of this Willamette River town from the days before the wagon trains, right on through the years when it was known as the Hop Center of the World.

Scio Depot Museum (503-394-2199), 39004 N. E. First Street, Scio. Many folks in Scio (pronounced *"SY-oh"*) can probably tell you that the town is the tenth oldest in Oregon and that it was named for Scio, Ohio, a great rhyme for any postal address. For the rest of the Scio story, however, visit its museum, which is housed in an 1890s train depot that stands on the edge of a shady park. Here you can trace the history of the community from its pioneer days—much of the collection has been donated by descendants of those pioneers—then go outside to have a picnic or climb on the caboose.

Albany Regional Museum (541-967-7122), 136 Lyon Street S. W. (in the basement of the Carnegie Library downtown), Albany. Dedicated to preserving the memory of a city whose historic buildings number at least 700, this museum has collected memorabilia and artifacts linked to, among other things, Albany's experiences with railroads, vaudeville, and World War II, especially with nearby Camp Adair.

Benton County Historical Museum (541-929-6230), 1101 Main Street, Philomath. Primary interests of this museum—whose building was once Philomath College, built in 1867 as one of the first colleges in the Oregon Territory—include its archaeological collection and depiction of early pioneer life and industrial development.

Linn County Historical Museum (541-466-3390), 101 Park Avenue, Brownsville. Housed in an 1890 depot complete with a display of seven railroad cars, this museum reflects the history of its location—Brownsville, one of Oregon's oldest towns, settled in 1846. One of its primary attractions is its collection of the relics of pioneer life, including a covered wagon that traveled the Oregon Trail in 1865.

HISTORIC HOMES **Hoover-Minthorn House** (503-538-6629), 115 S. River Street, Newberg. This is as close as Oregon has come to claiming a native son as President of the United States, for this was the 19th-century boyhood home of Herbert Hoover, who served as the 31st president from 1928 until 1932. The story of how he came to this corner of the state begins in 1881 when Henry Minthorn, Hoover's uncle, bought the house. But when Minthorn's young son died that same year, he wrote to Iowa and invited his 11-year-old nephew Herbert, then living with other relatives after the death several years earlier of his parents, to come to Oregon and join the family. Herbert accepted the invitation and lived with the Minthorns until 1891, when he entered Stanford University as a member of the school's first freshman class. In 1955, on his 81st birthday, the former president attended the opening of the restored home-turned-museum.

Newell House Museum (503-678-5537), 8089 Champoeg Road N. E. (exit 271 off Interstate 5), St. Paul. Robert "Doc" Newell was a fur trapper and trader turned settler, finally putting down roots here at Champoeg, near the Willamette River. Before long old Doc found himself getting involved in politicking, gold mining, store keeping, and house building before moving on to Idaho. This home is a replica of the house in Oregon he left behind—the only building in Champoeg to survive the great flood of 1861—though the stuff inside it is authentic to the time.

Dibble House (503-829-5521), 616 S. Molalla Avenue, Molalla. As local history tells it, Horace Dibble was roaming the hills around his homestead one day in 1856, searching for lost oxen, when he stumbled upon a piece of ground he wanted for his own. So using his homestead as payment, he bought the land and hired a carpenter, and three years later he moved into his new home. With hand-hewn timbers and a New England saltbox design, and with the interior looking much as though Mr. and Mrs. Dibble ought to be walking through the door any moment, the house stands today much as it did then.

Settlemier House (503-982-1897), 355 N. Settlemier Street (exit 271 off Interstate 5), Woodburn. This is one of those "Ooh! Ahhh!" houses, an 1891 Queen Anne Victorian mansion settled comfortably on its grounds like a queen on a green cushioned throne. On the outside, towers and gables and balconies seem to shout about the wealth of the home's original owner—Jesse Settlemier, who made his fortune in the nursery business but still had time to found the town of Woodburn—while the inside retains what the local newspaper in 1892 said was "every luxury that tends to make life easy." One of the three bathrooms even had a bidet, which one advertiser claimed could be "equally well adapted for use as a Foot Bath."

Abigail Scott Duniway Home, Highway 99W, Lafayette. Rooster Cogburn might say of Abigail Scott Duniway that here was a woman with sand, one with true grit—an Oregon Trail emigrant and Willamette Valley homesteader who for a half century fought for women's suffrage. Her tenacity paid off in 1912, when at the age of 79 she signed Oregon's "Proclamation of Woman's Suffrage in Oregon," which gave women in the state the right to vote. "Congratulations on the triumph of justice," said the telegram to Duniway from the National Suffrage Association. "Long live Oregon men." Two years later, Abigail Scott Duniway completed her triumph by becoming the first woman to cast a vote in an Oregon election.

Monteith House (1-800-526-2256), 518 Second Avenue S. W., Albany. After Walter and Thomas Monteith arrived in Oregon in 1847, they found their dream homesite on a half section of land located near the confluence of the Calapooya and Willamette Rivers—but a homesteader, Hiram Smead, already owned it. But that didn't stop the Monteiths. After buying the land from Mr. Smead for $400 and a Cayuse pony, the brothers purchased an adjoining half section, platted a town they named Albany (after the capital of their home state), and built a house that straddled the boundary between the two properties, satisfying the requirement that each brother sleep on his own claim. Today this 1849 house, one of the oldest surviving structures in the state, stands as a museum whose clock seems to have stopped in the mid-1850s.

Moyer House (541-466-3390), 204 Main Street, Brownsville. After arriving in Oregon in 1852, carpenter John Moyer found more than a job when he began building a house for Hugh Brown—he also found a wife in Brown's daughter, Elizabeth. When both their marriage and their business flourished, the Moyers built themselves a house that the local newspaper called "one of the most artistically arranged residences in the state." Today, thanks to years of restoration, visitors can still see one of the most elegant houses in one of the oldest pioneering communities in the state.

HISTORIC SITES **Tualatin Plains Presbyterian Church** (503-648-9573), 30685 N. W. Scotch Church Road, Hillsboro. Known locally as the "Old Scotch Church," this 1878 building with its eight-sided steeple and its arched windows is probably

DEEPWOOD ESTATE, AN 1894 QUEEN ANNE VICTORIAN, FEATURES SUCH TURN-OF-THE-CENTURY TECHNOLOGY AS ELECTRIC LIGHTS AND FLUSH TOILETS

the most photographed building in the area. In addition, former mountain man and U.S. marshall Joe Meek, one of Oregon's most famous and colorful characters, is buried in the church cemetery, as are many other early pioneers.

Silverton Walking Tour (503-873-5856), downtown Silverton. This 1-mile tour wanders through the downtown National Historic District of Silverton, a city that began with the mills powered by nearby Silver Creek and the farms started by Oregon Trail pioneers, and then grew when the railroad reached town, and logging operations spread through the hills.

Boon's Treasury (503-399-9062), 888 Liberty Street N. E., Salem. Built in 1860 and named for John Daniel Boon, Oregon's first state treasurer, this brick landmark has served as Oregon's first treasury building, a general store, and a tavern. If anything surpasses its history in importance, it's the hamburgers and beer now served at this **restaurant and pub.**

Elsinore Theatre (503-375-3574), 170 High Street S. E., Salem. Built in 1926 and designed in the Tudor Gothic image of Elsinore Castle that was home to Shakespeare's Hamlet, the Elsinore Theatre has served through the years as a site for films, vaudeville shows, live drama, and even the local Mickey Mouse Club. Today the tradition of diverse performances continues at the historic building, which draws more than 150,000 people a year to various events. Tours of the building, which are available the first Tuesday of each month or by appointment, can include an organ recital from the Elsinore's 1,644-pipe mighty **Wurlitzer organ.**

Waller Hall (503-370-6306), Willamette University, 900 State Street, Salem. Built in 1867, this is the oldest building on the oldest campus—it was established in 1842—west of the Mississippi River.

Bush House (503-363-4714), 600 Mission Street S. E., Salem. When it was completed in 1878, this 10,000-square-foot Victorian mansion was a marvel of technology, complete with central heating, gas lights, and even indoor plumbing with hot and cold running water. And today, because it contains many of the original furnishings, fireplaces, and wallpapers, the home remains relatively unchanged from the days it served as the family home of Asahel Bush II, founder of the capital city's first newspaper, the *Oregon Statesman,* as well as its first bank. So impressive was the finished house and grounds that the *Oregon Statesman*—remember that he owned it—called it "an elegant home surpassed by none in the state."

Deepwood Estate (503-363-1825), 1116 Mission Street, Salem. This 1894 Queen Anne Victorian—considered on of the finest in Oregon—probably looks almost as good as it did on the day its owner, Dr. Luke Port, moved into it: stained-glass windows, golden oak woodwork, electric lights, and (gasp) flush toilets. Located on 6 acres of landscaped grounds, the estate features the original carriage house, a 1905 gazebo built for that year's Lewis and Clark Exposition in Portland, and a quarter-mile nature trail that leads through a 1930s English garden designed by Elizabeth Lord and Edith Schryver, who constituted the Northwest's first firm of female landscape architects. The intended effect of the gardens, Schryver once said, was to create "an outdoor room in which we may have privacy and intimacy for work and relaxation."

Salem Walking Tour (1-800-874-7012), exit 253 or 256 off Interstate 5. Oregon's capital city offers two primary tours of historical neighborhoods: the **Court and Chemeketa Historic District**—in northeast Salem between 13th and 18th Streets—contains 37 historic homes dating from the 1860 to the 1930s; and the homes in the **Gaiety Hill/Bush's Pasture Park Historic District**—in south Salem between Mission, Liberty, and Cross Streets—include more than 100 houses built between 1880 and 1909. Both give you the chance to practice using such architectural terms as *Italianate.* In addition, from Memorial Day through Labor Day, and at other times by appointment, the **State Capitol and Mall** (503-986-1388; 900 Court Street N. E.) offers guided tours every hour. And if you feel like hiking 121 steps to the top of the Capitol, you can reach the base of the Golden Pioneer statue that watches over the city. The tower is open to visitors from 9 AM until 3:30 PM, Monday through Saturday. Beginning most springs and lasting until fall, guided tours head up the staircase every half hour. Adults must accompany children under the age of 16.

Brunk House (503-838-6603), 8 miles west of Salem off Highway 22 and near the junction with Highway 51. Open by appointment during summers, the Brunk House is a restored and furnished 1861 farmstead that belonged to the same family for three generations. The first generation of that family was Harrison and Emily Brunk, who came to Oregon in 1849 and found the Willamette Valley so fertile that they raised 12 children on their original 1,100-acre farm.

Dayton Historic Area (503-472-8075), near the junction of Highways 221 and 233. This tour takes an hour or two of walking and looking at such historic sites as the **Fort Yamhill Blockhouse** (see next listing), the **1880 Baptist Church,** the **Pioneer Cemetery,** and numerous homes and businesses.

Fort Yamhill Blockhouse (503-538-2014), city park, Dayton. This is the last remaining structure of Fort Yamhill, built in 1856 on the nearby Grand Ronde

Indian reservation, located some 28 miles southwest of here. The purpose of the post was to keep Indians on the reservation and settlers out, and it was the temporary home of Lieutenant Philip H. Sheridan, who would later win fame as a commanding officer in the Civil War.

McMinnville Walking Tour (503-472-3605), near the junction of Highways 18 and 99W. The downtown area comprising the city's historic district consists of 52 homes and buildings. The central core of this collection, especially of late-19th- and early-20th-century businesses, begins at the city park on Adams and stretches for seven blocks along Third Street.

Polk County Courthouse, 850 Main Street, Dallas. After almost two decades of political wrestling with nearby Independence, which was trying to take away the county seat, Dallas didn't waste any time when an 1898 fire tore through the town's county courthouse. (The county clerk and sheriff were suspected of, but never indicted for, arson.) Working from the idea that a new courthouse would settle the county seat's location once and for all, Dallas officials began almost immediately to plan a new building. Two years after the fire, almost to the week, Dallas proudly dedicated its new courthouse. Although the courthouse today is bordered on three sides by a U-shaped annex built in the 1960s, its exterior of sandstone blocks and its interior of tiled floors, paneled wainscoting, arched entrances, and sweeping stairs remain almost unchanged over the last century. In fact, former U.S. senator Mark Hatfield said the building "would compete" with any other in the world, "including the cathedral at Notre Dame." (And he wasn't running for reelection at the time, either.)

Fort Hoskins, 4 miles southwest of Kings Valley off Highway 223 and Hoskins Road. Built in 1856 and abandoned nine years later, Fort Hoskins stood in the foothills of the Coast Range and on the bank of the Luckiamute River, where its job was guarding the newly established Grand Ronde Indian Reservation. "When the military left this place, they left it a mess," says Oregon State University archaeologist David Brauner, "and archaeologists just love that." As a result, the artifacts left behind now help tell the story of this outpost on the old Oregon frontier.

Albany Walking Tour, exit 234A off Interstate 5. If it's stately elegance you're seeking in historic homes and buildings, you can't do much better than this: three historic districts spread across 140 blocks that contain more than 600 historic structures built in 13 architectural styles. "I would say that absolutely it is the best collection in Oregon," says Dave Skilton, preservation planner for the State Historic Preservation Office. "And you can walk to see them in one afternoon."

Hull-Oakes Lumber Co. (541-424-3112), south side of Dawson Road, Dawson (northwest of Monroe off Highway 99W). Even though this sawmill is on the **National Historic Register,** it still puts in a full day's work—yet it uses little electricity and no computers as it goes about its business of cutting approximately 18 million board feet of lumber each year. Instead, its power comes rumbling from out of the steel-riveted belly of an engine salvaged from a steamship in the 1930s, which makes this is the last **steam-driven sawmill** still operating in the Pacific Northwest and probably in the nation. "It's kind of the little engine that could," says Todd Nystrom, grandson of Ralph Hull, who started the mill in 1936. "It just keeps going and going."

Benton County Courthouse, 120 N. W. Fourth Street, Corvallis. When a crowd gathered for the laying of this courthouse's cornerstone on the Fourth of July in 1888, the ceremony began at dawn with the firing of a cannon. The muzzle blast, reported the local newspaper, "fired out nearly all the glass panes in the windows of the engine house and cracked and shattered a number of others." After that explosive awakening, the courthouse settled into more peaceful times, and today at the base of the 110-foot building, flowers and trees and benches give the landscaped grounds the beauty and quiet of a small park.

COVERED BRIDGES Even though only 53 of Oregon's original 450 covered bridges that existed in the 1920s still stand, the state can still boast of being the home of more covered bridges than anywhere else in the West. **Gallon House,** 2 miles north of Silverton off Highway 24 and Hobart Road (1916–17, 84 feet); **Harris Bridge,** 3 miles west of Wren off Highway 20 and Harris Road (1936, 75 feet); **Irish Bend,** in 1989 moved from northeast of Monroe to a site near the Oregon State University campus in Corvallis (1954, 60 feet); **Ritner Creek,** 2 miles southwest of Pedee off Highway 223 (1927, 75 feet).

Scio Area, south and east of Scio off Highway 226 and connecting roads. **Bohemian Hall Bridge** (built in 1947, 120 feet long); **Gilkey Bridge** (1939, 120 feet); **Hannah Bridge** (1936, 105 feet); **Hoffman Bridge** (1936, 90 feet); **Jordan Bridge** (1937, 90 feet); **Larwood Bridge,** also known as the **Roaring River Bridge** (1939, 103 feet); **Shimanek Bridge** (1966, 130 feet).

Sweet Home Area, east and west of Sweet Home off Highway 228 and connecting roads. **Short Bridge**, (1945, 115 feet), **Crawfordsville Bridge** (1932, 105 feet), **Weddle Bridge** (1937, 120 feet).

DRIVE-IN MOVIE THEATERS Ah, the drive-in movie—kids swinging on the playground, waiting for night to fall and the show to start; speakers hooked on car windows, spewing static until adjusted just so; folks shuffling to the snack bar as the giant white screen caught the first Technicolor flashes of the movie's trailers. Of the state's five drive-in movies, down from a high of 70 in the 1950s, three of them still operate in this region. (The state's other two drive-in movies are located in La Grande and Milton-Freewater, both in northeast Oregon; see *To See* in Pendleton–Hermiston–Milton-Freewater Area and La Grande–Union–Elegen Area.)

Motor Vu Drive-In (503-623-9346), 15 S. E. Fir Villa, Dallas. Of all the changes this venerable outdoor theater has witnessed since its opening in 1953, perhaps the most dramatic is the fact that it now sits next to a 300-acre suburban development. Even so, on some summer nights when the movie is right, the 13-acre drive-in fills to its capacity of 400 cars. Part of the draw may be what the drive-in advertises as "Oregon's Largest Movie Screen!!!" (45 x 90 feet), or maybe it's the bargain-basement rates. "Twelve bucks for a carload," says owner Ron Burch, "and you don't care how many people are in there."

99W Drive-In (503-538-2738), Highway 99, just west of the Springbrook Road intersection near Newberg. For three generations, beginning in 1953, the same family has owned and operated this drive-in. And today the drive-in reflects those earlier days, the golden years of drive-in movies, with posters, cartoons, trailers, and intermission reels all coming straight from the 1950s. In addition, the drive-in always runs double-feature family films. "And we have an Edsel night and a Volkswagen night," says Christine Francis, who joins her husband, Ted, as drive-in owner and operator. "People bring dogs and play Frisbee."

MotorVu Drive Drive-In (541-258-5432), South Santiam Highway, Lebanon. Here for 50 years on its 10-acre site, now next to Wal-Mart, owned for almost 30 years by Carl Hermanson, now in his seventies. "The only thing that shuts us down is fog and snow," he says. "We've sold out many times."

FOR FAMILIES **Enchanted Forest** (503-363-3060; www.enchantedforest.com), 7 miles south of Salem off Interstate 5 (exit 248). If you or the kids find yourselves fighting the urge to visit a haunted house or a Wild West town, duck into an Alice in Wonderland rabbit hole or the Seven Dwarf's mine, or even step into a witch's mouth and slide down her hair—then fight it no more. Instead, visit the Enchanted Forest, where childhood fantasies seem to come alive. "We never wanted to be a plastic, mass-produced park," says owner Roger Tofte, who began building the Enchanted Forest in 1964 and who, along with his family, has operated it since 1971. "We hope we've created an oasis where people can experience unique fun." That uniqueness includes streets and villages populated with animated people and animals, as well as rides through tunnels, up mountains, and down log flumes.

FERRY BOAT RIDES Before bridges spanned the Willamette River, ferries were the workhorses of river crossings. Their days, however, were numbered. "The cost of keeping men employed as ferrymen," bridge builder Nels Roney argued, "is much more than the interest on the money that will be expended on the building of bridges." And so bridges began replacing ferries. Nevertheless, three county-owned ferries still ride their cables and carry their passengers across the Willamette River. So if you want to pay a dollar or two fare for a five-minute ride, you can engage in a simple but rare river-crossing experience on one of the following: **Buena Vista Ferry,** 6 miles south of Independence off Buena Vista Road; **Wheatland Ferry,** 13 miles north of Salem between Wallace and Wheatland Roads; and **Canby Ferry,** 3 miles north of Canby off Mountain Road.

GARDEN TOURS **Swan Island Dahlias** (503-266-7711), 995 N. W. 22nd Avenue, Canby. With more than 40 acres under cultivation, this is the largest dahlia grower in the nation.

Wooden Shoe Bulb Company (503-634-2243), 33814 S. Meridian Road, north of Woodburn. More than 150 varieties of tulips and 40 acres of daffodils grow on this family farm. It's open daily during the height of growing season, usually from the end of March through the end of April, with the peak bloom coming around the first of April.

Schreiner's Iris Gardens (503-393-3232), 3625 Quinaby Road, Salem.

Schreiner's 250 acres of irises makes this company the nation's largest retail grower. And when the irises are blooming—from mid-May through the first week in June—the garden's 10-acre display area is open to the public every day from 8 AM until dusk.

Capitol Park and **Willson Park,** grounds of the Capitol Building, 900 Court Street N. E., Salem. Scattered across the grounds of the State Capitol are collections of trees, shrubs, flower beds, water fountains, and historical monuments and statues.

Willamette University (503-370-6300), 900 State Street, Salem. A rose garden, a Japanese garden, and a botanical garden are part of the campus of this university, the oldest institution of higher learning in the West.

Cooley's Gardens (503-873-5463), 2 miles west of Silverton off Highway 213. A family-owned operation since 1928, this 250-acre garden is the world's largest producer of bearded irises, and millions of them bloom here from mid-May until early June.

Oregon Garden (503-874-8100; www.oregongarden.org), 879 W. Main Street, Silverton. As far as gardens are concerned, this is just a sprout. But if the growth of the garden matches the vision of its creators, then one day soon this will be the premier garden in the state—240 acres containing virtually every flower, shrub, and tree that grows in Oregon, either commercial or wild. Throw in some trails and benches and arbors, some ponds and streams, and you've found a garden to write home about.

THE TRAILS AT PEAVY ARBORETUM LEAD PAST MORE THAN 200 SPECIES OF TREES AND SHRUBS

Delbert Hunter Arboretum and Botanic Garden (503-623-2564), entrance near the corner of Levens and Brandvold Streets, Dallas. A soft, winding trail leads walkers past a showcase of flowers, shrubs, and trees that constitute one of the largest collections of native plants in Oregon—almost 400 total species representing virtually all the regions in the state. Along the way the path dips to the edge of La Creole Creek and detours toward benches, where you can sit in sunlight or shade with the nearby sound of riffling water.

Peavy Arboretum (541-737-4452), 8 miles north of Corvallis off Highway 99W. More than 200 varieties of tree and shrub species collected from around the world grow on this 40-acre site. A stroll along the shaded trails introduces you to a number of them, and along the way you'll learn some interesting facts about trees, such as three-fourths of the world's pencil supply once came from southwest Oregon's incense cedar. In addition, the arboretum is on the edge of the **MacDonald-Dunn Research Forest** (see *To Do—Bicycling*), a 7,000-acre outdoor laboratory criss-crossed with miles of trees and trails.

SCENIC DRIVES **Highway 99,** 50 or 130 paved miles from Portland to Salem or from Portland to Eugene. Tucked away along the forests and fields that edge the whiz-bang traffic of Interstate 5 is the **old Pacific Highway,** once the major north–south route through Oregon and still a relatively quiet byway for travelers who want to escape the freeway rush. The old road had its start in 1913 as part of the highway that ran all the way from San Diego, California, to Blaine, Washington; it became US 99 in 1926 with the beginning of the U.S. Highway System; and it was divided in 1930 into US 99E and US 99W. Today **Highway 99E** stretches 50 miles between Portland (Interstate 5, exit 307) and Salem (exit 258); and **Highway 99W**, 130 miles from Portland (exit 306) to Eugene (exit 192). Both roads offer a glimpse of a slower, quieter time, traveling near oak groves and hazelnut orchards, vineyards and pastures, farmhouses and fruit stands. (One note of caution: On weekends, Highway 99W can stack up and slow down with the traffic leaving Portland and heading for the coast.)

North Willamette Valley Scenic Loops. In the northern stretches of the Willamette River's green, green valley, a series of short tour routes carry you along serene byways, past green fields, and over rolling hills. The countryside along the way includes wineries and nurseries, Christmas tree farms and hazelnut orchards. Although Wilsonville makes a good starting point, others include Aurora, Sherwood, or Canby.

East Loop, 33 paved miles. From Wilsonville, head east on Wilsonville Road, north on Stafford Road, south on Mountain Road and N. Holly Street to Canby; then southwest on Highway 99E to Aurora, north on Airport Road, and back to Wilsonville via Interstate 5. Special attractions along the way: the **Canby Ferry, Molalla State Park,** old **Aurora Colony Museum,** and **Aurora antiques shops** and malls.

West Loop, 38 paved miles. From Wilsonville, head south on Interstate 5 and turn west at exit 282B, then drive west on Butteville Road and Champoeg Road, north on Highway 219 and Springbrook Street, northeast on Highway 99W to Sherwood, south on Ladd Hill Road, and east on Wilsonville Road back to Wilsonville. Special attractions along the way: the **1863 Butteville General Store, Champoeg State Park, Newell House Museum,** and **Sherwood antiques shops** and malls.

Silver Falls Tour, 50 paved miles from Interstate 5, exit 248 south of Salem to Woodburn via Delaney Road and Highways 22 and 214. This is a lovely, winding road that passes through the small towns of **Turner, Aumsville,** and **Sublimity** before rolling over the hills and past the fields that lead the way into the foothills of the **Cascades** and **Silver Falls State Park.** Even though this is Oregon's most visited park, many travelers find the journey as beautiful as the destination.

"It's not just the park experience," says Mila Mohr, president of Friends of Silver Falls, "but the getting-to-the-park experience that's special." The same is true of the leaving-the-park experience, for the road from here wanders through more rolling hills and forests on its way to **Silverton, Mount Angel,** and **Woodburn.**

NATURAL WONDERS **Heritage Trees** (1-800-574-9397). For more than 40 years, Maynard Drawson, a retired Salem barber, has been tracking down trees tall, thick, rare, and historic. The result of his numerous discoveries is a collection of "Heritage Trees" that are living memorials to Oregon's history and culture. So if you should encounter one of these trees on your own journey, you may find yourself experiencing, as John Muir said he did when he first saw the baobab tree in Africa, "one of the greatest of the great tree days in my lucky life."

Ewing Young Oak, 3 miles west of Newberg off Highway 240. Beneath this oak tree lies the grave site of Ewing Young, former mountain man who settled in the Willamette Valley and who in 1837 rode to northern California and returned with Oregon's first herd of cattle. When he died in 1841 without leaving a will, the need to settle his estate led to the election of a judge to dispose of Young's property, a step that led indirectly to the eventual forming of a provisional government two years later.

Willamette Mission Cottonwood, 8 miles north of Salem off Wheatland Road. Standing taller than a 15-story building near the shore of Mission Lake at Willamette Mission State Park, this black cottonwood tree is the largest in the world. Its vital statistics include a height of 156 feet, a spread of 110 feet, a circumference of 26 feet 8 inches, and an age dating back to 1735.

Waldo Park Sequoia, corner of Summer and Union Streets, Salem. This is a tall tree with a big story, one that begins in the days of the California gold rush, when white Americans first encountered the giant sequoia. "When the people who found those trees described them," Maynard Drawson says, "people thought they were drunk or lying." But that didn't stop William Waldo of Salem from planting one at the corner of his property. As the tree grew, so did the town, and Waldo defended his sequoia from the surveyors and developers who would cut it down to widen the road. Then in the 1930s, with the tree once again threatened by the ax, the American War Mothers took up the fight, forcing the city council to designate the tree and the ground bordering it a park, the smallest in the world at the time. Today, Summer Street tightens from four lanes to three to skirt the 85-foot tree, which may reach more than 300 feet in height and more than 2,000 years in age before its days are over.

Hager Grove Pear Tree, north of Highway 22 and east of its junction with Interstate 5 southeast of Salem. What's now a busy interstate intersection was once an orchard planted by a family named Munkre; and what's left of that orchard is this pear tree, one of the oldest and largest in Oregon.

Erratic Rock, 6 miles east of Sheridan at Erratic Rock State Park. When the glaciers from the last Ice Age melted, the floodwaters washed huge rocks, known as *erratics,* across the continent. And when the floodwaters receded, many erratics were left strewn across valleys and hillsides. Here on the edge of the

Willamette Valley and near the foothills of the Coast Range, for instance, squats a 40-ton boulder that may have begun its journey in Canada.

Marys Peak, 23 miles southwest of Corvallis off Highway 34 and Mary's Peak Road. This might be a molehill when compared to many mountains, but it's still the giant of the Coast Range—almost 4,100 feet in elevation, its summit formed from the volcanic action of an ancient seafloor and its view reaching east to the Cascades and west to the Pacific.

McDowell Creek Falls, 14 miles southeast of Lebanon off Highway 20 and McDowell Creek Road. Here three waterfalls—20-foot **Crystal Pool,** 39-foot **Majestic Falls,** and 119-foot **Royal Terrace Falls**—plunge and splash their way through the forested canyon of McDowell Creek.

✷ To Do

BICYCLING **MacDonald-Dunn Research Forest** (541-737-4452), northwest of Corvallis and west of Highway 99W, with major entry points at Chip Ross Park on Lester Avenue, Sulphur Springs Trail on Sulphur Springs Road, and Peavy Arboretum on Arboretum Road. This 7,000-acre tract is used for research by forestry students at nearby Oregon State University, yet it's also open to bikers, hikers, and equestrians who use the more than 100 miles of trails crisscrossing the area.

CAMPING **Detroit Lake,** southwest of Detroit off Highway 22 and along Blowout Road. Even though the more than 300 campsites at **Detroit Lake State Park** can fill in a hurry when folks come streaming out of summertime Salem and into the mountains, three other more lightly used campgrounds located on the lake's perimeter—**Hoover, Cove Creek,** and **South Shore**—offer 130 additional sites; also, if you have a boat and a sense of adventure, **Piety Island,** located near the head of the lake, has a dozen campsites.

Breitenbush River Area, northeast of Detroit off Highway 22 and along Forest Road 46. More than 60 campsites divided among four camps—**Upper Arm, Humbug, Cleator Bend,** and **Breitenbush.**

Upper North Santiam Area, south of Idanha off Highway 22 and along the upper reaches of the North Santiam River. A total of 65 campsites at three camps—**Whispering Falls, Riverside,** and **Marion Forks;** in addition, **Big Meadows Horse Camp** offers 9 campsites along with horse facilities.

Sweet Home Area, near the town of Sweet Home and the South Santiam River, and off Highway 20 or connecting forest and county roads. **Foster Reservoir,** northeast of Sweet Home between Highway 26 and Quartzville Road, 4 camps—**Foster Reservoir, Sunnyside, Lewis Creek,** and **Whitcomb; House Rock,** 28 miles east of Sweet Home off Highway 20, 17 campsites near the confluence of Squaw Creek and Sheep Creek; along the southern edge of the **Menagerie Wilderness** east of Sweet Home and near Highway 20, 3 camps—**Trout Creek, Yukwah,** and **Fernview.**

See also **Champoeg State Park, Silver Falls State Park,** and **John**

Neal Memorial Park, North Santiam Parks, and **Cascadia State Park** under *Wilder Places—Parks.*

CANOEING **Cascade Lakes.** If you don't want to share a mountain lake with motorboats, scout out the following: **Breitenbush Lake,** northeast of Detroit off Highway 26 and Forest Roads 46 and 4220; **Daly Lake** and **Parish Lake,** south of Idanha off Highway 22 and Forest Road 2266; **Clear Lake,** southeast of Sweet Home off Highways 20 and 126.

GOLF **Elkhorn Valley Golf Course** (503-897-3368), 32295 North Fork Road, Lyons, 18 holes.

HIKING **Silver Creek Canyon,** 26 miles east of Salem off Highways 22 and 214. Through the canyon of Silver Creek leads one of the most remarkable hiking trails in the Northwest: the **Trail of Ten Falls,** a 7-mile loop that leads to what has been called "the greatest concentration of waterfalls in the U.S." Along this shaded, needle-softened path that smells of sun-warmed cedar, the air often thrums with the roar and splash of water that tumbles its white way over hillsides and down streams.

Mary's Peak, 23 miles southwest of Corvallis off Highway 34 and Mary's Peak Road. As far as the **Coast Range** is concerned, this is the top of the world, the 4,097-foot summit of the **highest mountain in the range,** and among its 12 miles of trail lie several routes that show different sides of the mountain: two short trails that lead to the summit—a three-quarter-mile gravel road (closed to all but power company vehicles) that takes off from the parking lot, and a slightly longer footpath that begins near the campgrounds; **Meadowedge Loop,** a 2-mile circle that starts from near the campground and passes through meadows and forests and over Parker Creek as it crosses the mountain's slope; and **North Ridge Loop,** a 3.5-mile trail that wanders through the woods and along the slopes and uses the **Tie Trail** as a link back to its starting point near the parking lot.

McDowell Creek Falls, 14 miles southeast of Lebanon off Highway 20 and McDowell Creek Road. A 2-mile walk along this creek and through its canyon takes you to three waterfalls that comes in sizes small (20-foot **Crystal Pool),** medium (39-foot **Majestic Falls),** and large (119-foot **Royal Terrace Falls**). Even without the falls, the forest, the stream, and the footbridges would still make this an enchanting hike.

See also *Wilder Places—Wilderness Areas.*

UNIQUE ADVENTURES **Our Lady of Guadalupe Trappist Abbey,** 3 miles west of Lafayette on Bridge Street. In the rolling farmland and hills outside the town of Lafayette stands this Trappist abbey, one of only a dozen such abbeys in the nation and the only one in Oregon.

Lafayette Schoolhouse Antique Mall (503-864-2451), Lafayette. If your idea of a good time is browsing through the goods and gear of the past, then drop by this three-story 1910 schoolhouse, where 100 antiques dealers stock more than 200,000 items.

Wine Country Tours (1-800-547-7842; www.oregonwine.org). For many people living in the hills of the Willamette Valley, their *Field of*

Dreams consisted of a fertile slope and a mysterious voice that said, "If you grow it, they will come." And so they planted their vineyards and harvested the grapes and turned them into wine—and sure enough, people came. Of Oregon's more than 170 wineries, second-most in the nation, the majority can be found in the Willamette Valley between Eugene in the south and Portland in the north, and a pastime growing in popularity is the wine tour, a visit to a series of wineries or vineyards that offers visitors a taste of their products. Probably the best route to follow in pursuing this tour is **Highway 99W,** which skirts the edge of some of the valley's best wine country, including areas near **Elmira, Cheshire, Monroe, Corvallis,** and **Amity.** But if you were to choose a single starting point for your first tour, you can't do better than **Dundee,** a small town that serves as the gateway to numerous wineries and vineyards in the valley's west hills. And if you're new to the wine-tasting circuit, you might find a couple of pointers helpful: Once the wine is poured, raise it slowly above eye level, gaze at it adoringly, and say, "Hmmm"; then lower the glass to your nose and sniff; finally, take a sip, tilt your head to the side and say, "Hmm, pernicious without being avuncular."

✷ Wilder Places

PARKS **Bald Peak State Park** (503-378-6305), 10 miles southwest of Hillsboro off Highway 219 and Bald Peak Road, day use only. A narrow, winding, climbing road leads past trophy homes and fir thickets to this park where the trees stand straight and spaced along a ridgeline, and where you can catch a view across to the Cascades and down to the Willamette Valley.

Molalla River State Park (503-378-6305), 2 miles north of Canby off N. Holly Street, day use only. Two worlds comprise this park: Down below, on the waters of the Willamette River, motorboats pull along skiers, long arcs of glistening spray soaring from the planing edge of their skis; up above, on the edge of Molalla River State Park, couples stroll and kids play and dogs wander across the lawns and through the forests that border farm fields and lead to river trails connecting the two worlds.

Champoeg State Park (503-678-1251), 4 miles southeast of Newberg off Highway 219, or 5 miles northwest of exit 278 on Interstate 5, day use and overnight. On a day in 1843, 102 men gathered here on the banks of the Willamette River to decide the future of the Oregon Country, and by a vote of 52-50 they made Oregon part of the United States. Since then, Champoeg (usually pronounced *"shamp-OO-ee"* or *"shamp-OO-ick"*) has seen the coming and going of stern-wheelers and towns and floods, leaving it today as a park whose square mile contains picnic sites, campgrounds, pioneers' buildings, and 10 miles of trails through one of the Willamette Valley's most historic sites.

Willamette Mission State Park (503-378-6305), 8 miles north of Salem off Wheatland Road, day use only. When Methodist missionary Jason Lee and four assistants arrived here from the east in 1834, they set to work building a mission that would serve as a school for the Indians of the Oregon Country. The missionaries constructed a log house and a barn, fenced and plowed 30 acres, and began raising enough food to make the mission self-sufficient. Over its first five years more missionaries arrived, pushing the local white population to almost 100, and the mission eventually grew to include a granary, a hospital, a school, and a blacksmith shop. In spite of its growth, the mission moved to a new home near today's Salem in 1840, and a flood in 1861 washed away most of the old site. What's left today is the history, a monument, and the park's roses, which are descendants of an 1837 cutting brought here by Rachel Beardsley Beers, wife of the blacksmith. Otherwise, the park serves as a huge riverside playground that contains miles of trails for walkers, joggers, bikers, and equestrians within its borders.

Maud Williamson State Park(503-378-6305), 12 miles north of Salem off Highway 221, day use only. Some folks might think this park doesn't invite long stays, that it lacks anything more than a few picnic tables and rest rooms. But they'd be missing the point, for this park's main attraction is its **fir trees:** tall trees, thick trees, straight trees; trees that invite staring, hugging, wondering; trees to run around or hide behind; trees to remind us of how majestic the centuries can be when they come wrapped in bark and grow themselves toward the sky.

Salem City Parks (503-364-4714), Interstate 5 exit 253 or 256. Even though Salem is a city with more than 40 parks covering almost 1,600 acres (in 1950 these figures were 8 parks and 113 acres), the following are especially inviting to visitors as well as residents.

Bush's Pasture Park, 600 Mission Street S. E. If the state's capital city has a communal backyard, this is it—almost 100 acres that once belonged to the Bush family, whose house and greenhouse, which date back to the 1870s and 1880s, still perch on the slope among the oak trees. Yet the draw here are the vast lawns, the tidy gardens, the numerous playgrounds, and the towering firs and widespread oaks that give adult and kids and dogs room to romp, a place to picnic away a summer evening among the scents of bark dust, mowed grass, and barbecue smoke.

Riverfront Park, west of Front Street, downtown. What used to be part of a ramshackle waterfront is fast becoming Salem's downtown parlor, a place where folks gather to spend sunny afternoons at the park's amphitheater, playground, pathways, or picnic tables, all on the edge of the Willamette River.

Minto-Brown Park, off Commercial Street S., Owens Street, and S. River Road. This tract devoted to wildlife and recreation is the wildest part of the city, almost 900 acres of forests and fields along a backwater of the Willamette River. Here you can take a walk, ride your bike, run your dog, fly a kite, or watch the birds and rabbits along miles of trails lined with blackberry brambles and cottonwood groves.

Bonesteele Park (503-378-6305), 2 miles northwest of Aumsville off the Aumsville Highway south of Highway 22. Before the first settlers arrived in the Willamette Valley, the landscape was a blend of prairie grasslands, wildflower meadows, and oak savannas, all of it kept tidy by the frequent fires set by the native Kalapuya people. Even though that landscape has almost disappeared from the valley, places such as this 30-acre park are being restored to their presettlement conditions. "We're simply trying to find some islands here and there," says Marion County Parks director Bob Hansen, "so 200 years from now people will have some idea of what this valley was like before it was settled."

Silver Falls State Park (503-873-8681), 26 miles east of Salem off Highways 22 and 214, day use and overnight. This park, Oregon's largest with more than 13 square miles, takes you to a world of towering fir trees and plunging waterfalls, a world glowing fern-green and mist-white along a trail gently winding beside canyons and streams. And it is this trail, which edges past and ducks behind **10 waterfalls,** that sets Silver Creek apart from other parks. After all, where else can you stand inside a mountain and watch water tumble over its edge?

John Neal Memorial Park(503-378-6305), Neal Park Road, Lyons, off Highway 22. With ponds and wetlands and forests, this 30-acre park on the bank of the **North Santiam River** is a wildlife haven for critters as various as frogs and beavers, rabbits and geese, raccoons and deer. In addition, smooth, packed walking paths wander through the area; a gentle current permits streamside wading or inner-tube floating; and a picnic site, playground, and primitive campground make longer stays a pleasant adventure.

Little North Fork Parks (503-378-6305), northeast of Mehama along the Little North Santiam River and North Fork Road. Head upstream along the **Little North Santiam River,** which flows clear and riffled from the western slope of the Cascades, and you'll find a series of shady riverside parks that offer amenities such as picnic areas, sandy beaches, swimming holes, hiking trails, or campsites. These parks include **Little North Fork, Canyon Creek, Bear Creek; Elkhorn Valley, Salmon Falls, Three Pools,** and **Shady Cove.**

BUSH'S PASTURE PARK

North Santiam Parks (503-378-6305), along the North Santiam River and Highway 22 between Mehama and Detroit Lake. **North Santiam State Park** is a destination of picnickers, steelheaders, and a few rafters drawn to the stream's clear green waters; **Fishermen's Bend** comes with a campground, a nature trail, a picnic area—that includes an 80-foot table cut from a single Douglas fir—and a good stretch of fishing water; **Minto County Park** offers picnic sites and a trail system within its 111 acres; **Packsaddle** has a picnic area and launch area popular with rafters and steelheaders; **Niagara County Park** is the site of an abandoned dam, a good stretch of fishing water, picnic tables, and hiking trails.

Sarah Helmick State Park (503-378-6305), 6 miles south of Monmouth off Highway 99W and Helmick Road, day use only. Only 10 of this park's 80 acres are devoted to the stuff of parks: sprawling lawns and towering trees, picnic tables and barbecue grills, parking lots and rest rooms. The rest is plowed and planted fields. Still, this site named for its donor, Sarah Helmick, who in 1845 traveled the Oregon Trail from Iowa to settle here along the banks of the Luckiamute River, is a green magnet during fair weather, drawing spring-feverish moms and dads and kids (as well as students from nearby Western Oregon University) to its back roads, old trees, and slow river.

Dallas City Park (503-378-6305), entrance near the corner of Levens and Brandvold, Dallas. Here you'll find 40 acres of rustling trees and flowing water, of kids loping through playgrounds and picnickers lounging at tables. Sure, a sunny Sunday at almost any other city park might be much the same, but this place carries the feel of a vortex, where time slows and maybe even backtracks a bit, carrying us away to the kind of world we expect to find in sepia-toned photographs. And even if we can't find our way all the way back to a Norman Rockwell past, this is still a snug place to spend a lazy afternoon, to snooze under a cottonwood tree or dangle your feet in the creek.

Corvallis City Parks (503-378-6305). Corvallis, home of Oregon State University, can boast of 30 city parks, many of which contain access to streams, hiking paths, or biking trails. Some of these include **Avery Park,** S. W. 15th Street and S. W. Avery Park Drive, located near Mary's River and containing a rose garden, a picnic area, and a playground that features an old locomotive; **Bald Hill Park**, N. W. Oak Creek Drive, with a hiking trail to a hilltop view of the city; **Chip Ross Park,** off N. W. Highland Drive on N. W. Lester Avenue, has views of the city and access to trails in **MacDonald-Dunn Research Forest** (see *To Do—Bicycling*); **Riverfront Park,** First Street and Madison Avenue, located close to downtown and along the bank of the Willamette River, with a trail leading to the Willamette's confluence with Mary's River; **Walnut Park,** 4905 N. W. Walnut Boulevard, featuring bike paths, hiking trails, and picnic areas.

Bellfountain Park (503-378-6305), 18 miles south of Corvallis off Highway 99W and Bellfountain Road. Established in 1851, this is Benton County's oldest park as well as the site of the **nation's longest picnic table** cut from a single piece of wood—85 feet. It was milled at the Hull-Oakes

Lumber Co. in Dawson (see *To See—Historic Sites*) and sits beneath one of the park's picnic shelters.

Waverly Lake (541-917-7777), Pacific Boulevard and Salem Avenue, Albany. Once a log pond for a sawmill and now a roadside oasis where families can picnic, fish, walk, or rent a paddleboat, Waverly Lake on a sun-warm afternoon can be a place that seems to hold time still enough, long enough that it's easy to slip away from whatever may be troubling you at the moment.

Monteith Riverpark (503-378-6305), on the bank of the Willamette River, Albany. Along a slow stretch of the Willamette River lies this park that beckons to those wanting to unload a picnic basket or cast a fishing line, take a stroll or read a book.

Roaring River Park (503-378-6305), 18 miles east of Albany off Highway 20 and Fish Hatchery Drive. Sitting along a country road and on the bank of Roaring River, this park offers visitors walking trails, playgrounds, and picnic areas.

Cascadia State Park (503-378-6305), 14 miles east of Sweet Home off Highway 20, day use and overnight. Once the site of a health spa and vacation resort that from the 1890s into the 1940s drew crowds of people to its soda springs, Cascadia had its start as a park when the state bought the resort during World War II. The park still draws crowds, though today they consist of campers, anglers, hikers, and swimmers who gather here near the **South Santiam River**'s riffles, pools, and trails.

WILDERNESS AREAS **Table Rock,** 20 miles southeast of Molalla off Highway 211 and Dickie Prairie Road and South Molalla Road, 9 square miles. Surrounded by private land logged for four decades beginning in the 1930s, Table Rock Wilderness lies in the forested foothills of the **Cascade Mountains.** The major entry points to the area's 16 miles of trails include **Old Bridge,** probably the most strenuous trail in the wilderness with an elevation gain of more than 3,200 feet in 6 miles; **Table Rock,** the highest but one of the shortest trails in the wilderness with a 1,000-foot climb in 2.3 miles; **Peachuck Lookout,** perhaps the flattest trail with an elevation gain of just 400 feet in the 2.6-mile route to **Rooster Rock;** and **Old Jeep Road,** which is really an old jeep road. Much of the area's human history is represented along the trail between Old Bridge and Peachuck, a path used for centuries first by Native Americans and then by homesteaders and miners.

Opal Creek, 45 miles east of Salem off Highway 22 and Little North Fork Road, 55 square miles. If you're not sure what qualifies as old-growth timber—one guideline is that "you'll know it when you see it"—then get thee to Opal Creek, where some of the **Douglas firs** and **western red cedars** are 10 centuries old. That's right—1,000 years old. In addition, the area holds **200 waterfalls, five lakes,** and miles of **salmon** and **steelhead streams.**

Menagerie, 22 miles east of Sweet Home off Highway 20, 7 square miles. Ten million years before the Cascade Mountains rose from the earth to stand as the backbone of what is today Oregon, a chain of volcanoes had long occupied their place. These **"Old Cascades"** were the

BASKETT SLOUGH NATIONAL WILDLIFE REFUGE EXISTS AS A WINTER HOME FOR CANADA GEESE

original creators of the region's rain shadow, stopping coastal rains from penetrating east of their summits and casting the land beyond in the clear skies and sunlight of desert. Time, however, has taken its toll on these old giants, eroding their towering volcanic peaks to the cliffs, pinnacles, and spires that now dot this canyonland wilderness.

Middle Santiam, 36 miles northeast of Sweet Home off Highway 20 or 22, Quartzville Road, and Forest Road 11, 12 square miles. In this old-growth forest along the Middle Santiam River, **firs and hemlocks and cedars** can reach 200 feet in height and 500 years in age, and **Chinook salmon** spawn in the stream's shaded pools. Among the trails are three easy day hikes—to **Daly, Parish, and Riggs Lakes,** each of which lies at the end of a half-mile walk.

WILDLIFE REFUGES **Kingston Prairie Preserve**, 3 miles southeast Stayton off Highway 22 and Kingston–Jordan and Kingston–Lyons Drives. Because this plateau rising above the North Santiam River was always too rocky for farming, its landscape has remained virtually unchanged through the years. In fact, it's one of the last surviving tracts of native prairie remaining in the Willamette Valley, part of the one half of 1 percent of what used to be more than a million acres of grasslands. Now managed by the Nature Conservancy, the 128-acre preserve is home to a wide variety of wildlife that seek out its meadows, especially the **western meadowlark,** Oregon's state bird, whose populations are declining in the central Willamette Valley though they still nest at Kingston Prairie.

Baskett Slough National Wildlife Refuge (541-757-7236), 4 miles northeast of Dallas off Highways 223 and 22. Major residents of this refuge in winter are **dusky geese,** which every year make the trip south from their nesting grounds in Alaska. The rest of the year, the refuge is more quiet but still a site that attracts and holds numerous species of wildlife. For a bird's-eye view of the place, visit the overlook off Highway 22, just west of its intersection with Highway 99W. For a closer look, take Colville Road into the refuge and its trailhead for a mile-long walk through the oak groves and along the grassy slopes of **Baskett Butte.**

Ankeny National Wildlife Refuge (541-757-7236), 10 miles north of Albany off Interstate 5 (take exit 243) and Ankeny Hill Road. Most of the 2,796 acres on this refuge, which lies just north of the confluence of the Santiam and Willamette Rivers, is open farmland, which suits the geese just fine. But even though human visitors are confined to the refuge's edges, a couple of places offer excellent viewing of the area's more than 300 species of wildlife, including **ducks, geese, swans, herons, shorebirds,** and **bald eagles.** One place is the information and viewing kiosk on Buena Vista Road; the other is the 1,300-foot **boardwalk** that serves as an elevated pathway into and over the refuge's wetlands. "It's a great achievement and good workmanship," said a man using the wooden trail for the first time. "Must've been quite difficult to build through the swamp, even in summer."

William L. Finley National Wildlife Refuge (541-757-7236),12 miles south of Corvallis off Highway 99W. Geese are grazers, cows with wings, and it was the grass of the Willamette Valley that once lured them from the sky and kept them happily nibbling the green prairies of the valley's bottom. But when those prairies were plowed under and the soil planted to crops, most of the grass disappeared and so did the geese. That's why in the 1960s this refuge was created, more than 5,000 acres of forests and marshes and ponds—but mostly of grass. And today the geese have returned by the tens of thousands, settling into these grasslands to wait out the winter. "Sometimes," says refuge manager Jim Houk, "it feels like you go back a hundred years in time around here."

E. E. Wilson Wildlife Area (541-745-5334), 9 miles north of Corvallis off Highway 99W. The former site of Camp Adair, where 15,000 soldiers trained during World War II, the E. E. Wilson Wildlife Area retains the old camp's road system, even though most of the grounds have been either restored to native trees, shrubs, and wetlands or invaded by blackberry brambles. The combination makes it one of the most accessible of the state's refuges, especially for those who want to explore by hiking or biking the gridwork of pavement and gravel.

♿ **Walton Ranch** (541-367-6186), 20 miles east of Sweet Home off Highway 20. From December through May a herd of **Roosevelt elk** graze on this 25-acre tract. A 400-yard, handicapped-accessible interpretive trail leads to viewing platforms that offer prime vantage points.

E. E. WILSON WILDLIFE AREA

✷ Lodging

BED & BREAKFASTS

Albany

Brier Rose Inn (1-888-848-4395; brierroseinn@cmug.com) 206 Seventh Avenue S. W., Albany 97321. As full as Albany seems to be with historic homes, this 1886 Queen Anne Victorian stands out with its turrets and towers, balconies and bay windows, wraparound porch and long front steps, all of it restored to its original noble elegance. Located in the center of Albany's historic districts, the inn is surrounded by other homes reminiscent of the days when Albany was the commercial hub and economic force of the mid–Willamette Valley. In addition, 15 antiques shops, as well as numerous stores and restaurants, lie only a stroll away. "We are a city inn," says owner Dick Evans. Of the inn's five guest rooms, three come with private baths ($69–125). A full breakfast, served in a dining room that retains its original beamed ceilings and pressed wallpaper, is included.

Country Oaks Farm (541-928-6375; stay@countryoaksfarm.com; www.countryoaksfarm.com), 35296 S. W. Riverside Drive, Albany 97321. Located along a quiet stretch of countryside, this B&B offers views of the Coast Range from its gazebo or patio, as well as two guest rooms that share 1-1/2 baths and come with a full breakfast ($55–65).

Aurora

Quilter's Inn at Aurora (1-800-246-1574; charw@teleport.com: www.quiltersinnataurora.com), 15109 Second Street N. E., Aurora 97002. Even though this two-story inn was built in 1995, both its exterior and interior are designed to match the historic architecture of the 1856 Aurora Colony as well as the Historic District in which it stands. The inn is also designed for those who follow some of the traditional crafts of the pioneer colony. "If you love anything about spinning, weaving, quilting, or handwork, then you'll enjoy your stay here," says owner Charlotte Wirfs. "Should you just happen to bring along a sewing machine, spinning wheel, quilting, or embroidery hoop, there is plenty of room at the inn to settle down and finish a project." The inn's three guest rooms all have private baths and come with a full breakfast, and the two upstairs rooms have private balconies ($95–110).

Willamette Gables Bed & Breakfast (503-678-2195; innkeeper@willamettegables.com; www.willamettegables.com), 10323 Schuler Road, Aurora 97002. On a forested hillside above the Willamette River lies this 5-acre estate and its grand home that seem transported from out of the Deep South: twin chimneys and white columns, gabled dormers and a long veranda, crystal chandeliers and a winding staircase, white wicker furniture and baby grand piano—it even has guest rooms named "Magnolia" and "Varina" (the latter named for Varina Howell, second wife of Jefferson Davis). A sense of southern serenity and hospitality also seems to be part of the amenities here. "Our location is perfect for those who are looking for a little bit of heaven here on earth," says owner Laurel Cookman, "peace and quiet, tranquillity and a chance to be spoiled rotten." All five of the guest rooms come with private baths, "a full from-scratch breakfast," and a nearby view of the easygoing

Willamette River flowing down below ($135–165).

Brownsville

Atavista Farm (541-466-5566; AtaVistaFarm@Centurytel.net; http://home.centurytel.net/Atavista/), 35580 Highway 228, Brownsville 97327. Standing in the middle of 70 acres of still-producing farmland and surrounded by an acre of gardens, this 1876 Italianate Victorian has two guest rooms with private baths ($105–115). A full breakfast is included.

Carlton

Lobenhaus Bed & Breakfast (1-888-339-3375; innkeeper@lobenhaus.com; www.lobenhaus.com), 6975 N. E. Abbey Road, Carlton 97111. If you find yourself with a hankering to surf the TV channels during a stay at the Lobenhaus, you're out of luck. The guest rooms at this trilevel lodge have no televisions. They have no telephones, either. What they do have are private baths, king or queen beds with down comforters, and doorways to decks that overlook the woods and pond of this 27-acre site ($120). A full breakfast is included. (Of course, if you really *must* see that show or make that call, the lodge has two common living rooms with television as well as an on-site private phone booth.) "A marvelous home to relax in," owner Shari Lobenstein says about her B&B. "A place for fresh-air strolling and fine dining." Children older than 10 are welcome when accompanied by "well-behaved parents."

Corvallis

A Bed & Breakfast on the Green (1-888-757-7321; neoma@bandbonthegreen.com; www.travelassist.com/reg/or17-26.html), 2515 S. W. 45th Street, Corvallis 97333. Standing on the edge of a golf course—hence, "on the green"—this 1952 two-story home features a wraparound porch, big decks, and an eclectic decor ranging from Victorian to Oriental. Its four guest rooms each come with a private bath and a full breakfast served on china and crystal ($70–87).

Chapman House (541-929-3059; bbhouse@peak.org; www.peak.org/~bbhouse), 6120 S. W. Country Club Drive, Corvallis 97333. Standing on 23 acres in the rolling hills 3 miles from downtown, this Tudor home is adjacent to the paved footpath running between Corvallis and Philomath, offering 30 miles of trails to walkers, joggers, and bikers. Its rooms come with private baths, a full breakfast, and enough glass to capture the views ($79–129).

The Courtyard Inn (1-800-647-7136; innkeeper@courtyard-inn.com; www.courtyard-inn.com), 2435 N. W. Harrison Boulevard, Corvallis 97330. When this four-winged Colonial building with its open courtyard was built in 1949, it was the largest sorority house at Oregon State University. Now it has been remodeled into a B&B containing 10 guest rooms with private baths ($69–147). In addition, the inn contains two living rooms, a parlor, and a library—along with grand pianos and fireplaces—and it serves a continental breakfast (included in rates).

Harrison House (1-800-233-6248; stay@corvallis-lodging.com; www.corvallis-lodging.com), 2310 N. W. Harrison Boulevard, Corvallis 97330. Check into this 1939 two-story Dutch Colonial home with its English cottage garden, and you'll find locally made chocolate truffles waiting for you in your room. Two of the rooms come with private baths and two with a shared bathroom ($90–100). The full breakfast can include local berries in season as well as such specialties as stuffed French toast with berry sauce or a stuffed croissant with smoked salmon and eggs.

Nutcracker Sweet Bed & Breakfast (541-752-0702; innkeeper@nutcrackersweetinn.com; www.nutcrackersweetinn.com), 3407 N. W. Harrison Boulevard, Corvallis 97330. As you approach this house situated in a tree-lined, historic neighborhood, you'll find nutcrackers awaiting your arrival. "A nutcracker-lined pathway leads to our 1927 French Provincial home," says owner Coy Scroggins, "and the home itself is filled with the warmth of old-world charm, gracious hospitality, and cordial friendship." Much of the charm appears in the form of antiques collected by Coy and his wife, Kathy, during the 20 years they spent serving in the U.S. Army in Europe. Today the home's guest room contains part of that collection, including traditional nutcrackers handcrafted from the Erzgebirge region of Germany. As far as the B&B aspect of the room is concerned, it comes with a four-poster bed, a private bath, and a full breakfast ($95). Other amenities include a sauna, hot tub, and backyard putting green. The entire package, Coy says, is designed to give guests "a relaxing and memorable experience."

Dayton

Wine Country Farm (1-800-261-3446; innkeeper@winecountryfarm.com; www.winecountryfarm.com), 6855 Breyman Orchards Road, Dayton 97114. If enthusiasm is a requirement of being an innkeeper, then Wine Country Farm's Joan Davenport might have been born to the role. "Can you tell I love doing this and guiding people around our beautiful wine country?" she says about accommodating guests in this 1910 hilltop inn that's surrounded by valley and mountain views as well as the farm's own vineyards. (You can sample the wines produced here in the wine-tasting room.) The seven guest rooms all come with private baths, and several are suites with living rooms and fireplaces ($95–135). "All of these rooms have spectacular views," Joan says, "and we serve a fantastic country farm breakfast." Children older than 12 are welcome.

Detroit

Repose and Repast (503-854-3204; berthels@open.org; www.reposeandrepast.com), 165 S. Detroit Avenue, Detroit 97342. At this B&B, the repose comes in the evening and the repast in the morning, and in between comes the opportunity to explore the forest and lake that make this part of the canyon of the North Santiam River something of an outdoor lover's playground. "Detroit Lake is Oregon's premier recreation lake," says owner Tee Berthel. "It has two marinas and a plethora of aquatic activities, and it's only a five-minute walk from the B&B in any of three directions. Hiking, bicycling, and other recreation are as close as walking out the front door." Guests here stay in either the Sunrise Room on the east or the Sunset Room on the west, which share a bathroom and come with a full breakfast ($55–60).

Grand Ronde

Granny Franny's Farm (1-800-553-9002; smithte@macnet.com; www.

sites.onlinemac.com/~smithte), 50730 S. W. Hebo Road, Grand Ronde 97347. Besides having one of the great names of any B&B anywhere, Granny Franny's gives guests the chance to stay at a family farm, critters and all. Yet because **Spirit Mountain Casino** is a short drive away, you can arrange to be shuttled back and forth. The farm's two guest rooms share two bathrooms ($65), and its full breakfast can include waffles, crêpes, or French toast (you can even get your coffee in bed). As a bonus, it's okay if you want to help feed the farm's animals.

Lafayette

Kelty Estate Bed & Breakfast (1-800-867-3740; jarwross@aol.com; www.keltyestatebb.com), 675 Third Street, Lafayette 97127. Standing on a sprawl of lawn growing 200-year-old trees, this 1872 Colonial home offers two rooms with private baths and a full breakfast that includes Oregon-grown products ($90–95).

McMinnville

Baker Street Inn (1-800-870-5575; cheryl@bakerstreetinn.com; www.bakerstreetinn.com), 129 S. E. Baker Street, McMinnville 97128. Located near downtown McMinnville but landscaped as a country home, this 1914 two-story Craftsman and its adjacent cottage have a total of five guest rooms with private baths ($95–125). All come with a full breakfast, which may include waffles, quiche, croissants, or French toast. Children are welcome in the cottage.

Brightridge Farm (503-843-5230; brightridge@brightridgefarmbnb.com; www.brightridgefarmbnb.com), 18575 Brightridge Road, McMinnville 97128. Standing on 10 acres of hillside in the foothills of the **Coast Range,** this B&B's nearest neighbors are farms and vineyards. Both guest rooms face the sunset side of the classic farmhouse and come with queen beds, private baths and decks, and a full breakfast that features locally grown, organic ingredients ($105–115).

Dielschneider Carriage House (503-472-9240; contact@dielschneider-carriagehouse.com; www.dielschneidercarriagehouse.com), 610 Cowls Street, McMinnville 97218. In case you wonder if this home was *really* a carriage house, you should know that when it was remodeled in 1977, two bales of hay were still upstairs. That upstairs today is an open loft bedroom that's part of a B&B suite located on the grounds of a 1905 home built by the son of an early McMinnville settler. "It's just a lovely, completely private cottage in a beautiful historical setting," says host Wayne Pyzer. The rest of the suite includes a sleeper sofa downstairs that sleeps two (maximum occupancy is four), a living room, an equipped kitchen, and a full breakfast selected from a menu and delivered to the suite ($125; children under 6 free).

Hotel Oregon (1-888-472-8427; www.hoteloregon.com), 310 N. E. Evans Street, McMinnville 97128. In Oregon, one of the best things that can happen to a building fading and wobbling with age is to be adopted by the McMenamin brothers, who are regionally famous for restoring historical buildings to their youthful elegance and then adding a first-class pub. The Hotel Oregon is just such a project. Built in 1905, the four-story hotel now incorporates modern comforts into its historic features, including 42 guest rooms in the upper three stories, a **pub and restaurant** on the ground floor, bars in the cellar and on the rooftop, and historical photographs of the old hotel lining the hallways. Rates range from $75–125 and breakfast is included. Guests have their choice of private or shared baths, and children under 6 stay free.

Mattey House (503-434-5058; seed@ matteyhouse.com; www.matteyhouse.com), 10221 N. E. Mattey Lane, McMinnville 97128. Key attractions of this Queen Anne Victorian farmhouse include stained-glass windows, high ceilings, a fireplace, and views of the orchards behind the house. Each of the four upstairs guest rooms has a private bath ($95–120) and comes with a multicourse breakfast that features Willamette Valley–grown food.

Orchard View Inn (503-472-0165), 16540 N. W. Orchard View Road, McMinnville 97128. Built as an octagon, sided with redwood, and overlooking some of the forests and meadows of the valley's wine country, this 1975 inn offers two rooms with a private bath ($80) and two with a shared bath ($75), all of which come with a full breakfast.

Steiger Haus (503-472-0821; stay@steigerhaus.com; www.steigerhaus.com), 360 S. E. Wilson Street, McMinnville 97128. Standing on a hillside above Cozine Creek, its sun-gathering windows and long deck overlooking a yard that resembles a park, the Steiger Haus counts birds, deer, and even pheasants among its neighbors, though it's still within walking distance of downtown McMinnville. The inn offers five guest rooms with private baths ($70–130), and its full breakfast includes specialties such as seasonal fruit, blueberry muffins, and Belgian waffles. Children older than 10 are welcome.

Youngberg Hill Vineyard Inn (1-888-657-8668; youngberghill@ netscape.net; www.youngberghill.com), 10660 S. W. Youngberg Hill Road, McMinnville 97128. High on a hilltop stands this expansive inn, its roof peaked with gables, its sides glazed with windows and hung with decks, all of it surrounded by acres of private vineyards and miles of mountain views that take in both the Cascades and the Coast Range. All four of its rooms and three of its suites come with private baths and a three-course breakfast that features a three-item entrée ($139–239).

Monmouth

Howell House (1-866-403-6951; howell@moriah.com; www.moriah.com/howell), 212 N. Knox, Monmouth, 97361. More than a historic Victorian in a small university town, the 1891 Howell House is home to a remarkable garden that contains 80 varieties of roses (both heirloom and modern) as well as a gazebo and covered spa; while inside, the gold-leaf wallpaper, original woodwork, claw-foot tubs, and antique furnishings are as historic as the house itself. Three of the guest rooms come with private bathrooms, and two share a bath for overnight rates ranging from $69 to $110. In addition, the breakfast menu can include Belgian waffles, blueberry French toast, or Pacific shrimp and cheddar omelets. You might even persuade hostess Sandra Boylan, a classical pianist, to furnish some breakfast music. Children older than 12 are welcome.

Mulino

Mulino House (503-349-9684; innkeeper@mulinohouse.com; www.mulinohouse.com), Highway 213, Mulino 97042. This old house's most recent story has a happy ending. "The house is an 1887 Victorian, owned by my grandparents for 50 years," says owner Roger Engle. "My brother and I purchased it in 2000 after it had suffered through 45 years of neglect, and after 2 years of work it's a showplace." It's also one of the region's newest inns, and its accommodations include three guest rooms with private baths ($85) and two rooms with shared baths ($60). These come with a full breakfast as well as the potential for an even fuller itinerary. "Plenty to see and do in the area," Roger says, "from fishing to skydiving and endless sight-seeing on paved roads."

Newberg

Avellan Inn (503-537-9161; innkeeper @avellaninn.com; www.avellaninn.com), 16900 N. E. Highway 240, Newberg 97132. Woods, orchards, gardens, and a pond lay scattered across the 12 acres that this inn calls home. Beyond its landscaped borders, among the hills that form the sloped walls of the valley, **20 wineries lie within a 10-mile radius.** The inn's two guest rooms ($98–115) come with private baths as well as a multicourse breakfast that can include homemade breads, jams, and granola.

Entheos Estate (503-625-1390; entheos@turbomgmt.com), 36280 N. E. Wilsonville Road, Newberg 97132. A stay at this home built in the style of a French chateau gives you the chance to wander its 5 acres located along the Willamette River and maybe stop a while at one of the sitting benches, the swing, or the hammock placed near the water. Its four rooms all come with private baths ($125) and a breakfast that can include entrées such as omelets, French toast, garden sausage, or fresh salmon.

Springbrook Hazelnut Farm (1-800-793-8528; ellen@nutfarm.com; www.nutfarm.com), 30295 N. Highway 99W, Newberg 97132. Age and authenticity—these are two distinguishing features of the Springbrook Hazelnut Farm. "The most wonderful thing about it is that it's the real thing," says owner Ellen McClure, "an intact Oregon nut farm from the turn of the century." The property includes the inn, a cottage, and a carriage house; 60 acres of orchards and 10 acres of vegetable and flower gardens; a pool and a tennis court; even a pond with a canoe and a barn with a **premium winery.** Guest accommodations include four rooms with private baths ($95–195) and two with shared baths ($95), and a full breakfast served in the dining room, the cottage, or the carriage house. "The proprietors are great cooks," Ellen says, "and breakfast is an event." Children older than 16 are welcome.

Salem

A Creekside Inn, the Marquee House (1-800-949-0837; rickiemh@open.org; www.marqueehouse.com), 333 Wyatt Court N. E., Salem 97301. Running through the heart of Salem is Mill Creek, and standing on its bank is this 1930s Mount Vernon Colonial that's within walking distance of Willamette University, the State Capitol, and downtown Salem. Of its five guest rooms, three come with private baths, one with a fireplace, and all with a full breakfast ($65–95). For film fans, a highlight of a stay here is the nightly movie with a bottomless popcorn bowl.

Sheridan

Bethell Lodging (1-866-842-2686; sandy@bethell-lodging.com; www.bethell-lodging.com), 17950 Highway 22, Sheridan 97378. A combination family estate, logging museum, and wine-country headquarters, this B&B stands on 10 acres of woods, lawn, and gardens. "We are only 30 minutes from the ocean beaches," says owner Sandra Boylan, "and near a variety of art galleries, museums, golf courses, and gardens." The guest rooms here come with private baths and entrances as well as a full breakfast ($90–110). In addition, guests have a spa at their disposal. "The outdoor hot tub is surrounded by tall firs and wildflower meadows," Sandra says, "and guests may choose a free bottle of wine from the home's wine rack."

Mill Creek Gardens Bed & Breakfast (1-877-792-4737; millcreekgardens-bb.com), 4430 Mill Creek Road, Sheridan 97378. Running water, flowering gardens, and towering firs are part of the landscape of this B&B located on the bank of Mill Creek. Its two antiques-furnished guest rooms come with private baths and entrances as well as a full breakfast ($125).

Silverton

East View Country Inn (503-508-6796; info@eastviewcountry.com; www.eastviewcountry.com), 5152 East View Lane N. E., Silverton 97381. Located a mile outside Silverton, this ranch-style home enjoys countryside quiet and valley views that are part of what owners Christine and Trevor Owen describe as "a gentleman's farm." The inn's two guest rooms come with private baths and a full breakfast ($65–75).

The Egg Cup Inn (1-877-417-1461), 11920 Sioux Road N. E., Silverton 97381. Named for its large egg-cup collection, this home in the country is distinguished by its 3-acre **arboretum.** Its two guest rooms have private baths and come with a full breakfast ($60–75).

Water Street Inn (866-873-3344; info@thewaterstreetinn.com; www.thewaterstreetinn.com), 421 N. Water Street, Silverton 97381. Downtown Silverton's 1890 Wolfard Hotel recently began a second life as this modern inn that retains its historic grandeur. Here you can sit on the porch swing or in front of the fireplace, take a stroll through the city or to the banks of Silver Creek. Its five guest rooms come with private baths and a full breakfast served in the formal dining room ($115–150).

Stayton

Our Place in the Country (1-888-678-2580; ourplace@wvi.com; www.oregon-bed-breakfast.com), 9297 Boedigheimer Road, Stayton 97383. So many birds flock to the gardens and grounds of this 1911 farmhouse and its 10 hilltop acres that owners Dave and Lynn Sweetland put out 10 *pounds* of seed every day. The inn's four guest rooms feature king or queen beds, private baths, and views of farmland, gardens, or the Cascade Mountains ($85–110). The full breakfast might include such house specialties as featherbed eggs, crab quiche, apple and sausage omelets, and freshly baked scones and bread.

Sweet Home

Santiam River Resort (541-367-4837; srr@relax-here.com; www.relax-here.com), 27945 Highway 20, Sweet Home 97386. Originally built in 1936 by a local lumber baron, this riverside lodge has been remodeled into what owner Pennie Farrington calls a "mini-resort B&B with the ambiance of the 1930s and the comforts of the 21st century." Included in the resort, which stands on the bank of the South Santiam River, are a heated pool and spa as well as three guest rooms that come with queen beds, private baths, and a full breakfast ($90–175). "What sets us apart from other resorts," Pennie says, is the special care we extend to our guests." One guest in particular, she says, summarized this care by commenting, "Somehow, magically, you know how to walk the line between giving your guests freedom and privacy and yet being accommodating."

COTTAGES

Corvallis

Brooklane Cottage (541-754-0258; riverkids@hotmail.com; www.brooklanecottage.com), 1923 S. W. Brooklane Drive, Corvallis 97333. Standing small and lovely in the shade of a tall sequoia, this 763-square-foot cottage is as much a tribute to a craftsman's skill as it is a guest house. The attention to detail that went into its construction also shows itself in the furnishings, which include everything you need for an extended stay, from a queen bed and large bathtub to equipped kitchen and laundry facilities ($115; breakfast extra).

Fischer House Cottage (541-752-3249; joeom@msn.com; www.visitcorvallis.com/fischer.html), 460 S. W. Jefferson Avenue, Corvallis 97333. Shaded by sycamore trees, this fully furnished guest cottage stands in downtown Corvallis, yet its landscaped grounds, which include a garden and koi pond, resemble a country estate ($80; no meals served).

McMinnville

Gahr Farm (503-472-6960; garhrfarm@moriah.com; www.gahrfarm.com), 18605 S. W. Masonville Road, McMinnville 97128. Guests at Gahr Farm have not only their own cottage but also a window to a 350-acre world managed as a native-plant and wildlife reserve. "The forest, wetlands, and grasslands have a broad range of native trees, shrubs, and flowering plants," says owner Ted Gahr, "which provide habitat for a wide diversity of birds and other wildlife—elk, deer, bobcats, ducks, hawks, frogs, butterflies, and on and on." In addition, miles of trails let you explore the farm as extensively as you'd like. The guest cottage is a small home in itself, complete with an equipped kitchen and laundry facilities ($65–95). "Our guests seem very enthused about their experience on the farm," Ted says. "Most say they plan to return, and many have."

✱ Where to Eat

DINING OUT

Corvallis

The Gables (541-752-3364), 1121 N. W. Ninth, Corvallis. A landmark of Corvallis dining for almost 50 years, the Gables seems to get even better with age. From its fresh soup and bread to its seafood and game dishes, everything served comes with a high degree of professional service.

Le Bistro (541-754-6680), 150 S. W. Madison, Corvallis. Even though in this university town the Left Bank refers to the Willamette River rather than to the Seine, Corvallis can still boast of being home to Le Bistro, a fine French restaurant in the mid-Valley. This downtown restaurant offers diners an intimate atmosphere, superb cooking, and fresh ingredients.

Dayton

Joel Palmer House (503-864-2995), 600 Ferry Street, Dayton. One thing you can bet on at the Joel Palmer House: Whatever you order, from the appetizers to the entrées, it's bound to include mushrooms, the signature ingredient of this formal restaurant that resides in the 1850s home of one of Oregon's most famous pioneers. Wild or domestic, sprinkled across the top or lying on the side, the mushroom is the star of chef Jack Czarnecki's culinary style.

Dundee

Dundee Bistro (503-554-1650), 100-A S. W. Seventh Street, Dundee. A bit of Italy settled down in the Willamette Valley's wine country, this bistro combines a Tuscan atmosphere with Northwest food and specialty pizzas.

Red Hills (503-538-8224), 276 Highway 99W, Dundee. This restaurant's Craftsman architecture, European dishes, and international wines combine to make an elegant dining experience for travelers along Highway 99W; in fact, many come especially for Red Hills's talked-about lunches and dinners.

Tina's (503-538-8880), 760 Highway 99W, Dundee. By combining locally grown ingredients with French-inspired dishes, Tina's has created a style and atmosphere some locals call "Oregon French." Homegrown herbs, homemade desserts, and regional wines add to the attraction of this cozy restaurant in its modest house.

Gates

Frontier Country Restaurant (503-897-2960), Highway 22, Gates. Some folks in the area call this restaurant "Bird Land," and a peek into the dining room will show you why: There behind a window stands an aviary all aflutter with pheasants, quail, ducks, pigeons, finches, parakeets, parrots, and other birds of a feather, sometimes more than two dozen species. "You learn what gets along," says owner Lee Reynolds. And oh yes, even though the birds steal the show, the food here is fine.

McMinnville

Nick's Italian Café (503-434-4471), 521 E. Third Street, McMinnville. A longtime tradition for Italian cooking in this part of the Willamette Valley, Nick's offers five-course dinners that carry diners from antipasto, soup, and salad through pasta, entrée, and dessert—a meal considered a classic in this part of the wine country.

Salem

Alessandro's 120 (503-370-9951), 120 Commercial Street, Salem. At this downtown favorite that specializes in pasta and seafood, a multicourse dinner can be served with a surprise: Simply let the staff show up with the dishes they've chosen for you.

Morton's Bistro Northwest (503-585-1113), 1128 Edgewater Street, Salem. An intimate atmosphere radiating from soft lights and wooden beams, a Northwestern menu featuring fresh foods and ingredients, and a friendly staff waiting tables as though they enjoy their work make Morton's a memorable dining experience on the west bank of the Willamette River.

Silverton

Silver Grille Café (503-873-4035), 206 E. Main Street, Silverton. With an elegance created by dim lights and wooden wainscoting, the Silver Grille matches its menu to the seasons and what the local farms produce. In addition, the café does double duty as a **wine shop,** ensuring a large and varied list. As a result, the meals served at this historic downtown location can be as refined as its decor.

EATING OUT

Canby

Jarboe's Grill (503-266-3805), 101 N. Elm Street, Canby. Owned and operated by a local fellow who seems to know what the town wants in a restaurant, Jarboe's Grill is a longtimer on the Canby food scene. Here it's tough to go wrong with any choice from either the lunch or dinner menu, and the big-house look with the wraparound porch adds to the homey feel of the place.

Tres Café (503-263-8737), 243 N. W. Second Street, Canby. This is a local favorite, a café that offers a gourmet lunch along with a wide variety of soups, sandwiches, and light meals.

Carlton

Café Bisbo (503-852-7248), 214 Main Street, Carlton. This small town that stands on the edge of the Willamette Valley's wine country can boast that its Café Bisbo serves some of the best authentic Italian food in the region. It's so traditional, in fact, that owner-chef Claudio Bisbocci spoke little English when he opened the café, which seems to breathe the wonderful aromas of basil and garlic and olive oil.

Corvallis

Big River (541-757-0694), 101 N. W. Jackson Street, Corvallis. Built something like a warehouse with its tall ceilings and open beams, Big River offers an original and changing menu, Northwest food that ranges from clams to duck, a variety of vegetarian dishes and wood-fired pizzas, and live jazz.

Bombs Away Café (541-757-7221), 2527 N. W. Monroe Avenue, Corvallis. Whether you're a carnivore or a vegetarian, the Bombs Away Café has a plate for you—even if you're a Tex-Mex aficionado. The food here is healthy, the service is fast, and the kids have a menu section of their own.

Magenta, 1425 N. W. Monroe Avenue, Suite A, Corvallis. Where you gonna go if you get a hankering for emu or buffalo steaks? Magenta. Located near the Oregon State University campus, this small hub of creative cookery is decorated with antiques and plants and specializes in unusual foods well prepared.

Detroit

Korner Post Restaurant (503-854-3735), 100 S. Detroit Avenue, Detroit. Located near the center of Detroit, a former logging and mill town whose giant reservoir has become a destination for Northwest boaters and campers, the Korner Post is home to an antique decor, a homey atmosphere, friendly service, and big servings of good food.

Idanha

Marion Forks Restaurant (503-854-3669), Highway 22, Idanha. Standing within a stone's throw of the confluence of Marion Creek and the North Santiam River, Marion Forks Restaurant is built and decorated in the tradition of the old-time mountain lodges. Here you'll find friendly service and moderate prices, as well as a view of one of the Cascade's pristine streams, especially if you sit on the deck.

Mulino

Mulino Airport Café (503-829-7555), 26687 S. Highway 213,

Mulino. If it seems strange to dine at an airport without catching a flight afterward, then consider that private planes land at the Mulino Airport every day specifically for the privilege of dining at its café. In fact, on weekends you can expect a crowd here. You can also expect good food served at all three meals as well as daily specials for lunch and dinner. "Always worth a stop," says a local resident who also says he does his fair share of stopping here.

Molalla

El Charrito (503-829-3017), 117 E. Main Street, Molalla. A local favorite, El Charrito serves authentic Mexican food and great margaritas.

Ricky D's Pizza and Ice Cream Parlor (503-829-8801), 111 E. Main Street, Molalla. Decorated with sports memorabilia from the local high school's teams, Ricky D's is a hometown favorite for its pizza as well as for a salad bar that some locals say earns the ranking of "one of the great ones if not the best."

Salem

The Arbor Café (503-588-2353), 380 High Street N. E., Salem. A bright spot of color and casualness that seems almost trapped in a downtown office building, the Arbor Café is a local favorite for its pastries and soups, sandwiches and salads. It also offers Oregon microwbrews and wines.

Fleur de Sel (503-363-3822), 1210 State Street, Salem. Even though it's French in its name as well as its cooking, you can expect American-style substance and portions at this downtown bistro. The combination, however, produces some outstanding results.

Silverton

Birdhouse Restaurant (503-873-0382), 211 Oak Street, Silverton. Named for the more than 300 birdhouses that decorate the place, the Birdhouse Restaurant offers a full menu but earns particular raves for its hamburgers and homemade chicken and dumplings.

✷ Special Events

March: **Amity Daffodil Festival** (503-835-2181), Amity.

May–June: **Strawberry Festival** (541-258-7164), Lebanon. Even though this festival began in 1909, its star attraction continues to make an annual appearance: "The World's Largest Strawberry Shortcake," whose ingredients include 382 pounds of flour, 254 pounds of sugar, 20.5 gallons of milk, and 110 dozen eggs. When the shortcake is finally put together, it's covered with 100 pounds of powdered sugar, 3,000 pounds of strawberries, and 60 gallons of whipped cream. Oh yes—it feeds 17,000 people, and it's all free.

July: **Salem Art Fair and Festival** (503-581-2228), Salem. **World Championship Timber Carnival** (541-928-0911; www.timbercarnival.com), **Fourth of July weekend,** Albany. Advertising itself as "the world's largest logging event," this timber carnival since 1941 has celebrated the muscle and the mythology of the logger. Over the course of three days, contestants grunt and sweat their way through competition based on traditional jobs of a premechanized timber industry: ax throwing, block chopping, log rolling, speed climbing, and tree topping.

July–August: **Great Oregon Steam-Up** (503-393-2424; www.antiquepowerland.com), Antique Powerland Museum, 3995 Brooklake Road N. E. (take exit 263 on Interstate 5), Brooks. It's one thing to read about or look at the machines that made our world possible, replacing horses in the fields and on the roads, but it's quite another to climb aboard such contraptions for a symbolic ride back to the days when muscle or steam power turned our wheels and gears. This event gives visitors the chance to take that ride.

August: **Oregon Jamboree** (541-367-8800), Sweet Home. **Mexican Fiesta** (503-982-8221), Woodburn. **Santiam Canyon Stampede** (503-769-2799), Stayton–Sublimity. **Scandinavian Festival** (541-998-9372), Junction City.

August–September: **Oregon State Fair** (503-947-3247) from the **third Thursday in August through Labor Day,** Salem. This is the annual party the state throws for itself, a celebration revolving like a Ferris wheel around hog barns and horse races, corn dogs and square dancing, flower gardens and bungee towers, and all the other stuff that can be squeezed onto midways, beneath big tops, and into the seats of rides that plunge and buck and whir their way across a summertime sky. It's enough to make many Oregonians believe, as the characters sing in the musical *State Fair,* that "our state fair is a great state fair, the best state fair in the state."

September: **Oktoberfest** (541-845-9440), Mount Angel. The traditional celebration of the summer's harvest, as well as the certainty that the darkness of winter is closing in, can spur those living in the northern climes to don Lederhosen, grab steins of beer, and dance the polka. And thus the reason for Oktoberfests, those Bavarian festivals that feature carnivals, barbecues, pony rides, bike races, and, of course, beer gardens and polka music. **Corvallis Fall Festival** (541-752-9655), Corvallis.

November: **Wine Country Thanksgiving** (503-646-2985), Yamhill County.

SOUTH WILLAMETTE VALLEY

GUIDANCE **Bureau of Land Management: Eugene District** (541-683-6600), 2890 Chad Drive, Eugene 97401.

Cottage Grove Chamber of Commerce (541-942-2411; www.cgchamber.com), 700 E. Gibbs Street, Suite C, Cottage Grove 97424.

Creswell Chamber of Commerce (541-895-5151; www.creswell-or.com), 55 N. Fifth Street, Creswell 97426.

Eugene Convention and Visitors Association (1-800-547-5445; www.VisitLaneCounty.org), 115 W. Eighth, Suite 190, Eugene 97401.

Junction City–Harrisburg Area Chamber of Commerce (541-998-6154; www.junctioncity.com), 235 W. Sixth Avenue, Junction City 97448.

Oakridge–Westfir Chamber of Commerce (541-782-4146; www.oakridgechamber.com), Greenwaters Park on Highway 58, Oakridge 97463.

Oregon State Parks (503-378-6305), State Parks and Recreation Department, 525 Trade Street S. E., Salem 97301.

Siuslaw National Forest (541-750-7000), 4077 S. W. Research Way, Corvallis 97330.

Springfield Area Chamber of Commerce (541-746-1651; www.springfieldchamber.org), 101 S. A Street, Springfield 97477.

Umpqua National Forest (541-672-6601), 2900 N. W. Stewart Parkway, Roseburg 97470; **Cottage Grove Ranger District** (541-942-5591).

Willamette National Forest: Headquarters (541-465-6521), 211 E. Seventh Avenue, Eugene 97401; **Blue River Ranger District** (541-822-3317); **McKenzie Ranger District** (541-822-3381); **Middle Fork Ranger District** (541-782-2283); **Middle Fork (Lowell) Ranger District** (541-937-2129).

GETTING THERE The South Willamette Valley can be reached from the east by Highways 242, 126, and 58; from the west by Highways 36 and 126; and from the north and south by Interstate 5 and Highways 99W and 99E.

MEDICAL EMERGENCY **Cottage Grove Community Hospital** (541-942-0511), 1340 Birch Avenue, Cottage Grove.

McKenzie–Willamette Medical Center (541-726-4400), 1460 G Street, Springfield.

Sacred Heart Medical Center (541-686-7300), 1255 Hilyard Street, Eugene.

* To See

MUSEUMS **Lane County Historical Museum** (541-0687-4239), 740 W. 13th Avenue, Eugene. With a collection dating back to the days of the Oregon Trail in the 1840s, this museum preserves the history of the area in the days when it was a destination of wagon trains.

Springfield Museum (541-726-3677; www.springfieldmuseum.com), 590 Main Street, Springfield. Because logging and farming have long been the two-part backbone of this town that lies between the rivers Willamette and McKenzie, that's also what you can expect to find as the focus of its museum, which is housed in a restored 1911 Oregon Power Company transformer station listed on the **National Register of Historic Places.**

Cottage Grove Historical Museum (541-942-3963), Birch and H Streets, Cottage Grove. Housed in a former Roman Catholic Church built in 1897 and said to be the "only octagonal-shaped public building in the Northwest," this museum features displays of the area's pioneer homes, farms, and industries.

Creswell Historical Museum (541-895-5161), Fifth Street and Oregon Avenue, Creswell. The area around Creswell has long made its living from the land—from what could be harvested from forests, orchards, and dairy and grain farms. Consequently, this museum, housed in a remodeled 1889 church, captures the life of the community as it grew from its farming and logging roots.

HISTORIC HOMES **Shelton-McMurphy-Johnson House** (541-484-0808), 303 Willamette Street (exit 194B off Interstate 5), Eugene. This is a twice-built home, a Victorian mansion that burned to the ground just before its completion in the early 1880s and was then built again from out of the ashes to become the family home of Eugene physician Thomas Shelton. Adding to the drama of the resurrection of this mansionesque phoenix was the deathbed confession of a former worker on the house who, angry from getting fired from his job, started the blaze. Today the house stands on a terrace of **Skinner Butte,** surrounded by trees and sporting all the traditional, decorative nooks and crannies that any Victorian could possibly want.

Springfield Depot (541-746-1651), 101 S. A Street, Springfield. Built in 1891 and moved to its present location in 1989, this former Southern Pacific Railroad station is the oldest two-story passenger depot in Oregon. Now fully restored, the depot is listed on the **National Register of Historic Places** and serves as the city's visitors center.

Cottage Grove Historic Homes, in Cottage Grove, exit 174 on Interstate 5. Cottage Grove can claim nine historic landmarks within the city, including five homes dating to the 1890s. Four of these are located on or near River Road: the 1892 **Hon. Robert Beatch House,** the 1895 **Young House,** the 1896 **Dr. Snapp House,** and the 1896 **Stone House;** the area's oldest home, the 1893 **George Lea House,** is located nearby off Highway 226.

HISTORIC SITES **Dorris Ranch** (541-736-4544), corner of S. Second and Dorris Streets, Springfield. On this ranch where Oregon's first commercial filbert orchard began growing in 1892, a 2-mile trail leads visitors through the orchards and pastures, wetlands and forests of a "living-history farm."

COVERED BRIDGES The reason for covering wooden bridges in western Oregon was rain: the drip and drizzle and drench that rotted the timbers and trusses and reduced the life of an uncovered bridge to a decade or so. As a result, builders sided their bridges with walls, topped them with roofs, and gave early travelers shelters from the storms. **Belknap Bridge,** 3 miles southwest of McKenzie Bridge off Highway 126 and King Road W. (1966, 120 feet); **Coyote Creek Bridge,** 12 miles south of Veneta off Highway 126, Crow Road, Territorial Highway, and Battle Creek Road (1922, 60 feet); **Earnest Bridge,** 4 miles north of Marcola off Marcola and Paschelke Roads (1938, 75 feet); **Wendling Bridge,** 5 miles northeast of Marcola off Marcola and Wendling Roads (1938, 60 feet); **Goodpasture Bridge,** western edge of Vida off Highway 126 (1938, 165 feet); **Office Bridge,** 1 mile north of Westfir off Highway 58 and Aufderheide Memorial Drive (1944, 180 feet), Oregon's longest covered bridge.

Cottage Grove Area, southeast of Cottage Grove off Interstate 5: **Mosby Creek Bridge** (1920, 90 feet) and **Stewart Bridge** (1930, 60 feet), both on Mosby Creek Road; **Dorena Bridge** (1949, 105 feet) on Government Road; and **Currin Bridge** (1925, 105 feet) on Row River Road. In addition, the **Centennial Bridge,** built in 1987 to mark the 100th birthday of Cottage Grove, incorporates components of three earlier covered bridges in its construction and stands near Cottage Grove's City Hall; and the **Chamber's Bridge,** a railroad covered bridge built in 1936, is located at Harrison and River Roads.

Lowell Area, southeast of Eugene near Highway 58 and the town of Lowell: **Lowell Bridge** (1945, 165 feet), **Parvin Bridge** (1921, 75 feet); **Unity Bridge** (1936, 90 feet); and **Pengra Bridge** (1938, 120 feet).

MARKET **Eugene Saturday Market** (541-686-8885; www.eugenesaturdaymarket.org), downtown Eugene at Broadway and Eighth Avenue. Operating since 1970 and featuring more than 150 local artists, craftspeople, and chefs in its two-block area, this is the nation's oldest weekly open-air festival. It's held every Saturday, rain or shine, from April through mid-November.

GARDEN TOURS **Hendricks Park Rhododendron Garden** (541-682-5324), Summit Avenue, Eugene. In 1906 when Martha and Thomas Hendricks donated most of the land for Eugene's first city park, they may have had no idea how their garden would grow, for today this ridgeline above the Willamette River sprouts groves of **white oaks,** stands of **Douglas firs**—some older than 200 years—and more than 5,000 **rhododendrons** as well as 1,000 or so **azaleas, magnolias,** and **viburnums.** (The rhodies, first planted more than 50 years ago, cover almost 15 of the park's 77 acres.) Leading through it all is a web of trails that meander through a friendly jungle of ferns, vines, and flowers both wild and domestic.

Owen Rose Garden (541-682-5333), near the Washington–Jefferson Street bridge, Eugene. If you can't get your fill of roses, this is the place to come—the 9-acre Owen Rose Garden, which contains more than 400 varieties of roses growing from more than 4,500 rosebushes. The garden also contains beds of perennials, stands of flowering trees, and views of the Willamette River. (See also **Owen Cherry Tree** under *Natural Wonders*.)

Mount Pisgah Arboretum (541-747-3817), 5 miles southeast of Springfield off Interstate 5 (take exit 189) and Seavey Loop Road. Spread across more than 200 acres of woods and meadows on the lower slope of Mount Pisgah and the east bank of the Willamette River's Coast Fork, this arboretum provides 7 miles of all-weather trails and 22 bridges to steer thousands of yearly visitors past the wildflowers, shrubs, and trees growing at the site.

SCENIC DRIVES **Highway 99,** 50 or 130 paved miles from Portland to Salem or from Portland to Eugene. Tucked away along the forests and fields that edge the whiz-bang traffic of Interstate 5 is the **old Pacific Highway,** once the major north–south route through Oregon and still a relatively quiet byway for travelers who want to escape the freeway rush. The old road had its start in 1913 as part of the highway that ran all the way from San Diego, California, to Blaine, Washington; it became US 99 in 1926 with the beginning of the U.S. Highway System; and it was divided in 1930 into US 99E and US 99W. Today **Highway 99E** stretches 50 miles between Portland (Interstate 5 exit 307) and Salem (exit 258); and **Highway 99W,** 130 miles from Portland (exit 306) to Eugene (exit 192). Both roads offer a glimpse of a slower, quieter time, traveling near oak groves and hazelnut orchards, vineyards and pastures, farmhouses and fruit stands. (One note of caution: On weekends, Highway 99W can stack up and slow down with the traffic leaving Portland and heading for the coast.)

South Fork Alsea River Back Country Byway, 12 paved and graveled miles from Alsea to Glenbrook. This is a slow road along a winding stream that slides from out of the Coast Range, carrying steelhead in its currents and growing wildflowers and fir forests along its banks. Along the way you might find reason to pause at hiking trails, picnic areas, campgrounds, and a **waterfall.**

Aufderheide Memorial National Scenic Byway, 65 paved miles from near McKenzie Bridge on Highway 126 to Westfir near Highway 58. This winding, slow-driving road connects the South Fork McKenzie River with the North Fork Willamette River, along the way passing by or through centuries-old firs and cedars and miles of woodland streams and their **waterfalls.**

NATURAL WONDERS **Owen Cherry Tree,** Owen Rose Garden (see Garden Tours), near the Washington–Jefferson Street bridge, Eugene. In the mid-1800s, Eugene Skinner made at least three lasting contributions to his community: He established the city that adopted his first name; he donated to it the 681-foot butte that was part of his homestead and that now bears his last name; and he planted this tree. For more information call **Heritage Trees** (1-800-574-9397).

McKenzie River Waterfalls, 22 miles northeast of McKenzie Bridge off Highway 126. Two waterfalls provide a primary attraction along the McKenzie River Highway: 150-foot **Sahalie Falls,** the highest falls on the river and, a 15-minute walk away, **Kosah Falls.**

H. J. Andrews Experimental Forest, 7 miles northeast of Blue River off Highway 126 and Forest Road 15. To figure out how life works in a forest—*all* life, everything with a microbe or molecule living from soil to treetops—scientists have been using this 25-square-mile ancient forest as a living laboratory. Established by the U.S. Forest Service in 1948, the forest is home to numerous 500-year-old trees that have been the subject of extensive research since the 1970s, making it one of the most-studied forests in the world. One of the best do-it-yourself tours of the site is provided by the 3.5-mile **Lookout Creek Old-Growth Trail.**

Waldo Lake, 36 miles east of Oakridge off Highway 58 and Forest Road 5897. The state's second-deepest lake at 420 feet—nothing in the nation rivals Oregon's Crater Lake at 1,932 feet deep—Waldo Lake is one of the purest bodies of water in the world. Carved by Ice Age glaciers and now nestled inside a moraine-enclosed basin, the lake covers almost 10 square miles, and visibility into its depths can reach 100 feet.

* To Do

BICYCLING **Eugene Riverfront Trail** (541-682-5218), in Eugene, exit Interstate 5 onto Interstate 105 W. With 26 miles of paved trails linked by 68 miles of biking lanes, Eugene is something of a bicycling Mecca. The most popular trail edges along both sides of the Willamette River, where every day as many as 2,000 bikers, walkers, joggers, and skaters travel along the 12-foot-wide paths. Two of the best access points are **Alton Baker Park** and **Skinner Butte Park,** both located off Interstate 105 W.

Row River Trail, 16 paved and graveled miles from Cottage Grove to Culp Creek. Part of the abandoned Oregon and Southern Eastern Railway, which began hauling freight and supplies along this route in 1902, the Row River Trail is now a mostly paved **Rails-to-Trails** project open to hiking, biking, and horseback riding. A series of parks and trailheads line the route, part of which follows the bank of Row River and the shoreline of Dorena Lake

CAMPING ♿ **McKenzie River Highway,** east of Eugene along Highway 126 or connecting county and forest roads. **Alder Springs,** 12 miles east of McKenzie Bridge off Highway 242, 7 campsites without water; **Cold Water Cove,** 20 miles northeast of McKenzie Bridge off Highway 126, 35 campsites on the shore of Clear Lake; **Delta,** 7 miles east of Blue River off Highway 126, 38 campsites along the South Fork McKenzie River, **handicapped-accessible rest rooms and nature trail; Fish Lake,** 22 miles northeast of McKenzie Bridge, 8 campsites near the lake as well as at the junction of Highways 126 and 20; **Ice Cap,** 17 miles northeast of McKenzie Bridge off Highway 126, 14 campsites near the river; **Lake's End,** 13 miles northeast of McKenzie Bridge off Highway 126, 17 campsites on Smith Reservoir, accessible by boat only; **Limberlost,** 5 miles east of McKenzie Bridge off Highway 242, 2 tent-only campsites; **McKenzie Bridge,** 1 mile west of McKenzie Bridge off Highway 126, 40 campsites; **Mona,** 7 miles northeast of Blue River off Highway 126 and Forest Road 15, 23 campsites on the shore of Blue River Lake and near the H. J. Andrews Experimental Forest (see *To See—Natural Wonders*); **Olallie,** 11 miles northeast of McKenzie Bridge off Highway 126, 17 campsites near the river; **Paradise,** 4 miles east of McKenzie Bridge off Highway 126, 64 campsites and one of the river's better boat ramps; **Trail Bridge,** 13 miles northeast of McKenzie Bridge off Highway 126, 26 campsites near the river.

Fall Creek State Recreation Area, 15 miles southeast of Eugene off Lowell–Jasper Road, 7 developed or primitive campgrounds located near the head of Fall Creek Reservoir and the adjacent **National Recreation Trail—Bedrock, Big Pool, Broken Bowl, Cascara, Dolly Varden, Fisherman's Point,** and **Puma,** each of which serves as a trailhead for the 14-mile-long pathway that runs through a narrow, forested canyon along fairly level terrain.

Cottage Grove Area, south and east of Cottage Grove off Interstate 5 or connecting county and forest roads. **Dorena Reservoir,** east of Cottage Grove between Row River Road and Government Road, more than 120 campsites divided between **Baker Bay** and **Schwarz Park,** both popular with the area's motorboaters and skiers; **Cedar Creek,** 24 miles southeast of Cottage Grove off Government Road and Forest Road 22, 8 campsites along Brice Creek; **Cottage Grove Lake,** 5 miles south of Cottage Grove off Interstate 5 and London Road, a total of 110 lakeshore campsites divided between a developed campground (including showers) at **Pine Meadows** and a primitive campground; **Rujada,** 21 miles southeast of Cottage Grove off Government Road and Forest Road 17, 10 campsites along the upper reaches of Row River.

Mapleton Area, south and east of Mapleton off Highway 126 or connecting county and forest roads. **Archie Knowles,** 4 miles east of Mapleton off Highway 126, 9 primitive campsites located adjacent to Knowles Creek and near the highway; **Turner Creek,** 7 miles east of Mapleton off Highway 126, 8 campsites; **Whitaker Creek,** 14 miles southeast of Mapleton off Highway 126 and the Siuslaw River Road, 31 campsites at the confluence of the Siuslaw River and Whitaker Creek, an important salmon spawning grounds, and near a trailhead to the **Old Growth Ridge National Recreation Trail,** which climbs to 1,000 feet above the river.

Oakridge Area, near the town of Oakridge off Highway 58 or connecting forest and county roads. Because these campgrounds lie in the foothills and up the slopes of the Cascade Mountains, you can expect clean air, cool nights, thick forests, and icy streams and lakes. Near the head of **Lookout Point Reservoir,** northwest of Oakridge along Highway 58, are **Black Canyon, Shady,** and **Hampton,** a total of 72 campsites and nearby access to the 2-mile **Goodman Creek Trail; Blair Lake,** 17 miles northeast of Oakridge off Forest Roads 24 and 1934, 7 campsite near the shore of this trout-stocked, 35-acre lake; **Blue Pool,** 9 miles east of Oakridge off Highway 58, 25 campsites along the bank of Salt Creek and near McCredie Hot Springs; **Gold Lake,** 28 miles southeast of Oakridge off Highway 58 and Forest Road 5897, 25 campsites, a log picnic shelter, and a hiking trail to nearby Marilyn Lakes on the slope of the Cascades; **Hills Creek Reservoir,** southeast of Oakridge, more than 50 campsites divided among three camps—**Packard Creek, Sand Prairie,** and **Salmon Creek Falls,** with 2-mile **Larison Cove Trail** nearby; **Timpanogas Lake,** 43 miles southeast of Oakridge off Highway 58 and Forest Road 21, 10 campsites along a small lake that prohibits motorboats and provides a milelong shoreline trail as well as a trailhead to **Cowhorn Mountain; Middle Fork Willamette River,** 21 to 31 miles south of Oakridge off Highway 58 and Forest Road 21, 34 total campsites available in four camps—**Camper Flat, Indigo Springs, Sacandaga,** and **Secret**—all located near the river; **Waldo Lake,** 36 miles east of Oakridge off Highway 58 and Forest Road 5897, more than 200 campsites divided among four camps that lie along Oregon's second deepest lake—**Islet, North Waldo, Harralson Horse Camp,** and **Shadow Bay**—with hiking and biking trails nearby, particularly to **Betty Lake, Bobby Lake, South Waldo Shelter, Islet Beach,** and **Rigdon Lakes.**

Aufderheide Memorial Drive, along the Aufderheide Memorial Drive or connecting forest roads between Highway 126 near Blue River and Highway 58 near Westfir. **Cougar Crossing,** 12 campsites; **French Pete,** 17 campsites near the confluence of French Pete Creek and the South Fork McKenzie River, with a creekside trail that leads toward the Three Sisters Wilderness; **Frissel Crossing,** 17 campsites; **Roaring River,** 1 group campsite; **Homestead,** 7 campsites near the South Fork McKenzie River; **Kiahanie,** 19 campsites in an old-growth forest and near the North Fork of the Middle Fork Willamette River; **Skookum Creek,** 9 campsites with horse facilities and a hiking trail; **Slide Creek,** 16 campsites along the shore of Cougar Reservoir. (See also **Aufderheide Memorial National Scenic Byway** under *To See—Scenic Drives.*)

See also **Timpanogas Lake** under *Canoeing.*

CANOEING **Clear Lake,** 20 miles northeast of McKenzie Bridge off Highway 126. On this mountain lake near the headwaters of the McKenzie River, motors are forbidden.

Cascade Lakes. If you want to avoid the whine of motors on mountain lakes, scout out the following: **Betty**

Lake, Bobby Lake, and **Gold Lake,** southeast of **Oakridge** off Highway 58 and Forest Road 5897.

Opal Lake and **Timpanogas Lake,** 45 miles southeast of Oakridge off Highway 58 and Forest Roads 21 and 2154. Tucked away near the summit of the Cascades and the southern edge of the Diamond Peak Wilderness, these two small lakes lie in glacial basins surrounded by hemlocks and firs. Timpanogas, at 40 acres some three times larger than the more secluded Opal, has a campground, a milelong shoreline path, and trailheads that lead to nearby lakes.

Alton Baker Park, off Centennial Boulevard in Eugene (take exit 194B off Interstate 5). Stretching alongside the Willamette River for 5 miles, Alton Baker Park has a canal system that runs for 3.5 miles to its source near the city of Springfield. Along the way you have a chance to see **great blue herons, Canada geese,** or **beavers.**

GOLF **Riveridge Golf Course** (541-345-9161), 3800 N. Delta Street, Eugene, 18 holes.

HIKING **Mount Pisgah,** 5 miles southeast of Springfield off Interstate 5 (exit 189) and Seavey Loop Road. Rising above the rolling hills, oak groves, and small farms along this stretch of the Willamette Valley is Mount Pisgah, its grassy, 1,500-foot summit standing at the end of a mile-and-a-half trail that looks out over the Willamette River drainage and its Coast Fork. But if you don't want to climb the mountain, more than 5 miles of trails lead you to other parts of this 208-acre park.

Clear Lake, 20 miles northeast of McKenzie Bridge off Highway 126. Five miles by foot may never pass so quickly, for this relatively flat shoreline trail circles a clear, cold mountain lake on its way through old-growth forests, past lava flows, around mountain springs, and across the **McKenzie River,** one of the Northwest's premier streams.

McKenzie River Waterfalls, 22 miles northeast of McKenzie Bridge off Highway 126. A 4-mile loop beginning near the McKenzie River Highway circles two waterfalls—**Sahalie** and **Kosah**—located near the river's headwaters.

Salt Creek Waterfall Loop, 25 miles southeast of Oakridge off Highway 58 and Forest Road 5893. A 3-mile circle through a countryside of forests and canyons and streams takes you to three waterfalls: 286-foot **Salt Creek Falls,** 200-foot **Lower Diamond Creek Falls,** and 86-foot **Diamond Creek Falls.**

See also *Bicycling* and *Camping;* and *Wilder Places—Parks* and *Wilderness Areas.*

UNIQUE ADVENTURES **British Excursions.** Granted, this will take you into the world of neither tea and crumpets nor tall-hatted guardsmen standing rigidly at palace gates, but it might be fun to tell people you've visited both London and Waterloo, even if you find those towns in the Willamette Valley.

London, 10 miles south of Cottage Grove off Interstate 5 and London Road. In the early years of the 20th century, London was a community thriving with visitors who came to use the health resort's mineral springs, to attend the local rodeos, or to play tennis, croquet, and polo on the hotel lawn.

Waterloo, 5 miles southeast of Lebanon off Highway 20 and Waterloo Road. Although this town, home to 240 people, began as Kees Mill, the name changed as the result of a local, contentious lawsuit over a property settlement that evidently reminded some residents of the British victory in the historic battle with Napoleon.

* Wilder Places

PARKS **Armitage State Park,** 5 miles north of Eugene off Interstate 5 and Coburg Road, day use only. Covering more than 50 acres of the McKenzie River's south bank, Armitage State Park is a city getaway and traveler's stop for those who would swap pavement for an afternoon of lawns and trees and stream.

Eugene City Parks. Alton Baker on Centennial Boulevard, along the bank of the **Willamette River** and the city's Riverfront Trail; **Hendricks Park,** on Summit Avenue, noted for its 12-acre garden where more than 6,000 rhododendrons grow; **Skinner Butte,** on High Street, with hilltop views and riverfront trails; **Spencers Butte,** on S. Willamette Street, a small, forested mountain built from ancient lava flows that looms on the city's southern skyline and offers trails to its open summit.

Richardson Park, 6 miles north of Veneta off Highway 126 and Territorial Highway. Located on the northern shore of **Fern Ridge Lake,** this county park offers campsites, picnic facilities, and a boat ramp as well as opportunities for fishing and swimming in the lake.

Elijah Bistow State Park, 10 miles southeast of Pleasant Hill off Highway 58 and Wheeler Road, day use only. Located along the Middle Fork Willamette River, this park contains just over a square mile of land but almost 16 miles of trails. Through forests and along creek banks and wetlands these trails wander, leading hikers and bikers and equestrians through a maze of valley bottomland.

Ben and Kay Dorris State Park, 31 miles east of Eugene off Highway 126, day use only. Along a slow bend of the **McKenzie River** stands this park popular with picnickers and anglers, the stream's clean green sheen (sorry, couldn't resist the Dr. Seussish rhyme) stroking up against the rocks stretching out from the banks.

Howard J. Morton State Park, 12 miles west of McKenzie Bridge off Highway 126, day use only. Hunkered down between the highway and McKenzie River, this 24-acre park is a mostly unlogged, undeveloped sanctuary donated by Winifred K. Morton as a memorial to her husband, Howard. A fellow can't do much better than to have his name live on through such a place.

WILDERNESS AREAS **Waldo Lake,** 16 miles northeast of Oakridge off Highway 58 and Salmon Creek Road, 58 square miles. One of the deepest and purest bodies of water in the Northwest, Waldo Lake is the main attraction in this forested wilderness of lake basins, small meadows, and steep slopes sprawled across the foothills of the Cascade Mountains. Its 84 miles of trails include a number of short day hikes, some as short as half-mile walks to **Betty and Upper and Lower Marilyn Lakes.**

WILDLIFE REFUGES **Fern Ridge Wildlife Area,** 6 miles west of Eugene off Highway 126. Bordered on three sides by 8 square miles of forest, marsh, and grass, this 20-square-mile reservoir supports 250 species of birds, including **ducks** and **geese, swans** and **ospreys, great blue herons** and **bald eagles.** In addition, as many as 600 **great egrets** have recently formed a winter colony here.

Buckhead Wildlife Area, 5 miles northwest of Oakridge off Highway 58 and W. Boundary Road. This is a small but lively refuge: 250 acres on the Middle Fork of the Willamette River, its willowy stream banks and fir forests home to wildlife ranging from **turtles** to **ospreys.**

✷ Lodging

INNS

Eugene

Excelsior Inn (1-800-321-6963, info@excelsiorinn.com; www.excelsior-inn.com), 754 E. 13th Avenue, Eugene 97401. Even though it's located just a block from the University of Oregon campus, this inn can give visitors something of a foreign lodging adventure. "The Excelsior Inn offers a classical European experience," says innkeeper Michele Wilson, "especially in its internationally recognized cuisine and award-winning desserts." Beyond the food, the inn has 14 guest rooms with private baths. Benvenuti!

BED & BREAKFASTS

Blue River

Drift Inn Bed & Breakfast (541-822-3822; driftnfish@aol.com), 51592 McKenzie Highway, Blue River 97413. A stay at this 1950 two-story home puts one foot into a world of outdoor adventure, for this inn specializes in making arrangements for excursions along the river. "We are on the McKenzie River with a beautiful view and access to the water," says owner Carolyn Gabriel. "My husband, Mel, is a river guide, so fishing and drifting is available." The inn has two guest rooms, one with a private bath and both with queen beds ($85). "We serve a hearty breakfast," Carolyn says, "and often chocolate cake with tea or coffee is available in the afternoons."

River's Edge Inn (541-822-3258; innkeeper@riversedgeinn.com; www.riversedgeinn.com), 91241 Blue River Drive, Blue River 97413. If you want to slumber to the sound of a wild river running past, try this contemporary Victorian, which stands close, very close, to the rush and roll of the **McKenzie River.** Its two guest rooms come with private baths and a full breakfast ($75–125).

Cottage Grove

Apple Inn (1-800-942-2393; kmcintir@lane.k12or.us; www.appleinnbb.com), 30697 Kenady Lane, Cottage Grove 97424. The WELCOME sign hanging at the entrance to this 190 forested acres is more than decoration. "We've had lots of lovely comments from our guests over the years," says Apple Inn owner Kathe McIntire, "and what most of them are in agreement on is that not only do they get a beautiful room that is comfortable and quiet, they also have hosts that make them feel warmly welcome." Both guest rooms come with queen beds, handmade quilts, private baths, a full breakfast, and an available hot tub ($80–100), while one of them has a private entrance and a gas fireplace. Yet it's *outdoors* where many guests choose to spend their time. "We have a secluded setting that includes a pretty garden and a large lawn surrounded by the forest," Kathe says, "and many guests choose to walk the forest trails before sitting down to breakfast."

Lily of the Field Bed & Breakfast (541-942-2049; huebner-sannes @juno.com; www.eugene-lodging. com/new /lily.html), 35712 Rose Lane, Cottage Grove 97424. Looking over meadows and toward mountains, this rambling two-story home with all its posts and beams, balconies and decks stands on 1,200 acres near **Lake Dorena.** Its guest suite has a private bath and entrance, and a full breakfast is included ($85). In addition, on the edge of the nearby woods stands a gypsy wagon used as a bedroom.

Elmira

McGillivray's Log Home (541-935-3564), 88680 Evers Road, Elmira 97437. Built of logs and decorated with pine furniture, this 1982 inn seems as woodsy as the 5 forested acres that surround it. Cathedral ceilings and log rafters, combined with the fact that breakfast is often cooked over an antique wood-burning stove, bring that same effect indoors. Its two guest rooms come with king beds, private baths, and that wood-cooked breakfast ($60–80).

Eugene

Campbell House (1-800-264-2519; innkeeper@campbellhouse.com; www.campbellhouse.com), 252 Pearl Street, Eugene 97401. Housed in a restored historic 1892 inn situated on 1 acre that overlooks the city of Eugene, the Campbell House is large enough to be many things to different people. "The Campbell House is a full-service bed and breakfast inn," says Emily Saylor, associate innkeeper. "It has the charm of a unique bed and breakfast, the amenities of a large hotel, and the class of a European inn." Its 18 rooms all come with private bathrooms ($80–375), and some rooms have claw-foot or Jacuzzi tubs, four-poster beds, or gas fireplaces. In addition, a full breakfast is served in the dining room. "Our desire," Emily says, "is to make sure our guests enjoy a memorable stay and fabulous accommodations."

🐾 ✎ **Chambers House** (541-302-3014; chambersinn@aol.com; www. chambersinn.com), 1006 Taylor Street, Eugene 97402. Standing in a historic neighborhood close to the University of Oregon campus, this Queen Anne Victorian was built in 1891 as a wedding gift for Frank and Ida Chambers, but then the early 20th century sent the house through several transformations. After the Chambers family sold the house around 1910, for example, it was used in the 1920s as a sanatorium and in the 1930s as a women's boardinghouse. "The women must have been quite adventurous," says current owner Darrell Hames, "because by the time World War II came around the house was suspected of being a bordello." Today the home retains a sense of its past not only in its 19th-century architecture and period furnishings but also in its picket fences, rosebushes, and mature trees. "Because the inn has been restored to its original glory," Darrell says, "it offers a unique opportunity to experience life as it was in the 1800s." (It enjoys a dual honor: It's listed on the **National Register of Historic**

Places and designated a **Eugene Historic Landmark.**) Three guest rooms and a suite, all with king or queen beds and some with private baths, come with a continental breakfast ($50–125). Children are welcome, as are "house-friendly" dogs.

Country Inn Bed & Breakfast (1-877-816-8757; cibab1@attbi.com; www.cibab.com), 4100 Country Farm Road, Eugene 97408. Take a five-minute walk from this 1874 home, and you'll be standing on the bank of the **McKenzie River.** Its two guest rooms come with private baths and a full breakfast ($95).

Enchanted Country Inn (1-877-465-1869; innkeeper@enchanted-countryinn.com; www.enchanted-countryinn.com), 29195 Gimpl Hill, Eugene 97402. Stands of firs and cedars and redwoods, a shaded path to the doorstep and homemade wine in the evening, gazebo and gardens in which to sit—these are some of the enchantments of the Enchanted Country Inn. To its guests it offers three rooms with queen beds as well as private baths and entrances ($75–100) and a fully furnished hillside cottage ($125). All accommodations include a full breakfast.

Fort Smith Bed & Breakfast (541-687-9079; esmith4645@aol.com), 2645 Emerald, Eugene 97403. Centrally located in Eugene, this 1910 two-story Craftsman home is decorated with period furnishings and offers one room with a private bath, one room that shares a bath, and a full breakfast ($40–60).

Kjaer's House in the Woods (541-343-3234; www.eugene-bedandbreakfast.com), 814 Lorane Highway, Eugene 97405. A blend of historic home and wildlife habitat that has been operating as a B&B since 1984, this 1910 Craftsman house stands in a parklike setting shaded by towering cedars, firs, and oaks. Its lead-glass windows and hardwood floors are original, while its Oriental rugs and European antiques are part of a decor that includes the Danish plate collection of owners Eunice and George Kjaer. Its two guest rooms with queen beds and private baths come with a full breakfast that can include freshly baked bread and locally grown food ($70–85).

McGarry House (1-800-953-9921; www.mcgarryhouse.com), 856 E. 11th Avenue, Eugene 97401. This 1939 home stands just a block from the University of Oregon campus. Its two guest rooms have private baths and come with a full breakfast that features freshly baked breads ($85–100).

The Oval Door (1-800-882-3160; ovaldoor@ovaldoor.com; www.ovaldoor.com), 988 Lawrence Street, Eugene 97401. If you stay in downtown Eugene at this 1990 inn, which is designed as a century-old farmhouse, you might find the breakfast more important than the bed. "Our bed and breakfast is special because it's owned and run by two young women who are both trained chefs," says Nicole Wergeland, one of the owners. "We make food a priority here." As a result, breakfast—which is served in the dining room, on the wraparound porch, or in your room—starts off with homemade breads and muffins and fresh Oregon fruit before moving on to the gourmet specialty of the day. When it does come time for the bed part of the stay, the inn has five guest rooms, all with private baths ($75–195). "We provide every amenity we can think of," Nicole says, "to make our guests happy."

Pookie's Bed 'n' Breakfast on College Hill (1-800-558-0383; pookiesbandb@aol.com; www.virtualcities.com/ons/or/e/ore4601.htm), 2013 Charnelton Street, Eugene 97405. Standing elegantly among firs and maples in a quiet neighborhood, Pookie's is a 1918 two-story Craftsman home furnished with antiques dating back to the time of its construction. Of its four guest rooms, two have private baths and two share a bath ($75–115). The full breakfast, served in the dining room, includes baked egg in puffed pastry and Great Aunt Sophie's Danish *aebelskivers*. Children older than 6 are welcome.

River Walk Inn (1-800-621-2904; innkeeper@ariverwalkinn.com; www.ariverwalkinn.com), 250 N. Adams Street, Eugene 97402. The River Walk Inn really does offer guests a walk by the river, for it stands next to Eugene's 20-mile **Willamette River Trail** that is so popular in this city of walkers, joggers, and bikers. The 1931 Dutch Colonial home, which retains its original wooden floors and coved ceilings, offers three guest rooms with private baths and a full breakfast ($70–98).

The Secret Garden (1-888-484-6755; innkeeper@secretgardenbbinn.com; www.secretgardenbbinn.com), 1910 University Street, Eugene 97403. This inn gets its name from a discovery made by a storybook girl when she comes upon a hidden doorway in her backyard fence. "Then she slipped through it and shut it behind her," Frances Hodgson Burnett wrote in her book *The Secret Garden*, "and stood with her back against it, looking about her and breathing quite fast with excitement, and wonder, and delight. She was inside the Secret Garden." Centrally located in a quiet neighborhood and a few blocks from the University of Oregon campus, this renovated 1918 three-story inn really is surrounded by a wondrous garden. All 10 of its guest rooms, decorated with international art and antiques, come with private baths and a full breakfast ($115–235).

Leaburg

Marjon Bed & Breakfast Inn (1-800-881-7120; www.moriah.com/marjon), 44975 Leaburg Dam Road, Leaburg 97489. This is an international inn, its exterior that of a Swiss chalet, its interior French and Asian, while running just 50 feet from its door is a river that's all Northwest—the **McKenzie.** The 2-acre site also grows 2,000 azaleas and 700 rhododendrons and includes a dock, grotto, and deck. Its two guest rooms come with private bathrooms and a buffet breakfast ($105–135).

Springfield

McKenzie River Trout House (1-877-611-1181; innkeeper@mckenzierivertrouthouse.com; www.mckenzierivertrouthouse.com), 41496 McKenzie Highway, Springfield 97478. Two highlights of this B&B are the **McKenzie River** flowing nearby and a landscaped yard and gardens surrounding the house. Its two guest rooms ($75–125) and two suites ($145–250) come with king or queen beds, private baths, and a full breakfast.

McKenzie View (1-888-625-8439; riverview@mckenzie-view.com; www.mckenzie-view.com), 34922 McKenzie View Drive, Springfield 97478. Furnished with antiques, decorated with original art, and located on 6 acres along a bend of the **McKenzie River,** this 1990 Cape Cod home has four guest rooms with private bathrooms that come with a full breakfast served either in the dining room or on the patio ($90–250).

Park View Bed & Breakfast (1-877-860-2100; stay@parkviewbedandbreakfast.com; www.parkviewbedandbreakfast.com), 311 G Street, Springfield 97477. Ponds, trees, flowers, and a **waterfall** make up the view through the cathedral windows of this custom-built home, whose history is as interesting as its landscaping. "Our B&B was originally built for a local doctor and later owned by a child movie actor attending the University of Oregon," says owner Wanda Berglund. "He rented rooms out to fellow students." Of the three guest rooms available today, one has a Jacuzzi and one a kitchenette, and all have private baths and come with a full breakfast ($79–149). "Our guests enjoy the tranquillity of our home," Wanda says, "and sharing experiences over breakfast." And yes, the Park View *does* have a view of a park, which lies across the street.

LODGES

McKenzie Bridge

Log Cabin Inn (1-800-355-3432; lci@ rio.com; www.logcabininn.com), 56483 McKenzie Highway, McKenzie Bridge 97413. This inn has lived at least two lives: built in 1886 as a resort that welcomed visitors who came seeking the green waters and valley of the McKenzie River; then built again as this three-story log house after a 1906 fire burned the original structure to the ground. (Guests at the resurrected inn through the years included Clark Gable, President Herbert Hoover, and the Duke of Windsor.) Today's visitors to the almost 7-acre resort have their choice of staying in one of the eight cabins that stand on a bluff above the **McKenzie River** ($90–110) or in one of the six tepees pitched in a meadow ($45). Either way, the river is nearby, for the inn has more than 900 feet of river frontage as well as a boat landing. In addition, the inn's **restaurant** specializes in meats and fish cooked slowly in a smoker barbecue and since 1900 has offered venison on the menu.

Vida

Eagle Rock Lodge (1-888-733-4333; eaglerock@nim-rod.com; www.nim-rod.com), 49198 McKenzie Highway, Vida 97488. Here at Eagle Rock Lodge, the **McKenzie River** is more than a view—it's a neighbor. With more than 450 feet of riverfront property running along the edge of its 4 acres, the lodge has an open door to one of the Northwest's great wild streams as well as to some of its tall timber and wildlife. Its eight guest rooms come with private baths, a full breakfast, and an angler's early start on the river's rainbow trout and steelhead ($75–195).

McKenzie River Inn (541-822-6260; innkeeper@mckenzieriverinn.com; www.mckenzieriverinn.com), 49164 McKenzie River Highway, Vida 97488. After beginning life as a homesteader's cabin in 1929, this riverside lodge starting offering rooms to travelers 50 years later. "It's the oldest B&B on the river," says host Bert de Klerk. "Today our bed and breakfast and cabins are located on a very unique, pristine piece of land: three acres with old-growth forest across the river and a gravel bar riverfront that stretches for over 1,200 feet, which makes it one of the best fly-fishing spots on the **McKenzie."** All three rooms in the lodge as well as the two adjacent cabins have private baths and come with what Bert (the cook) describes as "a real American breakfast with a European touch, from salmon omelets to Belgian hazelnut waffles to eggs Benedict."

Wayfarer Resort (1-800-627-3613; info@wayfarerresort.com; www.wayfarerresort.com), 46725 Goodpasture Road, Vida 97488. On 10 creekside acres near the **McKenzie** stand the 13 cabins of this mountain resort. "This is a lovely parklike setting," says manager Dorothy Hoffman, "with a large year-round creek and many gardens to linger over." The cabins ($85–230) include decks, fireplaces, equipped kitchens, and open-beamed ceilings—and they stand just steps away from an outdoor lover's paradise. "You can hike or bike right from our driveway," Dorothy says, "raft or fish from our beach, or just take in the spectacular Cascade foothills."

GUEST CABINS **Cedarwood Lodge** (541-822-3351; cwoodldg@aol.com; www.cedarwoodlodge.com), 56535 McKenzie Highway, McKenzie Bridge 97413. Roughing it easy seems part of the way of life here along the McKenzie River. At Cedarwood Lodge, for instance, the seven cabins are surrounded by cedars and firs, while the river runs as close as 50 feet from the doorsteps, yet they're also next door to a **restaurant** with a wine list and a full bar. In addition, the cabins come with equipped kitchens and bathrooms with showers; fireplaces and decks; even propane barbecues ($85–125).

✷ Where to Eat

DINING OUT For more dining options see the **Log Cabin Inn** under *Lodging*.

Eugene

Adam's Place (541-344-6948), 30 E. Broadway, Eugene. Dressed up in pillars and arches and other lavish trimmings of the carpenter's craft, Adam's Place matches the elegance of its meals to its decor, from appetizers to dessert, with appropriate stops at an award-winning wine list along the way.

Excelsior Inn Ristorante Italiano (541-342-6963), 754 E. 13th Avenue, Eugene. For more than three decades this restaurant has been ranked as one of the best in Eugene. With its Italian cuisine, walled courtyard, and skylit terrace, the Excelsior Inn has long carried a sense of European tradition in its food as well as its atmosphere.

Marche (541-342-3612), 296 E. Fifth Avenue, Eugene. Fresh, organic, and Northwest from the huckleberry sauce to the pork chops—that's what you can expect on the menu at Marche, a fine-dining restaurant located in Eugene's Fifth Street Public Market.

Ring of Fire (541-344-6475), 1099 Chambers Street, Eugene. In geographical terms, the "Ring of Fire" refers to the volcanic past and potential of the Pacific Rim nations; in Eugene dining circles, it means this restaurant that specializes in the food derived from those countries. The result is exotic food in a quiet, inviting atmosphere.

EATING OUT

Blue River

Holiday Farm Restaurant (541-822-3715), 54455 McKenzie River Drive, Blue River. Located along the old

McKenzie River Highway, this was once a hangout for President Herbert Hoover, Clark Gable, and other celebrities drawn to the magical blue of the McKenzie's waters. The restaurant's riverside deck gives you a chance to enjoy your meals near that same magic.

Eugene

Ambrosia (541-342-4141), 174 E. Broadway, Eugene. Even though its wood-burning ovens turn out some of the best pizzas in town, Ambrosia also serves first-class Italian food in an intimately inviting atmosphere.

Beppe and Gianni's (541-683-6661), 1646 E. 19th Avenue, Eugene. According to some longtime residents, this is the best Italian restaurant in Eugene—a small trattoria-style restaurant with authentic Tuscan cuisine and a crowded, boisterous atmosphere.

Café Soriah (541-342-4410), 384 W. 13th Avenue, Eugene. Small but comfortable and elegant, decorated with original art and beautiful woodwork, the Café Soriah serves excellent Northwest and Mediterranean cuisine that makes it a local favorite.

The Locomotive (541-465-4754), 291 E. Fifth Avenue, Eugene. The terms "upscale" and "organic vegetarian" don't always blend in restaurant descriptions, yet that's exactly what the Locomotive brings to the table—all organic, all vegetarian, all the time. (The portobello mushrooms in red wine sauce as well as the house-made ice creams are the stuff of local culinary legend.)

Zenon Café (541-343-3005), 898 Pearl Street, Eugene. Loud and happy is the sound of the Zenon Café, which fills with crowds hungering after . . . well, whatever happens to be on the menu, which changes constantly. From Italian to Northwest, Cajun to Greek, with some Thai and Chinese and vegetarian thrown in for good measure, the selections here are as varied as they are good.

Springfield

Crossroads Grill (541-741-3366), 737 Main Street, Springfield. A bright spot in a downtown that's still trying to recover from the closing of the area's woods and mills, the Crossroads Grill expertly juggles several distinct cooking styles of the South, including Cajun, Creole, and barbecue, from bouillabaisse to baby back ribs. In addition, many of the desserts are homemade, some nights feature live jazz, and a fireplace and a courtyard add atmosphere during the appropriate seasons.

Kuraya's (541-746-2951), 1410 Mohawk Boulevard, Springfield. Although the restaurant stands at a distance from the city's core, local residents and highway travelers who know about Kuraya's Thai cooking—especially its seafood specialties—hesitate not at all in making the drive to its door.

Mookie's Place (541-746-8298), 1507 Centennial Boulevard, Springfield. At Mookie's Place, doggy bags are almost as common as coffee cups, so large are the portions and so numerous the diners who flock here for the grilled salmon, the Cajun chicken, the prime rib, or almost any other item on the menu at this once-upon-a-time drive-in.

Vida

Mom's Pies (541-822-3891), 49647 McKenzie Highway, Vida. No doubt about the specialty at this roadside café—Mom's Pies, great pies. Just ask any of the thousands of rafters or fishermen or other river wanderers who've stopped here to find out what all the fuss is about.

Vida Café (541-896-3289), 45641 McKenzie Highway, Vida. If your journey along the McKenzie River carries you near Vida, stop at this small café for no other reason than to acquaint yourself with the McKenzie Monster Hamburger.

✱ Special Events

July: **Oregon Country Fair** (541-343-4298; www.oregoncountryfair.com), Veneta. Now in its fourth decade of celebrating 1960-ish uninhibited spirit, the Oregon Country Fair for three days each summer throws a drug- and alcohol-free party for families. When the doors open, the grounds fill with 300 booths selling art, crafts, or food; with people parading in costumes and masks; with vaudeville acts and amateur bands. Even though the fair can draw as many as 40,000 people to the former campsite of the native Kalapuya people, the fair retains a sense of intimacy and friendliness. "It's a one-of-a-kind experience that I can't get anywhere else," says a vendor from California. "There's beauty and art of all kinds being expressed here that other fairs just don't do."

Southwest

OAKLAND–ROSEBURG–MYRTLE CREEK AREA

GRANTS PASS–ROGUE RIVER AREA

ILLINOIS VALLEY AREA

MEDFORD–ASHLAND–APPLEGATE VALLEY AREA

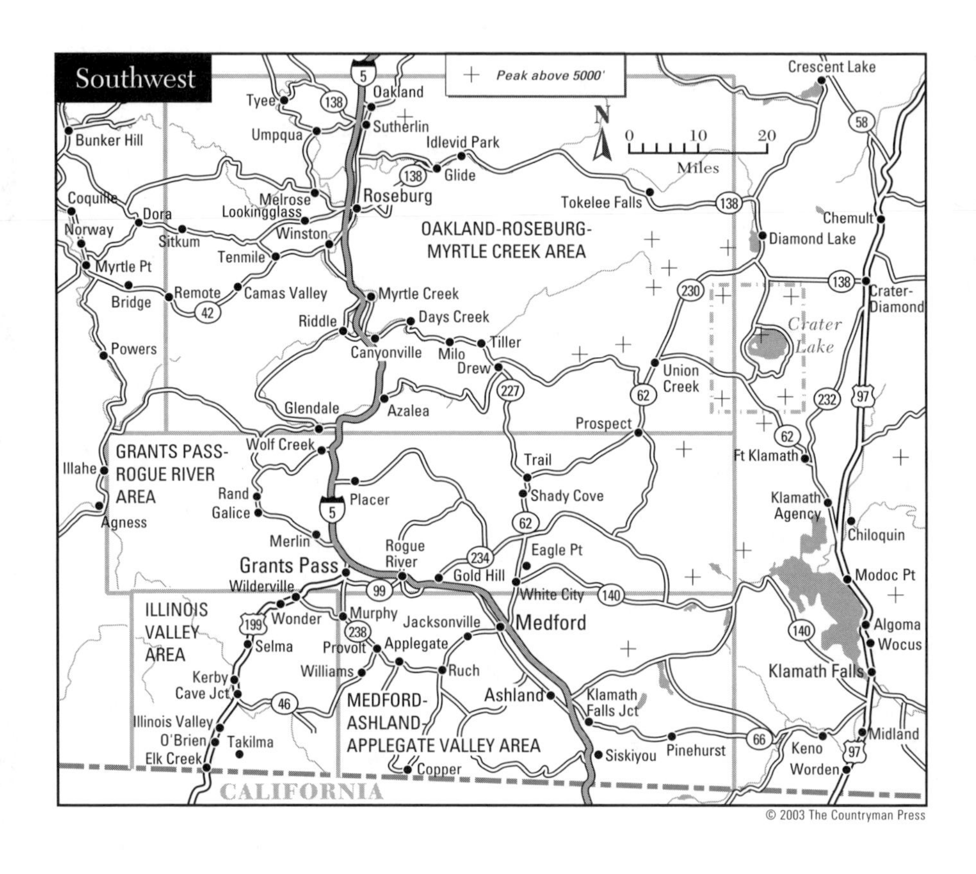

Southwest
Peak above 5000'
N
0 10 20
Miles
OAKLAND-ROSEBURG-
MYRTLE CREEK AREA
GRANTS PASS-
ROGUE RIVER
AREA
ILLINOIS
VALLEY
AREA
MEDFORD-
ASHLAND-
APPLEGATE VALLEY AREA
CALIFORNIA
Crater
Lake
Crescent Lake
Tyee
Oakland
Sutherlin
Umpqua
Bunker Hill
Idlevid Park
Glide
Melrose
Roseburg
Lookingglass
Coquille
Dora
Norway
Sitkum
Winston
Tokelee Falls
Chemult
Diamond Lake
Tenmile
Myrtle Pt
Remote
Camas Valley
Bridge
Myrtle Creek
Days Creek
Riddle
Canyonville
Milo
Tiller
Drew
Powers
Union
Creek
Crater-
Diamond
Glendale
Azalea
Prospect
Wolf Creek
Illahe
Trail
Ft Klamath
Rand
Galice
Agness
Placer
Shady Cove
Klamath
Agency
Chiloquin
Merlin
Rogue
River
Eagle Pt
Grants Pass
Gold Hill
Modoc Pt
Wilderville
White City
Wonder
Murphy
Jacksonville
Medford
Algoma
Wocus
Selma
Provolt
Applegate
Williams
Ruch
Klamath Falls
Kerby
Cave Jct
Ashland
Klamath
Falls Jct
Illinois Valley
O'Brien
Takilma
Midland
Elk Creek
Siskiyou
Pinehurst
Keno
Worden
Copper
5
138
58
42
230
227
62
232
97
234
99
140
199
238
46
66
© 2003 The Countryman Press

INTRODUCTION

"Here is a land of richness, a land of pure delight, where the joy of living and the need of making a living are not incompatible, a haven the like of which is hardly to be found."

—Commercial Club advertisement describing southwest Oregon's Rogue River Valley, 1910

All through this land stretch the mountainous scars of its birth—the millennia-long volcanic eruptions and the inch-by-inch continental collisions that created the Coast Range, the Cascades, the Klamaths, and the Siskiyous. Behind these ran the Umpqua and Coquille, the Rogue and Illinois, and others rivers that carved the canyons, drained the forests, and shaped the valleys across a region with enough ruggedness and seclusion to hold ancient treasures.

Gold was one such treasure, and it didn't take long for California's '49ers—the miners not the football team—to spill into the streambeds and hillsides of southwest Oregon. With picks and pans, cradle boxes and hydraulic hoses these men gobbled the gold and left behind a history of Indian wars and the seeds of settlements that grew into towns.

Plants were another prize, for within the region's mountains grows such a cornucopia of greenery that the U.S. Forest Service calls the segment it manages "the most floristically diverse national forest in the country." The age of the mountains, the extremes of its climate, and the variety of its rocks and soils are all given as reasons for the trove of plants that grows here. Botanists who quest after those plants, however, also discover the reason this region has been called the "wildest part of the United States."

"The rocky trails were so narrow that the burros caught their packs on the rocky cliffs and turned topsy-turvy while fording the many swift streams," botanist Lilla Leach wrote about her travels along the Rogue River in the late 1920s. "The rain descended in torrents and the water filled the extra space in our boots so that each step we made, the water went slush." Yet the rewards could justify the hardships, for Lilla also described the wildflower meadows and pine forests, the mountain lakes and wildlife that were part of the adventure.

In a sense, this region is every bit as untamed now as it was then, its rivers as wild, its mountains as rugged, its trails as lonely as in the days when both roads and travelers were few. As a result, the call to adventure still echoes loudly to those who seek solitude, beauty, and other treasures that lay across the scars of the land.

OAKLAND–ROSEBURG–MYRTLE CREEK AREA

GUIDANCE **Bureau of Land Management: Roseburg District** (541-672-4491), 777 Garden Valley Boulevard, Roseburg 97470.

Colliding Rivers Information Center (541-496-0157), 18782 N. Umpqua Highway, Glide 97443.

Oregon State Parks (503-378-6305), State Parks and Recreation Department, 525 Trade Street S. E., Salem 97301.

Rogue River National Forest: Headquarters (541-858-2200), 333 W. Eighth Street, Medford 97501; **Prospect Ranger District** (541-560-3400).

Roseburg Visitors and Convention Bureau (1-800-444-9584; www.visitroseburg.com), 410 S. E. Spruce Street, Roseburg 97470.

Sutherlin Visitors Center (541-459-5829), 1310 W. Central Avenue, Sutherlin 97479.

Winston Visitor Information Center (541-679-0118), 30 N. W. Glenhart Street, Winston 97496.

Umpqua National Forest: Headquarters (541-672-6601), 2900 N. W. Stewart Parkway, Roseburg 97470; **Diamond Lake Ranger District** (541-498-2531); **North Umpqua Ranger District** (541-496-3532); **Tiller Ranger District** (541-825-3201).

GETTING THERE The Oakland–Roseburg–Myrtle Creek area is reached from the east by Highway 138, from the west by Highways 138 and 42, and from the north and south by Interstate 5.

MEDICAL EMERGENCY **Mercy Medical Center** (541-673-0611), 2700 Stewart Parkway, Roseburg.

* To See

MUSEUMS **Oakland Museum** (541-459-4531), downtown Oakland. Lying on a glass counter in this museum is a poem that Oakland resident John Garrison carved in a rock, its verse opening with the lines, “In 1851 it was a new town /

Built among the oaks / By strong and sturdy folks." This was the Oakland of old, a farming and shipping center, an economic force in the region. Then came the fire. On the Fourth of July in 1899, virtually the entire downtown burned to the ground, and Oakland struggled to rebuild itself as both business and population dwindled through the years. Then in 1968 the town decided that one of its strengths was its past, for its downtown buildings—made of brick since the fire—have remained unchanged for more than a century, giving visitors the impression they've just stepped back to the 19th century. The museum is an extension of that impression, displaying the artifacts that tell the story of Oakland's past. This is why Mr. Garrison's poem concludes with the lines, "For it grew older and older / Stayed solid and sound / And now called / Historic Oakland Town."

DOWNTOWN OAKLAND HAS PRESERVED MANY OF ITS TURN-OF-THE-CENTURY BUILDINGS

Douglas County Museum of History and Natural History, 123 Museum Drive (exit 123 off Interstate 5),Roseburg. Since its beginning in 1969, this museum has expanded twice—in 1979 and again in 1989—so that it now consists of four wings of exhibits that capture a good deal of the human and natural history of the area. From a prehistoric saber-toothed tiger to a modern-day Roosevelt elk, and from the shattering eruption of Mount Mazama (which formed today's Crater Lake) to the pioneer treks along the **Applegate Trail** (which runs beneath today's Interstate 5; see *To See—Historic Sites* in Medford–Ashland–Applegate Valley Area), the museum traces the changes of the region's land and people.

Pioneer-Indian Museum (541-839-4845), 421 W. Fifth Street (exit 98 off Interstate 5), Canyonville. Canyonville prides itself on being "the third oldest town in Oregon," its roots stretching back to the passing of wagon trains in 1843 and its history collected in this museum.

HISTORIC HOMES **Drain House** (541-836-2223), 500 S. Main Street (Interstate 5 exit 150 from the north, exit 162 from the south), Drain. Here's another story of financial success from the Oregon Trail: After hoofing along with a wagon train to Oregon with his family, Charles Drain staked out a homestead, won election to the state legislature, dabbled in real estate, operated a mercantile, and started the town of Drain. By 1890 Charles was ready to splurge some of his wealth on a new home, which the local newspaper proclaimed to be the "finest and most costly ever built" in the area. The result today is the Drain House—some call it the Drain *Castle*—a Queen Anne Victorian with all the necessary towers, verandahs, and bay windows.

Floed-Lane House (541-459-1393), 544 S. E. Douglas Street (exit 124 off Interstate 5), Roseburg. What distinguishes this house is its 1866 origins and its pedigree, for its owner was the daughter of Joseph Lane, the first territorial governor of Oregon as well as a brigadier general and war hero during the Rogue Indian campaign of the 1850s. Even though the general lived down the street, he occasionally came here for dinner, and it's easy to imagine someone at the table asking him yet again to tell the story of that September day in 1853 when the general, still nursing the wound of a previous battle and accompanied by only 10 unarmed men, met at a peace council with 700 Takelma warriors. That's some story.

HISTORIC SITES **Scottsburg Walking Tour,** Main Street and its cross streets on the bank of the Umpqua Rive, Scottsburg. When gold mines and camps sprouted across southern Oregon and northern California in the 1850s, this town on the bank of the Umpqua River became one of the region's foremost supply centers. "It was a common sight," writes local historian Harold A. Minter, "to see five hundred pack animals in the streets waiting for their loads of supplies and mining machinery." Delivering those supplies were the numerous steamships that chugged their way upriver after crossing the Umpqua's bar. All that hustle and bustle brought with it a booming business to Scottsburg, which lasted all of five years, when new roads began to bypass the town and carry away the trade. Shops closed, people moved, and a flood in the winter of 1860–1861 washed away much of what remained. Today, however, a half-dozen historical structures—including homes, a store, and a grange—survive from those days as reminders of the community's golden years.

Oakland Walking Tour (541-459-4531). Established in 1851 on the bank of Oldam Creek, Oakland grew into a milling and business center—until potential disaster struck 21 years later when the Oregon and California Railroad bypassed the town by 2 miles. Unwilling to watch their city die, the citizens of Oakland loaded their shops and homes onto skids and moved the town to the tracks. What you see today, then, is the second Oakland, one whose appearance has remained virtually unchanged for more than a century. That's because in 1968 the city council passed an ordinance designed to preserve Oakland's historical qualities, a decision that led to the town's becoming Oregon's first designated Historic District. "We decided that this town is really unique," says former mayor Frieda Smith. "So let's not mess with it too much."

Stephens Community, 4 miles west of Sutherlin off Sutherlin–Umpqua Road. This historic district located along Calapooya Creek and on the former Donation Land Claim of Ebenezer Stephens is home to 10 simple but historical buildings constructed between 1870 and 1906.

Wilbur, 7 miles north of Roseburg off Highway 99 (exit 128 or 135 off Interstate 5). If he were still around, Mr. Ed might say this was his favorite town. It's a community whose beginnings date back to an 1851 home that stood along the **Applegate Trail** (see *To See—Historic Sites* in Medford– Ashland–Applegate Valley Area) and provided bed and board to travelers. That house, known as the Wilbur Tavern, as well as a nearby church and parsonage built in 1854, survive today as parts of the area's collection of historical structures.

Roseburg Walking Tour, Mill and Pine Streets along the Southern Pacific Railroad, Roseburg. When the railroad reached Roseburg in 1872, the young town became the southern terminus—and later a division point—of the Oregon and California Railroad Company, a situation that produced an influx of workers and businesses to the community. The subsequent demand for employee housing resulted in the construction near the rail yards of the Mill-Pine Neighborhood, whose 180 "working- class cottages" remain relatively unchanged since they were built in the 1880s and 1890s.

Winston Walking Tour (541-679-0118) on Highway 99 southwest of Roseburg. The two economic forces that shaped this area, orchards and cattle, are represented in the historic buildings standing on opposite edges of Winston. To the east, the **Winston Section Road Historic District,** comprised of homes built between 1887 and the 1920s, stands near orchards still producing. The oldest of these once belonged to the family of William C. Winston, a teacher for whom the city is named. To the west, the **Brockway** ranching community consists of barns that date between 1852 and the mid-1880s and houses between 1867 and 1900. In addition, the **Brockway Store,** which was moved to its present site at the junction of Brockway Road and Highway 42 to make room for road construction in 1922, still contains furnishings that date back to its opening in 1910.

Arthur Johnson Farm and Stage House, 15 miles west of Roseburg in Reston, at the junction of Coos Bay Wagon and Reston Roads. Built in 1911 by rancher Arthur Johnson, this house provided stagecoach passengers with meals and beds during their journey between Roseburg and Coos Bay. Behind the stage house stands the Reston Post Office, which closed in 1935.

Historic Barns. This area is home to least three barns listed on the **National Register of Historic Places,** whose purpose is to recognize "buildings, structures, objects, and sites that are over 50 years old and possess attributes architecturally, historically, or culturally significant to the nation, state or local community." These historical barns include the **David Hurst Barn** (4 miles west of Sutherlin off Sutherlin–Umpqua Road and County Road 32A; exit 136 off Interstate 5), part of an 1850 homestead; the **Peter Weaver Barn** (4 miles east of Canyonville off Tiller Trail Highway; exit 98 off Interstate 5), built in the late 1880s of hand-hewn timbers, beams, and braces; and the **James Wimer Barn** (8 miles southwest of Roseburg off Lookingglass Road and County Road 52; exit 123 or 124 off Interstate 5), an octagonal barn, one of only seven in the state, that is built of old- growth cedar, rests on stone footings, and was first used to house cattle and later to store fruit.

China Ditch, 10 miles northeast of Myrtle Creek off North Myrtle Creek Road, County Road 15, and Bureau of Land Management (BLM) Road 28. China Ditch is the result of a golden rule of hydraulic mining: If you're gonna find gold, you gotta have water. Heeding this rule in 1891, the Myrtle Creek Consolidated Hydraulic Gold Mining and Manufacturing Company hired as many as 200 Chinese laborers, paid them 25 cents a day and a bowl of rice, and put them to work digging a ditch that would bring the water of Little River, a tributary of the North Umpqua River, to the mining fields along North Myrtle Creek, some 33 miles away. And so with picks and shovels the Chinese began digging. They dug through rock. And roots. And stumps. For almost three years they dug, until the ditch ran 5 feet deep and almost 30 miles long and the company finally went broke. What's left of China Ditch today is an entrenched, serpentine scar that runs through the thickets and tangles of clear-cut hillsides and serves as a testament to the will and the muscle of men who worked to move a river.

Azalea General Store, Azalea (exit 86 or 88 off Interstate 5). When it started out in 1915, this building was a community center that held two necessities of early- 20th- century rural life: a store on the first floor and a dance hall on the second. Though the dance hall is gone the store remains—with the addition of a gas station and **café**—and it still serves as a commercial and social center for folks living in the upper Cow Creek Valley.

COVERED BRIDGES Oregon's first covered bridge was probably built in 1850, though its construction was based on a Chinese design dating back more than 2,000 years. Even though the bridge's roof and walls protected its beams and trusses from the weather and provided increased rigidity and strength, covered bridges remained vulnerable to decay and floods. (Floods in 1890 washed away virtually every major covered bridge in the state.) Consequently, steel began replacing wood as the preferred building material. Increased traffic, heavier loads, and wider roads finished off what steel began. The following are some of the covered bridges still to be found in this region, including their location, date of construction, and length:

Roaring Camp, 6 miles east of Drain off Highway 38 (1929, 88 feet); **Pass Creek,** First Street, Drain (1925, 61 feet); **Rochester,** 3 miles northwest of Sutherlin off Highway 138 and County Road 10-A (1933, 80 feet); **Cavitt Creek,** 6 miles southeast of Glide near the intersection of County Roads 17 and

CHINA DITCH, 30 MILES LONG, 5 FEET DEEP, AND DUG BY HAND

82A (1943, 70 feet); **Sandy Creek,** near the town of Remote, where Highway 42 crosses Sandy Creek (1921, 60 feet); **Neal Lane,** 2 miles southeast of Myrtle Creek off County Road 18-A and Neal Lane (1929, 42 feet); **Milo Academy,** 15 miles east of Canyonville off Highway 227 (1962, 100 feet).

FOR FAMILIES **Wildlife Safari** (1-800-355-4848; www.wildlifesafari.org), 6 miles south of Winston (off Interstate 5 exit 119) on Highway 42. At this 600-acre zoo, the people are confined and the animals free to wander. This means that from the seat of your car you can inch your way past lions and tigers, rhinos and bears, elephants and ostriches, and hundreds of other exotic animals—the population exceeds 600—that live at Oregon's only drive-through zoo.

Gold Panning, 22 miles southwest of Riddle off Cow Creek Road. The gold rush may be long gone, but that doesn't mean you can't stake a claim to some leisurely prospecting on a sunny afternoon. Along the roadside bank of Cow Creek, for example, more than 400 yards of stream is open to recreational gold panning. If you strike color, it's yours to keep; if not, you'll still be richer for the time spent along this sparkling creek.

SCENIC DRIVES **Coos Bay Wagon Road,** 35 paved miles in a loop beginning and ending in Roseburg, or 69 paved and graveled miles from Roseburg to Coos Bay. Completed in 1872 after crossing some of the roughest terrain in the state, the Coos Bay Wagon Road was the first overland connection to the port of Coos Bay. The modern version of this road, paved for all but a dozen or so miles, still follows most of the original route, giving travelers a chance to marvel at the country it passes through on its way over the Coast Range and on to the sea. (From Roseburg it starts out as Lookingglass Road.) If you'd like just a sampling of the historic wagon road, you can drive 15 miles of it to its junction with Reston Road, where you'll turn south to Tenmile and return to Roseburg by following Highway 42.

Scottsburg–Drain Historic Tour, 33 paved miles along Highway 38. Starting with its founding in 1850, the town of Scottsburg, located on the bank of the Umpqua River in the foothills of the Coast Range, served for a time as a vital port of entry to the interior of southwest Oregon during the region's gold- mining years. Here ships would dock and unload after crossing the Umpqua's bar and steaming upstream, and pack trains and freight wagons would then haul the supplies and equipment to the mining districts. The resulting pack trails and wagon roads eventually cut through the mountains to the east, linking the port to the railroad. Today's Highway 38 follows one such historical route to Drain, a stretch of road that includes a number of historical homes, bridges, landmarks, and markers.

♿ **Highway of Waterfalls,** 68 paved miles along Highway 138 from Glide to Diamond Lake. Part of the **Rogue–Umpqua National Scenic Byway** (see below), this stretch of highway stands as a scenic tour by itself, for it must be one of the splashiest roads in America, its pavement lined with the tumble of waterfalls coming off the North Umpqua River and its tributaries. A number of these falls are within rock-tossing distance of the highway, including **Susan**

Creek, Fall Creek, Toketee, Watson, Wasson, Horseshoe, and **Clearwater.** All have directional signs, parking areas, and handicapped access. In addition, a number of side roads lead to waterfalls more secluded and farther removed from pavement. For example, Forest Road 48, a paved road that branches to the north of Highway 38 near Steamboat Campground, leads to **Little Falls** and **Steamboat Falls.** Meanwhile, south of the highway, Little River Road runs southeast of Glide and heads toward **Cavitt Creek Falls** (off Cavitt Creek Road), **Wolf Creek Falls** (off Forest Road 2701), **Emile Falls** and **Grotto Falls** (off Forest Road 2703), **Hemlock Falls** and **Yasko Falls** (off Forest Road 27).

Rogue–Umpqua National Scenic Byway, 180 paved miles along Highways 138, 230, 62, and 234 from Roseburg to Medford. Follow the pavement along these two rivers famous for their trout and steelhead, and you'll find yourself skirting lakes high in the Cascades, including Oregon's one national park at Crater Lake, as well as wilderness areas, waterfalls, campgrounds, and hiking trails.

Myrtle Creek–Canyonville Scenic Historic Tour, 68 paved miles from Myrtle Creek to Canyonville along South Myrtle Creek Road and Tiller Trail Highway. Along this route that follows South Myrtle Creek and the South Umpqua River, you'll encounter thick timber and thin roads, historic towns and pioneer homes, picnic areas and mountain views, a giant Douglas fir log that holds enough wood to built a three-bedroom house, and a carved Smokey the Bear that dispenses local information and voices woodsy wisdom about forest fires.

Cow Creek Driving Tour, 49 paved miles from Azalea to Riddle along Cow Creek Road. On its way toward the South Umpqua River, Cow Creek bends its way into a lasso-shaped curve that passes through a canyon so steep and rugged that it took until the 1950s for a road to penetrate it. Today that canyon route passes through a mixture of scenery and history: forests of firs and oaks, groves of maple and oak, the remnants of pioneer homesteads, hydraulic mining, railroad tunnels, and bridges.

NATURAL WONDERS **Heritage Trees** (1-800-574-9397). For more than 30 years, Maynard Drawson of Salem has been tracking down the largest and most historic trees in the state, a record of exploration that eventually led to Oregon's Heritage Trees Program, the first such program in the country. Those trees making the list have been judged to be of special significance for their age, size, or connection to historical events. **Courthouse Elm,** 1036 S. E. Douglas Street (Douglas County Courthouse), Roseburg. U.S. congressman Binger Hermann gave this tree to the county near the turn of the 20th century. **Hinds Walnut Tree,** 12 miles northwest of Sutherlin off Highway 138 and near the Yellow Creek Bridge. Even though this tree isn't a native of the state, it began growing here before the first settlers arrived and is situated near what was probably a prehistoric campsite.

Myrtlewood Groves, north and south of Roseburg off Interstate 5. So rare are old groves of myrtlewood trees—and so limited is their range, which extends only from the coast of California to southwest Oregon—that you'll find yourself searching far and wide (not to mention high and low) for them. The reason for their scarcity is their beauty, which has long created a kind of wood lust in those who would turn them into bowls, carvings, and furniture. Left alone in good soil, myrtlewoods can reach heights of 150 feet and diameters of 5 feet. It may have been such a tree that provided the polished myrtlewood tie into which the golden spike was driven in the 1869 ceremony marking the completion of the transcontinental railroad. The national champion myrtlewood, however, has a circumference of greater than 41 feet, more than 5 feet larger than the girth of the largest Douglas fir. Visiting any of the following sites will give you a chance to explore these remarkable and beautiful trees: **Mill Site City Park,** Myrtle Creek, exit 108 on Interstate 5; **Amacher Myrtlewood Grove,** in a county park lying west of exit 129 on Interstate 5; **Singleton Park,** at the confluence of the North Fork and South Fork Umpqua River, 4 miles west of exit 125 on Interstate 5; **Myrtlewood Island,** in the middle of the Umpqua River, 4 miles west of exit 136 on Interstate 5 and off the Sutherlin–Umpqua Road, viewpoint near milepost 18.

Colliding Rivers, viewpoint off Highway 138 in Glide. This is a meeting of two rivers that can't seem to get along: Little River flowing from out of the southeast and then turning suddenly north, the North Umpqua River heading west and then veering due south, and the two of them finally crashing together at the town of Glide, the only place in the world where two rivers butt together this way. The watery collision creates churning whitewater that the deeper and faster North Umpqua eventually absorbs before turning its way west again, finishing its run to the sea.

✷ To Do

CAMPING **North Umpqua River,** between Winchester and Diamond Lake along Highway 138, 16 campgrounds strung along the bank of the North Umpqua: **Amacher, Whistlers Bend, Swiftwater, Susan Creek, Boundary, Bogus Creek, Williams, Island, Canton Creek, Apple Creek, Horseshoe Bend, Eagle Rock, Boulder Flat, Toketee Lake, Horseshoe Falls, Clearwater Falls;** in addition, two more campgrounds, **Scaredman** and **Steamboat Falls,** lie a short distance off the highway, north of Steamboat.

Rock Creek, northeast of Glide off Highway 138 and Rock Creek Road: **Millpond,** 12 campsites along with a ball field, pavilion, playground, and nearby fish hatchery; and **Rock Creek,** 17 campsites and a pavilion, but no fishing is permitted in the creek along this stretch.

Little River, southeast of Glide off Little River Road and Forest Road 27, 7 campgrounds near Little River, which collides with the North Umpqua River at the nearby town of Glide: **Wolf Creek, Emile Creek, Cool Water, White Creek, Lake in the Woods, Hemlock Lake,** and **Hemlock Meadows;** in addition, **Cavitt Creek** campground lies along adjacent Cavitt Creek Road.

Lemolo Lake, 78 miles east of Roseburg off Highway 138 and Basket Butte Road, 4 campgrounds on the shoreline of 100-foot-deep Lemolo Lake, with nearby hiking trails and a good chance to see bald eagles: **Poole Creek, Bunker Hill, Inlet,** and **East Lemolo.**

Diamond Lake, 80 miles east of Roseburg near the junction of Highways 138 and 230, more than 200 lakeshore campsites divided among

Broken Arrow, Diamond Lake, and **Thielsen View,** with various hiking trails leading into the Cascades.

Tyee, 16 miles northwest of Sutherlin off Highway 138, 15 campsites on the bank of the Umpqua River, with horseshoe pits and benches available courtesy of a recent Eagle Scout project.

South Umpqua River, east of Canyonville off Tiller Trail Highway and South Umpqua River Road. **Dumont Creek** and **Boulder Creek,** both near South Umpqua Falls, and **Camp Comfort,** in the shade of old- growth cedars and firs. In addition, **Threehorn** campground lies south of the Tiller Ranger District headquarters off the Tiller Trail Highway, and **Cover** campground lies along Jackson Creek, a tributary of the South Umpqua River, to the south off Forest Road 29 and near the world's largest sugar pine tree.

Devils Flat, 17 miles east of Azalea off County Road 36 and Forest Road 32, 2 primitive campsites on the bank of Cow Creek and near Cow Creek Falls. Hiking trails include short loops to the falls and a viewpoint as well as the 5-mile Devils Flat Trail, which leads to the top of Red Mountain.

See also *Wilder Places —Parks.*

CANOEING **Lake in the Woods** and **Hemlock Lake,** 27 and 32 miles southeast of Glide off Little River Road. It may be true that only God can make a tree, but people have made themselves some pretty good lakes, including these two along Little River: 4-acre **Lake in the Woods,** only 8 feet deep, and 28-acre **Hemlock Lake,** 33 feet deep. Both prohibit motors but offer campgrounds, boat ramps, and stocked rainbow trout, while nearby are waterfalls, hiking trails, and the **Boulder Creek Wilderness Area** (see *Wilder Places—Wilderness Areas*).

GOLF **Myrtle Creek Golf Course** (541-863-4653), Fairway Drive, Myrtle Creek, 18 holes.

Oak Hills Golf Club (541-459-4422), 1919 Recreation Lane, Sutherlin, 18 holes.

HIKING **North Umpqua River,** between Glide and Diamond Lake along Highway 138. Strung along the North Umpqua River is a 76-mile pathway broken into manageable segments for hikers who want to explore the countryside, especially its waterfalls: **Fern Falls,** 6 miles east of Glide, a 3.5-mile round -trip that begins at the Swiftwater Bridge and leads along the river, through a mossy forest, and toward **Deadline Falls** and Fern Falls; **Susan Creek Falls,** 12 miles east of Glide; a 2-mile round trip along forested Susan Creek to a 60-foot waterfall; **Fall Creek Falls,** 17 miles east of Glide, a 2-mile round trip along Fall Creek to its 100-foot falls; **Toketee Falls,** 40 miles east of Glide, a 1-mile round trip to this 90-foot falls whose Native American name means "graceful"; and **Watson Falls,** 43 miles east of Glide, 1-mile round trip to the highest falls in the area at 272 feet.

See also *Camping* and *Wilder Places—Wilderness Areas.*

UNIQUE ADVENTURES **Wine Country Tours** (1-800-547-7842; www.oregon-wine.org). **Umpqua River Valley** near **Roseburg: Henry Estate Winery** off Sutherlin–Umpqua Road (exit 136 off Interstate 5); **Hillcrest Vineyard** off Vineyard Lane; **Denino Umpqua**

River Estate off N. W. Valley Road; **Champagne Creek Cellars** off Busenbark Lane; and **Abacela Vineyard** and **La Garza Cellars,** both off Highway 99, (exit 119 off Interstate 5).

✷ Wilder Places

PARKS **Roseburg City Parks.** Two of the best parks in this city on the Umpqua River are **Riverside Park,** downtown between the Oak and Washington Street bridges, located on the bank of the river and featuring gardens that grow azaleas and rhododendrons; and **Stewart Park,** 230 acres located on Stewart Parkway and offering a playground, picnic pavilion, steam locomotive, duck pond, and a wildlife area left in its natural state.

Stanton County Park, 2 miles north of Canyonville off Interstate 5, exit 99 or 101. Visitors to this park on the bank of the South Umpqua River can take advantage of picnic areas with pavilions, and campgrounds with showers.

WILDERNESS AREAS **Boulder Creek,** 47 miles east of Roseburg off Highway 138, 30 square miles. With its southern edge nudging the north bank of the North Umpqua River, the Boulder Creek Wilderness is a land cut by a winding creek, bordered by rugged valleys, and studded with rock spires, mixed forests, and wildflower meadows. The trails, which follow or intersect Boulder Creek, total more than 30 miles, and one of its shortest (2 miles) and most accessible (off Highway 138) leads to an old-growth pine forest on Pine Bench.

Rogue–Umpqua Divide, 33 miles northeast of Shady Cove off Highways 62 and 230, 52 square miles. Lying along the western slope of the Cascades and the divide between the Rogue and Umpqua Rivers, this wilderness is a mosaic of lake basins, forested ridges and slopes, and the eroded remains of the ancient Cascades, which stood here millions of years before the current Cascades first inched their way up from the ground.

WILDLIFE REFUGES **Deadline Falls,** 20 miles east of Roseburg off Highway 138. A 400-yard trail that begins near the Swiftwater Bridge leads through an old-growth forest of fir and cedar to a viewing platform overlooking Deadline Falls. From here starting in June and lasting through October, visitors can watch **steelhead** and **chinook salmon** leaping the falls on the journey upriver to their spawning grounds.

✷ Lodging

BED & BREAKFASTS

Roseburg

House of Hunter (1-800-540-7704; walth@wizzards.net; www.magick.net/hunter/b&b.html), 813 S. E. Kane Street, Roseburg 97470. A strong sense of family pervades the 1900 Victorian Italianate home of Jean and Walt Hunter, perhaps because the guest rooms are named for the Hunters' daughters. Those four rooms come with king or queen beds, private baths, and a full breakfast ($70–90). Children older than 10 are welcome.

Riverview Bed & Breakfast (1-800-861-5655; www.riverview-bedandbreakfast.com), 5601 Sunshine Road, Roseburg 97470). This home stands so close to the Umpqua River that ospreys fly overhead and Canada geese and mallards stroll about the yard. The two guest rooms come with king beds, private baths, and a full breakfast ($55–65).

LODGES

🐾 **Elkqua Lodge** (1-888-862-7474), 221 Main Street, Elkton 97436. Because it's located at the confluence of Elk Creek and the Umpqua River—hence, the name—this 1964 lodge with its wood-beam ceilings can be a starting point for outdoor adventure, including either do-it-yourself or guided fishing and hunting trips. It offers two rooms with private baths and two with shared baths ($50–75). The full breakfast features such staples as biscuits and gravy, eggs and hash browns, pancakes and ham, and other items on a changing menu. Pets are welcome if "watched closely."

Steelhead Run Bed & Breakfast (1-800-348-0563; steelhead@steelheadrun.com; www.steelheadrun.com), 23049 North Umpqua Highway, Glide 97443. As the name implies, Steelhead Run stands along one of the Northwest's great steelhead streams, the North Umpqua. Taking advantage of that location, the home has two decks, and three of its four guest rooms ($58–88; buffet breakfast $10 extra) have river views and private entrances, so anglers can sneak away early to try their luck on the river they've been watching on the other side of the window. All four rooms come with private bathrooms.

* Where to Eat

EATING OUT

Roseburg

Roseburg Station Pub and Brewery (541-672-1934), 700 Sheridan Street, Roseburg. This is one of the good deeds the McMenamin brothers have done for lovers of good beer and historic buildings, converting the old Southern Pacific depot into a pub and brewery, one of many such restorations the brothers have undertaken across the state. Here a vaulted ceiling and wood wainscoting surround diners who dig into traditional but quality pub fare: burgers, sandwiches, salads, and some of the best beer in the Northwest.

Village Bistro and Bakery (541-677-3450), 500 S. E. Cass Avenue, Roseburg. Abundant space and a sunlit patio create the ambience for this bistro, while the stuff of salads and sandwiches makes up its memorable lunches that include both home-style and vegetarian dishes.

* Special Events

November–December: **Umpqua Valley Festival of Lights** (541-672-9731), Roseburg.

December: 🖍 **Wildlife Safari's Wildlights** (1-800-355-4848), Winston. View the animals at night. See also *To See—For Families*

GRANTS PASS–ROGUE RIVER AREA

GUIDANCE **Bureau of Land Management: Medford District** (541-770-2200), 3040 Biddle Road, Medford 97501.

Grants Pass Visitors and Convention Bureau (1-800-547-5927; www.visit-grantspass.org), 1995 N. W. Vine Street, Grants Pass 97526.

Oregon State Parks (503-378-6305), State Parks and Recreation Department, 525 Trade Street S. E., Salem 97301.

Rogue River Chamber of Commerce (541-582-0242), 8898 Rogue River Highway, Rogue River 97537.

Rogue River National Forest: Headquarters (541-858-2200), 333 W. 8th Street, Medford 97501; **Prospect Ranger District** (541-560-3400), Prospect.

Siskiyou National Forest:, Headquarters (541-471-6500), 200 N. E. Greenfield Road, Grants Pass 97526; **Galice Ranger District** (541-471-6500), Grants Pass.

GETTING THERE The Grants Pass–Rogue River area is reached from the east by Highway 234, from the south by Interstate 5 and Highway 199, from the west by Highway 199 and its connection to Highway 101 on the Oregon coast, and from the north by Interstate 5.

MEDICAL EMERGENCY **Three Rivers Community Hospital** (541-476-6831), 500 S. W. Ramsey Street, Grants Pass.

✷ To See

MUSEUMS **Applegate Trail Interpretive Center** (1-888-411-1846), Sunny Valley (exit 71 off Interstate 5). When the first wagon train traveling the Applegate Trail (see *To See—Historic Sites* in Medford–Ashland–Applegate Valley Area) camped near here in the fall of 1846, 16-year-old Martha Leland Crowley died of typhoid fever and was buried on the north side of the nearby stream, now named Grave Creek. Today this center tells the story of Martha and the other pioneers who took the southern route into Oregon. With displays spread across more than 5,000 square feet, this story has room to include chapters on gold mining, stagecoaches, and railroads.

HISTORIC HOMES **Whiskey Creek Cabin,** trailhead at Grave Creek Bridge, 24 miles northwest of Merlin off Merlin–Galice Road (exit 61 off Interstate 5). A remnant of the area's gold rush days, this miner's cabin started out in the 1880s as a shack with a dirt floor, but as the years passed and owners changed, the cabin began taking on some of the trappings of civilization: a plank floor and an extra room, a tool shed and a solar shower, even a sawdust-insulated pantry. That's pretty much the way it stands today on the north bank of the Rogue River near the mouth of Whiskey Creek, 3 miles from the nearest road and accessible only by foot or boat. In this isolation, the cabin remains much as it was in the beginning, as a distant outpost for those willing to work the canyon for the gold it held. "It's 12, 14 hours a day," said 82-year-old Lou Martin, who spent his last years living at the cabin and working his claim. "Couldn't be like a grasshopper, play around all summer, wouldn't have nothin.'"

HISTORIC SITES **Wolf Creek Inn** (541-866-2474), in the town of Wolf Creek, exit 76 off Interstate 5. Beginning in the 1860s, travelers on the Oregon Stage Line could make the 700-mile bone-jolting stagecoach journey between Portland and Sacramento in six days—six *long* days of 12 hours or more, an experience that might be compared to spending the same time tumbling in a dryer. (The price of a ticket was $50, more than two months' wages for many at the time.) Yet each night, passengers had the chance to unfold themselves from the stage and work out the kinks at one of the stops or inns standing every 15 or 20 miles along the way. Wolf Creek Inn, built in 1883, was such a place. With a parlor for the ladies and a sitting room for the men downstairs, 10 sleeping rooms upstairs, and no alcohol permitted on the premises, the inn offered gentile accommodations for the time. Through the years it continued serving travelers, compiling an impressive list of celebrity guests: Mary Pickford, Orson Welles, Carole Lombard, Clark Gable, and Jack London, to name a few. After falling on hard times and suffering through neglect, the 1883 inn was rescued and restored as an **Oregon State Park,** and today its rooms and **restaurant** are open once again to wayfaring strangers.

Golden, 6 miles east of Wolf Creek off Interstate 5 and Coyote Creek Road. The name says it all: Born in the late 19th century from out of the goldfields and destined to boom or bust with the mines, Golden today is a ghost town where only memories live and a few buildings remain. Yet the town may still have a future. "There are very few places left like this," says Sandy Henderson, member of a nonprofit group that has bought the town and plans to restore it. "It's absolutely precious."

Rogue River Ranch, 61 miles northwest of Merlin off Merlin–Galice Road and Bureau of Land Management (BLM)roads, turnoff at Grave Creek Bridge, 8 miles north of Galice. The history of this ranch, of its homestead houses and barns, shops and sheds, begins more than 9,000 years ago, when the native peoples of the Rogue River region began using the area for hunting, gathering, and camping. The white presence at the site, however, begins near the end of the 19th century with the arrival of the first homesteaders, miners, and millers. Between the turn of the 20th century and the Great Depression the community of **Marial,** named for the daughter of the first postmaster, reached a population as high as 100. "It was the spell of adventure," recalled one of Marial's residents, "the enchantment of the rugged canyon walls and wild river that clutched the souls of these early pioneers." Today this 200-acre ranch and its buildings—the complex is listed on the **National Register of Historic Places**—are what remain of the old community.

COVERED BRIDGES **Grave Creek,** 17 miles northeast of Grants Pass off Interstate 5 (take the Sunny Valley exit), built in 1920, 105 feet long; **Wimer,** 7 miles north of the town of Rogue River off Evans Creek Road and in the town of Wimer, built in 1927 (rebuilt in 1962), 85 feet.

FOR FAMILIES **Hellgate Jetboat Excursions** (1-800-648-4874), 966 S. E. Sixth Street, Grants Pass. Skimming the river's surface like a gigantic metallic water skipper, a jet boat can carry you away from the city, down the river, and into the wild, seemingly in moments. And once you leave the houses and lawns behind, the two-hour river ride along the Rogue opens an adventure in the world of ospreys and herons, beavers and deer.

Wildlife Images Rehabilitation and Education Center (541-476-0222), 13 miles west of Grants Pass off Lower River Road. A place of healing for injured, ill, or abandoned wildlife, this rehabilitation center offers twice-daily guided tours—call first for an appointment—that teaches visitors about animals ranging from hummingbirds to bears. Most of the 1,500 to 2,500 animals that arrive at the center each year are eventually able to return to the wild, though more than 100, including bears and wolves, become permanent residents of the 26-acre site. "These are all animals that were able to survive whatever got them here," says center director Dave Siddon, "but unfortunately cannot be in the wild again."

Fire Lookout Rentals (541-471-6516), Siskiyou National Forest, 200 N. E. Greenfield Road, Grants Pass. In the 1930s and 1940s, the U.S. Forest Service built hundreds of fire lookouts throughout the Northwest, but they fell into disuse with the extension of roads and the adoption of other fire- detection techniques. Those that remain are available to campers who want to spend time on the edge of untamed country. In this area, **Onion Mountain,** 20 miles west of Grants Pass, offers a view of the city's lights.

Yurt Camping (Oregon Parks and Recreation Department, 1-800-551-6949). Staying in a yurt makes it possible to make a reservation at a state park, show up without a tent and little camping gear, and still spend the night within sight of a starry, starry night. Usual yurt accommodations include beds and electricity inside, fire rings and picnic tables outside. In this region, yurt camping is available at **Valley of the Rogue State Park** (see *Wilder Places—Parks*), 12 miles east of Grants Pass off Interstate 5.

SCENIC DRIVES **Rogue River Loop,** 45 paved miles along the Lower River, Upper River, Merlin–Galice, Lower Grave Creek, and Lower Wolf Creek Roads from near Grants Pass to Wolf Creek. If you want to see a few stretches of the designated Wild and Scenic Rogue River, maybe stop along the way to have a picnic, take a walk, or wet a fishing line, then try this tour route: Start south of

Grants Pass on Lower River Road and drive northwest **along the Rogue** and past the park lawns stretching beneath the shade, the whitewater roaring through **Hellgate Canyon,** and the rafters clustering at the **Galice Resort** until you reach the bridge at **Grave Creek;** here you'll leave the river behind as your path veers to the northeast—along a hillside so curving and a road so narrow that every corner provides a reason to be thankful for the absence of traffic—and eventually carries you to **Wolf Creek,** where you can stop and have a beer at the inn.

Grave Creek to Marial Back Country Byway, 37 paved and graveled miles along Bureau of Land Management (BLM) roads, starting at Grave Creek Bridge, 26 miles northwest of Grants Pass off Interstate 5 (exit 61) and the Merlin–Galice Road. This rugged road leads you to the rim of the **Rogue River canyon** and the edge of the **Wild Rogue Wilderness** (see *Wilder Places—Wilderness Areas*). Near its end, where Mule Creek flows into the Rogue, you'll find yourself at a placed named **Marial** (see Rogue River Ranch under *Historic Sites*), a crossroads of cultures and their histories: a campsite and hunting area for native peoples, a homestead and mining center for early settlers, all of it still surrounded by miles of untamed country.

Grants Pass to Gold Beach, 98 paved miles along Lower River, Upper River, Galice–Merlin and Galice Access Roads, Forest Road 23, and Agness and Jerrys Flat Roads. Three forms of power will carry you along the designated Wild and Scenic portions of the Rogue River: travel by foot, by raft, or by car. The auto tour provides a more distant but a more comfortable experience, with the paved, sometimes single-lane road hugging river bank or canyon rim as it cuts through some of the wildest county in the Northwest.

NATURAL WONDERS **Siskiyou Mountains** (bordered by the Coast Range to the north, the Cascade Range to the east, and the California border to the south). This mountain range is the Oregon segment of the **Klamath Mountains** that extend into northern California and that were initially formed as the result of at least seven different collisions—the first occurring as long ago as 450 million years—between ocean islands and the North American continent. Comprising approximately 40 percent of the entire Klamath range, the Siskiyous' highest peak is **Mount Ashland** (7,533 feet) and its major river is the Rogue.

✷ To Do

CAMPING **Taylor Creek,** southwest of Merlin off Merlin–Galice and Taylor Creek Roads, 5 campgrounds, most with trailheads, stretch alongside Taylor Creek, a tributary of the Rogue River: **Tin Can,** 3 primitive campsites; **Myers Creek,** 2 primitive campsites; **Big Pine,** 12 campsites near one of the world's largest ponderosa pines, with an interpretive loop trail to show it off; **Sam Brown,** 42 campsites near a large meadow, flush toilets, and nearby horse facilities; and **Secret Creek,** 2 primitive campsites and the nearby Secret Way Trail.

Bearcamp, 21 miles northwest of Galice off the Galice Access Road, a campground almost a mile high that offers a viewpoint above the Rogue River as well as a 1.5-mile ridgeline trail.

See also **Rogue River Parks** under *Wilder Places—Parks.*

HIKING **Rainie Falls,** 24 miles northwest of Merlin off Merlin–Galice Road (exit 61 off Interstate 5). One way to experience the Rogue River's whitewater without getting wet is to hike its south bank 2 miles to Rainie Falls. Here the entire river squeezes through a narrow chute and then plunges 12 feet over a vertical ledge of basalt. It's an impressive show. That's why folks line the bank here to watch kayaks and rafts take on the tumbling river. In fact, Rainie Falls—named for a fellow called Old Man Rainie, who lived in a cabin below the falls and made his living gaffing salmon from the river—represents that portion of the Rogue that has remained relatively unchanged in its wildness since before the time of the area's native people, the Takelma, who called the falls *Taktamaykh,* part of which translates to "a big waterfall way down Rogue River."

Whiskey Creek Cabin, trailhead at Grave Creek Bridge, 24 miles northwest of Merlin off Merlin–Galice Road (exit 61 off Interstate 5). This 3-mile walk along the north bank of the Rogue River does two things: gives you a taste of the 40-mile **Rogue River National Recreation Trail** as well as a segment of this designated Wild and Scenic river, and leads you to a historic miner's cabin, one of the last standing from the later years of the area's gold rush days.

RAINIE FALLS

Limpy Botanical Interpretive Trail, 10 miles southwest of Grants Pass off Highway 99, Riverbanks Road, and Limpy Creek Road. Much of the southwest corner of the state is a botanist's delight for the number and variety of plants growing here, and this 1-mile loop and interpretive trail provides visitors with a sample of the region's offerings, as well as some stunning views of the Rogue River Valley.

See also *Camping.*

✷ Wilder Places

PARKS **Riverside Park,** next to Caveman Bridge on the bank of the Rogue River, Grants Pass. The main attraction here is the Rogue River, on whose bank the park lies, providing visitors to the city with picnic sites, playgrounds, rose gardens, and sites for occasional music festivals.

Valley of the Rogue State Park, 12 miles east of Grants Pass off Interstate 5, day use and overnight. For more than 2 miles this park stretches itself in a shady green line between Interstate 5 and the Rogue River. As a result, the place seems to grow calmer the farther you move from the traffic and the closer you get to the water. So it's the freeway that brings people here (it's one of the most visited of Oregon's inland parks) and the river that keeps them (it's a calm span of the Rogue, famous for its whitewater).

Rogue River Parks, along the Rogue River from east of Grants Pass to north of Galice. A series of county parks lining the Rogue River offer campgrounds as well as a wide range of recreational facilities, especially those connected to almost anything you can do in the water. The closer the park is to the city of Grants Pass, the more sophisticated are its offerings; the farther away, the more primitive. So from east to west, these parks include the following: **Tom Pearce Park,** 107 acres and facilities that include picnic shelters, horseshoe pits, a volleyball court, softball diamond, playground, and even a disc golf course; **Schroeder Park,** similar to Tom Pearce Park with the addition of boat rentals; **Whitehorse Park,** primitive areas along the river that serve as wildlife habitat and bird-watching areas; **Griffin Park,** a smaller park with easy access to the river; **Indian Mary Park,** located on the Wild and Scenic portion of the river, once the nation's smallest Indian reservation and now an area where rafters and anglers gather; **Almeda Park,** a primitive campground popular with rafters.

Palmerton Park Arboretum, W. Evans Creek Road (exit 48 off Interstate 5), Rogue River. This green, leafy corner of the world is a gift from the family of Orin Palmerton, who in the 1930s began planting trees, shrubs, and flowers at the landscape nursery business he operated from his home. Those plantings, acquired from all over the world, now line the pathways of this park and arboretum.

WILDERNESS AREAS **Wild Rogue Wilderness,** 27 miles northwest of Grants Pass off Interstate 5 (exit 80), Cow Creek Road and Mule Creek–Marial Road, 56 square miles. A wild river running through rough country, the Rogue spent millennia cutting its way through mountains to reach the sea, and it has calmed down little since then. With its whitewater rapids tumbling through towering canyons, the river seems ever restless in its race to the Pacific, not so much pristine as it is primitive, as is the land it drains.

* Lodging

See also **Fire Lookout Rentals** and **Yurt Camping** under *To See—For Families*.

INNS **Wolf Creek Inn** (541-866-2474; innkeeper@state.or.us; www.wolfcreekinn.com), 100 Front Street, Wolf Creek, 97497. Innkeeper Dean Kasner calls the Wolf Creek Inn "among the best preserved and oldest active traveler's inns in Oregon." The inn's history goes back to 1883, when it began serving as a stage stop along the Portland to Sacramento route. Today it still offers travelers a break from the road, providing eight guest rooms ($55–75) and a suite ($100), furnished as in the days of the stagecoach, with period antiques (or reproductions), braided rugs, and quilts. Private baths and a full breakfast are part of the package. "We define the cuisine at the Wolf Creek Inn as 'country elegant,'" Dean says, "and there's something on the menu for everyone."

BED & BREAKFASTS

Azalea

Havenshire Bed & Breakfast (541-837-3511), 1098 Hogum Creek Road, Azalea 97410). On 60 acres bristling with forests and wildflowers stands this 1981 inn built in the style of an English Tudor home. It offers two guest rooms, one with a private bath, both with a full breakfast served in the dining room ($60–65).

Grants Pass

Chateau Le Bear Bed & Breakfast (541-471-6269; innkeeper@chateaulebear.com; www.chateaulebear.com), 1219 Summer Lane, Grants Pass 97526. A relative newcomer to the B&B scene—it opened in the summer of 2002—the Chateau Le Bear began with the dream of owner Daisy Franks. "The original concept for the bed and breakfast was to allow cancer patients to come and stay for a night or two without paying and to be pampered," Daisy says, "to relax and enjoy the atmosphere and food, and not have to think of the problems at hand." Even though financial realities have postponed that goal, the B&B has opened its doors on almost 2 acres along the Rogue River, and now offers guest suites that come with private baths, river views, gas fireplaces, jetted tubs, queen feather beds, and a full breakfast ($95–150). "I'm hoping," Daisy says, "that the saying 'Let the stress of life flow down the Rogue River at Chateau Le Bear Bed and Breakfast' comes true for all."

Flery Manor (541-476-3591; flery@flerymanor.com; www.flerymanor.com), 2000 Jumpoff Joe Creek Road, Grants Pass 97526. Family antiques and original artwork decorate this modern three-story inn that stands on 7 acres near the Rogue River. Its five guest rooms all have private baths; suites have king beds, fireplaces, Jacuzzis, and private balconies ($85–150). Guests are invited to share the living room with its two-story fireplace and windows as well as the library; outside, they can wander the paths leading to the ponds and gardens, gazebo and waterfall, and stream and koi pond. The three-course gourmet breakfast might feature orange blossom French toast, wild apple and blackberry crêepes, or baked potato pancakes, among many items developed specifically for the inn, some of which have appeared in *Chef* magazine. Children older than 10 are welcome.

The Ivy House (541-474-7363), 139 S. W. I Street, Grants Pass 97526. Listed on the **National Historic Register** and located in the city's historic district, this 1905 two-story English "arts and crafts" brick home offers one guest room with a private bath ($80) and four rooms that share baths ($55–75). In addition, the home's breakfast is as English as its design, serving tea, crumpets, and bangers along with entrées that can include bacon, tomatoes, mushrooms, and eggs.

Ponderosa Pine Inn (866-299-7463; pondpininn@chatlink.com; www.ponderosapineinn.com), 907 Stringer Gap Road, Grants Pass 97527. Location is a primary feature of this inn situated between the Rogue and Applegate Rivers—not only in its proximity to the Oregon Caves, Crater Lake, and area wineries, but also in its quiet 5 acres that adjoin a hiking trail and border a country road suitable for sight-seeing by car or bicycle. But you don't have to leave the place to enjoy it. "This is a real country inn," says owner Shelly Clary, "with a wraparound porch and a swing to enjoy in the cool evenings." Its two guest rooms have separate baths and come with breakfast. "We always have fresh flowers in the rooms," Shelly says, "and we offer a wonderful breakfast."

Merlin

Pine Meadow Inn (1-800-554-0806; pmi@pinemeadowinn.com; www.pinemeadowinn.com), 1000 Crow Road, Merlin 97532. Take a modern two-story midwestern farmhouse with a wraparound porch, decorate it with turn-of-the-20th-century antiques, set it down near the wild Rogue River, surround it with meadows and woods, sprinkle in some paths and benches and a koi pond with a waterfall—and you've got yourself Pine Meadow Inn. "We do have a very unique and special property," says Nancy Murdock, who, along with her husband, Maloy, owns and operates the inn. The four guest rooms all have private baths ($80–100) and come with a three-course breakfast that can include seasonal fruits and vegetables from the inn's garden. Children older than 10 are welcome.

LODGES **Weasku Inn** (1-800-493-2758; riverinn@budget.net; www.weasku.com), 5560 Rogue River Highway, Grants Pass 97527. If you've ever wanted to stay in a log cabin built when Calvin Coolidge was president, this is your chance. Yet the Weasku Inn has always been more than a cabin. After Alfred Smith toppled the timber to build this log lodge at his newly established fishing camp, opening its doors in 1924, guests could rent a room for a dollar a night. Before long, word got out about the great fishing, and celebrities such as Walt Disney, Bing Crosby, Herbert Hoover, Clark Gable, and Zane Grey—Gable and Grey seem to have visited virtually every fishing lodge in the state at one time or another—made their way here, rods in hand. Today the inn offers 17 guest rooms and suites, all of them with king or queen beds and private baths and entrances and some of them with fireplaces, decks, and whirlpool tubs ($110–350). A continental breakfast is included.

* Where to Eat

EATING OUT

Grants Pass

Hamilton River House (541-479-3938), 1936 Rogue River Highway, Grants Pass. Doug Hamilton's River House features a bright decor, river views, and good food. Various fish and chicken dishes are popular for dinner, as are the hamburgers and wood-fired pizzas for lunch.

Matsukaze (541-479-2961), 1675 N. E. Seventh Street, Grants Pass. Even though Interstate 5 lies nearby, this Japanese restaurant retains a sense of serenity. Its offerings include tempura and teriyaki, sushi and sukiyaki, and fish and seafood dishes.

Summer Jo's (541-476-6882), 2315 Upper River Road Loop, Grants Pass. Surrounded by acres of flowers and shrubs and trees, Summer Jo's is something of a Garden of Eden when it comes to its scenic qualities and lunch offerings. Sandwiches and salads are the mainstays, with the produce and herbs grown fresh on-site.

* Special Events

May: **Amazing May** (541-476-7717), Grants Pass. Through the month of May each year, Grants Pass is the host of a series of events the entire family can either watch or join: art shows, horse races, golf tournaments, farmer's markets, ethnic festivals, hot-air balloon rides, and a bunch more.

ILLINOIS VALLEY AREA

GUIDANCE **Bureau of Land Management: Medford District** (541-770-2200), 3040 Biddle Road, Medford 97501.

Illinois River Valley Visitor Center (541-592-2631), 201 Caves Highway, Cave Junction 97523.

Oregon State Parks (503-378-6305), State Parks and Recreation Department, 525 Trade Street S. E., Salem 97301.

Rogue River National Forest: Headquarters (541-858-2200), 333 W. Eighth Street, Medford 97501.

Siskiyou National Forest: Headquarters (541-471-6500), 200 N. E. Greenfield Road, Grants Pass 97526; **Illinois Valley Ranger District** (541-592-4000).

GETTING THERE The main road through the Illinois Valley area is Highway 199, which connects to Highway 101 on the Oregon coast and to Interstate 5 near Grants Pass.

MEDICAL EMERGENCY **Three Rivers Community Hospital** (541-476-6831), 500 SW Ramsey Street, Grants Pass.

✷ To See

MUSEUMS **Kerbyville Museum** (541-592-5252), 24195 Redwood Highway, Kerby. The old mining town of Kerby could once boast of a population of more than 500 miners, giving it enough size and influence in 1858 to make it the county seat. Even though the town faded away when the mines played out, the museum remains to tell its story. In addition, the museum surrounds the **Naucke House,** which was built in 1883 by Prussian immigrants William and Nannie Naucke, stands on its original site, and offers a look back at the days of sitting rooms, kerosene lamps, and hand pumps inside and equipment for farming, mining, and logging outside.

FOR FAMILIES ✐ **Fire Lookout Rentals** (541-471-6516), Siskiyou National Forest, 200 N. E. Greenfield Road, Grants Pass. Some of the fire lookouts built by the U.S. Forest Service in the 1930s and 1940s are now available to campers who want to spend time on the edge of untamed country. In this area, **Bolan,** located 30 miles southeast of Cave Junction, offers a tippity-top view of the world, including the **Red Buttes Wilderness** (see *Wilder Places—Wilderness Areas* in Medford–Ashland–Applegate Valley) along the California border, from a perch 6,242 feet above sea level.

SCENIC DRIVES **Redwood Highway,** beginning south of Cave Junction along Highway 199. If this land is my land and this land is your land, then the redwood forest part of it stretches between San Francisco and southwest Oregon. Even though the *big* trees are south of the border, beginning near Jedediah Smith Redwood State Park, you can get a start on them by heading south of Cave Junction on Highway 199.

NATURAL WONDERS **Oregon Caves National Monument,** 20 miles southeast of Cave Junction off Highway 46. The size of these caves is awe-inspiring and their origins baffling, for they're composed of a marble that originated as a limestone coral reef somewhere in the South Pacific. Then more than 100 million years ago, that reef collided with the landmass that is now southern Oregon, and the caves formed as the result of the earth faulting, folding, and eroding. More recently, in 1874, an area settler named Dijah Davidson was tracking a bear when he followed his dog Bruno to the site and stumbled upon the caves. (Recently discovered grizzly bear bones date back more than 50,000 years, making it, says the cave's resource manager John Roth, "the oldest known grizzly in the Americas.") Today 3 miles of these marble caves, located beneath 480 acres of forest, are the home of **nine species of bats** and the destination of thousands of visitors who come to see for themselves what can hardly be described.

✷ To Do

CAMPING **Cave Junction Area,** north, south, and east of Cave Junction off Highways 101 or Highway 46. **Bolan Lake,** 29 miles southeast of Cave Junction off Highway 199 and Waldo Road (turn east at O'Brien Road), 12 campsites at a small stocked lake that prohibits motorized boats, with a nearby fire lookout and hiking trail; **Cave Creek,** 16 miles east of Cave Junction off Highway 46, 18 campsites near the Oregon Caves National Monument; **Deer Creek,** 12 miles northeast of Cave Junction off Highway 99 and Reeves Creek Road, 16 creekside campsites near the community of Dryden and Lake Selmac; **Grayback,** 12 miles east of Cave Junction off Highway 46, 39 campsites near the Oregon Caves National Monument; **Lake Selmac Park,** 10 miles northeast of Cave Junction off Highway 199 and Reeves Creek Road, 73 campsites scattered across 5 camps that surround this lake known for its bass fishing; **Spaulding Pond,** 26 miles northwest of Cave Junction off Highway 199 and Forest Road 25, 5 primitive campsites near a historic mill site and a pond stocked annually with rainbow trout.

Illinois River (west of **Selma** on Highway 199 and along the Illinois

River Road and intersecting designated Forest Roads), 3 campgrounds: **Sixmile, Store Gulch,** and **Briggs Creek.**

HIKING **Oregon Caves Big Tree Loop,** 19 miles south of Cave Junction on Highway 46. Even though the Oregon Caves (see *To See—Natural Wonders*) attract crowds who come to ponder the wonder of all that cavernous space underground, at least one marvel grows in the sunlight and shade of a nearby hillside: Big Tree, Oregon's **second-largest Douglas fir,** more than 12 feet in diameter and possibly 15 centuries old. This loop trail, stretching a bit more than 3 miles along the slope rising above the caves, will take you to it.

UNIQUE ADVENTURES **Wine Country Tours** (1-800-547-7842; www.oregonwine.org). In **Cave Junction: Bear Creek Winery/Siskiyou Vineyards** off Highway 46, **Bridgeview Vineyard** off Holland Loop Road, and **Foris Vineyards Winery** off Kendall Road.

* Wilder Places

PARKS **Illinois River State Park,** 1 mile south of Cave Junction off Highway 199, day use only. This park lies on the edge of things—the confluence of the East and West Forks of the Illinois River, the boundary of the Siskiyou National Forest, and the turnoff to the famous **Oregon Caves National Monument** (see *To See—Natural Wonders*).

WILDERNESS AREAS **Kalmiopsis,** 33 miles southwest of Grants Pass off Highway 199 and the Illinois River Road and its spur roads, 281 square miles). Once upon a time, some 200 million years ago, what is now the Klamath Mountain range was the shoreline of North America, a continent that couldn't hold still. Restless but slow, it drifted along on a westward path at a rate of an inch per year. Not a fast journey, of course, but a persistent one: Multiply that yearly inch by millions, calculate the mass and the weight behind it, and you'll see that something had to give. In this case, it was the seafloor, which buckled into canyons, rose into ridges, and formed the rumpled landscape that today holds this wilderness area.

* Lodging

See also **Fire Lookout Rentals** under *To See—For Families.*

RESORTS **Out 'n' About Treesort** (1-800-200-5484; treesort@treehouses.com; www.treehouses.com), 300 Page Creek Road, Cave Junction 97523. One thing's for sure: You'll have to travel a *long* ways before you find anything else like this, if you can find anything at all. That's because here the accommodations are out on a limb, stuck up in a tree. Literally. The rooms and suites and cabins at Out 'n' About Treesort are perched in the branches and fixed to the trunks of trees on this 36-acre resort at the edge of the Siskiyou National Forest. But don't expect these tree houses to resemble something from a Tarzan movie, for they can contain queen beds, kitchenettes, even a full bath, though most of the rest-room facilities remain nearby at ground level ($90–160, including a full breakfast). In addition, two suspension bridges of 45 and 90 feet provide treetop walkways.

INNS ✐ **Kerbyville Inn** (1-877-273-4843; bvw@bridgeviewwine.com; www.bridgeviewwine.com), 24304 Redwood Highway, Kerby 97531. Get down around the California neck of the woods along the Redwood Highway, and at this inn you'll find a guest room ($59) and four suites ($75–99) that come with private baths and entrances, king or queen beds, access to a deck and garden, and a continental breakfast. Children younger than 8 stay free.

LODGES ✐ **Erin Lodge** (541-592-4253; erin77@intenetcds.com; www.erinlodge.com), 2905 Redwood Highway, Cave Junction 97523. As peaceful as the stretch of Illinois River that flows past it, Erin Lodge is built from logs and stones yet offers accommodations far from rustic. Five guest rooms include Queen ($60), King ($70), Deluxe King ($80), Double Queen ($110), and Family ($170) suites that come with a continental or full breakfast. Kids are welcome.

✱ Special Events

August: **Wild Blackberry Festival** (541-592-3326), Cave Junction.

MEDFORD–ASHLAND–APPLEGATE VALLEY AREA

GUIDANCE **Bureau of Land Management: Medford District** (541-770-2200), 3040 Biddle Road, Medford 97501.

Central Point Visitor Center (541-664-5301), 27 S. Seventh Street, Central Point 97502.

Jacksonville Chamber of Commerce (541-899-8118; www.jacksonvilleoregon.org), 185 N. Oregon Street, Jacksonville 97530.

Medford Visitor and Convention Bureau (1-800-469-6307; www.visitmedford.org), 101 E. Eigth Street, Medford 97501.

Oregon State Parks (503-378-6305), State Parks and Recreation Department, 525 Trade Street S. E., Salem 97301.

Rogue River Chamber of Commerce (541-582-0242), 8898 Rogue River Highway, Rogue River 97537.

Rogue River National Forest: Headquarters (541-858-2200), 333 W. Eighth Street, Medford 97501; **Applegate Ranger District** (541-482-3333); **Ashland Ranger District** (541-899-1812); **Butte Falls Ranger District** (541-865-2700).

GETTING THERE The Medford–Ashland area is reached from the north by Highways 62 and 234 and Interstate 5, from the east by Highways 140 and 66, and from the south by Interstate 5. In addition, Highway 199 connects the area to the Oregon coast. The Applegate Valley is linked to the Medford–Ashland area by Highway 238 and the Applegate River Road.

MEDICAL EMERGENCY **Ashland Community Hospital** (541-482-2441), 280 Maple Street, Ashland.

Providence Medford Medical Center (541-732-5000), 1111 Crater Lake Avenue, Medford.

Rogue Valley Medical Center (541-608-4900), 2825 E. Barnett Road, Medford.

✷ To See

MUSEUMS **Southern Oregon History Center** (541-773-6536; www.sohs.org), 106 N. Central Avenue, Medford. The past of southwest Oregon is wrapped in layers of native tribes and gold camps, Indian wars and fruit growers, railroads and sawmills—and this museum's more than 80,000 artifacts seem to cover much of it. In addition, its collection of historical photographs is considered one of the finest in the Northwest.

Jacksonville Museum of Southern Oregon History (541-773-6536; www.sohs.org), 206 N. Fifth Street, Jacksonville. Located in the 1883 former Jackson County Courthouse, this museum traces the changes in the region, the historical transitions that saw native Takelmas and Hudson's Bay trappers give way first to gold miners and homesteaders and eventually businessmen whose visions created towns such as Jacksonville.

Children's Museum (541-773-6536; www.sohs.org), 206 N. Fifth Street, Jacksonville. Although it's probably not meant as a symbolic gesture, this museum devoted to children is housed in the former county jail. Hmm.

Applegate Valley Historical Society Museum (541-846-7565), junction of Highway 238 and North Applegate Road, Applegate. The age and history of this museum building match that of its contents, for the hand-hewn pine-log cabin dates back to the 1870s when the Applegate Valley was the site of homestead farms and gold mines.

HISTORIC HOMES **Beekman House** (541-773-6536), 406 E. California Street, Jacksonville. Like many men lured to California during the gold rush, Cornelius Beekman, originally of New York, found it was easier to make money from the miners than from the mines. As a result, he found himself easing his way into the banking and express business in Jacksonville, and in the 1870s he and his wife, Julia, built this Gothic Revival house there. Nowadays this simple home with the steep gables and railed balcony still contains the Beekmans' furniture and appliances as well as their outbuildings, including a woodshed and outhouse. (Perhaps the house's most significant feature, however, is the presence of the "Beekman family," portrayed by performers in period costumes.) After Cornelius died in 1915 of what the local newspaper reported as "hemorrhage of the bowels," his son Ben adopted as his motto "Trust in God and keep your bowels open."

HISTORIC SITES **Applegate Trail,** Highway 66 and Interstate 5, from east of Ashland to west of Myrtle Creek. In the home stretch of their journey along the Oregon Trail in 1843, the families of Lindsay and Jesse Applegate each lost a 10 year-old-son in a whirlpool of the Columbia River. Vowing to spare other families the same tragedy, the brothers searched for a new route into the Willamette Valley, and three years later the Applegate Trail opened through the southern Cascades. Even though most of the Oregon portion of the trail today lies beneath the pavement of Highway 66 and Interstate 5, you can still find remnants of the old wagon route, including its ruts, at **Tubb Spring State Wayside,** 18 miles east of Ashland off Highway 66, and along **Dole Road,** west of Myrtle Creek and east of Interstate 5.

Butte Creek Mill (541-826-3531), 402 Royal Avenue N., Eagle Point. Since 1872 this four-story water-powered grist mill on the banks of Little Butte Creek has been grinding grain into flour the same methodical way: The creekwater enters the millrace and flows into a penstock; the weight of the water turns the wheels and belts and pulleys that turn the millstones; the grain pours into a hopper that feeds it to the stones. Like the operation, the mill itself has remained unchanged through the years, featuring the same two millstones—quarried near Paris and assembled in Illinois, eventually shaped into a matched set, with each stone measuring 4 feet in diameter and weighing 1,400 pounds, then shipped around Cape Horn and hauled by horse-drawn wagon to Oregon—housed in the same mill building, with walls of whipsawed lumber fastened with square nails to a frame of mortised and pegged beams. Now listed on the **National Register of Historic Places,** the mill is the only one like it still operating in Oregon.

Prospect Hotel, 391 Mill Creek Drive, Prospect, off Highway 62. When it opened to guests in 1892, the Prospect Hotel had no difficulty luring travelers to its doors. After all, the hotel stood on the old Fort Klamath military and wagon road, near the banks of the Rogue River, and on the route to Crater Lake. As a result, the guest register through the years came to include the names of celebrities such as Teddy Roosevelt, Zane Grey, Jack London, and Herbert Hoover. After falling on hard times, the hotel has been recently restored as a B&B.

Southern Pacific Railroad Depot, 147 Front Street, Medford. Southwest Oregon's largest city was born along the railroad tracks, the train bringing to life an isolated community and an engineer from Medford, Massachusetts, giving it its name. As the Oregon and California Railroad—later the Southern Pacific—grew, so did Medford, until the city in 1909 became the state's second-largest rail point, a distinction that resulted in the construction of this brick depot the following year. Even though Medford's golden years of busy rails lasted only until the late 1920s—when the railroad shifted its main line to Klamath Falls and businesses began transporting their freight by truck—the depot remains as a reminder of those days.

Hanley Farm (5451-773-6536), Hanley Road, Medford. For more than a century, beginning with a Donation Land Claim in 1856, this farm was the home of the Hanley family. Today the 38-acre site is a working farm and a historical landmark whose features range from prehistoric campsites to 19th-century buildings.

Jacksonville Walking Tour (541-899-8118). After its beginning in the early 1850s as a center of the region's gold rush, Jacksonville soon grew into a city of 1,000 people, the county seat, and an anticipated major stop between Portland and Sacramento on the Oregon and California Railroad. But when the city refused to pay the railroad its "fee" of $25,000 to be included on the line, the O&C laid its tracks to the north, and the depot there soon gave rise to the town of Medford. Before long, Jacksonville's people and businesses began following the railroad to Medford, which eventually became the county seat. Because of Jacksonville's decline, however, more than 100 buildings escaped the detriments

ONE OF THE THREE BUILDINGS LEFT AT THE GHOST TOWN OF BUNCOM

of rapid growth, and today it stands as a **National Historic Landmark Town,** one of only eight in the country.

Beekman Bank, California and Third Streets, Jacksonville. Born during the southern Oregon gold rush and named for banker C. C. Beekman (see *Historic Homes*), this 1863 bank, the first in the region, was an important stop for Wells Fargo express stages carrying gold between Oregon and California. Today the building retains many of its 19th-century qualities, including the original furnishings.

Buncom, 14 miles south of Jacksonville off Highway 238 and Applegate and Little Applegate Roads. When 2,500 people showed up in 1996 for Buncom's centennial celebration—the main event was the Famous Chicken Splat Contest (see *Special Events*), which involved chicken droppings on numbered squares—it increased the population of the town by exactly 2,500 people. That's not surprising when you consider that this collection of three 19th-century buildings—a cookhouse, a bunk house, and a combination post office and general store—has been celebrated in a book, a song, and a poem as well as on postcards and T-shirts. Folks just seem to go bonkers for Buncom, a former gold- mining boom town and then a farm supply center. In fact, during the 100th-year celebration of this town with a population of zero, the governor, a U.S. senator, and even President Clinton wrote letters wishing Buncom a happy birthday.

Gin Lin Trail, 18 miles south of Jacksonville off Highway 238 and Applegate and Palmer Creek Roads. High on a slope above the Applegate River, the Gin Lin Trail helps explain two chapters in the story of the region's gold rush days: Chinese miners and hydraulic mining. Gin Lin, for example, was a Chinese "boss" who brought laborers from China and hired them out to white miners in the days when laws prohibited Chinese from staking claims. When those laws were relaxed in the 1880s, however, Gin Lin had saved enough money to start his own hydraulic mining operation here near Palmer Creek. The result of that operation, in which gravity-fed water surged through giant hoses and nozzles to wash away hillsides and uncover their gold, is evident today in the gouges and ravines and rubble that scar the land along this three-quarter-mile trail.

Auto Camp Cabin, Lithia Park, off Siskiyou Boulevard, Ashland. When the open road called to motorists in the days before motels and RV parks, they answered by packing up their canvas tents and picnic baskets and setting out for distant auto camps, which consisted of parking spaces, rest rooms, and, occasionally, small cabins where travelers could bunk for the night. A reminder of those days now stands next to the Parks and Recreation Department headquarters in Ashland's Lithia Park: a 200-square-foot cabin restored to its original 1916 condition, when it was part of Ashland's free auto camp, the nation's first. "This is the last remaining evidence of the very, very first free auto camp in the nation," says Margaret Watson of the Southern Oregon Historical Society. "It's got true national significance."

COVERED BRIDGES **Antelope Creek,** 10 miles northeast of Medford off Highway 62 and Antelope Road, built in 1922, 58 feet long; **Lost Creek,** 23 miles northeast of Medford off Highways 62 and 140 and South Fork Little Butte Road, built in 1919, 39 feet (and, it is said, saved from destruction in the 1964 floods by a neighborhood prayer vigil, after which the storm broke); **McKee,** 8 miles south of Ruch off Applegate Road, built in 1917, 122 feet.

FOR FAMILIES **Oregon Vortex** (541-855-1543), 4303 Sardine Creek Road, Gold Hill. When you enter this place the Indians named "the Forbidden Ground," check your sense of reality at the gate, for you probably won't believe what you see. Here on this three-quarter-acre creekside plot, magnetism and perception spin in a whirlpool that has balls rolling uphill, brooms balancing on end, plumb bobs hanging at a slant, and people growing or shrinking as they move locations. Call it mystery, magic, science, or hoax—but when you finally walk out the gate and leave the Vortex behind, you'll call it unforgettable.

AT THE OREGON VORTEX, ALMOST EVERYTHING SEEMS TILTED

Dogs for the Deaf (541-826-9220), 10175 Wheeler Road, Central Point. This is off the usual tourist route, but those who wonder at the intelligence and dedication of hearing dogs can't find a better place to watch these remarkable animals and their trainers than here, at Dogs for the Deaf, the nation's only facility for training and placing hearing dogs.

THE UPPER VALLEY OF THE APPLEGATE RIVER

Every year from May through September, the facility opens for tours, going so far as to provide demonstrations of the dogs in action. Great stuff.

SCENIC DRIVES **Highway 99,** 128 paved miles from the California border to Eugene. Even though the yellow lines of Interstate 5 now stitch together the distance lying between the borders of California and Washington, the old Pacific Highway once performed the same task in a quieter way: the pavement narrower, the cars slower, the road gentler in the way it curved around farm fields and woodlands, yet still seemed to find the main street of every small town along the way. Well, the old highway is still there, running parallel to the interstate from Siskiyou south of Ashland to the Columbia River north of Portland. And following any part of the segment that connects this region to the southern end of the Willamette Valley near Eugene can seem to steer you through days gone by.

Applegate Valley, 40 paved miles along North Applegate Road and Highway 238 from Grants Pass to Central Point. The heart of this byway is the upper valley of the Applegate River, a tributary of the Rogue River that begins in the Siskiyou Mountains near the California border. From here it heads north and then bends west, following flowing water and green fields through the quiet communities of Ruch, Applegate, and Murphy; the historic city of Jacksonville; and the area's old gold diggings and modern vineyards.

Rogue–Umpqua National Scenic Byway, 180 paved miles along Highways 234, 62, 230, and 138 from Medford to Roseburg. Follow the pavement along these two rivers famous for their trout and steelhead, and you'll find yourself skirting lakes high in the Cascades, including Oregon's one national park at **Crater Lake,** as well as wilderness areas, waterfalls, campgrounds, and hiking trails.

Mountain Lakes Tour, 40 paved miles along Dead Indian Memorial Road, Hyatt Prairie Road, and Highway 66, beginning and ending at Ashland. This loop carries you away from Ashland, into the southern Cascades, and past three mountain lakes—Howard Prairie, Hyatt, and Emigrant—before steering you back toward your starting point.

Dead Indian Memorial Road, 40 paved miles from Ashland to Highway 140. Although it may seem to be a most politically incorrect place-name, Dead Indian Memorial Road—as well as the mountain and the creek of the same name—were actually named for the discovery by local settlers in 1854 of two dead Rogue River Indians. The bodies were found in a tepee, and the settlers assumed the deaths resulted from a fight with Klamath Indians. The route named for the event leads through forests and past lakes in the Cascade Mountains. (See also *To Do—Camping.*)

NATURAL WONDERS **Siskiyou Mountains,** bordered by the Coast Range to the north, the Cascade Range to the east, and the California border to the south. This mountain range is the Oregon segment of the **Klamath Mountains** that extend into northern California and were initially formed as the result of at least seven different collisions—the first occurring as long ago as 450 million years—between ocean islands and the North American continent. Comprising approximately 40 percent of the entire Klamath range, the Siskiyous' highest peak is **Mount Ashland** (7,533 feet) and its major river is the Rogue.

Table Rocks, north of Medford off Table Rock Road. These two flat-topped, horseshoe-shaped plateaus looming to the west above the Rogue River were once the river's channel. But when the Cascade Mountains erupted some 7 million years ago and clogged that channel with lava, the river moved and the old streambed, protected beneath layers of volcanic rock, endured through the ages as the ground around it eroded away.

AVENUE OF THE BOULDERS ON THE UPPER ROGUE RIVER

Agate Desert, 6 miles north of Medford off Table Rock Road. Sprawling across 32 square miles of the Rogue River Valley floor, the Agate Desert is a gravely plain of prairie grasslands, rainwater pools, and spring wildflowers that is a rare survivor of what was once widespread habitat across southwest Oregon. But because less than 20 percent of the Agate Desert's native habitat is still intact, the Nature Conservancy is trying to restore a portion of it. Their 53-acre preserve, at the intersection of Table Rock and Antelope Roads, is probably the best place to visit the area, though you'll find neither trails nor signs there.

Avenue of the Boulders, south of Prospect off Highway 62 (turnoff near milepost 42) and Mill Creek Drive. Just south of the town of Prospect, several short trails lead to viewpoints, streamsides, and riverbanks of the upper Rogue River in an area strewn with the tumbled piles of boulders and the mist of waterfalls. Here **Mill Creek, Barr Creek,** and **Pearsoney Falls** topple from ledges or pour over rocks in their rush to feed the Rogue.

Cascade–Siskiyou National Monument, southeast of Ashland between Interstate 5, Highway 66, and the California border. Oregon's newest monument, designated by President Bill Clinton in 2000, consists of more than 80 square miles considered to be one of North America's most ecologically diverse landscapes. It contains more than 600 species of plants and wildlife, including a number of threatened or **endangered species,** that range from **lilies** to **snails** and **mollusks** to **elk.** "The Siskiyous are the Noah's ark of botanical diversity in the West," says Dave Willis, who spent 17 years working to protect the area that surrounds 6,000-foot **Soda Mountain.** "This is the loading dock of the ark."

Heritage Trees (1-800-574-9397). **Lonesome Hickory,** 1 miles south of Shady Cove off Highway 62. When Mary Louisa Black left Missouri in 1865 and headed west on the Oregon Trail, she carried along the nuts of a hickory tree, which she planted here in 1866. **Britt Sequoia,** Britt Gardens, First Street, Jacksonville. On the day his son Emil was born in the spring of 1862, noted pioneer photographer Peter Britt planted this tree in his yard (see also Britt Gardens under *Wilder Places—Parks*). **Waldo Tree at Island Lake** (near the intersection of two Sky Lakes Wilderness trails—the Pacific Crest Trail and Forest Service Trail 982—and accessible only by foot). While traveling through the area in 1888, Judge John B. Waldo carved his name on this tree.

✷ To Do

CAMPING **Fish Lake,** 34 miles northeast of Medford off Highway 140. More than 40 campsites divided between **Doe Point** and **Fish Lake.** In addition, **North Fork** campground lies nearby to the west off Big Elk road, and **Willow Springs** lies north of the highway off Butte Falls–Fish Lake Road.

Butte Falls Area, northeast of Butte Falls off Forest Road 34 and its spur roads, or southeast of Butte Falls–Fish Lake Road and its spur roads). To the northeast: **South Fork, Big Ben,** and **Parker Meadows;** to the southeast: **Willow Lake, Whiskey Spring, Fourbit Ford,** and **Snowshoe.**

Crater Lake Highway, between Shady Cove and north of Union Creek along Highways 62, 230, and the Rogue River: **Rogue Elk County Park, Mill Creek, River Bridge, Woodruff Bridge, Natural Bridge, Union Creek, Farewell Bend,** and **Hamaker.** In addition, **Imnaha** campground lies southeast of Prospect off Forest Road 37, and **Huckleberry Mountain** east of Union Creek off Forest Road 6050. (See also *Hiking.*)

See also *Wilder Places—Parks.*

Applegate River, south of Jacksonville along the Applegate River or its tributaries or reservoir, at least 8 campgrounds, all located on or near water: **Flumet**

Flats, Jackson, and **Beaver Sulpher;** and at Applegate Reservoir: **Hart-Tish, Watkins, Carberry, Copper,** and **Seattle Bar.**

Dead Indian Memorial Road, 26 miles northeast of Ashland, 9 campsites divided between **Beaver Dam** and **Daley Creek.**

Emigrant Lake, 5 miles southeast of Ashland off Highway 66, 42 campsites near an 800-acre lake whose features include playgrounds, ball fields, and, perhaps the main attraction, two 280-foot water slides.

Hyatt Reservoir, 15 miles east of Ashland off Highway 66 and Hyatt Prairie Road. More than 20 campsites divided between **Wildcat** and **Hyatt Lake.**

Howard Prairie, 21 miles east of Ashland off Highway 66 and Hyatt Prairie Road. More than 200 campsites divided among four camps: **Lily Glen, Grizzly Creek, Howard Prairie,** and **Willow Point.**

See also *Canoeing.*

CANOEING **Squaw Lakes,** 27 miles south of Jacksonville off Highway 238, the Upper Applegate Road, and Forest Road 490. The motors can get loud at nearby Applegate Reservoir, but the waters at Squaw Creek, some half-dozen miles away, remain relatively calm and quiet. In addition, the lake can lay claim to stocked **rainbow trout** as well as a shoreline hiking trail and campground.

GOLF **Eagle Point Golf Course** (541-826-8225), 100 Eagle Point-Drive, Eagle Point, 18 holes.

Quail Point Golf Course (541-857-7000), 1200 Mira Mar, Medford, 9 holes.

HIKING **Upper Table Rock,** 5 miles north of Medford off Table Rock Road. Looming 750 feet above the Rogue River Valley, Upper Table Rock keeps some tough company—rattlesnakes, ticks, and poison oak to name a few. But if you stay on the trail and keep your eyes open, your reward will be spectacles of wildflowers in the spring and panoramic views all year long. You'll also have the chance to walk in the steps of Joseph Lane (see **Flood-Lane House** under *To See—Historic Homes* in Oakland–Roseburg–Myrtle Creek Area), who as a brigadier general in command of volunteer troops during the Rogue River War, climbed to the top of this rock on a September day in 1853 with 10 other unarmed men to negotiate a peace treaty with 700 armed Takelma warriors.

Grizzly Peak, 13 miles southeast of Ashland off Interstate 5 (exit 14) Dead Indian Memorial Road, and Shale City Road. A 3-mile up-and-back hike takes you upward to the highest peak and the best views near Ashland.

Crater Lake Highway, between Shady Cove and Union Creek along Highway 62 and the Rogue River. If you get the urge to stop the car and follow part of the river or see the countryside, you have your choice of several trails: **Upper Rogue River Trail,** a 48-mile riverside pathway that begins near the town of Prospect and ends near the boundary of Crater Lake National Park, giving hikers the chance to explore various sections of the overall route; **Natural Bridge,** 2 miles south of Union Creek off Forest Road 300, a 2-mile loop along an interpretive trail that demonstrates what happens to the Rogue River when it disappears into the channel's lava tubes; **Takelma Gorge,** 7 miles southwest of Union Creek off Forest Road 68,: a 3- or 4-mile round -trip to the basalt columns and cliffs that roil the Rogue River to whitewater.

UNIQUE ADVENTURES **Wine Country Tours** (1-800-547-7842; www.oregonwine.org). **Medford: Griffin Creek Vineyards** near the junction of Voorhies and South Stage Roads; **Talent: Paschal Winery** off Suncrest Road (exit 21 off Interstate 5). **Ashland: Ashland Vineyards** off E. Main Street and **Weisinger's of Ashland** off Siskiyou Boulevard (exit 14 off Interstate 5 for both). **Applegate Valley: Academy of Wine of Oregon** off Highway 238 and **Valley View Winery** near the junction of Highway 238 and Applegate Road.

✷ Wilder Places

PARKS **Tou Velle State Park,** 6 miles north of Central Point off Interstate 5 (exit 32) and Table Rock Road, day use only. Lying on both sides of the Rogue River, its two sides linked by a bridge, Tou Velle can count **hawks** and **herons, salmon** and **steelhead** as welcome neighbors or frequent visitors. A paved trail shows you around, taking you to wetlands, meadows, and wildlife areas.

Britt Gardens, First Street, Jacksonville. This park is the former home of Swiss-born Peter Britt, who arrived in Oregon by ox cart in 1852, tried his hand at gold mining for a while, and finally turned to photography. For a half century, until his death in 1905, Britt amassed a photographic record of the region, capturing on film the landscapes, the people, and the changes of the area. Of particular note is Britt's 1874 photograph of Crater Lake, the first ever taken. It was an image that helped win the campaign to make the lake a national park. The gardens were designed as part of the nation's bicentennial celebration in the mid-1970s and now serve as the home of the **Britt Music Festival** held each summer (see *Special Events*).

Cantrall-Buckley Park, 8 miles southwest of Jacksonville off Highway 240. Located on the bank of the Applegate River, this day-use park

UPPER TABLE ROCK IN THE ROGUE RIVER VALLEY IS THE RIVER'S ANCIENT STREAMBED

offers opportunities for picnicking, fishing, swimming, and camping (it even has showers).

Casey State Park, 6 miles northeast of Shady Cove off Highway 62, day use only. Once the Rogue River spills over the Lost Creek Dam, it sheds it slack water and gets itself set near this park for another whitewater run toward the sea. Located near the river's confluence with Big Butte Creek, Casey State Park offers shady picnic sites and a riverside seat for **migrating salmon.** For a bigger view, a hiking trail connects to the 75-mile **Rogue River Trail** (see Crater Lake Highway under *To Do—Hiking*) that follows the river to its headwaters.

Joseph H. Stewart State Park, 12 miles northeast of Shady Cove off Highway 62, day use and overnight. Near the upper end of **Lost Creek Lake,** which is the holding tank for the waters of Lost Creek and the Rogue River, stands this park consisting of more than 200 campsites and a half-dozen miles of paved trails that lead hither and yon to points around the lake and that connect to other trails leading to distant parts and other parks.

Lithia Park, off Siskiyou Boulevard, Ashland. One of the first city-owned parks on the West Coast, Ashland's Lithia Park rose from the rubble that was once a flour mill built on the site of the city founder's homestead. Since that time the park has grown to include 100 acres of walking paths, nature trails, picnic areas, and playgrounds. Special features include its **Japanese Garden** and locally famous **Sycamore Grove,** a drinking fountain that dispenses mineral water from **Lithia Springs** (stout stuff!), and tennis courts where it seems almost everybody wears white.

WILDERNESS AREAS **Red Buttes,** 34 miles southwest of Medford off Highway 238, Applegate Road, and Forest Road 1030, 31 square miles with 6 square miles in Oregon. Straddling the border between Oregon and California and the ridgeline of the Siskiyou Mountains (see *To See—Natural Wonders*), Red Buttes is a land of dense forests, open meadows, and steep slopes. Its system of ridgeline trails leads to panoramic views—sometimes all the way to the Pacific—and connect to the **Pacific Crest Trail.** This is also an area known for more than a century of bigfoot sightings.

WILDLIFE REFUGES **Denman Wildlife Area,** 7 miles north of Medford off Highway 62 and between Agate and Table Rock Roads. Bordered by the Rogue River and Table Rocks (see *To See—Natural Wonders*), this wildlife area is divided into two parcels totaling almost 1,800 acres that attract a variety of wildlife to its hedgerows, marshes, hardwood groves, and rocky grasslands that are near or part of the Agate Desert (see *To See—Natural Wonders*). In addition, 20 ponds speckle the area, while 5 miles of irrigation ditches run through it.

* Lodging

INNS

Ashland

Ashland Creek Inn (541-482-3315; reservation@ashlandcreekinn.com; www.ashlandcreekinn.com), 70 Water Street, Ashland 97520. "A jewel in

Ashland's crown" is how the inn's Ardis Fraser describes this establishment located two blocks from downtown and at the upscale end of the B&B world. The newly renovated inn has seven luxury suites decorated with period antiques and international art and provided with private entrances, shaded decks, fully equipped kitchens, and chef-prepared breakfasts served in the terraced gardens or on the creekside deck ($175–400).

Peerless Hotel and Restaurant (1-800-460-8758; info@peerlesshotel.com; www.peerlesshotel.com), 243 Fourth Street, Ashland 97520. The same year that Americans observed the changing of centuries and wondered about Y2K—remember that?—the Peerless Hotel was marking a quiet 100th birthday. Located in Ashland's historic railroad district and just three blocks from downtown, the hotel stands today as a restored red-brick inn that offers six guest rooms ($95–200) as well as a restaurant run by executive chefs.

Pinehurst Inn at Jenny Creek (541-488-1002; www.boxrranch.com/Pinehurst.html), 17250 Highway 66, Ashland 97520. Standing some two dozen miles east of Ashland, this inn was built in the 1920s as a roadhouse to serve travelers along then-new Highway 66. Today it's a two-story inn that retains the look of it past—wooden floors, stone fireplace, antique furnishings, handmade quilts—and offers six guest rooms with private baths and views of either the inn's garden or Jenny Creek ($69–89 for bed and continental breakfast, $10 extra for dinner). The first-floor **restaurant** serves breakfasts, lunches, and dinners.

Shrew's House (1-800-482-9214; innkeeper@shrews.com; www.shrews.com), 570 Siskiyou Boulevard, Ashland 97520. Owner Barbara Simard calls her Shrew's House "a bed and breakfast alternative." The reason is that each of its four guest rooms ($95–125) are almost self-contained, with a private entrance and bath, refrigerator, wet bar, TV, and telephone (some even have fireplaces and whirlpool tubs). When you do venture outside, you'll find a candlelight breakfast served in the dining room and a swimming pool and gardens in the yard.

Winchester Country Inn (1-800-972-4991; AshlandInn@aol.com; www.winchesterinn.com), 35 S. Second Street, Ashland 97520. This is an inn with many lives through many years: businessman's mansion, regional hospital, sanatorium, boardinghouse, low-rent apartments, and finally, almost a century after its construction, a country inn and restaurant. All of the inn's 18 rooms or suites, which are divided among the main house and three separate cottages, offer private baths, and some come with balconies, patios, bay windows, or garden entrances ($110–225). The **restaurant** employs two chefs and specializes in fine dining. Children are welcome.

Jacksonville

Jacksonville Inn (1-800-321-9344; jvinn@mind.net; www.jacksonvilleinn.com), 175 E. California Street, Jacksonville 97530. Even though this venerable two-story brick inn has roots running deep into Jacksonville's past, it keeps up with the modern world just fine, thank you very much. Built in 1861 and restored to offer guests the services of 11 rooms with private baths ($125), three honeymoon cottages ($150–245), a wine cellar (more than 2,000 selections), and a **gourmet restaurant,** the inn is every bit as functional as it is historical. For breakfast, guests may order from the menu.

Prospect

Prospect Hotel (1-800-944-6490; prospect@cdsnet.net; www.prospecthotel.com), 391 Mill Creek Drive, Prospect 97536. Once a stage stop on the road to Crater Lake, this 1889 renovated inn can boast of a long record of hospitality. "What sets us apart is probably our attention to our guests," says owner Jo Turner. "We're focused on their overall experience and hope they walk away feeling well cared for and refreshed." In addition, the hotel, which stands within walking distance of the Rogue River and three waterfalls, serves as a headquarters for those wanting to explore the forests or waterways of the Cascades as well as nearby **Crater Lake National Park.** "We provide more than enough information about the local area to keep guests busy for a week," Jo says, "even if they're staying only one night." The hotel's 10 guest rooms ($80–135) have private baths and antique furnishings and come with a full breakfast.

PROSPECT HOTEL

BED & BREAKFASTS

Ashland

Adams Cottage Bed & Breakfast (1-800-345-2570; emerald-spalding@hotmail.com; www.ashland-oregon-inns.com), 737 Siskiyou Boulevard, Ashland 97520. A tree-lined road and a picket fence frame this Victorian farmhouse that retains the architectural details and quality craftsmanship of a century ago. Its two upstairs guest rooms have queen beds and private baths ($105–115), while its two cottage suites include fireplaces, kitchens, patios, and balconies ($125). In addition, the breakfasts, according to owners Billy and Emme Spalding, are "legendary," and children are welcome.

A-Dome Studio Bed & Breakfast (541-482-1755; adome@mind.net;, www.mind.net/adome), 8550 Dead Indian Memorial Road, Ashland 97520. Standing on 23 acres in the grassy, oak-studded hills above Ashland, this geodesic dome is only a 15-minute drive from town but a world away from the scurry of the city. "A-Dome Studio," says owner Barbara Schoonover, "is a delightful surprise." Part of that surprise comes in the sense of country living that often seems to belong to another time. Outside, horses graze and geese squawk and a creek passes by; inside, knotty-pine walls, antique furnishings, and a rock fireplace are cradled within the curves of the dome. Each of the two guest suites—they're contained within an A-frame attached to the dome—have private bathrooms and entrances ($120). In the morning, you can help collect the eggs for your omelet from the resident hens. Children are welcome.

A Midsummer's Dream B&B (1-877-376-8800; info@amidsummer.com; www.amidsummer.com), 496 Beach Street, Ashland 97520. Even though it's past its 100th birthday, this Victorian home with its landscaped gardens and grounds looks as good as ever. Its five guest suites all come with fireplaces, private baths, spas, and a full breakfast ($140–220), as well as names that will put you in the mood for the nearby Oregon Shakespeare Festival (see *Special Events*): Romeo, Juliet, Desdemona, Othello, and Falstaff.

Anne Hathaway's Cottage (1-800-643-4434; annehathaway@ashlandbandb.com; www.ashlandbandb.com), 586 E. Main Street, Ashland 97520. Since 1908, guests have found their way to this former boardinghouse, and since 1994 they've been able to enjoy it as a newly renovated inn with private rooms. "We have just recently launched our innkeeping careers, having come to Oregon in voluntary exile from more than 20 wildish years in politics, journalism, and nonprofit work in Washington, D.C.," says owner Deedie Runkel. "With us came a houseful of interesting art, antiques, files full of fascinating recipes, and a seven-year-old chocolate Lab named Hattie." With a Lab around the place, you know this is going to be a friendly inn. Its four guest rooms and one suite all come with private baths and a full breakfast ($75–180). Children of "well-behaved parents" are welcome in the suite. "So far we've gotten great feedback from guests," Deedie says. "We're trying to do Anne Hathaway proud."

Arden Forest Inn (1-800-460-3912; aforest@afinn.com; www.afinn.com), 261 W. Hersey Street, Ashland 97520. With views of Mount Ashland and Grizzly Peak in the distance, this 1890 Victorian farmhouse and its adjoining carriage house seem to blossom with the flowers of its gardens. The main house offers two guest rooms, while the carriage house has three rooms, all with outside entrances and two with private patios ($80–190). The two-course breakfast is served family style and can feature dishes with such intriguing names as Arden's breakfast pie and bird's nests.

Ashland's Tudor House (1-800-760-4428; innkeeper@ashlandbb.com; www.ashlandbb.com), 271 Beach Street, Ashland, 97520. Sitting off the street and deep in its lot, this is a house that survived the 1970s and the paint job that gave it the nickname "The Purple House." After living down that shame, the 1940 Tudor home has been remodeled (and repainted) into a B&B surrounded by gardens and flower beds. Its five rooms ($79–140) all have private baths and come with a full breakfast cooked and served by host Raleigh Grantham, described by some guests as *lively.* "What I think sets my inn apart is my energy level," Raliegh says, "which may have to do with my age. I'm only 30, which is very young by innkeeper standards. Also, I hear my food has a pretty good reputation."

Bayberry Inn (1-800-795-1252; harriet@bayberryinn.com; www.bayberryinn.com), 438 N. Main Street, Ashland 97520. This 1925 Craftsman home has plenty of room for the family heirlooms and fresh flowers that grace it. The inn's five guest rooms, three of which have queen beds, all come with private baths and a full breakfast ($115). In addition, its veranda and deck open to views of the mountains. "It is our desire," says owner Harriet Maher, "that your stay with us be a memorable, relaxing, fun-filled experience."

Blue Moon Bed & Breakfast (1-800-460-5453; innkeeper@bluemoon-bandb.com; www.mousetrapinn.com), 312 Helman Street, Ashland 97520. A restored 1890s Victorian farmhouse, the Blue Moon offers four rooms ($90–115), a suite ($100–125), and a cottage ($125–150), some with views of Mount Ashland or the inn's garden and all with private baths and a full breakfast.

Chanticleer Inn (1-800-898-1950; innkeeper@ashlandbnb.com; www.lashland-bed-breakfast.com), 120 Gresham Street, Ashland 97520. Since its opening in 1981, this 1920 Craftsman home settled along a quiet street in a peaceful neighborhood has been on the receiving end of numerous "Best Places" awards, and it shows no signs of resting on its laurels. "For more than 20 years, the Chanticleer has been one of Ashland's premier B&Bs," says owner Ellen Campbell. "We took over the inn last year and are carrying on the tradition of providing our guests a superb experience of warm and caring hospitality, full gourmet breakfasts, and an elegant and comfortable place to rest and rejuvenate." The inn's six guest rooms all come with private baths as well as views of the Cascades, the sunrise, the city, or the garden ($85–195). A stay here also includes a breakfast that Ellen calls "an art form." Yet one of the strongest points remains its location. "We are away from the noise of downtown but still close to everything," Ellen says, "a rare combination in Ashland."

Colonel Silsby's Bed & Breakfast Inn (1-800-927-3070; colonel@silsbysinn.com; www.silsbysinn.com), 111 N. Third Street, Ashland 97520. Even though it has been a while since Colonel Silsby, a veteran of the Civil War, has lived in this Queen Anne Victorian, the house was built for him in 1896. "It's been lovingly restored and is one of the finest preserved Victorians in Ashland," says owner Rosemary Silvan. "It's also just a five-minute stroll into the charming downtown." The inn's six guest rooms all come with private baths, while some include Jacuzzis, fireplaces, kitchenettes, or refrigerators ($100–175). A stay here also includes what owner Rosemary calls the "best breakfast in town."

Coolidge House Bed & Breakfast (1-800-655-5522; info@coolidgehouse.com; www.coolidgehouse.com), 137 N. Main Street, Ashland 97520. Built in 1875 by Orlando Coolidge, the Rogue Valley's first commercial nurseryman, this Victorian home was once surrounded by nursery stock that grew along the surrounding hills. Today it offers guests five suites with private bathrooms ($85–175) as well as a separate cottage with a kitchenette, fireplace, and patio ($120–175).

Country Willows B&B Inn (1-800-945-5697; willows@willowsinn.com; www.willowsinn.com), 1313 Clay Street, Ashland 97520. Located on 5 acres of countryside lined with white fences, this is an inn with two sides—historic and modern. The historic comes from the 19th- century home and barn; the modern, from what guests find waiting for them to do. "It offers resortlike amenities," says owner Dan Durant, "such as a heated swimming pool, Jacuzzi, hiking trails, and complimentary bicycles." The inn's accommodations include nine guest rooms with private baths and a full breakfast ($115–245), and its permanent residents include ducks and geese on the pond and horses in the pastures. Children older than 12 are welcome.

Cowslip's Belle Bed & Breakfast (1-800-888-6819; stay@cowslip.com; www.cowslip.com/cowslip), 159 N. Main Street, Ashland 97520. What sets this B&B apart, says owner Carmen Reinhardt, are its "teddy bears, chocolate truffles, and scrumptious breakfasts" waiting for guests during a stay here. It must be the right combination, for since its opening in 1984 Cowslip's Belle has won a series of "Best Places" and "Favorite Inns" awards. The B&B's five guest rooms and private baths ($115–195) are housed in a 1913 Craftsman bungalow that's decorated with antique furnishings and Oriental rugs and features an adjacent carriage house and a pond with a waterfall. In addition, guests receive courtesy use of the Ashland Racquet and Fitness Center, and pets can be accommodated at a nearby kennel.

GrapeVine Inn (1-800-500-8463; innkeeper@thegrapevineinn.com; www.thegrapevineinn.com), 486 Siskiyou Boulevard, Ashland 97520. A blend of two qualities, says owner Susan Yarne, distinguishes the lodging here. "The GrapeVine Inn is special," she says, "because it's an intimate inn—only three rooms—that's a short walk to theaters, shopping, and dining." It's also probably the only inn around offering what Susan calls "intimate grape-inspired rooms." Hmm. Those three rooms, contained within a 1909 Dutch Colonial fronted by a wraparound front porch and surrounded by gardens, come with private baths, fireplaces, and a three-course breakfast served in either the dining room or the garden's gazebo ($95–160). "My rooms and house are very inviting and comfortable," Susan says, "my breakfasts are delightful, and the gardens peaceful." Children older than 12 are welcome, and pets can be kept in a nearby kennel.

Hersey House and Bungalow (1-888-343-7739; innkeeper@hersey-house.com; www.herseyhouse.com), 451 N. Main Street, Ashland 97520. The Hersey House is a 1904 two-story Craftsman that features a sitting porch, hardwood floors, period furnishings, and antiques, while the Bungalow is a 1940 guest cottage that was renovated in 1992. Together they offer guests their choice of five rooms, all with queen beds, private bathrooms, and either a full or continental breakfast ($125–150).

The Iris Inn (1-800-460-7650; innkeeper@irisinn.com; www.iris-innbb.com), 59 Manzanita Street, Ashland 97520. A picket fence, flower beds, and a sitting porch are what guests first see when arriving at this 1905 Victorian home that opened its doors to travelers for the first time in 1982. The inn's five antiques-decorated five guest rooms come with private baths and a full breakfast ($80–135).

Lithia Springs Inn (1-800-482-7128; lithia@mind.net; www.ashlandinn.com), 2165 W. Jackson Road, Ashland 97520. Located on 8 acres of lawn and gardens, Lithia Springs can boast of one amenity you're unlikely to find elsewhere: each of its guest rooms comes with a hot springs–fed whirlpool. Its accommodations include suites ($145) or cottages ($165) with private baths, king beds, double whirlpools, and small kitchens. In addition, guests sit down to a breakfast that includes fresh-baked breads and Starbucks coffee.

McCall House Bed & Breakfast (541-482-9296; mccall@mccallhouse.com; www.mccallhouse.com), 153 Oak Street, Ashland 97520. After making his fortune in the gold mines and becoming a prominent citizen of Ashland, John McCall had this Italianate manor built in 1883, just in time to host some of the biggest celebrities of the day. Under this roof, for example, slept such dignitaries as William Jennings Bryan, General William T. Sherman, and even President Rutherford B. Hayes. Today these names are attached to three of the home's nine guest rooms, which come with private baths and a two-course breakfast that changes daily ($115–225).

Morical House Garden Inn (1-800-208-0960; innkeeper@garden-inn.com; www.garden-inn.com), 668 N. Main Street, Ashland 97520. Surrounded by 2 acres of landscaped grounds—which include gardens, ponds, waterfalls, and a bird sanctuary—this 1882 Eastlake Victorian farmhouse offers guests eight rooms (five in the main house and three in a converted carriage house), private bathrooms, garden rooms, a sun porch, and three-course breakfasts featuring Northwest fare ($120–200). "Morical House is a small luxury inn and garden retreat hallmarked by its cool metropolitan styling and sophisticated Eurasian design," says proprietor Alicia Hwang, "truly a step apart from the traditional Victorian and country inns of old." Kids older than 12 are welcome; pet boarding is available at a nearby kennel.

Neil Creek House (1-800-460-7860; bnb@neilcreek.com; www.neilcreekhousebnb.com), 341 Mowetza Drive, Ashland 97520. The 5 acres in the Siskiyou Mountain foothills that hold this ranch-style home has what owner Gayle Negro calls "lots of open space and an air of casualness." Here you'll find a creek, a pond, a pool, and a gazebo on grounds landscaped smoothly enough for lawn bowling, croquet, or badminton—yet this is also one of the wildest places around. "Neil Creek House has received its certificate as a **Backyard Habitat for Wildlife,"** Gayle says. "Over 100 species of birds migrate through our property, and many others are year-round residents. In addition to our feathered friends, many four-legged critters live in the area." She goes on to list raccoons, coyotes, bobcats, cougars, deer, and "an occasional black bear" as neighbors or visitors. Yet human visitors will find the accommodations here completely tame. "Once guests arrive and are settled, their every need is anticipated," Gayle says. "For the remainder of their stay they're free to roam the grounds of this beautiful parklike setting and rest or relax at several tranquil areas throughout the property." Once they head inside, visitors will find that the home's two guest rooms come with queen beds, private baths, and a full breakfast ($90–120). "Being a guest at Neil Creek House is a unique experience," Gayle says. "We feel that we truly live in a paradise that has been 'loaned' to us to make beautiful."

Oak Hill Country Bed & Breakfast (1-800-888-7434; innkeeper@oakhillbb.com; www.oakhillbb.com), 2190 Siskiyou Boulevard, Ashland 97520. As far as their B&B is concerned, Tom and Pat Howard have a simple goal: "We want you to remember your stay here," they say, "as a high point of your visit to Ashland." To that end, they extend their hospitality throughout this quiet, comfortable 1910 farmhouse that contains six guest rooms with fireplaces and private baths ($89–159). In addition, the menu for breakfast, which in nice weather is served family style on the garden deck, can range from homemade granola to smoked salmon roulade with grilled asparagus. (If you haven't tried grilled asparagus, you'll be glad if you give it a chance.)

Pedigrift House (1-800-262-4073; www.pedigrift.com), 407 Scenic Drive, Ashland 97520. More than a century after its construction in 1888, this Queen Anne Victorian underwent major restoration, though owners Dorothy and Richard Davis were careful to retain the traditional features of a classic Victorian—including the high ceilings, double-hung windows, and four-panel doors. Now the home offers guests their choice of four rooms with queen beds, private baths, and views from their windows of the nearby mountains or the home's gardens ($85–135). A full breakfast is served in the dining room.

Romeo Inn (1-800-915-8899; innkeeper@romeoinn.com; www.romeoinn.com), 295 Idaho Street, Ashland 97520. Standing in a quiet neighborhood and surrounded by flower gardens and pine trees—some of them as old as 200 years—this 1932 two-story Cape Cod home offers guests a choice of six rooms with king beds and private bathrooms ($95–185), as well as the use of an outdoor swimming pool. The three-course breakfast menu changes daily. Kids older than 12 are welcome.

Wolfe Manor Inn (1-800-801-3676; sybil@wolfemanor.com; www.wolfemanorcom), 586 B Street, Ashland 97520). Set in a historic district near downtown Ashland and surrounded by an English garden, this 1910 two-story Craftsman house looks as though Mamie and Julius Wolfe, the original owners, could be coming home any moment. So do some of the inn's five guest rooms and private baths, with their early-20th-century decorations, antique furniture, and brass fixtures ($99–145). In addition, full breakfast is served in the grand ballroom, where Mamie and Julius used to love to throw parties.

The Woods House (1-800-435-8260; woodsinfo@woodshouse.com; www.woodshouse.com), 333 N. Main Street, Ashland 97520. The setting for this 1908 two-story Craftsman is a half acre of flowering, manicured grounds. "The comment I most hear from my guests, over 60 percent of whom return year after year, is that they feel so very comfortable and 'at home' here," says Francois Roddy, who has owned Woods House since 1990. The inn's six guest rooms all have private bathrooms ($100–140, with off-season discounts). In addition, breakfast is memorable enough that popular demand prompted Francois to compile 53 favorites of her recipes into the book *Treasures of the Woods House*. "Guests rave about the exceptionally wonderful, full breakfasts we serve each morning," Francois says, "as well as the fresh cookies, which are always in the cookie jar."

Gold Hill

Rogue River Guest House (1-877-764-8322; www.rogueriverguesthouse.com), 41 Rogue River Highway, Gold Hill 97525). With its namesake flowing just across the road, the Rogue River Guest House is a restored 1890s farmhouse that offers two guest rooms. One faces the river and has a private deck and Jacuzzi, and both come with king or queen beds and a full breakfast ($70–125). In addition, picnic lunches and gourmet dinners are available by request.

Jacksonville

Historic Orth House (1-800-7007301; orthbnb@orthbnb.com; www.orthbnb.com), 105 W. Main Street, Jacksonville 97530). Decorated with enough antique toys and teddy bears that it's nicknamed "the Teddy Bear Inn," this 1880 two-story Italianate villa is listed on both the **State and National Historic Registers.** "What makes our B&B unique is the fact that it allows our guests to 'step back in time,'" says owner Marilyn Lewis. "We've worked hard to restore the house to its original elegance, and guests feel relaxed and pampered when they visit." Three of its guest rooms come with private baths, one shares a bathroom, and all include a full breakfast ($95–250) as well as the casual company of all those toy bears. "Our teddy bear collection," Marilyn says, "adds to the welcoming, friendly feeling."

Laurelwood Manor (1-800-846-8422; laurelwood@wave.net; www.laurelwoodmanor.com), 540 E. California Street, Jacksonville 97530. When this Queen Anne Victorian was built, the country was still carrying the scars of the Civil War and Andrew Johnson was trying to finish out his troublesome term as president. Today, however, the 1868 house seems stronger and more stately than ever, its door open to guests who can choose from six antiques-furnished guest rooms (two with private baths and four with shared), lounge on the covered patio or in front of the fireplace, or stroll the perennial gardens ($105–135).

The Touvelle House (1-800-846-8422; info@touvellehouse.com; www.touvellehouse.com), 455 N. Oregon Street, Jacksonville 97530. Its 1916 Craftsman style with a hilltop view and an English garden, its venerable oaks and stone steps give this home, like so many in Jacksonville, a sense of belonging in an earlier time. Yet the amenities here, from its heated pool to its three-course breakfast, make this a most modern B&B. Its six guest rooms all have private baths, scenic views, and antique furnishings ($145–195).

Medford

Under the Greenwood Tree Bed & Breakfast (541-776-0000; grwdtree@internetcds.com; www.greenwoodtree.com), 3045 Bellinger Lane, Medford 97501. You have to respect the originality of a B&B that names its guest rooms after different pears, brings in 10 bouquets of flowers every day from the garden, and proclaims its qualities with these lines: "At this B&B the birds aren't just on the stationery nor the bunnies made of plaster. Here the gardens aren't stamp size and breakfast isn't just something greasy with a hole in it." Such is how it is at Under the Greenwood Tree, a home settled on

10 acres of roses and honeysuckle and rhododendrons. Its five guest rooms all come with private baths and a full breakfast that features fruits and herbs from the garden ($115–160).

GUEST HOUSES **The Wells Ranch House** (541-899-1942; www.bbonline.com/or/wellsranch), 126 Hamilton Road, Jacksonville 97530. When you stay at this ranch house in the Applegate Valley, you'll have the guest accommodations to yourself, including the single pine-lined guest room, private bath, and adjacent den with fireplace ($95, including a continental breakfast). The views of grazing cattle and flying geese, however, you'll be sharing with the horses, llamas, and other residents of the 40-acre ranch.

LODGES

Applegate

Applegate River Lodge (541-846-6690; info@applegateriverlodge.com; www.applegateriverlodge.com), 15100 Highway 238, Applegate 97530. With a view of the Applegate River and the historic Pioneer Bridge, this two-story log and timber lodge offers seven guest rooms, each with a private bath, a two-person Jacuzzi tub, a deck with a river view, and a continental breakfast ($125–145). A large lobby area with a balcony and sitting room is available to guests. For an outdoor adventure, the lodge offers raft trips on the river with free pickup downstream. They'll even lend you fishing rods.

Ashland

Green Springs Inn (1-800-572-9172; info@greenspringsinn.net; www.greenspringsinn.net), 11470 Highway 66, Ashland 97520. Green Springs Inn straddles a world of contrasts, both cultural and natural. "We are perched up in the southern Cascades, close to the cultural divide between the cowboy and logger communities of the Klamath Basin and the academics and Shakespeareans of Ashland," says owner Diarmuid McGuire. "A couple of years ago, our neighborhood was incorporated into one of our nation's first ecological preserves, the **Cascade-Siskiyou National Monument.** As the political dust settles around this designation, more visitors are coming to explore the unique biology of this area, which forms a high-elevation bridge between the Cascades and the Coast Range." To supply the comforts of the open road, some of these explorers look to the inn with its **restaurant** and two-story cedar lodge, which consists of eight rooms with private baths ($59–99). "The incentives that seem to keep them coming back," Diarmuid says, "are outstanding food (the simple, tasty kinds of meals that one might find in an Italian village) and a few creature comforts (such as the jetted tubs that we have added to most of our rooms)." In addition, lodging and meal packages are available, and kids are welcome to this still often overlooked area. "Our roads are still lightly traveled," Diarmuid says, "and the treasures of these mountains are still relatively unrecognized."

Mt. Ashland Inn (1-800-830-8707; stay@mtashlandinn.com; www.mtashlandinn.com), 550 Mount Ashland Road, Ashland 97520. After they bought this three-story cedar-log lodge in 1995, owners Chuck and Laurel Biegert went to work making it into what Laurel calls "a breath of fresh wilderness" for guests who want to stay near the top of Ashland's world. "The inn," Laurel says, "is perched on the crest of the Siskiyou Mountains, with spectacular views." On the outside the Biegerts added a spa and sauna, and on the inside they created five guest suites, all of which come with Jacuzzi tubs, gas fireplaces, handmade quilts, and mile-high views ($135–200). In addition, a stay here comes with a multicourse breakfast as well as the chance to play with the Biegerts' two golden retrievers.

✷ Where to Eat

DINING OUT

Ashland

Chateaulin (541-482-2264), 50 E. Main Street, Ashland. A local and visitors' favorite both before and after the theater, Chateaulin serves a blend of contemporary and traditional French cuisine that earns "excellent" ratings from almost everyone who has dined here.

Cucina Biazzi (541-488-3739), 568 E. Main Street, Ashland. In this small house converted to an Italian restaurant, a taste of Tuscany comes in the form of multicourse dinners served on linen-covered tables. Antipasti and cheese and olives, pasta and rice and mushrooms, some Northwest entréees thrown in to balance out the Mediterranean—it all comes together into memorable dinner.

Monet (541-482-1339), 36 S. Second Street, Ashland. Considered one of the best restaurants in town with one of the best chefs in the region, Monet features French cuisine that ranges from shrimp to pasta, veal to vegetarian.

The Winchester Country Inn (1-800-972-4991), 35 S. Second Street, Ashland. With a view of an English garden through the window, with a waiter in a top hat pouring the wine, and with *two* chefs orchestrating the evening's fare, it's no wonder the Winchester Inn is considered one of the most elegant restaurants in Ashland.

Also see the **Green Springs Inn, Peerless Hotel and Restaurant**, **Pinehurst Inn at Jenny Creek,** and **Winchester Country Inn** under *Lodging.*

Jacksonville

Gogi's (541-899-8699), 235 W. Main Street, Jacksonville. Another local favorite, especially among those preferring a fine dining experience, Gogi's reputation is based in part on the inventiveness and skills of owner William Prahl, who some consider one of the best chefs in Oregon. Fresh ingredients, a changing menu, nightly specials, dinner-sized appetizers, and specialty dishes are some of the reasons for the restaurant's well-earned reputation for quality and creativity.

Jacksonville Inn (541-899-1900), 175 E. California Street, Jacksonville. The state of Oregon is just four years older than the 1863 building that houses the Jacksonville Inn, which is regionally famous for its historic but intimate atmosphere; its multicourse dinners that feature steak, seafood, pasta, and vegetarian entrées; and its wine cellar containing some 1,500 labels from around the world.

Also see the **Jacksonville Inn** under *Lodging.*

EATING OUT

Ashland

Geppetto's (541-482-1138), 343 E. Main Street, Ashland. With a storefront outside and a 1950s-diner inside, Geppetto's is a local favorite for café cooking that reaches as far as eggplant burgers.

Lela's Bakery Café (541-482-1702), 258 A Street, Ashland. Locals and tourists alike are drawn to Lela's, where fresh ingredients and scratch cooking distinguish the meals and a local guitarist provides the entertainment.

Natural Café (541-488-5493), 358 E. Main Street, Ashland. As you might gather from the name, this café provides healthful, wholesome food, and its quality is high enough to make the place a local hangout. Even though its focus is on vegetarian food, you can also get fish and chicken, all of it reasonably priced.

Omar's (541-482-1281), 1380 Siskiyou Boulevard, Ashland. This is one of Ashland's longest-operating restaurants, so you know they must have been doing something right all these years. If it has a drawback for the theater crowd, it may be too far from downtown for a comfortable walk to the play, especially if you're behind schedule.

Pangea (541-552-1630), 272 E. Main Street, Ashland. Pangea specializes in wraps good enough to fill the eatery's 8 or 10 tables and to make it wise to call your order ahead.

Pilaf (541-488-7898), 10 Calle Guanajuato, Ashland. Ashland's only 100 percent vegetarian restaurant, Pilaf offers diners fresh ingredients, large portions, and simple decor.

Quinz Mediterranean (541-488-5937), N. Main Street, Ashland. Specializing in Middle Eastern and Mediterranean fare, Quinz is locally known for two things: providing extra plates at each table so diners can share one another's selections and cooking excellent soups, including what one diner calls "the best clam chowder in town, maybe in your lifetime."

Wiley's World of Pasta (541-488-0285), 1606 Ashland Street, Ashland. Wiley's is a small popular deli that specializes in homemade pasta and sauce, including the best ravioli in town.

Jacksonville

Back Porch (541-899-8821), 605 N. Fifth Street, Jacksonville. Way down here in southern Oregon is where ya'll can find great Texas barbecue, which comes from a cooking process that takes place close enough that the smell of smoke and sauce will get you thinking about the ribs before they ever arrive at your table.

Bella Union (541-899-1770), 170 W. California Street, Jacksonville. Located in a historic saloon, the Bella Union is something of a local hangout known for its pizza, pasta, and hamburgers; its outdoor dining; and, during the winter, its Thursday-night oysters and ale.

Country Cottage Café and Bakery (541-899-2900), 230 E. C Street, Jacksonville. Folks who try the Country Cottage's chocolate and carrot cakes usually get stuck on the same word to describe them: "Incredible!"

La Fiesta (541-899-4450), 150 S. Oregon Street, Jacksonville. When the locals want Mexican food, this is where many of them go. Two brick fireplaces, a patio deck, and a balcony overlooking downtown Jacksonville give La Fiesta a blended sense of romance, coziness, and history. But it's the food that keeps diners coming back.

McCully House (541-899-1942), 240 E. California Street, Jacksonville. During an evening of dining at the McCully House, you can imagine yourself transported back to the 1860s, when this mansion served as the elegant home of the town's first doctor. In this world of lace curtains, antique furnishings, and flowering gardens, diners pull up to tables in the house's four dining rooms, where they can order from menu selections that range from homestyle cooking to fine dining.

✷ Special Events

February–November: **Oregon Shakespeare Festival** (541-482-2111; www.osfashland.org), Ashland. This celebrated festival of drama began in 1935, when Angus Bowmer, a professor of English and drama at Ashland's Southern Oregon Normal School—now Southern Oregon University—came across the city's abandoned Chautauqua Tabernacle and figured the domed building, built in 1893 to hold the city's highly popular programs of traveling lectures and entertainment, resembled Shakespeare's Globe Theatre. (The first production, *Twelfth Night,* was held in July of that year; general admission was 50 cents and reserved seats a dollar.) Today the festival is world-renowned for its performances.

May: **Buncom Day,** Buncom, 14 miles south of Jacksonville off Highway 238 and Applegate and Little Applegate Roads **(Saturday of Memorial Day weekend).** Even though it has a population of zero, the town of Buncom has its own Historical Society, which sponsors an annual celebration for "Southern Oregon's Last Remaining Ghost Town." The all-day celebration, which is intended for the family and draws as many as 500 people, features live music, crafts booths, a barbecue, and the locally famous chicken-splat contest, in which the droppings from a caged chicken determine the winning number. (See also Buncom under *To See—Historic Sites.*)

August: **Britt Music Festival** (1-800-882-7488), Jacksonville. On summer nights, some of the world's renowned musicians perform here beneath the stars, raising their voices, strumming their strings, and tooting their horns to the southern Oregon sky. (See also **Britt Gardens** under *Wilder Places—Parks.*)

October: **Medford Jazz Jubilee** (541-770-6972), Medford.

November–December: **Festival of Lights** (541-482-3486), Ashland.

December: **Victorian Christmas** (541-899-8118), Jacksonville.

North Central

MID–COLUMBIA RIVER

COLUMBIA PLATEAU

REDMOND–PRINEVILLE–MADRAS AREA

BEND–SISTERS–LA PINE AREA

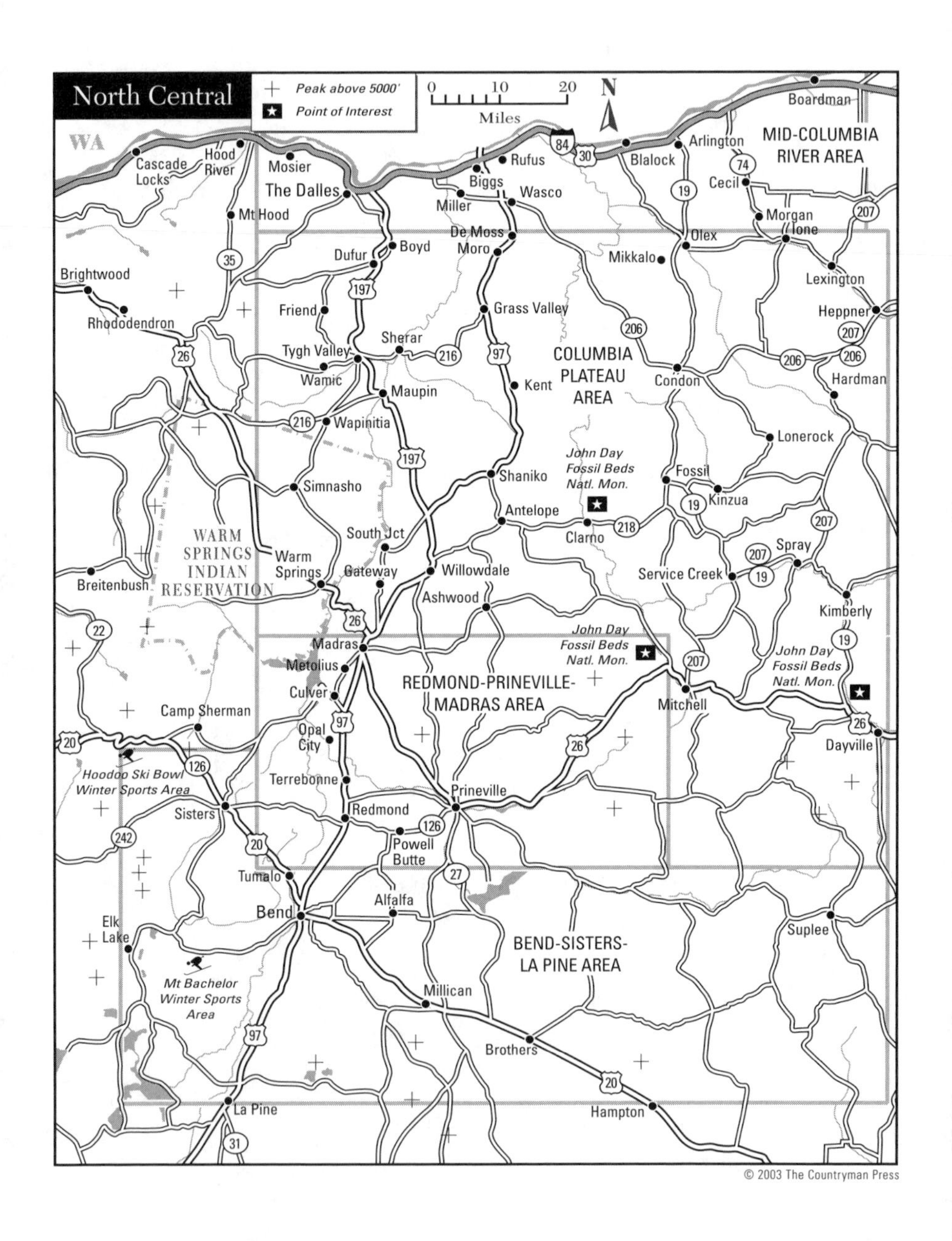

North Central
Peak above 5000'
Point of Interest
0 10 20
Miles
N
WA
Cascade Locks
Hood River
Mosier
The Dalles
Mt Hood
Rufus
Biggs
Wasco
Miller
Blalock
Arlington
Boardman
MID-COLUMBIA RIVER AREA
Cecil
Morgan
Ione
Olex
Mikkalo
De Moss
Moro
Boyd
Dufur
Lexington
Heppner
Brightwood
Rhododendron
Friend
Grass Valley
Tygh Valley
Sherar
Wamic
Maupin
Kent
COLUMBIA PLATEAU AREA
Condon
Hardman
Wapinitia
Lonerock
John Day Fossil Beds Natl. Mon.
Shaniko
Fossil
Kinzua
Simnasho
Antelope
Clarno
WARM SPRINGS INDIAN RESERVATION
South Jct
Warm Springs
Gateway
Willowdale
Service Creek
Spray
Breitenbush
Ashwood
Kimberly
Madras
Metolius
Culver
REDMOND-PRINEVILLE-MADRAS AREA
Mitchell
Camp Sherman
Opal City
Dayville
Hoodoo Ski Bowl Winter Sports Area
Terrebonne
Prineville
Sisters
Redmond
Powell Butte
Tumalo
Alfalfa
Bend
Elk Lake
BEND-SISTERS-LA PINE AREA
Suplee
Mt Bachelor Winter Sports Area
Millican
Brothers
La Pine
Hampton

INTRODUCTION

"Still in memory, I hear the thunder of the hoofs of wild horses rushing to corrals in spring roundups. I feel the tremor of blasts in the Deschutes Gorge when two railroad giants raced to Bend. I recall many nights when my blankets were spread under summer stars."

—Phil F. Brogan, longtime central Oregon journalist and author

The line of slope-shouldered, white-crowned giants that stand their ground between Oregon's high desert and rain forest is more than a chain of alpine peaks beloved by hikers and skiers and sightseers, for these Cascade Mountains are the state's Great Divide that shapes the character as well as the climate of the state. Think of it [au: Reword as "the landscape on either side" or some such rather than say "it"?—pb] as the difference between green and brown.

West of the Cascades, on the green side of Oregon, lie the thick-forested foothills and deep-soiled valleys that catch the coastal rains and carry the mountains' streams past bustling cities and busy roads. People living here might spend some of their time looking for a way to escape crowds, picking slugs from their gardens, worrying about too many people moving to town, or cussing the rain.

Meanwhile, folks living on the brown side of the mountains, especially along the sagebrush plains and flat-topped wheat fields of the north-central region, might spend the same time looking for company, picking ticks from their dogs, worrying about too many people leaving town, or praying for rain. The Dry Side, they call this sprawl of distance, and through the years it has retained many of the qualities that a century ago made early settlers fall in love with it.

"Stretching away for hundreds of miles to the east . . . was a vast expanse of semi-arid, rolling plateau country," Bend physician Urling C. Coe wrote about the country he knew in 1905, "covered with sagebrush, bunchgrass, and occasional small patches of scrubby juniper trees, and dotted here and there with large stock ranches."

Those ranches were built upon a landscape shaped by the volcanoes and glaciers of the Cascades, a rock-hard land of scarce water where the region's first towns grew out of the west side's need for wool, wheat, and lumber. Now settled into their wheat and sage surroundings, many of the small communities scattered throughout the region retain a quiet sense of their age, a dignity arising from enduring dry years, bad crops, or closed mills.

Yet in spite of the difficulties the region faces in making a living from its farms and forests, the lure of open spaces, sunlight, and pine trees—along with what Dr. Coe called "clear mountain lakes and sparkling streams"—keeps a steady flow of traffic passing over the snow-clad Cascades and into this land of long summers and blue skies.

MID–COLUMBIA RIVER

GUIDANCE Boardman Chamber of Commerce (541-481-3014; www.visit-boardman.com), 206 N. Main Street, Boardman 97818.

Central Oregon Visitors Association (1-800-800-8334; cova@empnet.com; www.empnet.com/cova), 63085 N. Highway 97, Suite 94, Bend 97701.

Columbia River Gorge National Scenic Area: Headquarters (541-386-2333), 902 Wasco Avenue, Suite 200, Hood River 97031.

The Dalles Area Chamber of Commerce (1-800-255-3385; www.thedalleschamber.com), 402 W. Second Street, the Dalles 97058.

Mount Hood National Forest: Headquarters (503-668-1771), 16400 Champion Way, Sandy 97055.

Oregon State Parks (503-378-6305), State Parks and Recreation Department, 525 Trade Street S. E., Salem 97301.

GETTING THERE The Mid–Columbia River area is reached from the east and west by Interstate 84 and from the south by Highways 74, 19, 97, and 197.

MEDICAL EMERGENCY Mid-Columbia Medical Center (541-296-1111), 1700 E. 19th Street, the Dalles.

Providence Hood River Memorial Hospital (541-386-3911), 811 13th Street, Hood River.

✷ Towns

Boardman. Seemingly always on the move, Boardman is now occupying its third site. It got its start when Sam Boardman, a civil engineer from Massachusetts, homesteaded here in 1903, though it took another 13 years for concrete canals to bring water from the Umatilla River to his farm. That same year he sold 40 acres, on which the town was platted, and in 1922 the Columbia River Highway finally reached the fledgling community, now named Boardman. But the town moved approximately a mile south in 1952, following the new interstate highway, then south again in the 1960s to make way for the backwaters of the new John Day Dam. Today it sits between the Columbia River and Interstate 84, accommodating a flow of commercial traffic through the region.

Mosier. Soon after arriving in the Dalles by wagon train in 1852 and then building a sawmill along a tributary of the Columbia that would one day carry his name, Jonah Mosier discovered, as the old country-western song says, that if it hadn't been for bad luck he'd have had no luck at all. That's because over the course of five years, from 1854 to 1858, spring floods washed away his mill three times. Even though he got out of the lumber business, Mosier continued living on his homestead, which after his death in 1894 became part of the town that now bears his name.

The Dalles. If a crossroads of Oregon history exists, you can probably find it near the Dalles. In this place, tribes gathered and traded for thousands of years; Oregon Trail pioneers rested both their stock and themselves before tackling the rapids of the Columbia River or the slopes of Mount Hood; and soldiers watched over a country whose boundaries reached to the summit of the Rockies. As a result, the Dalles is one of the oldest inhabited locations in North America and one of the oldest incorporated cities west of the Mississippi River. (For more on the Dalles, see **Lewis and Clark Trail** and **The Dalles** under *To See—Historic Sites.*)

✷ To See

MUSEUMS **Fort Dalles Museum** (541-296-4547), 500 W. 15th Street, The Dalles. In the days when the old Oregon Country stretched from the Pacific to the Rockies, Fort Dalles stood as the center of an 1850s world of wagon trains and Indian wars. Located on a hilltop overlooking the Columbia River, this army

FORT DALLES

outpost once consisted of two dozen buildings, though fire or neglect claimed all of the major structures except for the surgeon's quarters, which houses most of the museum's collection of 19th-century pioneer and military artifacts. Yet the simple elegance of the surgeon's quarters—once described as "one of the loveliest little buildings in the state"—emanates such a strong sense of the past that at times it seems still to be standing guard over the land it was built to protect.

Anderson House Complex (541-296-4547), 500 W. 15th Street (adjacent to Fort Dalles Museum; see previous listing), The Dalles. To step inside this hand-hewn log house is to step for a moment into a homesteader's world, for Lewis Anderson built it in 1895 on his homestead in the dryland wheat country of Pleasant Ridge, a dozen miles from the Dalles. "Among my fondest childhood memories is my Grandpa's farm," writes Helen Saunders, Anderson's granddaughter. "There was a rather imposing log house with a big kitchen, and a pantry which always held a supply of fresh sour-cream cookies."

Columbia River Gorge Discovery Center–Wasco County Museum (541-296-8600), 4 miles west of the Dalles off Interstate 84, exit 82 or 84. Housed in the same 50,000-square-foot building that perches on a ledge above the Columbia River, these two historical centers attempt to store the memories and record the changes of the river and its people as the mighty River of the West was transformed from the region's wildest river into its electrical generator. To tell this story, the centers follow the modern trend of interpreting history through technology rather than preserving it through artifacts. As a result, you can expect video presentations, audio recordings, fiberglass replicas, and sound effects. Its most remarkable and rare feature, however, is film footage of Celilo Falls, the ancient fishing grounds that in 1957 drowned beneath the backwaters of the Dalles Dam.

HISTORIC HOMES **Rorick House** (541-296-1867), 300 W. 13th Street, The Dalles. If you had been at the raising of the Rorick House and stood on its stoop and gazed toward the river, you'd have seen the Columbia River rolling through rapids and frothing with falls, the canoes of the Wasco people beached along the banks and their villages spread across the islands; you'd have seen emigrants unloading their wagons, packing their rafts, and calming their families for the last dreadful run of the Oregon Trail, down the Columbia and into the Willamette Valley. And now, even though the world has changed around it, the old house still stands. Built in 1850 by a noncommissioned officer from nearby Fort Dalles, the Rorick House, named for two longtime residents, is not only the oldest house in The Dalles but also one of the oldest surviving homes from the days of the Northwest frontier.

HISTORIC SITES **Lewis and Clark Trail** (Irrigon to Memaloose Island). Making their way in pirogues down the Columbia, Lewis and Clark's Corps of Discovery found the river wild with rapids and the islands filled with Indian villages. Today the whitewater is drowned and the people are gone, yet lying along the river near Interstate 84 is a series of sites visited by Lewis and Clark during their journey:

Columbia River Campsite, October 19 and 20, 1805 (Sand Island near Irrigon Marine Park, on the northern outskirts of Irrigon off Highway 730). After their 1-mile-per-hour trip through the Umatilla Rapids, the Lewis and Clark's Corps of Discovery pitched camp on the south bank of the river, downstream from the site of this small riverfront town. Soon visitors arrived. "About thirty-six canoe loads [from a nearby village] came over to see us," Sergeant Patrick Gass wrote, "but we could not have much conversation with them as we did not understand their language." But everybody did seem to understand music. "The highest satisfaction they enjoyed was the music of two of our violins," Captain Lewis wrote, "with which they seemed much delighted: they remained all night at our fires."

John Day River, October 21, 1805 (LePage Park, 27 miles east of the Dalles off Interstate 84 at exit 114). After leaving their camp located near today's Irrigon, the Corps of Discovery floated through a series of seemingly endless rapids, some of which Captain Clark found to be "Very bad . . . a chain of rocks . . . nearly choking the river up entirely with huge black rocks." The whitewater continued past the mouth of the John Day River, which the captains named for the corps' Private Baptise LePage. "Between three and four miles below the last rapid occurs a second, which is also difficult," Captain Lewis wrote, "and three miles below it is a small river . . . we gave it the name of Lepage's river from Lepage one of our company." That night when they camped nearby, the corps prepared its usual fare of "Dog meat and fish," but they also had a welcome addition to their dinner. "One of our party, J. Collins," Captain Clark wrote, "presented us with very good beer made of the [camas] bread."

Deschutes River, October 22, 1805 (Deschutes River State Recreation Area, 14 miles east of the Dalles off Interstate 84 and old Highway 30; see also *To Do—Camping*). The next morning's journey continued through rapids and past islands and villages, until the corps encountered what Captain Clark described as "several Indians in canoes killing fish with gigs [spears]." The captain wrote that nearby, "we discovered the entrance of a large river . . . We landed at some distance above the mouth of this river and Captain Lewis and myself set out to view this river above its mouth." This was the Deschutes, just upstream and around a bend from "the great falls" of Celilo (see next listing).

Celilo Falls, October 22 and 23, 1805 (Celilo Park, 10 miles east of the Dalles off Interstate 84, exit 97). To see the great falls of Celilo, you'll have to use your imagination, for they vanished in 1957, drowned beneath the slack water of The Dalles Dam, some 12 miles downstream. Still, this is a place so important in the mythology and history of the Northwest that it's worth your time to stop here and gaze at the water and imagine how it used to be: the river plunging over basalt in a roaring, churning froth where slab-sided salmon and nimble-footed fishermen joined in a food-gathering dance older than memory. When Captain Clark counted the stacks of dried, pounded fish on some rocks, he figured they "must have contained 10,000 [pounds of salmon]." And this was in October, well past the peak of the season.

The Dalles, October 24 and 25, 1805 (the Dalles Dam off Interstate 84, exit 88). The next set of falls was downstream at the Dalles. "At this place the water of this great river is compressed into a channel between two rocks not exceeding forty five yards wide," Captain Clark wrote. "The whole of the current of this great river must at all stages pass though this narrow channel." In spite of the river's ferocity at this point—which Captain Clark described as "this agitated gut swelling, boiling and whorling in every direction"—the captains decided to shoot the rapids in their canoes rather than portage around it. To the astonishment of the Indians, who lined the rocks above the falls to watch the spectacle, the Corps of Discovery passed safely through the whitewater.

Fort Rock Camp, October 25–27, 1805 (port area along the Columbia River, the Dalles). After running the rapids at The Dalles, the expedition camped here for two days. They spent the time repairing their boats, drying their gear, and hunting for fresh game, the first they'd had since entering Oregon. "We hauled up all our canoes to dress and repair them, as they had been injured in passing over the portage, round the falls," Sergeant Patrick Gass wrote. "Some hunters went out and killed 6 deer and some squirrels." On their return trip the following April, the Corps of Discovery camped here again.

Memaloose Island, October 29, 1805 (Memaloose State Park, 11 miles west of the Dalles off Interstate 84; see also *Wilder Places—Parks*). Lewis and Clark named this rocky island Sepulcher Island, one of the oldest surviving Indian burial grounds in the Northwest. Because of Bonneville Dam's backwaters, however, it now measures only about one-eighth of its original 4 acres. Victor Trevitt, an early settler in The Dalles as well as a former state legislator and senator, is also buried on the island because he asked to be placed "among honest men." "In the resurrection," he is reported to have said, "I'll take my chances with the Indians."

The Dalles (Chamber of Commerce 1-800-255-3385) has long been cloaked in layers of human history: a gathering place of Northwest tribes, a campsite of the

THE DALLES

Lewis and Clark expedition, a rendezvous point for fur trappers and traders, a temporary home to missionaries and soldiers, the initial end of the overland Oregon Trail, a river port to stern-wheelers, and a supply center to gold-mining towns and camps, among other things. As a result, the city's streets are lined with historical buildings, monuments, and other reminders of the town's early days. The following sites are of particular interest:

Wasco County Courthouse, 410 W. Second Street, the Dalles. Constructed in 1859, the year of Oregon's statehood, this wood-frame, two-story building is the original courthouse for what was once the largest county ever established in the nation. It stretched for 130,000 square miles, from the Cascades to the Rockies, and reached as far east as today's Wyoming. When county officials decided to raze the old building in 1973, city residents rescued it, restored it, and moved it here, its sixth home.

Pulpit Rock, intersection of 12th and Court Streets, the Dalles. Now surrounded by pavement, this 20-foot-high stone pillar once served as the pulpit from which the region's earliest Methodist missionaries preached to the Indians.

FOR FAMILIES **The Dalles Dam Tour Train** (541-296-9778), the Dalles Dam near the Dalles on Interstate 84, exit 87. A small train scoots visitors past the fish ladder and powerhouse of the Dalles Dam, which drowned the upstream ancient fishing grounds at Celilo Falls (see **Lewis and Clark Trail** under *Historic Sites*) in 1957. This guided tour attempts to explain the operation of the dam as well as the cultural history that now lies underwater.

SCENIC DRIVES **Historic Columbia River Highway—eastern segment,** 18 paved miles from Mosier to the Dalles, exits 69 to 84 on Interstate 84. This stretch of the famous road built in the days of the Model T—then the first scenic road built in the United States and now one of only 15 designated **All-American Roads** in the nation—climbs through apple orchards and across arched-span bridges, winding its way past views of the Columbia River and basalt-walled canyons before topping out at **Rowena Crest** (see *Natural Wonders*). It then begins the descent back toward the river. This is an unhurried road designed for thoughtful travelers, so if you find yourself stunned by the beauty you discover along the way, you can thank Samuel Lancaster, the road's engineer. His goal, he said, was "to find the beauty spots, or those points where the most beautiful things along the line might be seen in the best advantage, and if possible to locate the road in such a way as to reach them." Yet the call of this particular road seems to extend beyond the beauty of the countryside. "It's not necessarily the road itself that's important," one state park ranger says. "It's the journey you experience while you're driving on it, what you experience that will make you want to drive it again."

NATURAL WONDERS **Columbia River Gorge,** along the Historic Columbia River Highway (see *Scenic Drives*) or Interstate 84 from the Dalles to Troutdale. Along its entire length, which stretches from British Columbia to northern California, the Cascade Mountain Range is naturally breached but once: in the

ROWENA CREST, FORMED FROM BASALT AND SHAPED BY THE COLUMBIA RIVER

Columbia River Gorge, which was created by some of the most catastrophic floods ever documented. The story of those floods began some 30,000 years ago when a chunk of the continental ice sheet slid far enough south to block the westward-flowing streams of the Rocky Mountains. Behind the ice dam, in what is today western Montana, Lake Missoula formed, eventually covering as much as 100,000 square miles at a depth of 4,000 feet. (To put that in perspective, imagine the entire state of Oregon submerged beneath three-quarters of a mile of water.) Through the millennia, this lake may have flooded more than 100 times. But it was the most recent floodings, which came near the end of the last Ice Age some 12,000 years ago, that shook this part of the world the most. For then when the lake broke its dam, walls of water gushed across the Northwest and roared down the Columbia River, reaching depths of 1,000 feet and sweeping icebergs and boulders along for the ride. The flood scoured the land and stripped the rock—carving what had been a V-shaped river valley into a wide, steep-walled gorge—before filling the Willamette Valley with a lake 400 feet deep and covering as much as 3,000 square miles.

Rowena Crest, 14 miles west of the Dalles off Interstate 84, exit 76. When the latest and greatest of the Missoula floods hit the Columbia River Gorge some 13,000 years ago, the waters reached depths of 1,000 feet, leaving Rowena Crest beneath 200 feet of water while scouring away the area's topsoil and stripping away its rock. Today this overlook offers both viewpoints and trails that let you examine what the floods left behind. (See also *Scenic Drives* and *To Do—Hiking.*)

TOM McCALL POINT

✷ To Do

BICYCLING **Historic Columbia River Highway,** 5 paved miles from Hood River to Mosier, exits 64 to 69 on Interstate 84. Open to foot and bicycle traffic only, this segment of the historic highway leads through the **Mosier Twin Tunnels,** an engineering marvel from the 1920s. Bored through basalt and framed with cedar, the original tunnels were 17 feet wide, roomy enough to accommodate two lanes of Model T traffic, but too narrow for later, larger automobiles. So the tunnels were widened in 1938 then closed and filled with rubble in the 1950s. Trailheads are located south of Hood River off Highway 35 and southwest of Mosier on Rock Creek Road.

Atiyeh Deschutes River Trail, 14 miles east of The Dalles off Interstate 84 and old Highway 30. This 17-mile (one way) biking trail begins north of the campground (see *Camping*) at the Deschutes River State Recreation Area and follows a gravel service road along the bank of the Deschutes River. The road is closed to motor vehicles, so you'll be mostly alone with the water and the wildlife, sharing the bank with only a few fishermen and rafters.

CAMPING **Deschutes River State Recreation Area**, 14 miles east of the Dalles off Interstate 84 and old Highway 30. More than 100 campsites with just about every accommodation except RV hookups.

Marine Parks, along the Columbia River off Highway 730 in **Irrigon** and off Interstate 84 in **Boardman.** Irrigon and Boardman can each boast of a riverside park offering campgrounds and picnic areas, ball fields and boat docks, playgrounds and trails.

See also **Memaloose State Park** under *Wilder Places—Parks.*

HIKING **Tom McCall Point** and **Tom McCall Preserve,** 14 miles west of The Dalles off Interstate 84 exit 76. Both trails begin at the viewpoint on **Rowena Crest** (see *To See—Natural Wonders*). (That lovely bridge in the distance is Dry Canyon Creek Bridge, built in 1921.) The **Point trail** (1.7 miles one way) climbs to a 1,700-foot hilltop meadow that offers a panoramic downstream view of the **Columbia Gorge;** the **Preserve trail** (2.2 miles round trip) wanders across a prairie of wildflowers where the shadows of golden eagles and red-tailed hawks sometimes soar on sunny days.

See also **Umatilla National Wildlife Refuge** under *Wilder Places—Wildlife Refuges.*

✷ Wilder Places

PARKS **Boardman Marina Park,** on the Columbia River edge of Boardman off Interstate 84. An oasis of lawns and trees that invites picnicking or swimming, this riverside park contains campgrounds (see *To Do—Camping*), beaches, and trails.

Interstate-84 Parks, from west of the Dalles to east of Hood River. If you need to save your eyes from the road, your nerves from the traffic, or your kids from each other, these roadside parks give you the chance to stretch your legs and see the sights. **Mayer State Park,** 10 miles west of the Dalles, offers riverside swimming, picnicking, and boating, as well as access to **Rowena Crest Overlook** and its two hiking trails (see *To Do—Hiking*). **Koberg Beach State Recreation Site**, 3 miles east of Hood River, has a sandy beach and swimming area on the Columbia River, as well as ghosts of the 1920s, when a stone and concrete dance pavilion stood here at the water's edge (two steel girders and parts of the retaining walls remain at the site).

Memaloose State Park, 11 miles west of the Dalles off Interstate 84, offers day-use and overnight facilities. With more than 100 campsites sprawled across a bank of the Columbia River and near historic **Memaloose Island** (see **Lewis and Clark Trail** under *To See—Historic Sites*), this park serves as a campground and recreation area for freeway travelers along the Columbia River Gorge.

WILDLIFE REFUGES **Lower Deschutes Fish and Wildlife Area,** 14 miles east of the Dalles off Interstate 84. Beginning approximately a mile south of Deschutes River State Recreation Area (see *To Do—Camping*) and stretching along the lower 17 miles of both banks of the river, this rugged wildlife area is open to travel only by boat, bike, or foot. With sagebrush and bunchgrass growing on the uplands and alder and hackberry along the river, this corridor is home to a variety of game birds—including **quail, doves,** and **chukars**—as well as **waterfowl.**

Willow Creek Wildlife Area, 11 miles east of Arlington off Interstate 84, exit 151. Located near the mouth of Willow Creek just upstream from where it crosses beneath the interstate and flows into the Columbia River, this 1-square-mile wildlife area consists of uplands spotted with big sagebrush and streamsides thick with willows and cattails.

Umatilla National Wildlife Refuge, 4 miles west of Irrigon off Washington Lane. This refuge is so large, covering almost 14 square miles, that it contains a spectrum of native habitats, including shrub-steppe desert, wet woodlands, and marshlands. As a result, it's at least a temporary home to a dizzying variety and number of birds, from **burrowing owls** to **bald eagles;** fall flights of **waterfowl** can number in the hundreds of thousands. To help you get a glimpse of what it has to offer critters both feathered and furred, the refuge offers 1- and 4-mile hiking trails.

Irrigon Wildlife Area, along the Columbia River and Highway 730 between Irrigon and Umatilla. For 6 miles this 940-acre refuge stretches in a narrow strip of bogs and hollows and marsh where the underbrush twitches with the skittering of **quail** and **rabbits.** The makeshift trails—none are maintained—are as wild as the country, leading nowhere in particular but instead wandering through sagebrush and

IIRRIGON WILDLIFE AREA

woods before nuzzling up beside the slack water of the Columbia. You'll find several entry points along the highway as well as at the east end of Irrigon's city park. And because the area is squeezed between river and road, you'll also find it difficult to get lost.

✳ Lodging

BED & BREAKFASTS **The Columbia House** (1-800-807-2668), 525 E. Seventh Street, the Dalles 97058. Surrounded by an acre of forested grounds that shade its patio and deck, this 1939 home sits high enough on a bluff to overlook the Columbia River and far enough from the street to maintain a woodsy quiet. Its den and living room each have a fireplace and its rec room a pool table. Three of its guest rooms come with a private bath and one shares a bathroom ($85). A full breakfast is included.

GUEST HOUSES **The Guest House at Stone House Farm** (1-800-211-1202 ext. 02745; info@stonehousefarm.ws; www.stonehousefarm.ws), 6700 Mill Creek Road, the Dalles 97058. The setting for this three-room cottage is 54 acres of pastures and trees, all of it covered with that lovely Columbia Gorge sky, and all of it open to families. "Our cottage is set up to cater to families with children," says owner Ann-Gale Peterson. "It embodies the relaxing atmosphere of a small farm with plenty to do to keep everyone happy." Besides the three rooms, which sleep seven, the cottage contains antique furnishings, a full kitchen, and laundry facilities ($70, includes no charge for as many as two children younger than 12). "There are lots of toys for all ages inside," Ann-Gale says, "plus the fun of a small farm outside with a lighted sport court; a barn loft for hay forts; always lots of loving, tame kittens; horses who are always interested in apples and carrots; and, in summer, big juicy blackberries down by the pond. In fact, some of the best blackberries are only accessible from the paddleboat on the pond."

✵ Where to Eat

DINING OUT **Bailey's Place** (541-296-6708), 515 Liberty Street, the Dalles. In this 1865 Victorian home, lace curtains frame the windows, white linen covers the tables, and prime rib and seafood dominate the menu selections made by diners who come for the food and the wine as well as the upstairs lounge with a view.

EATING OUT

Boardman

Lynrd's Spud Cellar (541-481-4855), 102 Boardman Avenue N. W., Boardman. With its pool balls clacking and its poker machines pinging, Lynrd's might seem more like a typical tavern than what it truly is—a destination lunch stop and the home of some of the Northwest's great sandwiches, most of them stacked so thick you'll have to carry home half.

The Dalles

Baldwin Saloon (541-296-5666), 205 Court Street, The Dalles. After more than 125 years of switching careers—of working with people who ran steamboats, assembled coffins, or made saddles—the 1876 Baldwin Saloon is back in business doing what it was born to do, offering a gathering place to those seeking food, drink, and comfort along the upper reaches of the Columbia Gorge. Consequently, the old building's fir floors, brick walls, and mahogany bar are reminiscent of older days, but the diners from those days probably never tasted anything like the restaurant's trademark seafood specials and homemade desserts.

Big Jim's Drive In (541-296-2938), E. Second Street, the Dalles. It's a drive-in, sure, but Big Jim's also serves some of the best hamburgers you'll find anywhere. In fact, a stop here is something of a tradition with some Columbia Gorge travelers. The drive-in also offers a large menu, fresh ingredients, and regionally famous Umpqua ice cream.

Orient Café (541-296-4653), 1222 W. Second Street, the Dalles. Though its appearance can be rough enough to prompt some local diners to use the term "hole in the wall" affectionately when referring to the Orient Café, this is where they go for the best Chinese food in town.

✵ Special Events

April: **Northwest Cherry Festival** (1-800-255-3385), the Dalles.

November: **Starlight Parade** (1-800-255-3385), the Dalles.

COLUMBIA PLATEAU

GUIDANCE **Central Oregon Visitors Association** (1-800-800-8334; cova@empnet.com; www.empnet.com/cova), 63085 N. Highway 97, Suite 94, Bend 97701.

Heppner Chamber of Commerce (541-676-5536), W. May Street, Heppner 97836.

Mount Hood National Forest: Headquarters (503-668-1771), 16400 Champion Way, Sandy 97055.

Ochoco National Forest: Headquarters (541-447-6247), 3000 E. Third, Prineville 97754.

Oregon State Parks (503-378-6305), State Parks and Recreation Department, 525 Trade Street S. E., Salem 97301.

Sherman County Visitors Association (541-565-3232), 200 Dewey Street, Moro 97039.

Umatilla National Forest: Headquarters (541-278-3716), 2517 S. W. Hailey Avenue, Pendleton 97801; **Heppner Ranger District** (541-676-9187).

GETTING THERE The Columbia Plateau region is reached from the north by Interstate 84's connections to Highways 74, 19, 97, and 197. The area is also linked by Highways 207, 206, 216, and 218.

MEDICAL EMERGENCY **Mid-Columbia Medical Center** (541-296-1111), 1700 E. 19th Street, the Dalles.

Pioneer Memorial Hospital (541-676-9133), 564 E. Pioneer Drive, Heppner.

✷ Towns

Shaniko. With its days as the Wool Capital of the World long gone, the old railroad terminus of Shaniko has seen some hard times but still holds onto enough life to escape the fate Oregon writer Virgil Rupp describes as "close enough to a ghost town that you can hear the bones rattle when the wind blows." Possibly thinking that "close enough" is good enough, this historic community advertises itself as "Oregon's Best Known Ghost Town," which is reason enough to stop for a look at what's left of Shaniko's Wild West past (for more on Shaniko, see also *To See—Historic Sites*).

Moro. Night descends here like a soft blanket, the sunset laying wisps of pink clouds across a darkening blue sky that holds silhouettes of hay silos, grain elevators, and distant trees. On the outskirts of town, rooster pheasants call from the edges of plowed fields. Unfortunately, truckers with rumbling rigs and hissing brakes often speed through town in their frenzy to put another milepost behind them. Nevertheless, Moro's spirit seems as calm and constant as her wheat fields.

Condon. A student at Condon High School described the closeness of her hometown in one sentence. "Everyone knows everything about you," she said, "before you know it yourself." For the 750 people who live in Condon—a town where the *Time-Journal* newspaper has come out every week since 1886 and where the local radio station (KGAB) reports the news, predicts the weather, and spins its country-western records from the living room of a single wide trailer—prosperity rises and falls with the price of wheat. "There's no lumber here and no industry," a local teacher said. "There's just grain." Nevertheless, Condon endures.

Ione. Folks in Ione seem to possess that rare quality of genuine happiness. They're happy to live here, to work here, to share their town with those who visit. This shows in their smiles and their conversation, in their hospitality and their openness. Walk down the street, and people wave from their porches; drop into the store, and people greet you as though you've just come home from a long trip. Don't be surprised if someone offers you a tomato from their garden or a beer from their fridge. Don't try to figure it out, either—just smile and wave and say, "Howdy." You'll fit in just fine.

Fossil. Things here in Fossil are gentle: the slopes of the hills, the smiles of the people, the waves from the pickups. But even gentleness has its limits. For example, when a writer for the *Oregonian,* the Northwest's largest newspaper,

IONE

reported in a 1970 story that as far as Fossil was concerned, "you had to want to be there because it's not on the way to anywhere else," residents rushed to their town's defense. One of the more temperate responses came from Clarence Asher, county judge at the time. "Fossil is a quiet community . . . with no drug problems, no juvenile delinquency, no smog, no traffic jams, no riots," Asher wrote the paper. "Just plenty of good clean air and good clean living with plenty of Americanism and patriotism to be found." (See also *To See—Historic Sites.*)

Mitchell. Like so many towns on the dry side of the state, Mitchell enjoyed a youth characterized by rapid growth and boundless optimism before settling into a quiet middle age. After getting its start as a stage stop on the Dalles–Canyon City road, the town's growing years, mostly from the 1870s to the turn of the 20th century, sprung from the area's grass and water, which lured the farmers and ranchers who brought the families that brought the businesses. Today Mitchell leads a quiet country life in the canyon of Bridge Creek along Highway 26.

Spray. Small towns have long memories. At commencement ceremonies for Spray High School in 1945, for example, the mother of graduating senior Marvin Britt stood on the stage behind his chair—and she was crying because the chair was empty. Marvin was with the U.S. Army in the Philippines, training for the invasion of Japan. After the war Marvin returned to Spray, logged and ranched and got himself elected mayor, but he never received his diploma. Not until 1999. That spring when the graduating class made him an honorary senior at the age of 72, Marvin Britt donned a cap and gown, received his diploma, and then wept as the audience of 250 people gave him a standing ovation.

See also *To See—Historic Sites.*

✷ To See

MUSEUMS **Sherman County Museum** (541-565-3232), 200 Dewey Street, Moro. Here in a former American Legion hall resides the story of the birth and growth of this region bordered by rivers, bristled with wheat, and carved by the tracks of wagons and trains, threshers and combines. Yet perhaps its most impressive display involves the spirit of the people who built the museum. Of this county's 1,800 people, 100 of them volunteer at the museum and another 400 belong to the historical society. The result is an award-winning collection that preserves more than a century of local history.

Gilliam County Museum (541-384-04233), Highway 19, Condon. If you want to know about this sunbaked country where the wheat fields roll to the horizon, then visit this museum housed in a 1905 railroad depot. "We want people to walk through here, touch the displays, feel the charm," says Karen Wilde, the museum's one-woman staff. "We want to keep this history alive and let people enjoy it." The museum is arranged as an early-1900s home with family portraits hanging from walls, cookbooks lining shelves, and high school yearbooks gathering dust. The history continues outside, where there stands a collection of historical buildings, including a one-woman brothel that eventually evolved into a barbershop in the days when a haircut cost two bits; a settler's cabin complete with homestead certificate signed by President Theodore Roosevelt; and a one-room schoolhouse, one of the last of more than 40 that were once scattered throughout the hills and hollows of the region.

Fossil Museum (541-763-2698), downtown Fossil. A bird-watcher in New York City's Central Park once said something about birds that also helps describe this town of 500 people in north-central Oregon: "What we understand we come to love," she said, "and what we love, we want to care for." And because many people in Fossil care about the community's past, they built this museum in the old Odd Fellows Hall to store the memories of those who came before, those who fought wars, played football, raced horses, built schools, cut timber, preached sermons, wrangled horses, cured diseases, pulled teeth, cut hair, kept books, taught school—in short, those who through the years brought life to this small town. Yet in a sense, the collection extends beyond the museum's walls, to the streets outside where historic homes line the sidewalks, where the one-room Pine School stands on a street corner and serves as a reminder of its 1889 world, and where a wall mural commemorates the old mill town of Kinzua with scenes of days gone by as well with the words "May the memories live forever."

Morrow County Museum (541-676-5545), next to the city park in Heppner. If you want to get a sense of what it was like in the homesteading years of eastern Oregon, if you want to peek into the lives of the people who worked the land and raised their families and built their communities on the dry side of the state, then this is the place for you—all 5,000 square feet of it. Probably one of the finest regional museums anywhere, this one is distinguished by the breadth of its collection and the care with which it's displayed, both coming together in a way that makes you feel you can reach out and grab hold of a moment from the past.

HISTORIC SITES **Oregon Trail** (Well Spring to Mount Hood). It was a trip of two days from the Umatilla River to Willow Creek, then two days more between Willow Creek and the John Day River. These were days of heat and thirst and bone-deep weariness for both people and animals. "Over rocks, gravel and sand we plod along all day," Harriet Loughary wrote about her journey through here in 1864. "Nothing indicates life except an occasional juniper tree." After that, especially for those who followed the Barlow Road, the trail grew even worse.

Well Spring, 14 miles east of Cecil off Immigrant Road. Once they left Echo Meadows and entered this span of desert, Oregon Trail emigrants faced more than 30 miles between streams, 30 miles of heat and sand, 30 miles without water—except at Well Spring. "We found a great hole of water 12 or 15 feet across," emigrant Elizabeth Dixon Smith wrote about the spring in 1847, "had to water a hundred and fifty head of cattle with pails." But the traffic soon took a toll. "A mud hole it maybe have been," emigrant Amelia Steward Knight wrote in 1853," but . . . it was essential to the survival of both emigrants and livestock." Used for centuries by the Cayuse and their horses, the spring today stands empty, drained by the sinking of modern irrigation wells. The gaping, rock-lined hole, however, still seems to hold the memories of centuries. (Less than a half mile away stands a pioneer cemetery dating back to 1848.)

Willow Creek, at Cecil on Highway 74, 14 miles south of Heppner Junction, exit 147 on Interstate 84. This creekside campsite marked the emigrants' first clean, reliable source of water since leaving Echo Meadows. For emigrant William Cecil, however, it became something even more when he stopped here to repair his wagon; other emigrants saw his knack for fixing what was broken, and he settled down on the banks of the creek to doctor wounded wagons and eventually build the area's first store, which still stands.

Fourmile Canyon, 6 paved and graveled miles west of Cecil off Fourmile Canyon Road. To retrace Mrs. Loughary's steps over the hills and through the hollows that roll through this country leading to the John Day River, head north from Cecil and then turn west onto a gully-edged road bordering wheat fields and hilltops until you reach the junction with Fourmile Road. At the nearby **Fourmile Historic Site,** wagon ruts still lie carved into the earth.

John Day River Crossing, 23 paved and graveled miles southwest of Arlington off Highway 19, Cedar Springs Road, and Lower Rock Creek Road. When it leaves Fourmile Canyon (see previous listing), the Oregon Trail crosses private land; the best way to pick up the trail again is to make your way northwest to Highway 19, where nearby Cedar Springs Road leads to Rock Creek Station and the 7-mile road that ends at the ford on the John Day River. Here near a power line and water pump, a rail fence surrounds a granite marker carved with the message, OLD OREGON TRAIL, 1843–1882.

The Fork, 12 paved miles east of Wasco on McDonald Ferry Lane. After crossing the John Day River, wagon trains squeezed themselves into the rocky bottom of a V-wedged ravine and began creaking their way uphill. "The worse peace of road we had yet to encounter," Philip Condit wrote in 1854. On top of the plateau, less than 3 miles from the ford, lay a fork in the trail: The right fork led to the Dalles and the Columbia River route to the Willamette Valley; the left fork followed the Barlow Road that swung south around Mount Hood, cutting off 100 miles and avoiding the perils of the Columbia. You can still follow both routes from the crossing, though the fork is now at Wasco, where you can drive either 10 miles north toward Biggs, where much of the remaining Oregon Trail now lies beneath the asphalt of Interstate 84; or 19 miles south to Grass Valley, the Deschutes River, and the old Barlow Road, parts of which still require a pioneer spirit to tackle.

Deschutes River Crossing, 17 miles east of the Dalles off Interstate 84. If a wagon train chose the Columbia River Route, here would be its last major river crossing before reaching the Dalles, where the emigrants would break down their wagons, load them and their supplies onto rafts, and face the rapids and falls of the wild Columbia.

Barlow Road, 87 paved miles west of Grass Valley off Highway 216 and Forest Roads 48 and 3550. In 1845 the conventional wisdom of the day held that building a road around Mount Hood was impossible—but emigrant Sam Barlow took a different view. "God never made a mountain that He didn't make a way to get over it," he said. So in 1846 he and Joel Palmer finished hacking out a road around the mountain, then Sam built some gates and began charging tolls to those who followed. "I never could have imagined such roads," Esther McMillan Hanna wrote about the Barlow Road in 1853. "Over roots and branches, fallen trees and logs, over streams, through sloughs and marshes, up hill and down—in short, everything that could possibly make it intolerable!" Emigrant Isom Cranfill, however, was more succinct in his description of the route: "Desperate bad beyond Discription." Today's route starts out easily enough—a cruise south and west from Wasco along Highways 97 and 216 to Grass Valley, the Deschutes River, and Tygh Valley. But soon after leaving the pavement for the gravel and dirt that leads up the ever-steepening slope toward Mount Hood, you might wonder how anybody ever made the trip with wagon and oxen.

(You'll also find Oregon Trail historical markers near **Arlington** off Interstate 84 exit 137; on **Highway 19,** 8 miles south of Arlington; and in **Grass Valley** on Highway 97.)

Kinzua Site, 10 miles east of Fossil off Highway 19 and Forest Road 21. The old Kinzua Corporation sure knew how to take care of its people. Named for a river in its founder's native state of Pennsylvania, Kinzua (pronounced *"KIN-zoo")* in 1929 built a company town in the forests of north-central Oregon. And what a town it was, complete with library and church, restaurant and tavern, barbershop and gas station, grocery store and post office—even a trout lake and a golf course. "It's a beautiful life," said the man who drove the company garbage truck, "with everything for the person who doesn't want to live in a city." For almost a half century, as many as 150 people worked at the town's sawmill and lived in its 125 houses, until the day came in 1978 when the town of Kinzua closed and the company moved away. Today the only traces of the old town are a sign that says KINZUA LANE, an old railway with tracks and ties missing, and seedlings growing in rows where ancient pines once stood.

Smock Prairie Schoolhouse, 5 miles west of Tygh Valley off Highway 197 and Wamic Market Road. When it closed in 1956 after a half century of service to its community, the Smock Prairie grade school was one of the last of its kind in the region, a one-room school for the first eight grades. Built in 1906, the school today is a reminder of yesterday; its collections of historical books and furniture and photographs trigger memories of days when children walked or rode horses to school and when the local district permitted only unmarried women to teach, paid them $11 a month salary, and required them to board with local families.

Shaniko, 38 miles north of Madras off Highways 97 and 218 (see also *Towns*). In the first years of the 20th century, when the grasslands of north-central Oregon seemed to be one vast sheep pasture, Shaniko stood at its hub as the largest wool-shipping center in the United States. The town's Wild West days, however, lasted little more than a decade, and the reason for its bust was the same as that for its boom: the train. For in 1900 the Southern Columbia Railroad built Shaniko as its southern terminus where freight would be loaded for the trip to the Columbia River, and in 1911 the Great Northern and Union Pacific bypassed Shaniko on its way to Bend, taking away the traffic and the business. Today this town of some two dozen people—once it was home to more than 600—calls itself "Oregon's Best Known Ghost Town." Buildings left over from the town's wilder days include its water tower, city hall, post office, livery stable, and schoolhouse as well as the restored 1902 Shaniko Hotel.

Sherman County Courthouse, 500 Court Street, Moro. In the 1860s when settlers crossed the Cascades in search of grass for their sheep and homes for their families, they found what they were looking for here in the rolling bunchgrass hills of the Columbia Plateau. And when the bunchgrass was gone, they found even greater prosperity in the wheat that replaced it. "Few counties in the state are better off financially than Sherman," a local paper reported in 1899, "and it certainly is in condition to build a temple of justice that will be a credit to the county." The resulting brick courthouse, completed that same year, still stands, its arched windows and corner tower reminders of its 19th-century origins.

Fossil Walking Tour (541-763-2400). In this town of quiet streets and friendly people (see also *Towns*), some buildings bear the dates of their construction, the years marking the growth of the town from its time of settlement to its role as a ranching and logging center. Even though the passing of those years has led to some hard times in a changing world, Fossil seems to face its future with the same sense of pride with which it remembers its past.

Wheeler County Courthouse, 701 Adams Street, Fossil. In the 1890s, folks in Gilliam County got riled when they heard that some of their neighbors to the south wanted to strike out on their own. "Everyone about here is kicking like a mule downhill," reported a county newspaper, "against the proposition to cut off a slice of Gilliam County for the purpose of benefiting a little two by four locality." Nevertheless, by 1899 Wheeler County was on its own, and by 1902 it had built itself a courthouse of local brick and stone. Standing on the edge of Fossil (see previous listing), the building is entering its second century while retaining its sense of quiet and simple elegance.

Morrow County Courthouse, 100 Court Street, Heppner. Built of locally quarried basalt in 1902, this courthouse arrived just in time to survive Oregon's worst natural disaster, the 1903 flood that killed almost 250 people, more than one-fifth of Heppner's population. "The water was 15 feet high in Heppner's streets," a local paper reported. "Many people slept in the courthouse last night, any place they can make a bed." Because this hilltop building has changed little in more than 100 years, it's one of the most photographed courthouses in the state. Its appearance, however, isn't its only intriguing quality, for some believe the courthouse is haunted. "Some of the dispatchers who worked the graveyard shift swore they heard noises," says county clerk Barbara Bloodsworth. "The only thing I ever heard was the creak of an old building."

WHEELER COUNTY COURTHOUSE

Hardman, 20 miles south of Heppner on Highway 207. A former stage stop and freight center on a main road connecting two rivers—the Columbia to the north and the John Day to the south—Hardman is another ghost town that isn't. Sure, some of its buildings go all the way back to the town's beginnings in the 1870s (it was once known as Raw Dog and then Dog Town), and the cemetery on the hill could tell tales of old sadnesses (Sina Emry, for instance, died in childbirth at the age of 31, one day after the death of her newborn son), but this town is still home to a handful of people who, according to a former resident, "take their independence very seriously." Still, if you take a stroll past the ramshackle buildings and down the deserted streets, the rustle of grass on the treeless hillsides may be the only sound you hear.

Richmond, 20 miles northeast of Mitchell off Highway 207. Back in the days when 20 miles was a day's travel by horse, the ranchers living just that distance north of Mitchell and south of Spray found themselves getting tired of shuttling back and forth for supplies. So in 1890 they built themselves this town. Before long its residents had their own school, church, and stores; their own post office, community center, even an Odd Fellows Lodge. The coming of the automobile, however, brought the rest of the world closer to Richmond even as it emphasized the community's isolation. The result was the town's slow abandonment and final decay into a classic ghost town.

FOR FAMILIES ✐ **Public Fossil Digging Beds,** Fossil. Behind an end zone at the football field at Wheeler County High School in Fossil lies a unique treasure: a 30-million-year-old fossil bed, one of the richest in this fossil-rich area, and it's open to public exploration. That's right—you can dig 'em, pick 'em, and pack 'em home with you (daily limit: what you can carry by hand in one trip to your car). First exposed in 1949 during construction of the school, the bed attracts a steady flow of people who come to dig deep into the past but not into the ground. "The fossils aren't tough to find," says a woman visiting the site for the first time. She picks through the shale strewn across the hillside as she sings, "Let's go fossilin' now, everybody's learnin' how, come on a safari with me!" She stops, stoops, picks up a flat white stone. "Here's one," she says, then stoops again. "And here's another. They're everywhere." She rises and runs her fingers across one stone's finely etched imprint of a leaf, left there millions of years ago. "This is just fascinating. It's worth the drive just to do this."

SCENIC DRIVES **Arlington Loop,** 54 paved and graveled miles along Highway 19 and Clem, Barnett, and Cedar Springs Roads, beginning and ending at Arlington. Wheat may still be king in north-central Oregon, but his royal majesty has fallen on hard times. In this land where wealth was once measured in bushels, towns sprouted across the hills like . . . well, like wheat. But hard times and low prices have reduced the number of the region's communities as well as its people. Olex, Clem, Mikkalo, Rock Creek, and Shutler—these are among the once-thriving towns along the route that faded through the years so that only their names are left. Nevertheless, a visit to the old places takes you across a rolling countryside glowing golden and blue with its wheat and sky.

Gordon Ridge Road, 15 mostly graveled miles lying west of Moro and Wasco off Highway 97. If you want to see this country, *really* see it, then drive up to Gordon Ridge, where golden wheat and snowy peaks and whitewater rivers come together in a panoramic view.

Condon to Lonerock, 18 paved and graveled miles along Highway 206 and Lonerock Road. Folks who live in Lonerock probably wish writers and historians would stop calling their community a ghost town. Granted, it *is* quiet, so quiet that some scholars believe it was Shakespeare's visit here in 1606 that prompted him to revise Macbeth's famous "To be or not to be" speech by adding the lines, "Ah, languid Lonerock, thy aloneness is the rub / For here there stands no deli, no car wash, no pub." Just kidding—about the bard's visit, not about the quiet. But even if you won't find a store or café here, even if the school has been made into a home and the church holds services only once a year, even if the population is only about one-tenth of the 230 it reached during its peak years at the turn of the 20th century, this town of tidy homes still has plenty of life left in it. Perhaps the best reason for visiting Lonerock, however, is its seclusion, its silence, and its lingering sense of a nostalgic past.

Blue Mountains Scenic Byway—northwest segment, 91 paved miles along Highway 74 and Forest Road 53, from Heppner Junction—exit 147 on Interstate 84—to Ukiah. One end of this 130-mile byway lies on an interstate highway near the slack water of the Columbia River and the wheat fields of its inland plateau; the other, on a forest road near a tumbling mountain stream that has carved its way through the Blue Mountains. The segment that lies in this region leads first through the narrow **Willow Creek Valley,** with its low-slung, sunbaked hills of sagebrush and basalt and wheat overlooking hayfields glittering with the lines of sprinkler pipes. At Heppner, however, the land begins to change, to ease its way onto the timbered slopes of the **Blue Mountains,** its smells shifting from sun and wheat to shady pine, the valley narrowing and the road climbing and curving its way into mountaintop forests before plunging down the other side to the open meadows, the **Camas Valley,** and Ukiah.

THE BLUE MOUNTAIN SCENIC BYWAY PROVIDES A BACKCOUNTRY ROUTE BETWEEN THE COLUMBIA RIVER AND THE BLUE MOUNTAINS

Journey Through Time Scenic Byway—western segment, 166 paved miles from the junction of Highways 26 and 19 near Dayville to Biggs on Interstate 84 via Highways 19, 218, and 97. History is the main attraction along this route that cuts through the north-central heartland of the state. Beginning with the prehistoric remains at the **John Day Fossil Beds** (see *Natural Wonders*), the byway bends its way past an **old ferry crossing** at Spray and a **stage stop** at Service Creek, **more fossils** near Fossil and the former Rolls Royce cruising area of the Rajneeshpuram at Antelope, the onetime **"Wool Shipping Center of the World"** at Shaniko, the **Oregon Trail**'s Barlow Road at Grass Valley and Moro, the old wheat center of Wasco, and the ancient **Native American fishing site** at Biggs.

NATURAL WONDERS **John Day Fossil Beds** (Three units—**Clarno Palisades, Painted Hills,** and **Sheep Rock**—spread across 14,000 acres lying near Fossil, Mitchell, and Dayville. Cast in stone within the 22 square miles of this world-famous national monument established by Congress in 1974 is a record of life on earth dating back 50 million years. "There just is not any other place on earth like it," says park supervisor Jim Hammett. First studied in the 1860s, the fossil beds not only contain evidence of the exploding volcanoes and tropical jungles that once dominated this landscape but also hold the remains of a bewildering zoo of critters. "If it was not for the fossils," says staff paleontologist Ted Fremd, "one might think that many of the creatures that used to live in the Northwest were about as believable as Paul Bunyan's big blue ox." The list includes "beavers the size of black bears and lions the length of cars" as well as ground sloths as large as grizzly bears, "Nevada vultures" that stood as tall as a man and had wingspans of more than 15 feet, and 8-foot "saber-toothed salmon" with 2-inch fangs. "Fishing might have been a lot more interesting then," Fremd says, "even hazardous."

CLARNO PALISADES

Clarno Palisades, 18 miles west of Fossil off Highway 218. One of three units of the famous John Day Fossil Beds. Erupting volcanoes, sliding mud, and 40 million years of erosion created these ragged red spires that thrust 200 feet toward the sky. Three short trails, each only a quarter-mile or so, steer visitors to some of the best views and most informative sites: **Trail of the Fossils** loops along a slope and past boulders to 10 fossil sites; **Arch Trail** climbs the hill toward the base of the cliffs of the Palisades; and the paved **Geologic Time Trail** offers a series of interpretive signs that attempts to put a perspective on 50 million years of changes.

PAINTED HILLS

Painted Hills, 9 miles northwest of Mitchell off Highway 26 and Bridge Creek Road. If you're able to sense poetry in the movements and moods of a changing earth, you'll feel it here at the Painted Hills Unit of the John Day Fossil Beds. And if you're here during the early-morning glow when these rounded hills brighten into curves and stripes of red and blue and green and yellow, you might even feel thankful, as the poet e. e. cummings phrases it, "for most this amazing day" with its "blue true dream of sky." (Or at least you might agree with Tom Selleck's comment in *Quigly Down Under:* "You sure look pretty in the morning sun.") For in this landscape that began forming with the belching of volcanoes some 30 million years ago lies the quiet calm that comes with age. To see it from its best perspective, take any or all of four trails: the three-quarter-mile **Carroll Rim Trail** that lifts you to a hilltop summit; the quarter-mile **Painted Hills Overlook Trail** that lets you gaze across at the rumples and stipples of sweeping slopes; or the even shorter **Painted Cove** and **Fossil Leaf Hill Trails,** each of which gives you a glimpse of what the earth was doing here millions of years ago.

Sheep Rock, 6 miles northwest of Dayville along Highway 19. This unit of the John Day Fossil Beds was once the hunting grounds of saber-toothed tigers and stabbing cats and sharp-toothed dogs as well as the grazing lands of animals perhaps best described as tiny horses, hornless rhinoceroses, and grazing hogs, all of which had to keep an eye on the cats and dogs. Oh my. A series of trails in the area can help give you a perspective on both the country and its changes. In the Blue Basin area—yes, the basin really is blue—the **Blue Basin Trail** takes a 3-mile loop up hillsides and across rims to reveal panoramic views of red rock and blue sky, while the half-mile interpretive **Island in Time Trail** follows a stream along the basin's blue-green walls. Meanwhile, the Foree Area, some 5 miles north of Blue Basin, has two quarter-mile interpretive trails whose names describe what you'll find here: **Flood of Fire** and **Story in Stone.** On your drive between the two areas, look toward the left side of the highway for **Cathedral Rock,** which slid into the John Day River, forcing the river's course into a horseshoe bend to get around it.

Picture Gorge, 6 miles northwest of Dayville along Highway 26. The John Day River bends its way through this gorge where at least a dozen layers of 16-million-year-old basalt form walls that tower above the highway.

Sherars Falls, 17 miles northeast of Maupin off Highways 197 and 216; alternate 9-mile gravel route north of Maupin on Deschutes River Access Road. Here at the bottom of a canyon and between ledges of basalt, the Deschutes River froths and spews itself into a tumbling roar of whitewater that squeezes through a narrow, rocky trough. The ancient fishing grounds of native tribes, the falls spill their way toward **Sherars Bridge** (pronounced shears), an important river crossing since the time of the pioneers. Both were named for John Sherar, who in 1871 built a three-story, 33-room motel near the site. "The grade down to Sherars Bridge was [miles of switchbacks and drop-offs]," Herbert P. Eby wrote about his family's journey by wagon in 1905, "but at the bottom there was a fine modern hotel."

✷ To Do

BICYCLING **Ione and Heppner Wheat Country,** various rides originating near Ione or Heppner on Highway 74). If you get the hankering to take your bicycle for a spin across a vast, open country of wheat and sky, this is the place for you. But be warned: You're not in Kansas. Even though the wheat fields may seem relatively flat, with few exceptions this terrain buckles and wobbles and rolls from horizon to horizon; shoulderless roads run down into ravines, then up onto crests and rims, with nary a flat piece of ground in sight. That said, you can count on the fact that most highways see light use, many side roads are paved, and routes of varying lengths can be planned to circle back to the starting point.

Willow Creek Valley, 32 paved miles from Cecil to Heppner along Highway 74. This route follows a graceful, winding asphalt road through a narrow farm valley, the slopes of the hills bristling with sagebrush, the fields green with alfalfa and brushy with willows, the cows and horses lounging by the creek, slow and sleek in the sun. Two friendly towns along the way, Ione and Lexington, give you places to rest or turn around.

Rhea Creek, 3 miles east of Ione on Highway 74. This 22-mile paved route, one of the relatively flat roads in the wheat region, traces the banks of Rhea Creek, winding upstream past small farms and green fields before reaching Ruggs, where a Pepsi machine and a pay phone stand at a highway junction, and where the distant peaks of the snow-streaked Cascades shine white against a blue sky. If you want to make a loop from here, pedal up Highway 207 to Heppner and its junction with Highway 74.

Fossil–Kinzua Loop, 20 paved and graveled miles along Highway 19, Forest Road 21, and Black Butte Lane, beginning and ending in Fossil. This mountain-bike route takes you winding and climbing through a microcosm of the region, over hills and through forests and up to far-reaching views of a rolling countryside studded with junipers and basalt and pines. A shorter version of the route is the **Fossil–Hoover Creek Loop,** which begins at Fossil and goes 12 miles along Black Butte Lane, Hoover Creek Road, and Highway 19 before coming back to Fossil.

CAMPING **Mount Hood—east slope,** south of the Dalles between Highways 35 and 26 to the west and Highway 197 to the west: **Bonney Meadows,** 32 miles west of Tygh Valley off Highway 197 and Forest Roads 48 and 4891, 6 campsites near Boulder Lake; **Eightmile Creek**, 17 miles west of Dufur off Highway 197 and Forest Road 44, 27 campsites divided among **Eightmile Crossing, Lower Crossing,** and **Pebble Ford,** all located near Eightmile Creek; **Fifteen Mile,** 23 miles west of Dufur off Highway 197 and Forest Roads 44, 4420, and 2730, 3 campsites near Fifteenmile Creek; **Forest Creek,** 26 miles southwest of Tygh Valley off Highway 197 and Forest Road 48, 5 campsites along Frog Lake; **Knebel Springs,** 24 miles west of Dufur off Highway 197 and Forest Road 1720, 8 campsites; **McCubbins Gulch,** 25 miles west of Maupin off Highway 216, 5 campsites; **Rock Creek Reservoir,** 19 miles west of Tygh Valley off Highway 197 and Forest Road 48, 33 campsites along the reservoir with handicapped-accessible fishing; **Underhill Site,** 17 miles west of Dufur off Highway 197 and Forest Road 44, 2 campsites near Rainy Creek.

Bonney Crossing, 10 miles west of Tygh Valley off Highway 197 and Forest Roads 27 and 2710, 8 campsites near Badger Creek and the Badger Creek Wilderness (see *Wilder Places—Wilderness Areas*).

Bear Springs, 25 miles west of Maupin off Highway 216, 21 campsites, fishing at nearby Clear Creek.

Deschutes River, north and south of Maupin along or near the Deschutes River Access Road. More than a dozen riverside campgrounds make this stretch of the Deschutes River easily accessible for rafting (by permit) and fishing: **Beavertail,** 17 campsites; **Blue Hole,** 5 campsites; **Devils Canyon,** 3 campsites; **Harpham Flat,** 9 campsites; **Jones Canyon,** 10 campsites; **Long Bend,** 4 campsites; **Macks Canyon,** 19 campsites; **Maupin City Park,** 77 campsites; **Oak Springs,** 5 campsites; **Oasis,** 12 campsites; **Rattlesnake Canyon,** 10 campsites; **South Junction**, 7 campsites; **Trout Creek,** 23 campsites; **Twin Springs,** 7 campsites; **Wapinitia,** 2 campsites; **White River,** 3 campsites.

Heppner Area: Anson Wright, 26 miles south of Heppner off Highway 207, 14 campsites, some with full RV hookups, and a stocked trout pond; **Bull Prairie,** 36 miles south of Heppner off Highway 207 and Forest Road 2039, 28 campsites near 24-acre Bull Prairie Lake, which has a handicapped-accessible trail; **Fairview,** 18 miles southeast of Spray off Highway 207, 26 campsites, fishing at nearby Bull Prairie Reservoir; **Willow Reservoir Park and RV Campground,** 1 mile north of Heppner off Willow Creek Road, 24 campsites, fishing and boating on Willow Creek Reservoir; **Penland Lake,** 28 miles southeast of Heppner off Willow Creek Road and Forest Road 5321, 5 campsites along a lake that permits boating with electric motors.

Shelton State Wayside, 10 miles southeast of Fossil off Highway 19, 36 primitive campsites.

Wildwood, 30 miles northeast of Prineville off Highway 26 and Forest Road 2210, 5 campsites, fishing and hiking at nearby Walton Lake and the Bridge Creek Wilderness Area, close to **John Day Fossil Beds** (see *To See—Natural Wonders*).

Barnhouse, 18 miles southeast of Mitchell off Highway 26 and Forest Road 12, 5 campsites, fishing at nearby Rock Creek Lake.

Service Creek Area: Service Creek, just south of Service Creek, 6 campsites and a boat ramp on the bank of the John Day River **Mule Shoe,** 1 mile east of Service Creek off Highway 19, 10 campsites and a boat launch on the bank of the John Day River.

CANOEING **Rock Creek Reservoir,** 19 miles west of Tygh Valley off Highway 197 and Forest Road 48. This small lake is motor-free and has a campground with 33 tent sites.

Penland Lake, 28 miles southeast of Heppner off Willow Creek Road and Forest Road 5321. A mountain lake, a boat launch, and an absence of gasoline motors (though small electric motors are permitted) make Penland Lake a good place to dip a paddle.

Bull Prairie, 36 miles south of Heppner off Highway 207 and Forest Road 2039. Motors are prohibited on this 24-acre lake, making it prime water for canoes and rafts.

GOLF **Kinzua Hills Golf Course** (10 miles east of **Fossil** off Highway 19 and Forest Road 21). Built by the Kinzua Corporation in the 1930s for its sawmill employees—parts of the site were once used as a millpond and log yard—Kinzua Hills is Oregon's only U.S.G.A.-approved six-hole golf course; more telling, however, is that it is perhaps the most secluded course anywhere, tucked away in a mountain valley on the edge of a pine forest, a seasonal creek, and a gravel road. "If your putt goes awry, you can blame it on the high-pitched buzz of cicadas," says Oregon journalist and golfer Jeff Petersen. "Or maybe a bull elk's growing enthusiasm over fall rut."

HIKING **Bald Mountain Loop,** 20 miles southeast of Heppner off Willow Creek Road. The 7-mile-long Bald Mountain Loop is divided into three connected trail sections of approximately equal lengths: the **Bald Mountain Trail** (2.2 miles), **Hells Half Acre Trail** (2.5 miles), and **Willow Creek Trail** (2.6 miles). The entire loop begins and ends at either Cutsforth County Park or Coalmine Hill Park, and even though each leg has a distinct personality—as well as gives you the chance to stretch your legs or

THE BLUE BASIN OF JOHN DAY

walk the dog, see grouse or deer—all three take you to some historical curiosities: the cave where a fellow named Gibson lived in the 1930s and 1940s while he cut firewood to sell, the remnants of an old coal mining operation that fizzled out soon after the area was touted as a potential giant of coal production, and an irrigation ditch hand-dug by Civilian Conservation Corps (CCC) crews in the 1930s.

Blue Basin, 11 miles northwest of Dayville off Highways 26 and 19, in the **John Day Fossil Beds** (see *To See—Natural Wonders*). How do you describe a place both beautiful and blessed, a place where it seems you can reach out, grip a rock and shake hands with eternity? "Time is lost and years are but the pulse beat," is the message on a sign standing beside the Fossil Beds' **Blue Basin Trail.** And along this 3-mile route that skirts the tops or rimrocks and cuts the slopes of hills, the pulse of this fire-forged land throbs across the mountainous waves and the deep-wrought colors of an ancient and unsettled earth, where humanity is its least important element. Does wonders for your perspective.

See also *Wilder Places—Wilderness Areas.*

✷ Wilder Places

PARKS **White River State Park,** 5 miles east of Tygh Valley off Highway 216, day use only. At this quiet, shaded park you'll discover two fascinating qualities—90-foot **White River Falls,** which plunge over a basalt ledge; and the remnants of on old power plant, built in 1901 to provide electrical streetlights for the town that once occupied the site of today's park.

DeMoss Springs, 3 miles north of Moro off Highway 97. Flanked by hills of grass and sage and the rumble of trucks on the nearby highway, this park was once the homestead of the DeMoss family—James, Elizabeth, and their five children—who spent more than six decades singing to packed houses in both America and Europe. In the 1880s, weary of their travels and searching for a place to rest between tours, the family platted a town on this site, naming the streets for famous musicians and poets. Before long the community had a school, a church, a store, a post office, and a blacksmith shop as well as plans for a college. In 1921 they donated this land to the county as a park, though today nothing remains of the old streets and buildings.

Cutsforth County Park, 20 miles southeast of Heppner off Willow Creek Road. After the road leading to this park takes you from rolling wheat fields to mountainside forests, the sign hanging at the entrance lets you know right away this is a friendly place: COME IN, it says, WE'RE OPEN. Beyond the sign are a shady campground and picnic area, fishing ponds, and trailheads. And if it's one of those summer days so common around here, one with a blue sky shining and a soft breeze blowing, you'll probably also find kids swinging and sliding on the playground and trout rising in the ponds.

WILDERNESS AREAS **Badger Creek,** 12 miles northwest of Tygh Valley off Forest Road 27, or 25 miles south of Hood River off Highway 35; 45 square miles. Even though it measures just 12 miles from end to end, the Badger Creek Wilderness holds a world of differences: wet highlands and dry lowlands, alpine ridges and glacier-cut valleys, stands of ponderosa pines and white oaks, pinnacles and gorges, wildflowers and scablands. **Trailheads** located at a number of campgrounds on the perimeter—including **Robinhood** off Highway 35, and **Bonney Crossing** and **Little Badger** off Forest Road 21 and 2110—lead into the wilderness.

Bridge Creek, 20 miles south of Mitchell off Highway 26 and Forest Road 22; 8 square miles. Even though this land of open meadows, plateau forests, and steep slopes is Oregon's smallest designated wilderness area, it's also the most undeveloped: only a faded trail and a couple of old jeep tracks lie within its boundaries. One of those tracks leads a mile to the top of **North Point** and a view of hills and sky.

WILDLIFE REFUGES **White River Wildlife Area,** 10 miles west of Tygh Valley off Highway 197, Wamic Market Road, and Dodson Road. Herds of **black-tailed deer** and **Rocky Mountain elk** roam here, as well as the highest populations of **wild turkeys** in the region. But because this wildlife area consists of almost 65 square miles—which includes almost 50 lakes and ponds and 15 miles of year-round streams—it's best seen by car in a drive that will take you through mixed forests of fir, pine, and oak as well as along sagebrush flats.

Oak Springs Fish Hatchery, 3 miles north of Maupin off Highway 197 and Oak Springs Road. Located on more than 200 acres bordering the Deschutes River, the hatchery grounds are near a series of springs that flow from the canyon walls and feed the oak, alder, and cottonwood trees so rare in this sagebrush desert. The trees and blackberry thickets create a habitat that lures a wide range of both birds and mammals to the area. It also contains a show pond for the **steelhead** and **rainbow trout** raised here.

* Lodging

RESORTS

Maupin

Imperial River Company (1-800-395-3903; irc@deschutesriver.com; www.deschutesriver.com), 304 Bakeoven Road, Maupin 97037. What distinguishes this resort is that one of the Northwest's premier rivers almost runs through it. "We offer a very unique lodging experience," says owner Rob Miles. "The Deschutes River runs right across the edge of our yard, providing fantastic trout and steelhead fishing. From our swing in the yard, you can watch fish rise on the evening hatch or catch a glimpse of a slow freight train pulling its way up the canyon to central Oregon." To make sure that you're really getting away from it all, the resort's 12 guest rooms contain neither TVs nor telephones ($75–110). In addition, guided whitewater raft trips leave from the lodge daily, and an adjacent restaurant is open seven days a week. "In short," Rob says, "it's a great little place to get away from the world all year long."

The Oasis Resort (541-395-2611; mmalefyt@deschutesriveroasis.com; www.deschutesriveroasis.com), 609 Highway 197 S., Maupin 97037. Since 1928 the Oasis Resort has been a destination of people who come from around the world carrying their fly-rods to test the trouty waters of the Deschutes River. "We offer professional guide service for wild trout and steelhead," says owner Mark Malefyt, "comfortable accommodations, great food, and hospitality." The accommodations include 11 private cabins that surround a shaded, woodsy lawn and contain coffeemakers, refrigerators, and microwave ovens ($59–75). The food is served at the nearby **Oasis Café,** which contains "the world's smallest **fly-fishing museum."**

INNS ✐ **Hotel Condon** (1-800-201-6706; info@hotelcondon.com; www.hotelcondon.com), 202 S. Main Street, Condon 97823. Built in farming's happier times when wheat prices were high, the Hotel Condon faded along with the price per bushel, until it had accumulated so many years of neglect that it seemed it might not recover. But then in 1999 a group of investors took notice of the 1920 hotel, and over the next two years raised enough money and devoted enough labor to restore it. "The efforts of more than 30 local craftsmen and the support of the community brought Hotel Condon back to life," says Marion Weatherford, a Condon attorney who helped spearhead the restoration. The renovated hotel now offers 14 guest rooms and four suites on its three floors ($70–110, including a continental breakfast; kids six and under stay free). In addition, the hotel's restaurant offers a full menu, and its lounge contains a replica of the 1900 bar that once graced the town's Buckhorn Saloon.

BED & BREAKFASTS

Dufur

🐾 ✐ **Dufur Valley Bed & Breakfast** (1-800-846-7313; suzi@dufurvalley.com; www.dufurvalley.com), 82439 Dufur Valley Road, Dufur 97021. The tradition at this B&B is as long as the views from its porch, for the land was first homesteaded in 1861 and the home built in 1912, and the farm stayed in the same family until 2000. That's when current owners Suzi and Dennis Smith bought it, restored it, and opened it as a B&B. "Our theme is 'Welcome Home,' and we mean that in every meal we serve and in every amenity we provide," Suzi says. "The atmosphere is quiet, serene, peaceful, and relaxing. When you come here, you really are 'away from it all' and yet just a short drive from all kinds of activities." In keep with their theme, the Smiths provide five guest rooms that "give you the feeling of being home." Each comes with a private bathroom and a full breakfast ($95–145). Children older than 12 are welcome at an extra charge, and pets (also at an extra charge) can stay in an outside area if you bring your own kennel. "We try to set our inn apart from the rest," Suzi says. "We provide spectacular scenery, great hospitality, and fabulous food—and our guests know we're glad they're here."

Fossil

Bridge Creek Flora Inn B&B (541-763-2355; fossilinn@centurytel.net; www.fossilinn.com), 828 Main Street, Fossil 97830. This inn has two pasts, one that goes back to its 1905 construction as the home of one of Fossil's founding families, and one that goes *way* back to a world of more than 50 million years ago. "Our most unique feature," says owner Lyn Craig, "is that we're the closest lodging to the only free public fossil digging beds in the continental U.S., located four blocks away" (see *To See—For Families*). In fact, the 9,000-square-foot inn takes its name from those fossils. "Bridge Creek Flora," Lyn says, "is the general scientific term used to describe the plant fossils found across north-central and east-central Oregon." Besides access to the nearby fossils—Lyn and her husband, Mike, will even lend you digging tools—the inn offers a total of 10 guest rooms. Four of these are inside the Victorian-style home: a downstairs room with private bath, entry, and porch ($65), and three upstairs rooms that share a bath ($60); the other six rooms, all with shared bathrooms ($60), are next door at the rustic **Fossil Lodge,** which was built in 1927 by the son of the original homeowner. Together the two structures occupy an entire city block. All rooms come with an all-you-can-eat breakfast. "We have a lot of repeat guests," Lyn says, "who tell us they come back for the breakfasts."

Service Creek Stage Stop Bed & Breakfast (541-468-3331; info@servicecreekstagestop.com; www.servicecreekstagestop.com), 38686 Highway 19, Fossil 97830. Originally Tilly's Boarding House in the 1920s, this inn, which stands on 26 acres along the bank of the John Day River, is part of a country that's changed little through the years. "Today Service Creek is an oasis nestled deep in ancient canyons," says Mark Miller, who's been part of the Stage Stop for about 30 years. "In the evenings, the rims, bathed in alpenglow, drape a mercurial backlight of intense clarity. In the mornings, the quiet is broken by the raucous songs of birds welcoming the day." Its six guest rooms, which come with four bathrooms and a full breakfast, feature such traditional, comfortable furnishings as quilts, rocking chairs, ceiling fans, and wood-burning stoves ($40 single, $60 double). But Service Creek goes beyond the duties of a B&B to serve as an outpost to adventure. **"A store, restaurant, and raft rental business** are next door," Mark says. "The store carries groceries, beverages, and camping, rafting, and fishing supplies. The restaurant features a full menu, from hand-cut New York steaks to hamburgers and locally grown produce in season. The raft rental and vehicle shuttle business has boats for rent, will shuttle your vehicle from river put-in to take-out, and provides guided fishing and eco-tour trips." In addition, Service Creek is located close to all three units of the **John Day Fossil Beds** National Monument (see *To See—Natural Wonders*). "It's a natural base of exploration," Mark says. "It offers rest for the weary traveler and a haven for the intrepid explorer."

Wilson Ranches Retreat B&B (1-888-968-7698; npwilson@wilsonranchesretreat.com; www.wilsonranchesretreat.com), 16555 Butte Creek Lane, Fossil 97830. Space on this working cattle ranch located 2 miles west of Fossil is measured in thousands, including both its land—9,000 acres—and its guest house, a 4,300-square-foot former ranch house that holds seven rooms (two with private baths) named for homesteads, hideouts, and bunkhouses as well as pioneers, wranglers, and buckaroos ($65–100). "The bed and breakfast gives us a great opportunity to share our pioneer values and western hospitality with guests who want a special lodging experience," says owner Phil Wilson. "Many of our guests are repeat customers that enjoy the solitude, quiet, and unique scenery that surrounds the ranch." Part of the ranch experience lies beyond the rooms, however, for the Wilsons also offer trail riding, cattle drives, and truck tours. "The ranch is rich in history and geological diversity," Phil says, "and has a large population of wildlife to view." What it comes down to, he says, is that guests stay here because of their love for "the land, scenery, fresh air, blue sky, and stars that we tend to take for granted."

Ione

Woolery House Bed & Breakfast (541-422-7218), 170 E. Second Street, Ione 97843. If during your travels you're looking for a home away from home, then this is the place to stay. Owner Faith Jordan, one of the nicest people you'll ever meet, treats her guests as though they're family, maybe better. The restored 1898 Victorian house, the home of Ione's first mayor, generates the same sense of friendliness and charm, inviting guests to plop down on the living-room couch or hang out in the kitchen with a cup of coffee. Rates for the six guest rooms with shared bathrooms are $45 to $55, which includes a breakfast that Faith calls "continental" but that guests say is like Mom used to make.

Mosier

The Mosier House (541-478-3640; innkeeper@mosierhouse.com; www.mosierhouse.com), 704 Third Avenue, Mosier 97040. Built in 1904 by town founder Jefferson Newton Mosier and restored in the late 1980s, this historic Victorian home stands on a hilltop high above the Columbia River and near cherry orchards, oak groves, and pine woods. Its grounds contain a garden, creek, and pond, and its accommodations include one room with a private bathroom ($100) and four rooms with a shared bath ($85). A full breakfast is included.

MOTELS **Condon Motel** (541-384-2181; condonmt@oregonvos.net), 216 N. Washington Street, Condon 97823. Across the vast land of the Columbia Plateau's amber waves of grain, it can sometimes be tough to find a night's lodging. The Condon Motel, however, is a clean, quiet, and friendly stop along the road (18 rooms, $42–50).

Fossil Motel and RV Park (541-763-4075), 105 First Street, Fossil 97830. On the edge of Fossil stands a sign saying that travelers who stop at this motel can "Sleep in a Fossil Bed." Can't argue with that. Although the rooms were probably at their peak during the shag carpet days of the past, the motel is quiet, the rates are low, and the managers—as well as their dogs—are friendly (10 rooms, $34–55).

Northwestern Motel (541-676-9167), 389 N. Main Street, Heppner 97836. 16 rooms, $45–50.

Deschutes Motel (541-395-2626; dmotel@centurytel.net), 616 Mill Street, Maupin 97037. 12 rooms, $45–60.

Skyhook Motel (541-462-3569), 101 Highway 26, Mitchell 97750. If your impression of the Skyhook is that it resembles a series of connected cottages rather than a motel, you'd be right. This structure was salvaged from the old World War II shipyard workers' town of Vanport that once stood near Portland as the largest housing project in the nation, but that was mostly swept away during a 1948 flooding of the Columbia River. As a result, the rooms today retain a sense of the cozy and calm built for those families of the 1940s, as well as separate living rooms, bedrooms, and kitchens.

Tall Winds Motel (541-565-3519), 301 Main Street, Moro 97039.

Spray Asher Motel (541-468-2053), Highway 19, Spray 97874.

Where to Eat

EATING OUT **Elks Temple** (541-384-3331), 117 S. Main Street, Condon. As the people in town will tell you when you ask where to find a good place to eat, you don't have to be a member of the lodge to dine at the Elks. In fact, this might be Condon's most popular restaurant because of its good food, modest prices, and friendly service.

Dufur Pastime Saloon (541-467-9248), S. Main Street , Dufur. In both its cooking and hospitality, the Pastime Saloon offers visitors a taste of small-town living. The family-style dining, heaping servings, and friendly staff might leave you with the impression that you wandered into someone's home for dinner.

Fossil Café (541-763-4328), 540 1st Street, Fossil. This is something of a communal kitchen where the locals gather for coffee, news, conversation, and meals. In addition, a back room contains what must be one of the smallest and most cheerful bars in Oregon.

Imperial River Company (1-800-395-3903), 304 Bakeoven Road, Maupin. Located near the edge of the famous Deschutes River, the whitewater grail of river runners and fly-fishermen from across the country, the Imperial River Company offers a menu whose offerings range from steaks to seafood, all of it benefiting from good cooking and decent prices.

✱ Special Events

March: **St. Patrick's Day Celebration** (541-676-5536; www.heppner.net), Heppner. Irish blood runs in many and many a vein in this part of Oregon, a fact of intense and glowing pride among the descendants of the first Irish stockmen who found their way here in the 1870s. (How many towns have you seen with a shamrock painted in the middle of Main Street?) "The image by which the community knew the Irish," writes local historian John F. Kilkenny, "[was that they were] first to reach a helping hand, utter a kindly word, partake of a friendly drink, or engage in a worthwhile fight." To celebrate that heritage, Heppner throws an annual St. Patrick's Day bash, complete with Mrs. O'Leary's Stew Feed and Little Leprechaun Carnival, a Kuma Coffee Hour and an Irish Parade, an O'Ducky Race and an O'Farley Social Hour, right on through homemade Irish soup and bread at the O'Senior Center, a chicken and ribs O'Barbecue at the city park, and a Lads and Lassies Teen Dance at the high school.

August: **Dufur Threshing Bee** (541-467-2349), Dufur. In the wheat country of days gone by, neighbors combined their labor and their horses to bring in the wheat, a tradition celebrated each summer at the Dufur Threshing Bee. In this two-day festival devoted to an older way of getting things done on the farm, horses weighing more than a ton each provide the muscle that powers the antique threshing equipment, while blacksmiths, spinners, and makers of soap, ropes, and knives demonstrate their crafts.

REDMOND–PRINEVILLE–MADRAS AREA

GUIDANCE **Bureau of Land Management: Prineville District** (541-447-4115), 185 Fourth Street, Prineville 97754.

Culver Visitors Information Center (541-546-6032), 411 First Avenue, Culver 97734.

Central Oregon Visitors Association (1-800-800-8334; cova@empnet.com; www.empnet.com/cova), 63085 N. Highway 97, Suite 94, Bend 97701.

Deschutes National Forest: Headquarters (541-388-2715), 1645 Highway 20 E., Bend, 97701.

Greater Maupin Area Chamber of Commerce (541-395-2599; www.maupinoregon.com), Maupin 97037.

Madras–Jefferson County Chamber of Commerce (541-475-2350), 197 S. E. 5th Street, Madras 97741.

Ochoco National Forest: Headquarters (541-447-6247), 3000 E. Third Street, Prineville 97754; **Big Summit Ranger District** (541-447-9645), **Paulina Ranger District** (541-477-3713); **Prineville Ranger District** (541-477-9641); **Crooked River National Grasslands** (541-447-9640).

Oregon State Parks (503-378-6305), State Parks and Recreation Department, 525 Trade Street S. E., Salem 97301.

Prineville–Crook County Chamber of Commerce (541-447-6304), 390 North Fairview, Prineville 97754.

Redmond Chamber of Commerce (541-923-5191; redap@empnet.com), 446 S. W. Seventh Street, Redmond 97756.

GETTING THERE The Redmond–Prineville–Madras area is reached from the north by Highways 97 and 26, from the east by Highways 26 and 126, from the south by Highway 97, and from the west by Highway 126.

MEDICAL EMERGENCY **Central Oregon Community Hospital** (541-548-8131), 1253 N. Canal Boulevard, Redmond.

Mountain View Hospital (541-475-3882), 470 N. E. A Street, Madras.

Pioneer Memorial Hospital (541-447-6254), 1201 N. Elm Street, Prineville.

✷ Towns

Maupin. This town standing in the canyon of the Deschutes River is named for Howard Maupin, an early rancher and ferry operator said to be the man who in 1867 killed the infamous Chief Paulina, a Shoshone known by some settlers of the time as the Executioner of the Ochoco. Today the town is a center of white-water rafting and steelhead fishing.

Redmond. When Frank Redmond and his wife, both schoolteachers from North Dakota, moved to Oregon in 1904 and pitched a tent in a sprawl of sagebrush between the Deschutes and Crooked Rivers, they were betting their future on an act of Congress and a set of blueprints. The act set aside land in central Oregon for irrigation projects and opened it to homesteading, and the blueprints showed that an irrigation ditch would soon be built through the Redmonds' newly claimed property. While they waited for the water, the Redmonds cleared their land, built a home, and hauled water from the Deschutes River, 4 miles away. But their gamble paid off—the main canal eventually made its way to the Redmonds' ranch, and the irrigation company decided to build a town beside it and to name it for the two pioneers who had seen in the desert what H. G. Wells called "the shape of things to come."

Prineville. You had to be self-reliant and independent to live in early Prineville because for a long time—beginning in 1868 with the arrival of the first settlers, Barney and Elizabeth Prine—it was the only town in more than 10,000 square miles. With the nearest telegraph and railroad 120 miles away in the Dalles, Prineville remained one of the state's most isolated communities until Bend and Redmond came along in the first years of the 20th century. Today, this first town established in central Oregon is the only incorporated city in Crook County.

✷ To See

MUSEUMS **Museum at Warm Springs** (541-553-3331), Highway 26, Warm Springs. With 27,000 square feet of floor space, this museum brings together under one roof a comprehensive collection of artifacts and displays whose purpose is to preserve the history and culture of the Confederated Tribes of the Warm Springs Reservation: the Wasco, Paiute, and Warm Springs peoples. The museum's permanent collection, one of the largest in the nation, includes heirlooms handed down from generation to generation in tribal families.

Jefferson County Museum (541-475-3808), 34 S. E. D Street, Madras. Housed in three rooms of the old City Hall's upper floor, this museum displays artifacts, photographs, and restorations that recall the days of the Oregon Trail, gold mines, cattle ranches, sheep camps, railroads, and other eras in Jefferson County's past. And while a restored Victorian bedroom—complete with authentic plumbing, furniture, and dresses—gives you a sense of what the great indoors was like a century ago, the 1913 county jail standing near the museum shows a less genteel side of life in the Northwest.

Farrell Homestead, Jefferson County Fairgrounds in Madras. On display at Farrell Homestead are two historic buildings from the region: a pioneer homestead cabin and a one-room schoolhouse, both of which have been restored and furnished.

A. R. Bowman Memorial Museum (541-447-3715), 246 N. Main Street, Prineville. When you walk into this museum, an old county bank constructed in 1910 of locally quarried stone, you might swear you stepped back in time. Marble counters, etched glass, mahogany paneling, alabaster chandeliers—these and other original furnishings give the impression that the old bank is ready to open its doors for an early-20th-century business day. In fact, when those doors did first open, the local paper announced the building to be "finer than anything in any city in the United States which is not on a railroad." The sense of antiquity is prevalent throughout the museum, with its displays preserving the memories as well as the artifacts of the area's ranching and logging past.

HISTORIC SITES **Crook County Courthouse,** 300 E. Third Street, Prineville. It would be tough to finder a wilder Wild West in the Northwest than what you'll find in Crook County's past. Folks who survived the Indian raids, range wars, and vigilante lynchings might wet their whistles at establishments such as the Bucket-O-Blood Saloon. Obviously, what the place needed was some law and order and a darn fine courthouse to hold it all. After a long struggle with finances and public relations, the county in 1909 unveiled this three-story stone courthouse that is still one of the most unique and attention-grabbing buildings in central Oregon.

Ashwood, 28 miles northeast of Madras off Highway 97 and Pony Butte Road. In a Wild West town, you knew the days of the "wild" were numbered when its saloon was converted to a Baptist church. That's what happened in Ashwood, which was established in the 1890s and soon grew into a ranching center and then a mining boomtown with a population of some 300 people. "When I walked past the open doors of saloons on warm summer days, I saw inside men standing at bars back of which were big mirrors," writes journalist and regional historian Phil F. Brogan, whose father owned a nearby stock ranch at the turn of the 20th century. "I have other memories of freight trains moving through town, headed for the end of the rails at Shaniko." And today, long after the boom left the town, even the memories of Ashwood are fading.

TRAIN TOURS It's not too late to hop aboard a train, still plenty of time to see the countryside pass by the window, moving in time to the clack of steel wheels and rails.

City of Prineville Railway (541-447-6251), Prineville. Perhaps the only city-owned railroad in the nation, the Prineville Railway began with a sense of desperation. It happened in 1911 when the Union Pacific decided to bypass Prineville and build its line through Bend. Fearing the economic death of their town, Prineville's citizens in 1917 voted 358 to 1 to pay for the building of a spur line that would connect to the main line near Redmond. The result was a 19-mile railway that's still in use today, including a 4-mile tour that's available from June through October.

Crooked River Railroad Company (541-548-8630; www.crookedriverrailroad.com), 526 S. Sixth Street, Redmond. A "theme train" that attempts to give passengers a feel for the drama of the Wild West as it serves them either brunch or dinner, this train runs 38 miles past the rimrocks and farm fields and sagebrush of the Crooked River Valley between Redmond and Prineville.

SCENIC DRIVES **Lower Crooked River Back Country Byway,** 43 paved and graveled miles along Highway 27 from Prineville to Highway 20. Follow the Crooked River, a designated Wild and Scenic River, as this byway leads you from basalt canyons to sagebrush plains.

Lower Deschutes River Back Country Byway, 39 graveled miles along Deschutes River Access Road, north and south of Maupin. This route bends through the canyon of the Deschutes River, one of the great rivers of the Northwest—just ask any trout fisherman or whitewater rafter. But early in the last century it was also a battleground, the site of a railroad war between James J. Hill of the Great Northern and Edward H. Harriman of the Union Pacific. The goal was to lay tracks from the Columbia River to California, and the shortest route lay across central Oregon and along the Deschutes River. And so in the summer of 1909, with Hill's crews on the east bank and Harriman's on the west, the race up the river and toward Bend began. Separated by only the width of the water and working with picks and shovels, the two crews fought the heat and snakes and each other. By the following spring, when the battle grew too expensive, a truce was called and the two crews worked together on the final stretch into Bend, where in the fall of 1911 a golden spike fastened the last rail.

NATURAL WONDERS **Crooked River Gorge,** 15 miles south of Madras on Highway 97. This is where the bottom seems to fall out of the desert, where the sagebrush plains come to an abrupt halt at the edge of a 300-foot canyon with almost vertical lava walls and a deep, deep drop to where the Crooked River snakes its way along. As impressive as the gorge is, however, some folks might be even more impressed with the **arched bridge** that spans it, for stretching itself over this 535-foot gap in the earth is 32 million tons of concrete and 132 miles of steel bar blended together into an elegant structure designed to last 100 years.

Smith Rock, 9 miles north of Redmond off Highway 97 and Smith Rock Road (see also *To Do—Hiking*). The famous rock formation that serves as the centerpiece of this park as well as a Mecca for rock climbers from around the world formed from volcanic eruptions some 17 million years ago. Ash and steam, gas and rocks did the building up; wind and water the tearing down. The result is a craggy collection of jags and spires that holds as many faces as do breeze-blown clouds.

Stein's Pillar, 18 miles northeast of Prineville off Highway 26 and Forest Road 33 (see also *To Do—Hiking*). In a long-ago time when ocean waves washed against the Blue Mountains, volcanic eruptions buried what is now Mill Creek Valley in lava and ash. After more than 40 million years of erosion, one of the few remnants of that age is Stein's Pillar, a spire 40 yards wide and darn near as tall as a four-story building.

✷ To Do

BICYCLING **Trout Creek Trail,** 16 miles north of Madras off Highway 97 and Clark Drive via Gateway. Beginning at the Trout Creek Campground, this trail runs approximately 5 miles along the east bank of the Deschutes River, upstream from the mouth of Trout Creek and through a land that is often loaded with deer, chukars, and coyotes.

CAMPING **Haystack Reservoir,** 10 miles south of Madras off Highway 97, 24 campsites on the east end of Haystack Reservoir, groceries and a restaurant, nearby fishing and hiking, and boat ramps.

Pelton, 8 miles south of Warm Springs off Highway 26 and Forest Road 6630, 100 campsites on the Deschutes River, nearby fishing and hiking, boat ramps, and play area.

Prineville Area: Allen Creek, 33 miles northeast of Prineville off Highway 26 and Forest Road 22, 6 campsites near Allen Creek Reservoir; **Antelope,** 43 miles southeast of Prineville off Highway 380 and Forest Road 17, 25 campsites near Antelope Reservoir; **Deep Creek,** 49 miles east of Prineville off Highway 26 and Forest Road 42, 8 campsites, nearby fishing and hiking; **Elkhorn,** 37 miles southeast of Prineville off Highway 380 and Forest Road 16, 4 campsites, nearby fishing and hiking; **Ochoco Divide,** 31 miles northeast of Prineville off Highway 26, 28 campsites, nearby hiking, 10 miles from John Day Fossil Beds (see *To See—Natural Wonders* in Columbia Plateau); **Prineville Reservoir,** 18 miles southeast of Prineville off Highway 26, 70 campsites along the shoreline, with everything from showers to slide shows available to campers; **Scott's Camp,** 34 miles northeast of Prineville off Highway 26 and County Road 23, 3 campsites, fishing and hiking at nearby Walton Lake and the Bridge Creek Wilderness Area (See *Wilder Places—Wilderness Areas* in Columbia Plateau), close to John Day Fossil Beds; **White Rock,** 36 miles northeast of Prineville off Highway 26 and Forest Road 3350, 3 campsites, fishing and hiking at nearby Walton Lake and the Bridge Creek Wilderness Area, close to John Day Fossil Beds.

See also **Cove Palisades State Park** and **Ochoco Lake State Park** under *Wilder Places—Parks.*

GOLF **Eagle Crest Resort** (541-923-4653), 1522 Cline Falls Road, Redmond, 18 holes.

Kah-Nee-Ta Resort (541-553-1112), Highway, Warm Springs, 18 holes.

Meadow Lakes (1-800-577-2797), 300 Meadow Lakes Drive, Prineville, 18 holes.

HIKING **Smith Rock State Park,** 9 miles north of Redmond off Highway 97 and Smith Rock Road (see also *To See—Natural Wonders*). This small park contains 7 miles of hiking trails that follow the bank of the Crooked River, climb onto rock formations, or circle the park itself. Trailheads are located near the parking area, the picnic area, and the bivouac area. For those who want an introduction to the place, two of the best trails are **River Path** and **Misery Ridge.**

Stein's Pillar, 18 miles northwest of Prineville off Highway 26 and Forest Road 33 (see also *To See—Natural Wonders*). A 2-mile trail leads through shaded forests and along sunlit hillsides to 350-foot Stein's Pillar, a leftover landmark from an age when volcanoes buried the region in lava and ash.

See also *Wilder Places—Parks* and *Wilderness Areas.*

✱ Wilder Places

PARKS **Cove Palisades State Park,** 15 miles southwest of Madras off Highway 97 and the Culver Highway, day use and overnight. Sometimes called the "Grand Canyon of Oregon," Cove Palisades is a vast complex of cliff-lined picnic areas, campgrounds, boat ramps, hiking trails, and reservoir water—lots of water, courtesy of the **Round Butte Dam,** which in 1963 stopped the flow of the Metolius, Deschutes, and Crooked Rivers and formed 72 miles of shoreline. As a result, the park pulls to its shores every year as many as a half-million campers, boaters, skiers, fishermen, and other folks with a hankering for the wet side of this sun-baked land.

Smith Rock State Park, 9 miles north of Redmond off Highway 97 and Smith Rock Road, day use and overnight. Since the 1940s rock climbers from around the world have come here to test their skill along some of the park's 600 routes, but in the 1980s the place grew into a rock climber's Mecca; they all come to tackle what many experts say are among the most challenging climbs in North America.Yet this small park, less than a square mile along the banks of the Crooked River, also beckons hikers, bikers, birders, picnickers, and sightseers. "This is a showpiece of central Oregon," one rock climber says, "a good slice of what central Oregon has to offer all in one little area."

Cline Falls State Park, 4 miles west of Redmond off Highway 126, day use only. A small park with a big swimming hole, Cline Falls sits on a slow stretch of the Deschutes River, where picnickers, anglers, and swimmers gather on summer days.

Ochoco Lake State Park, 7 miles east of Prineville off Highway 26, day use and overnight. Even tame water can have its wild side. Take this reservoir, for instance, an impoundment of Ochoco Creek whose waters sprinkle the area's farms and ranches, but whose shoreline offers primitive campsites and makeshift hiking trails.

WILDERNESS AREAS **Mill Creek,** 20 miles northeast of Prineville off Highway 26 and Forest Road 33. This tract of 26 square miles includes a 21-mile trail system that leads through old-growth pines, deep canyons, and towering rocks. Perhaps the most popular

STEIN'S PILLAR, A 350-FOOT REMNANT OF THE VOLCANIC AGE

of the three hiking routes here stretches less than 2 miles between the Bingham Prairie Campground and **Twin Pillars,** the 200-foot plugs of an ancient volcano.

WILDLIFE REFUGES

Crooked River National Grasslands, east and south of Madras near Highways 26 and 97. This 174 square miles of rolling grasslands was homesteaded at the turn of the 20th century before the farms folded beneath the dust bowl drought and the Great Depression of the 1930s. After the land reverted to federal ownership under the management of the U.S. Forest Service, Congress created the National Grasslands—one of only 19 in the country and the only one in Oregon—in 1960. With much of its native sagebrush, juniper, and grasses restored, the area today provides habitat for **deer, pronghorns,** and **upland game.**

Rimrock Springs Wildlife Area, 10 miles south of Madras off Highway 26. Surrounded by the Crooked River National Grasslands (see previous listing), this 430-acre site contains a cross section of the region's habitats—from sagebrush and juniper uplands to marsh, meadows, and ponds—and wildlife. A 1.5-mile trails leads to two observation decks and various mountain viewpoints.

✷ Lodging

BED & BREAKFASTS 🖍 **The Elliot House** (541-416-0423), 305 W. First Street, Prineville 97754. Once you see this three-story, antiques-furnished 1908 Queen Anne Victorian, you won't be surprised to learn it's listed on both the National and State Historic Registers. With Tuscan columns, bay windows, a wraparound porch, and a scrolled iron gate, this home is an elegant example of early-20th-century architecture. Of its three guest rooms, one comes with a private bathroom and the other two share a bath ($70–100). The full breakfast may be even more impressive than the architecture, for its highlights include fresh-ground coffee and fresh-squeezed orange juice, homemade applesauce, and fresh strawberry crêpes, all served by candlelight. But wait—there's more: Owners Andrew and Betty Wiechert offer the use of golf clubs and bicycles, and you might even get the chance to crank up the 1906 Edison phonograph or the 1916 Wurlitzer player piano standing in the parlor. Children older than 12 are welcome.

Seeder's Desert Rose Bed & Breakfast (541-923-8575), 6724 W. Highway 126, Redmond 97756. Located 5 miles from downtown Redmond, this B&B offers two guest rooms that share a bath, with a private bath available by request ($75–85).

✷ Where to Eat

EATING OUT

Brand Dinner House (541-548-3168), 5876 S. Highway 97, Redmond. Nothing fancy about the food or atmosphere of the Brand, and it's that simplicity that's probably its best quality. Here all the dinners—everyday specialties include prime rib, pot roast, and barbecued ribs—are served family style; the food is good and the prices decent.

BEND–SISTERS–LA PINE AREA

GUIDANCE **Bend Visitor and Convention Bureau** (1-800-905-2363; bend@empnet.com; www.empnet.com/bchamber), 63085 N. Highway 97, Bend 97701.

Bureau of Land Management: Prineville District (541-447-4115), 185 4th Street, Prineville 97754.

Central Oregon Visitors Association (1-800-800-8334, cova@empnet.com; www.empnet.com/cova), 63085 N. Highway 97, Suite 94, Bend 97701.

Deschutes National Forest: Headquarters (541-388-2715), 1645 Highway 20 E., Bend 97701; **Bend–Fort Rock Ranger District** (541-383-4000); **Sisters Ranger District** (541-549-2111).

La Pine Visitor Information Center (541-536-9771; www.lapine.org), 51425 Highway 97, Suite A, La Pine 97739.

Ochoco National Forest: Headquarters (541-447-6247), 3000 E. Third Street, Prineville 97754; **Paulina Ranger District** (541-477-3713).

Oregon State Parks (503-378-6305), State Parks and Recreation Department, 525 Trade Street S. E., Salem 97301.

Sisters Area Visitors Center (541-549-0251; www.sisterschamber.com), 164 N. Elm Street, Sisters 97759.

Sunriver Area Chamber of Commerce (541-593-8149), Sunriver Village, Building 15, Sunriver 97707.

GETTING THERE The Bend–Sisters–La Pine area is reached from the north by Highway 97, from the east by Highway 20, from the south by Highways 31 and 97, and from the west by Highways 242 and 20.

MEDICAL EMERGENCY **St. Charles Medical Center** (541-382-4321), 2500 N. E. Neff Road, Bend.

✱ Towns

Bend. First named Farewell Bend for a Deschutes River ford where wagon trains crossed before departing central Oregon for the Willamette Valley, the frontier town of Bend grew up near the end of a dead-end road, its free land and irrigation canals drawing early-20th-century homesteaders to the sagebrush of the high desert and the pine trees of the Cascade slopes. Even though it was the train's arrival in 1911 that made Bend a mill town by connecting the city to the Northwest's lumber markets—between 1910 and 1920 the city's population grew to more than 5,000, an increase of almost 1,000 percent—the area's sunlight, space, and seclusion have long pushed Bend toward its modern position as an outdoor playground and retirement vacation land. "If anyone knows of a more delightful climate than Bend, we should like to have it pointed out," reported a 1903 issue of Bend's *Bulletin.* "Bend can't be beaten as a pleasant and beautiful abiding place."

Sisters. When a company of Oregon volunteer infantrymen marched across the Cascades from the Willamette Valley on an 1865 patrol, they didn't find the Indians they were looking for, but they did find a place to spend the winter—near a forested mountain stream where they built **Camp Polk** (see *To See—Historic Sites*). In the years following the soldiers' departure, homesteaders began moving into the area, and the camp became the site of a store and post office, which eventually moved 3 miles south to join the fledgling community of Sisters. Located near the mountain passes leading to the Santiam and McKenzie Rivers, Sisters grew up as a regional crossroads and timber town. But after its last sawmill closed in 1963, the town resurrected itself in the 1970s with a false-front, Old West architecture that caught travelers' attention and turned the community into one of the best-known tourist towns in the state. "There's nothing like living in Central Oregon and Sisters in particular," says Vaunell Temple, who owns the Blue Spruce Bed & Breakfast. "Here the air is clear and crisp and there seem to be more stars in the evening sky. More than 300 days of sunshine a year is what brings people here and makes them want to stay."

Sunriver. Even though this planned residential and resort community, which covers approximately 5 square miles of meadowland along the Deschutes River, didn't start taking shape until the early 1970s, it has a long history. Its landscape began with a long-ago eruption of lava from Lava Butte, which blocked the Deschutes River and formed a lake that lasted until the river cut a new channel. When the lake finally drained into the rerouted river, the old lake bed became a meadow that became a campsite for native people and a pathway for trappers, explorers—Kit Carson and John Frémont stayed here—and railroad surveyors. "Our course this morning lay through a fine prairie," Henry Abbot wrote about the meadow in 1855 while conducting a survey, "from half a mile to two miles in width, and bordering with pine timber." The army post built here during World War II carried Abbot's name. "Hundreds of new trainees may be seen daily," the *Bulletin* reported at Camp Abbot's 1943 opening, "marching and countermarching amidst swirls of dust from the camp streets." Today, the biggest share of the community's population live here only part-time.

La Pine. The businesses of La Pine—the state's largest unincorporated community with a population of more than 14,000—s-t-r-e-t-c-h along the shoulders of Highway 97 while its homes hunker back in the pines. First platted in 1910 in anticipation of the coming of the railroad, La Pine was advertised as the commercial center of a potentially rich homesteading area, though the local newspaper warned that farming here required "courage and hard work [and] at least a small surplus of ready cash." (Yet those who came so equipped still found only frustration in the area's dry soil and cold climate.) Even though the railroad never materialized, the construction of Highway 97 brought steady growth to the community, and people drawn to the area's rural life and recreational opportunities still find their way to La Pine.

✷ To See

MUSEUMS **Deschutes County Historical Center** (541-389-1813), 129 N. W. Idaho Street, Bend. Inside this old stone school building with an arched door is collected the story of the area's past: native peoples and fur trappers, pioneers and homesteaders, loggers and soldiers.

High Desert Museum (541-382-4754; www.highdesert.org), 6 miles south of Bend off Highway 97. One of the most educational museums in the Northwest, especially as far as natural history is concerned, the High Desert Museum attempts to capture 10,000 years of life in the land lying between the Rockies and the Cascades. Here you can view Indian artifacts and pioneer relics, examine a sheepherder's wagon and a sawmill, walk through a settlers cabin and past an otter pond.

HISTORIC SITES **Camp Polk Site,** 3 miles north of Sisters off Camp Polk Road. This was the first "settlement" in the area, the winter quarters of a company of mounted Oregon Volunteers who crossed the Cascades from the Willamette Valley on an 1865 patrol to squelch the threat of Indian uprisings and didn't return until spring. Named by the commanding officer in honor of his home county, Camp Polk eventually had a post office, but it was moved to the fledgling town of Sisters in 1888. The last of the camp's eight buildings was razed in 1940, and only a pioneer cemetery remains near the site.

FOR FAMILIES **Pine Mountain Observatory** (541-382-8331), 9 miles south of Millican off Pine Mountain Road. This is the only major observatory and one of the largest telescopes in the Pacific Northwest. Although it's open to the public, please call first.

SCENIC DRIVES **McKenzie Pass–Santiam Pass Scenic Byway,** 82 paved miles along Highways 242 and 20, beginning and ending at Sisters. Toward the top of a rock-hard world of volcanic peaks and lava flows this winding road climbs, then takes you along glacier-fed rivers, through mountain passes, and near the top of a world that carries the scars earned in ancient battles with fire and ice.

McKenzie Pass Scenic Highway, 40 paved miles along Highway 242 from Sisters to Highway 126. Part of the larger McKenzie Pass–Santiam Pass Scenic Byway (see previous listing), this route leads through country so wild that snow can close it for more than eight months each year, so steep and winding that trailers or motor homes longer than 35 feet are prohibited. So if it's untamed mountains and forests and streams you seek, you can't do much better than this.

Cascade Lakes Highway, 87 paved miles along Forest Roads 46 and 42 and Highway 97, beginning and ending at Bend. In the early years of the 20th century, Sparks Lake, some 30 miles east of Bend, was said to be a "sportsman's paradise and perhaps the most beautiful to be found on the eastern slopes of the Cascades." Consequently, the U.S. Forest Service approved the construction of a lodge at the lake as well as a road that led there. Well, it took more than 10 years and 6,000 pounds of TNT—for blasting through lava rock—but by 1920 a wagon road at last connected Bend and Sparks Lake, and the road builders kept right on going. When they finally finished 36 years later, they had dug and blasted and graded a road that connected many of the lakes along a route they named Century Drive because of its 100-mile length. Even though improvements through the years have straightened and shortened the road to 87 miles, the new version of the old road is the Cascade Lakes Highway, often called Oregon's "Highway in the Sky" because it leads you through a world where everything—desert and forest and mountain—seems to stand high enough to tickle the clouds. The main attraction, however, remains the dozen or so alpine lakes nuzzling the flanks of the Cascades. (The U.S. Forest Service's 66-mile **Cascade Lakes Scenic Byway** follows the same road west and south but continues on to the junction of Highway 58.)

NATURAL WONDERS **The Cascade Peaks.** This is the backbone of Oregon, the range that separates east from west, that divides the state's topography, climate, and culture. And standing above the rest of the range, some at elevations of 2 miles, are giants that carry on their shoulders and flanks the memories and the mythology of the volcanic fire and glacial ice that created this landscape.

Standing 11,235 feet high, **Mount Hood** is not only Oregon's tallest peak but also one of the most active, voted by many geologists as the Oregon mountain most likely to erupt again. In spite of its age, approximately 730,000 years, the old-timer found enough oomph to erupt most recently in 1790.

Until glaciers chewed away at it, eroding its summit as well as a third of its western flank, 10,495-foot **Mount Jefferson** may have towered more than 12,000 feet. Even now, however, it rises almost a mile above its surroundings, far enough that Lewis and Clark named the mountain when they saw its peak from the mouth of the Willamette River, more than 80 miles away as the crow flies.

The region's best-known and most easily seen landmarks are the **Three Sisters,** a trio of 10,000-foot peaks that fill the western skyline with their snowy pinnacles. Once known as Faith, Hope, and Charity, today's North Sister, Middle Sister, and South Sister still hold some of the state's largest glaciers.

Keeping close company with the Three Sisters is 9,165-foot **Broken Top,** whose ragged crater exposes the inner structure of an old volcano. Those splinters and spires, however, formed as the result of glacial erosion rather than volcanic eruption.

Even though its 15,000 years makes it a youngster by mountain standards, 9,065-foot **Mount Bachelor** has gone by many names, including Brother Jonathan, the Bachelor, Old Baldy, Snow Mountain, and Bachelor Butte. Its youth is also reflected in its temperament, for it's one of the most active volcanoes in the Cascade Range. Even so, its powdery snow and long slopes make the mountain one of Oregon's premier ski areas.

See also *Wilder Places—Wilderness Areas.*

Headwaters of the Metolius River, 2 miles south of Camp Sherman off Forest Road 14. When 6,000-foot Black Butte began rising along a fault line a million years or so ago, it blocked the ancient channel of the Metolius River, and the river, seeing nowhere else to go but down, began percolating through sand and gravel until it found an opening near the base of Black Butte. As a result, today you can stand at the headwaters and watch the Metolius River emerge from the ground at a rate of approximately 50,000 gallons per minute. Here the emerging water forms a channel 30 yards wide and is ready to begin its 35-mile journey to the Deschutes River. (PS: *Great* view of **Mount Jefferson** from here.)

Lava River Cave, 12 miles south of Bend off Highway 97. In 1889 a local hunter discovered this mile-long lava tube and used it as a cooler for his venison. Today, Lava River Cave, Oregon's longest lava tube, gives visitors a peek at the inside of the earth along a dark (flashlights or lanterns necessary) and cool (40 degrees year-round) path.

Lava Cast Forest, 14 miles southeast of Bend off Highway 97 and Forest Road 9710. After nearby Newberry volcano erupted about 6,000 year ago, the hot molten lava buried this forest, flowing around tree trunks and forming molds around them. Today a mile-long nature trail shows you the lava casts left behind by ancient trees and stumps.

Newberry Crater, 20 miles northeast of La Pine off Highway 97 and Forest Road 21. Still active with rumblings and steam, this 500-square-mile volcano with its 17-square-mile caldera is the largest Ice Age volcano in Oregon. Within its crater lie **East and Paulina Lakes,** which hold more than 2,500 total acres of water, as well as **Big Obsidian Flow,** which supplied Native Americans with material for spear points and arrowheads for close to 10,000 years. In fact, an archaeological site near Paulina Lake recently yielded the remains of a 9,400-year-old wickiup that some researchers call "the oldest home discovered in western North America."

✷ To Do

BICYCLING **Deschutes National Forest** (541-388-2715), 1645 Highway 20E, Bend. With its western boundary riding the summit of the Cascade Mountains, the Deschutes National Forest contains a network of gravel and dirt trails presenting various degrees of difficulty. Trails rated "Easy" include the **Deschutes River Trail,** 6 miles along the Deschutes River between Lava Island Falls and Dillon Falls; **Inn Loop,** 13 miles through pine forest; **Kiwa Butte Loop,** 9 miles with big pines and fine views along the way; **Swampy Lakes Loop,** 2.5 miles along a single-track dirt road to Swampy Lakes and back; **Tangent Loop,** 6 miles through pine forests; and **Sunriver to Benham Falls,** 4.3 miles that begins at the

Sunriver resort area and follows a loop along flat dirt roads.

Newberry Crater Trail, 21 miles northeast of La Pine off Highway 97 and Forest Road 21. Beginning near the outlet of Paulina Lake, this 8.5-mile route runs parallel to Forest Road 21, past the **Big Obsidian Flow** (see **Newberry Crater** under *To See—Natural Wonders*), and to the eastern edge of East Lake. From here you can either return by the same route or make a steep climb to the lake's rim. Here the trail joins the **Newberry Crater Rim Loop,** a route that rises and dips and circles the crater, ending back at your starting point.

CAMPING ♿ **Bend Area: Big River,** 22 miles south of Bend off Highway 97 and Forest Road 43, 15 campsites along the Deschutes River; **Dillon Falls,** 10 miles southwest of Bend off Forest Roads 46 and 41, nearby fishing and hiking; **Fall River,** 30 miles south of Bend off Highway 97 and Forest Road 43, 12 campsites, nearby fishing and hiking, handicapped accessible with barrier-free toilets and trails; **Tumalo Falls,** 16 miles west of Bend off Forest Road 4603, 4 campsites, nearby fishing and hiking.

Sisters Area: Big Lake, 18 miles west of Sisters off Forest Road 2690, 2 campgrounds. **Black Pine Spring,** 8 miles south of Sisters off Forest Road 16, 7 campsites with nearby fishing; **Cold Springs,** 4 miles west of Sisters off Highway 242, 27 campsites, nearby fishing and hiking as well as excellent bird-watching opportunities; **Graham Corral,** 9 miles northwest of Sisters off Highway 20, 10 campsites, nearby fishing, corrals, horse and hiking trails; **Indian Ford,** 5 miles northwest of Sisters off Highway 20, 25 campsites, nearby hiking; **Three Creek Lake,** 17 miles south of Sisters off Forest Road 16, 3 separate campgrounds—**Three Creek, Driftwood,** and **Three Creek Lake**—located along Three Creek Lake, with nearby fishing and hiking; **Sheep Spring,** 22 miles northwest of Sisters off Highway 20 and Forest Roads 14 and 1260, 10 campsites, nearby trails for hiking and horseback riding.

Suttle Lake, 14 miles northwest of Sisters off Highway 20, 4 campgrounds—**Link Creek, Scout Lake, Blue Bay,** and **South Shore**—with nearby fishing and hiking.

Upper Metolius River Campgrounds, 16 to 23 miles north of Sisters off Highway 20 and Forest Road 14. The banks along the Metolius River, one of the loveliest rivers in the Northwest, contain at least 11 campgrounds. From south to north: **Riverside,** 22 campsites; **Camp Sherman,** 15 campsites; **Allingham,** 10 campsites; **Smiling River,** 46 campsites; **Pine Rest,** 8 campsites; **Gorge,** 18 campsites; **Lower Canyon Creek,** 4 campsites; **Allan Springs,** 17 campsites; **Pioneer Ford,** 20 campsites; **Lower Bridge,** 12 campsites; and **Candle Creek,** 4 campsites.

Cascade Lakes, southwest of Bend along Highway 56. You can find numerous campgrounds along the alpine lakes scattered along this byway, including some that border designated wilderness areas. The general rule is the bigger the lake, the greater the number of campgrounds. Larger lakes include **Crane Prairie, Cultus, Davis, Elk, Hosmer, Lava,** and **Wickiup,** but don't overlook smaller lakes such as **Todd, Devil,**

Little Cultus, North Twin, and **South Twin.**

Newberry National Volcanic Monument Campgrounds, 20 miles northeast of La Pine off Highway 97 and Forest Road 21. Located near Paulina Lake: **Paulina Lake Campground,** 69 campsites; **Chief Paulina,** 13 campsites; and **Little Crater,** 50 campsites; near East Lake: **East Lake Campground,** 29 campsites; **Hot Springs,** 21 campsites; and **Cinder Hill,** 110 campsites. In addition, **Prairie** and **McKay Crossing** are located along Forest Road 21, which connects Highway 97 to Newberry Crater.

La Pine Area: China Hat, 34 miles east of La Pine off Highway 97 and Forest Road 22, 14 campsites; **Rosland** and **Pringle Falls,** 5 and 9 miles northwest of La Pine off Highway 97, 17 campsites, nearby fishing and hiking.

CANOEING **Cascade Lakes.** With so many lakes, with so many rivers, with so much water running and falling and just lying there flat, the Cascade Range is a seductress to those with an urge to grip and stroke a paddle. Yet some lakes are more inviting than others. Those that forbid motors, for instance, include the following located southwest of Bend off Forest Road 46: **Todd** off Forest Road 370; **Devils, Irish,** and **Taylor** off Forest Road 600; **Lucky, North Twin,** and **South Twin** off Forest Road 42; and **Charlton** off Forest Road 4290. Along the same road, **Hosmer Lake** permits electric motors only. In addition, motor-free lakes located off Highway 20 include **Dark** and **Scout,** south of Suttle Lake off Forest Roads 2067 and 2068; **Round Lake,** northeast of Suttle Lake off Forest Road 1210; and **Three Creek,** south of Sisters off Forest Road 16. Lakes popular with paddlers that place speed and wake restrictions on motors in the same area include **Sparks, Davis,** and **Crane Prairie Reservoir,** all located near Forest Road 46. Farther north, along the south slope of Mount Hood, lakes that prohibit motors include **Trillium Lake,** southeast of Government Camp off Highway 26 and Forest Road 2656; **Frog Lake,** southeast of Government Camp off Highway 26; and **Summit Lake,** southeast of Government Camp off Highway 26 and Forest Road 42.

Link Creek Basin, 26 miles west of Sisters off Highway 20 and Forest road 2076. Located west of Suttle Lake and south of the highway, this mountain basin contains four lakes—**Island, Link, Meadow,** and **Torso**—that offer easy access, good fishing, and no motors.

GOLF **Aspen Lakes** (541-549-4653), 16900 Aspen Lakes Drive, Sisters, 18 holes.

Black Butte Ranch (1-800-452-7455), Black Butte: **Big Meadow,** 18 holes; **Glaze Meadow,** 18 holes.

Broken Top (541-383-8200), 61999 Broken Top Drive, Bend, 18 holes.

High Desert Golf and Learning Center (541-389-3919), 20420 Robal Lane, Bend, 68 hitting stations, 33 heated stations.

Quail Run Golf Course (1-800-895-4653), 8 miles south of Sunriver, 9 holes.

The Riverhouse, River's Edge Golf Course (541-389-2828), 400 Pro Shop Lane, Bend, 18 holes.

Sunriver Resort (1-800-386-2243),

Sunriver: **Crosswater** 18 holes; Meadows, 18 holes; **Woodlands,** 18 holes.

HIKING **Black Butte,** 28 miles northwest of Sisters off Highway 126 and Forest Roads 11 and 1110. Along this 2-mile trail you'll pass through forests of pine and fir on your way to views of Mount Washington, the Three Sisters, and Smith Rock before topping out on the 6,400-foot summit of Black Butte. Two of the mountain's old fire lookouts—one built in 1924 and the other 10 years later—still stand as reminders of Black Butte's days as a fire watch.

Metolius River, 18 miles northwest of Sisters off Highway 126 and Forest Roads 14 and 1420. Beginning at Lower Canyon Creek Campground and ending 2.7 miles away near Wizard Falls Fish Hatchery, this 2.7-mile trail follows the Metolius River for most of its length, bypassing the springs and rapids and shallows that make this one of Oregon's loveliest streams.

Deschutes River Trail, between Sawyer Park and N. W. First Street, Bend. For 3 miles this community pathway follows the Deschutes River through town, carrying walkers, joggers, bikers, and anglers along a bark-dust ribbon that skirts one of the premier streams in the Northwest.

Lava Butte and **Lava Lands Visitor Center,** 11 miles south of Bend off Highway 97. A paved road climbs 500 feet to the top of Lava Butte, a volcanic cinder cone. From here a series of interpretive trails wanders around craters, across lava flows, and into a pine forest.

Benham Falls, 15 miles south of Bend off Forest Roads 46 and 4120. A short trail leads to a series of rapids and a waterfall.

Todd Lake, 27 miles southwest of Bend off Forest Road 46. This 2.4-mile trail circles 45-acre Todd Lake, tracing the shoreline as it crosses springs, seeps, and soggy meadows where wildflowers grow.

Newberry National Volcanic Monument, 20 miles northeast of La Pine off Highway 97 and Forest Road 21. Even though this area contains over 150 miles of hiking trails throughout its more than 50,000 acres of mountain lakes and lava flows, two trails are especially good for those wanting a pleasant stroll. The shorter of the two is **Paulina Creek Falls,** a mile-long loop between the Paulina Creek Falls Picnic Area and Paulina Lake Lodge, edging along the creek and leading to the waterfalls. The longer route is the lower section of the **Paulina Creek Trail,** which stretches 1.5 miles from Ogden Group Camp to McKay Crossing Campground. If you want a longer hike and a bigger view, try the **Paulina Lake Trail,** a 7.5-mile path that circles the lake.

See also *Wilder Places—Wilderness Areas.*

UNIQUE ADVENTURES **Geographical Center of Oregon**, near Post, 25 miles southeast of Prineville off Highway 380. This probably won't make your heart flutter with excitement, but if you drive to the community of Post, which consists of a grocery store on the shoulder of Highway 380, you'll encounter the geographical center of the state. Actually, the center lies in a field just north of the store—a stake marks the spot—but two signs hanging on the false front of the Post General Store announce it to be "The Center of Oregon." Close enough.

✷ Wilder Places

PARKS **Bend City Parks.** In 1903 the local newspaper said that even though Bend was "growing up in the virgin forest," it was still necessary to plan a park system. "In our old age," the paper said, "we can be very thankful that we had foresight enough to plan a pleasant place in which to spend a Sunday afternoon with our grandchildren." That foresight has made Bend a city of parks—more than 20 of them. Two of the most accessible because of their nearness to downtown and their location along the east bank of the Deschutes River are 11-acre **Drake Park,** once the site of a homesteader's log cabin but now a place to feed geese and ducks along the shores of Mirror Pond; and 6-acre **Pioneer Park,** a city-owned auto campground in the 1920s but now a tree-shaded, garden-blooming span of lawn that attracts picnickers. Bend's largest park is **Shevlin Park** (5 miles west of town off Shevlin Park Road), which consists of more than 500 acres of forest beside Tumalo Creek. "The stream is very swift and deep," John C. Frémont wrote about the creek in 1843. "Among the timber here are larches 140 feet high and over 3 feet in diameter." In addition, **Sawyer Park** (a half mile northwest of Bend River Mall) contains more than 60 acres of riverside picnic areas as well as one end of the Deschutes River Trail.

Tumalo State Park, 5 mile northwest of Bend off Highway 20, day use and overnight. Located on the bank of the Deschutes River, this is a big park built to handle big crowds—more than 80 campsites along with four yurts, two tepees, and a hiker/biker camp. The park's personality, however, also has a quiet side, which you can find along one of its riverside hik-

POST GENERAL STORE, LOCATED NEAR THE GEOGRAPHICAL CENTER OF THE STATE

ing trails or fly-fishing stretches of water.

Pilot Butte State Park, on the eastern edge of Bend off Highway 20, day use only. On the eastern skyline of Bend stands Pilot Butte, the 500-foot cinder cone of an extinct volcano that could be as old as 50,000 years. A road to the summit leads to panoramic views stretching as far as the Cascades. "Beyond the green hills are other hills that are blue," a Bend resident wrote about the view from here in 1918. "Those are also covered with forest, and they roll higher and higher, hill beyond hill, and bluer and bluer, until they end in the snow-capped peaks of the Cascade Mountains."

E. R. Corbett State Park, 14 miles west of Sisters off Highway 20, day use and overnight. This is a one-of-a-kind state park in Oregon, for it lies beyond the end of the road and can be reached only by muscle-power—by foot, bike, or horse. Once there you'll find a wilderness setting near the southern shore of Blue Lake with a network of shoreline and forest trails looping the water and connecting to nearby Suttle Lake.

La Pine State Park, 14 miles northwest of La Pine off Highway 97 and Forest Road 43, day use and overnight. In spite of the size of its campgrounds—145 campsites, five log cabins, three yurts—the stars of the show at this park located on the Upper Deschutes River are its small waterfall (15-foot **Fall River Falls**) and its big tree, named appropriately enough Big Pine, a **state Heritage Tree** and the largest ponderosa pine in Oregon. It stands 191 feet tall with a circumference of more than 28 feet and a diameter of 9 feet.

WILDERNESS AREAS **Mount Jefferson,** 17 miles northwest of Sisters off Highway 20, 174 square miles. The centerpiece of this wilderness sprawling beside the spine of the Cascades is an extinct volcano that is Oregon's second-highest mountain, the 10,497-foot Jefferson, which Lewis and Clark named for the president that sent them on their way. With more than 190 miles of trails, 150 alpine lakes, and five glaciers mixed in with talus slopes and alpine meadows, this wilderness and its adjacent areas can draw summertime crowds of hikers, climbers, and sightseers. Shorter hikes (2 to 3 miles) in the area include trails to **Pamelia Lake, Marion Lake, Square Lake, Canyon Creek Meadows,** and **Triangulation Peak.**

Mount Washington, 15 miles west of Sisters off Highway 242 or 18 miles west of Sisters off Highway 20 and Forest Road 2690, 82 square miles. Unlike its mountainous neighbor Jefferson to the north (see previous listing), this wilderness sees only occasional hikers and sightseers, probably because this is a land of lava-strewn rubble that sprawls across most of its area and gives it the nickname the "Black Wilderness." Nevertheless, it holds more than two dozen small lakes, some of which are connected by short trails. Relatively short and easy hikes in the area, all of them beginning at the southern end near Highway 242, include trails to **Hand Lake, Scott Lake,** and **Benson Lake.** Near its edge to the north, a short drive off Highway 20 and Forest Road 2690, is **Big Lake** with its two campgrounds.

Three Sisters, 26 miles west of Bend off Forest Road 46 or 15 miles west of

Sisters off Highway 242, 446 square miles. This is Oregon's most-visited wilderness, with miles of snowy peaks and alpine lakes, waterfalls and lava fields, glacial moraines and obsidian flows, cones and craters. The most numerous trailheads for the area's 260 miles of trails begin near Forest Road 46, the Cascade Lakes Highway, but the shortest hikes—to **Proxy Falls** and **Linton Lake,** round trips of 1 and 4 miles, respectively—begin near Highway 242.

Mount Hood, 6 miles north of Government Camp off Highway 26 and Timberline Road, 74 square miles. Oregon's tallest mountain—and the second most often climbed peak in the world—commands one of the state's most beautiful and untamed landscapes: glaciated peaks, forested slopes, alpine meadows, winding streams roiling blue gray with snowmelt and sometimes tumbling over ledges as cascading waterfalls. No wonder the mythologies of the land's earliest people saw the mountain as a god.

WILDLIFE REFUGES **Metolius Fish Overlook,** near Camp Sherman bridge, 13 miles northwest of Sisters off Highway 20 and Forest Road 14. Beneath the observation platform overlooking the Metolius River, lunker **rainbow trout** lurk in the pools and gulp down the food that heads their way. If you think "trout as long as your arm" is a fisherman's fantasy, then pay this site a visit.

Sunriver Nature Center, at Sunriver, 13 miles south of Bend off Highway 97. This facility squeezes a miniature world into its 7 acres: forest and lake, marsh and wetlands, observatory and nature trail, **waterfowl** and **songbirds,** and central Oregon's only **botanical garden.** In addition, it comes with interpretive programs and exhibits to help visitors understand it all.

Crane Prairie Reservoir, 45 miles southwest of Bend off Forest Road 46. On the west shore of this reservoir stands Osprey Point, established in 1969 as one of only a few scattered **osprey** nesting sites in the nation. From here you can watch these "fish hawks" circle the lake, hunting for trout. In addition, a quarter-mile nature trail leads to where you can see their nests, which perch at the tops of tall poles.

* Lodging

BED & BREAKFASTS

Bend

Cricketwood Country (877-330-0747; innkeeper@cricketwood.com; www.cricketwood.com), 63520 Cricketwood Road, Bend 97701. What Cricketwood Country owners Jim and Tracy won't do for their guests probably hasn't been thought of yet. After all, they custom-build the breakfasts, stock the guest refrigerator, provide free dinners, and set out chocolate chip cookies at bedtime. Besides the amenities, this two-story contemporary home standing on 10 acres close to downtown Bend offers four guest rooms, including two suites and a cottage, that come with private baths ($90–130).

Juniper Acres Bed & Breakfast (541-389-2193; juniper@moriah.com; www.juniperacres.com), 65220 Smokey Ridge Road, Bend 97701. Even though it's located just 6 miles from Bend, this 1991 two-story log lodge seems far from city and suburbs. "We're completely in the country and surrounded by woods," says Vern Bjerk of the 10-acre site he and his wife, Della, own. "And we overlook seven mountains of the Cascade Range." Both guest rooms come with private bathrooms and a gourmet breakfast ($89). "Della serves a *full* breakfast," Vern says, "which many guests have said is the best they've ever had."

Lara House (1-800-766-4064; innkeeper@larahouse.com; www.larahouse.com), 640 N. W. Congress Street, Bend 97701. As it heads toward its second century of life, this 1910 Craftsman home has already entered its third decade of service as a B&B, a notable accomplishment for this thriving central-Oregon city. "Lara House was established in 1982," says innkeeper Susan Schaffer, "and was the first bed and breakfast in Bend." Named for A. M. Lara, one of Bend's pioneer merchants, this three-story, 5,000-square-foot house offers five guest rooms with private baths ($95–150). A stay here includes a full breakfast—entrées include items such as sun-dried tomato quiche with fruit bread or stuffed French toast with fruit sauce, served in the dining room or sun room—a hot tub available on the deck, and one of Bend's premier parks, Drake Park on the shore of **Mirror Pond,** as a neighbor (see Bend City Parks under *Wilder Places—Parks*). "Our other major attraction to visitors," Susan says, "is the fact we're just two blocks from downtown, which has many shops and fine restaurants."

✐ **Mill Inn Bed & Breakfast** (541-389-9198; innkeeper@millinn.com; www.millinn.com), 642 N. W. Colorado Avenue, Bend 97701. After starting out in 1917 as a hotel and boardinghouse, this home in 1990 was rebuilt into a B&B with 10 guest rooms (5 with private baths) that include a full breakfast ($59–89). In addition, a hot tub stands on the back deck and a fireplace in the living room. Children are welcome.

The Sather House (1-888-388-1065; satherhouse@aol.com; www.satherhouse.com), 7 N. W. Tumalo Avenue, Bend 97701. For 75 years the Sather family lived in this 1911 Craftsman house located near downtown Bend and within a few blocks of Drake Park and Mirror Pond. And today, even though the Sathers are gone, the elegance of their old house remains. Its four guest rooms come with private baths and a full breakfast ($99–126).

Swallow Ridge Bed & Breakfast (541-389-1913; bluesky@teleport.com; www.teleport.com/~bluesky), 65711 Twin Bridges Road, Bend 97701. If you've got something good going, people ought to know about it. So Swallow Ridge owner Ted Keener doesn't hold back. "We consider ourselves the Best Little B&B in Central Oregon!" he says. He has a good case. For starters, the one guest room in this home located on the edge of Deschutes River Canyon encompasses the entire second floor. It comes with a private entrance, a full bath and kitchen, a covered deck facing the canyon and another facing the Cascades, and the reason for bragging rights—a 360-degree panoramic view of the area, a rim of glass that gives your eyes as many fell swoops as it can stand of river and mountains and forests. The room ($50–70) also comes with a make-your-own breakfast. "We stock the refrigerator with breakfast ingredients," Ted says, "and Lark [Ted's wife] makes homemade bread, which allows our guests to eat whenever they like." One thing you won't find here, however, is noise. "Bird and river sounds," Ted says. "That's what our guests can expect."

Sisters

Big Red Barn Bed and Breakfast (1-888-257-1275; innkeeper@bigredbarnbb.com; www.bigredbarnbb.com), 69482 Squaw Creek Drive, Sisters 97759. This big red barn really *is* a big red barn, built more than a century ago but recently renovated into a 4,000-square-foot inn that comes with a tennis court, solar swimming pool, and 5 acres of natural beauty. "It's surrounded by an oasis of wildlife and huge ponderosa pines and green plant life," says owner Lynne Myers. "Then when people step inside, it's totally different from what they expect." The unexpected includes the wooden floors, granite counters, and wraparound windows, along with three guest rooms that contain queen beds and private baths ($95). "Add to that our love for this place," Lynne says, "and it's truly felt throughout your stay."

Blue Spruce Bed & Breakfast (1-888-328-9644; vbtemple@outlawnet.com; www.blue-spruce.biz), 444 S. Spruce Street, Sisters 97759. Surrounded by the pines and junipers of a quiet residential neighborhood four blocks south of Sisters' main street, this contemporary house stands near the edge of the area's forest and desert playgrounds. "We can set up everything from massages to horseback riding, raft trips to guided fishing tours," says owner Vaunell Temple. "We have deer that visit our backyard and a family of large gray squirrels who are peanut fiends." Each of the inn's four guest rooms comes with a private bath, king bed, gas log fireplace, jetted tub, and a full breakfast ($125). In addition, Vaunell provides bicycles and maps so guests can tour the area. "I really try to make this a home away from home for my guests," she says, "and enjoy seeing their excitement as they discover Sisters and the beauty of central Oregon."

🐾 🖍 **Conklin's Guest House** (1-800-549-4262; www.conklinsguesthouse.com), 69013 Camp Polk Road, Sisters 97759. Surrounded by trees and distinguished by its wraparound porch, post-and-rail fence, and resident flocks of chickens and ducks, this 1910 white farmhouse offers five guest rooms, all with private bathrooms and with a full breakfast included ($90–150). In addition, the home's grounds include a swimming pool as well as two trout ponds where catch-and-release fishing is available for guests. Pets must be leashed outside, but children older than 12 are welcome even without a leash.

Lazy Rockin' B 'n' C Ranch (1-888-488-0178; innkeepers@sistersbedandbreakfast.com; www.sistersbedandbreakfast.com), 69707 Homes Road, Sisters 97759. Owners Cindy and Burt Murray call their 40-acre ranch an "illusion of seclusion" because of the calm beauty that surrounds it. "The opportunity for serenity is magnified by the beauty of the mountains, open vistas, and breathtaking sunsets," Cindy says, "all from the covered porch next to the pond with a melodious waterfall—truly a magical place." The ranch house is new but its furnishings are traditional, including its leather furniture and stone fireplace. All four of its guest rooms come with private entries and bathrooms (with jetted tubs), antique furniture and handmade quilts, and a full breakfast ($95–120).

Rags to Walkers Guest Ranch (1-800-422-5622; rags@ragstowalkers.com; www.ragstowalkers.com), 17045 Farthing Lane, Sisters 97759. With the Three Sisters looming nearby and green pastures sprawling around it, the B&B portion of this 125-acre guest ranch contains three suites that come with private baths, queen beds, and a full breakfast ($150). In addition, the ranch offers the use of bicycles for exploring and trout-stocked ponds for fishing.

GUEST HOUSES

Sunriver

Blue Heron Hideaway (541-389-6035; bendjudy@aol.com; www.sunriver-direct.com/ryan), 17035 Guss Way, Sunriver 97707. Located 3 miles from Sunriver along the Deschutes River, this home accommodates as many as 12 people ($175–225, cleaning deposit required). Amenities include river views, hot tub, woodstove, picnic tables, and barbecue. In addition, a large yard and small dock make the river easily accessible for fishing or boating.

Sunriver Getaway (541-673-2241; sjhenry@wizzards.net; www.magick.net/ sjhenry). This two-bedroom house includes fireplace and hot tub, propane barbecue, and laundry facilities, even bicycles ($110 per night and a nonrefundable $50 cleaning fee).

Sisters

Squaw Creek Ranch (541-549-4072; kathyd@sistersoregon.net; www.squawcrkranch.com), Bradley Road, Sisters 97759. Standing near Squaw Creek on one of central Oregon's oldest homesteads, this ranch house celebrated its 100th birthday in 2000. "Squaw Creek Ranch is a lovingly restored old historic ranch house, all original wood floors and antiques mixed into the decor," says owner Kathy Deggendorfer. "Our guests love the seclusion and the peaceful setting that is so close to town." The ranch's three guest rooms come with shared bathrooms, queen beds with handmade quilts, and views of the iris gardens, pine trees, Squaw Creek, or the Cascades ($100–125, with a refundable $200 security deposit). In addition, your neighbors will probably include deer in the woods, horses in the pasture, and geese on the creek. "You've got to see it to believe it," Kathy says. "It's a whole different place down by the creek—plenty of wildlife and beautiful wildflowers."

RESORTS AT NEWBERRY NATIONAL MONUMENT Before it was a lake-filled caldera, Newberry Crater was a shield volcano spanning 30 miles in diameter and standing 10,000 feet above sea level. Through the millennia it spilled lava, sprouted cinder cones, and generally wreaked its volcanic havoc on a landscape that still carries its fiery brand. But because those fires have been banked for 1,300 years or so, visitors today have a rare chance to spend time in the depths of an ancient volcano.

East Lake Resort (541-536-2230; www.eastlakeresort.com). Located on the east shore of 1,000-acre East Lake, this resort started in 1915 as a health spa that tapped into the lake's hot springs for its bath water. Nowadays, from May through September, it offers rental cabins ($65–125) as well as rooms ($45). Eastlake Resort also offers campgrounds for RVs and tents, public showers and a Laundromat, and a café that serves breakfast and lunch. The greatest appeal of the resort, however, is its location on the shore of a lake that sprawls for almost a mile across the caldera of Newberry Crater.

LODGES **Australian Outback Country Lodge** (1-800-930-0055; australianoutback@sisterslodging.com; www.australianoutback@sisterslodging.com), Sisters 97759. Surrounded by 9 acres of ponderosa pines and quaking aspens and within sight of the Three Sisters mountains, this creekside lodge seems to blend into the wild around it. "Our acreage has a magical feel to it," says owner Margaret Mason. "Sometimes the mule deer appear as if by magic from behind a tree, and at night you can hear the coyotes howl." Its guest rooms all have private bathrooms and entrances, and are decorated with antique furnishings and handmade Oriental rugs ($89–149). "But we are not 'stuffy,'" Margaret says. "There is a great water hole in the creek to play in, if you can brave the glacier water on a hot day." And when it comes to breakfast, the Australian Outback lives up to its name. "We use a lot of Australian cookbooks to make our breakfasts," Margaret says, "as Richard [Margaret's husband] is from Australia."

Diamond Stone Guest Lodge and Gallery (1-800-600-6263; diamond@diamondstone.com; www.diamondstone.com), 16693 Sprague Loop, La Pine 97709. Standing on 5 acres located near the doorway to the Newberry Crater National Volcanic Monument and on the edge of Quail Run Golf Course, this two-story lodge is Western right down to its boots. Western art decorates its walls, wildlife sculptures stand on its shelves, and pine furniture invites you to settle in for a while. Its two guest suites come with king or queen beds, private baths, mountain views, and a full breakfast ($80–135). In addition, the lodge offers a hot tub and sauna to its guests. Children are welcome, as are pets with prior approval.

✷ Where to Eat

DINING OUT

Bend

Broken Top Restaurant (541-383-8210), 62000 Broken Top Drive, Bend. Named for the mountain that looms in the distance beyond the dining room's window, Broken Top offers fine dining to go along with an even finer view, especially the sun setting behind the Cascades. Although the menu selections can include New York steak and New Zealand lamb, it's the Northwest specialties that attract much of the attention.

Café Rosemary (541-317-0276), 222 N. W. Irving Avenue, Bend. When it opened in the early 1990s, Café Rosemary didn't mince words in explaining its purpose: "To bring grace and beauty to this gastronomical wasteland." The result is a restaurant offering fine dining to those whom owner and executive chef Robert Brown calls "a certain part of the population." This "certain part" evidently enjoys such Café Rosemary offerings as escargot salad, sautéed ahi tuna, and honey-roasted duck breast, while thinking nothing of paying $11 for a beef tenderloin sandwich.

Merenda Restaurant and Wine Bar (541-330-230), 4900 N. W. Wall Street, Bend. With wood-fired cooking that emphasizes French and Italian cuisine, 65 wines by the glass, one of the state's largest selections of spirits, and nice people seemingly everywhere, Merenda is a local favorite in Bend. As one resident puts it, "It's the best we have!"

Suttle Lake Resort, the Boat House Restaurant (541-595-6662), 13300 Highway 20, 14 miles east of Sisters. With a view of the lake, an opportunity for outside dining, and excellent food that includes filet mignon you can cut with a fork and pizza baked in a brick oven, this restaurant is worth the drive.

Sisters

Bronco Billy's (541-549-7427), 190 E. Cascade Street, Sisters. A local favorite, Bronco Billy's offers appealing food and friendly service, an attractive presentation, and an atmosphere resembling a late-19th-century hotel. (In fact, it was once the Hotel Sisters, whose upstairs rooms are now available as private dining rooms.) Menu selections include steak, seafood, and chicken, all of which are cooked remarkably well and then served with a smile.

Kokanee Café (541-595-6420), Camp Sherman, 15 miles northwest of Sisters off Highway 20 and Forest Road 14. Often included among the best gourmet restaurants in the state and the best in central Oregon, the Kokanee Café specializes in Northwest atmosphere and cuisine. "Lots of atmosphere," says one diner from nearby Sisters. "Not much around here compares."

EATING OUT

Bend

Alpenglow Café (541-383-7676), 1040 N. W. Bond Street, Bend. If food so fresh it seems to have just come from the farm is a factor, then the Alpenglow may very well be the breakfast capital of central Oregon. Here you'll find the bread homemade, the meat smoked nearby, the orange juice squeezed in the kitchen, and your plate otherwise piled with some of the best food in town.

Deschutes Brewery (541-382-9242), 1044 N. W. Bond Street, Bend. At this pub, some of the friendliest help in town serves decent to darn good pub fare along with some of the best microbrew beer in the Northwest. This is a place where it's okay to spill the salsa.

Hans (541-389-9700), 915 N. W. Wall Street, Bend. At Hans, sunlight streaming through big windows brings out the shine on the wooden floors as the waitresses hustle their way back and forth across a dining room that seems always full. The selection of salads and sandwiches rival the windows in size, while dinners feature seafood, steaks, and pizza.

Pilot Butte Drive In (541-382-2972), Ninth and Greenwood Streets, Bend. This is one of those places where—breakfast, lunch, or dinner—a line of people seems always to be winding out the door. But the wait is worth it, for the Pilot Butte Drive In offers some of the best café food in the region, including hamburgers that many believe to be the best in the world. In spite of the crowds, however, the service is fast and genuinely friendly.

Pine Tavern (541-382-5581), 967 N. W. Brooks Street, Bend. A dining tradition in Bend since 1936, the Pine Tavern is a standard destination for locals and a new experience for visitors who come to see what all the fuss is about. Although the restaurant's reputation for quality food is deserved, some come for the view from the dining room of Mirror Pond, while others come to see if it's true that a 200-year-old Ponderosa pine grows through the restaurant and out the roof. (It's true.)

Tumalo Feed Co. (541-382-2202), 64619 Highway 20, Bend. The food, the atmosphere, and the friendliness of the place make the Tumalo Feed Co. a favorite steak house in the area. The restaurant also serves seafood and chicken specialties as well as some pleasant Western hospitality.

Sisters

Angeline's Bakery and Café, 121 W. Main Street, Sisters. Known for its extraordinary bagels, fresh salads, and friendly atmosphere, Angeline's offers healthful food and reasonable prices as well as live music on weekends.

Depot Deli (549-2572), 351 W. Cascade Street, Sisters. With a model train circling the room near the ceiling and with knotty-pine lumber lining the walls, this deli combines locomotive entertainment and a warm Western atmosphere with its offerings of salads, breads, and sandwiches. On sunny days—of which they have many in Sisters—you cans sit at the picnic tables outside.

The Gallery (541-549-2631), 220 W. Cascade Street, Sisters. A local favorite that has become something of an institution in Sisters, the Gallery is an old-timey café known for its big breakfasts and friendly help as well as its halibut fish-and-chips. The place is popular enough that lines can form outside the door—probably the best endorsement any restaurant can earn.

Papandreas (541-549-6081) 325 E. Hood Street, Sisters. Specializing in locally famous pizza and calzones, Papandreas might make you wait for your order, but remember that quality takes time.

Seasons (541-549-8911), 411 E. Hood Street, Sisters. At Seasons you can probably find a sandwich you haven't even thought of before, such as the Summer Santa, made of turkey, cream cheese, and cranberry sauce. Salads can be just as inventive, just as good. An extra attraction comes with summer's outdoor seating near a small creek.

Sisters Bakery (541-549-0361), 120 E. Cascade Street, Sisters. The Sisters Bakery, which turns out some of the best bread and pastries in the region, has been part of Sisters since long before the first hordes of RVs swept through town. "No trip to Sisters would be complete with out a stop at the Sisters Bakery," says a 30-year resident. "In fact, I don't think anyone drives through Sisters without stopping there first."

South Central

KLAMATH BASIN–CRATER LAKE AREA

LAKEVIEW–PAISLEY–BLY AREA

SILVER LAKE–CHRISTMAS VALLEY–FORT ROCK AREA

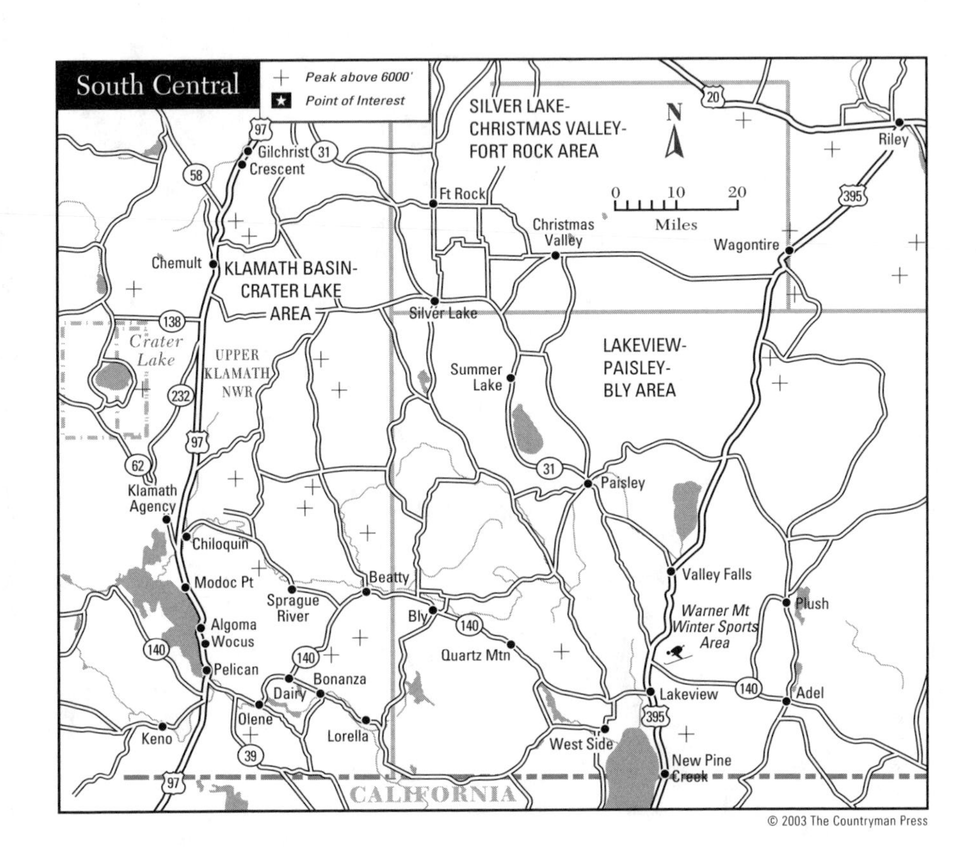
South Central
Peak above 6000'
Point of Interest
SILVER LAKE-
CHRISTMAS VALLEY-
FORT ROCK AREA
KLAMATH BASIN-
CRATER LAKE
AREA
LAKEVIEW-
PAISLEY-
BLY AREA
UPPER
KLAMATH
NWR
Crater
Lake
N
0 10 20
Miles
Gilchrist
Crescent
Chemult
Ft Rock
Christmas
Valley
Wagontire
Riley
Silver Lake
Summer
Lake
Paisley
Klamath
Agency
Chiloquin
Modoc Pt
Sprague
River
Beatty
Bly
Quartz Mtn
Algoma
Wocus
Pelican
Dairy
Bonanza
Olene
Lorella
Keno
Valley Falls
Plush
Warner Mt
Winter Sports
Area
Lakeview
Adel
West Side
New Pine
Creek
CALIFORNIA
97
31
58
138
232
62
140
39
20
395

INTRODUCTION

"I never saw a more beautiful country. It was covered with bunch grass. Cattle were fat. Grass and crops were good and the people content."

—Homesteader in south-central Oregon's Fort Rock Valley, 1910

Before the Cascade Mountains give way to the high desert along the south-central edge of the state, they leave parts of their green, wet selves scattered across the borderlands. Forests and dunes, lakes and playas, grasslands and sage-brush stand almost near enough to nuzzle each other. The result is a mingling of open spaces and timbered slopes, of freshwater lakes and alkali flats in a world straddling such vastly different geological and historical eras that only a strong imagination can reconcile the contrasts.

Some differences began near the end of the last Ice Age, in the millennia that saw melting glaciers flood what are now desert basins. Across the region now, for example, you'll see irrigated alfalfa growing across the floors of evaporated inland seas, wave-carved rock formations looming above sagebrush valleys, and cattle herds grazing near the oldest prehistoric homesites in the Northwest.

Other changes, however, are more recent, for here you'll also find bare ground where towns, homesteads, or sawmills once stood. "To the south and east," home-steader S. M. Findley wrote in 1909, "the houses and tents and newly plowed fields dot the land as far as the eye can see."

Weather and time, of course, changed the world Mr. Findley knew—shriveled the crops and closed the towns and sent the homesteaders packing. Yet some parts of it seem to remain timeless: the sun shining most days of the year; the wildfowl migrating every fall and spring through the Klamath and Summer Lake basins; the bunchgrass and sagebrush, junipers and pines sprouting from layers of volcanic debris; the distant saunter or casual stare of mule deer or pronghorns; and the hori-zons so distant they seem to smooth earth and sky into a slender, wavering line.

It's enough to make you feel that in this world of change, the most important things have never really changed at all.

KLAMATH BASIN–CRATER LAKE AREA

GUIDANCE **Deschutes National Forest: Headquarters** (541-388-2715), 1645 Highway 20 E., Bend 97701; **Crescent Ranger District** (541-433-2234).

Klamath County Department of Tourism (1-800-445-6728; www.klamath-county.net), 507 Main Street, Klamath Falls 97601.

Northern Klamath County Visitor Center (541-433-2348; www.klamath-county.net), 138351 Highway 97 N., Crescent, 97733; Gilchrist Mall, Highway 97 S., Gilchrist 97737.

Oregon State Parks (503-378-6305), State Parks and Recreation Department, 525 Trade Street S. E., Salem 97301.

Winema National Forest: Headquarters (541-883-6714), 2819 Dahlia Street, Klamath Falls, 97601; **Chemult Ranger District** (541-365-7001); **Chiloquin Ranger District** (541-783-4001); **Klamath Ranger District** (541-885-3400).

GETTING THERE The Klamath Basin–Crater Lake area is reached from the north and south by Highway 97, from the east by Highway 140, and from the west by Highways 66, 140, 62, 230, and 138.

THE KLAMATH COUNTY MUSEUM IS A STOREHOUSE OF REGIONAL HISTORY

MEDICAL EMERGENCY **Merle West Medical Center** (541-882-6311), 2865 Daggett Street, Klamath Falls.

* To See

MUSEUMS **Klamath County Museum** (541-883-4208), 1451 Main Street, Klamath Falls. The region's history is housed here in collections that include Native American artifacts, pioneer relics, and natural history. The most powerful displays, however, feature the images, reports,

COLLIER MEMORIAL STATE PARK LOGGING MUSEUM

and memorabilia from the Modoc War of 1873, from photographs of Modoc prisoners to mortar rounds of the U.S. Army.

Favell Museum of Western Art and Indian Artifacts (541-882-9996), 125 W. Main Street, Klamath Falls. Established in 1972 as the creation of Gene Favell, who as a young boy during the 1930s had developed a passion for collecting Indian artifacts found along the shores of the high desert's drying lakes, the Favell Museum has been called "one of the three best Western museums in the United Sates." Its collection includes tens of thousands of artifacts—including arrowheads, stonework, basketry, pottery, and carvings—and perhaps one of the best displays of contemporary Western art in the world, consisting of more than 850 paintings by almost 500 artists.

Collier Memorial State Park Logging Museum, 30 miles north of Klamath Falls off Highway 97. Timber beasts and river pigs, flume herders and skid greasers, pond monkeys and donkey punchers—yes, the Oregon woods were once full of such critters during the early days of logging. And for more than 50 years this outdoor museum, which contains probably the largest and finest collection of logging equipment in the nation, gives you a peek into a world run by the muscle of men and the power of steam. (See also *Wilder Places—Parks.*)

HISTORIC SITES **Baldwin Hotel,** 31 Main Street, Klamath Falls (541-883-4207). Built in 1906 as a lodging house for train passengers traveling from San Francisco to the outdoor playground of the Klamath Basin, this hotel now houses original furnishings as well as thousands of artifacts from the early 1900s.

THE GUARDHOUSE AT FORT KLAMATH, WHERE MODOC LEADERS WERE TRIED AND HANGED AFTER THE MODOC WAR OF 1872–73.

Fort Klamath, 2 miles south of Fort Klamath. This frontier fort was built in 1863 to protect the area's settlers and control the Klamath and Modoc Indians. For almost a decade the troops stationed here had little to struggle against other than bad food, harsh officers, and dull routines. But then, led by a man the whites called Captain Jack, a group of Modocs left the reservation, and in 1872 a company of cavalry rode to Captain Jack's camp (see next listing) to bring them back. When shots were fired and a battle erupted, war followed. The Modocs fled to nearby lava fields, and from there 50 warriors and their families fought the U.S. Army to a standstill for six months. When it was over, the Modoc prisoners were marched to the fort, where Captain Jack and three other warriors were hanged. Today, a replica of the fort's guardhouse contains displays from the fort's history. Yet the most moving, even eerie, remnants of its past are located outside—the grave sites and head markers of the hanged Modocs.

Captain Jack's Stronghold, 43 miles southeast of Klamath Falls off California Highway 139. Okay, this is cheating because you have to travel south of the border and into the land of California to see this—but if you've come this far, you can't miss the Stronghold, which was the main battleground of the 1873 Modoc War and the site of some of the most dramatic events in Oregon history. "Roughest battlefield ever fought over," a local rancher wrote at the time. "Ten square miles of lava rock, all crisscrossed and cut up with ridges eight or ten feet high." If you tread the trail that winds through this labyrinth of lava, you'll sense the ghosts born of desperate and enduring courage, for this was the land of the Modocs, a proud people who played out the tragedy of their war with the U.S. Army in a story of sacrifice, betrayal, murder, and exile. "I never realized what a horrible thing war is," wrote a second lieutenant who fought at the Stronghold, "until I came out on this trip." And now this lava field holds the spirits of warriors from both sides.

FOR FAMILIES **Edison's Village,** 4 miles north of Chiloquin off Highway 58. Along one bank of the Sprague River where the stream flows slow and shining in the sun, stands the land of a man who defeated the U.S. government with one word. The man is Edison Chiloquin, a Klamath Indian. The word was *NO*. The two were pulled together in the 1970s after Congress passed legislation dissolving the Klamath tribe and buying out the lands of their reservation. More than 2,000 Klamaths accepted the government checks that went as high as a quarter-million dollars. Only Edison Chiloquin refused. Instead, he waged a legal battle for years to keep his land—and he won. On the road leading to his village today, you'll find signs pointing the way, like a series of "Welcome" mats, until you reach the entrance, where there hangs one last sign, which says THE EARTH IS OUR MOTHER. MOTHER EARTH IS TO BE LOVED AND RESPECTED.

Upper Klamath Lake Jetboat Tours (Klamath Excursions; 541-850-6391; www.klamathexcursions.com). Explore the wildlife and history of Upper Klamath Lake in jetboat tours lasting one hour (20 miles), two hours (40 miles), or four hours (60 miles and can include lunch or dinner).

Crater Lake Tours (541-594-2511), Crater Lake Lodge. From July through early September, regularly scheduled two-hour boat tours cruise Crater Lake's 25-mile perimeter. Joining this tour, however, requires a milelong hike down to the lakeshore and back. (The ensuing trip, however, is well worth the effort, for the lake is almost as pristine today as it was a century ago. In fact, the preservation of this beauty was a primary goal of William Steel, the lake's "father" who, when he first visited here in 1885, discovered "that no point around this wonderful cauldron had the hand of man yet desecrated with peanut stands or other marks of desolation, and that something should be done to save it forever for the people of this great country." Even when the vast majority of people leave in the winter, the park remains open for those who want to try skiing or snowshoeing. Trails range from 1- and 2-mile beginners' loops to the three-day journey around the lake rim.

SCENIC DRIVES **Volcanic Legacy Scenic Byway,** 140 paved miles along Highways 62 and 97 from Diamond Lake Junction to California border. This **All-American Road**—one of only 15 in the nation—travels through a land of superlatives: deepest, largest, greatest, highest, and most of it built up or torn apart by ancient volcanic eruptions. It starts near **Crater Lake** (see *Natural Wonders*), the deepest lake in America; skirts **Upper Klamath Lake** (see *Natural Wonders*), the largest body of freshwater west of the Rockies; and passes through the **Klamath Basin,** home to the greatest numbers of migrating waterfowl in the West as well as the highest population of wintering bald eagles in the Lower 48. Can't do much better than that.

Outback National Scenic Byway, 171 paved miles along Highway 31 from La Pine to California border. Carrying you from ponderosa pine forests to sagebrush basins, from alkaline lakes to basalt silhouettes, this route dips and rises past white-barked aspens and chisel-faced rims, past puddles of water that once were lakes and that now hold the flutter and gabble of ducks and geese. On some of the more lonesome stretches, the road is straight and flat, a sleep-inducing, mind-numbing, fantasy-evoking drive. Along the way you'll have the chance to come face-to-face with such Oregon landmarks as **Fort Rock, Summer Lake, Winter Ridge,** and **Abert Rim.**

Crater Lake Rim Road, 32 paved miles around Crater Lake (see *Natural Wonders*). It's a remarkable thing to drive the rim of a volcano that 7,000 years ago blew its innards across the Northwest in a roaring spew that blotted out the sun. With those days of darkness long gone and with a crystal-blue sheen of lake water now cupped in the volcano's crater, it's an adventure to cruise around this mythological force and geological wonder that has remained relatively unchanged through the past century. "Were the founders of the national park system to come back today and looked at Crater lake, I think they would smile," says Chuck Lundy, Crater Lake National Park's superintendent. "The lake is every bit as magnificent today as it was 100 years ago."

State Line Road, 20 paved miles along Highway 161 (the Oregon–California border) from Highway 97 to Highway 39. Surrounded by farm fields and bordered by a **wildlife refuge,** this highway lies in a major flight path for waterfowl. Take this drive in the evening, especially during the spring or fall migrations, and you'll find yourself craning your neck and peering through the windshield at soaring flights of birds. Luckily, numerous pullouts along the shoulder are there just for the gawking.

Upper Klamath Lake Loop, 93 paved miles along Highways 97 and 62; Weed Road, Sevenmile Road, and West Side Road; and Highway 140, beginning and ending at Klamath Falls. In a loop around Upper Klamath Lake (see *Natural Wonders*), the largest freshwater lake in the West, this route carries you past marshes and forests before showing you the history of logging at one park and of the Modoc War at another.

NATURAL WONDERS **Upper Klamath Lake,** northwest of Klamath Falls along Highways 97 and 140. With a length of almost 30 miles and a width of as much as 8 miles, this lake is the largest body of freshwater west of the Rockies.

Crater Lake, 62 miles north of Klamath Falls off Highway 62. Some 7,000 years ago, Mount Mazama was a giant of the southern Cascades, 500,000 years old and 12,000 feet high. Then it exploded. "It was like taking the lid off a well-shaken pop bottle," says Ellen Bishop, an Oregon geologist. Before the series of eruptions ended, the mountain sent 14 cubic miles of itself gushing onto the ground or hurtling into the sky, burying parts of eastern Oregon in ash as deep as 10 feet, falling as far away as Saskatchewan, Canada, and blocking sunlight around the world. After flinging off so much of its rock and emptying itself of magma, the mountain collapsed, leaving a hole—a *caldera*—4,000 feet deep that began filling with rain and snow until it formed a lake more than 6 miles across and 1,900 feet deep. Today, an average annual snowfall of 45 feet—enough to reach the roof of the four-story Crater Lake Lodge—keeps the lake filled and people coming to see one of the wonders of the nation. "There are only a few places . . . that everyone in the nation knows about, and this is probably one," says Steve Mark, Crater Lake National Park historian. "This is one of those scenic places thought to embody the greatness of the nation."

✱ To Do

BICYCLING **OC&E Woods Line,** 100 paved and graveled miles from Klamath Falls to Bly and Sycan Marsh. This old railbed of the Oregon, California and Eastern Railroad (OC&E) has been converted to Oregon's longest linear park, a Rails-to-Trail system dedicated to hiking, biking, skiing, and other forms of nonmotorized propulsion. Constructed between 1917 and 1929, the rail line eventually included more than 400 miles of tracks, its spurs leading to the logging camps and sawmills that once thrived in the region.

CAMPING **Winema National Forest** (541-883-6714), 2819 Dahlia Street, Klamath Falls. Once part of the Klamath Indian Reservation, the Winema National Forest includes two designated wilderness areas among its more than 1,700 square miles.

Klamath Ranger District (541-885-3400). **Fourmile Lake,** 41 miles northwest of Klamath Falls off Highway 140 and Forest Road 3661, 25 lakeside campsites; **Odessa,** 22 miles northwest of Klamath Falls off Highway 140 and Forest Road 3639, 5 campsites near Upper Klamath Lake; **Rocky Point,** 28 miles northwest of Klamath Falls off Highway 140 and West Side Road, 33 campsites with many amenities near the resort on the shoreline of Upper Klamath Lake.

Chemult Ranger District (541-365-7001). **Corral Springs,** 4 miles north of Chemult off Highway 97 and Forest Road 9774, 7 campsites; **Jackson Creek,** 30 miles southeast of Chemult off Highway 97 and Forest Road 49, 12 campsites; **Digit Point,** 12 miles west of Chemult off Highway 97 and Forest Road 9772, 64 campsites on Miller Lake; **Scott Creek,** 30 miles southwest of Chemult off Highway 97 and Forest Roads 623 and 2310, 6 campsites.

Klamath Falls Area, near Klamath Falls off Highway 58, 66, or 97 and connecting designated Forest Roads. **Crescent Lake,** 103 miles northwest of Klamath Falls off Highway 58, 5 camping areas containing a total of 136 sites, boat ramp and nearby fishing, hiking trails; **Hagelstein,** 12 miles north of Klamath Falls off Highway 97, 10 campsites near Upper Klamath Lake, hiking trail and boat launch; **Oux Kanee,** 33 miles north of Klamath Falls off Highway 97, 10 campsites near the Wood River, hiking trails and nearby fishing; **Summit Lake,** 130 miles northwest of Klamath Falls off Highway 58, 3 campsites at this primitive camp (with difficult access for RVs), hiking trails and nearby fishing; **Surveyor,** 34 miles west of Klamath Falls, 6 campsites, hiking trails and nearby fishing; **Topsy,** 20 miles southwest of Klamath Falls off Highway 66, 15 campsites, hiking trails and nearby fishing; **Williamson River,** 31 miles north of Klamath Falls, 10 campsites, hiking trails, and nearby fishing.

Chiloquin Area, near Chiloquin off Highway 97 or the Williamson River Road and connecting designated Forest Roads. **Head of the River,** 25 miles northeast of Chiloquin off Williamson River Road, 6 campsites at the head of the Williamson River, hiking trail and nearby fishing; **Spring Creek,** 5 miles north of Chiloquin off Highway 97 and Forest Road 9732, 5 campsites, nearby fishing and canoe launch.

Lake of the Woods, 35 miles northwest of **Klamath Falls** off Highway 140, 2 campgrounds—**Aspen Point** and **Sunset**—with a total of more than 60 campsites, and hiking trails and boat ramps.

Crater Lake National Park, 62 miles north of Klamath Falls off Highway 62: 200 sites for RV camping only, open June through mid-October; 16 sites for tent camping only, open July through mid-September.

Odell Lake, 102 miles northwest of **Klamath Falls** off Highway 58, 4 lakeside camping areas contain a total of 126 sites, and hiking trails and boat ramp.

See also *Wilder Places—Parks.*

CANOEING **Lake Ewauna,** at Klamath Falls, take Oregon Avenue exit from Highway 97. The lake along with the adjoining Klamath River offers 16 miles of flatwater paddling through **Lake Ewauna Wildlife Refuge** (see *Wilder Places—Wildlife Refuges*), favored by bald eagles.

Upper Klamath Lake, 28 miles northwest of Klamath Falls off Highway 97 and West Side Road. This might be one of the best canoe routes in the country—a marked trail of 6 miles, which includes a shortcut that reduces it to 3.5 miles, takes you into the heart of **Upper Klamath Lake National Wildlife Refuge** (see *Wilder Places—Wildlife Refuges*). Side trips extend into backwaters, streams, and marshes. Launch point: Rocky Point Resort.

Spring Creek, 30 miles north of Klamath Falls off Highway 97. This 3-mile loop takes you upstream to the headwaters of cold, clear Spring Creek. Launch point: Collier State Park Spring Creek Day Use Area.

Williamson River, 30 miles north of Klamath Falls off Highway 97. From near its confluence with Spring Creek (see previous listing), this route is a 5-mile, round-trip paddle through pine forest and along willow-shaded shorelines to **Williamson Campground** (see Williamson River in Klamath Falls Area under *Camping*). Launch

THE CANOE TRAIL ON UPPER KLAMATH LAKE

point: Collier Memorial State Park Rest Area.

Lake of the Woods, 35 miles northwest of Klamath Falls off Highway 140. The centerpiece of this timbered resort area, one of the region's most popular, is a 1,100-acre lake that is home to **trout** and **kokanee** and shares the mountain slopes with nearby Fourmile and Fish Lakes. "Lake of the Woods, Four Mile, Fish Lake," wrote a cowboy riding through the area in the late 19th century, "all lost in the big silence."

See also **Klamath Marsh National Wildlife Refuge** under *Wilder Places—Wildlife Refuges.*

HIKING **Link River Trail,** take Oregon Avenue exit off Highway 97 in Klamath Falls. For approximately a mile, this trail follows a hillside of blackberry brambles and a stream bank of willow thickets along the Link River, a gentle stream that now connects **Upper Klamath Lake** with **Lake Ewauna,** but that once ran wild with a series of rapids that tumbled over a reef at Upper Klamath's outlet, forming the now-drowned Klamath Falls. Also gone is the ancient settlement of Klamath Indians, who built fish traps near the foot of the falls.

Lake of the Woods, 35 miles northwest of Klamath Falls off Highway 140. This long-used resort and recreation contains a number of trail systems, including three located near the lake: **Sunset Trail, Family Loop Trail,** and **Lake of the Woods Trail.**

Crater Lake National Park, 62 miles north of Klamath Falls off Highway 62. Even with a half-million visitors a year, it's still easy to find little-used trails in the park, especially in the park's backcountry. But for those looking only to stretch their legs and see the sights, three half-mile interpretive trails offer a look at the country as well as the history of the area: the **Ties Through Time Trail** (railroad logging), the **Open Forest Trail** (old-growth pine), and the **Pines in the Pumice Trail** (volcanic deposits). On the other hand, if you're looking for something more, try the **Cleetwood Trail,** a 1-mile path that descends to the lake's shore and ends at the boat dock where **boat tours to Wizard Island** begin.

Jackson F. Kimball State Park, 3 miles north of Fort Klamath off Highway 232. This park offers two trails: a 1.5-mile path leading from its primitive campground at the head of the **Wood River** to the spring that feeds a nearby lagoon, and a 1-mile trail leading to the south gate of **Crater Lake National Park.**

Pacific Crest National Scenic Trail. Not that you'd hike the entire 2,650-mile trail that stretches from Mexico to Canada, not even the Oregon portion of it—but you if you get a hankering to at least step foot on this world-famous, sky-high pathway, you'll find some of the more accessible points at **Miller Lake, Fourmile Lake,** and **Lake of the Woods.**

See also *Camping, Wilder Places—Parks,* and *Wilder Places—Wilderness Areas.*

✷ Wilder Places

PARKS **Jackson F. Kimball State Park,** 3 miles north of Fort Klamath off Highway 232, day use and overnight. Lying near the head of the pristine Wood River, this park offers

10 primitive campsites and a canoe launch as well as nearby hiking trails and fishing opportunities.

Eagle Ridge Park, 14 miles northwest of Klamath Falls off Highway 140. Take a sun-bright morning on the watery edge of this park, add a swoop or two of flying ducks that glide along the bay, then mix it all with a chorus of chirps and whistles from the songbirds hovering near the shoreline's grassy thickets, and you'll know you've wandered into one of the region's special places. Located along a peninsula of Klamath Lake, Eagle Ridge Park remains one place where the birds still outnumber the people.

Collier Memorial State Park, 30 miles north of Klamath Falls off Highway 97, day use and overnight. Located near the confluence of Spring Creek and the Williamson River, this park offers days worth of entertainment, from campgrounds and picnic sites to hiking trails and a **logging museum** (see *To See—Museums*).

Crater Lake National Park, 62 miles north of Klamath Falls off Highway 62. When Crater Lake was established in 1902 as Oregon's only national park, William G. Steel, who devoted years of his life to establishing the park, called it "a grand awe-inspiring temple the likes of which the world has never seen before." Today many of the half-million annual visitors probably agree. After all, where else can you stare into a volcano and see one of the deepest lakes and some of the bluest water in the world? (See *To See—Natural Wonders.*) And because most of these visitors stay fairly close to the pavement, the majority of the park's 280 square miles still offers a backcountry experience for those who seek quieter trails.

WILDERNESS AREAS **Mountain Lakes,** 15 miles northwest of Klamath Falls off Highway 140 or County Road 603, 36 square miles. Like Mount Mazama's Crater Lake, its famous brother (or sister, it's hard to tell with mountains) to the north, Mountain Lakes may have been created by volcanic explosions that collapsed its peak, forming a caldera that gathers rain and snow. (Some estimates say the original mountain was one of the giants of the southern Cascades, sprawling 85 square miles and rising 12,000 feet.) The 9-mile **Mountain Lakes Loop Trail** now traces the caldera's rim and connects with other trails. Two of its major trailheads are **Varney Creek Trail** (the most used) from the north and **Clover Creek Trail** (the least used) from the south.

Sky Lakes, 22 miles northwest of Klamath Falls off Highway 140 and connecting designated Forest Roads, 177 square miles. The name of this wilderness area that straddles the southern Cascades is accurate as well as lovely because more than 200 ponds or lakes spot the area. The most popular—and probably the most difficult—hike in the wilderness is the 5-mile trail to the summit of **Mount McLoughlin,** where you can catch a view of most of southern Oregon. Three basins receive much of the foot traffic—**Seven Lakes Basin, Sky Lakes Basin, Blue Canyon Basin**—but quieter, shorter trails lead to **Heavenly Twin Lakes, South Puck Lake,** and **Blue Lake.**

Mount Thielsen, 89 miles north of Klamath Falls off Highway 97 and 138, 86 square miles. Even though it has been extinct for at least 100,000 years,

EAGLE RIDGE PARK ON KLAMATH LAKE

Mount Thielsen still attracts a different kind of fire: lightning strikes its spire so often that its nickname is the "lightning rod of the Cascades." One of the more popular trailheads leading to shorter trails is located at **Miller Lake;** for those who seek longer hikes, the area contains a segment of the **Pacific Crest Trail.**

Diamond Peak, 25 miles northwest of Crescent off Highway 58, 82 square miles. Even though four summits of pre–Ice Age volcanoes soar to elevations over 7,000 feet in this wilderness, it was Diamond Peak that Oregon Trail emigrant John Diamond climbed and named in 1852, searching for a shortcut through the Cascades. Today 48 miles of trails, including 14 miles of the **Pacific Crest Trail,** crisscross this land shaped by the plowing and gouging of glaciers. Numerous access points are available on the north and east from Highway 58 as well as from Odell and Crescent Lakes, and shorter hikes—from a half mile to 3 miles—are available on the west and south sides of the wilderness with trails to **Hemlock Butte, Blue Lake, and Happy Lake.**

WILDLIFE REFUGES **Lake Ewauna,** at Klamath Falls take Oregon Avenue exit from Highway 97. This is a wetland and a wildlife interpretive area on the edge of Lake Ewauna. A stroll along the milelong trail on the western shore of the lake gives you the chance to see numerous species of birds, with the highlight being the eagle perch that is used year-round by either wintering or nesting **bald eagles.**

Miller Island, 6 miles south of Klamath Falls off Highway 97. Part of the **Klamath Wildlife Complex,** 2,400-acre Miller Island lies within sight of the silhouettes of towers and buildings belonging to the city of Klamath Falls but still receives as many as a million waterfowl visitors in the fall and about half that number in the spring. A nature trail that begins at the parking area loops through wetlands and ponds, and a gravel road leads across the upland.

Bear Valley National Wildlife Refuge, 15 miles southwest of Klamath Falls off Highway 97. Established in 1978 to protect a wintering site for **bald eagles**—now the largest in the Lower

WETLANDS AT MILLER ISLAND, PART OF THE KLAMATH WILDLIFE COMPLEX

48—this area every year can receive as many as 300 eagle visitors, which use the site's old-growth trees as shelter and the nearby Lower Klamath National Wildlife Refuge as hunting grounds. Morning and evening you can see them fly out in search of breakfast or dinner.

Klamath Marsh National Wildlife Refuge, 22 miles north of Chiloquin off Silver Lake Highway. Almost 60 square miles of marshes and meadows and forest that is home to myriad critters both feathered and furred. A **700-acre canoe area** lets you paddle in close for a bird's-eye view (the launch area is in the southeast segment of the refuge, 4 miles down Forest Road 690).

Upper Klamath Lake National Wildlife Refuge, 28 miles west of Klamath Falls off Highway 140. This is much of what's left of ancient Lake Modoc, which once covered nearly 1,000 square miles of the Klamath Basin, its shallow lakes and freshwater marshes holding as many as 6 million **waterfowl** at a time. But after the Bureau of Reclamation drained much of the basin and channeled most of the water to create farmland, less than a quarter of the wetlands remain. Nevertheless, the majority of waterfowl migrating along the **Pacific Flyway** visit here at one time or another. "The basin is a major birding area for people from all over the world," says a state biologist. "You can see more pure species here than almost anywhere else in the western United States."

✷ Lodging

RESORTS **Agency Lake Resort** (541-783-2489; agncylke@kfalls.net; www.kfalls.net/~agncylke), 37000 Modoc Point Road, Chiloquin 97624. Standing at the edge of Agency Lake, this resort offers four cabins (starting at $45) situated along 750 feet of shaded shoreline. Its accommodations also include showers, a general store, and boat rentals—yet it's biggest draw is probably its trout fishing.

Crater Lake Resort (541-381-

2349; crtrlkrst@aol.com; www.craterlakeresort.com), 50711 Highway 62, Fort Klamath 97626. With ponderosa pine forests and almost a mile of stream frontage along Fort Creek, this resort resides in a world of natural wonder. "Our resort has a very beautiful setting," says owner Babe Hamilton, "with huge grassy areas, mature pine trees, and crystal clear Fort Creek." It also offers nine cabins, large and small, with kitchens and without ($45–65; you can bring along pooch for an extra $7 per day). "It's an affordable place to stay for families," Babe says, "because the price you pay includes all activities, even the canoe for the creek."

Diamond Lake Resort (541-793-3333; dlresort@rosenet.net; www.diamondlake.net), 350 Lake Front Drive, Diamond Lake 97731 (80 miles northwest of Klamath Falls off Highways 97 and 138). This is more like a mountain village than a resort because accommodations and amenities include not only a total of 98 rooms ($69–75; cabins $125–195), but also a cocktail lounge and pizza parlor, a grocery story and gas station, a laundry and marina, even a post office; it also rents boats and bikes and provides shuttle service from regional airports.

Lake of the Woods Resort (541-949-8300; lowoffice@aol.com; www.lakeofthewoodsresort.com), 950 Harriman Road, Klamath Falls 97601 (36 miles northwest of Klamath Falls off Highway 140 and Dead Indian Memorial Road). Once a fishing camp that grew into a destination for weekend and vacation getaways, Lake of the Woods today is the site of a resort with many facets: marina, general store, lodge with a restaurant and bar, and 15 guest cabins. Even though these cabins come in a wide range of sizes, amenities, and prices ($45–249), they all have views of the lake. In addition, you can rent mountain bikes for the trails and motorboats, paddleboats, and canoes for the lake. For some people, however, the lure of the lake lies beyond its recreational opportunities. "It has been my privilege to live, work, and raise my children in what I consider to be one of the most beautiful places in Oregon," says George Gregory, general manager of the resort. "I am constantly asked by our customers how I managed to end up living and working in paradise, where so many people pay to come and play for just a little time. I usually just smile and tell them I just happened to be in the right place at the right time."

Rocky Point Resort (541-356-2287; rvoregon@aol.com; www.rockypointoregon.com), 28121 Rocky Point Road, Klamath Falls 97601 (28 miles northwest of Klamath Falls off Highway 140 and Rocky Point Road). With a shoreline seat on the Upper Klamath Lake National Wildlife Refuge, this resort is close to almost everything wild in this neck of the woods, including canoeing, hiking, birding, and fishing. Accommodations include cabins with furnished kitchens ($89–129, with refundable cleaning deposit) and guest rooms with private baths ($55, neither cooking nor pets permitted). Also available to guests are a store and laundry, a boat ramp and canoe rentals.

BED & BREAKFASTS

Fort Klamath

Sun Pass Ranch (866-381-2259; sunpass@aol.com; www.virtualcities.com/or/sunpass.htm), 52125 Highway

62, Fort Klamath 97626. Located 15 minutes from Crater Lake National Park and on the bank of the Wood River, this bed & breakfast is a working cattle and horse ranch almost surrounded by state and national forest. As a result, hiking, mountain biking, and horseback riding begin near the front door. The two-story guest house features three guest rooms with private baths and two rooms with shared baths ($75). A full breakfast is included, and a special "Guest Package" (lunch and dinner, horseback rides and other activities) is available.

Klamath Falls

🐾 **Crystalwood Lodge** (866-381-2322; info@crystalwoodlodge.com; www.crystalwoodlodge.com), 38625 Westside Road, Klamath Falls 97601. Surrounded by the **Winema National Forest** in the southern Cascades, Crystalwood Lodge has a door that opens onto a mountain vacation—and you can bring your dog. "We're not your typical B&B," says owner Liz Parrish. "Our focus is being pet welcoming and providing personalized service, outstanding cuisine, and opportunities for everyone to enjoy the wonderful recreation opportunities in the area." Some of those opportunities—in the form of forest trails, golf courses, scenic byways, mountain lakes, and wildlife areas—lie within less than an hour's drive of the lodge. Seven guest rooms all have private baths and far-reaching views ($105–245), and a "continental plus" breakfast is included.

Iron Gate Estate Bed & Breakfast (1-888-884-4184), 2035 Portland Street, Klamath Falls 97601. This 1912 home features an interior of old English furnishings, a landscape of more than 250 varieties of flowers, and a pool heated by an unlimited supply of hot water piped from a geothermal well. Each of the two guest rooms comes with a private bath and a full breakfast ($65–95).

Thompson's Bed & Breakfast (541-882-7938; tompohll@aol.com), 1420 Wild Plum Court, Klamath Falls 97601. This contemporary two-story cedar home overlooks **Upper Klamath Lake** and stands next door to Moore Park, which has tennis courts and hiking trails near the water. Its four guest rooms all come with private bathrooms as well as a nearby common room equipped with refrigerator and microwave ($70–80).

LODGES

Chemult

Dawson House (1-888-281-83754; dawson@presys.com; www.dawson-house.net), Highway 97 N., Chemult 97731. In 1929 when a new railroad and highway were pushing through central Oregon and workers needed a place to stay, Dick Dawson built the 12-room Hotel Chemult as a boardinghouse, which has since gone several owners and transformations. "The lodge has been completely renovated in the past six years," says owner Pam Stayner, "and is a comfortable, homey place to stay," The Dawson House actually has two kinds of accommodations for guests: The original hotel contains five rooms that come with private baths as well as a pastry and fresh fruit breakfast ($40–55), and a motel addition contains three rooms that do not include breakfast ($40–55). "We have lots of surprised remarks from our guests when first viewing our rooms, Pam says. "'Ooooo, wow, isn't this wonderful,' is often the first thing they say, followed by, 'I never expected this!'"

Crater Lake National Park

Crater Lake Lodge (541-830-8700; info-cl@xanterra.com; www.craterlakelodges.com) on Highway 62. This historic four-story lodge, dedicated in 1915 and restored in 1995 (at a cost of $15 million), perches at an elevation of more than 7,000 feet on the south rim of the caldera of old Mount Mazama, which blew its top some 7,000 years ago, leaving behind a gaping hole that now holds a 1,932-foot-deep lake, the deepest in the country. The lodge offers a sense of elegance in both its rooms and meals, but the view remains its most memorable feature. In fact, the rates on the lodge's 71 rooms ($117–227, with no telephones, televisions, or air conditioning) are determined in part by that view: the more you can see, the more you pay. In addition, 7 miles away lies the 40-unit Mazama Village Motor Inn, which offers queen beds and private baths ($98, with no telephone, televisions, or air conditioning).

Fort Klamath

Horseshoe Ranch (866-658-5933; mayflydi@aol.com; www.thehorseshoeranch.com), 52909 Highway 62, Fort Klamath 97626. No doubt about it, this lodge appeals to anglers lusting after huge rainbow trout, for through this ranch runs the Wood River, one of the world's gifts to the fly-fishing set. Here lies private access to 6 miles of the stream, which flows past the ranch's red Craftsman lodge with its tall pines and big deck, its fireplace and leather chairs, and its six guest rooms. (When he stayed here, President Jimmy Carter slept in, of course, the President's Room.) A continental breakfast is included with the room ($79–150) and dinners are available by request.

Wilson Cottages and Camp (541-381-2209), 57997 Highway 62, Fort Klamath 97626. Built in the 1930s from pine trees cut and milled on the property, these 10 cabins ($50–60) stand on 135 acres of land located in the vicinity of Crater Lake, Lake of the Woods, and Diamond Lake.

✷ Where to Eat

EATING OUT **Fiorella's** (541-882-1878), 6139 Simmers Avenue, Klamath Falls. When Fiorella and Renato Durighellois left Venice for Klamath Falls almost 20 years ago, they brought part of Italy with them and put it into their restaurant. As a result, Fiorella's today imparts a sense of Mediterranean style in this former home with its plaster walls and wooden beams, white tablecloths and filled flower vases, and old-world menu selections, including homemade pastas and ravioli.

Home Run Pizza Parlor (541-365-2304), Highway 97, Chemult. Sure, the pizza here is great, but so are the barbecued pork ribs. You'll also find a decent salad bar, deli sandwiches, and homemade soups.

✷ Special Events

February: **Bald Eagle Conference** (1-800-445-6728), Klamath Falls.

August: **Dixieland Jazz Festival** (541-433-2793), Crescent Lake.

December: **Snowflake Festival** (1-800-445-6728), Klamath Falls.

LAKEVIEW–PAISLEY–BLY AREA

GUIDANCE **Bureau of Land Management**, Lakeview District (541-947-2177), 1000 Ninth Street S., Lakeview 97630.

Fremont National Forest: Headquarters (541-947-2151), 524 N. G Street, Lakeview 97630; **Bly Ranger District** (541-353-2427); **Paisley Ranger District** (541-943-3114).

Lake County Chamber of Commerce (1-877-947-6040; info@lakecountychamber.org; www.lakecountychamber.org), 126 N. E Street, Lakeview 97630.

Oregon State Parks (503-378-6305), State Parks and Recreation Department, 525 Trade Street S. E., Salem 97301.

GETTING THERE The Lakeview–Paisley–Bly area is reached from the north by Highways 31 and 395, from the east and west by Highway 140, and from the south by Highway 395.

MEDICAL EMERGENCY **Lake District Hospital** (541-947-2114), 700 S. J Street, Lakeview.

* Towns

Lakeview. Lakeview is not only a community of quiet streets and shady lawns and slow summer evenings, but also the tallest town in Oregon, 4,800 feet above the watery blue of the distant Pacific. To commemorate that fact, the town has long marked its entrance with the cutout of one t-a-a-a-l-l-l cowboy. But as weather and age took its toll on this towering buckaroo with the eastern Oregon scowl, the city put up a grinning version of the t-a-a-a-l-l-cowboy, which makes some residents long for the old gunslinger look.

Bly. The large sawmills that once drew families to the area and let them make a living from the nearby forests are now missing, their absence creating gaps in the landscape as well as in the local economy. Now what's left from the old timber-rich days is a historic ranger station built in the Civilian Conservation Corps (CCC) years of the 1930s, though some people in town expect at least a partial return to lumber days. "Folks are always going to need two-by-fours," says one ranger at the station. "And the only way you make them is by cutting trees."

BLY RANGER STATION

Paisley. Once part of the homeland of the Paiute, Modoc, and Klamath Indians—rock paintings and cave artifacts indicate native people may have lived in the area as long ago as 10,000 years—the open range surrounding Paisley caught the eyes of cattle ranchers soon after the first wagon trains creaked into Oregon. It's been mostly cowboy country ever since. "Cowboys ride through the streets," said the *WPA Guide to Oregon* as late as 1950, "and the water trough and hitching post still stand." Even though the troughs and the posts are gone, this town of "249 friendly folks and one old grouch" is still headquarters to the 2,500-square-mile ZX Ranch, the second largest in the nation.

Summer Lake. The valley that holds the small community of Summer Lake can glisten white with alkali and blue with sky as it spreads out between the rimrocks and ridges that mark its boundaries. In addition to the lodge that makes up the bulk of the town, here and there you'll find ranches or pastures, but most of the valley is taken up with miles of marsh that draw birds by the thousands during the spring and fall migrations.

✱ To See

MUSEUMS Lake County Museum (541-947-2220), 118 S. E Street, Lakeview. Located in a house built in 1927, the museum holds displays that tell the story of the region's life and development, from native people to homesteaders, from pioneer kitchens to Civilian Conservation Corps (CCC) camps. Perhaps the most valuable articles in the collection are Indian artifacts—including a sandal, a basket, and ropes—that date back more than 9,000 years.

LAKE COUNTY MUSEUM

Schminck Memorial Museum (541-947-3134), 128 S. E Street, Lakeview. Dalpheus Schminck, for more than 50 years a clerk in a Lakeview mercantile, and his wife, Lula, were devoted collectors of the stuff of pioneer life. As a result, their collection of more than 5,000 pieces is now on display in this museum operated by the Daughters of the American Revolution. Toys and tack, buggies and bustles, goblets and guns—they all contribute to a wide perspective of life in the West.

HISTORIC SITES **Lakeview Walking Tour,** downtown Lakeview (1-877-947-6040). The climb into Lakeview, "the Tallest Town in Oregon" with an elevation of 4,800 feet, shows you plenty of the stuff from which it was made: cattle and timber. The beginnings of the city's downtown, however, burned away in a 1900 fire—only the county courthouse and a Methodist church survived—and the brick buildings that rose from the ashes have entered their second century of service to the community. A stroll along the downtown sidewalks will introduce you to the architecture of the days that began the *last* century.

Bly Ranger Station, off Highway 140 in Bly. This complex of stone and wood buildings was a project of the Civilian Conservation Corps (CCC) in the late 1930s and early 1940s. Today, still used as a ranger station, it demonstrates the craftsmanship that was the trademark of the CCC.

Mitchell Monument, 11 miles east of Bly off Highway 140 and Forest Road 34. As monuments go, this one is modest: no pigeons perching on the shoulders of bronze generals, no sunlight glistening from the flanks of marble horses. No, the Mitchell Monument is only a simple monolith of stone and mortar that stands at the end of a short gravel path and in the shade of copper-barked pines. The names on its brass plaque, however, hold the story of a Saturday morning in 1945 when war visited this Oregon forest. For on that day Archie Mitchell, a minister from nearby Bly, and his pregnant 26-year-old wife, Elsie, stopped here to have a picnic with five children who attended their church. While he was unpacking the car, Mitchell heard one of the children call from nearby, "Look what I found!" And when Elsie and the other children ran over to investigate, a Japanese balloon bomb, one of thousands launched in an attempt to ignite Northwest forests, exploded. Only Reverend Mitchell survived. The other six became the only World War II deaths known to have occurred on American soil as a result of enemy action.

MITCHELL MONUMENT

FOR FAMILIES ✐ **Fire Lookout Rentals,** Fremont National Forest, Lakeview (541-947-2151). In 1931 the U.S. Forest Service loaded up a fire lookout kit, all its pieces precut to no more than 6 feet so it would fit a pack horse, and hauled it to the top of **Bald Butte** (southwest of Paisley off Forest Road 28). Abandoned 61 years later but preserved for its history, the old lookout is now available for overnight rentals; the forest service even provides the table and chairs, stove and lights. Just pack along food and water, some camping gear and a sense of adventure. The same accommodations are also available at **Fremont Point** (southwest of Summer Lake off Forest Road 2901), which stands more than 7,000 feet high on Winter Ridge, high above Summer Lake.

SCENIC DRIVES **Lakeview to Steens Back Country Byway,** 91 paved and graveled miles from Lakeview to Highway 205 south of Frenchglen. Through land both wet and dry, green and brown this road wanders, from **Goose Lake Valley** and through the **Warner Wetlands,** then up toward the sky and across **Hart Mountain,** where it enters a long span of desert that holds hardly a memory of water. "A gateway to other worlds you will remember for years to come" is what the Bureau of Land Management says about this stretch of gravel and dust. But some folks, especially those who tire of a steady view of sagebrush and cows, might prefer Longfellow's description of "the sea-like, pathless, limitless waste of the desert." Either way, it's guaranteed to be an adventure.

NATURAL WONDERS **Old Perpetual Geyser,** 1 mile north of Lakeview off Highway 395. Oregon's only geyser, Old Perpetual spouts a stream of hot water 60 feet into the air every 30 seconds

Sunstone Gem Collection Area, 23 miles north of Plush off County Road 3-10 and connecting Bureau of Land Management roads. If you get a rockhound's hankering to pluck shining gems from the desert sand, then head north from Plush until you reach the Sunstone Collection Area, 4 square miles of high desert set aside for the gathering of Oregon sunstones. This is land as gritty as its gravel roads, yet the folks who come here to pick or dig these rocks—the crystallized remnants of volcanic basalt—are so intense in their search that they don't seem to mind that in the entire 2,560 acres there stands only one vault toilet.

Abert Rim, 30 miles north of Lakeview off Highway 395. Standing 2,500 feet above the valley floor, the 30-mile-long Abert Rim is the highest scarp in North America. Its west side rises abruptly from Lake Abert (see *Wilder Places—Wildlife Refuges*), while its east side slopes gradually from Warner Valley. And on top, a 600-foot cliff, which you can reach by driving a dirt road, offers a viewpoint of both sides.

Slide Mountain, 21 miles south of Summer Lake off Highway 31 and Forest Road 29. Several thousand years ago, the north face of this old volcano slid away, exposing its insides, which you can see from the highway. If you want a closer view of the mountain, as well as of Winter Ridge, Summer Lake, and the Diablo Mountains, you can hike to the summit if you're willing to forgo a maintained trail.

✷ To Do

BICYCLING **Summer Lake Wildlife Area,** various graveled routes beginning 1 mile south of the town of Summer Lake off Highway 31. One of the best places in Oregon to watch the spring and fall migrations of waterfowl—especially the **snow geese;** gosh, you won't believe the snow geese—Summer Lake also has more than 8 miles of roads along the dikes that control the water and the wetlands at this 29-square-mile refuge. So if you park your car and saddle up your bike, you'll find yourself taking a memorable spin down a timeworn trail. Be sure to leave your watch behind.

Fremont National Forest Trail System (541-947-2151), 524 North G Street, Lakeview. Fremont National Forest, which lies north and south of Highway 140, contains a network of trail systems presenting various degrees of difficulty. Trails suitable for family rides include **Cottonwood,** 7 miles one way; **Cox Pass,** 6 miles one way; **Bull Prairie,** 9 miles round trip; and **Rogger Meadow,** 3 miles round trip. Trails for experienced riders include **Vee Lake,** 4 miles one way; **Black Cap,** 10 miles round trip; **Bullard Canyon,** 17 miles round trip; and **Crane Mountain,** 16 miles round trip.

See also *Hiking*.

CAMPING **Fremont National Forest** (541-947-2151), 524 N. G Street, Lakeview. Named for John C. Frémont, early explorer of the Oregon Country, this national forest consists of almost 2,700 square miles of some of the most rugged and secluded lands in Oregon. Its numerous campgrounds border streams and lakes, forests and mountains.

Lakeview Ranger District (541-947-3334). **Can Springs,** 25 miles northeast of Lakeview off Highway 140 and Forest Roads 3615 and 3720, 3 campsites; **Cottonwood Meadows,** 26 miles northwest of Lakeview off Highway 140 and Forest Road 3870, 21 campsites along the shore of Cottonwood Meadow Lake; **Deep Creek,** 28 miles southeast of Lakeview off highway 140 and Forest Roads 3915 and 4015, 5 campsites; **Dismal Creek,** 27 miles southeast of Lakeview off Highway 140 and Forest Road 3915, 3 campsites; **Dog Lake,** 25 miles southwest of Lakeview off Highway 140 and Dog Lake Road, 8 campsites; **Drews Creek,** 14 miles southwest of Lakeview off Highway 140 and Forest Road 4812, 5 campsites near Drews Reservoir; **Mud Creek,** 18 miles northeast of Lakeview off Highway 140 and Forest Road 3615, 7 campsites; **Overton Reservoir,** 26 miles northeast of Lakeview off Highway 140 and Forest Roads 3615 and 3624, 2 campsites; **Twin Springs,** 15 miles southeast of Lakeview off Forest Roads 017 and 3910, 3 campsites; **Willow Creek,** 22 miles southeast of Lakeview off Forest Road 4011, 8 campsites.

Paisley Ranger District (541-943-3114). **Campbell Lake** and **Deadhorse Lake,** 26 miles southwest of Paisley off Highway 31 and Forest Road 33, a total of 34 lakeshore campsites; **Slide Lake,** 10 miles west of Paisley off Forest Roads 3315 and 3360, 3 campsites.

Bly Ranger District (541-353-2427), Highway 140, Bly. **Holbrook Reservoir,** 18 miles southeast of Bly off Highway 140 and Forest Road 3715, 1 campsite; **Lofton Reservoir,** 21 miles southeast of Bly off Highway 140 and Forest Road 3715, 26 campsites; **Deep Creek,** 28 miles southeast of Lakeview off Highway 140 and Forest Roads 3915 and 4015, 5 campsites; **Dismal Creek,** 27 miles southeast of Lakeview off Highway 140 and Forest Road 3915, 3 campsites.

Lower Cottonwood, 14 miles northwest of Lakeview off Highway 140 and Forest Road 3870, 2 campsites on the shore of Cottonwood Reservoir, boat ramp and nearby fishing.

Paisley Area. Sycan River, between 16 and 20 miles southwest of Paisley off Forest Roads 29 and 30: **Pikes Crossing** and **Rock Creek,** each with 6 campsites; **Dairy Creek,** between 21 and 25 miles southwest of Paisley off Forest Road 33: **Dairy Point,** 4 campsites; **Deadhorse Creek,** 5 campsites; **Happy Camp,** 9 campsites. **North Fork Sprague River**, between 26 and 29 miles southwest of Paisley off Forest Road 3411: **Lee Thomas,** 8 campsites; **Sandhill Crossing,** 5 campsites.

Chewaucan River Area, between 7 and 9 miles south of Paisley off Forest Road 33. **Chewaucan Crossing,** 2 campsites; **Jones Crossing,** 8 campsites; **Marsters Spring,** 11 campsites; **Upper Jones,** 2 campsites; **Upper Marsters,** 1 campsite.

Bly Area. **Gerber Reservoir,** 18 miles south of Bly off Forest Roads 3752 and 3814, more than 50 total campsites divided among the following five camps: **Gerber Potholes, Gerber Recreation Site North, Gerber Recreation Site South, Stan H. Springs,** and **Miller Creek; Wildhorse Creek,** 23 miles south of Bly off Forest Road 3752, 3 campgrounds located near Wildhorse Creek and Horse Camp Rim and holding a total of some half-dozen campsites, including **Basin Camp, Pitch Log,** and **Wildhorse Camp.**

CANOEING **Dog Lake,** 25 miles southwest of Lakeview off Highway 140 and Dog Lake Road. The lake that shines from the center of this 5,000-acre blend of desert, forest, and marsh is one of the few natural freshwater lakes in this part of Oregon. **Pelicans** and **osprey,** even **bald eagles** and **turkey vultures,** might look on as you paddle the waters here.

Cottonwood Meadow Lake, 26 miles northwest of Lakeview off Highway 140 and Forest Road 3870. Created by an earthen dam built across Cottonwood Creek in 1961, this lake prohibits motors and offers fishing for **stocked rainbows** and **brookies.**

Campbell and Deadhorse Lakes, 38 miles northeast of Bly off Highway 140 and Forest Roads 34, 28, and 033. Located a mile apart, these two high-elevation lakes (7,200 feet) come with campgrounds (see *Camping*), hiking trails, and **rainbow trout** as well as quiet waters.

HIKING **Fremont National Recreation Trail,** in the Fremont National Forest located roughly north and south of Highway 140 between Lakeview and Bly. When this trail is finished, it will run the entire length of Fremont National Forest—approximately 175 miles through virtually every kind of landscape the forest offers, from high desert to pine forest. But you don't have to hike the whole darn thing. Right now, with more than 120 miles completed, look on your map for these trailheads that offer access points: **Bear Creek, Chewaucan Crossing, Cox Pass, Mill, Moss Pass, Swale,**

Vee Lake, and **Walker.** Open to foot, horse, and bike traffic.

Crane Mountain National Recreation Trail, east of Lakeview in Fremont National Forest, extending south to the California border. This 36-mile trail cuts across the steep slopes of Crane Mountain, whose summit is one of the highest points in the region at an elevation of almost 8,400 feet. It's open to foot, horse, and bike traffic, and motorized vehicles are permitted in the southernmost 8 miles. Trailheads include **Crane Mountain, Rogger Meadow,** and **Walker.**

Cottonwood Meadows Trail System, northwest of Lakeview. Three trails make up this system: **Cottonwood Creek** and **Cougar Peak Trails,** each 5 miles long, and **Cottonwood Loop,** 2 miles long. All three are limited to traffic by foot, horse, or bike.

Hanan Trail, southwest of Paisley. This trail—which consists of two connected segments, the **Hanan/Sycan** and the **Hanan/Coffeepot**—is a historical pathway that served Native Americans as well as early settlers. Today it offers access to the headwaters of the **Sycan River,** a National Wild and Scenic River, as it crosses the divide that separates the Great Basin from the Pacific Ocean.

Lakes Loop, southwest of Paisley and sometimes called the **Lakes Trail System.** With upper and lower, eastern and western segments, this system of connecting loops offers hikes of various difficulties and lengths (up to 9 miles) between **Campbell Lake** and **Deadhorse Lake** with links to **Dead Cow**, **Dead Horse Rim,** and **Cache Cabin Trails.** Open to foot, horse, and bike traffic.

See also **Campbell and Deadhorse Lakes** under *Canoeing,* and **Gearhart** under *Wilder Places—Wilderness Areas.*

✷ Wilder Places

PARKS **Goose Lake State Park,** 15 miles south of Lakeview off Highway 395, day use and overnight. Even though it lies in Oregon, this park with 48 campsites shares its lake with California. And, yes, **geese** really *do* flock to the waters here, making it a prime bird-watching site, especially for waterfowl.

WILDERNESS AREAS **Gearhart,** 36 miles northwest of Lakeview off Highway 140 and Forest Road 34 or 3660, 35 square miles. Three major trailheads lead into this wilderness named for the craggy, volcanic dome that serves as its major landmark: **Lookout Rock, North Fork Sprague,** and **Boulder Springs.** Perhaps the easiest trail is the **Gearhart Mountain Trail,** less than 2 miles long and leading to 18-acre **Blue Lake,** the area's only lake and its most popular destination and campsite. (Don't be surprised to find cows keeping you company on your hike; the entire wilderness is open to grazing.)

WILDLIFE REFUGES **Warner Lakes**, off County Road 3-10 and Hart Mountain Road north of Plush. During the last Ice Age, the Warner Valley held a lake that covered 500 square miles at a depth of 360 feet. Today, however, the valley acts as a giant basin that holds the runoff from nearby mountains without letting it run to the sea. As a result, years of high water link the lakes into a giant wetland, while periods of low water shrink them into marshlands.

HART MOUNTAIN NATIONAL WILDLIFE REFUGE

Hart Mountain National Antelope Refuge, 65 miles northeast of Lakeview off Highways 395 and 140, and Hart Mountain Road. Established in 1936 to help save the region's vanishing herds of **pronghorn antelope,** this refuge covers more than 760 square miles of rimrock and rangeland and sagebrush spread across a fault-block mountain that stands almost a mile above the floor of adjacent Warner Valley and more than a mile and a half above sea level. Keeping the pronghorns company these days are critters ranging from **kangaroo rats** to **bighorn sheep** and from **burrowing owls** to **golden eagles.**

Lake Abert, 3 miles north of Valley Falls off Highway 395. Spanning 180 square miles—18 miles long and 10 miles wide—Lake Abert is the third largest body of salt water on the continent—and it's full of life. Here millions of brine shrimp feed thousands of waterfowl and shorebirds during the spring and fall migrations. In addition, this is the home of one of the world's largest breeding populations of **western snowy plovers.**

Summer Lake, east of Highway 31 near the town of Summer Lake. Come spring and fall, this high-desert basin clamors with the flurry of **waterfowl** voices and wings. From distant lands and across vast skies they fly, and when at last they reach Summer Lake they find what William Cullen Bryant describes as *the welcome land:* "Soon shalt thou find a summer home, and rest, / And scream among thy fellows; reeds shall bend, / Soon, o'er thy sheltered nest." The migrating multitudes of ducks and geese, swans and cranes that settle for a spell here in this blue-sky basin are following a genetic trail that began even before the days when this part of Oregon was a land of mammoths and camels and flamingos, of belching volcanoes and roiling lakes.

Winter Ridge, west of Highway 31

SUMMER LAKE, RESTING PLACE FOR THOUSANDS OF MIGRATING WATERFOWL

near the town of Summer Lake. This is the ridge that looms above Summer Lake. Both ridge and lake were named by the same man, John C. Frémont who, when exploring the area in 1845, found his party struggling in a snowstorm. "The air was dark with falling snow which everywhere weighed down the trees," he wrote. "Toward noon, we found ourselves on the verge of a vertical and rocky wall of the mountain. At our feet, more than a thousand feet below, we looked into a green prairie country in which a beautiful lake was spread along the foot of the mountain, its shores bordered with green grass . . . Shivering in snow three feet deep and stiffening in a cold north wind, we exclaimed at once that the names of Summer Lake and Winter Ridge should be applied to these two proximate places of sudden and violent contrast." Then, deciding that his mama didn't raise no fool, Frémont led his men to the lake and the sunlight below.

Gerber Reservoir, 18 miles south of Bly off Forest Roads 3752 and 3814. Nine stops along the **Gerber Area Watchable Wildlife Tour** take you to islands and creeks, potholes and nesting sites, but mostly to a chain of reservoirs scattered throughout the area. Although these were built for irrigation, they attract a variety of **shorebirds** and **waterfowl, ospreys** and **eagles.**

✷ Lodging

See also *Fire Lookout Rentals,* under *To Do—For Families.*

Aspen Ridge Resort (1-800-393-3323; aspenrr@starband.net; www.aspenrr.com), Fishhole Creek Road, Bly 97622. Located on a 14,000-acre ranch surrounded by the **Fremont National Forest,** Aspen Ridge stands firmly planted in cattle country. Its guest accommodations total nine units divided between log cabins that come with complete furnishings, including a full kitchen ($140) and lodge rooms ($75–95). In addition, the resort's restaurant serves breakfast and specializes in mesquite-barbecued dinners.

INNS 🐾 ✐ **Summer Lake Inn** (1-800-261-2778; dseven@summerlakeinn.com; www.summerlakeinn.com), 31501 Highway 31, Summer Lake 97640. Between highway shoulder and lakeshore stands Summer Lake Inn, whose neighbors are more likely to be geese than people. "Our location is part of what makes us unique in that we are in the Oregon Outback and a long distance from any cities," says owner Darrell Seven. "This gives our clients an opportunity to enjoy the Outback country in luxury cabins and with good food." Most of the nine cabins come with soft chairs and big beds, air-conditioning and Jacuzzis, fully equipped kitchens and built-in fireplaces, all surrounded by wood-paneled walls decorated with Western and Native American art ($105–165; meals, kids, and pets extra). Perhaps the best reason to stay at the inn, however, is for the chance to explore the Summer Lake area (be aware, however, that this is an alkali lake unsuitable for swimming). "Our grounds are beautiful, the view spans over a distance from 30 to 50 miles," Seven says, "and the quiet gives peace to the soul."

BED AND BREAKFASTS **Heryford Inn Bed & Breakfast** (1-888-295-3402), 108 S. F Street, Lakeview 97630. When this Victorian home was built in 1911 by pioneer cattleman William Heryford, the local newspaper called it the "first modern residence to be built in Lakeview" because of its central heating, electrical wiring, and telephone service. Now restored to its early glory, the brick house, which is located near the courthouse in downtown Lakeview, offers three guest rooms with a shared bath ($65–85).

LODGES **Honker Inn Lodge** (530-946-4179; honkerinn@att.net; www.honkerinnlodge.com), Snow Goose Lane, New Pine Creek 97635. Standing so near the border that its address is in Oregon but its phone number Californian, the Honker Inn is a lodge that specializes in hunting but also welcomes guests who'd rather spend their time exploring. Accommodations include either rooms or cabins with shared baths and a large dining room where meals are served family style ($75 per person).

The Lodge at Summer Lake (866-943-3993; smlk31@presys.com; www.thelodgeatsummerlake.com), 36980 Highway 31, Summer Lake 97640. Built from two army barracks that the owners trucked in and set up across the road from the **Summer Lake Wildlife Refuge** (see *Wilder Places—Wildlife Refuges*), this lodge first opened its doors in 1947 and, in spite of its distance from a city, it has been going strong ever since. Since 1994 it has been owned and operated by four people who take care of the building, baking, cooking, cleaning, greeting, and guiding parts of the business. "We love the high desert and helping people explore this beautiful area," say Gary, Marie, Jan, and Gil. (They don't speak in unison, though they prefer all their names be used.) "We also enjoy spending time with our guests, hearing about their lives and what they like about Summer Lake." Although the lodge offers several categories of guest accommodations, ranging from **tent camping** and **RV parking** to a **vacation house,** many travelers take advantage of the seven-unit **motel** ($54–60). In addition, the lodge's **restaurant** offers a complete menu. "We promise to always give you our best," say the owners. "Delicious food, comfortable lodging, and, most important of all, the peace and quiet that only Summer Lake has to offer."

COTTAGES Summer Lake Hot Springs (1-877-492-8554; www.summerlakehotsprings.com), Highway 31, Summer Lake 97640. Here at Summer Lake Hot Springs, where the snow clings through summer to the upper escarpment of Winter Ridge and hot springs bubble from the ground at temperatures that would make a water heater proud, lies what owners Duane Grahama and Suzy Vitello call "an Oregon you've never seen." Located near milepost 92 on Highway 31, the hot springs is part of a 143-acre site that borders Summer Lake, one of the Northwest's prime bird refuges. Its guest accommodations include seven "vintage" Airstream trailers—complete with kitchen, dishes, and linens—that visitors can rent by the day ($40), as well as the hot-spring-fed swimming pool that's been in operation since 1927.

* Where to Eat

EATING OUT Aspen Ridge Resort (541-884-8685), Fishhole Creek Road, Bly. This is one of those "secret" places that requires a drive along a back road to find. But once you get there, you'll also find some of the area's best cooking, including mesquite-barbecued beef, chicken, and fish. You won't leave hungry.

The Lodge at Summer Lake (541-943-3993), Highway 31 N., Summer Lake. Out here beneath the wide and starry sky where eagles soar and snow geese fly, you can pull into the Lodge at Summer Lake for a dinner that might include coastal salmon or jumbo prawns, Icelandic white fish or filet mignon, all of it coming with fresh-baked bread.

Special Events

July: **Mosquito Festival,** Paisley. Begun in 1984 as a way to raise funds to control mosquitoes in Paisley, this celebration has grown into a two-day event that includes some activities you might not expect in a small town, such as shows for classic cars and acrobatic airplanes. But it also offers the more traditional parade and rodeo, crafts market and art show, dunk tank and quilt auction, beef barbecue and horseshoe tournament. Perhaps the most memorable event, however, occurs after dark, when telescopes are provided for gazing at Paisley's big sky during the sky watch.

August: **Summer Lake Blues Festival,** Summer Lake. Hard to say whether the music or the sky is bluer at this festival, but it's definitely the surroundings that set this music festival apart: Summer Lake, Winter Ridge, and the big sky of the high desert serving as a backdrop to it all.

SILVER LAKE–CHRISTMAS VALLEY–FORT ROCK AREA

GUIDANCE **Bureau of Land Management,** Lakeview District (541-947-2177), 1000 Ninth Street S., Lakeview 97630.

Christmas Valley Chamber of Commerce (541-576-2166), Christmas Valley 97641.

Fremont National Forest: Headquarters (541-947-2151), 524 N. G Street, Lakeview 97630; **Silver Lake Ranger District** (541-576-2107).

Lake County Chamber of Commerce (1-877-947-6040; info@lakecounty-chamber.org; www.lakecountychamber.org), 126 N. E Street, Lakeview 97630.

Oregon State Parks (503-378-6305), State Parks and Recreation Department, 525 Trade Street S. E., Salem 97301

GETTING THERE The Silver Lake–Christmas Valley–Fort Rock area is reached from the north and south by Highway 31, from the east by county roads connecting to Highway 395, and from the west by county roads connecting to Highways 97 and 140.

MEDICAL EMERGENCY **Lake District Hospital** (541-947-2114), 700 S. J Street, Lakeview.

✱ Towns

Silver Lake. In Oregon history, Silver Lake's fame is its tragedy. The disaster struck on Christmas Eve 1894, when 200 people crowded into the second floor of the town's general store for a dance, a kerosene lamp tipped over, and the ensuing fire and panic killed 43 people. (Their ashes were placed in one coffin and buried in the community's cemetery, where a marble monument still marks the grave.) At the time, according to a newspaper of the day, Silver Lake was "an important town on the dusty road of pioneer days, a stopping place of freighters and range men and a shopping center for a region larger than some eastern states." But like other settlements that seemed to sprout from the desert during the early-20th-century rush of land-hungry homesteaders, Silver Lake learned that you can't grow crops without water. Even so, when electricity arrived in

1955, it brought with it the pivot irrigation needed to grow alfalfa and hay, and the community endures as a ranching center.

Christmas Valley. This is one of the Northwest's youngest towns, born in 1961 when a California developer paid a cattle company 10 dollars an acre for 108 square miles of desert, then sold homesites to several thousand people, many of whom demanded their money back when they first saw their "sagebrush subdivision." Enough stayed, however, so that today Christmas Valley can boast of an airport, a business strip, and a nine-hole golf course, as well as a fledgling community park and a thriving kitty-litter industry. "It's very exciting," says a local alfalfa farmer, "to be on the ground floor of a community that's springing up out of the desert."

✷ To See

MUSEUMS **Homestead Village Museum** (541-576-2251), downtown Fort Rock. Cattlemen began moving into the Fort Rock Valley soon after the Civil War, but it was the new homestead acts in the first decade of the 20th century—along with railroad propaganda of the valley's "rich black loam" that would grow 60 bushels of wheat per acre—that began luring homesteaders here. "The houses and tents and newly plowed fields," wrote a Fort Rock farmer in 1909, "dot the land as far as the eye can see." Then a drought took the crops, World War I took the men, and the Depression took most of what was left. Some of the buildings and equipment from those days, however, are gathered at the 10-acre Homestead Village Museum, whose mission is "preserving the past and never forgetting the pioneers who once lived here."

HISTORIC SITES **Fort Rock Cave,** near Fort Rock State Park, but its archaeological value leaves it unmarked on most maps. It was here in 1938 that Luther Cressman, a University of Oregon anthropology professor leading an archaeological dig, made a discovery that rewrote history. "As we dug," he wrote, "we went through a bed of volcanic ash from an ancient eruption and suddenly, under this, came upon a sandal." Woven of sagebrush bark, this sandal turned out to be more than 9,000 years old, a date that more than doubled scientists' previous estimates of when the first humans lived in North America.

FOR FAMILIES ✐ **Fire Lookout Rentals,** Fremont National Forest, Lakeview, 541-947-2151. Built in the 1920s, **Hager Mountain** (south of Silver Lake off Forest Road 28) is still used as a fire lookout, which means the snow is usually flying before the site opens to campers. So plan on showshoes or skis.

SCENIC DRIVES **Christmas Valley National Back Country Byway,** 102 paved miles southwest of Christmas Valley to the west of Fort Rock. This byway skirts the edges of lava flows and cinder cones, sand dunes and sage flats, rises to the crests of viewpoints and wanders past juniper forests and hayfields. "People came here to be isolated," says a Fort Rock alfalfa farmer. Yet running through this isolation is the sense of more than 10,000 years of history, from cave people to homesteaders, found along the ancient shores of what was once an inland sea.

FORT ROCK, FORMED A THOUSAND CENTURIES AGO, WAS ONCE SURROUNDED BY A VAST LAKE

NATURAL WONDERS

Fossil Lake, 16 miles northeast of Christmas Valley off County Roads 5-14 and 5-14D. The water of Fossil Lake is long gone, gone as long as 8,000 to 9,000 years, an age when some mighty interesting critters lived hereabouts. For example, when paleontologist Thomas Condon explored the area in 1876, he listed among his findings the fossilized remains of "a great sloth as large as a grizzly bear, four kinds of camels, a mammoth elephant and three species of the modern type of horse." First discovered by cattlemen searching for lost stock, the site is now one of the continent's most important for the study of Ice Age mammals, birds, and fish. (You're welcome to walk through the area—a span of sand that stretches as long as four or five football fields laid end zone–to–end zone—but it's illegal to collect fossils.)

Sand Dunes, 18 miles northeast of Christmas Valley off County Roads 5-14 and 5-14D. A hundred centuries or so ago, Christmas Valley was a watery world, a lakeside home to flamingos and mammoths and camels. But then the lakes dried, Mount Mazama erupted, and ash and pumice began piling up. The result in this area today is 25 square miles of sand dunes that reach windblown heights as tall as a six-story building, making it the largest inland shifting dune in the Pacific Northwest. Yet in spite of the area's seclusion, the dunes often buzz with the whine rising from swarms of off-road vehicles scurrying across the sand.

Lost Forest, 21 miles northeast of Christmas Valley off County Roads 5-14 and 5-14D. This 9,000-acre stand of ponderosa pines isn't so much lost as it is misplaced—40 miles from the nearest pine forest in a land where summertime temperatures rise near 100 and annual rainfall is less than 10 inches (ponderosas typically require at least 14 inches). So go figure. One theory says the grove is a survivor from the Ice Age, its taproots reaching through the sand of an ancient lake bed to drink the rainfall collected on the hardpan there.

Crack in the Ground, 8 miles north of Christmas Valley off County Roads 5-14 and 6109D. When lava flowed from four nearby cinder cones to the north about 1,100 years ago, the release of underground pressure forced an older block of lava to collapse, forming a basalt slot 2 miles long and from 10 to 70 feet deep. "We followed a well-worn trail leading into the very bowels of the earth," writes Oregon explorer and author Maynard Drawson about his journey into the crack. "From the dark, eerie depths it appeared we were looking up at a crack in the sky."

Fort Rock, 2 miles north of the town of Fort Rock off China Hat Road. This rock fortress that looms above the desert sage was formed by fire and shaped by water and wind. Its beginning came perhaps 100,000 years ago, when a volcanic eruption spewed up through the lake that once covered this basin, resulting in molten rock and muddy ash plopping itself down around the circular vent, eventually rising more than 300 feet to form an island. Through the centuries, the wind-tossed waves of the lake wore away part of the wall and sculpted the rock into its present shape.

Hole in the Ground, 10 miles northwest of Fort Rock off County Roads 5-14 and 5-14D. Hole in the Ground is a . . . well, it's a big hole in the ground, its rim almost a mile wide and its bottom 500 feet deep. Although often mistaken for a meteorite crater, this circular pit in the desert floor is now thought to be the result of volcanic steam explosions.

CRACK IN THE GROUND

✷ To Do

CAMPING **Fremont National Forest: Silver Lake Ranger District** (541-576-2107). **Alder Springs,** 16 miles south of Silver Lake off Highway 31 and Forest Road 27, 3 campsites; **Bunyard Crossing,** 4 miles south of Silver Lake off Forest Roads 28 and 2917, 3 campsites; **Farm Well,** 15 miles southeast of Silver Lake off Forest Roads 28 and 2916, 2 campsites; **Lower Buck,** 11 miles southwest of Silver Lake off Highway 31 and Forest Roads 27 and 2804, 3 campsites; **Trapper Spring,** 20 miles northwest of Silver Lake off Highway 31, County Road 410, and Forest Road 2516, 2 campsites; **Upper Buck,** 12 miles southwest of Silver Lake off Highway 31 and Forest Roads 27 and 2804, 5 campsites.

Silver Lake Area, near Silver Lake off Highway 31 and connecting county or forest roads: **Duncan Reservoir,** 10 miles southeast of Silver Lake off Highway 31 and County Road 4-14, 5 primitive campsites along the shore of the 33-acre rainbow trout–stocked reservoir; **Silver Creek,** 9 miles southwest of Silver Lake off Highway 31, 16 campsites, hiking trails and nearby fishing; **Thompson Reservoir,** 16 miles south of Silver Lake between Forest Roads 27 and 28: **East Bay,** 17 campsites; **Thompson,** 19 campsites.

Cabin Lake, 10 miles north of **Fort Rock** off Highway 31, 14 campsites in the area of Fort Rock.

✷ Wilder Places

WILDLIFE REFUGES **Oatman Flat Deer Viewing Area,** 8 miles north of Silver Lake off Highway 31. Although this site appears on few maps because it's private land, if you find yourself driving this stretch of country some spring evening, use the pullout on the west side of the highway and keep an eye on the roadside alfalfa fields. Herds of **mule deer,** from 500 to 1,000, often gather here.

✷ Lodging

The only lodging options available in this area are a handful of motels. See also **Fire Lookout Rentals** under *To Do—For Families.*

MOTELS

Christmas Valley

Christmas Valley Desert Inn (541-576-2262).

Lakeside Terrace Motel (541-576-2309).

Silver Lake

Silver Lake Mercantile and Motel (541-943-2131), Highway 31, Silver Lake 97638.

✷ Where to Eat

EATING OUT **Cowboy Dinner Tree** (541-576-2426), South Hagar Mountain Road, Silver Lake. Folks from all around the region make the drive to Silver Lake to eat at this restaurant built of poles and planks. And once they do, they probably don't have to eat again for a day or two. The menu offers but one dinner that features either a 2-pound steak or a whole chicken, which is added to soup and salad, potatoes and rolls, and a homemade dessert. Be prepared to carry home a doggie bag or two because they ask you not to split the dinner. As far as ambience is concerned, you can believe the sign hanging on the wall that says, NO ELECTRICITY—NO CREDIT CARDS—NO KIDDING.

✷ Special Events

September: **Fort Rock Valley Homestead Days,** Fort Rock. In the Fort Rock Valley, the memory of homesteading has lasted longer than the homesteading itself ever did. For the 10 years between 1905 and 1915, as many as a thousand homesteaders filed their claims, tilled the soil, and prayed for rain during an era when great faith was put into dryland crops. But the faith ended when the drought began, and today the village of Fort Rock is the site of an annual reunion of people who remember or want to know about those days.

Northeast

PENDLETON–HERMISTON–MILTON-FREEWATER AREA

LA GRANDE–UNION–ELGIN AREA

WALLOWA VALLEY–SNAKE RIVER AREA

POWDER RIVER–SUMPTER VALLEY–UKIAH AREA

JOHN DAY RIVER AREA

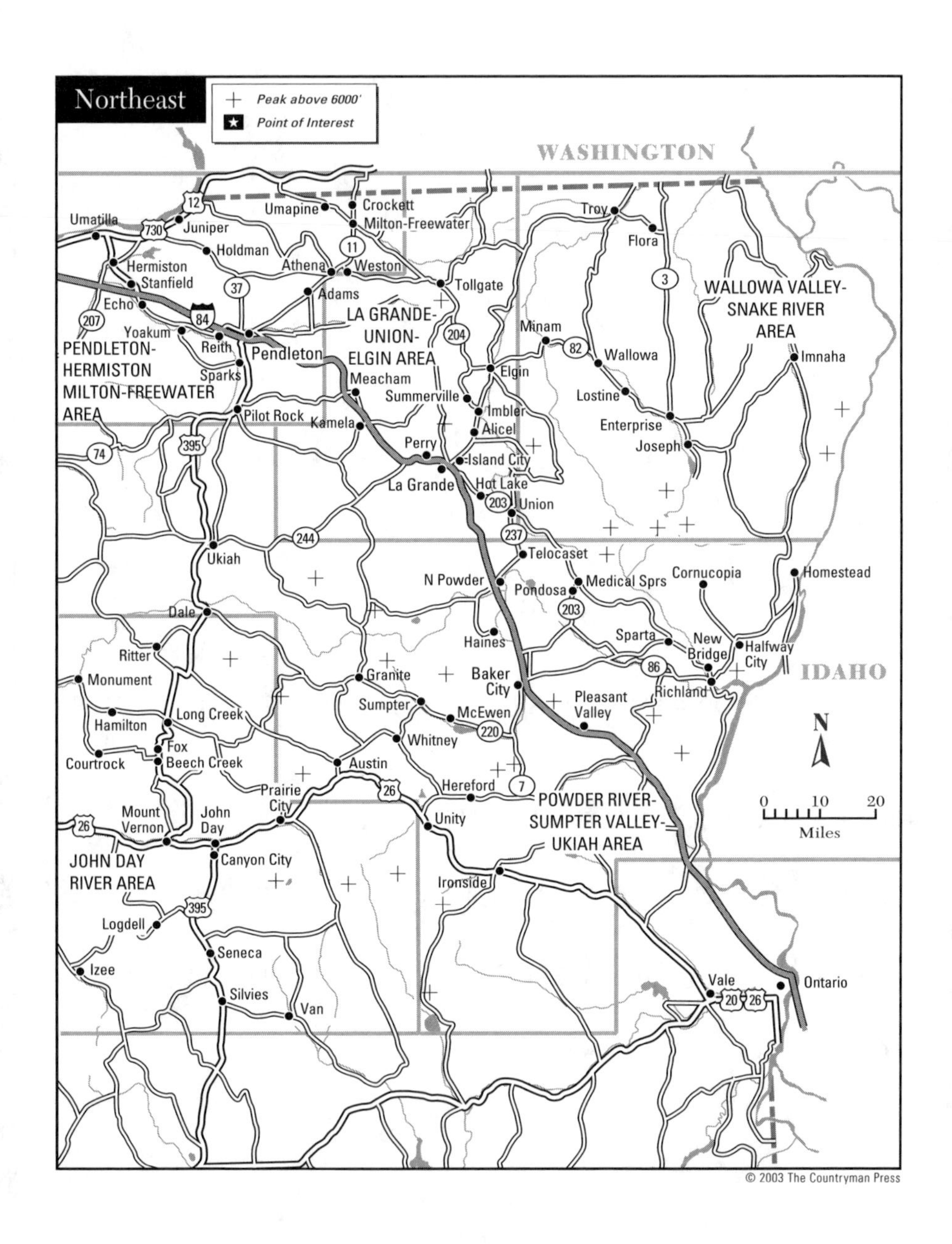
Northeast
Peak above 6000'
Point of Interest
WASHINGTON
IDAHO
PENDLETON-HERMISTON MILTON-FREEWATER AREA
LA GRANDE-UNION-ELGIN AREA
WALLOWA VALLEY-SNAKE RIVER AREA
POWDER RIVER-SUMPTER VALLEY-UKIAH AREA
JOHN DAY RIVER AREA
Umatilla
Juniper
Umapine
Crockett
Milton-Freewater
Holdman
Hermiston
Stanfield
Echo
Athena
Weston
Adams
Tollgate
Yoakum
Reith
Pendleton
Sparks
Meacham
Pilot Rock
Kamela
Summerville
Imbler
Alicel
Elgin
Minam
Wallowa
Lostine
Enterprise
Joseph
Troy
Flora
Imnaha
Perry
La Grande
Island City
Hot Lake
Union
Telocaset
Ukiah
N Powder
Pondosa
Medical Sprs
Cornucopia
Homestead
Dale
Haines
Sparta
New Bridge
Halfway City
Richland
Ritter
Monument
Granite
Baker City
Pleasant Valley
Hamilton
Long Creek
Sumpter
McEwen
Whitney
Fox
Beech Creek
Courtrock
Austin
Hereford
Prairie City
Unity
Mount Vernon
John Day
Canyon City
Ironside
Logdell
Seneca
Izee
Silvies
Van
Vale
Ontario
N
Miles
0 10 20
© 2003 The Countryman Press

INTRODUCTION

"I hear music. When I am real still and look at the mountains,
I hear it."

—Daisy Wasson, who grew up on a late-19th-century
homestead in northeast Oregon

On the sunrise side of the state, in Oregon's northeast corner, the land holds the memories of ancient seas and fiery volcanoes, of mountains that rose from its earth and glaciers that plowed out its valleys, and of footsteps belonging to the people who have called this place home. Getting to know this far-reaching country of blue mountains and big sky, however, means leaving behind the traffic and following the bends of the back roads that take you into its heart. So keep your eyes wide open and your cruise control turned off, and you'll find yourself traveling through a world that still remembers a frontier Oregon.

Depending on the route you choose, such a journey can carry you along roads winding past furrowed fields and through small towns, beneath sky-high summits and along steep-walled canyons. "I love that land more than all the rest of the world," Chief Joseph of the Nez Perce said more than a century ago about his home here. It's easy to see why—blue-black mountains hunched shoulder-to-shoulder, forested slopes slanting toward snow-layered peaks, bunchgrass- and wheat-field-covered hills rippling in brown waves across green valleys.

The beauty of the region as a whole, in fact, may be rivaled only by the drama of its parts. Prime examples include the ruggedness of the Eagle Cap Wilderness, the largest wilderness area in the state; the grandeur of Hells Canyon, the deepest gorge on the continent; and the history of the Blue Mountains, a barrier to the wagon trains traveling the Oregon Trail and the center of the gold-mining era that settled and shaped the lands east of the Cascades.

The area's communities also have their dramas to share, their stories to tell from memories of an older West: The winter when the citizens of Adams held up a train and stole its coal, though they paid for it the next morning. The bully in

Athena who liked to shoot at the bullet-dodging feet of townspeople, until the day someone shot back. The murder in Wallowa that helped trigger the Nez Perce War, which General William Tecumseh Sherman called "the most extraordinary of Indian wars." The governor's visit to Huntington, a crusade that put at least temporary padlocks on the doors of the wild town's "open saloons, gambling tables, and dance halls." The fire that destroyed Sumpter, leaving the town known as "the Queen City" to rebuild itself from the ashes.

This isn't all you'll find, of course. The direction you head, the places you stop, the people you meet—these can make your discoveries as varied as the landscape itself as you wander across this land where each morning the sun first shines upon the state.

PENDLETON–HERMISTON–MILTON-FREEWATER AREA

GUIDANCE **Milton-Freewater Chamber of Commerce** (541-938-5563; www.mfchamber.com), 505 Ward Street, Milton-Freewater 97862.

Oregon State Parks: Headquarters (503-378-6305), State Parks and Recreation Department, 525 Trade Street S. E., Salem, 97301.

Pendleton Chamber of Commerce (1-800-547-8911; info@pendleton-oregon.org; www.pendleton-oregon.org), 501 S. Main Street, Pendleton 97801.

Umatilla Chamber of Commerce (1-800-542-4944; chamber@umatilla.org; www.umatilla.org/chamber), 1530 Sixth Street, Umatilla 97882.

Umatilla National Forest: Headquarters (541-278-3716), 2517 S. W. Hailey Avenue, Pendleton 97801; **Heppner Ranger District** (541-676-9187); **North Fork John Day Ranger District** (541-427-3231).

GETTING THERE The Pendleton–Hermiston–Milton-Freewater area is reached from the north by Highway 11 and roads connecting to Highway 730, from the east and west by Interstate 84, and from the south by Highways 395 and 207. In addition, Highway 37 and Interstate 82 provide links within the area.

MEDICAL EMERGENCY **Good Shepherd Medical Center** (541-567-6483), 610 N. W. 11th Street, Hermiston.

St. Anthony Hospital (541-276-5121), 1601 S. E. Court Avenue, Pendleton.

* To See

MUSEUMS **Tamastslikt Cultural Institute** (541-966-9748), 7 miles east of Pendleton off Interstate 84 exit 216. On the edge of a wheat field that rolls to the edge of the mountains stands the Tamastslikt Cultural Institute, which tells the story of the region's earliest people, its oldest culture. Owned and operated by the Confederated Tribes of the Umatilla Indian Reservation, the interpretive center's artifacts, photographs, and replicas capture a history involving almost 200 years of trappers and missionaries, settlers and soldiers during a time when the resident Cayuse, Umatilla, and Walla Walla peoples saw their lives change

THE FRAZIER FARMSTEAD MUSEUM PRESERVES MEMORIES OF THE REGION'S FARMING PAST

forever. "We're a small group of people with a big story to tell," says Bobbie Conner, a tribal member and the institute's director. "Tamastslikt uses native voices to tell our history, which is rarely heard anywhere else. But we want to open hearts and minds to the rest of the story."

Umatilla County Historical Society Museum (541-276-0012), 108 S. W. Frazer Street, Pendleton. Located in a 1909 railroad depot, this museum weaves together the human strands of local history: Indians, trappers, missionaries, pioneers, ranchers, loggers. From Native American beadwork to Oregon Trail tack to a restored and furnished one-room school, the museum traces the region's roots into the far past.

Echo Historical Museum, 230 W. Main Street, Echo. Even though this museum has impressive displays of historic photographs, Native American artifacts, and period furnishings, its centerpiece and biggest attraction is probably the building itself. Designed by a local architect and built in 1920 as the Bank of Echo, the two-story structure is constructed of glazed brick and terra-cotta and still contains the original marble floors and counters as well as wrought-iron tellers' cages.

Frazier Farmstead Museum (541-963-4636; www.museum.bmi.net), 1403 Chestnut Street, Milton-Freewater. When ex-confederate soldier William Samuel Frazier left Texas and arrived in this farming community in 1867, he built a farm that not only stayed with the family for 115 years but also retained its appearance and authenticity. (Frazier planted the **shagbark hickory** in the yard, now a state **Heritage Tree.)** Even though the land itself has been whittled down to 6 acres, today a restored version of the farm is so thorough in its preservation of pioneer artifacts and a 19th-century lifestyle that you might still be able to smell the hay and hear the clop of hooves in the farm's big red barn.

Maxwell Siding Railroad Museum (541-567-8532), 200 W. Highland Avenue, Hermiston. Even though its name explains exactly what it is—a museum situated on a railway siding, devoted to railroads, and located in a town formerly known as Maxwell—this museum is often overlooked by residents and visitors alike. "Maxwell Siding is Hermiston's best-kept little secret," says Connie Maret, museum president and former railroad maintenance worker. "There are people who have lived here for years and are unaware of the museum." Yet for railroad buffs, this museum located on six tracks near Hermiston's downtown offers a rare collection of railroad snowplows as well as a 1912 passenger car, a 1913 diner car, and various motor cars, cabooses, and railroad equipment.

HISTORIC SITES **Lewis and Clark Trail** (Hat Rock to Umatilla Rapids). After entering what is now Oregon on October 18, 1805, Lewis and Clark's Corps of Discovery spent the day meeting with leaders of the Walla Walla tribe, learning what they could about the Columbia River and buying 40 dogs to take along as food. The next day they pushed on downriver.

Hat Rock, October 19, 1805 (Hat Rock State Park, 9 miles east of Umatilla off Highway 730). When the corps passed near this spot, the captains noted in their journals the presence of four islands, 12 houses, and "a bad rapid . . . At the foot of this rapid is a rock, on the left shore, which . . . resembles a hat in its shape." Although the rapids and islands now lie under the backwater of McNary Dam, Hat Rock remains as the centerpiece of this state park.

Umatilla Rapids, October 19, 1805 (McNary Dam Overlook, 1 mile east of Umatilla off Highway 730). Downstream from Hat Rock lay the once dreaded and now drowned Umatilla Rapids. "It is a very dangerous rapid, strewed with high rocks and rocky islands," Captain Lewis wrote, "and in many places obstructed by shoals, over which the canoes were to be hauled, so that we were more than two hours in passing through the rapids, which extend for the same number of miles."

Oregon Trail (Emigrant Hill to Echo Meadows). You'll find an **Oregon Trail interpretive site** in **Pendleton** near the Umatilla Historical Society Museum (exit 209 off Interstate 84).

Emigrant Hill, east of Pendleton on Emigrant Hill Road. In the first years of the western migration, wagon trains descended this hill outside today's Pendleton, crossed the Umatilla River, and then either continued their journey west along a route that ran roughly parallel to today's Interstate 84 or turned north toward the Whitman Mission (near

HAT ROCK, NAMED BY LEWIS AND CLARK

today's Walla Walla) for much-needed supplies. After the Cayuse killed the Whitmans at their mission in 1847, however, the trail moved farther south, keeping distance from the Cayuse and staying closer to the Umatilla.

Corral Springs, 5 miles southeast of Echo off Umatilla River Road. Even though this site is located on private property, the owners permit public access to a segment of the wagon ruts that lie to the east and north. When the spring was flowing, this was probably a much-used campsite on the way to the next crossing of the Umatilla River. "Numbers were camped around us," Amelia Knight wrote in 1853. "No feed for our poor stock. It is quite warm."

Koontz Grave, 1 mile east of Echo off Umatilla River Road. This marks the gravesite of David Koontz, who began his westward journey in Iowa with his family in 1852, contracted cholera in Oregon, and died near here.

Echo Meadows, 7 miles west of Echo off the Lexington–Echo Highway. Beneath a blue sky and near irrigated fields lies Echo Meadows, where a 15-minute walk along an asphalt path leads you past tumbleweeds and sagebrush and finally to a bench facing a horizon reaching so far it vanishes in haze. And nearby lay almost a mile of wagon ruts. "Over rocks, gravel and sand we plod along all day," Harriet Loughary wrote in 1864. "After a hard day's work, we of course were hungry, but to cook with a fire made of green sagebrush with the sand driving in your eyes, ears and mouth, being mixed in our dough, meat and coffee was a task that we seldom want repeated. We finally abandoned the fire part and crouched into our wagons and nibbled hardtack."

Pendleton Walking Tour (541-276-7411). Although Pendleton prides itself on being part of the Old West of cowboys and cattle drives, the city has long thrived as a business center for wheat and wool. And because prosperity followed the arrival of the train, Pendleton's "Old Town" consists of buildings dating back to about 1900, a time when both business and the population were booming. You can find this Historic District downtown between S. W. First and S. E. First Streets and between Dorion and Frazer Avenues.

Echo Walking Tour (541-376-8411). Home of the Cayuse tribe, campsite on the Oregon Trail, location of Fort Henrietta, and railroad town and sheep center—Echo has evolved through the years into its position today as a quiet farming community on the bank of the Umatilla River. The town's past, however, is becoming increasingly more apparent in the restoration of its buildings and the celebration of its heritage.

Utilla Agency and **Fort Henrietta,** W. Main Street, Echo. Near the Oregon Trail crossing on the west bank of the Umatilla River once stood the Utilla Indian Agency, built in 1851 as the region's first agency for the Cayuse, Umatilla, and Walla Walla tribes. According to emigrants' diaries, the building was "the first frame house [we've seen] since leaving the Missouri River" and "painted white as snow." Its major impact, however, appears to have been the hope it gave pioneers. "The sight of the house standing out here in the wilderness," E. W. Conyers wrote in 1852, "proves to be a great stimulant to the poor emigrants worn out by their long trip." But when hostilities followed the signing of a contentious 1855 treaty, 100 troops of the Oregon Volunteer Cavalry arrived to find the agency burned to the ground. Almost immediately they began building a fort. Using split cottonwood logs, the soldiers erected a stockade 100 feet square and 7 feet high, with two log blockhouses standing at opposite corners. The following year Fort Henrietta, named for the wife of an army officer—was ordered abandoned and its equipment and supplies destroyed. The replica blockhouse that now stands on the edge of Echo is on the original site.

FOR FAMILIES **Underground Tours** (1-800-226-6398), 37 S. W. Emigrant Avenue, Pendleton. (Note: Reservations required for the 90-minute tour.) More than a century ago, Pendleton was a honky-tonker's delight. Why, when cowboys and sheepherders rode into town looking to blow off a little steam, they could choose from 32 saloons and 18 bordellos—some of them sprawled out beneath the city's streets. Besides whiskey and women, this underground network of tunnels and rooms also offered card rooms, a meat market, and an ice cream parlor, as well as a Chinese laundry, jail, and opium den. Today you can step into this subterranean world, where actors re-create a sense of what life was like underground 100 years ago.

Drive-In Movies. Even though today's drive-in lacks the digital sound and sophisticated screens of the multiplex, it remains for some people the ultimate movie experience. "I think there will be some around for a number of years," says one of Oregon's drive-in owners, "until there's so dadgum much technology."

M&F Drive-In (541-938-4327), Highway 11 north of Milton-Freewater. This drive-in movie not only has been showing films since 1954, it can almost make you believe it *is* 1954. After all, you'll pay just $8 per carload, see a double feature (both second-run movies), listen to the soundtrack over your car radio, and have the chance to buy homemade pizza—some people come just for the pizza—at the snack bar.

SCENIC DRIVES **Emigrant Hill Road,** 36 paved miles from Interstate 84's exit 248 north of La Grande to Mission, north of Pendleton. Ignored by many maps and bypassed by most motorists, Emigrant Hill Road bends and climbs and dips its way along what a 1923 travel guide calls "one of the finest scenic roads in Oregon." For three dozen miles this byway follows where the wheels of wagon trains and steam locomotives once rolled, edging along forests and cutting across hillsides, passing old stagecoach stops and emigrant campsites before slanting down to Pendleton. In more modern times it was a segment of Highway 30, once the region's major east–west road.

Umatilla River Road, 23 paved miles from Pendleton to Echo, access points on Interstate 84 at exits 207 and 188. This is a lovely run of road, this old byway that wriggles its way along the bank of the Umatilla River. Though you wouldn't know it to see it now, this stretch of shoulderless asphalt was once the most important route in the region, a link that helped connect the Blue Mountains with the Columbia River for wagon trains and pack strings and freight wagons. Today, however, it's used mostly by local farmers moving between fields or heading to town, or by freeway travelers seeking relief from the numbing whiz of traffic.

✷ To Do

BICYCLING Lake Wallula River Trail, 9 miles east of Umatilla off Highway 730. Lake Wallula is the name they've given the backwaters of McNary Dam, though beneath all that slack water is the old channel of the Columbia River, running 5 feet deep and 100 feet wide. The graveled trail follows an old railroad grade that edges along the water for 5 miles before ending near the dam. In that stretch it manages to wander past sagebrush, wildflowers, and rimrocks, all the while offering views of Cascade Peaks, especially Mount Hood and Mount Adams.

CAMPING Indian Lake, 19 miles southeast of Pilot Rock off East Birch Creek Road, 42 campsites near Indian Lake, fishing for stocked rainbow trout, boating but no gas motors (see *Canoeing*).

CANOEING Indian Lake, 19 miles southeast of Pilot Rock off East Birch Creek Road. Operated by the Confederated Tribes of the Umatilla Indian Reservation, 80-acre Indian Lake—*Lake Hump-Ti-Pin: Grizzly Bitten*—lies at the southern edge of the Utilla Indian Agency (see *To See—Historic Sites*) and near the crest of the Blue Mountains. Only electric motors are permitted, and even though the camping season (see *Camping*) lasts only from May 15 through September 30, the lake itself is open year-round.

GOLF Wildhorse Resort Golf Course (1-800-654-9453), 72787 Highway 331, Pendleton, 18 holes.

HIKING Pendleton River Parkway, between Westgate and S.E. Eighth Street in Pendleton. For 2.5 miles, this paved path follows the south bank of the Umatilla River, bending its way past a fascinating combination of wild and domestic habitats: backwaters and back porches, bird nests and dog kennels, groves of cottonwoods and piles of auto parts. Along this route kids

UMATILLA RIVER ROAD

pedal to school, retirees stroll for exercise, and dogs take their people for walks.

UNIQUE ADVENTURES **Echo Library,** City Hall, corner of Bonanza and Bridge Streets, Echo. If you don't think a visit to a library can be a unique adventure, then step inside this one—elegant and bright, with ceiling fans turning and soft music playing and upholstered chairs inviting you to plop down long enough to open a book. With its carpets and drapes, its rocking chairs and couch, the library resembles someone's living room. In fact, the resident cat—named City Kitty for his presence in adjoining city hall—will rise from his chair, its green cushion layered with his white fur, and insist that you pet him.

✷ Wilder Places

PARKS **Hat Rock State Park,** 9 miles east of Umatilla off Highway 730, day use and overnight. Named for the landmark that Lewis and Clark thought resembled a man's top hat, Hat Rock edges along the slack water of the dam-tamed Columbia River. The park's green spans of shaded lawn and its placid pond give picnickers and campers relief from the sagebrush steppe.

Umatilla Marine Park, along the Columbia River off Highway 730, Umatilla. This riverside park serves as an oasis and playground for residents and visitors alike, offering picnic areas, ball fields, boat docks, swimming beaches, and walking trails.

WILDLIFE REFUGES **Cold Springs National Wildlife Refuge,** 7 miles east of Hermiston off Stanfield Loop Road. This 3,000-acre refuge, basically an irrigation reservoir, might be easily accessible for birds—as many as 30,000 **ducks** and 10,000 **Canada geese** can gather here in winter—but people will find neither trails nor viewpoints. Still, if you care to work your way through the sagebrush to wander the sandy shoreline beneath cottonwoods with 10-foot-high flood stains on their trunks, you'll find thickets and backwaters where **beavers** work at night and mallards rest during the day.

McKay Creek National Wildlife Refuge, 6 miles south of Pendleton off Highway 395. Most of this refuge's more than 1,800 acres is an open-water reservoir used for irrigation. Visited mostly by hunters, fishermen, and migrating **waterfowl,** McKay (pronounced *Ma-KYE*) has a boat ramp but no trails, viewpoints, or even picnic tables.

McNary Wildlife Area, 1 mile east of Umatilla off Highway 730. When the folks who built McNary Dam took away the rapids along this stretch of the Columbia, they set aside a 500-acre chunk of land that's crossed by streams, spotted with ponds, and rippling with grass and brush and trees. The result is that a small wilderness is not only a close neighbor to all that concrete and steel but also a home to creatures great and small, from **pond turtles** to **tundra swans.** To catch a peek at them, you can follow a system of trails softened with grass or bark and leading to woods and meadows.

Power City, 3 miles north of Hermiston off Highway 395 and Bensel Road. This 100-acre refuge is a secretive patchwork of tree-lined marshes and meadows where **deer** and **ducks** and **rabbits** carry on with their business, seemingly oblivious to the fact that they're mere steps from a whizzing highway. A ragged trail leads you to potholed ponds created in the last Ice Age, though the walking can get soggy at times.

Umatilla Chemical Depot, near exit 177 on Interstate 84. No, this isn't a joke: This sprawl of barren ground all humped up with 1,000 dirt igloos storing chemical bombs and missiles and rockets is a great place to spot **pronghorn antelope** as you're cruising along the interstate. Well, actually, it's only safe if you do one or the other—spot or cruise—but pronghorns often wander the roadside perimeter of the 25-square-mile depot. In fact, they seem to be thriving here in the prime shrub-steppe habitat that remains untouched by modern development or agriculture.

Wanaket Wildlife Mitigation Area, between McNary Wildlife Area (see listing, above) and Hat Rock State Park (see *Parks*) along Highway 730. Managed by the Confederated Tribes of the Umatilla Indian Reservation, this 2,800-acre strip of shrub-steppe grasslands bordering the Columbia River is financed by the Bonneville Power Administration's attempts to compensate for habitat lost to the river's dams. Most of the land is dry—summer temperatures can top 100 degrees—though you'll find some ditch-fed wetlands and ponds. The area requires mostly cross-country travel, though the **Lake Wallula River Trail** runs along its northern edge. From both the trail and the highway, some signs identify this area as the **"Columbia Basin Wildlife Area."**

✷ Lodging

BED & BREAKFASTS

Pendleton

A Place Apart Bed & Breakfast (1-888-441-8932; pkmatteri@yahoo.com; www.aplace-apart.com), 711 S. E. Byers, Pendleton 97801. Standing near the Umatilla River and its paved walking trail, this 1901 two-story Colonial-revival inn features Doric columns and beadwork cornices, balconies and a fireplace, and a garden with a gazebo. Its two guest rooms share a bathroom and include a full breakfast ($60–100). Children older than 12 are welcome.

The Parker House Bed & Breakfast (1-800-700-8581; www.parkerhousebnb.com), 311 N. Main Street, Pendleton 97801. Listed on the **State Historic Register** and located just one block from the center of downtown Pendleton, the Parker House is a 1917 three-story, 6,000-square-foot Italian Renaissance inn that retains its original hardwood floors, imported Chinese silk wallpaper and draperies, ornate plaster ceiling, and curved staircase. "Nothing has been spared in providing one of the best B&B experiences in the state," says Gerry Frank, columnist for the *Oregonian.* "The house itself is breathtaking." Accommodations consist of one guest room with a private bathroom and four other rooms that share a bathroom ($75–135). All the rooms contain French double doors that lead to outside balconies, and an elevator takes guests to upstairs rooms. A full breakfast is included.

✵ Where to Eat

DINING OUT **Raphael's** (541-276-8500), 233 S. E. Fourth Street, Pendleton. Considered by many Pendleton residents to be the best restaurant in town, the award-winning Raphael's serves some of the finest food in the region. And even though its menu offers many traditional Northwest dishes, some of its specialties include ingredients—such as rattlesnake or Rocky Mountain elk—that would be difficult to find anywhere else.

EATING OUT

Milton-Freewater

JP's on the Green (541-938-0911), 299 Catherine Street, Milton-Freewater. Standing on the edge of the town's golf course, JP's offers a varied menu, daily specials, and a short stroll to the first tee.

La Casita (541-938-3508), 6 S. Columbia, Milton-Freewater. In this town with a large Hispanic population, La Casita is a local favorite for Mexican food.

Pendleton

Cookie Tree Bakery and Café (541-278-0343), 30 S. W. Emigrant Avenue, Pendleton. At breakfast and lunch, the Cookie Tree bustles with folks who appreciate the café's fresh-baked bread, homemade dishes, and memorable sandwiches.

Wildhorse Casino and Resort (1-800-654-9453), 72777 Highway 331, Pendleton. As part of the casino operated by the Confederated Tribes of the Umatilla Agency, this café is often overlooked in the rush for the slots, cards, and dice. Yet its menu, though limited, offers well-cooked meals at modest prices.

✵ Special Events

July: **Caledonian Games** (541-566-3880; www.oregontrail.net/~caledonian), Athena. Drop by this festival devoted to Scottish heritage and tradition, and you'll see caber tossing and stone putting, hear pipe bands and Celtic harps, and even get the chance to say *Ceud mile failte,* which means "100,000 welcomes" in Gaelic. (Kilts at the festival are optional.)

August: **Muddy Frogwater Festival** (541-938-5563), Milton-Freewater. With bluegrass music and frog-jumping contests, square dances and fun runs, barbecued chicken and homemade pie, this is a summer celebration in which the entire community makes residents and visitors alike feel welcome.

September: **Fort Henrietta Days** (541-376-8411), Echo. Steeped in the history of the Oregon Trail and Northwest Indian wars, this town steps back into its past during this summertime rendezvous of buckskin-clad, tomahawk-tossing, muzzle-loader-shooting trappers and mountain men who bring their tepees with them. If you want to sense what the West was like in the 1850s, this is an event to attend. (For more on Fort Henrietta, see *To See—Historic Sites.*) **Pendleton Round-Up** (1-800-457-6336), Pendleton. Begun as a Fourth of July celebration in 1909—when it featured fireworks, sack races, and greased pig contests as well as bronc riding and horse races—the Pendleton Round-up has grown into one of the world's largest rodeos.

LA GRANDE–UNION–ELGIN AREA

GUIDANCE **Elgin Visitors Center** (541-437-3456), 104 N. 8th Street, Elgin 97827.

Oregon State Parks: Headquarters (503-378-6305), State Parks and Recreation Department, 525 Trade Street S. E., Salem 97301; **La Grande office** (541-963-6444).

Umatilla National Forest: Headquarters (541-278-3716), 2517 S. W. Hailey Avenue, Pendleton 97801.

Union County Visitors and Conventions Bureau (1-800-848-9969; visitlg@eoni.com; www.visitlagrande.com), 1912 Fourth Street, #200, La Grande 97850.

Wallowa-Whitman National Forest: Headquarters (541-523-6391), 1550 Dewey Avenue, Baker City 97814; **La Grande Ranger District** (541-963-7186).

GETTING THERE The La Grande–Union–Elgin area is reached from the north by Highway 204 and its connection to Highway 82, from the east by Highway 82, from the south by Interstate 84 and Highways 203 and 237, and from the west by Interstate 84 and Highway 244.

MEDICAL EMERGENCY **Grande Ronde Hospital** (541-963-8421), 900 Sunset Drive, La Grande.

✷ Towns

La Grande. When the railroad finally crossed the Blue Mountains and reached this tree-lined town, it was reason to celebrate. "The children went wild," said a woman who saw the first train chug into La Grande on the Fourth of July in 1884, "and the older people were not very far behind them in the matter of thrills." Thanks to the train, La Grande grew into a city of brick buildings and shady parks, the valley's commercial center, and the home of Eastern Oregon University.

Union. At the foot of one timbered hill, with its back to the Wallowa Mountains and its face to the Blues, stands the town of Union, home to some of Oregon's finest Victorian architecture, the Northwest's oldest rodeo, and one grand old hotel.

✱ To See

MUSEUMS **Union County Museum** (541-562-6003), Main Street, Union. Among the collections in this museum that tells the story of the region's natural and human history, perhaps the most often visited is the segment that honors "Cowboys Then and Now." The "Then" part of this exhibit teaches visitors about cowboys that are legendary (Wild Bill Hickock and Buffalo Bill Cody), real (John Devine and Pete French), and televised (Hopalong Cassidy and the Lone Ranger). The exhibits "Now" portion, however, is less extensive. "We have just a few displays featuring contemporary ranchers," says Kathleen Almquist, once the museum's director and now a volunteer. "Times have changed. The branding and the roundups still go on—and we still have cattle drives through town—but most of today's working cowboys hold jobs off the ranch to support their cowboying habit."

HISTORIC SITES **Oregon Trail** (Grande Ronde Valley to Emigrant Springs). You'll find Oregon Trail interpretive sites at the following Interstate 84 rest areas: south of **La Grande,** between exits 270 and 268; **Hilgard State Park,** exit 252; and **Emigrant Springs State Park,** exit 234 or 236.

Grande Ronde Valley, Foothill Road to La Grande; exit 268 off Interstate 84. "The worst hill we have had on the trip" is how emigrant Jared Fox described the descent into the Grande Ronde Valley. The route was so steep and rocky that drivers dragged logs behind the wagons or locked the rear wheels with chains, and then braced themselves in their seats and rode the brakes as the wagons skidded downhill. "Most drivers," emigrant Samuel James wrote in 1850, "quaked in getting their wagons down." Even the rough trip, however, couldn't deter the emigrants' wonder at the valley's beauty. "At last we arrived in the middle of this famous plateau called 'La Grand Rond,'" wrote Honore-Timothee Lempfrit in 1848. "It is really one of the loveliest places in the whole world." But because most of the valley floor consisted of marshes and wetlands—remnants of the Ice Age lake that once filled the valley—the wagon trains edged along the foothills to the south and west, camping along today's Foothill Road and the city of La Grande before beginning the journey across the Blue Mountains.

Blue Mountain Crossing, 15 miles northwest of La Grande off Interstate 84 (exit 248) and Forest Road 1843. Steep slopes, thick forests, and rocky ground made the crossing of the Blue Mountains just as bad as the emigrants expected. Maybe worse. Probably the best place to get a close look at what they faced is at Blue Mountain Crossing. Here you'll find some of the best-preserved wagon ruts on public land in Oregon, and the paved walking paths reveal their story a few steps at time. You can read that story in the interpretive signs; see it in the wheel-worn swales and the rim-scarred pines; even hear it at an emigrant's camp, where Elizabeth and her husband, Andrew—"living-history characters"—

BLUE MOUNTAIN CROSSING, WHERE ACTORS RECREATE THE EMIGRANTS' DAYS ON THE OREGON TRAIL

tend a fire next to a covered wagon as they explain the hardships of the trail and their longing to reach the end of it when, Elizabeth says, there will be "no more plains to cross, no more burials to endure."

California Gulch, adjacent to Blue Mountain Crossing (see previous listing). Beginning at the picnic area of Blue Mountain Crossing, a 1-mile trail follows a ridge to a campsite and water source used by the wagon trains. "Good water in abundance," John Fothergill wrote about California Gulch in 1853, "but too steep and thick to turn stock to." So the emigrants hiked down into the gulch and hauled the water back out. Interpretive information about the Oregon Trail as well as later logging operations steers hikers through a history of the area.

Emigrant Springs, 26 miles southeast of Pendleton off Interstate 84. This park lies close enough to the interstate to absorb much of its noise, yet it retains a sense of quiet intrigue because wagon trains camped on this same site and filled their water barrels from its spring. At this point the emigrants were probably two days into their three-day trip across what emigrant Maria Parsons Belshaw called "such hills as never were viewed by us poor mortals before."

La Grande Walking Tour (1-800-848-9969). After struggling along the Burnt and Power Rivers to the south, many Oregon Trail emigrants were overjoyed to find a change of scenery. "They urged their toilsome way among the hills, half famished and faint at heart," one pioneer wrote of his wagon train, "when they came to where a fair valley spread out before them." That fair valley was the Grande Ronde, and its first settlement would eventually become its most important city. "We should pull together," the local newspaper said in 1904 when La Grande won the county seat, "and then and only then will La Grande grow as it should and become the leading town in Eastern Oregon." Much of that spirit, as well as many of the buildings, are the same now as they were then, especially in the downtown core.

Hot Lake Resort, 8 miles southeast of La Grande off Highway 203. Used for centuries by native tribes, fur trappers, and Oregon Trail pioneers, Hot Lake is Oregon's largest, and possibly hottest, hot spring, with 2.5 million gallons of 205-degree water feeding the 8-acre lake every day. (In comparison, your water heater is probably set at 120 to 160 degrees.) In 1864 a resort hotel was built near the lakeshore, and in 1900 a larger hotel replaced it. Then with the 1906 addition of a luxury spa, people began flocking to the resort for the curative powers of its hot baths, and by the 1920s Hot Lake was known as the "Mayo Clinic of the West." Before a 1934 fire destroyed most of it, the resort at its peak employed 175 people and served more than 2,000 meals per day. Today the abandoned building, which is said to be haunted, is looking for a new owner to restore it to its glory days.

Elgin Opera House, 104 N. Eighth Street, Elgin. This two-story Colonial-style brick building was built in 1912 as a combination city office and theater, a role it served until recently when a new city hall was built next door, and a regional museum moved in to take its place. Today the opera house still draws audiences to see movies, plays, and other performances. One of the building's most interesting features, however, remains backstage, where there hangs a 1912 canvas backdrop containing the signatures of more than 200 people who performed here from 1914 to 1992.

Whitman Overlook, 17 miles northwest of La Grande off Interstate 84 (exit 248) and Forest Road 31. In 1836 when Marcus and Narcissa Whitman traveled 3,000 miles from their home in New York to establish a mission among the Cayuse Indians in the Oregon Country, they reached the toughest part of their journey just miles from its end—the Blue Mountains. The first people ever to cross the continent in a wagon, the husband and wife missionaries found crossing the mountains to be a difficult challenge. "Before noon we began to descend one of the most terrible mountains for steepness and length I have yet seen," Narcissa wrote in her diary. "It was like winding stairs in its descent and in some places almost perpendicular." Yet Narcissa, pregnant and riding sidesaddle, still found beauty in these mountains. "Indeed," she wrote, "I do not know as I was ever so affected with any scenery in my life." From this viewpoint and its half-mile trail you can look out at the mountain slopes and valleys the Whitmans crossed—and you'll understand why later wagons took a different route.

Meacham, 24 miles northwest of La Grande off Interstate 84 exit 238. Because it was such a job getting over the Blue Mountains on the old Oregon Trail, a fellow named Lee in 1844 established "Lee's Encampment" near the midway point in a clearing that offered grass, water, and firewood. When gold was discovered on the eastern slopes of the mountains, Harvey and Alfred Meacham bought the place, built a stage stop, and provided meals and beds and even hay—at 10 cents a pound—to the miners passing through. The town grew to include some 500 people by the turn of the 20th century, and even President Warren Harding stopped by in 1923 to mark the 80th anniversary of the beginning of the Great Migration.

FOR FAMILIES **Drive-In Movies.** Following World War II, growing families seeking entertainment that included the kids found what they were looking for at the drive-in movie. At the height of the drive-in's popularity in the 1950s, 5,000 of them were strung across the country, including 70 in Oregon; now, only 500 are still doing business nationally, only 5 in the state. Today much of the technology remains in the 1950s, lacking the digital sound and sophisticated screens of the multiplex. Yet for some people, the drive-in remains the ultimate movie experience.

La Grande Drive-In (541-963-3866), 20th Street near Bi-Mart, La Grande. Family-owned and-operated since the 1950s, the La Grande Drive-In plays first-run movies, charges just $11 per carload, and gives you a view of the Blue Mountains while you're waiting for the show to begin.

U.S. FOREST SERVICE CABIN RENTALS Instead of demolishing the abandoned fire lookouts, guard stations, and work-camp cabins that once stood scattered across the national forests as temporary living quarters for rangers and crews, the U.S. Forest Service has opened them to the public. Most are available year-round—accessible by car in summer and by skis, snowshoes, or snowmobile in winter—and are available on a first-come, first-served basis.

Moss Springs Guard Station (La Grande Ranger District; 541-963-7186), 6 miles east of Cove on Forest Road 6220. Built in 1927, this guard station sat unused for almost two decades before the U.S. Forest Service restored it and opened it to the public. The small cabin offers accommodations that would be considered downright plush by the rangers who once stayed here: a propane-powered heater and refrigerator, a queen-sized couch-bed, and even a new outhouse just 20 steps from the door.

Two Color Guard Station (La Grande Ranger District; 541-963-7186), 30 miles southeast of Union off Highway 203 and Forest Roads 77 and 7755. This cabin, which sleeps as many as 12, stands in wild country, almost a mile high on the edge of the Eagle Cap Wilderness and along the designated Wild and Scenic segment of Catherine Creek.

SCENIC DRIVES **Emigrant Hill Road,** 36 paved miles from Interstate 84's exit 248 north of La Grande to Mission, north of Pendleton. Ignored by many maps and bypassed by most motorists, Emigrant Hill Road bends and climbs and dips its way along what a 1923 travel guide calls "one of the finest scenic roads in Oregon." For three dozen miles this byway follows where the wheels of wagon trains and steam locomotives once rolled, edging along forests and cutting across hillsides, passing old stagecoach stops and emigrant campsites before slanting down to Pendleton. In more modern times it was a segment of Highway 30, once the region's major east–west road.

Grande Ronde Valley, 77 paved and graveled miles around the Grande Ronde Valley. Suggested route: Beginning at La Grande, southwest to Union on Foothill Road and Highway 203; north to Elgin on Highway 237, Lower Cove Road, Gray's Corner Road, Rhinehart Lane, and Clark Creek Road; southwest to La Grande on Highway 204, Summerville Road, Hunter Lane, and Highway 82.

The great circle. A valley nestled below the cloud-crowded peaks of rumple-sloped mountains. Here the world shines golden or green with the change of the seasons, swirls with the furrows of fields and with the wheels and water of sprinkler lines glinting from the stubble. So special is this valley cut by the wriggling flow of the Grande Ronde River that its first inhabitants—the Umatilla, Cayuse, Walla Walla, and Nez Perce peoples—shared it as a place to hunt, fish, and gather; so beautiful is it that the weary-footed pioneers of the Oregon Trail, with 1,700 miles of the West lying behind them, described the valley as "a perfect gem—an oasis in a desert" and "one of the loveliest valleys the eye ever rested upon." And today, for the people who live and visit here, the feeling is much the same. This valley loop—bounded by Union to the south, Cove to the east, Elgin to the north, and La Grande to the west—shows you why.
Hells Canyon Scenic Byway, 208 paved miles along Highway 82, Forest Road 39, and Highway 86 from La Grande to Baker City—the long way around. One of three **All-American Roads** in Oregon and one of 15 in the nation, the Hells Canyon Scenic Byway leads travelers through some of the most beautiful scenery in the country: the valleys and fields of the Grande Ronde, Wallowa, and Powder Rivers; the ridges and slopes of the Blue, Wallowa, and Elkhorn Mountains; the rimrocks and canyons of the Minam, Snake, and Imnaha drainages. It's a land tough enough to show the scars of grinding glaciers and raging wildfires, gentle enough to sprout wildflowers—and the road shows you both aspects.

NATURAL WONDERS **Blue Mountains,** between Prineville to the west and Hells Canyon to the east, perhaps best viewed from either the Grande Ronde or Powder River Valley. Hard to believe, but these rolling Blue Mountains—which geologically include the Ochoco, Strawberry, Elkhorn, and Wallowa ranges—were once part of a tropical sea's shoreline. "Before the Blue Mountains there was no Oregon," writes Oregon geologist Ellen Bishop, "and ocean waves broke on Idaho beaches." But then when an island system that later became the Blue Mountains joined North America about 100 million years ago, it became part of the continent's western coastline.

✷ To Do

BICYCLING **Spring Creek,** 15 miles west of La Grande off Interstate 84 (exit 248) and Forest Road 21. Logging roads in this forested area, which is home to a thriving population of **great gray owls,** provide two relatively flat loop rides. The beginning point for each is the intersection of Forest Roads 21 and 2155, located approximately 3 miles from exit 248 on Interstate 84. From here, a 5-mile loop begins on your right, a 7-mile loop on your left. These loops lead toward the Grande Ronde River, owl nesting platforms, elk calving areas, bat ponds, signs of 19th-century logging operations, an aspen generation project, and some old-growth ponderosa pines. (See also *Wilder Places—Wildlife Refuges.*)

CAMPING **Grande Ronde River Campgrounds,** southwest of La Grande off Highway 244 and Forest Road 51. The Nez Perce who lived here called it *Welleweah:* "River that

Flows into the Far Beyond." Local legend has it that writer and outdoorsman Zane Grey loved this river so much that when he wrote about it, he never used its name—Grande Ronde. With its headwaters flowing from the snowpacks of the Elkhorn Mountains, this stream winds its way almost 200 miles through forest and canyons until it reaches the Snake River. And the campgrounds lining its upper stretches give you a chance to sleep beside this river that still flows into the far beyond: **Bird Track Springs** (see *Wilder Places—Wildlife Refuges*), 13 miles southwest of La Grande off Interstate 84 (exit 252) and Highway 244, 10 campsites, rest rooms, water, and a nature trail popular with birdwatchers; **Hilgard Junction State Park,** 9 miles west of La Grande off Interstate 84, 18 sites along the Grande Ronde River with nearby water and rest rooms as well as historical information about this former campground along the Oregon Trail; **Red Bridge State Park,** 16 miles southwest of La Grande off Highway 244, 5 sites and a rest room along a good stretch of trout water; **River,** 32 miles southwest of La Grande off Interstate 84, Highway 244, and Forest Road 51, 6 campsites; **Spool Cart,** 27 miles southwest of La Grande off Interstate 84, Highway 244, and Forest Road 51, 16 campsites.

Eagle Cap Wilderness Campgrounds, south of Cove or Union. **Boulder Park,** 38 miles southeast of Union off Highway 203 and Forest Roads 77 and 7755, 11 campsites near Eagle Creek; **Moss Springs,** 10 miles east of Cove off Forest Road 6220, 11 mile-high campsites at the end of a steep gravel road; **North Fork Catherine Creek,** 15 miles southeast of Union off Highway 203 and Forest Road 7785, 6 campsites near the creek; **Two Color,** 29 miles southeast of Union off Highway 203 and Forest Roads 77 and 7755, 14 campsites near Eagle Creek; **West Eagle Meadow,** 26 miles southeast of Union off Highway 203 and Forest Road 77, 22 total sites, including walk-in and horse camps on West Eagle Creek. (See also *Wilder Places—Wilderness Areas*.)

Umatilla National Forest: Headquarters (541-278-3716), 2517 S. W. Hailey Avenue, Pendleton 97801. **Umatilla Forks,** 33 miles east of Pendleton off Cayuse Road and Forest Road 32, 15 sites located near the edge of the North Fork Umatilla Wilderness; **Target Meadows,** 2 miles north of Tollgate off Forest Roads 64 and 6401, 20 campsites on the edge of a large meadow; **Woodward,** 18 miles east of Weston off Highway 204, 18 campsites near the highway. **Woodland,** 23 miles east of Weston off Highway 204, 7 campsites near the highway; **Jubilee Lake,** 12 miles northeast of Tollgate off Forest Road 64, 50 campsites near the lake that permits electric motors only and is circled by a hiking trail; **Mottet,** 14 miles northeast of Tollgate off Forest Roads 64 and 6403, 7 campsites near the breaks of the South Fork Wenaha River.

CANOEING **Morgan Lake,** 3 miles southwest of La Grande off Morgan Lake Road. This is a city-owned reservoir that began its second century of life in 2001. (And long before that, its hilltop lay along the route of the Oregon Trail.) Except during the height of fishing season, when folks like to hunker with their rods along the shoreline, the lake is a quiet place to launch a canoe or raft.

Jubilee Lake, 12 miles northeast of Tollgate off Forest Road 64. If you avoid the weekends when crowds of fishermen congregate here, you'll find this forest- and wetland-lined lake to be a place of placid waters where the rings of rising trout ripple the surface.

GOLF **Buffalo Peak Golf Course** (541-562-9031), 1224 E. Fulton Street, Union, 18 holes.

La Grande Country Club (541-963-4241), 10605 S. McAlister Road, Island City, 9 holes.

HIKING **Catherine Creek,** 14 miles southeast of Union off Highway 203. Through the shade of pine trees runs this 1.5-mile loop trail, leading hikers past panoramic mountain views—as well as deer and grouse—on its way to the top of a small mountain rising near the park's southern boundary. Because this trail is so new, however, it appears on few maps; but you'll find it by crossing the creek on the park's west bridge.

Jubilee Lake National Recreation Trail, 12 miles northeast of Tollgate off Forest Road 64. Circling this quiet mountain lake is a hiking trail that bends its way for 2.7 miles around the shoreline and its adjacent wetlands and forest. The farther you travel this path and the farther you leave the campground behind, the more you'll feel you have the place to yourself.

See also *Wilder Places—Parks* and *Wilderness Areas.*

SWIMMING **Cove Hot Springs Pool** (541-568-4890), Highway 237, Cove. Open daily from May through Labor Day.

UNIQUE ADVENTURES **Geographical Center of the United States,** 12 miles southeast of Union on Highway 203. Now don't get too excited about this—you'll feel nary a tingle nor a shiver when you get here—but ever since Alaska and Hawaii joined the union in 1959, America's geographical center shifted from Kansas to a spot near where Highway 203 crosses Catherine Creek. Even though the exact point is approximately 9 miles northeast of here as the crow flies, this is probably close enough for most folks who want to tell their friends they stood smack-dab in the middle of the United States.

* Wilder Places

PARKS **La Grande City Parks.** Because this is a community that loves trees and lawns and flowerbeds, 65 acres of parks lie inside the city limits and more than 216 acres outside. **Gangloff Park,** for instance, greets travelers entering town from the west on Interstate 84. This 2.5-acre site offers an aerial view of the city as well as a historic log cabin and a nature trail that leads through native grasses and wildflowers from the pre-settlement era of the valley. A different kind of landscape, however, grows down the hill and across the river at the corner of Spruce Street and Fruitdale Lane, where **Riverside Park** contains more than 12 acres of lawn and riverbank as well as an Oriental garden. On the other side of town, **Birnie Park,** located on the corner of B Avenue and Gekeler Street, now occupies a site that once served as an Oregon Trail campground. As a result, a walking path bends its way past works of art and an interpretive site that honor the memory of the wagon trains and the trail's westward trekkers. And if you were to follow that trail into the hills above town, you'd soon find yourself at **Morgan Lake,** more than 240 acres that include woods, trails, and a pond.

Minam State Park, 13 miles northwest of Wallowa off Highway 82, day use and overnight. Just downriver from the confluence of the Wallowa and Minam Rivers, this park's campground and picnic area occupy a flat, grassy bench where a slope of pine tapers off toward the river. Highlights include a nearby swimming hole and a stretch of trout water.

Catherine Creek State Park, 8 miles southeast of Union off Highway 203, day use and overnight. Here beside this mountain creek that flows through a forest near the edge of a wilderness, even the nearby road is quiet, easing its few cars on their gently winding way toward towns that used to be, such as Medical Springs and Pondosa. An arched bridge connects the campground and picnic area with a hiking trail, and in between runs a stream almost begging for the giggling splash of wading kids.

Emigrant Springs State Park, 26 miles southeast of Pendleton off Interstate 84, day use and overnight. If you could arrange the eras to assemble the people who have visited this campground near the summit of this Blue Mountain pass, your guests would arrive on Cayuse ponies and in fur brigades, by wagon trains and freight wagons, in Model Ts and SUVs. Today, however, is certainly the most comfortable time to visit, with the park offering electric hookups and flush toilets. Nevertheless, if you find yourself hankering for the good old days, you can still spend the night in a covered wagon, available by reservation.

WILDERNESS AREAS **Eagle Cap,** between La Grande, Halfway, and Joseph, 541 square miles. The largest wilderness area in the state, Eagle Cap is bigger than two of Oregon's counties—Hood River and Multnomah—and contains approximately 500 miles of trails that wander beneath granite peaks and ridges, past more than 70 alpine lakes and numerous meadows, and through U-shaped valleys carved by glaciers.

North Fork Umatilla, 30 miles east of Pendleton off Interstate 84 and County Road 900, or 1 mile south of Tollgate off Highway 205 and Forest Roads 3715 or 3719, 31 square miles. This segment of the Blue Mountains swaps alpine peaks for timbered canyons, bunchgrass-covered plateaus, and small streams pristine enough to hold **native trout** and **steelhead.** A breeding, calving, and rearing area for **elk** as well as a winter range for **deer,** the wilderness has 27 miles of trails divided into eight spurs, all of them climbing steep ground whose elevations range from 2,000 to 6,000 feet.

WILDLIFE REFUGES **Bird Track Springs Wildlife Area,** 15 miles west of La Grande off Interstate 84 (exit 252) and Highway 244. This floodplain of the Grande Ronde River, where springs and ponds and forests mingle, is a popular **bird-watching area,** especially during the late spring and early summer. Sprouting cottonwoods and willows, hawthorn and alder, meadow grass and giant pines—the place's hold on nature lovers is so strong they built a campground here (see *To Do—Camping*) so you can stay a spell. When it comes time for exploring, you'll find a riverside loop trail that crosses footbridges and leads to viewing platforms.

LADD MARSH

Ladd Marsh, 6 miles southeast of La Grande between Foothill Drive and Highway 203 (exit 265 or 268 on Interstate 84). The 3,000 acres of this wildlife area contains most of what's left—approximately one-tenth—of the Grande Ronde Valley's original wetlands that settlers began draining and converting to farm fields in the 1860s. Today it's home to the largest native tule marsh in the region as well as to populations of **deer, elk, songbirds, raptors,** and **waterfowl.** Although access to the refuge is limited except during hunting seasons, its perimeter presents good viewing opportunities, including an **observation and photo blind** near Highway 203 and a viewpoint and nature trail near Foothill Road.

Spring Creek, 15 miles west of La Grande off Interstate 84 (exit 248) and Forest Road 21. This area is notable for what is perhaps the densest population of **great gray owls** in the world. With one exception, the owls have nested here every year since their discovery in the early 1980s, reaching numbers of at least eight pairs per 4 square miles. The area's open stands of pine provide the owls with hunting areas while dense stands of fir—supplemented with artificial platforms—offer protection for nesting. The best time to spot the owls is between mid-May and early June, when the young are leaving their nests. A good way to explore the area is by bicycle (see also *To Do—Bicycling*).

Starkey Elk Project (541-963-7122), 28 miles southwest of La Grande off Highway 244. This project is the only one like it in the world: a 25,000-acre experimental forest designed to study how elk respond to human activities in general, and to the management of forests and rangelands in particular. To accomplish this, an 8-foot-high fence of woven wire surrounds the 40-square-mile plot so elk can't get out, but people can come in. So if you should hike, bike, or camp here, you not only have a chance of seeing elk but also of becoming part of the experiment.

✳ Lodging

See also **U.S. Forest Service Cabin Rentals** under *To Do—For Families.*

HOTELS **Historic Union Hotel** (541-562-6135; info@theunionhotel.com; www.theunionhotelcom), 326 N. Main Street, Union 97883. When it first opened in 1921, the Union Hotel was widely considered the best hotel between Portland and Boise. Situated near downtown Union along Highway 30—then advertised as "the finest and most scenic highway and the only all year route to the Pacific Coast"—the hotel offered travelers 76 guest rooms with private baths. But through the years, the Great Depression and a new interstate carried away enough business that the hotel fell on hard times until being rescued in 1996. Now restored to its former elegance, the hotel today has 13 guest rooms, all with private bathrooms but, like the 1920s, none with telephones or televisions ($39–89). In addition, a **restaurant** sits next to the hotel's lobby.

BED & BREAKFASTS **Pinewood Bed & Breakfast** (1-888-731-8889; stay@pinewoodbb.com; www.pinewoodbb.com), 72333 Darr Road, Elgin 97827. Among the pine trees on the outskirts of Elgin stands this small B&B with a big reputation. "We may be the smallest—some tell us 'the best'—destination resort in Oregon," says owner Anndell Thompson. "Our forte is total seclusion and tranquillity in the forest." That seclusion is the result of the B&B's booking only one party at a time, Anndell says. "This gives our guests complete privacy on the ground level of our log home." The two-bedroom suite includes an outside entrance, a patio with hot tub, a kitchenette, and a bathroom with a spa ($85). And then comes breakfast (included in the rates). "I bake all of my own breads, rolls, scones, and muffins," Anndell says. "Fresh fruit with a white chocolate sauce is a favorite. Also soufflés, quiches, sourdough Belgian waffles, and home-smoked ham and bacon fill the menu." She'll even serve you breakfast in bed.

Stang Manor Bed & Breakfast (1-888-286-9463; innkeeper@stangmanor.com; www.stangmanor.com), 1612 Walnut Street, La Grande 97850. Surrounded by an acre of lawn and roses and once owned by a local timber baron, this restored 1923 Georgian Colonial inn is listed on both the **National and State Historic Registers.** Its four guest rooms come with private baths and a full breakfast ($85–98). Children older than 9 are welcome.

Tamarack Inn Bed & Breakfast (1-800-662-9348; innkeeper@tamarackinnbb.com; www.tamarackinnbb.com), 62388 Highway 204, Weston 97886 (19 miles east of Weston off Highway 204, in Tollgate). An A-frame lodge built originally as a restaurant, the Tamarack Inn now provides guests with a home away from home near the summit of the Blue Mountains. "We pride ourselves on being friendly, helpful, and flexible," says owner Wally Quast. "Our best advertising comes from good word-of-mouth comments from past guests." Many of those guests seem to have been just as impressed with what they discover on the *outside* of the inn as what they find on the inside. "We're located deep in 'the piney woods,'" Wally says. "Deer are often seen around the inn, and bears and elk are often seen within a quarter mile of us." The outdoor attractions may be even more appealing in winter, especially for those involved in snow sports. "We're located at the center of 250 miles of groomed snowmobile trails," Wally says, "and the snowmobiling here is great. Within a few miles is the Spout Springs ski area, a downhill ski resort with several lifts and tows. And close to Spout Springs is the Horseshoe Prairie cross-country ski area." The inn's four guest rooms all have king or queen beds, and two have private bathrooms ($70–120). A full breakfast served family style is included. "My wife, Sharon, is the head cook," Wally says, "and her breakfasts are quickly becoming famous here on the mountain." Children are welcome and small pets can be accommodated with advance arrangements.

✷ Where to Eat

DINING OUT **Foley Station** (541-963-7443), 1011 Adams Avenue, La Grande. When chef Merlyn Baker made the 1997 move from the prestigious Jake's in Portland to Foley Station in La Grande, he brought to his new restaurant some of the polish of the big city and mixed it with foods produced locally. The result is a dining experience and menu selection unique to the region, a blend of Northwest food and metropolitan elegance.

EATING OUT **Jefferson Street Depot** (541-963-3292), 1118 Jefferson Avenue, La Grande. It can sometimes seem thick with cigarette smoke and gaudy with video poker machines, but Jefferson Street Depot still serves up some of the best German food you'll find this side of Heidelberg. So if a dinner of bread and bratwurst with sauerkraut and potatoes is your idea of a culinary delight, then find a seat and ask for the menu.

Mamacita's (541-963-6223), 110 Depot Street, La Grande. Known for its casual atmosphere, friendly service, and original Mexican food, Mamacita's is something of a tradition in the La Grande area. In fact, owner Sandy Sorrels runs a weekly feature in the local newspaper, announcing the latest specials and revealing the house recipes.

Ten Depot Street (541-963-8766), 10 Depot Street, La Grande. You can't be in a hurry when dining at Ten Depot—nor do you want to be. The atmosphere of this old brick building with its antique furnishings can be as warm and comfortable as an old coat, inviting diners to stay a while longer, to order one more pint of beer or glass of wine before the blue plate special finally arrives.

✷ Special Events

June–July: **Regional Rodeos** (1-800-332-1843). **Eastern Oregon Livestock Show,** June, Union. **Elgin Stampede,** July, Elgin.

August: **Oregon Trail Days Pioneer Celebration** (1-800-848-9969), La Grande. The old Oregon Trail still runs through La Grande—it's buried beneath the pavement on B Avenue—and a summertime reminder of those wagon-train days happens at this pioneer encampment featuring fiddling and dancing, buffalo barbecuing, and Dutch-oven cooking. The biggest event of the weekend is probably the old-time fiddle contest, which draws fiddle fans from throughout the Northwest.

WALLOWA VALLEY–SNAKE RIVER AREA

GUIDANCE **Oregon State Parks: Headquarters** (503-378-6305), State Parks and Recreation Department, 525 Trade Street S. E., Salem 97301.

Wallowa County Chamber of Commerce (1-800-585-4121; wallowa@eoni.com; www.wallowacountychamber.com), 936 W. North Street, Enterprise 97828.

Wallowa-Whitman National Forest: Headquarters (541-523-6391), 1550 Dewey Avenue, Baker City 97814; **Wallowa Mountains Visitors Center** (541-426-5546).

GETTING THERE The Wallowa Valley–Snake River area is reached from the north by Highway 3, from the south by Forest Road 39 and its connection with Highway 86, and from the west by Highway 82.

MEDICAL EMERGENCY **Wallowa Memorial Hospital** (541-426-3111), 401 N. E. 1st Street, Enterprise.

* To See

MUSEUMS **Wallowa County Museum** (541-432-6095), 110 S. Main Street, Joseph. Because the first settlers didn't arrive in the Wallowa Valley until more than a decade after Oregon became a state, the memory and the heritage of the pioneers still pack a wallop around here. As a result, the county museum is a storehouse of photographs and artifacts that capture a way of life that seems to have happened not very many yesterdays ago.

HISTORIC SITES **M. Crow & Co.** (541-569-2285), Highway 82, Lostine. Open the squeaky screen door and step inside M. Crow & Co., and the next feeling you'll have is of passing through a time warp. For spread out along the walls and shelves are the posters and paraphernalia and knickknacks of earlier eras, including advertisements for products no longer made at prices no longer believable. But because Crow's is a working store in the grand tradition of the old mercantiles, selling everything from bolts to bread and socks to sausage, you can stock up for a picnic as you wander the aisles of this 1880s building.

Wallowa County Courthouse, 101 S. River Street, Enterprise. It was a happy day when the county courthouse opened for business in the spring of 1910. The county sheriff, according to the local newspaper, "appeared on the scene . . . beaming like a 60-candle incandescent light and almost happy enough to sing." The feeling was typical in the county seat of Enterprise, for its citizens saw the brand-new building made of local stone as a symbol of the town's promising future. "The building itself, showing in concrete form the progressive spirit of Wallowa County," the local paper reported, "will be one of the biggest advertisements Enterprise and Wallowa County could have." Even though the years have worn away at the building's grandeur, and an expanded government has squeezed its space, recent plans for its restoration ensure its future.

Chief Joseph Cemetery Historical Monument, 1 mile south of Joseph off Highway 82. According to Young Chief Joseph, leader of the Wallowa Band of Nez Perce during the years of conflict and war that began in the 1870s, the dying words of his father warned of trouble to come. "White men . . . have their eyes on this land," Old Chief Joseph told his son. "This country holds your father's body. Never sell the bones of your father and your mother." Yet the bones of the old Nez Perce chief faced a difficult journey before they found a final resting place near the foot of Wallowa Lake. In the years following the 1871 burial of Old Joseph at the traditional Nez Perce summer camp near the forks of the Wallowa and Lostine Rivers, white men robbed the grave twice; the second time, in 1886, a dentist from Baker City stole Old Joseph's skull. "He took the skull down to the river . . . built a fire and boiled it clean," writes local historian Grace Bartlett. "He kept this skull in his office in Baker, marked 'Joseph's Skull,' for many years." In the fall of 1926, the headless body of Old Joseph was exhumed and then reburied at its present site in a ceremony that drew a crowd the local newspaper estimated at 4,500 people. "Arriving at the monument, the Indians formed around the stone memorial," reported the *Enterprise Record Chieftain.* "As they came up the hill they wailed the accents of a dirge perhaps familiar only to the old men and reminiscent of the days of their old free life."

Nez Perce National Historical Park. It's a national park without cabins or campgrounds, rest rooms or picnic tables; you can't rent a boat or hire a guide—but you can see some of the land the Nez Perce called home at the 38 sites of the Nez Perce National Historical Park. Four of these sites that pertain specifically to the Wallowa Band Nez Perce are located in or near the Wallowa Valley:

Traditional Homesite, 2 miles south of Wallowa off Highway 82, near the confluence of the Wallowa and Lostine Rivers, the traditional summer camping site of the Wallowa Band. If you're willing to do some bushwhacking and stream wading, the best approach is to hike upstream from the Spring Branch Wildlife Area (see *Wilder Places—Wildlife Refuges)* to the rivers' confluence; other access is across private land, and you might have to settle for a distant view from Baker Road.

Joseph Canyon Viewpoint, 30 miles north of Enterprise off Highway 3, overlooks the Nez Perce's winter home, where Young Chief Joseph was reputedly born.

Old Chief Joseph's Grave, 1 mile south of Joseph off Highway 82, a traditional burial place of the Nez Perce and the final resting place of Old Chief Joseph, revered head man of the Wallowa Band and father of Young Chief Joseph.

Dug Bar, 27 miles north of Imnaha on the Imnaha River Road. Dug Bar is the traditional Snake River crossing, which marked the Nez Perce's 1877 passage from their homeland to the battlefield.

Hells Canyon Sites, north and west of Imnaha along the Snake River. For thousands of years the Nez Perce made their winter homes along the Snake River here in the deepest gorge in North America. Through the years the canyon's rugged terrain bewildered explorers, lured miners, wore out homesteaders, and frustrated cattlemen and sheepmen. Nevertheless, by 1910 more than 100 families lived in the canyon along the Snake River. Within eight years, however, more than 95 percent of them had abandoned their homes. "The government bet you 160 acres," said one homesteader, "that you couldn't live there three years without starving to death." Strung along the river today are reminders of the canyon's earlier days.

Eureka Bar, 4 miles downstream from Dug Bar, accessible either by foot along the **Imnaha River Trail**—located 15 miles north of Imnaha off the Imnaha River Road—or by boat along the Snake River. When copper ore was discovered near here in 1898, this gravel bar located near the confluence of the Imnaha and Snake Rivers began drawing lots of attention. Crews of the Eureka Mining Company began digging tunnels and building roads, and before long a town started taking shape. "Eureka has been selected as the name of the new town," the Wallowa County chieftain reported in 1903, "which ought to become a place of considerable importance in the near future." Yet the mine was too isolated and its deposits too small for the town to last, and it closed in 1906. What's left today is one of its mining tunnels, the cellar of its hotel, and the terraced foundations of the stamp mill.

Nez Perce Crossing, near Dug Bar, on the Imnaha River Road, 27 miles north of Imnaha;, accessible by car, high-clearance vehicles recommended. After a treaty they never signed took away their homeland, the struggle of the Nez Perce to stay in the Wallowa country came to an end in the spring of 1877 when U.S. Army General O. O. Howard gave them 30 days to move to the Lapwai Reservation in Idaho, which would force the Nez Perce to cross the Snake River during the spring runoff. "Why are you in such a hurry?" asked Joseph, the leader of the Wallowa Band. "Our stock is scattered and the Snake River is very high. Let us wait till fall, then the river will be low." But Howard was firm. "If you let the time run over one day, he said, "the soldiers will be there to drive you on the reservation." So the Nez Perce rounded up their stock, packed their belongings, and crossed the Snake River during the spring flood—and soon after reaching the other side, they found themselves fighting a war that changed their lives forever.

Chinese Massacre Site, 4 miles upstream from Dug Bar (see Nez Perce National Historical Park) on the Snake River, accessible by boat. It was here on a day in May 1887 that a gang of seven horse thieves rode into a camp of Chinese miners and murdered as many as 31 of them. "The most cold-blooded, cowardly

MOUNT HOWARD TRAMWAY

treachery I have ever heard tell of on this coast," said J. K. Vincent, who investigated the murders. "Every [victim] was shot, cut up, and stripped and thrown in the river." Risking his life to work undercover, Vincent gathered enough evidence to bring the seven to trial for murder, but a Wallowa County jury quickly found them "not guilty" of the deed.

Kirkwood Historic Ranch, 24 miles upstream from Dug Bar (see Nez Perce National Historical Park) accessible either by foot on the **Snake River National Recreation Trail** or by boat. Most homesteaders found Hells Canyon to be a land of too many *toos*—too much isolation and loneliness, too few roads and neighbors, too little rain and grass. As a result, virtually nobody lives here anymore. That's why the Kirkwood Ranch preserves some of the homesteading chapters in the canyon's story by displaying settlers' cabins and houses, barns and corrals, lambing sheds and shearing pens.

SIGHTSEEING TOURS **Jet-boat Rides** (Hells Canyon National Recreation Area Snake River Office; 509-758-0616), Snake River. If you're looking for a tour of Hells Canyon without the heat, the steep, or the strain of a long hike, then a jet boat tour might be your passageway to adventure. Planing across the flat stretches and thumping through the whitewater, these boats can give you a daylong glimpse at the canyon's river, wildlife, and history from the comfort of a padded seat. Virtually all outfitters operate from the downstream cities of Lewiston, Idaho, or Clarkston, Washington.

Mount Howard Tramway (541-432-5331; www.wallowalaketramway.com), Wallowa Lake State Park, 6 miles south of Joseph on Highway 82. Exploring the wilderness doesn't have to result in foot blisters or saddle sores—not when you can ride the Wallowa Lake tramway to the top of 8,000-foot Mount Howard and the edge of the Eagle Cap Wilderness (see *Wilder Places—Wilderness Areas*). Even though this is the steepest and longest tram in North America, it carries passengers to the mountaintop in about 15 minutes, unloading them at the **Summit Grill** and near a network of mountain trails that leads to top-of-the-world views.

SCENIC DRIVES **Imnaha River Loop,** 90 paved and graveled miles along Forest Road 39, Upper Imnaha River Road, and Highway 350, beginning and ending at Joseph. This loop contains a trinity of symmetry, a trio of 30s: the first 30 miles (paved) east and south from Joseph along Forest Road 39 to the Imnaha River, the middle 30 miles (graveled) north along the Imnaha River Road (Forest Road 3955) to the town of Imnaha, and the final 30 miles (paved) southwest along the Little Sheep Creek Highway and back to Joseph. When put together, this three-part journey climbs toward ridgelines and dips into forests, edges along salmon streams and drops into canyons, and wanders into Imnaha and pauses at the **Store and Tavern,** where the hamburgers are grilled and the beer is cold.

Wallowa Mountain Loop Road, 72 paved miles along Forest Road 39 from Joseph to Halfway. Part of the **Hells Canyon Scenic Byway** (see below), this road is often shown on maps as the Wallowa Mountain Loop and known by locals as the Loop Road. (*Loop* derives from the fact that once travelers reach

IMNAHA RIVER CANYON

Halfway, they can following Highway 86 back to Baker City, and then Interstate 84 and Highway 82 back to the Wallowa Valley.) But no matter what you call it, this stretch of pavement bends its way through some of the most rugged country in the region, skirting the Eagle Cap Wilderness before dropping toward the Snake River.

Imnaha River Canyon, 27 mostly dirt miles from Imnaha to Dug Bar (see Nez Perce National Historical Park), along Forest Road 4260 (Dug Bar Road). Steppe and desert, rims and river, hillsides and ridgetops, wildflowers and sagebrush, prickly pear and Douglas fir—the canyon of the Imnaha River seems to have it all. Containing one of the most diverse landscapes in the country, the canyon serves as home to as many as 350 species of wildlife, and the road, following the river, penetrates the heart of it.

Hat Point Scenic Drive, 24 graveled miles on Hat Point Road (Forest Road 4240) from Imnaha to Hat Point. The site of a fire lookout, Hat Point stands at an elevation of almost 7,000 feet on the edge of Hells Canyon (see *Natural Wonders*), the deepest gorge in North America. Peer over that edge, and you'll see the Snake River more than a mile below, flowing free and running wild, shrugging off the slack water of its upstream dams as it makes its whitewater way toward the Columbia. The drive to reach this point—which follows a steep, single-lane gravel road suitable for passenger cars but *not* for trailers and large RVs—offers views almost as striking, reaching out toward the Imnaha River and the Wallowa Mountains.

Hells Canyon Scenic Byway, 208 paved miles along Highway 82, Forest Road 39, and Highway 86 from La Grande to Baker City—the long way around. One of three **All-American Roads** in Oregon and one of 15 in the nation, the Hells Canyon Scenic Byway leads travelers through some of the most beautiful scenery in the country: the valleys and fields of the Grande Ronde, Wallowa, and Powder Rivers; the ridges and slopes of the Blue, Wallowa, and Elkhorn Mountains; the rimrocks and canyons of the Minam, Snake, and Imnaha drainages. It's a land tough enough to show the scars of grinding glaciers and raging wildfires, gentle enough to sprout wildflowers—and the road shows you both aspects.

NATURAL WONDERS **Wallowa Mountains,** bordered by the Grande Ronde River to the west, the Wallowa River to the north, the Snake River to the east, and the Powder River to the south, perhaps best viewed from the Wallowa Valley. The rocks of the Wallowa Mountains originated as coral reefs that first bordered and eventually covered volcanic South Sea islands. "Some 200 million years ago," writes Oregon geologist Ellen Bishop, "tropical fish swam at Sacajawea Peak." The coral reef became mountains as the result of faults that lifted the land more than 7,000 feet and glaciers that carved the peaks and valleys.

Wallowa Lake, 1 mile south of Joseph along Highway 82. Thousands of years ago when ancient glaciers ground their way out of the Wallowa Mountains and toward the valley below, they scooped out this lake bed and piled the rubble into ridges, or *moraines.* The result is a lake 4 miles long, a mile wide, and almost 300 feet deep—large enough to harbor an ages-old legend of a monster lurking

THE HELLS CANYON OVERLOOK PROVIDES THE MOST EASILY-REACHED VIEWPOINT OF THE DEEPEST GORGE IN NORTH AMERICA

in its depths. With the moraines rising more than 800 feet above the lake's surface, the great gouges of the glaciers reach almost a quarter mile from lake bottom to moraine crest.

Buckhorn Springs, 43 miles northeast of Enterprise off Highway 82, Zumwalt Road, and Forest Roads 46 and 780. How do I see thee? Let me count the ways. I see thee to the depth and breadth and height thy ripple-ridged canyons can reach, when fading from sight the wildflower slopes that plunge seeking the silver waters winding—gosh, apologies to Elizabeth Barrett Browning, but writing sonnets must be a tough business. Describing this land that overlooks the Imnaha River Canyon, however, demands more than the flimsy adjectives usually tossed at it: vast, deep, beautiful, stunning. Sure, it's all those things—but still so much more. Maybe it's as Edna St. Vincent Millay wrote, "Lord, I do fear / Thou'st made the world too beautiful this year." And from high on top of the world at Buckhorn Springs, you'll see what she was talking about.

Hells Canyon, along the Snake River between Oregon and Idaho with best Oregon access downstream from Imnaha. Forget what you might've heard about the Grand Canyon—*this* is the deepest gorge in North America, plunging more than a mile from rim to river in some of its more vertigo-inducing spots. Yet in spite of its heat and sagebrush and its sense of rock-solid permanence, the canyon formed from ancient South Sea volcanoes. Probably the two best viewpoints are at **Hat Point** (24 miles south of Imnaha on Forest Road 4240; see *Scenic Drives)* and at the **Hells Canyon Overlook** (30 miles northeast of Halfway or 43 miles southeast of Joseph off Forest Roads 39 and 3965).

Joseph Canyon, 30 miles north of Enterprise off Highway 3. From the Joseph Canyon Viewpoint off Highway 3, you look across and down at layers of basalt stacked from canyon floor to ridgetop, the walls ragged and buckled with cliffs and crags. The canyon bottom was the winter home of the Wallowa Band Nez Perce, and a combination of legend and history says Chief Joseph was born in one of its caves.

✷ To Do

CAMPING **Lostine River Campgrounds,** south of Lostine off Highway 82 and Lostine River Road. This string of campgrounds lies near a road that stretches 18 miles along the edges of the Eagle Cap Wilderness and the banks of the Lostine River. In order of their location from Lostine they include **Williamson,** 9 sites along as pretty a stretch of river as you've ever seen; **Walla Walla,** 4 campsites at a place local tribes called "Dead Dog," though that's no reflection on either its beauty or character; **Irondyke,** 5 campsites where a miner once worked a nearby iron mine; **Bowman and Frances Lake Trailhead,** 2 campsites used mostly by equestrians heading into the high country; **Turkey Flats,** 5 campsites at a spot that might have been named for some turkeys that escaped just before they were to become the main course at an early-20th-century dinner, but that were then captured near this bend in the river; **Arrow,** 3 campsites and picnic tables near an old Nez Perce hunting area; **Shady,** 12 campsites at a former sheep camp; **Two Pan,** 8 campsites at a location that the road didn't reach until 1955, named for the two frying pans left hanging on a tree by long-ago sheepherders.

Imnaha River Campgrounds, southeast of Joseph off Highway 350 and Forest Roads 39 and 3960. Because the upper stretches of the Imnaha River lie only a few tumbles and splashes away from its headwaters in the Eagle Cap Wilderness, the campgrounds along this segment enjoy a riverside relationship with a wild-flowing stream. Pitch a tent or park a trailer at one of the following sites, and you'll be neighbors with trout water and wilderness trailheads: **Blackhorse,** 16 sites; **Coverdale,** 11 sites; **Evergreen,** 15 sites; **Hidden,** 13 sites; **Indian Crossing,** 14 sites; **Ollokot,** 12 sites.

Wallowa-Whitman National Forest, Wallowa Valley Ranger District (541-426-4978), 88401 Highway 82, Enterprise. Its 3,700 square miles makes the Wallowa-Whitman not only the largest national forest in the Pacific Northwest but also one of the most dramatic in Oregon. After all, this is home to some of the highest mountains (the Blues and Wallowas) and the biggest designated wilderness area (Eagle Cap) in the state, as well as the deepest canyon on the continent (Hells Canyon). The forest's campsites include **Buckhorn,** 43 miles northeast of Enterprise off Highway 82, Zumwalt Road, and Forest Roads 46 and 780, 6 campsites near one of the most scenic overlooks in the Northwest, with views of the Imnaha River Canyon and Idaho's Seven Devils mountains; **Coyote,** 40 miles northeast of Enterprise off Highway 3 and Forest Road 46, 29 campsites near the breaks of Joseph Creek; **Dougherty Springs,** 45 miles northeast of **Enterprise** off Highway 3 and Forest Road 46, 12 campsites near Billy Meadows, the initial home of Oregon's first reintroduced elk herd in 1912; **Lick Creek,** 24 miles southeast of Joseph, 12 campsites along Lick Creek.

HIKING **Imnaha River Trail,** 15 miles north of Imnaha off the Dug Bar Road. A walk along this relatively flat 4-mile trail, which follows the Imnaha River on its way to join the Snake River, is one of the easiest ways to reach the bottom of Hells Canyon (see *To See—Natural Wonders*), the deepest gorge in North America. Sharp-eyed hikers might spot along the bank the ancient tepee pits of the Nez Perce, who for thousands of years used the canyon as a winter home. Be alert to an amazing variety of wildlife, including river otters, and be aware of poison oak and rattlesnakes.

Nee Mee Poo National Recreation Trail, 17 miles north of Imnaha off the Dug Bar Road. This 3.7-mile trail that cuts across the hillsides on its way to the Snake River follows a traditional route the Nez Perce used on their travels through the Imnaha and Snake River country. Perhaps the most historically significant of those travels came in the spring of 1877, when the U.S. Army ordered the Wallowa Band to move to the reservation at Lapwai, Idaho. But soon after crossing the Snake River near the end of this trail, the Nez Perce found themselves fleeing toward Canada in the Nez Perce War of 1877.

See also *Wilder Places—Parks* and *Wilderness Areas.*

HORSEBACK RIDING **Horseback Trips** (Eagle Cap Wilderness Pack Station; 1-800-681-6222), Wallowa Lake, 6 miles south of Joseph on Highway 82. For an hour or a day or somewhere in between, you can sway in time to the creak of saddle leather and the clop of hooves as you ride a trusty—and mostly docile—steed along mountain trails leading into the

THE IMNAHA RIVER TRAIL LEADS TO THE CONFLUENCE OF THE IMNAHA AND SNAKE RIVERS

Eagle Cap Wilderness (see *Wilder Places—Wilderness Areas*). Starting at Wallowa Lake, these guided trips are designed for greenhorns who may not know a gelding from a mare—it's usually important only to the horses, anyway—or their saddle's cantle from its pommel. (When you mount up, just remember the horse's *head* should be in front.)

UNIQUE ADVENTURES **Buffalo Viewing,** Enterprise. To see a herd of buffalo is to move back in time, "to hear water at night and the wind in the trees, to take the mountains and the plains sharp and lasting into [your] mind," as A. B. Guthrie wrote in his novel, *The Big Sky*. And even though these descendants of the great herds that once roamed the continent may lounge in corrals or graze in fenced pastures, their shaggy presence stirs a powerful image of a wilder West. The largest herd in Oregon, approximately 500 buffalo, lives on the 3,000-acre **Stangel Buffalo Ranch** north of Enterprise off Highway 3. Even though the herd is the ranch's cash crop rather than a tourist attraction, the buffalo are usually visible to drivers on the highway, though it's difficult to pinpoint exactly where they'll be. "We have a saying in this business," says owner Bob Stangel, "that you can make a buffalo go anywhere it wants to go."

U.S. FOREST SERVICE CABIN RENTALS Instead of demolishing the abandoned fire lookouts, guard stations, and work-camp cabins that once stood scattered across the national forests as temporary living quarters for rangers and crews, the U.S. Forest Service has opened them to the public. Most are available year-round—accessible by car in summer and by skis, snowshoes, or snowmobile in winter—and are available on a first-come, first-served basis.

Lostine Guard Station (Wallowa Valley Ranger District; 541-426-4978), 12 miles south of Lostine off Highway 82 and Lostine River Road. Because it's used in the summer by forest service volunteers working in the nearby **Eagle Cap Wilderness** (see *Wilder Places—Wilderness Areas*)—the wilderness boundary is just 200 yards from the door—this 1930s-era cabin built by the Civilian Conservation Corps (CCC) is a winter-only destination for cross-country skiers or snowmobilers able to travel the 6 miles of road that the snowplows don't touch.

✷ Wilder Places

PARKS **Wallowa Lake State Park,** 6 miles south of Joseph on Highway 82, day use and overnight. A glacier-carved lake cupped in moraines and reflecting alpine peaks, Wallowa Lake blends rugged topography with natural and human history, and then for good measure tosses in a dose of civilized comfort. The result is one of the nation's most famous parks, a curious blend of wilderness trails and miniature-golf greens.

WILDERNESS AREAS **Eagle Cap,** between La Grande, Halfway, and Joseph, 541 square miles. Although Eagle Cap is the most heavily used wilderness in northeast Oregon, 90 percent of its visitors start at one of three trailheads—Wallowa Lake, Hurricane Creek, and Two Pan—and most camp at just a few lake basins, especially Lakes Basin, leaving most of the remaining wilderness in relative solitude.

Hells Canyon, east of Imnaha off Highway 350 and the Imnaha River Road, 334 square miles with 198 square miles in Oregon. Topped by alpine mountains and cut by a wild river, this canyon that straddles the Oregon–Idaho border has some of the steepest, deepest, toughest country on the continent. Home to **mule deer, bighorn sheep,** and **Rocky Mountain elk,** the canyon is too remote and rugged to offer anything but long, slow drives to trailheads and long hikes into an untamed country.

Wenaha-Tucannon, 28 miles north of Elgin off Highway 204 and Forest Road 62, 277 square miles with 104 square miles in Oregon. Spreading across the Oregon–Washington border, this wilderness area is a land of steep, basaltic canyons and long ridgelines that support the nation's densest population of **Rocky Mountain elk.** Keeping the elk company are **whitetail and mule deer, bighorn sheep, black bears,** and **cougars.** Of its more than 200 miles of trails, the only riverside trailhead in Oregon—the others begin high on the ridge along Forest Road 62—lies near the town of Troy, at the confluence of the Grande Ronde and Wenaha Rivers.

WILDLIFE REFUGES **Enterprise Wildlife Area,** 1 mile west of Enterprise off Highway 82 and Fish Hatchery Road. This is one of those places you could zip right past without giving a sidelong glance—a small corner of the world left alone with its own quiet wildness. Located in the backyard of the Enterprise fish hatchery, this 32-acre site has small streams, dense cover, and a large pond often filled with gabbling duck and squawking geese. In addition, part of the wildlife area borders the Wallowa River, one of the few riverside tracts not privately owned and open to public access. A few local residents come here for quiet strolling or sitting, but mostly its left to the birds.

Spring Branch Wildlife Area, 2 miles southeast of Wallowa off Highway 82. Except for a few steelhead fishermen who venture here for the winter runs, this 8-acre wildlife area receives few visitors. One reason is its obscurity; no signs mark it from the highway, where a gap in the guardrail and a graveled slope leading toward the Wallowa River are the only clues to its entrance (though a sign in the small parking area is assurance you've found the right place). Another reason is its accessibility—or lack of it. Stream-wading and bushwhacking are part of the adventure here, but if you can endure wet feet and tangled ground, you'll find deer trails leading into the shade of towering cottonwoods and beside quiet backwaters.

Wenaha Wildlife Area, near Troy, 48 miles north of Enterprise off Highway 3 and down the Redmond Grade from Flora. In the bottom of this canyon carved by the Grande Ronde River may have been where Noah finally parked his ark. **Bald eagles** and **Canada geese** and **wild turkeys, bighorn sheep** and **Rocky Mountain elk** and **mule deer**—as well as a whole passel of other creatures great and small—hang out here on mountaintops, hillsides, and river bottoms, especially on the 13,000 acres that the state manages as a wildlife area. The journey here, however, is not for the faint of heart when it comes to navigating steep, winding, narrow roads.

✱ Lodging

See also **U.S. Forest Service Cabin Rentals** under *To Do.*

RESORTS **Zeller's Resort** (541-828-7786; www.zellersresort.com), 90219 Troy Road, Enterprise 97828 (a mile upstream from Troy). Located on the sloped bank of the Grande Ronde River, Zeller's Resort is reminiscent of the old fishing camps that tired executives would slink off to for a week or two of fresh air, blissful quiet, tall timber, and feisty trout. Its accommodations include four older and two newer cabins furnished with bunk beds, small refrigerators, microwave ovens, and showers ($50–75). If you don't want to do your own cooking, meals are available at the restaurant a mile away in Troy.

BED & BREAKFASTS

Imnaha

Imnaha River Inn Bed & Breakfast (1-866-601-9214; sandy@imnahariverinn.com; www.imnahariverinn.com), 73946 Rimrock Road, Imnaha 97842. On the edge of land into which few venture stands an inn that seems to glow with the patina of its wood and the intricacies of the craftsmanship that created it. "We did all the work," says Nick Vidan, who, along with his wife, Sandy, owns and operates the 7,000-square-foot, seven-bedroom B&B that doubles as their home. "We even harvested the trees that gave us this wood." Near the stone fireplace and leather furniture, gnarled and polished juniper posts glisten in the sunlight streaming through windows that look out toward the slopes and ridges of the Imnaha River canyon, which lie stacked like a giant layered cake against a blue sky. "Last fall we had 11 bighorn sheep on that hill," Nick says, "and we might see elk on all those ridges." After first visiting the canyon on hunting and fishing trips with his father and "falling in love with the country," Nick decided to find a way to live here. The result is a destination inn that's not far from the end of the road. All rooms share bathrooms ($65–105), a full breakfast is included, and lunch and dinner are available at an extra charge. Children are welcome.

Joseph

Bronze Antler Bed & Breakfast (1-866-520-9769; info@bronzeantler.com; www.bronzeantler.com), 309 S. Main Street, Joseph 97846. Heather Tyreman, innkeeper at the Bronze Antler B&B, poses a remarkable rhetorical question to potential guests: "How often is it," she asks, "that you can travel to a unique, artistically minded community with towering mountain views, the deepest canyon in the United States nearby, a pure, snow-fed glacially formed lake within walking distance, and some of the lushest open grasslands and farms replete with interesting birds and plants?" For Heather and her husband, Bill Finney, the answer lies through the windows of their Joseph home. "Sometimes we have to pinch ourselves that we can actually look out of the dining-room window with Chief Joseph Mountain and the rest of the Wallowas looking back at us," she says. "It's amazing that we actually live here and are pursuing what we desire." That pursuit led Heather and Bill to remodel their 1925 Craftsman bungalow home and then open it to guests. As a result, the home today offers three rooms that come with private baths, a "fantastic" breakfast, and views to write home about. "Once you've stayed with us," Heather says, "you're bound to be drawn back again."

LODGES **Wallowa Lake Lodge** (541-432-9821; info@wallowalake.com; www.wallowalakelodge.com), 60060 Wallowa Lake Highway, Joseph 97846—6 miles south of Joseph off Highway 82. Built in the 1920s when the best way to travel to the head of Wallowa Lake was by passenger boat, the lodge was originally part of a resort area that included an amusement park, a bowling alley, a dance hall, campgrounds, and other trappings of the tourist trade. Today, even though it was renovated beginning in 1988, the lodge retains a sense of its earlier days in its period antiques, furniture, and prints as well as in its lobby, which serves as a communal living room where guests settle into overstuffed chairs in front of a stone fireplace. The lodge offers 22 guest rooms ($65–145) and eight nearby cabins ($95–190), and its restaurant serves breakfast and dinner (not included in rates).

MOTELS AND CABINS **Imnaha Motel** (541-577-3111), Main Street, Imnaha 97842. When the owners say it's quiet here, you can believe them (four rooms, $45).

Shilo Oasis (541-828-7741), 84570 Bartlett Road, Troy 97828. On the main street of Troy stands the one place for miles around that you can find food and lodging while exploring the canyon of the Grande Ronde River—Shilo Oasis, a combination restaurant, motel, and gathering place for anglers, hunters, and rafters as well as for the locals who live in or near this unincorporated town. Accommodations are divided between upstairs rooms in the hotel that share a bathroom and separate cabins ($35–110).

* Where to Eat

EATING OUT

Enterprise

Cloud 9 Bakery (541-426-3790), 105 S. E. First Street, Enterprise. If you can make it past the fresh-baked pastries to save your appetite for lunch, you'll find at Cloud 9 some of the area's best sandwiches and soups as well as some of its friendliest service.

Joseph

Old Town Café (541-432-9898), 8 S. Main Street, Joseph. Its casual atmosphere, friendly service, and darn good food—much of it homemade—make the Old Town Café a favorite among locals and visitors alike. Even when the summertime crowds of travelers thin out in this tourist town, the café is popular enough to continue drawing wait-for-a-table seating at breakfast and lunch.

R & R Drive In (541-432-64020), Imnaha Highway, Joseph. Definitely not just another hamburger joint, the R & R is something of a local secret, a drive-in whose food is distinguished by its quality.

Wildflour Bakery (541-432-7225), 600 N. Main Street, Joseph. Tucked back off the street behind a wildflower garden, the Wildflour Bakery is the local choice for morning-baked bread, fresh-brewed coffee, lively conversation and eavesdropping, and homemade fixings at breakfast and lunch. In fair weather, most patrons prefer to sit outside, near the garden and within sight of the Wallowa Mountains' peaks, which seem to ripple across the sky.

Lostine

Lostine Tavern (541-569-2246), 125 Highway 82, Lostine. Affectionately known as the LT, the Lostine Tavern is a local watering hole, dining spot, and gathering place where you can get the latest news about darn near everything there is to know about Lostine. In fact, nearly everybody in town probably drops by at one time or another, especially during Wednesday's Taco Night, a tradition for more than 20 years. Also popular are Steak Night on Fridays, breakfast on any day, and hamburgers and beer after a hiking, hunting, or fishing trip in the neighboring Wallowa Mountains.

✷ Special Events

June: **Old Time Fiddlers Contest** (541-886-7885), Enterprise. For more than 30 years, fiddlers young and old have gathered annually for this celebration of traditional music. Some of the musicians have been playing since early in the 20th century, while others aren't much bigger than their fiddles, but everyone, professionals excluded, is welcome and encouraged to play. **Oregon Mountain Cruise Car Show** (541-432-2215), Joseph. If you ever find yourself with a 1950s itch to roll up your cuffs, slick down your hair, and cruise down a Saturday-night street with Buddy Holly singing on the radio, then this festival devoted to our automobiling past might be the scratch you need. With more than 200 vintage, restored, and custom cars lining Joseph's main street, this event triggers a sense of nostalgia that can go back as far as the Model T.

July: **TamKaLiks Celebration** (541-886-3101), Wallowa. Since time before memory the Wallowa Band of Nez Perce called this valley home—but then an 1877 war took it away from them. When they finally returned more than a century later, they bought a piece of land that catches the light of the rising sun, and there they built a dance arbor where every summer they invite visitors to join them in celebrating their homecoming. The celebration consists of traditional ceremonies and dancing as well as a community potluck feast and an unstated certainty: Here you will discover a rare experience and an enduring memory in feeling your heart beat in time to the thumping of a Nez Perce drum. **Chief Joseph Days** (541-432-1015), Joseph. The highlight of this annual summer celebration is the rodeo, considered one of the best in the Northwest.

August: **Wallowa Valley Barn Tour** (541-426-0219; ehig@uwtc.net), Enterprise. If our fascination with old barns sprouts from farming roots planted deep in our collective memory of fresh-tilled soil and new-mown hay, then it's no wonder that this August event is considered one of the best of its kind in the Northwest. A tour of historic barns, a display of antique tractors and implements, and a country barbecue topped off with, of course, a barn dance are all part of the festivities. In addition, if you can't make it to the organized event, several outlets in the area provide a guide that will steer you along on a self-guided driving tour of the barns.

September: **Bear and Rattlesnake Feed** (541-577-3105), Imnaha. You can bet a snake sirloin that an event like this doesn't happen anywhere else. "We might be in the 20th century, but that don't mean we have to live that way," says Dave Tanzey, owner of the **Imnaha Store and Tavern,** the town's only business and the site of the annual celebration. Throughout the summer, residents of this riverside town collect the rattlers they dispatch in their yards and along the road, then donate them—along with the bears shot during hunting season—to the cookout, which raises money for local scholarships and draws a crowd that in the past has pushed Imnaha's population from 18 to as many as 600.

POWDER RIVER–SUMPTER VALLEY–UKIAH AREA

GUIDANCE **Baker County Unlimited** (1-800-523-1235; info@visitbaker.com; www.visitbaker.com), 490 Campbell Street, Baker City 97814.

Huntington Chamber of Commerce (541-869-2019), 210 W. Washington, Huntington 97907.

Oregon State Parks: Headquarters (503-378-6305), State Parks and Recreation Department, 525 Trade Street S. E., Salem 97301.

Umatilla National Forest: Headquarters (541-278-3716), 2517 S. W. Hailey Avenue, Pendleton 97801.

Wallowa-Whitman National Forest: Headquarters (541-523-6391), 1550 Dewey Avenue, Baker City 97814; **Baker Ranger District** (541-523-4476); **Pine Ranger District** (541-742-7511); **Unity Ranger District** (541-446-3351).

GETTING THERE The Powder River–Sumpter Valley–Ukiah area is reached from the north and south by Interstate 84, from the east by Highway 86, and from the west by Highway 7 and Forest Road 52.

MEDICAL EMERGENCY **St. Elizabeth Health Services** (541-523-6461), 3325 Pocahontas Road, Baker City.

✷ Towns

Halfway. Originally named for its position halfway between Pine and Cornucopia, this small community that lies at the edges of **Hells Canyon** and the **Eagle Cap Wilderness** (see *Wilder Places—Wilderness Areas* in Wallowa Valley–Snake River Area) gained national attention when it decided in 2000 to change its name for a year to Half.com to accommodate a scheme devised by an Internet company. "We're a small community where all of our industry's been taken away," said town mayor Dick Crow, referring to the area's decline in logging, ranching, and mining. "We've got to do something to survive or we're going to be a dead community."

For historic mining towns and ghost towns, see *To See—Historic Sites* and **Blue Mountain Ghost Towns** under *To See—Scenic Drives.*

✷ To See

MUSEUMS Pioneer Park (541-856-3366), Highway 30, Haines. Advertising itself as "the Biggest Little Town in Oregon," Haines—population 400—might pack more history per square foot into its streets than any other place in the region. A quarter-mile stretch of its roadside, for example, holds Pioneer Park, an outdoor museum containing a collection of cabins that date back to the early 1860s and were once used by miners, settlers, or cowboys.

HAINES GENERAL STORE

Eastern Oregon Museum (541-856-3233), 610 Third Street, Haines. In this age of interpretive centers and discovery centers, loud and glaring with their audio sound tracks and video big screens, a museum with real stuff is becoming as rare as some of the real stuff itself. This old high school gymnasium, however, is a cavernous grandma's attic filled with relics from days gone by in eastern Oregon. In shadowy corners and on dusty shelves rest the piles of our past, reminders of the way we worked and lived and played in a time of unpaved roads and sitting porches: from coffee grinders to threshing machines, Indian arrowheads to muzzle-loading rifles, horse-drawn buggies to ghost-town bars. "Our purpose is to show how settlers lived when they first got here," says Marge Loennig, a volunteer at the museum. But for some residents, such items are more than artifacts. "The miners in the hills still use the same kind of sluice boxes as we have in the museum," says Marge, whose husband's family settled here in 1863. "Some also use kerosene lamps and iceboxes. I still use a butter churn and a 100-year-old quilting frame." Grandma herself would be proud.

Adler House Museum (1-800-523-1235), 2305 Main Street, Baker City. Every town ought to have a Leo Adler—but it was Baker City's good fortune that he belonged here. After all, this was a man who began selling magazines on the city's streets when he was just nine years old, and by the time he died in 1993 at the age of 98, his magazine distributorship, the largest in the Northwest, had earned him $20 million. And he left it all to his hometown. The result of that money, now grown to more than $32 million, is that Baker City enjoys a new firehouse, parkway, and athletic complex; and its parks, hospital, library, golf course, city hall, and fairgrounds have received funds for expansion or restoration. In addition, any student ever to have graduated from the local high school is eligible to receive a scholarship for further education. A more personal contribution to the community was Leo Adler's house. Built in 1889 and bought by Leo's father a year later, the house remained virtually unchanged during the 94 years that Leo lived in it. Now restored with its original Victorian furnishings, the home serves as a museum for the community as well as a tribute to the man who gave his town so much.

Oregon Trail Regional Museum (541-523-9308), 2480 Grove Street, Baker

City. This 1920 building, originally a natatorium and a community center that featured a ballroom, was scheduled for demolition in 1977 until its listing on the **National Register of Historic Places** saved it. Today the restored building's displays help capture the history of the community as well as that of the region, going back as far as the 1840s. Perhaps its most notable exhibit is a collection of rocks, minerals, and fossils considered to be one of the finest in the United States.

National Historic Oregon Trail Interpretive Center (541-523-1843), 7 miles east of Baker City on Highway 86 (exit 302 off Interstate 84). From this hilltop, where the Oregon Trail Interpretive Center perches on the sagebrushed crest of Flagstaff Hill, Oregon Trail emigrants gazed upon the rumpled slopes of the Blue Mountains, one of the last barriers on their dusty trek. "The dust is even worse than . . . storms, or winds, or mosquitoes, or even wood ticks," emigrant Jane Gould wrote in her 1852 diary. "Dust. If I could just have a bath!" With a movie theater, interpretive displays, and living-history performances, the center examines the Oregon Trail from a number of different angles. Yet probably its most significant feature is the trail system that lets you walk along the same ground, feel the same heat, see the same mountains as the pioneers did as you make your way to the wagon ruts that lead toward the valley below.

Power of the Past Museum (541-523-4003), on Highway 86 northeast of Baker City (exit 302 off Interstate 84). This is a private museum with a widespread appeal for those with an appreciation of the mechanical past. Displayed on this ranch that has been in the same family for more than six decades is a collection of wagons, tractors, crawlers, and combines powered by steam, diesel, or gas. Whether these wheeled machines plowed fields, threshed grain, hauled grain, bladed dirt, or carried people, they provided the power of the past.

Pine Valley Community Museum (541-742-2921), 155 E. Record, Halfway. This community museum attempts to limit its collection to within a 16-mile radius of Halfway. The result is a main building that houses a collection of equipment and gear from the area's tribes, mines, farms, businesses, and families. Outside you'll find an 1882 schoolhouse, an 1885 smokehouse, and even a 1909 jail.

Sumpter Museum (541-894-2362), 150 N. Mill Street, Sumpter. Don't look for a fancy building housing the memories of this former mining and timber town; in fact, don't even look for a *separate* building. That's because this museum is housed in a back room of the Gold Post, a general store and post office on Sumpter's Main Street. But don't let the size fool you—when judged by the square foot, this might be one of the best museums in the Northwest, for its collection seems to make the past come alive again.

HISTORIC SITES **Oregon Trail** (Farewell Bend to Powder River Valley). Once they reached Farewell Bend on the Snake River, emigrants left behind 300 miles of sagebrush plains and scarce water, but still faced river canyons and crossings as well as the Blue Mountains. "'Tis the long road," wrote one emigrant, "that has no end."

Pioneer Cemetery, a half mile south of Huntington on Highway 30. Between Farewell Bend and Huntington, 4 miles to the north, runs Highway 30, once the area's major highway and before that the route of the Oregon Trail. Wagon ruts survive as roadside depressions on both sides of the highway. On the west side, near the summit of Huntington Hill and several hundred yards from the road, stands a white cross that marks the grave of eight emigrants killed in an 1860 Indian attack. By the time cavalry troops arrived—almost seven weeks after the attack—some of the survivors had fled across 100 miles of desert on foot. "The awful madness of hunger was upon us," wrote survivor Emeline Fuller, who was 13 years old at the time, "and we cooked and ate the bodies of each of the poor [dead] children."

Burnt River Canyon, Huntington to Durkee along Interstate 84 exits 345 to 330, and Durkee to Pleasant Valley along Highway 30 exits 330 to 317. It took as many as six days for emigrants to slug their way over the rocks, through the brush, and along the hillsides of this tight canyon. "The creek and road are so enclosed by the high mountains," emigrant Joel Palmer wrote in 1845, "as to afford but little room to pass along, rendering it in some places as almost impassable." The result was numerous tipped and broken wagons.

Flagstaff Hill, 7 miles northeast of Baker City off Highway 86. Once free of the Burnt River, the wagon trains headed north (near milepost 320 on today's Interstate 84) toward Virtue Flats and then Flagstaff Hill, where they got their first daunting views of the soon-to-be-crossed Blue Mountains. "They struck us with terror," emigrant Medorem Crawford wrote in 1842, "their lofty peaks seemed a resting place for the clouds." Where the wagons began their descent toward the Powder River now stands one of the country's finest educational monuments to the westward migration—the **National Historic Oregon Trail Interpretive Center** (see *Museums*). Inside the center, the emigrants' story appears through exhibits of such detailed craftsmanship that you can examine the flies in the eyes of the stuffed oxen hitched to the replica wagons; outside, the ruts of real wagons lay carved in the earth.

Powder River Valley, Baker City to North Powder along Highway 30. Along this stretch of streamside valley bottom, some emigrants made note of the grass

FLAGSTAFF HILL, WHERE WAGON TRAINS BEGAN THEIR DESCENT INTO THE POWDER RIVER

and water they found here, of the good campsites and the relatively level road. Others, however, found the going rough. "The worst possible road," one emigrant wrote, "too much for man or beast." Up ahead, however, the road got even worse.

You'll also find interpretive sites at the following Interstate 84 rest areas: **Weatherby,** exit 335; north of **Baker City,** 4 miles north of exit 298.

Haines Walking Tour (541-856-3366). You wouldn't know it to look at this small town sitting in the sunset shadow of the Elkhorn Mountains, but it has seen its share of excitement through the years: wagon trains, gold miners, cattle drives, and freight trains all stopped here on a regular basis at one time or another. So did travelers bustling along Highway 30, once one of the state's major roads and still the town's main street. This means that a slow stroll around town will take you to buildings and sites that played a role in a number of chapters in the region's history.

Baker City Walking Tour (1-800-523-1235). Baker City's Historic District, one of the largest in Oregon, comprises 110 buildings, most of them standing in a downtown constructed during the city's days on the edge of the frontier but at the center of the region's gold-mining activity. Even though the city tried to "modernize" its look in the years following World War II, little damage was done to the historical structures. "If they could have torn [the old buildings] down and built new," says Bev Calder, president of the Historic Baker City organization, "they would have." As a result, many of the buildings were simply covered with stucco, plaster, and (shudder) aluminum. Today those facades are being torn away to reveal the original stone, brick, and wood.

Chinese Cemetery, Allen Street, Baker City, just off exit 304 on Interstate 84. The gold strikes that lured white miners to the region also enticed Chinese immigrants to towns such as Baker City. As a result, Chinatowns were common in parts of northeast Oregon. "Chinatown was a series of little wooden shacks," said Marjorie Fong, who lived in Baker City's Chinese community in the early years of the 20th century. "We had our temple and our own community life." They also had their own cemetery, where 46 burials took place between 1894 and 1948. Today, however, only one marked grave is left at the site; the other remains were exhumed and returned to China. That return seems to have been the fulfillment of many wishes. "They dreamed about going back to their homeland," Mrs. Fong said, referring to the Chinese immigrants. "That's all they thought about. Some saved enough money and went back. Others didn't make it and were buried here."

Auburn, 13 miles southwest of Baker City off Highway 7 and Auburn Road. Life was short for Auburn, once Oregon's second-largest town. "Auburn is fast going to decay," a regional newspaper reported in 1864. "Today the total population does not exceed one hundred and fifty. The chief occupation there is said to be tearing down the vacant houses that adorn a street once a mile in length, and cutting them up for firewood." Ah, but at its peak—in 1862, the same year it was founded—Auburn was home to some 5,000 residents, many of whom spent their days lustily questing after the gold that had been discovered only the previous spring. Today almost nothing is left of those times but the scars: the pockmarks and potholes and rubble piles of mining. The tilted headstones in the hilltop cemetery hold some of the last reminders of the townspeople, for here is buried Henry Griffin, who discovered the gold that led to the founding of Auburn, as well as H. M. Labaree and J. Desmond, killed during a poker game one winter night in 1862, the victims of the long knife and short temper of Spanish Tom, who soon after was lynched from the community's hanging tree.

See also **Blue Mountain Ghost Towns** under *To See—Scenic Drives.*

Cornucopia, 11 miles north of Halfway on County Road 413. In spite of the fact that Cornucopia was a latecomer to the eastern Oregon gold rush—miners made their first strikes here in the 1880s—it enjoyed a much longer life than did most other boomtowns. With its 36 miles of tunnels, some of them more than a half mile deep, producing more than $20 million in gold, silver, copper, and lead, Cornucopia was the most productive mine in eastern Oregon and one of the six largest mines in the United States. Although deserted now, the mines employed 700 men in the early days, and the town's closure in the 1940s marks the end of the gold-rush era in Oregon.

Sparta, 32 miles northeast of Baker City off Highway 86 and Sparta Road. What's left of Sparta, where gold was discovered in 1863 and which grew into a town of 3,000 people by 1869, is the stone building of the town's store, once called "the finest building erected this side of Portland," and the road that takes you there. "This route was only 10 miles long, yet there were dozens of terrible curves and many steep grades," said a stagecoach passenger of the time. "The name given to one hairpin turn—Deadman's Curve—symbolized the entire road."

Durkee, 23 miles southeast of Baker City off Interstate 84 exit 327. This ramshackle town was once a thriving community—first a camping place for emigrants and freighters, then an important relay station on the freight route between the Columbia River in Oregon and the Boise Basin in Idaho, and finally a ranching center. "I've seen long strings of mules and horses tied to the hitching racks," says Tom Sheehy, who grew up on a ranch outside Durkee. "And the trains shipped lots of livestock before trucks. Thousands of lambs to Omaha, cows to Portland. In the fall the trains were nothing but cattle cars going to Portland." When automobiles came along, Sheehy says, the town's businesses seemed to come in pairs: two gas stations, two cafés, and two stores with "anything anybody could want." What's left today is a post office, a 1912 school converted to a grange, and the long, lonely wail of an occasional passing freight train. "As far as I know," Sheehy says, "there's nothing alive in Durkee."

Granite, 15 miles northwest of Sumpter off the Elkhorn Drive Scenic Byway (see *Scenic Drives*). After a miner struck gold in these now-scarred hills on the Fourth of July in 1862, Granite, first named Independence, boomed with the times. Moved to its present location in 1900 to be closer to the mines—the original town stood about 1.5 miles south of where it stands today—the community thrived with commerce and sin, its five saloons, three stores, and two hotels doing a brisk business, as did the drugstore, dance hall, newspaper, and other assorted businesses that lined Granite's streets. Of course, when the gold was gone so was the business, and the town began to sag beneath the weight of its emptiness. Today, however, it's making a small comeback, with some of its old-timey buildings and shacks still standing (or at least leaning) adjacent to a modern store, café, and lodge that open their doors to those who come here for the mountain quiet and seclusion.

Chinese Walls, 2 miles north of Granite on County Road 24 (Elkhorn Drive Scenic Byway; see *Scenic Drives*). Even though 19th-century laws prohibited Chinese immigrants from owning American mines, they often bought nearly exhausted claims from white miners, then laboriously worked them by hand. The Chinese Walls, elongated humps of rock mounded along the edges of a roadside stream, is an example of such work: Every rock was lifted and stacked by hand.

Malheur City, 18 miles northwest of Brogan off Highway 26. A ghost town, writes Marc Faulconer, an editor at *The Bulletin* in Bend, is "where the streets are empty and the graveyards full." In that case, Malheur City, once a gold-mining boomtown beginning with its first strike in 1863, qualifies because its streets are empty even of buildings: They all burned in a 1957 range fire. So what's left are a few foundations and the cemetery—and the memories of a town perhaps best remembered by the few descendants who occasionally return to tend the graves.

Sumpter Valley Dredge, 27 miles southwest of Baker City off Highway 7 and County Road 410. To visualize a dredge, imagine a mechanical monster more than 100 feet long and 50 feet wide with 72 mouths. Working 24 hours a day, the monster gobbles the streambed and guzzles the water of the Powder River. Every minute it swills 3,000 gallons of river; every 90 seconds it swallows a dump-truck-sized chunk of earth, chomping its way to a depth of 30 feet, ripping its way through the valley floor. This monster is a dredge. And its job is digging gold. To see what it does, watch the roadside after you pass Sumpter Valley's Phillips Lake. The tailing piles—the hills of rocks stacked across the valley—is the waste spewed from the dredge after it extracted the gold. To see how it looks, drive to Sumpter, where the Sumpter Valley Dredge—the third and largest to work the valley between 1913 and 1954—stands in the state park built for it. Step aboard to the smells of oil and grease, to the hulk of steel welded, bolted, or riveted from fore to aft, from the buckets that ate the rock to the stacker that disgorged it. Nearby is the **Dredge Loop Trail,** a gravel path of less than a half mile that follows the Powder River and gives you a close-up view of its tailings.

Whitney, 10 miles southwest of Sumpter Junction (junction of Highway 7 and County Road 410) off Highway 7. The tilted, fractured buildings you see in the meadow south of Highway 7 are what's left of Whitney, built along the Sumpter Valley Railway in 1901 by the Oregon Lumber Company to serve as the hub of railroad logging in the region, especially as a source of lumber for nearby gold-mining towns. With its spur lines stretching as far as 14 miles into the ponderosa pine forests, Whitney pulled in enough lumber to keep 75 men working in its sawmill and 14 crews stationed near its railway. The town faded along with the mining camps and finally closed when the railway was abandoned in 1947.

Battle Mountain State Park, 10 miles north of Ukiah off Highway 395. During the Bannock-Paiute Indian War of 1878, this was near the site of a July Eighth Battle of Birch Creek, which pitted troops from Fort Vancouver led by

General O. O. Howard against Bannock and Paiute Indians under Chief Egan. "The advance [toward the Indian's hilltop position] was made along several approaches in a handsome manner, not a man falling out of ranks," General Howard wrote. "The troops, though encountering severe fire that emptied some saddles and killed many horses, did not waver, but skirmished to the very top."

FOR FAMILIES **Elk Feeding** (541-898-2826; 541-856-3356), Anthony Creek site of the **Elkhorn Wildlife Management Area** (see *Wilder Places—Wildlife Refuges*), 8 miles east of North Powder off North Powder River Lane (exit 285 off Interstate 84 and follow the binocular signs). Sitting on the wooden seat of this horse-drawn wagon is as close as most people will ever come to a herd of Rocky Mountain elk: with the winter air sharp against your face, hay strewn on the snow nearby, more than 100 bulls and cows and calves strolling out of the foothills and onto the feeding grounds, their breath steaming as they settle in for breakfast as close as 30 feet from the wagon, and the sounds of voices and the clicks of cameras causing not a stir among them. "I think the elk genuinely are entertained by people," says Alice Trindle, who, along with Susan Triplett, drives the feeding wagon and runs the tour, the only one of its kind in Oregon. "The word is out in the elk world, 'if you want to see some crazy humans, this is the place to come.'"

Horse-Drawn Trolley Tours (Oregon Trail Trolley; 1-800-523-1235), Baker City. On Friday and Saturday from June through September, these horse-drawn trolleys roll up and down the streets of Baker City, giving visitors a glimpse of the past as well as a tour of the city's historic homes and buildings.

Sumpter Valley Railroad, 24 miles southwest of Baker City off Highway 7 and Dredge Loop Road. This is a train that came back from the dead. First linked to Sumpter in 1896, the Sumpter Valley Railroad brought mining equipment into the valley and hauled logs out of it. Then when trucks began replacing trains in the 1930s, the railroad first withered, then died. But five decades after that death, thousands of hours of volunteer labor resurrected the old train, which now hauls passengers on hour-long round trips through the heart of the mine tailings left behind by the **Sumpter Valley Dredge** (see *Historic Sites*). "We try to give people the experience of what it was like a hundred years ago," says Jim Ross of Boise, who serves as a volunteer conductor on the train. Once you enter the old goldfields and settle into the rumble and lurch of the train, you might be surprised at what you find, for tucked away in this land of stone is a wildlife haven of ponds and sloughs, of backwaters and wetlands fed by the Powder River, which slides through the piles like a watery snake.

A RESTORED TRAIN OF THE SUMPTER VALLEY RAILROAD

Gold Panning (Cracker Creek Mining Company; 541-894-2510; www.dk-nugget.com), Cracker Creek Road, Sumpter. If you feel yourself struck with gold fever, if your hands tingle for the grasp of a pan and its swirl of water and gravel, then you can still stake a claim at the Cracker Creek Mining Camp. This outfit provides you with shovel, a pan, and a place to work, then turns you loose to prospect for the mother lode. Of course, just like during the gold rush days, you'll need a grubstake, for the charge is $50 per day per person or $85 for the family.

Lehman Hot Springs (541-427-3015), 17 miles east of Ukiah off Highway 244. Open year-round.

Hells Canyon Bison Ranch (541-742-6558), Halfway. Outside Halfway, visitors can pay to hitch a ride on the hay wagon that feeds these critters that were once the monarchs of the plains.

U.S. FOREST SERVICE CABIN RENTALS Instead of demolishing the abandoned fire lookouts, guard stations, and work-camp cabins that once stood scattered across the national forests as temporary living quarters for rangers and crews, the U.S. Forest Service has opened them to the public. Most are available year-round—accessible by car in summer and by skis, snowshoes, or snowmobile in winter—and are available on a first-come, first-served basis.

Antlers Guard Station (Unity Ranger District; 541-446-3351), 15 miles southwest of Sumpter off Highway 7 and County Road 529. Constructed by the Civilian Conservation Corps (CCC) in the 1930s, this two-room guard station is located along the **North Fork Burnt River** and just a couple of miles from the historic ghost town of **Whitney** (see *Historic Sites*).

Peavy Cabin (Baker Ranger District; 541-523-1932), 31 miles west of North Powder off Anthony Lakes Road (Forest Roads 73 and 380). Oregon Agricultural College (now Oregon State University) forestry professor George Peavy built this one-room log cabin in 1934 as an outdoor forestry laboratory for his students. Out its front door lie trails leading to the **North Fork John Day Wilderness** and the **Elkhorn Crest National Recreation Trail** (see *Wilder Places—Wilderness Areas*).

SCENIC DRIVES **Blue Mountain Ghost Towns,** southwest of Baker City along roads branching off Highway 7. When the 1860s began, eastern Oregon was still the domain of native tribes, still empty of settlers, cabins, and towns. But that changed in a hurry. When Henry Griffin struck gold in the fall of 1861 near today's Baker City, the following spring thaw brought hordes of miners across the Cascades and into the Blue Mountains. "Everybody are in a hurry but us," E. S. McComas wrote while driving a wagon through the area in the fall of 1862. Mining camps sprung up, grew into boomtowns, and finally faded and then vanished along with the supply of gold. Yet what's left behind to tell the story of those days is still scattered across the landscape. "It is a history recorded not just in words on paper," writes Baker City journalist Jayson Jacoby, "but in square nails rusting in a quiet meadow, and in wood frayed and grayed by a thousand blizzards." Today, Highway 7 from Baker City leads you toward the relics of that history.

Griffin Gulch, 4 miles south of Baker City off Highway 7 and Griffin Gulch

Road. This is not only where Henry Griffin first struck gold to begin the 1862 rush but also the site of the region's first cabin, in which Griffin and a partner spent the winter. No marker commemorates the location of either Griffin's strike or cabin, but on quiet mornings you can still sense the history of the place.

Auburn (see also *Historic Sites*), 13 miles southwest of Baker City off Highway 7 and Auburn Road. The region's first boomtown, Auburn grew so fast that its estimated 1862 population of 5,000 made it the second-largest city in Oregon at the time. The only thing remaining from those days are the mine tailings and the hilltop cemetery, whose deceased residents include Henry Griffin, whose gold strike opened the region to settlement (see Griffin Gulch, above), and H. M. Labaree and J. Desmond, who were stabbed to death in Auburn during an 1862 card game.

Bourne, 7 miles north of Sumpter off County Road 410 and Cracker Creek Road. Because its few surviving buildings are boarded up—a 1937 flash flood down Cracker Creek destroyed most of the town—Bourne has that classic "ghost-town" look, though a few nearby mines are still producing small quantities of gold.

Greenhorn, 24 miles west of Sumpter Junction (junction of Highway 7 and Forest Road 1035). This old mining town, home to more than 1,000 miners in 1865, is Oregon's highest (6,200-foot elevation) and smallest incorporated city. With seven houses but no year-round residents, Greenhorn had an official 2000 population of *zero.* But perhaps the town's most distinguishing characteristic dates from 1912. That's when the town wanted to build a school but found itself blocked by the fact that U.S. Forest Service land surrounded it and by the law that decreed schools couldn't be built within a quarter mile of a saloon (Greenhorn had a few). So when mayor Simeon C. Richardson asked President Taft to loosen these restrictions, Greenhorn received a U.S. patent granting that 53.58 acres be put "in trust for the use and benefit of the occupants of the townsite of Greenhorn." This act in effect made the town the nation's only "principality," though the school was never built.

Susanville and **Galena,** 20 miles northwest of Austin Junction (junction of Highways 7 and 26) off Highway 7 and Middle Fork Road. The story goes that when strong winds toppled trees along the Middle Fork Burnt River and its tributary Elk Creek, the upturned roots held chunks of gold. The resulting 1864 gold rush crowded the streams so much that the miners agreed that a man's claim would be only as wide as he could reach with his pick without moving his feet. The mining camps of Susanville and Galena popped up as competitors just 2 miles from each other, and their saloons could draw as many as 1,000 thirsty miners into town on a Saturday night.

Blue Mountains Scenic Byway—southeast section, 39 paved miles along Forest Road 52, from Ukiah to the North Fork John Day Campground north of Granite. The two ends of this 130-mile byway—one near the Columbia River and the other in the Blue Mountains—are connected by a blend of the pastoral and the wild in a string of farmland and forests, small towns and wilderness areas, trout streams and mountain peaks. This segment of the road climbs out of the Camas Valley at Ukiah, into the Blue Mountains, and through the heart of the **North Fork John Day Wilderness** (see *Wilder Places—Wilderness Areas*).

Elkhorn Drive Scenic Byway, 106 paved miles along Highway 7, Forest Road 73, and Highway 30, beginning and ending in Baker City. From the hayfields of the Powder River Valley to the alpine peaks of the Elkhorn Ridge, this road climbs over, curls around, and dips into a cross section of the region's landscape and history. Along this drive you'll find a striking blend of skyline views, old towns, granite peaks, abandoned mines, and elk herds.

Journey Through Time Scenic Byway—eastern section, 116 paved miles along Highways 7 and 26 from Baker City to Dayville and the junction of Highways 26 and 19. Although the scenery along this byway is wildly beautiful, its special feature is the history that visitors encounter along the way. The route steers you past the remnants of the **Oregon Trail** (see *To See—Historic Sites*) near Baker City, **gold mining** near Sumpter and Canyon City, **steam trains** at Whitney (see *To See—Historic Sites*) and Prairie City, and prehistoric fossils at the **John Day Fossil Beds** (see *To See—Natural Wonders* in Columbia Plateau in the North Central region).

Hells Canyon Scenic Byway, 208 paved miles along Highway 82, Forest Road 39, and Highway 86 from La Grande to Baker City—the long way around. One of three **All-American Roads** in Oregon and one of 15 in the nation, the Hells Canyon Scenic Byway leads travelers through some of the most beautiful scenery in the country: the valleys and fields of the Grande Ronde, Wallowa, and Powder Rivers; the ridges and slopes of the Blue, Wallowa, and Elkhorn Mountains; the rimrocks and canyons of the Minam, Snake, and Imnaha drainages. It's a land tough enough to show the scars of grinding glaciers and raging wildfires, gentle enough to sprout wildflowers—and the road shows you both aspects.

Old Highway 30, 80 paved miles along Highway 30 from North Powder to Durkee. Even though most of venerable Highway 30, once one of Oregon's major east–west thoroughfares, now lies beneath the asphalt of Interstate 84, portions of it survive to offer travelers a slower and more serene alternative to the freeway rush. One good entry point is at the town of **Union,** where the old highway climbs through **Pyles Canyon,** once a pathway for fur brigades before Fred Nodine and "Three Fingered" Smith blazed a better trail in the 1860s. To accomplish this, the two men first sunk willow stakes to mark the way, then steered a series of pack trains from stake to stake to tromp out a path toward the gold mines in the mountains outside Baker City. Today the old highway follows a similar path as it crosses beneath the interstate at **North Powder,** bends its way through **Haines** and **Baker City,** and leaves the **Elkhorn Mountains** behind for the orchards and pastures, the meadows and hills that line the road to **Durkee.**

Sumpter Valley Railway Route, 65 paved miles from Baker City to Prairie City along Highways 7 and 26. Through the foothills of the Blue Mountains she once ran, her steam engine chugging and her steel wheels clacking as she snaked her slow way over mile-high passes and water-roiling streams. The **Stump Dodger,** they called the old narrow-gauge train of the Sumpter Valley Railway, a line that for more than 50 years linked people and businesses across some 80 miles of northeast Oregon's backcountry. And even though the tracks are long gone, you can still follow the memory of the Stump Dodger through the country she once ruled. "After breakfast we walked to the [Baker City] station and the eight o'clock train," said David Eccles, grandson of the man who started

THE SNAKE RIVER PORTION OF THE SNAKE RIVER–MORMON BASIN BACK COUNTRY BYWAY

the Sumpter Valley Railway. "Father got off at his south Baker office, but we rode on to adventure." That adventure today takes you through the mine tailings of the **Sumpter Valley** and past the ghost town of **Whitney,** over a mile-high pass at **Tipton** and to the old stage stop at **Austin House** before sending you over **Dixie Pass**—look for the roadside **Sumpter Valley Railroad** Interpretive Site (see *For Families*)—and then down into **Prairie City,** the end of the old line.

Burnt River Road, 40 paved and graveled miles from Unity on Highway 26 to Durkee on Highway 30. Cutting through pasturelands and canyon country, this byway follows the Burnt River through the small communities of **Hereford, Bridgeport,** and **Durkee.** This is a land of grass and cows and sprinkler pipes, of zigzag rail fences lining alfalfa fields, willow thickets spotting narrow valleys, and mine tailings littering stream banks.

Snake River–Mormon Basin Back Country Byway, 150 paved and graveled miles beginning and ending in Baker City. You can drive this loop in two parts. The first part is a journey along the **Snake River Road,** which begins near **Richland,** 39 miles east of Baker City off Highway 86, and from there runs upstream along the hills and banks of the slackwater **Snake River,** which is impounded behind **Brownlee Dam.** This stretch follows a river tamed into a reservoir, appreciated mostly by irrigators, water-skiers, and catfishermen, but the neighboring countryside can be as wild as the river once was, its sky wide enough for hawks, its slopes steep enough for chukars, its draws deep enough and its ridgetops secluded enough for mule deer. Not far from where this road ends—at **Huntington** near Interstate 84—the second part of the route begins. From the Dixie turnoff on the interstate (exit 340), a rough road heads west toward **Mormon Basin,** a gold-mining community of the 1860s that was once home to more than 300 people and that produced gold into the early years of the 20th century. Today, however, nothing remains of this once thriving settlement. The return route follows Highway 245 and 7 back to **Baker City.**

NATURAL WONDERS **Blue Mountains,** between Prineville to the west and Hells Canyon to the east, perhaps best viewed from either the Grande Ronde or Powder River Valley. Hard to believe, but these rolling Blue Mountains—which geologically include the Ochoco, Strawberry, Elkhorn, and Wallowa ranges—were once part of a tropical sea's shoreline. "Before the Blue Mountains there was no Oregon," writes Oregon geologist Ellen Bishop, "and ocean waves broke on Idaho beaches." But then when an island system that later became the Blue

Mountains joined North America about 100 million years ago, it became part of the continent's western coastline.

Hole in the Wall Landslide, 9 miles northwest of Richland off Highway 86. If you've never seen what happens when a hillside crumbles and its slope sluffs off, then pull the car over between mileposts 30 and 31 and take a look across the way at that jumbled mass of rock; beneath it lies what used to be the highway, until the 1984 slide buried it forever.

✷ To Do

BICYCLING **Phillips Lake,** 17 miles southwest of Baker City along Highway 7. At this reservoir in the Sumpter Valley, you have your pick of two 6-mile mountain bike routes that lie on opposite shores and that are almost, but not quite, connected. The more secluded and primitive of the two is the **South Shoreline Trail,** a dirt path that stretches between Mason Dam to the east and Southwest Shore Campground to the south as it wanders along the curved edge of the lake, past pine trees and wildflowers and views of the Elkhorn Mountains. On the other hand (and on the other shore) lies **North Shoreline Trail,** the South Shoreline's homely brother, for the view from this side is of camp trailers, motorboats, and logging scars, though it does offer a couple of miles of pavement and a number of friendly campers and boaters. If you want to make a **shore-to-shore loop,** the connections include Hudspeth Lane and Highway 7, though you may do a bit of bushwhacking and head-scratching on the north side of the lake.

CAMPING **Powder River Valley Reservoirs.** The following irrigation reservoirs provide fishing, boating, and camping opportunities for flatwater fishermen: **Thief Valley,** 12 miles south of Union off Highway, 12 camping sites, boat ramp and no motor restrictions; **Pilcher Creek,** 9 miles west of North Powder off North Powder River Lane, 10 campsites, boat ramp, and trolling motors only; **Wolf Creek,** 6 miles northwest of North Powder off Interstate 84 (exit 283) and Wolf Creek Road.

Phillips Lake, 19 to 27 miles southwest of Baker City off Highway 7 and Hudspeth Lane. This lake, a dammed portion of the Powder River, offers two campgrounds, one on each major shoreline. Along the north shore lies **Union Creek Campground,** the larger and more developed of the two, with 76 campsites (58 of them with RV hookups), rest rooms with flush toilets, a paved boat ramp, even a security gate that's closed during the night. Across the lake lies **Southwest Shore Campground,** a more primitive campground that contains 18 lakeside sites that see light use. Just a mile away

PHILLIPS LAKE, LOCATED IN THE POWDER RIVER VALLEY AND AT THE BASE OF THE BLUE MOUNTAINS

lies **Millers Lane,** another primitive camp that features 7 sites near the lakeshore. For some travelers, however, the most appealing campsites are the 3 scattered more deeply along the mostly roadless south shore, where a few picnic tables and outhouses mark the spots where those willing to use foot- or bike-power can pitch their tents in the grassy shade of pine trees.

Wallowa-Whitman National Forest (541-523-6391), 1550 Dewey Avenue, Baker City. Consisting of more than 3,700 square miles divided between Oregon and Idaho, the Wallowa-Whitman is the largest national forest in the Pacific Northwest. As a result, many campgrounds lie near the edge of country yet untamed.

Baker Ranger District (541-523-4476), 3165 10th Street, Baker City. **Anthony Lakes,** 18 miles west of North Powder off Anthony Lakes Highway (Forest Road 73), 37 campsites near the lakeshore at an elevation of 7,100 feet; **Deer Creek,** 28 miles southwest of Baker City off Highway 7, County Road 656, and Forest Road 6550, 6 campsites near the creek and north of Phillips Lake; **Grande Ronde Lake,** 19 miles west of North Powder off Anthony Lakes Highway (Forest Road 73),8 campsites near the lake that serves as the headwaters of the Grande Ronde River; **McCully Forks,** 33 miles southwest of Baker City off Highway 7 and County Roads 410 and 520, 6 campsites northwest of Sumpter and near a tributary of the Powder River; **Mud Lake,** 18 miles west of North Powder off Anthony Lakes Highway (Forest Road 73), 8 campsites near a shallow lake and near Anthony Lakes.

Pine Ranger District (541-742-7511), Halfway. **Duck Lake,** 30 miles north of Halfway off Forest Road 66, 2 campsites near the lake; **Eagle Forks,** 10 miles northwest of Richland off Forest Road 7735, 7 campsites along Eagle Creek; **Fish Lake,** 29 miles north of Halfway off Forest Road 66, 15 campsites near the lake; **Lake Fork,** 18 miles northeast of Halfway off Highway 86 and Forest Road 39, 10 campsites near Elk Creek; **McBride** 10 miles northwest of Halfway off Highway 86 and Forest Road 77, 11 campsites along Summit Creek; **Tamarack,** 36 miles northwest of Richland off Forest Roads 7735, 7720, and 77, 24 campsites near the confluence of Eagle Creek and its West Fork; **Twin Lakes,** 35 miles north of Halfway off Forest Road 66, 6 campsites near the lakes.

Umatilla National Forest: North Fork John Day Ranger District (541-427-3231). The Umatilla National Forest consists of almost 2,200 square miles that are fairly evenly divided between Oregon and Washington, with Interstate 84 serving as a rough dividing line. Although its mountain elevations can reach as high as 8,000 feet, much of the forest's landscape consists of canyons and valleys, ridges and plateaus, where you can expect warm summers and cool evenings at the following campgrounds: **Bear Wallow,** 10 miles east of Ukiah off Highway 244, 6 campsites near Bear Wallowa Creek and its interpretive trail; **Big Creek,** 22 miles southeast of Ukiah off Forest Road 52, 2 campsites near the creek, which offers fishing and a hiking trail, but which is also near an off-highway vehicle (OHV) staging area and its adjacent motorized routes; **Divide Well,** 20 miles west of Ukiah off Forest Roads 53 and 5327, 3 campsites and a nearby trail open to OHVs; **Drift**

Fence, 7 miles southeast of Ukiah off Forest Road 52, 3 campsites; **Frazier,** 16 miles east of Ukiah off Forest Roads 52 and 5226, 32 campsites near an OHV staging area and its adjacent motorized routes; **Gold Dredge**, 7 miles east of Dale off Forest Roads 55 and 5506, 42 campsites near an OHV staging area and its adjacent motorized routes; **Lane Creek,** 9 miles east of Ukiah off Highway 244, 4 campsites near Bear Wallow Creek; **North Fork John Day,** 10 miles north of Granite off Forest Road 52, 19 sites along the North Fork John Day River; **Olive Lake,** 24 miles southeast of Dale off Forest Roads 55 and 10, 3 campsites along the shore of Olive Lake; **Oriental Creek**, 12 miles east of Dale off Forest Roads 55 and 5506, 5 campsites near the North Fork John Day Wilderness; **Tollbridge,** 1 mile northeast of Dale off Highway 395 and Forest Road 55; 7 campsites near North Fork John Day River.

See also **Powder River Accessible Fishing Facility** under *To Do—Hiking* and **Ukiah–Dale Forest State Park** under *Wilder Places—Parks.*

CANOEING **Anthony Lakes,** 18 miles west of North Powder off Anthony Lakes Highway (Forest Road 73).This is quiet water that glistens deep with sunlight and the reflections of the granite peaks that surround it. From out of the nearby pines, ospreys soar out over the lake and circle the water, swoop low and touch their talons to the surface, then rise again, clutching a trout and soaring back to their trees. On the lake, fly-fishermen in float tubes or rowboats or canoes cast their lines to the dimpled rising of the trout the ospreys leave behind.

GOLF **Baker City Golf Course** (541-523-2358), 2801 Indiana Avenue, Baker City. 18 holes.

HIKING **Anthony Lakes,** 18 miles west of North Powder off Anthony Lakes Highway (Forest Road 73). This alpine setting is high enough for mountain goats—the lake's elevation is 7,100 feet—wild enough for granite mountains and glassy waters, and friendly enough to offer a series of hiking trails that leads you through it all. **Anthony Lake Shoreline Loop:** a 1-mile gravel path that circles the lake, bypassing leaping trout, casting fishermen, and diving ospreys; along the way you'll see beaver chewings, cross footbridges, glimpse granite peaks, and skirt the watery edges of a grassy shore. **Hoffer Lakes Trail:** a half-mile (one way) climb along a winding mountain stream that slides and splashes its way down the slope before the trail straightens, steepens, and finally ends at an alpine meadow holding a couple of dimpled ponds; a nearby spur (Forest Road 185) gives you an optional loop back to Anthony Lake. **Black Lake Trail:** a 1-mile (one way) trail leading through mead-

ANTHONY LAKES, THE ALPINE HOME OF MOUNTAIN GOATS

ows and forests that smell of soil and sunlight as it climbs its way to the shoreline of a mountain-rimmed lake where small trout rise to the whine of mosquitoes.

Three short but sometimes steep hikes requiring drives to nearby trailheads include **Crawfish Lake** (1.6 miles one way) off Forest Road 216, **the Lakes Lookout** (0.7 mile one way) off Forest Road 187, and **Van Patten Lake** (0.5 mile one way) off Forest Road 130.

♿ **Powder River Accessible Fishing Facility,** 14 miles southwest of Baker City off Highway 7. Along this lovely, trout-laden, pine-shaded stretch of river lies 3 miles of paved or graveled trail stretching along both sides of the river and connected by five bridges and containing fishing platforms, sitting benches, picnic areas, camping sites, and rest rooms—*all of it handicapped accessible.* Is this a great country or what?

See also **North Fork John Day Wilderness** under *Wilder Places—Wilderness Areas.*

✷ Wilder Places

PARKS **Farewell Bend State Park,** 24 miles north of Ontario off Interstate 84, day use and overnight. This is a place so big in regional history that its guest book would include the signatures of missionaries Marcus and Narcissa Whitman, explorers Benjamin Bonneville and John Fremont, fur traders Nathaniel Wyeth and Wilson Price Hunt, and countless pioneers who camped here and said good-bye to the Snake River plains.

Ukiah–Dale Forest State Park, between Ukiah and Dale along Highway 395, day use and overnight. Consisting of almost 3,000 acres stretched along 14 miles of Camas Creek, this park offers a total of 27 primitive campsites and uncountable fishing spots scattered across the bottom of this forested canyon.

WILDERNESS AREAS **North Fork John Day Wilderness,** 15 miles southeast of Ukiah off Highway 244 and Forest Road 52, 190 square miles. Encompassing two mountain ranges—the Elkhorns and Greenhorns—and divided into four segments across two national forests, this is the largest wild area in the Blue Mountains. With more than 100 miles of trails and 130 miles of streams, the area is famous for its populations of **elk, deer, trout,** and **steelhead.** Its trail system ranges from the 24-mile **Elkhorn Crest National Recreation Trail** to half-mile trails near Anthony Lakes.

WILDLIFE REFUGES **Bridge Creek Wildlife Area,** 5 miles south of Ukiah off Forest Road 52. Because this 20-square-mile refuge is a wintering area for **deer** and **elk,** roads are few and vehicle access is limited. But those who don't mind traveling by foot will find the grasslands and meadows and forests along Bridge Creek to be a good place to spot **deer, grouse,** and **songbirds.**

Elkhorn Wildlife Management Area, 8 miles west of North Powder off North Powder River Lane and 10 miles south of Baker City off Highway 7 and Auburn Road. Established to provide a winter feeding range for Rocky Mountain elk, this wildlife area consists of 12 square miles divided into two separate segments, both located in the foothills of the Elkhorn Mountains and featuring habitats of mixed meadows, sagebrush, and forest. Although traveling by foot through either area is prohibited during the feeding season—December 1 through April 15—both sites have roadside viewing areas from which elk and deer are often clearly visible.

Sumpter Valley Wildlife Area, 24 miles southwest of Baker City off Highway 7 and Dredge Loop Road. The Sumpter Valley saw its share of hard times from the dredges that tore its meadows into rock piles. "We were never completely out of debt until we tolerated gold dredging in 1940," writes Brooks Hawley, who once ranched in the valley. "For 30 years Powder River ran muddy to Baker, so muddy that fish could not live in it." Today, however, the river runs clear and the valley shows signs of healing, especially if you look at it from the 3-mile trail of the Sumpter Valley Wildlife Area. Starting near the depot of the **Sumpter Valley Railroad** (see *To See—For Families*), the trail loops through a landscape of mine tailings, wetlands, potholes, willow groves, and streambeds.

✷ Lodging

See also **U.S. Forest Service Cabin Rentals** under *To See.*

BED & BREAKFASTS

Baker City

Baer House Bed & Breakfast (541-523-1812; baerhouse@triax.com; www.triax.com/baerhouse), 2333 Main Street, Baker City 97814. Near the old Oregon Trail stands this 1882 two-story Victorian that offers one room with a private bath ($65–80) and two others that share a bath ($55–65), all coming with a full breakfast that may include "decadent French toast." A kitchenette and laundry are available upstairs, and a historic walking tour of the city's homes and businesses begins nearby (see **Baker City Walking Tour** under *To See—Historic Sites*). Children older than 12 are welcome.

Grant House Bed & Breakfast (1-800-606-7468; www.neoregon.com/granthouse.htm), 2525 Third Street, Baker City 97814. Carpenter Tom Grant built this structure in 1881 as a Catholic parish hall, then bought it in 1908 (for $20) when the church wanted to make room for a new rectory, and finally finished remodeling it into the family home in the 1920s. Today the 12-room English Tudor home offers three guest rooms with a shared bath and a full breakfast ($68–78). Well-behaved dogs (an extra $10) and children are welcome.

Powder River Bed & Breakfast (1-800-600-7143; powdergs@eoni.com), Highway 7, Baker City 97814. This B&B, located on the edge of Baker City and near the Powder River, caters to all travelers but specializes in serious fishermen, with host Phil Simonski offering guided fishing trips and a full-line tackle shop. Its two-story guest house, which comes with antique furnishings and a large yard, offers two rooms, both with private baths ($50–60). A specialty entrée of Danae Simonki's full breakfast is sourdough waffles with barbecued sausage. Children and pets are welcome.

Halfway

Birch Leaf Farm Bed & Breakfast (541-742-2990; www.thebirchleaf.com), 47830 Steele Hill Road, Halfway 97834. Situated between the **Eagle Cap Wilderness** (see *Wilder Places—Wilderness Areas* in Wallowa Valley–Snake River Area) and the Snake River, Birch Leaf is a working farm of gardens and orchards, chickens and horses. It's also a farm that offers visitors their choice of two kinds of accommodations: the Guesthouse, built in 1906 from a Montgomery Ward's mail-order kit, has four upstairs bedrooms that share two baths (one upstairs, one downstairs) as well as a downstairs living room, dining room, and kitchen ($65); and the Bunkhouse, which contains two bedrooms, a loft, bathroom, and kitchen ($125). Dogs are welcome for an additional $15.

Sumpter

Sumpter Bed & Breakfast (1-800-287-5234; sumpbb.eoni.com; www.sumpterbb.com), 344 N. Columbia Street, Sumpter 97877. A stay at this inn comes with a connection to local history. "Our bed and breakfast started life as a hospital in 1900, in the bustling gold town of Sumpter," says owner Barb Phillips. "In 1912 the doctors moved on to Baker City, and the building sat empty and survived the fire of 1917 that devastated the town." After serving for 55 years as the lodge for the area's Masons, the old hospital eventually found a new life with the Phillipses. "We are the third private owners," Barb says. "We purchased it in 1997 and renovated it into a lovely Victorian period home containing many antiques and lots of collectibles for guests to view and enjoy." Its six guest rooms ($70–85) share three bathrooms and come with a breakfast that may trigger memories of the home's past. "We prepare scrumptious full breakfasts—consisting of huckleberry pancakes, or hot biscuits and sausage gravy and homemade jams—in the operating room–turned-kitchen," Barb says. "We serve our guests in the former ward, which is now a large dining room." In addition, deer are usually constant visitors, and children are always welcome. "We love large groups and family gatherings."

LODGES **Lehman Hot Springs** (541-427-3015; info@lehmanhotsprings.com; www.lehmanhotsprings.com), Milepost 17, Highway 244, Ukiah 97880 (17 miles east of Ukiah off Highway 244). The Blue Mountains is a complicated place—a land of ridges and canyons, plateaus and basins, as though it can't decide what it wants to be. Included in this mosaic is a place of restless earth that pushes a stream of scalding water down a hillside leading to Lehman Springs, one of the largest hot springs in the Northwest. First developed into a resort in the 1880s, the springs drew numerous travelers willing to take a two-day buggy ride from Pendleton to reach it. Today's resort includes two rental cabins, an RV park, a bunkhouse that sleeps 48, and a 9,000-square-foot complex containing four pools. What separates it from other resorts, however, is that it's surrounded by almost 4 million acres of national forest, a situation that often brings deer, and sometimes bears, onto the grounds. Accommodations include lodge rooms ($75–95), A-frame and log cabins ($95), and a log home ($145).

The Lodge at Granite (541-755-5200), 1575 McCann Street, Granite. According to a legend in these mountains, if on a moonless night when the wind is right you stand on the edge of this old gold-mining town and gaze into the dark and lonely distance, you can hear the ghosts of long-departed miners moaning in the branches of the trees. Well, now you can be frightened in comfort, peering into the star-spangled mountain sky from the big deck of a new log lodge, the newest member of the community in one of Oregon's smallest incorporated towns (population 45, many of them part-time). Although the lodge offers nine guest rooms ($50 double, with children 12 and younger $12.50 each), most of the attraction around here lies beyond, in the forests and along the streams and trails of the Blue Mountains that surround Granite. "Our goal," say owners Mitch and Pat Fielding, "is to make you feel that you hate to leave and cannot wait to return."

✷ Where to Eat

EATING OUT **Baker City Café Pizza a Fetta** (541-523-6099), 1915 Washington Avenue, Baker City. This is the place to go for pizza made the Old-World way, the dough twirled into a crust, the cheese and toppings spread in layers, the resulting combination slid into an oven to fill the café with the warmth and aroma of one of the best pizzas you'll ever eat.

Haines Steak House (541-856-3639), Highway 30, Haines. A longtime eastern Oregon favorite, the Haines Steak House serves up a sense of cowboy tradition with the two mainstays of its menu: giant steaks from grain-fed cows and the chuck-wagon salad bar. Sure, you can also order chicken or seafood—but it's the steak that has earned this small-town restaurant its statewide reputation.

✷ Special Events

May–September: **Sumpter Flea Markets** (541-523-1845), Sumpter. For nine days each year (Memorial Day, Fourth of July, and Labor Day weekends) this small town in the Blue Mountains sheds its "ghost-town" label—honest, it ain't dead yet; just ask the 175 people who live here—and welcomes several thousand visitors who come to prowl for bargains and treasures among the tables of the 300 to 400 vendors set up here, making these holiday events some of the largest flea markets in the Northwest.

July: **Haines Stampede** (541-856-3366), Fourth of July, Haines. **Miners' Jubilee** (541-523-5855), Baker City. Behind the chutes at the rodeo grounds, beneath the gleam of a July sun and within sight of the twirls and loops of carnival rides, slope-shouldered cowboys in dusty jeans buckle their chaps, tape their wrists, and get ready to ride. "When it comes to bronc ridin' and bull ridin,'"the announcer drawls into his microphone, "you gotta be tough just to *watch.*" And when the chute gate swings open, out charges the wilder side of Baker City's annual summer festival—the **Bronc- and Bull-Riding Blowout.** A gentler side to the Miners' Jubilee, however, hovers near the city park, its air filled with the smells of buttered popcorn and grilling ribs, its lawn clustered with vendors' tents and food stands, its sidewalks busy with the steps of sandaled feet and the roll of baby strollers. Here among the strums of guitar strings and the giggles of kids comes the sense that this is a sepia-toned version of a slower, calmer world.

August: **Durkee Steak Feed** (541-523-3356), Durkee. During World War II when labor-strapped ranchers had problems bringing in the crops, their neighbors got together and pitched in to help. In gratitude, the ranchers rounded up some cows, started up a barbecue, and threw the community a steak feed. Today this gathering of neighbors and the sizzling of steaks continues in the annual Durkee Steak Feed, which the local grange sponsors as a fundraiser.

JOHN DAY RIVER AREA

GUIDANCE **Canyonville Information Center** (541-839-4258), 250 N. Main, Canyonville, 97417.

Grant County Chamber of Commerce (1-800-769-5664; www.grantcounty.cc), 281 W. Main, John Day 97845.

Malheur National Forest: Headquarters (541-575-1731), 431 Patterson Bridge Road, John Day 97845; **Bear Valley Ranger District** (541-575-3000); **Long Creek Ranger District** (541-575-3089); **Prairie City Ranger District** (541-820-3311).

Oregon State Parks: Headquarters (503-378-6305), State Parks and Recreation Department, 525 Trade Street S. E., Salem 97301.

Umatilla National Forest: Headquarters (541-278-3716), 2517 S. W. Hailey Avenue, Pendleton 97801; **North Fork John Day Ranger District** (541-427-3231).

Wallowa-Whitman National Forest: Headquarters (541-523-6391), 1550 Dewey Avenue, Baker City 97814; **Unity Ranger District** (541-446-3351), 214 Main Street, Unity.

GETTING THERE The John Day River area is reached from the north and south by Highway 395, from the east by Highway 7, and from the west by Highway 19.

MEDICAL EMERGENCY **Blue Mountain Hospital** (541-575-1311), 170 Ford Road, John Day.

✷ To See

MUSEUMS **Dewitt Museum** (541-820-3605), Depot Park, Prairie City. The old depot that once served as the western terminus for the **Sumpter Valley Railroad** (see *To See—For Families* in Powder River–Sumpter Valley–Ukiah Area) is now filled with train and pioneer memorabilia and furnishings. The depot's waiting and baggage and freight rooms, the station agent's parlor and kitchen—all are so genuine it's easy to believe you hear the whistle and chug of an approaching train.

Grant County Historical Museum, Highway 395, Canyon City. Canyon City was one of the first Oregon settlements east of the Cascades, a mining camp born in 1862 from the nearby gold-bearing creek, a boomtown where as many as 10,000 miners lived along its Whiskey Gulch Street. Yet unlike so many other towns forged from the heat of gold fever, the town and the county that grew from it refused to die when the mines played out. As a result, the history housed in this museum includes far more than artifacts from the region's mining days, displaying memorabilia that traces decades of change through ranching and logging and commerce.

Ox Bow Trade Co., Highway 395, Canyon City. Housed in an 11,000-square-foot historic dance hall, this is a museum of horse-drawn vehicles, displaying more than 100 buggies, wagons, and carriages as well as the tools of the trades that kept them on the road—blacksmiths and wheelwrights, woodworkers and harness makers.

HISTORIC HOMES **Joaquin Miller Cabin,** Highway 395, Canyon City. When he arrived in Canyon City in 1864, a time when the town's population bulged toward 10,000 during the height of its gold-fever years, Cincinnatus Heiner Miller was already well on his way to becoming one of Oregon's most eccentric characters. Arriving in Oregon with his family by covered wagon in 1852 at the age of 15, Miller soon ran away to the California goldfields, where he worked as a cook in mining camps. "I cooked all winter for 27 men," he once said, "and every man was alive in the spring." Subsequent years found him living with Indians, attending college, stealing some horses, opening a law practice, teaching school, riding for the pony express, running a newspaper, drinking in saloons, writing poetry, and fabricating such stories of his exploits and his past that the writer Ambrose Bierce called Miller "the greatest liar this country has ever produced." During his stay at this cabin in Canyon City, Miller not only wrote poetry but also was elected the first judge of Grant County, a position he held for several years before moving back to California. There he continued writing as he altered his image: changing his name to Joaquin—and later Agricola and Professor Bones—as well as wearing sombreros and carrying a riding quirt. "It helps sell the poems, boys," he said. One literary critic, however, said that as far as Miller's literary talents were concerned, "We fear Mr. Miller lacks the power of growth, unless it is the power to grow worse."

HISTORIC SITES **Eldorado Ditch,** crosses various Forest Roads in the Wallowa-Whitman National Forest, interpretive site at Unity on Highway 26. During the region's gold rush in the 1860s, some of the mines lacked enough waterpower to work the sluice boxes and hydraulic hoses. Consequently, in 1863 some businessmen financed the digging of a ditch that would carry water to the mines. With most of the muscle supplied by as many as 1,000 Chinese laborers—who were paid 10 cents an hour for a 10-hour day—crews armed with picks and shovels began digging at South Fork Burnt River, and for the next 17 years they worked their way east, eventually digging a ditch 110 miles long. But local ranchers, angered by the fact that the area's creeks were diverted into the ditch, began waging war, going so far as to use dynamite to blow up a flume. Nevertheless, the ditch saw use until almost 1900 and then was abandoned in 1925 as the result of legal battles with ranchers. Almost 40 miles of the ditch now lies within U.S. Forest Service boundaries.

Austin House, 17 miles northeast of Prairie City at the junction of Highways 26 and 7. This roadhouse that combines the duties of restaurant–tavern–grocery store–post office is all that's left of the town of Austin, once a thriving community of 400 people and three sawmills. But even standing alone, this former stage stop on the run between Baker City and Prairie City hangs on to its self-reliance. "It really is like going back in the past," one former owner said. "I don't dial 9-1-1 because by the time they get up here, it's over." The tavern's back bar made the trip west from Chicago in 1866 and served some time at the Elkhorn Saloon in Sumpter before making its way here.

Kam Wah Chung and Co. (1-800-551-6949), adjacent to the city park in John Day. This stone building with its thick walls, steel door, and barred windows was built in the late 1860s as a trading post that could withstand Indian attacks. But when Chinese immigrants Ing Hay and Lung On bought the building in 1887, it evolved in to a general store, doctor's office, Chinese temple, and opium parlor—opium was legal in the United States until 1909—and the site became a gathering place for many of the area's more than 1,000 Chinese who worked the gold mines. Perhaps the business's main attraction, however, was Ing "Doc" Hay, who served as doctor, advisor, herbalist, priest, and fortune-teller to the Chinese, though it's said he also cured the ills and saved the lives of numerous Anglos. Today the old stone building displays not only Doc Hay's medicines—including tiger bone and rhino horn, bear paws and deer hooves, rattlesnakes and lizards—but also the utensils and tools and gear of everyday life in the good doctor's home.

SCENIC DRIVES **Strawberry Mountain Loops,** three possible paved routes in the vicinity of **Seneca, John Day, Prairie City,** and **Unity.** Here's a chain of roads that circles a mountain range, wrapping its asphalt around one of the tallest peaks in Oregon as it passes over streams, beside meadows, and through forests. You have your choice of two loops: one small, one big. The **small loop** is a 75-mile circle involving Highways 26 and 395, County Road 62 and Forest Road 16; good starting and ending points include Prairie City or John Day on Highway 26 and Seneca or Canyon City on Highway 395. The **big loop** is almost twice the size of the small loop, 155 miles. This circle, of course, encompasses much more than the **Strawberry Mountains** (see *Natural Wonders*) stretching wide enough to cross the drainages of the Burnt River and to curl past the **Monument Rock Wilderness** (see *Wilder Places—Wilderness Areas*). Good starting and ending points include the same towns listed for the small loop, as well as Austin Junction or Unity on Highway 26. A **third option** includes following Forest Road 16 for 70 miles between Eldorado Pass, 12 miles south of Unity on Highway 26, and Seneca on Highway 395.

South Fork John Day River Back Country Byway, 35 graveled miles along County Road 42 and the South Fork John Day River from Dayville to Izee

Road. This is a sometimes rocky road notable for the diversity of its countryside, from cow-gnawed pastures to pine-lined canyons in a vague patchwork of public and private land. This makes it difficult to know when it's all right to get out of the car and sniff the flowers and sit by the stream, or when you're legally bound to stay on the road.

NATURAL WONDERS **Strawberry Mountains,** south of John Day and Prairie City on Highway 26. The crest of this range, part of which drifted here from the Pacific Ocean between 200 and 250 million years ago, marks the northernmost boundary of the Great Basin: Rain falling on the north slope makes its way into the John Day River and eventually to the sea, while rain falling on the south slope heads for the Silvies River drainage, where it will end its days at land-locked Malheur Lake.

✷ To Do

BICYCLING **Prairie City Loop,** along County Roads 61 and 62, beginning and ending at Prairie City. This route, which consists of 14 relatively flat miles of paved and graveled roads, leads into the cattle country of the upper John Day River Valley. If you want an easier return ride, first follow mostly graveled County Road 61 out of town toward the Strawberry Mountains, and then take all-paved Road 62 back.

Strawberry Mountain Trails, south of Prairie City off County Road 62 and Forest Roads 13 and 16. Although these mountain-bike trails are relatively short excursions that pass through prime wildlife habitat and lead to spectacular views, the ground they cover can be quite steep, disqualifying them for casual family trips. In addition, be aware that hikers, horses, and even motorcycles may be using the same trail. With that in mind, the following are paths not often taken: **Sunshine Flat Trail**—3.7 miles of ridgetops and forest slopes with an elevation change of 2,500 feet; **Elk Flat Trail**—2.5 miles with an elevation change of 1,550 feet and one river crossing (North Fork Malheur) along the way, but because they don't call it Elk Flat for nothing, you might happen upon elk in the flat; **Horseshoe Trail**—6 miles of steep ground, an incline averaging almost 500 feet per mile, that leads to big views, as tough climbs almost always do; **Sheep Creek Trail**—stands of timber and some steep climbs along this 5.4-mile trail that sees an elevation change of 3,000 feet; **North Fork Malheur Trail**—less than 900 feet in elevation change along this 12.5-mile trail that follows the west bank of the North Fork Malheur River, a designated Wild and Scenic River; **Crane Creek Trail**—6.5 miles of trail located near the North Fork Malheur River and in the old roadbed of the historic Dalles Military Road.

Big Creek Loops, 20 miles east of Seneca off Forest Road 16. This area offers two loops, one of 6 miles and one of 8. Both begin at Big Creek Campground in the foothills of the **Strawberry Mountains** (see *To See—Natural Wonders*) and then follow two-track roads, an abandoned railroad line, and some pavement through meadows and forest. Both routes also start out following Forest

Roads 815 and 307 north to Lake Creek Camp. But from here the 6-mile loop turns south to Forest Road 16—which heads east back to the starting point, passing the **Logan Valley Interpretive Viewpoint** along the way—while the 8-mile circle continues north to Murray Campground, then returns to the starting point via Forest Road 1648.

Magone Lake, 13 miles northwest of Prairie City off Highway 395 and Forest Road 3620. This is an out-and-back ride along a 2-mile stretch of closed, two-track forest road leading to views of the **Strawberry Mountains** (see *To See—Natural Wonders*).

CAMPING **Wallowa-Whitman National Forest: Unity Ranger District** (541-446-3351), 214 Main Street, Unity. Two group camping sites are **Long Creek,** 10 miles south of Unity off Forest Road 1680, and **Eldorado,** 12 miles south of Unity off Highway 26 and Forest Road 16; southwest of Unity along South Fork Burnt River, three more group sites lie between 6 and 8 miles off Highway 600 and Forest Road 6005—**Elk Creek, Mammoth Springs,** and **Steven's Creek.** Nearby is **South Fork,** which has 9 individual campsites; another clump of camps lies between 10 and 12 miles northwest of Unity off Highway 26, near the Middle Fork Burnt River—**Wetmore,** 12 campsites, and **Yellow Pine,** 21 campsites, lie only a mile apart with a barrier-free trail connecting them; and a mile down the road, **Oregon** campground has 7 campsites near off-highway vehicle (OHV) trails.

Malheur National Forest (541-575-3000), 431 Patterson Bridge Road, John Day. The landscape of the Malheur National Forest, which covers almost 2,300 square miles of northeast Oregon, ranges from alpine peaks to sagebrush flats with forests and streams and lakes in between. Most of the following campgrounds are open from late May through October, and many offer access to fishing, boating, and hiking (more than 250 miles of trails cross the area). **Big Creek,** 20 miles east of Seneca off Forest Road 815, 15 campsites with nearby fishing and biking; **Canyon Meadows,** 20 miles east of John Day off Highway 395 and Forest Road 1520, 18 campsites near Canyon Creek; **Crescent,** 17 miles southeast of Prairie City off Highway 26 and Forest Road 14, 5 campsites and nearby fishing; **Dixie,** 8 miles northeast of Prairie City off Highway 26, 11 campsites and a picnic area; **Elk Creek,** 25 miles southeast of Prairie City off Highway 26 and Forest Road 16, 5 campsites with nearby fishing; **Little Crane,** 30 miles southeast of Prairie City off Highway 26 and Forest Road 16, 7 campsites with nearby fishing; **Magone Lake,** 13 miles northwest of Prairie City off Highway 395 and Forest Road 3620, 23 lakeside campsites, boating and fishing in the lake, nearby hiking and biking; **McNaughton Spring,** 8 miles south of Prairie City off Highway 26 and Forest Road 6001, 4 campsites with nearby fishing and hiking; **Middle Fork,** 9 miles northwest of Austin off Highway 26 and County Road 20, 10 campsites with nearby fishing; **Murray,** 21 miles east of Seneca off Highway 395 and Forest Road 924, 5 campsites with nearby fishing, hiking, and biking; **North Fork Malheur,** 29 miles southeast of Prairie City off Highway 26 and Forest Road 1675, 8 campsites with nearby fishing and hiking; **Parish Cabin,** 11 miles east of Seneca off Highway 395 and Forest Road 16, 20 campsites; **Slide Creek,** 9 miles south of Prairie City off Highway 26 and Forest Road 6001, 4 campsites with nearby fishing and hiking; **Starr,** 16 miles south of John Day off Highway 395, 8 campsites; **Strawberry,** 11 miles south of Prairie City off Highway 26 and Forest Road 6001, 11 campsites on the edge of the **Strawberry Mountain Wilderness** (see *Wilder Places—Wilderness Areas*), nearby fishing and hiking; **Trout Farm,** 15 miles southeast of Prairie City off Highway 26 and Forest Road 14, 10 campsites along Trout Farm Pond, a stocked pond encircled by a half-mile trail; **Wickiup,** 18 miles southeast of John Day off Highway 395 and Forest Road 15, 9 campsites near Canyon Creek.

Kimberly Area. **Lone Pine** and **Big Bend,** 2 and 3 miles northeast of Kimberly off Highway 402, a total of 9 primitive campsites along the North Fork John Day River.

See also *Wilder Places—Parks.*

GOLF **Bear Valley Meadows Golf Course,** Seneca. "Pasture golf" some people call it, for the greens look grazed and the hazards can include fence lines and manure piles. The roughness, however, is what makes golfing on a course such as this an adventure. Built in 1991, owned by the city and maintained by the community, Bear Valley Meadows Golf Course lies along the willow thickets that line the Silvies River. "It's really new and not very perfect," the waitress in a Seneca café says about the course. "You don't want to play with your best balls."

HIKING **Summit Trail—Strawberry Mountain,** south of Prairie City off County Road 62 and Forest Roads 16 and 1640. If you'd like to catch the view from a sky-high mountain peak, or if you'd like to tell your friends that you climbed a 9,000-foot mountain without breaking a sweat, then this is the hike for you: a quarter-mile trail that climbs less than 500 feet—but remember this translates to a *steep* 2,000-foot-per-mile incline—on its way to the top of 9,038-foot Strawberry Mountain. Even though much of the land surrounding the mountain is designated wilderness, the southern boundaries come so close to the peak that **Road's End Trailhead** takes you mighty close to it. (See also *Wilder Places—Wilderness Areas.*)

Cedar Grove National Scenic Trail, 26 miles southwest of Mount Vernon off Highway 26 and Forest Roads 21 and 2150. Even though this trail is only a mile long, in a sense it carries you far away. That's because it leads to a 60-acre grove of Alaska cedar trees—a grove that is 130 miles away from the next nearest Alaska cedars, a fact that makes the origin of these trees something of a mystery.

♿ **Swick Creek Old Growth Trail,** 8 miles north of Seneca off Highway 395. This is the home of straight-trunked, round-bellied, orange-barked ponderosa pines that were just seedlings when Lewis and Clark were crossing the Northwest. Two routes—a 0.75-mile "universal-access" path and a 1.5-mile "native-surface" trail—loop through the forest, leading you past these towering fellows and their scent of pine needles and pitch.

Table Rock Trail, 34 miles southeast of Prairie City off County Road 62 and Forest Roads 13 and 1370. A trail

SWICK CREEK OLD GROWTH TRAIL, SITE OF 200-YEAR-OLD PINE TREES

of less than 2 miles takes you through elk and deer country to views of the Little Malheur River and **Monument Rock** (see *Wilder Places—Wilderness Areas*).

See also *Camping* and *Wilder Places—Wilderness Areas.*

HOT SPRINGS Here's how it works: First, magma, the molten matter under the earth's crust, works its way toward the earth's surface; next, groundwater comes in contact with hot rock, carrying the heat with it as it discharges from the ground in the form of hot springs; and finally, you take the plunge into the hot springs, following a millennia-long tradition of immersion that produces a pleasant and healthy stupor from what's called hydrotherapy, which results from your body's reaction to water (buoyancy) and heat (relaxation). If this sounds good to you, then you can take a soak at **Blue Mountain Hot Springs** (541-820-3744), 10 miles southeast of Prairie City off County Road 62, open year-round, call for appointment; or at **Ritter Hot Springs** (541-421-3846), 21 miles north of Long Creek off Highway 395 and County Road 20, located on the Middle Fork John Day River, open May through September.

U.S. FOREST SERVICE CABIN RENTALS Instead of demolishing the abandoned fire lookouts, guard stations, and work-camp cabins that once stood scattered across the national forests as temporary living quarters for rangers and crews, the U.S. Forest Service has opened them to the public. Most are available year-round—accessible by car in summer and by skis, snowshoes, or snowmobile in winter—and are available on a first-come, first-served basis.

John Day–area camps and lookouts (Bear Valley Ranger District; 541-575-3000). A half-dozen facilities lay scattered across this segment of the region, including **Bear Valley Work Center,** 20 miles south of John Day; **Sunshine Work Center,** 35 miles east of John Day on the middle fork of the John Day River; **Fall Mountain Lookout,** 14 miles southwest of John Day; **Murderer's Creek Work Center,** 27 miles southwest of John Day; **Deer Creek Work Center,** 34 miles southwest of John Day; **Flagtail Lookout,** 33 miles south of John Day.

✷ Wilder Places

PARKS **Unity Lake State Park,** 4 miles north of Unity off Highway 245, day use and overnight. Even though its water is an irrigation reservoir, Unity Lake borrows its scenery from the nearby sagebrush desert and mountain slopes to generate a sense of wildness. Sharing the shoreline in the shade of its trees are 21 campsites with hookups along with a hiker/biker camp and two tepees.

Clyde Holliday State Park, 2 miles east of Mount Vernon off Highway 26, day use and overnight. Bordering a tree-lined 20 acres of the John Day River and looking out toward Strawberry Mountain to the south and Mount Vernon Butte to the north, Clyde Holliday stands near the scenic heart of the John Day Valley. And if gazing at grasslands and mountain slopes isn't enough entertainment, the park also offers horseshoe pits near its campground.

WILDERNESS AREAS **Black Canyon,** 10 miles south of Dayville off Highway 26 and Forest Road 42, 21 square miles. This is a wilderness of thick forests and steep canyons with such diverse vegetation it supports almost 300 species of wildlife, including year-round populations of **deer, elk, cougars,** and **bears.** The area has 18 miles of maintained trails, including the 12-mile **Black Canyon Trail,** which is joined by a number of side trails.

Monument Rock, 10 miles southwest of Unity off Highway 26, 31 square miles. Winter snowstorms and summer thundershowers seems to love this elevated area so much that it receives twice the precipitation (40 inches) of the surrounding lowlands. The result is a mixture of forests, wildflowers, and alpine meadows that is home to 100 species of **birds.** Trails follow ridgelines and streambeds, ranging from relatively flat 2-mile strolls along Bullrun or Reynolds Creek to a 10-mile hike along the Little Malheur River, which requires a number of stream crossings.

Strawberry Mountain, 10 miles south of Prairie City off Highway 26 and County Road 60, 107 square miles. Rising craggy-flanked and snowy-capped from the green pastured floor of the John Day River Valley, Strawberry Mountain Wilderness contains the headwaters of nine creeks and is the home of five of the continent's seven life zones. In addition, it contains seven mountain lakes and a 125-mile network of trails that leads to most of them. Hikes range from a 1-mile walk to **Strawberry Lake** to an ascent to the peak of 9,038-foot Strawberry Mountain (see *To Do—Hiking*).

WILDLIFE REFUGES **Logan Valley,** 17 miles east of Seneca off Forest Road 16. After creeks flow down the south slope of the Strawberry Mountains, they gather here, in this valley's meadows, to form the headwaters of the Malheur River. Part of the Malheur Indian Reservation in the 1870s and 1880s—with segments recently returned to the management of the Northern Paiutes—the valley's landscape is a mix of meadows, marsh, and pine forest that is home to **pronghorn antelope** and **mule deer, songbirds** and **shorebirds,** including the largest population of **upland sandpipers** in the western United States.

Phillip W. Schneider Wildlife Area, south of Dayville on Highway 26 and mostly east of County Road 42. First homesteaded in the late

1850s, this area first became a state wildlife refuge in 1929, and at one time was the winter home of 40,000 **mule deer**, the largest wintering herd in Oregon. Through the years, however, heavy grazing by domestic stock depleted both the grass and the soil until the land today can support only about 2,000 deer. Consequently, rehabilitation efforts are underway to restore habitat in this 66 square miles lying in scattered parcels between the John Day River and its South Fork. In the meantime, some scattered **grouse, elk, wild turkeys,** and **bighorn sheep** continue to live nearby.

✷ Lodging

See also **U.S. Forest Service Cabin Rentals** under *To Do*.

INNS **Holmes River Ranch Inn** (541-934-2833; sholmes97848 @ yahoo.com; www.holmesriver-ranchinn.com), Kimberly 97848. Located on the North Fork of the John Day River, this ranch provides a green swath of wildlife habitat 70 miles from the nearest traffic light. "We have a large brush pile in our yard where quail live and hatch their young, and big horned owls roost in our maple trees during the day," says owner Steve Holmes. "In the early evening, deer come into the alfalfa fields to feed, and by the end of August the elk rutting season starts." The inn's four guest rooms come with king or queen beds and a full breakfast ($55–85), yet the inn's greatest attraction is for those who love the call of the wild. "The bull elk bugle up and down the John Day River most nights through September," Steve says. "Some evenings, when it's clear and cold, you can hear the horns hit while the bulls are fighting. This makes the Holmes River Ranch Inn somewhat unique."

BED & BREAKFASTS **Fish House Inn** (1-888-286-3474), 110 Franklin Highway 26, Dayville 97825. With its green lawn, shaded trees, and flower beds, the Fish House Inn is something of an oasis in the John Day country, where strong summertime sunshine comes with the territory. The 1908 Craftsman home, which was renovated in 1992, offers five guest rooms, three on the main house's second floor—which has an outside entrance—and two more in a separate cottage ($50–65). Outside, a barbecue area and horseshoe pits are on the grounds, a city park and the John Day River down the street, and a unit of the **John Day Fossil Beds** (see *To See—Natural Wonders* in Columbia Plateau in the North Central region) a short drive away.

Sonshine Bed & Breakfast (541-575-1827; cstout@orednet.org), 210 N. W. Canton, John Day 97845. Located on the edge of the city park in John Day and only two blocks from downtown, this B&B is more than a business to the people who run it. "Sonshine B&B is a home stay rather than an inn," says owner Carolyn Stout. "Our home is your home when you stay with us." During that stay, Sonshine offers two rooms that share a bathroom and come with breakfast ($55–65). "We serve a full breakfast," Carolyn says, "consisting of food you will not find offered in any restaurant." Specialties include homemade bread and oatmeal buttermilk pancakes, elk steak, and venison sausage.

Land's Inn Bed & Breakfast (541-

934-2333; landsinn@oregontrail.ne; www.landsinn.net), 45457 Dick Creek Lane, Kimberly 97848. Nestled among the pinnacles, rimrocks, and swales of the John Day country, this 1,000-acre spread seems a lovely illustration of the slogan owners Tom and Carol Bruce have devised for their lodging venture: "The middle of nowhere can be surprisingly hard to find." Once you find it, however, you'll carry memories of it home with you. "We offer a place for people to come and just get away from it all," Carol says. "We don't offer extra activities, but people seem to enjoy the solitude, taking walks, scenery, getting to know our family, lots of space, wildlife, and quiet." The inn offers guests private cabins that include breakfast, but some are furnished with kitchens and everything else you'll need for an independent stay ($55–75). In addition, the inn's dining room serves three meals a day on weekends.

Riverside School House Bed & Breakfast (541-820-4731, jjacobs@ortelco.net, www.riversideschoolhouse.com), 28076 N. River Road, Prairie City 97869. Located 6 miles east of town on a working cattle ranch near the headwaters of the John Day River, this century-old former schoolhouse is remote enough to count deer, elk, and mountains as some of its nearest neighbors. "My B&B is not your 'usual bed and breakfast,'" owner Judy Jacobs says about her renovated one-room school. "We offer complete privacy with a spectacular view of Strawberry Mountain." One reason for the privacy is that you'll have the schoolhouse all to yourself; another is the sense of timelessness that comes from the sound of the nearby river and the presence of the school's original barn and bell. A stay here also includes a full breakfast ($95).

LODGES 🐾 ✐ **Oxbow Ranch** (1-888-820-8434; candy@oxbowranch.com; www.oxbowranch.com), Strawberry Road, Prairie City. It's tough not to stare at your neighbor if it happens to be 9,000-foot Strawberry Mountain. "The view of the mountain range is absolutely breathtaking," says Candy Stewart, who operates the lodge at Oxbow Ranch. "Most who come here sit quietly in the morning, sip their coffee, and take it all in." That can take a while, for this working cattle ranch spreads across 17,000 acres of the Strawberry Mountains foothills. Even though its 7,000-square-foot lodge includes two fireplaces and four guest rooms ($90), the main attraction remains outside. "It's one of the most beautiful ranches in Oregon," Candy says. "It's so relaxing and wonderful to be where there's so much beauty and solitude." Breakfast is served when and where you want it (including in bed), pets can stay at the ranch's **pet motel** ($10 per day), and "children are very welcome."

✷ Where to Eat

Because a number of local favorites have recently closed down or changed hands, specific dining recommendations are missing from this area. This situation, however, is changing rapidly, and you can be assured that most restaurants and cafes in the region provide decent meals. In addition, some travelers are likely to encounter those eateries emerging as "new" local favorites.

Southeast

ONTARIO–NYSSA–VALE AREA

JORDAN VALLEY AREA

HARPER–JUNTURA–DREWSEY AREA

BURNS AREA

MALHEUR REFUGE–STEENS MOUNTAIN AREA

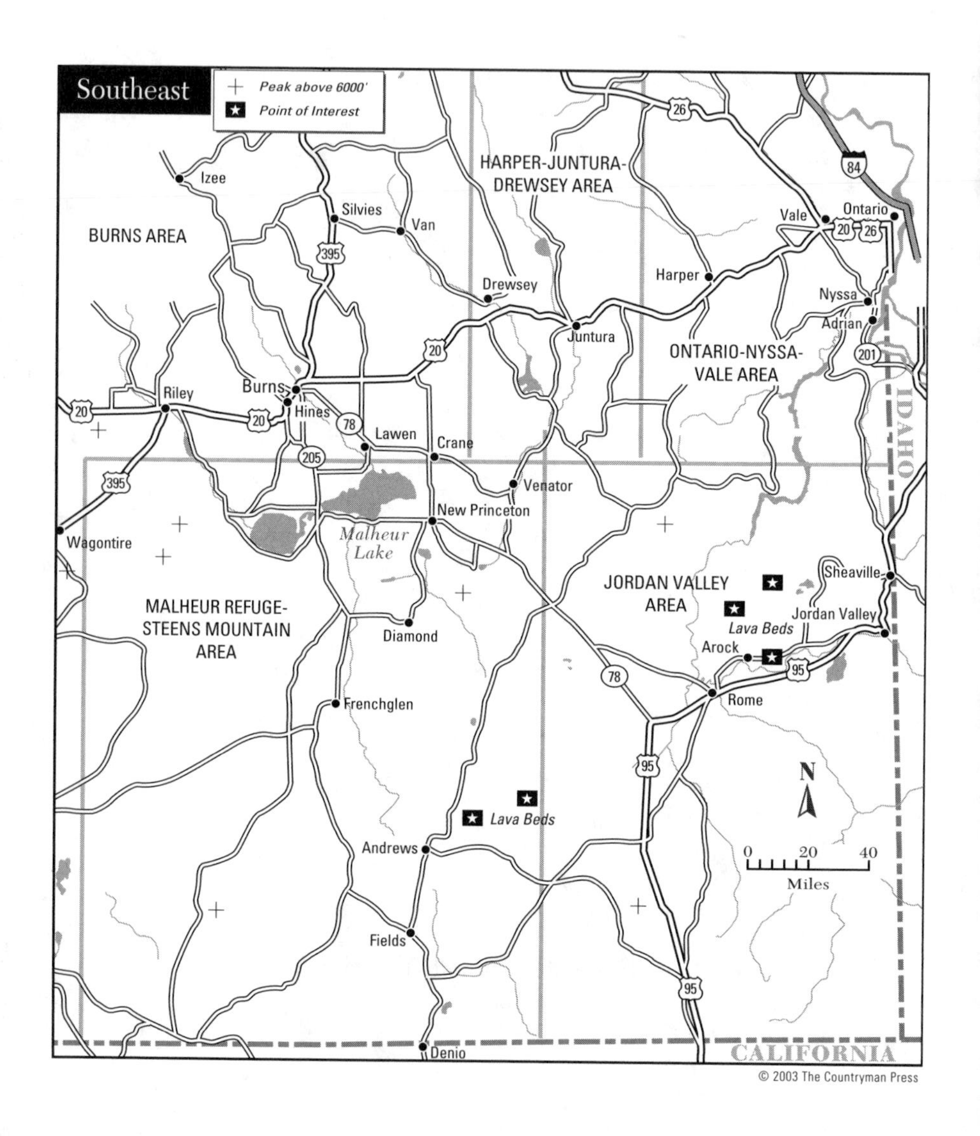

Southeast
Peak above 6000'
Point of Interest
BURNS AREA
HARPER-JUNTURA-DREWSEY AREA
ONTARIO-NYSSA-VALE AREA
JORDAN VALLEY AREA
MALHEUR REFUGE-STEENS MOUNTAIN AREA
Izee
Silvies
Van
Drewsey
Juntura
Harper
Vale
Ontario
Nyssa
Adrian
Burns
Hines
Riley
Lawen
Crane
Venator
New Princeton
Wagontire
Malheur Lake
Diamond
Frenchglen
Andrews
Fields
Denio
Sheaville
Jordan Valley
Arock
Rome
Lava Beds
Lava Beds
IDAHO
CALIFORNIA
N
0 20 40
Miles

INTRODUCTION

"Now, sure enough, you are heading into the Never Never land: a trail which winds and twists through sagebrush, volcanic buttes and shallow valleys in seemingly endless profusion."

—Edward M. Miller, describing his 1933 automobile journey across southeast Oregon

In a time so distant that it defies human understanding, the earth here cracked and rumbled and heaved and mountains rose towering toward the sky. And when the land finally settled, when the glaciers had melted and the rivers had dried and the sagebrush had sprouted across the sand, a sprawl of desert lay stretched between the horizons.

"In Oregon a quarter of our state is desert, and we'd better be getting proud of it," E. R. Jackman writes. "There are twenty-four thousand square miles of it, the size of West Virginia."

The high desert—that's what travel brochures like to call this corner of Oregon lying in the northern Great Basin, though the English writer Joseph Addison may have been more accurate when he referred to such country as "a wild of sand." For your journey here takes you across a high plateau, its crust in places broken and squeezed upward into tilted ridges, its rain dribbling into sand, its streams trickling into alkali lakes but never reaching the sea. As a result, space, sky, and sagebrush are your constant companions—along with the distant scurries or stares of pronghorns, deer, and coyotes—as you travel through this land of sprawling distances and solitary roads.

In fact, this region is so vast that one of its two counties, Harney, is about the same size as Maryland while the other, Malheur, is bigger than either New Hampshire or Vermont; overall, the area's more than 28,000 square miles could hold almost two each of the combined states of Connecticut, Delaware, Rhode Island, and Hawaii, yet its entire population wouldn't fill half the seats in the Rose Bowl.

Because of its size and seclusion, the region once sprouted towns 20 or 30 miles apart, a day's ride by stagecoach, freight wagon, or horseback. Even though the coming of the newfangled automobile drove away most of the traffic and stranded many of the settlements, the surviving communities serve as outposts to a modern frontier that still holds the remnants of eras ranging from mastodon hunters to homesteaders and as gateways to Alvord Desert, Diamond Craters, Leslie Gulch, Malheur National Wildlife Refuge, Steens Mountain, and other natural wonders formed by volcanoes, glaciers, or time.

So if you're looking for jostling crowds or busy streets, follow the shimmer of neon to the city. But if you want to find a corner of life that refuses to be subdued, then this is the place for you.

ONTARIO–NYSSA–VALE AREA

GUIDANCE **Bureau of Land Management** (541-573-5241); **Vale District** (541-473-3144).

Nyssa Chamber of Commerce (541-372-3091; www.nyssa.or.us), 14 S. Third Street, Nyssa 97913.

Ontario Chamber of Commerce (1-888-889-8012; www.ontariochamber.com), 676 S. W. Fifth Avenue,Ontario 97914.

Oregon State Parks: Headquarters (503-378-6305), State Parks and Recreation Department, 525 Trade Street S. E., Salem 97301.

Vale Chamber of Commerce (541-473-3800; abutler@fmtc.com; www.valeoregon.org), 275 N. Main Street, Vale 97918.

GETTING THERE The Ontario–Nyssa–Vale area is reached from the north by Interstate 84 and Highway 26, from the south by Highway 201, and from the west by Highway 20.

MEDICAL EMERGENCY **Holy Rosary Medical Center** (541-881-7000), 351 S. W. 9th Avenue,Ontario.

* Towns

Ontario. Some local folks once bragged that Ontario had one of the largest stockyards west of the Mississippi River, and on Thursday nights before weekend cattle auctions, you could smell the truth of that claim. But then somewhere along the line Ontario grew citified, outgrew its cowboy boots and donned a merchant's apron, and today it's the population center and business hub for the agricultural-rich **Treasure Valley.** Here the landscape is furrowed and watered and planted with onions and potatoes, corn and beets, and the business of the region is still linked to the soil.

Nyssa. Nyssa (pronounced *NISS-uh*) grew up along a Snake River run of railroad tracks, blossomed beside the valley's farmland, and stuck it out as times changed and rumbling machines replaced callused hands as the source of labor in the fields. But agriculture and its related business, especially the processing plant that turns beets into sugar, are still the cornerstones in the foundation of the town's economy. "Old-timers around here [don't mind the smell of the beets]," says the town's police chief. "Around here they call it the smell of money."

✷ To See

MUSEUMS **Four Rivers Cultural Center** (541-889-8191), 676 S. W. Fifth Avenue, Ontario. At this center the joining of the area's four rivers (Snake, Malheur, Owyhee, Payette) and five cultures (Northern Paiute, Basque, Hispanic, Japanese, and European) is celebrated as "a cultural melting pot that's been simmering for nearly 200 years." From replica Paiute villages to Basque boardinghouses to Japanese internment camps, the museum at the center tells part of the story about the people who have called this valley home.

Oregon Trail Agricultural Museum (541-372-5069), corner of Good and S. Second Avenues, Nyssa. This is a museum that begins in a former feed and seed store but then wanders out the door as a **walking tour** along the streets of Nyssa, stopping at the Western Hotel, the Green Lantern Saloon, the Vinsonhaler Blacksmith Shop, and other historic landmarks in this town where the Oregon Trail entered Oregon. The result is a blend of the old West and the new, a tribute to pioneers and farmers, and a sense of history still alive here on the banks of the Snake River.

HISTORIC SITES **Oregon Trail** (Snake River to Farewell Bend). If you travel this segment of the Oregon Trail in summer, you'll most likely feel the same kind of heat, breathe the same kind of dust the emigrants did on their trudge through the Snake River country. Here the long distances between water sources, as well as the scarcity of drinkable water, taxed both emigrants and their animals.

Snake River Crossing, 5 miles south of Nyssa off Highway 201. After leaving Fort Boise on the east bank of the Snake River, the pioneers and their oxen struggled across the river and into Oregon. "It was a very long tedious task," emigrant Martha Hill Gillette wrote about her family's 1853 crossing, "and when finished, men and stock would both be almost exhausted."

Keeney Pass, 6 miles south of Vale on Lytle Boulevard. Once on the Oregon side, the wagons headed into a stretch of winding desert road that squeezes through a dusty, sagebrushed hollow. At the interpretive site a short trail leads along wagon ruts and to a hilltop overlooking the slopes and gullies the emigrants had to cross in one day. "Had an unusual allowance of dust to the mile today," John T. Kerns wrote about these miles in 1852; "460 more miles will get us dirty-faced boys and girls out of this dirty-faced kingdom."

Henderson Grave, 1 mile south of Vale off Lytle Boulevard. The thirst produced by those waterless miles also created a tall tale symbolized by this gravestone located approximately a mile south of Vale. "Died of Thirst August 9, 1852," the marker says about John Henderson. "Unaware of Nearness of the Malheur River." Because the river is only a few hundred yards away, the story has been part of local legend since the 1930s, when a Vale third-grader invented

KEENEY PASS, THE LINK BETWEEN THE SNAKE AND MALHEUR RIVERS ON THE OREGON TRAIL

the tale for a class assignment. (A different marker nearby explains that Mr. Henderson actually died of black measles.)

Malheur Crossing, on the eastern edge of Vale off Highway 20. The nearby river not only ended the day's journey but also gave the emigrants a chance to wash their clothes in its hot springs. "Temperature of the water was 193 degrees," John C. Frémont wrote in 1843. "The ground, which was too hot for the naked foot, was covered above and below the springs with an encrustation of common salt, very white and good."

Alkali Springs and **Tub Mountain** turnoff, 6 miles north of Vale off Highway 26 and Fifth Avenue. From here a 22-mile route along dirt roads heads northwest, past Alkali Springs and around Tub Mountain before connecting with Interstate 84 near the **Birch Creek interpretive site.** (This is *not* a casual drive; roads can be rugged and directions unclear.) On this long stretch of dusty trail, emigrants and their animals struggled against dust, wind, heat, and thirst. "Traveled until nearly dark last night, when we stopped to get supper," Esther Belle McMillan Hanna wrote in 1852. "This done, we started on again, intending to go as far as we could, but the wind rose very high, whirling the dust about so that we could not see the road. We were obliged to stop by the road side and tie up our cattle, as there was no grass. There was a sulphur spring near but it was not fit to drink."

Farewell Bend, 24 miles northwest of Ontario off Interstate 84. Here is where the pioneers said good-bye to the Snake River country. Some were happy to leave it behind. "The roads have been very dusty," Amelia Knight wrote in 1853, "no water, nothing but dust, and dead cattle all day, the air filled with the odor from dead cattle." But others had a different perspective. "There the road leaves Snake River and we see it no more," George Belshaw wrote the same year. "I was sorry for that for we have caught a number of fish. Willie gets his hook and line in a morning and soon catches enough for breakfast for us."

You'll also find an interpretive site at the **Oregon State Visitor Center** near Ontario, off Interstate 84 and south of exit 376.

Union Pacific Train Depot, downtown Ontario. "The Good Book tells us that God made the world out of nothing," an early resident of Ontario once remarked, "but the town of Ontario emerged from sand clouds." Some historians, however, would argue that Ontario emerged with the arrival of the railroad, an 1884 event that not only connected the region to the rest of the world but also made Ontario its commercial hub. In 1907 the city built itself this sandstone and brick depot to note that fact.

Rinehart Stone House, downtown Vale. Built in 1872, this sandstone building was not only the first permanent building in the area but also the source for Vale's original name: Stone House. Through its early life it served as a private home, a stage stop, a community center, and even as a refuge for settlers during the Bannock raids of 1878. Today it houses exhibits and displays relics that help tell the story of the Oregon Trail.

Vale Walking Tour (541-473-3800). Because it was once an important stop on the Oregon Trail and the early center of regional business, this agricultural community is home to more than a dozen historical homes and businesses, as well as a series of **Oregon Trail murals** that decorate its downtown area.

Owyhee Dam, 33 miles southwest of Nyssa off Owyhee Lake Road. When it was completed in 1932 as part of an irrigation project to divert the waters of the Owyhee River to the farms of Malheur County, this 502-foot dam—some recent figures have shrunk it down to 417 feet—was the highest in the world. "The day will soon be over," wrote a journalist attending the dam's dedication, "and you have the feeling that you have been present at something that will never happen again." Behind the dam lurks the **Glory Hole,** the reservoir's funneled overflow valve like a giant bathtub drain, whose roaring whirlpool of whitewater can induce a sense of vertigo in those who venture onto the viewing walkway to stare into its depths.

RINEHART STONE HOUSE

FOR FAMILIES **Horse and Buggy Tours** (Wilcox Horse and Buggy; 1-888-879-8253; www.wilcoxhorse-buggy.com), Vale. During the summer, beginning at eight o'clock each Friday evening, these one-hour tours by horse-drawn buggies steer you around Vale, where 25 **historical murals** painted on some of the town's buildings depict scenes from the old Oregon Trail. "We stop at each mural," says owner Jerry Wilcox, "and explain what each scene represents to the history of the Oregon Trail or to Vale and how they interrelate."

SCENIC DRIVES **Oregon Slope,** 26 paved miles on Highway 201, from Ontario to Interstate 84 near Farewell Bend. A peaceful alternative for travelers wanting a respite from the buzz and blur of Interstate 84, this route follows the Snake River with its tall blue hills, edging past cherry and apple trees growing on the slopes and onions and alfalfa in the fields.

✷ To Do

CAMPING **Bully Creek State Park,** 8 miles west of Vale off Highway 20 and Bully Creek Road, 33 campsites, most with full hookups, rest rooms with showers, boat ramp with dock, 10 acres of lawn with trees, and a 1,000-acre reservoir.

Twin Springs, 37 miles southwest of Vale off Highway 20 and Dry Creek Road, 5 campsites, a quiet alternative to the Lake Owyhee State Park sites (see *Wilder Places—Parks*), located just 4 miles to the west.

CANOEING **Snake River,** Ontario to Farewell Bend, exits 374 to 353 on Interstate 84. This is a do-it-yourself, Huckleberry Finn kind of slow float by either canoe or raft down the sluggish waters of the Snake. Don't mistake this two-dozen-mile stretch of the river for its whitewater, raft-bending lower end; this is the limp and poolish segment that feeds farm ditches and wanders past islands. More than 16 of these islands are part of the **Deer Flat National Wildlife Refuge** (see *Wilder Places—Wildlife Refuges*), and are closed to the public from February 1 through May 31 to protect nesting sites. The rest of the year, however, they're open for exploring.

✷ Wilder Places

PARKS **Ontario State Park,** 1 mile north of Ontario. This riverside stretch of lawn is a good place to find some shade on a hot day, or to watch catfish and carp slurp at the surface of the Snake River on a summer evening when the heat of the day is falling slack as the river rolls languidly along.

Lake Owyhee State Park, 33 miles southwest of Nyssa off Owyhee Lake Road. Probably the most heavily used state park in the region during the late spring and early summer (for a quieter nearby alternative, see *To Do—Camping*), Lake Owyhee lures campers and boaters, skiers and fishermen with its 53 miles of slack water backed up behind Owyhee Dam. With over a square mile of space, the park offers 40 campsites (30 for tents and 10 with hookups) featuring some of the only shade trees and green lawns you'll find in this sunbaked land. Most of the lake's shoreline—150 miles of it—is public land that provides secluded camping for boaters who want to explore deeper into this remote country.

WILDLIFE REFUGES **Deer Flat National Wildlife Refuge,** along the Snake River from Adrian, 24 miles south of Ontario on Highway 201, to Farewell Bend, 24 miles north of Ontario off Interstate 84 exit 353. Scattered along the river for more than four dozen miles are 16 islands that make up the "Snake River Sector" of the Deer Flat Refuge. (Boat launches are available at Adrian, Ontario, and Farewell Bend.) Ranging in size from less than 1 to more than 4 acres, the islands contain a wide variety of wildlife habitat, including sagebrush and shrubs, willows and cottonwoods. Visited mostly during hunting season, the islands remain secluded throughout most of the summer and are closed to the public from February 1 through May 31 to protect nesting sites.

Lower Owyhee River Canyon, 20 miles southwest of Nyssa off Highway 201. This 13-mile paved road that follows the Owyhee River to Owyhee Dam bends through rock-craggy country that seems to glow rose and orange in the early-morning light. If you make the drive near sunrise or sunset, you have a chance of seeing a menagerie of wild critters, both feathered and furred, as they visit the river and its banks.

* Lodging

BED & BREAKFASTS **The Creek House** (541-823-0717; lodging@creekshouse.com; www.creekshouse.com), 717 S. W. Second Street, Ontario 97914. When owner Wilson Creek wants to say something about the Creek House, he lets his guests do the talking. *Lovely, great, beautiful,* and even *awesome* and *magical* are some of the comments that seem to rise from the pages of the guest book that Wilson's proud of. He has good reason. With most of its charm and beauty enduring from its earlier days, this 1908 Victorian home offers four guest rooms with private baths and a variety of interesting features: a cast-iron bed that survived the San Francisco earthquake, original Victorian light fixtures, a gas fireplace, a private balcony ($69–89). A full breakfast is included. How good is it? "Your food was soooo good!" writes one satisfied visitor. "With guests like these," Wilson says, "being an innkeeper has been wonderful fun."

MOTELS **Stockman's Motel and General Store** (541-889-4446), 81 S. W. First Street, Ontario 97914. As you might guess from its closeness to the interstate, Ontario has its share of chain motels that edge the zip and whiz of the pavement. So if you want to get away from that, Stockman's is located downtown, sidled up close to stores, restaurants, with the chance for a quieter sleep.

Bates Motel (541-473-3234), 1101 A Street W., Vale 97918. Nothing fancy about the Bates, but if you need a motel for the night in Vale this is the one to choose. (Note: this is *not* the motel of *Psycho* fame; the owner's name is Steve, not Norman, Bates.)

* Where to Eat

EATING OUT

Adrian

Mirage (541-372-2338), 605 First Street, Adrian. Although it looks like many other small-town cafés—distinguished only by its replica outhouse that's labeled "Far Eastern State Capitol Building"—the Mirage has become locally famous for its Friday-night prime rib special, a meal that draws some folks from as far away as Boise, Idaho.

Ontario

Casa Jaramillo (541-889-9258), 57 S. E. Second Street, Ontario. It might be difficult to find a local resident who remembers the town before Casa Jaramillo, the oldest restaurant in Ontario. Its longevity is the result of authentic Mexican food that has drawn generations of diners to its doors.

Cheyenne Social Club (541-889-3777), 4 N. W. First Street, Ontario. Even though it has been an Ontario dining fixture for so long that it's beginning to show its age, the Cheyenne Social Club continues to do a steady business, especially among those who believe this is *the* place in town for a steak dinner.

Fiesta Guadalajara, 336 S. Oregon Street, Ontario. A place of bustling waiters and cheerful noise, Fiesta Guadalajara offers not only first-rate Mexican food, but also one of the liveliest dining atmospheres in the region.

✵ Special Events

July: **Thunderegg Days,** Nyssa. During this five-day festival, thousands of rockhounds gather in this town that describes itself as the "Thunderegg Capital of the World"—a reference to the abundance hereabouts of the volcanic agate that is Oregon's "official state rock"—to buy, sell, trade, admire, discuss, and collect all things rock.

JORDAN VALLEY AREA

GUIDANCE **Bureau of Land Management** (541-573-5241); **Burns District**, 12533 Highway 20 W., Hines 97720; **Vale District** (541-473-3144).

Oregon State Parks: Headquarters (503-378-6305), State Parks and Recreation Department, 525 Trade Street S. E., Salem 97301.

GETTING THERE The Jordan Valley area is reached from the north and south by Highway 95 and from the west by Highways 95 and 78.

MEDICAL EMERGENCY **Holy Rosary Medical Center** (541-881-7000), 351 S. W. Ninth Avenue, Ontario.

* Towns

Jordan Valley. During the Northwest's gold-rush years starting in the 1860s, when miners swarmed through eastern Oregon like locusts, some of the folks in Jordan Valley figured they might make out even better if they stayed put and raised the cattle and sheep that fed those miners. Turns out they were right. The result was another rush, but this one was for grass. "Hundreds of homesteads were take up [around Jordan Valley]," a local historian writes. "Dugouts and small shacks, along streams or by a spring of water, dotted the landscape." Today this town of about 300 people still serves as a crossroads to travelers and a center for ranchers. Something about the mix of open spaces, cowboy traditions, and Basque culture (see **Pelota Fronton** under *To See—Historic Sites*) seems to give Jordan Valley a genuine friendliness. As an old city motto once put it: "Where smiles are wide and frowns are few, where cattle are numerous and friends are, too!"

* To See

HISTORIC SITES **Pelota Fronton,** downtown Jordan Valley. From out of the Pyrenees Mountains on the border of France and Spain they came, heading to the Northwest near the turn of the 20th century, searching for a better life and finding it on the open ranges of the high desert, where millions of sheep grazed.

Euskaldunak, they called themselves. But because that tripped on the American tongue, they became known as Basques, and one of their cultural centers in Oregon is Jordan Valley. Here you'll find a Basque restaurant as well as a phone book listing names such as Acordagoitia and Calzacorta, Lequerica, and Mendiata. And near the center of town you'll find a **pelota fronton,** the only Basque handball court in the state. Built by Basque immigrants in 1915, the court is constructed of locally quarried and hand-hewn stones mortared into walls standing 30 feet tall. As the immigrants aged, the games at the court slowed until they died out in the 1930s. Today, however, the court is restored and a new generation is returning to the game of **pelota.**

Inskip Station, 18 miles west of Jordan Valley on Danner Loop Road. Broken chimneys and toppled walls are almost all that's left of this old way station that in the 1860s and 1870s provided refuge to travelers headed for the gold mines in western Idaho. Built in 1863 by Edward "Doc" Inskip and Frank Osgood from lava collected nearby, the station furnished food and lodging as well as protection from Indian attacks. In the spring of 1866, for instance, a local newspaper reported that "Frank Osgood and the Inskip Ranch were attacked by probably twenty-five savages . . . They kept indoors and were besieged at 8:00 in the evening and continued until 8:30 the next morning." As a result, "The house is completely riddled with bullets and quite a quiver of arrows." And today, even with the walls crumbling, you can still take a peek through the rifle ports used in that battle.

Charbonneau Grave Site, 18 miles west of Jordan Valley on Danner Loop Road. For Jean Baptiste Charbonneau, son of Sacajawea, life began and ended

SUCCOR CREEK ROAD

LESLIE GULCH

as an adventure. The beginning was spent riding along on his mother's back as she accompanied the Lewis and Clark Expedition to the sea; the end came more than 60 years later at this lonely outpost on the Oregon frontier where—after spending his life in the company of European royalty and American mountain men, after working at one time or another as a trapper, guide, miner, and magistrate—Jean Baptiste died of pneumonia on his way to the Montana gold fields. And today in this small cemetery, a stone-mounted plaque commemorates this man who now lies "under the wide and starry sky" of the Oregon desert.

Arock, 30 miles west of Jordan Valley off Highway 95 and Arock Road. Hunkered down on the edge of this community—which consists of a school, a post office, a Catholic church, and a few houses—is the Sheep Ranch, a stone building that's the oldest structure in the area. Built in 1868 as a stage stop on the road to the Idaho gold mines, the building features 2-foot walls that contained eight rifle ports as defense again Indian raids. In addition, a high stockade surrounded the building, enclosing 10 or 15 acres where horses could be safeguarded. The U.S. Army helped build a two-story addition in 1865, then used it as headquarters during Indian uprisings in 1866–67 and again during the Bannock War of 1878. (This site, visible from the road, is on private land.)

SCENIC DRIVES **Succor Creek Road,** 34 graveled miles, from Highway 201 south of Nyssa to Highway 95 north of Jordan Valley. Succor Creek cuts though a lonely land that breathes the scent of sage as it sprawls its dusty, grassy self toward a rimrock horizon. Hard to say what makes the squint-eyed distance, the far-stretching silence so appealing. English poet Edward Young defined solitude as a "Divine retreat"; Charles Cotton, another English poet, called it "the soul's best friend." If they're right, then you might find more divine friendship on this desert drive than on any other road in Oregon.

NATURAL WONDERS

Jordan Craters, 36 miles northwest of Jordan Valley off Highway 95, Cow Creek Road, and Blowout Reservoir Road. This is your chance to walk the rim of a volcano, to stare down into its vent, to ponder the volcanic belly that belched out enough lava to cover 30 square miles of desert in times so recent that the mythologies of the native peoples of the Great Basin include stories of the smoke and fire that once covered this land.

Leslie Gulch, 31 miles north of Jordan Valley off Highway 95, Succor Creek Road, and Leslie Gulch Road. In 1926, when he drove a Model T Ford into Leslie Gulch to sketch the country, Melville T. Wire found a bewildering land of volcanic debris, of spires and chasms and honeycombs that shifted colors with the changing sunlight. "Many of the cliffs," he wrote, "are hollowed and eaten out into tiny caverns, the holes looking like the work of some Gargantuan woodpecker." Even though it's the result of volcanic eruptions and 15 million years of erosion, Leslie Gulch seems more the creation of a fiery sculptor.

Walls of Rome, 5 miles north of Rome off Highway 95. It's a matter of debate just how impressive these blocks and spires of rocks are that rise from the desert in the Owyhee Canyon country and that were named for their resemblance to the pillars of ancient Rome (maps label them the "Pillars of Rome"). Some describe them as "imposing and fantastic" and "one of the most impressive

JORDAN CRATERS

formations in all the Pacific Northwest." A local rancher, however, calls them "a little old low chain of hills that some outside folks got excited about." So see them for yourself and make up your own mind.

✷ To Do

CAMPING **Antelope Reservoir,** 12 miles west of Jordan Valley off Highway 95, 4 campsites near the reservoir, boat ramp, fishing, and swimming.

Cow Lakes, 18 miles northwest of Jordan Valley off Highway 95 and Lower Cow Creek Road, 10 campsites located between two small lakes, lava fields and wild horses nearby.

Slocum Creek, 40 miles north of Jordan Valley off Highway 95, Succor Creek Road, and Leslie Gulch Road, 12 campsites in the heart of **Leslie Gulch** (see *To See—Natural Wonders*) and near the shore of Lake Owyhee.

See also *Wilder Places—Parks.*

✷ Wilder Places

PARKS **Succor Creek State Park,** 23 miles south of Adrian off Succor Creek Road. Even though this site has 19 primitive campsites (toilets but no water and little shade), people come here not for the camping but for the wildness and seclusion of this rough-and-tumble canyon. Here and there a few rockhounds explore for thundereggs while an occasional hunter searches for chukars; sightseers wander along the stream and others through the hills. But in the first years of the 20th century, people came for the land, for this was once part of the homestead belonging to Ida and Willard Dutcher. "It was months at a time that I never saw another woman," Ida wrote. "The coyotes howled every night and of course I had to watch the sheep and corral them each night." The Dutchers left in 1927, but the coyotes—as well as quail and hawks, pronghorns and mule deer—still thrive here.

✷ Lodging

BED & BREAKFASTS **Ridgeview Bed & Breakfast** (541-586-2370, pkmatteri@yahoo.com), 1888 Highway 95 W., Jordan Valley 97910. Perched on the edge of a ridge overlooking the Danner Valley, this B&B offers a panoramic view of valley and mountains, a patio room with piano and pool table, and a private nine-hole golf course that sends guests on a 2-mile walk of the countryside. In addition, the guest room comes with a full breakfast ($60–100), and dinner is available by request.

HARPER–JUNTURA–DREWSEY AREA

GUIDANCE **Bureau of Land Management** (541-573-5241); **Burns District**, 12533 Highway 20 W., Hines 97720.

Harney County Chamber of Commerce (541-573-2636; lijohnso@oregonvos.net; www.harneycounty.com), 18 W. D Street, Burns 97720.

Oregon State Parks: Headquarters (503-378-6305), State Parks and Recreation Department, 525 Trade Street S. E., Salem 97301.

GETTING THERE The Harper–Juntura–Drewsey area is reached from the east and west by Highway 20.

MEDICAL EMERGENCY **Harney District Hospital** (541-573-7281), 557 W. Washington, Burns.

* Towns

Juntura. "This was the end of the tracks," says longtime Juntura resident Beulah Corns, referring to the railroad spur that once ran from Ontario on the Snake River to Juntura on the Malheur. The train's arrival brought a boom to this small ranching center located where the river's two forks join. Today the tracks are gone and the boom is past, and Juntura serves as a community center for residents and a rest stop for travelers.

Drewsey. First named Gouge Eye, supposedly a reference to the favored fighting tactic of local cowboys involved in saloon brawls, the town of Drewsey started out in the 1880s as the site of a squatter's shack and a tent saloon but soon grew into a cow town and freight center perched high in the sagebrush hills of Stinkingwater Pass. Over the next four decades settlers moved in and buildings went up and buckaroos rode into town for Saturday-night sprees. But in the 1920s the railroad and the highway both bypassed the town, and Drewsey's bloom began to fade.

✱ To See

HISTORIC SITES **Stallard Stage Stop,** 4 miles east of Drewsey off Highway 20. In 1906, a time when stagecoaches still connected the far-flung towns of the frontier, Lorenzo Stallard opened a stage stop along the major route between Ontario and Burns. Here a dining-room table could accommodate 14 hungry travelers at once—a meal cost a freighter 25 cents and a drummer, a traveling salesman, 50 cents—and a bunkhouse offered drivers a bed for the night. The station faded with the coming of the auto age, but some of its buildings, as well as Lorenzo's hand-hewn log house, remain at the site.

SCENIC DRIVES **Harper to Westfall,** 12 paved miles along the Harper–Westfall Road, off Highway 20. This is a route that leads through a dozen miles of chalky cliffs and green pastures and blue sky, where grazing cattle and soaring ravens provide most of the company—even when the pavement ends at Westfall. The smallest incorporated town in America in the early 1960s with a population of three, Westfall today is slipping away into the sage, the community's school and stores and homes baking in the sun, bowing to the sand. Still surviving, however, is a post office that serves the ranches scattered through the hills. Stop by and you might hear the stories of older times, when the town was a thriving hub of business—until the railroad bypassed it in 1913 in favor of Harper, and Westfall began to wither away until only the memories were left.

Juntura to Crane, 38 graveled miles along the Juntura–Riverside Road, the Crane–Venetor Road, and other Bureau of Land Management (BLM) roads. Astronaut Buzz Aldrin, the second man to walk on the moon, described the lunar surface as "magnificent desolation." This may also be a fitting description for the vast countryside this route follows as it traces the South Fork of the Malheur River across sage flats and past scattered ranches, offering travelers the opportunity to experience a relatively untouched piece of the Oregon high desert. Along the way you're almost certain to see reminders of days gone:

THE 12-MILE DRIVE FROM HARPER TO WESTFALL IS A JOURNEY BACK TO AN OLDER WEST

CROWLEY ROAD

maybe pronghorn herds or cattle drives—but always the sense of freedom that's a part of so much space.

Crowley Road, 83 graveled miles, Highway 78 to Harper Valley. If you crave long, lingering hours with sagebrush, sky, and solitude, this graveled route shows you how lonesome the high lonesome can be. Even though you're almost guaranteed to see more pronghorns than cars, some folks might get a bit jumpy at so much space, might start humming more county-western tunes than they ever thought they knew, especially those by Hank Williams or the Sons of the Pioneers. By the time you reach pavement again, you'll probably have discovered a new perspective of distance as well as an urgent fondness for the smoothness of asphalt.

* To Do

CAMPING **Chukar Park,** 6 miles north of Juntura off Beulah Road, about midway between Juntura and Beulah Reservoir, 19 campsites near North Fork Malheur River.

Beulah Reservoir, 12 miles north of Juntura off Beulah Road, 19 campsites near this 1,900-acre reservoir, fishing and swimming.

WILDLIFE REFUGES **Riverside Fish and Wildlife Area,** 17 miles south of Juntura off Juntura–Riverside Road. A public area consisting of more than 4,000 acres along the Malheur River, the desert oasis at Riverside is a place where **chukars** live in the rimrocks, **quail** in the sagebrush, and **rainbow trout** in the stream. In addition, flights of **ducks** can speckle the skies of spring and autumn.

* Lodging

BED & BREAKFASTS **Blue Bucket Inn** (541-493-2375; www.moriah.com/bluebucket; Judyahmann@cs.com), #3 E Ranch, HC 68-536, Drewsey 97904. Here at the Blue

Bucket Inn, located near the banks of the Malheur River some 13 miles northwest of Drewsey, you'll find plenty of space and quiet. "Around here," says owner Judy Ahmann, "rush hour is a cow on the road." Once the ranch house of a cattle empire and still part of a working ranch, the inn offers opportunities for hiking nearby trails, fishing the Malheur's waters, or experiencing part of the ranching life, especially during haying and calving seasons. Accommodations include four bedrooms ($65–85) in a house that retains a sense of its cowboy past, right down to the longhorns mounted over the fireplace. In addition, Maria, the inn's cook, fixes traditional ranch breakfasts that feature combinations of pancakes, waffles, eggs, bacon, sausage, and toast. (Dinners available with advance notice.) Children older than 12 are welcome.

MOTELS **Oasis Café and Motel** (541-277-3605), Highway 20, Juntura 97911. If you want to spend your evenings clicking through 181 channels, don't stay here. Depending on the season, the TV reception at this motel might come from a coat hanger twisted into a set of rabbit ears. But if night catches you on the desert highway that runs between Vale and Burns, and if you want to spend an evening in a friendly town where you can awaken to the sounds of meadowlarks, then this is the place for you. The motel offers seven rooms (starting at $32), and next door at the **café** you can buy a buffalo burger or some homemade fudge, then trade in your old cap for a dollar discount on a new one.

✷ Where to Eat

EATING OUT **Drewsey Café** (541-493-2427), Main Street, Drewsey. When Linda Redding first bought the Drewsey Café and began to remodel it, she ran out of money before it could open. So, she says, the neighbors "pitched in" enough labor and materials to make sure the café opened its doors for business. After all, this is the social center of the community as well as the only place in town to eat, and it seems to be a toss-up whether the café's biggest draw is the friendly people or the excellent food. "One man came all the way from Boise because he heard the macaroni salad here was good," Linda says. "So he ate the salad and left."

See also **Oasis Café and Motel** under *Lodging*.

BURNS AREA

GUIDANCE **Bureau of Land Management: Burns District** (541-573-5241), 12533 Highway 20 W., Hines 97720.

Burns Chamber of Commerce (5410573-2636; burnscc@centurytel.net; www.el.com/to/burns), 76 E. Washington Street, Burns 97720.

Harney County Chamber of Commerce (541-573-2636; lijohnso@oregonvos.net; www.harneycounty.com), 18 W. D Street, Burns 97720.

Malheur National Forest: Headquarters (541-575-1731), 431 Patterson Bridge Road, John Day 97845; **Burns Ranger District** (541-573-7292).

Oregon State Parks: Headquarters (503-378-6305), State Parks and Recreation Department, 525 Trade Street S. E., Salem 97301.

GETTING THERE The Burns area is reached from the north by Highway 395, from the east by Highway 20, from the south by Highways 78 and 205, and from the west by Highways 20 and 395.

MEDICAL EMERGENCY **Harney District Hospital** (541-573-7281), 557 W. Washington Street, Burns.

✷ Towns

Burns. You gotta admire a frontier town named for a Scottish poet. "This was the heart of a big country of magnificent distances" was how Burn's first postmaster, and the man who named the town after Robert Burns, described the area. But the big country also caused hardships. "The citizens were not very interested in . . . the outside world," writes a local historian. "They had more serious concerns—their personal tasks of surviving in a land that was isolated . . . They lived their lives a day at a time. To do otherwise would be folly on the unpredictable frontier." Today the distances are still magnificent, but the frontier is more predictable.

Hines. When the Edward Hines Lumber Company set out to build the largest covered sawmill in the world on the outskirts of Burns (see previous listing) in

1929, it built the subdivision of Hines with it. Called "one of the first scientifically planned cities" in America, Hines had a park at its center and variety in its neighborhoods (adjacent homes had different designs and colors). Then when the city of Burns couldn't come up with the money to buy the subdivision from its developers, the people of Hines voted in 1930 to incorporate as a city. Soon after, the mill opened its doors and the workers moved into their homes, but then the Great Depression hit. (That giant concrete structure standing near the park is a leftover from those days, a hotel project abandoned for lack of money.) Nevertheless, the town has continued to grow through the decades, all the way to the edge of Burns.

Crane. Today its claim to fame is that it's home to one of Oregon's two public boarding schools—its students come from as far away as 100 miles—but in the early years of the 20th century, Crane was such a thriving town that one of its stores advertised "Everything for Everybody." That about covers it. The railroad brought in prosperity, but distant jobs and devastating fires carried it away again.

Wagontire. If the folks who live in Wagontire, either of them, need a loaf of bread or a gallon of milk, they drive 112 miles round trip to get it. Perhaps for this reason, the 16 acres that make up this high-desert town of two has been called "a blip in the middle of nowhere." But it's more than a blip; more accurately, it's a café, a six-room motel, two gas pumps, an RV park, and a landing strip that sports a sign saying WAGONTIRE INTERNATIONAL AIRPORT.

✷ To See

MUSEUMS **Buchanan,** 23 miles east of Burns off Highway 20. For more than 30 years this roadside store and gas station located on the northern edge of the Great Basin has been the domain of Mavis Oard, a relentless collector of the stuff of the region's past. Inside this free museum are displayed items and artifacts ranging from spinning wheels to cavalry gloves, crank telephones to Paiute cradle boards. Worth a stop, whether you want to fill your cooler or browse the collection—and you really *can't* miss it; just look for the Model T Ford perched on the roof.

Harney County Historical Museum (541-573-2636), 18 W. D Street, Burns. The collection here tells stories or shows images of soldiers and sailors and school boards, of sawmills and saloons and stores, of war veterans and postmasters, of Paiute camps and basketball players, of stagecoaches and jackrabbit drives, of fields of hay and flights of geese and herds of pronghorns. "I suppose, says Emery Ferguson, vice president of the museum board and a Burns resident since 1929, "that we have everything from salt and pepper shakers to African hunting." So be prepared to spend some time here.

HISTORIC SITES **Buchanan Site,** 24 miles east of Burns off Highway 20. On Highway 20 near the top of the hill lying north of the Buchanan store is the site of the former **Buchanan Stage Station.** (The old Buchanan school was located at what is today the highway's Buchanan Springs rest area.) Established in the

1880s by the Buchanan family, the stage stop provided meals for passengers (50 cents per meal) and freighters (35 cents per meal and 25 cents per horse for feed and water) traveling the road between Ontario and Burns. "We never knew what it was to be alone," said Lilah Olean, daughter of George Buchanan, one of the station's owners. "We'd never spend an evening or a night without someone coming in."

Camp Harney site, 16 miles east of Burns off Highway 20 and North Harney Road. In the 1860s and 1870s this field stretching along the banks of Rattlesnake Creek held Camp Harney, where U.S. Army troops were stationed during the years of the Bannock and Paiute raids. "It was the only thing in the whole big country that looked like civilization," wrote a local cattleman who visited the fort in the 1870s. "There was a long row of officers' quarters, soldiers' barracks, and the guardhouse conspicuous—all painted white, shining in the sun. And there was a settlers' store and big commissary buildings." When the camp was finally abandoned in 1880, nearby settlers salvaged lumber from the buildings, and today nothing remains of the old camp.

Harney City Site, 15 miles east of Burns off Highway 20 and North Harney Road. The fear of Indian attacks in the 1860s and 1870s prompted many settlers to seek refuge near Camp Harney in the Rattlesnake Creek Valley. Then, even after the camp closed, enough settlers stayed that the town of Harney grew up a mile from the abandoned army base. Serving as Harney County's first county seat—until losing an election to the city of Burns, which then had to steal the county records from Harney in the middle of the night—Harney City at its peak could boast of a dance hall and a church, two stores and two hotels, and three saloons. (The intense rivalry among the saloons resulted in a 1912 Main Street shoot-out.) The town, however, began to wither when its citizens and businesses began moving to the up-and-coming Burns, and all that's left of it today is a home, a barn, and a cemetery.

Lawen Store, 16 miles southeast of Burns off Highway 78. This 1896 white frame building that now serves as a post office is all that's left of the old town of Lawen, which was established in 1887 approximately 1 mile south of here on the shore of Malheur Lake. Reaching a population of about 100 during its peak, the town included a saloon and hotel, a livery stable and blacksmith shop, a dance hall and drugstore, a schoolhouse and a doctor's office (run by Dr. Minnie Iland, a woman who moved from the East Coast to open a practice in the area). A new main road, now Highway 78, bypassed the town in 1920, and the store was moved to its present site nine years later.

I and C Hotsprings, 4 miles west of Crane off Highway 78. Evoking a "what the heck is *that*?" response from travelers who catch a glimpse of its ruins in the sagebrush along Highway 78, the I and C Hotsprings was the joint business venture of Dr. Minnie Iland (see Lawen Store, above) and Ralph Catterson in the 1920s. Here the partners built a resort complex that included a restaurant and dance hall as well as the concrete pool that still grabs travelers' attention. The water from the nearby hot springs—you can still see them steaming—was so hot that it had to be cooled for 24 hours before people could soak in it. After a fire destroyed the resort's buildings and the owners declined to rebuild, local women used the pool to wash their clothes and ranchers to scald their hogs (though probably at different times).

SCENIC DRIVES **Burns to Seneca,** 45 paved miles on Highway 395. Along this portion of Highway 395 you'll cruise beneath the basalt rims of Devine Canyon, past the pines of the Malheur National Forest, and into the grasslands and sage flats of Silvies Valley. The major route between the Harney Basin and the John Day Valley since the days of the first settlers, the road today is gentle and smooth even in its dips and bends, but the terrain is so rugged that stagecoaches and freight wagons used to stop every 15 to 20 miles to rest and water their horses.

Riley to Wagontire, 27 paved miles on Highway 395. For folks who want to get a feel for big country, this road stretches along in sways and humps through miles of sagebrush where fence lines reach toward a hill-lined horizon and the world spreads out in rolls of green and brown and yellow. Ravens perch on fence posts. A trailer or two squat in the sage. Some towers prop up power lines. And the clatter of your tires rolling across highway cattle guards is often the only sound to break the silence. Of course, it has always been a mite lonesome out here. "Wagontire was not so much of a center for cattle as it was a meeting place out of the desert," wrote a cowboy who herded cattle here in the 1870s. "Here for a week we had feasts, lassoing the mountain sheep that were plentiful around Wagontire and killing mule-tail deer, then we had bucking contests and horse races. This was just the social life of the range riders."

NATURAL WONDERS **Wright's Point,** 12 miles south of Burns on Highway 205. This 6-mile-long, lava-capped ridge goes a long way in teaching a lesson in what's called "inverted topography"; that is, this 250-foot ridge was once a streambed at the bottom of a valley. But then a couple of lava flows oozed down the valley, forming a layer of lava over its floor and making it resistant to erosion. As a result, when the surrounding land wore away over the next couple of million years, the old stream bed was left to meander across the skyline.

✷ To Do

BICYCLING **Craft Cabin Trail,** 25 miles northeast of Burns off Forest Road 28. For 8 miles this trail edges along Pine Creek through a steep canyon. Along the way, streamside pools hold redband trout.

Myrtle Creek Trail, 32 miles north of Burns off Forest Road 31. This route follows Myrtle Creek for almost 8 miles through deer and elk country.

CAMPING **Idlewild Campground,** 17 miles north of Burns off Highway 395, 23 campsites, 2 trails (see *Hiking*).

Falls Camp, 33 miles northwest of Burns off Highway 20, County Road 127, and Forest Road 43, 6 campsites near Emigrant Creek, fishing and hiking and tall pine trees.

Yellowjacket Campground, 30

miles northwest of Burns off Highway 395, County Road 127, and Forest Roads 47 and 3745, 20 campsites near Yellowjacket Lake and Yellowjacket Creek, boating and fishing.

Emigrant Creek, 35 miles northwest of Burns off Highway 20, County Road 127, and Forest Road 43, 7 campsites bordering Emigrant Creek.

Buck Springs, 45 miles west of Burns off Highway 20, 8 campsites.

Delintment Lake, 50 miles northwest of Burns off Highway 20 and Forest Road 41, 29 campsites, fishing, boating, and hiking (see *Hiking*).

Chickahominy Reservoir, 5 miles west of Riley off Highway 20, 28 campsites without hookups along the shore of this 491-acre reservoir that has a boat ramp.

See also **Crystal Crane Hot Springs** under *Lodging*.

HIKING **Idlewild Loop Trail,** 17 miles north of Burns off Highway 395. A 1-mile footpath circles Idlewild Campground (see *Camping*) through pines and past meadows, making it an ideal evening stroll or pedal—bikes are permitted—before settling down to the campfire.

Devine Summit Trail, 17 miles north of Burns off Highway 395. Beginning and ending at Idlewild Campground (see *Camping*), this trail wanders for less than 2 miles along a low ridge and through the thickets and groves and clearings of a pine forest. "This place sure has a lot of personalities," says a woman along the trail with her Labrador retriever. She breathes deeply, sniffs the air. "This is the fresh-pine scent they always promise in the commercials." Back at the trailhead, a box holds a guest book that recent visitors have signed. "Never been to Oregon before," writes a woman from Maine. "This is a good place to start."

West Myrtle Creek, 40 miles north of Burns off Forest Road 37. For approximately 2 scenic miles this trail descends into the canyon of West Myrtle Creek.

Delintment Creek Trail, 50 northwest of Burns off Forest Road 41. Beginning near Delintment Lake, this trail wanders for a bit more than 3 miles through old-growth ponderosa pine and Douglas fir forests.

Sagehen Hill Nature Trail, 18 miles west of Burns off Highway 20. To the multitudes of travelers who stop within a few yards of the trailhead when they visit the rest area located at milepost 114 along Highway 20, this nature trail remains darn near a secret. But if you'll step behind the rest rooms there, you'll find the beginning of a half-mile path that leads through a desert world of sagebrush and wildflowers, juniper trees and volcanic rock as it gives you a lesson in the beauty of distance and silence.

See also *Camping*.

✷ Lodging

BED & BREAKFASTS

Burns

Lone Pine Guest Ranch (541-573-2103), Lone Pine Road, Burns 97720. From high atop its rimrock perch, this B&B gazes over a sprawling view of sage and sky, across the Silvies River and all the way to Steens Mountain. Each room has a private bath and kitchenette, fireplace, and deck ($75). Children are welcome and horse corrals available (though not for the kids; they can stay in the room).

Sage Country Inn (541-573-7243; mchuseby@centurytel.net; www.sage-countryinn.com), 351 W. Monroe Street, Burns 97720. Owner Mike Huseby calls his inn "a peaceful, restful oasis," a 1907 home on 2 acres where quail and deer are almost daily visitors, and where flowers and shrubs and apple trees thrive. In addition, the inn can serve as a starting point for exploring the nearby—in southeast Oregon miles—Diamond Craters, Steens Mountain, or Malheur National Wildlife Refuge (see Malheur Refuge–Steens Mountain Area for all three locations). Of course, you don't have to do anything at all beyond the yard. "Guests can relax on the front porch or on a swing under a spruce tree," Mike says, "or curl up with a good read in front of a roaring fire." Three of the home's four guest rooms have private baths, and a full breakfast is included ($85). Children older than 6 are welcome.

RUSTIC RESORTS **Crystal Crane Hot Springs** (541-493-2312), Highway 78, Burns 97720. Even though it has a Burns address, this rustic resort is located much closer to Crane. It offers travelers five cabins ($30), camping areas for both tents ($8) and RVs ($12), and a swimming pool and bathhouse fed by natural springs. It doesn't pretend to be fancy. "We don't have television or telephones in the cabins," the managers say, "and the bathroom is a short stroll down the boardwalk." If you want to drop in for a quick soak in the hot springs, they're open from 9 till 9 seven days a week.

MOTELS **Silver Spur Motel** (1-800-400-2077), 789 N. Broadway Avenue,Burns 97720. Because Burn's is located 130 miles from the next towns of any size—Bend to the west and Ontario to the east—it contains a number of motels. Yet the Silver Spur stands out for its special sense of friendliness: The manager will give you free popcorn upon your arrival, and some of its visitors—especially road crews and government workers stationed in the area—might haul chairs out to the balcony in the evening and settle down to socialize with the neighbors.

✷ Where to Eat

EATING OUT

Burns

El Toreo (541-573-1829), 239 N. Broadway Avenue, Burns. When people in Burns get a hankering for authentic Mexican food, this is the first choice of many.

Pine Room (541-573-6631), 543 W. Monroe Street, Burns. Probably the best restaurant in town, the Pine Room is so popular among locals that the more popular dishes can sell out on a busy evening. You should, however, always find enough homemade bread and hand-cut steaks to go around.

Ye Old Castle (541-573-6601), 186 W. Monroe Street, Burns. This is a local favorite for breakfasts, burgers, and sandwiches, as well as for the intriguing collection of antique toys that decorate the interior.

Hines

The Worst Food in Oregon (541-573-3760), 212 Hines Boulevard, Hines. If this restaurant's name arouses your curiosity, then consider the signs standing outside its door: COME IN AND SIT WITH THE FLIES! says one; FOOD IS TERRIBLE—SERVICE IS WORSE, says another. Even the owner, Bernie Hannaford, does what he can to live up—er, down—to the café's reputation. "I'm a lousy cook," he says, "and my father always told me to tell the truth, no matter what." And so you have the basis of a regional legend, a restaurant with good food and service that seems determined to drive away customers but instead pulls them in by the carload to see what all the fuss is about.

✷ Special Events

April: **John Scharff Migratory Bird Festival,** Burns. If you've ever had a hankering to watch sage grouse strut upon their leks or to go dizzy with the fluttering whir of thousands of snow geese, then come April this is the place for you. Here you can take tours, attend workshops, hear speakers, find art and books, and delve deeply into the world of all things birds. And it all happens near the peak of spring migration at nearby **Malheur National Wildlife Refuge** (see *Wilder Places—Wildlife Refuges* in Malheur Refuge–Steens Mountain Area).

MALHEUR REFUGE–STEENS MOUNTAIN AREA

GUIDANCE **Bureau of Land Management** (541-573-5241); **Burns District,** 12533 Highway 20 W., Hines 97720.

Burns Chamber of Commerce (5410573-2636; burnscc@centurytel.net; www.el.com/to/burns), 76 E. Washington Street, Burns 97720.

Harney County Chamber of Commerce (541-573-2636; lijohnso@oregonvos.net; www.harneycounty.com), 18 W. D Street, Burns 97720.

GETTING THERE The Malheur Refuge–Steens Mountain Area is reached from the north and south by Highway 205, from the east by roads connecting with Highways 78 and 95, and from the west by Highway 140.

MEDICAL EMERGENCY **Harney District Hospital** (541-573-7281), 557 W. Washington, Burns.

* Towns

Diamond. Back in the days when homes and ranches lay scattered like stray stars across southeast Oregon, small villages sprung up to fill some of the gaps. Diamond was one such center, a place where people gathered to buy groceries and mail letters, swill whiskey and play cards. "Its special charm for people accustomed to solitary living attracted many clients," writes one historian. But when fires burned down some of the buildings and cars carried away most of the customers, Diamond began slipping away into what it is today: a collection of abandoned buildings, a few homes, and a surviving hotel.

Frenchglen. On your way to Frenchglen, don't be surprised if you encounter one end or the other of a highway cattle drive. After all, this is buckaroo country, pardner, a land settled by cowboys and shaped by cows. It started in 1872 when Pete French began turning the Blitzen Valley into a cattle empire, and it ended 25 years later when an angry homesteader with an itchy trigger finger shot French dead. The town of Frenchglen—10 people, one school, one store, no gas pump—is a remnant of that empire.

Fields. To find Fields on a map, look toward Nevada; trace your finger along its northern border until it hits Denio, then slide it north for an inch or two along the highway until it stops at Fields. That's why Fields is there: It's a stop, first for stagecoaches and freight wagons and ranch hands on the line between the cow country of Burns and the railhead at Winnemucca, Nevada, now for road-weary travelers looking for food, fuel, or sleep.

✷ To See

MUSEUMS **Malheur Refuge Headquarters,** 34 miles southeast of Burns off Highway 205 and Princeton–Narrows Road. Within this one-room museum is contained a remarkable display of the feathered and furred wildlife that live or visit the nearby Malheur National Wildlife Refuge (see *Wilder Places—Wildlife Refuges*). Visiting it before venturing onto the refuge, especially during the spring or fall migrations, gives you an introduction to the world you're about to enter.

HISTORIC SITES **Harney Lake Sand Reef,** 20 miles south of Burns, west of Highway 205. Along the eastern edge of Harney Lake stretches a long, thick sand reef that acts as a barrier to the waters of Malheur Lake and that served once as the main route across the lake beds for those who wanted to avoid skirting the shorelines. Through the years, native tribes, fur trappers, cavalry patrols, cattlemen, and settlers all used the sandy road. It seems, however, that the occasional opening of a large channel in the reef, and the subsequent flowing of Malheur Lake into Harney Lake, sometimes made the reef impossible to cross. One story from local lore says that in the spring of 1881, when the waters of Malheur Lake approached the top of the reef, Martin Brenton, a cowboy working for cattle king Pete French (see Frenchglen under *Towns*), kicked an opening in the sand. This caused Malheur Lake to begin draining into Harney Lake, which eventually breached the reef, lowered Malheur's water level by a foot, and exposed 10,000 acres of new shoreline.

The Narrows, 22 miles south of Burns on Highway 205. The narrow channel that connects Malheur and Harney Lakes, the area's only crossing when the lakes are full, was once the site of the Narrows, a town established in 1889. With travelers funneled past its door and with the construction of a bridge in 1893, the town sprouted into a social and business hub of the area. At one time it could boast of three saloons, two hotels and livery stables, a school, and a restaurant. In addition, its general store and dance hall drew people from miles around. After declining in the 1920s and 1930s, the town was finally abandoned in 1940, and today only part of the store's storage room and some graves remain.

Sod House, 34 miles southeast of Burns off Highway 205 and Princeton–Narrows Road. Near the shores of Malheur Lake, on the grounds of the headquarters of the Malheur National Wildlife Refuge (see *Museums* and *Wilder Places—Wildlife Refuges*), stands a low rock wall that was part of the foundation for the Sod House, the area's first permanent structure and a reminder of the days of the mountain men. Built of willows and sod during a winter trapping expedition as early as 1862—36 years after the first trappers arrived—the building served as a shelter for those drawn to the lake and the river and the beaver they held. In 1860, for instance, a fellow named Trapper Bill caught more than 500 beavers along a 15-mile stretch of the nearby Blitzen River.

PETE FRENCH ROUND BARN

Sod House Ranch, 33 miles southeast of Burns off Highway 205 and Princeton–Narrows Road. Located within the boundaries of the Malheur National Wildlife Refuge (see *Wilder Places—Wildlife Refuges*), this 10-acre site was once a major part of the Pete French cattle empire (see Frenchglen under *Towns*) and is now one of the oldest ranches in eastern Oregon. A dozen structures still standing—including fences, corrals, barn, bunkhouse, carriage shed, and main house—were constructed by French's crews in the 1880s and 1890s.

Pete French Round Barn, 13 miles north of Diamond off Lava Bed Road. Designed by cattle king Pete French (see Frenchglen under *Towns*) and built by his P Ranch (see next listing) crew in the late 1870s or early 1880s, this barn was used to break horses during the winter. The structure, which is 100 feet in diameter, features a lava corral, juniper posts, and a domed roof with 50,000 shingles, though it's unclear why anyone decided to count the shingles in the first place.

P Ranch, 2 miles east of Frenchglen off Steens North Loop Road and Center Patrol Road. On an early-summer day in 1872, a young cowboy leading six Mexican vaqueros and 1,200 cows sat on his horse and took his first look at the Blitzen River Valley sprawling its grassy green way southward from the foot of Steens Mountain. The cowboy's name was Pete French (see Frenchglen under *Towns*), and before his death 25 years later at the hands of a homesteader packing a pistol and a grudge, French turned this valley into a 250-square-mile cattle empire, and the P Ranch would serve as its headquarters. "There was a great white house among the willows," wrote cattleman Bill Hanley, "and it had a fireplace about which more big cattlemen had gathered than perhaps any other spot in the world." Even though fire destroyed the ranch house years ago—leaving behind only the fireplace chimney—a long barn, a willow fence, and a beef wheel survive from the days of the region's first buckaroos.

REMNANTS OF THE OLD P RANCH

Catlow and Roaring Springs Caves, in the Catlow Valley, south of Frenchglen off Highway 205. Located approximately 30 miles apart along the basalt rim bordering the eastern edge of Catlow Valley, these two caves have yielded a trove of prehistoric treasures left by people who lived along what was once the shore of a prehistoric lake. Beginning in the 1930s, archaeological diggings have uncovered woven mats and sandals, nets and ropes, bags and baskets; atlatls and darts, bows and arrows, knives and scrapers. Archaeologists believe that people lived in Catlow Cave (near the valley's southern end) as early 9,500 years ago and in Roaring Springs Cave (near its northern end) as recently as 800 years ago.

Blitzen, 22 miles south of Frenchglen off Highway 205. Toppled buildings and rusting cars and a hotel that leans its way ever closer to the sagebrush that surrounds it—this is what's left of the old town of Blitzen, a relic from the first decade of the 20th century, a time when this desert teemed with the dreams of homesteaders who came West for the chance at some free land and a better life.

Borax Lake, 7 miles northeast of Fields off Fields–Denio Road. For 10 years, beginning in 1898, Chinese laborers worked seven days a week near the hot waters of this desert lake fed by geothermal springs. After raking boron from the ground and then boiling it in steel vats fired by sagebrush, they poured the residual crystals into 90-pound sacks that they loaded onto freight wagons pulled by 20-mule teams to the railhead at Winnemucca, Nevada, 130 miles away. Before boron deposits and sagebrush fuel ran low enough to close the mine in 1907, workers produced more than a ton a day of refined borax, the stuff that went into laundry detergent. For this they received a buck and a half a day—good wages for the time—and a bunk in a sod hut. What's left today are the sulfuric air, the alkali soil, and the rusting vats.

BORAX LAKE WITH STEENS MOUNTAIN IN THE BACKGROUND

KIGER MUSTANG OVERLOOK, THE RANGE OF WILD HORSES BELIEVED TO BE DESCENDANTS OF THOSE RIDDEN BY SPANISH CONQUISTADORS

Andrews, 14 miles north of Fields off the Fields–Denio Road. Out here the road is long and the ranches lonesome, and the folks who call this place home wouldn't change any of that. "This is the last frontier in America," says a rancher who lives nearby. From 1898 to 1918, the town of Andrews, once named Wildhorse, served as a gathering place for the region's ranchers, farmers, sheepherders, and buckaroos—and some of those gatherings could be boisterous. "Of all rough places, this town of Wildhorse takes the cake," wrote a woman visiting in 1914. "Here we dressed gun wounds, knife wounds and broken heads." Today, however, it would be difficult to gather enough people for a friendly scuffle, though the town still has a school and a couple of homes.

Whitehorse Ranch, 37 miles southeast of Fields off Highway 292 and Whitehorse Ranch Road. When John Devine rode out of California into this corner of the state in 1868, he brought with him only a cook, a supply wagon, a few vaqueros, and 2,500 cattle—but it was enough to establish what was to become the region's first cattle empire. (He built his headquarters at the site of the abandoned army post, Camp C. F. Smith, built in 1866 to protect the nearby Oregon Central Military Road from Indian attacks.) Once he was established, Devine's reputation for gaudy dress and arrogant attitude soon spread through the region. "John Devine himself was a long-bodied man of unusual height and size, and he generally traveled through the country with his buggy and team," wrote Bill Hanley, a rancher and contemporary of John Devine. "He was a splendid horseman, and setting up in his high rig, with picked driving horses, he was a figure to arouse admiration." Even though Devine accumulated more than 20,000 head of stock by 1882, his love seemed to have been racehorses, for which he built a giant barn that still stands as the centerpiece of this more than 100-square-mile ranch.

SCENIC DRIVES **Diamond Loop Back Country Byway,** 69 paved and graveled miles, Diamond Valley and beyond. Follow this route to discover slices of the area's natural and human history: the volcanic debris of **Diamond Craters** (see *Natural Wonders*) and the ancient migrations of the birds of **Malheur**

National Wildlife Refuge (see *Wilder Places—Wildlife Refuges*), the cowboy legacy of the **Pete French Round Barn** (see *Historic Sites*) and the legendary presence of the **Kiger Mustangs** (see next listing), the century-long endurance of the towns of **Diamond** and **Frenchglen** (see *Towns*)—all are stopping points on this tour through time.

Kiger Mustang Overlook, 15 graveled miles southeast of Diamond off Diamond Loop Road. Like the country they roam, the Kiger Mustangs are wild enough to carry with them an aura of the mythical. In fact, some people believe they are the direct descendants of the continent's first modern horses that escaped from Spanish conquistadors some four centuries ago, while others say that's bunk. No matter—out here the herd has 100 square miles of sagebrush and rimrock to wander, and a quest to spot them will lead you into the heart of wildness.

Malheur National Wildlife Refuge, 42 graveled miles along Center Patrol Road, from refuge headquarters (see *Museums*) to Frenchglen. Through the length of the Blitzen Valley and the heart of the refuge, this tour leads from **Malheur Lake** (see *Natural Wonders*) to **Steens Mountain** (see *Natural Wonders* and *Wilder Places—Wilderness Areas*), following a route that passes through a springtime land of sage and grass, of buttes and basalt, of sun-speckled streams and cloud-layered skies that seem to soar and dip, glide and flutter with the wings of birds. Even though the refuge contains almost 290 square miles, Center Patrol Road is the only route consistently open to the public. (See also *Wilder Places—Wildlife Refuges.*)

Frenchglen to Fields, 52 paved miles along Highway 205. From Frenchglen, located on the edge of the Malheur National Wildlife Refuge (see previous listing), the asphalt bends its way up **Steens Mountain** (see *Natural Wonders*) and into **Catlow Valley** (see *Historic Sites*), a far-reaching country, deep and lonesome, flat and sagebrushed, its rimrock caves the home of the region's first people 10,000 years ago, its grasslands a lure to cattlemen in the 1870s. "It was then, as now, one of the most beautiful valleys in southeastern Oregon," wrote David Shirk, Catlow Valley's first settler, "the bunch grass waving over its broad

CATLOW VALLEY WITH BEATYS BUTTE IN THE DISTANCE

stretches like a grain field." At the southern end of the valley lies Long Hollow, a pass that leads you to catch-your-breath views of the **Pueblo and Trout Creek Mountains** (see *Natural Wonders*) before easing you down toward the eastern base of **Steens Mountain** (see *Natural Wonders*) and the community of Fields.

Steens Mountain Back Country Byway, 66 paved and graveled miles, beginning and ending at Frenchglen. Also called the **Steens Mountain Loop Road** and sometimes divided into the South Loop and the North Loop, this circular path leads through some of the wildest country in Oregon, reaching elevations of almost 10,000 feet while passing near high mountain lakes and glacier-gouged valleys, wildflower meadows and sagebrush slopes.

NATURAL WONDERS **Malheur Lake,** 20 miles southeast of Burns, east of Highway 205. To the east of the highway between Burns and Frenchglen lies Malheur Lake, once the dimple at the bottom of a vast body of water that flowed from the melt of Steens Mountain glaciers. At the end of the last Ice Age, approximately 15,000 years ago, water sprawled across almost 1,500 square miles of this basin, reaching depths of more than 200 feet and overflowing into the Malheur River's south fork near the present site of Princeton. In contrast, the landlocked water of today's lake covers less than 100 square miles at a maximum depth of 10 feet, making it one of the largest freshwater marshes on the continent.

Harney Lake, 20 miles southeast of Burns, west of Highway 205. This dry, alkali playa that may occupy an ancient caldera is the lowest point in Harney Basin. Usually nothing more than a vast salt flat, the lake's waters can cover almost 40 square miles during high-water years when Malheur Lake (see previous listing) drains into it.

Diamond Craters, 10 miles northwest of Diamond off Lava Bed Road. Here lies more than 26 square miles of the stuff the earth spews and spits and shakes loose during some of its more volcanic moments. The result is a pocked land of craters and cones, tubes and spires spread out beneath a wide desert sky.

Blitzen River, from near Frenchglen to Malheur National Wildlife Refuge Headquarters. From the snowfields of Steens Mountain to the marshes of Malheur Lake this desert stream flows, watering the grasslands and feeding the marshes of the Malheur National Wildlife Refuge (see *Museums* and *Wilder Places—Wildlife Refuges*). Formally named the Donner und Blitzen—German for "thunder and lightning"—by cavalry troops who crossed the river during a thunderstorm in 1864, the Blitzen is a designated Wild and Scenic River, though access to it is limited; rafting and canoeing are prohibited along its entire 42-mile length, and fishing is limited to its upper end. The rest is reserved for the birds. Probably the best way to see segments of the river is to follow the Center Patrol Road through the Malheur National Wildlife Refuge.

Steens Mountain, adjacent to Frenchglen, 60 miles south of Burns on Highway 205. Here it is, the snow-white crown jewel of the high desert, a block of rock 30 miles long, its summit rising almost 10,000 feet above sea level and a mile above the basin floor, its flanks tapering or plunging to the valleys crouching at its base. Even though it has seen people come and go around here for more than 10,000

STEENS MOUNTAIN STANDS ALMOST A MILE ABOVE THE DESERT AT ITS BASE

years, that's just a blink of an eye to this 15-million-year-old mountain. (See also *To Do—Hiking* and *Wilder Places—Wilderness Areas.*)

Alvord Desert, 18 miles north of Fields off the Fields–Denio Road. This desert, which lies as flat and tan as a swimmer's belly, is the driest spot in Oregon with 5 inches of annual rainfall. And as you drive along in the rain shadow of Steens Mountain, beneath the folds and creases of its eastern slope, you'll pass through a region of greasewood thickets and barbed-wire fences. Here distant cars shine as metallic specks in the dust plumes that billow out from the backs of rigs and then drift off toward the sage, and the loudest sounds come from the click of gravel beneath your tires and the rattle of cattle guards as you cross them.

Malheur Cave, 16 miles southeast of New Princeton off Highway 78. Over the last century, this 3,000-foot lava tube has seen archaeologists digging Indian artifacts from its floor, townspeople boating on its lake (which fills the cave's lower end, starting about 300 yards from the entrance and reaching depths of more than 20 feet), and Masons holding meetings near its entrance. Used by bats, tree frogs, and barn swallows—as well as by an occasional freshwater fish whose presence so far defies explanation—the cave is the site of continuing scientific and environmental research.

Pueblo Mountains and **Trout Creek Mountains,** south of Fields near the Nevada border and along Highway 292 and its adjacent roads. Steens Mountain to the north might be higher and more famous, but these two ranges of fault-block mountains standing to the south are older, perhaps by as much as 180 million years. Yet it's not their age but their drama—their peaks, snow-clad until late spring or early summer, towering above the surrounding sagebrush and seeming to brush the wide blue sky—that may be their greatest appeal.

✸ To Do

BICYCLING **Frenchglen Loop,** beginning and ending at Frenchglen, 60 miles south of Burns on Highway 205. To get close to the wildlife of the **Malheur National Wildlife Refuge** —*really* close—start off some early spring or fall morning and pedal your way along this 30-mile route east from the Frenchglen Hotel to the P Ranch (see *To See—Historic Sites*), then turn north along the Center Patrol Road to Krumbo Road, and finally head west to Highway 205 and back to Frenchglen. The almost-flat terrain of the refuge (see *Wilder Places—Wildlife Refuges*) through which the road passes, as well as the bird life that fills the sky and water and grasslands, makes this trip seem much shorter than it is.

CAMPING **Page Springs,** 4 miles southeast of Frenchglen off Steens North Loop Road, 36 campsites near the Blitzen River and the Malheur National Wildlife Refuge.

Fish Lake, 20 miles east of Frenchglen off Steens North Loop Road, 23 lakeside campsites on the south slope of Steens Mountain, fishing dock and boat ramp (no motors permitted).

Jackman Park, 22 miles east of Frenchglen off the Steens North Loop Road, 6 campsites on the south slope of Steens Mountain.

South Steens, 28 miles southeast of Frenchglen off Steens South Loop Road, 21 family campsites and 15 equestrian campsites near the Little Blitzen River, with two nearby trailheads—Little Blitzen and Big Indian Gorge—that can lead you deeper into the heart of the mountain.

Mann Lake, 40 miles north of Fields off Fields–Denio Road. A year-round primitive campsite with two vault toilets, two boat ramps, and a reputation for big trout lurking in the 400-acre lake.

HIKING **South Coyote Butte,** adjacent to the Malheur Field Station, 31 miles southeast of Burns off Highway 205 and Princeton–Narrows Road. This is one of the few hiking trails in the **Malheur National Wildlife Area** (see *Wilder Places—Wildlife Refuges*). Even though it's short and follows a relatively easy grade to the top of the butte's low, flat summit, in springtime it offers a front-row seat to the flights and noises emerging from the nearby wetlands, as well as distant views of the refuge and Steens Mountain.

Steens Mountain, adjacent to Frenchglen, 60 miles south of Burns. A variety of trails, from short strolls to demanding hikes, wander throughout the range of this massive, 30-mile fault-block mountain. Almost all trailheads border the **Steens Mountain Back Country Byway,** a 66-mile loop open to vehicles (see *To See—Scenic Drives*). Some of the more easily accessible trails include a half-mile walk down a spur road to **Kiger Gorge Overlook,** which offers a view of a deep, glacier-cut canyon, the bottom of which you reach by a nearby trail; a mile-long trail that descends a steep, rocky slope to **Wildhorse Lake,** which lies in a hanging valley; and a half-mile path that leads to **East Rim,** Steens's summit at 9,733 feet, where you can catch a glimpse of the **Alvord Desert** (see *To See—Natural Wonders*) almost a mile below. More demanding hikes include one along the **Little Blitzen River** (9 miles) and through **Big and Little Indian Canyons** (11 miles each).

See also **South Steens** under *Camping.*

✷ Wilder Places

WILDERNESS AREAS **Steens Mountain,** adjacent to Frenchglen, 60 miles south of Burns, 266 square miles. After years of wrangling between cattlemen, environmentalists, and politicians about who gets which part of the mountain, at least 100,000 acres of Steens Mountain (some folks don't count an additional 70,000 acres left open to grazing) is now Oregon's newest designated wilderness. "If you want to think of it as just your grandfather's wilderness area, it's not," says Oregon congressman Greg Walden. "This is the first cow-free wilderness area in the nation." Once you see this fault-block mountain that was squeezed from the earth and now soars toward the sky—once you travel its roads, hike its trails, visit its campgrounds; once you see its aspen groves and wildflowers, its **bighorn sheep** and **golden eagles**—you'll understand what all the fuss was about, why folks fought so hard for their share of this sacred land. (See also *To See—Natural Wonders* and *To Do—Hiking.*)

WILDLIFE REFUGES **Malheur National Wildlife Refuge,** south of Burns between Malheur Lake and Steens Mountain. "Life began with the darkness," Bruce Catton wrote in *A Stillness at Appomattox.* This is also true of the stillness at Malheur: Settle yourself down on a springtime hilltop before the eastern sky turns red and rumpled with light and clouds, and you'll see a world first take form, then take flight. The form begins with the voices of the thousands of birds that have followed their genetic maps and compasses to this place to mate and nest and raise their young. The flight comes on wings that stir the air as those birds lift themselves into soaring flight from these ancient wetlands.

MALHEUR NATIONAL WILDLIFE REFUGE FROM THE BUENA VISTA OVERLOOK

Do this, and you might feel in those wingbeats the heartbeat of the world. Do this, and you might understand why some say there are no atheists at Malheur Refuge.

✷ Lodging

INNS Diamond Hotel (541-493-1898; www.central-oregon.com/hotel-diamond), Diamond 97722. Quiet and seclusion fit the Diamond Hotel like a soft old coat. Built in 1898 as a stop for travelers and restored in 1986 as a destination for vacationers, the hotel stands near the edge of the Malheur National Wildlife Refuge, Diamond Craters, and the historic P Ranch of 19th-century cattle king Pete French. Outside the hotel, mule deer gather in the yard and great horned owls live in the old poplars lining the road; inside, rooms are decorated with antique furnishings, hand-stitched quilts, and historical photographs and prints. The hotel is open from March 15 through November 15 ($55–90) and breakfast and dinner are available at an extra charge, as are box lunches, by request. Restrictions include no children and no meals for anyone but hotel guests. (If you stop for a quick look at the place, be aware that the hotel's hospitality may be reserved for paying guests only.)

BED & BREAKFASTS McCoy Creek Inn (541-493-2131), HC 72 Box 11, Diamond 97722. For five generations the same family has run this cattle ranch that nudges up against the foothills of Steens Mountain. Here a term such as "secluded setting" is more than a nice line in a brochure, for the ranch house—now converted to a B&B—sits at the dead-end edge of a 2-mile driveway where the most frequent visitors are Canada geese. This leaves visitors with plenty of time to stroll along the creek, read on the deck, soak in the spa, or hang out at the corrals. Accommodations include three guest rooms that come with a private bath and a full breakfast ($60–75). In addition, dinner is available by reservation—a good idea, unless you want to eat from your cooler. Besides, owners Shirley Thompson and Gretchen Nichols no sooner get the dinner dishes washed before they're baking bread for breakfast, and that kind of effort shows up in the quality of their meals.

Frenchglen Hotel (541-493-2825; fghotel@ptinet.net), Highway 205, Frenchglen 97736. The hotel was established in 1916 to house guests visiting the nearby P Ranch, Pete French's old headquarters (see *To See—Historic Sites*). Today it's a **State Heritage Site** that is open from March 15 through November 15 and offers eight rooms—pessimists call them "cramped" while optimists say they're "cozy"—that average about $60 a night with meals extra (see *Eating Out*). "Our amenities are few," says manager John Ross. "We don't

FRENCHGLEN HOTEL

have TV or telephones, and the bathrooms are down the hall." Yet that simplicity attracts many guests who want to experience the hotel's atmosphere of casual living. For instance, the lobby, with its easy chairs and bookcases, serves as a living room where guests staying for breakfast can pull a mug off the shelf and help themselves to morning coffee. And the screened front porch, which gathers the morning sun, is a place to sit and read and gaze toward the edges of the Malheur National Wildlife Refuge and Steens Mountain.

FIELD STATIONS **Fields Station** (541-495-2275), Fields. The old roadhouse is now the **store** and **restaurant** (see *Eating Out*) here at Fields Station, which sits on the site of Charles Fields's 1881 homestead. In the adjoining motel, two people and their dog (or cat) can get a room for the night for about $40. And if you should happen to need anything during your stay—anything at all, from toilet-tank balls to licorice sticks, frying pans to shaving cream—the store next door probably carries it.

Malheur Field Station (541-493-2629; mfs@burnsnet.com), 31 miles southeast of Burns off Highway 205 and Princeton–Narrows Road, Malheur. What is now the Malheur National Wildlife Refuge was hunted for millennia and grazed for centuries, but now it belongs to the birds. Even so, part of the refuge is open to visitors who follow the migrations of waterfowl and shorebirds across this desert basin that long ago ran deep with water. A former Job Corps camp built during the Kennedy administration, the Malheur Field Station stands on the edge of the refuge and serves as an educational center for the teaching, housing, and feeding of refuge explorers. Accommodations include dorm rooms (many with the beds and mattresses from the 1960s), RV sites, and trailers. Daily rates range from $18 for one person in the dorm to $54 for four people in a trailer. No matter where you stay, though, bring your own drinking water unless you've developed a taste for alkali. Low-priced meals—whose quality fluctuates between good and excellent, depending on the cook of the season—are also available in the **cafeteria.** Although the housing can be a bit rough around the edges, waking to a red-sky sunrise that brings with it the smell of sage and the calls of birds can make this one of the most memorable stays in the state.

✱ Where to Eat

EATING OUT **Fields Café** (541-495-2275), Highway 205, Fields. The sign on the wall tells you almost everything you need to know about the food at the Fields Café: HOME OF WORLD FAMOUS MILKSHAKES AND HAMBURGERS it says, and an accompanying chart shows that every year the café sells more than 6,000 of each. And this is in a town where, by unofficial count, the dogs outnumber the people.

Frenchglen Hotel (541-493-2825), Highway 205, Frenchglen. Sit down for a breakfast or dinner at the Frenchglen Hotel, and you're almost guaranteed to return again someday for another meal. In fact, while some travelers come to this area for the nearby Malheur National Wildlife Refuge or Steens Mountain, others make the hotel a destination for the home-style cooking and the family-style meals.

INDEX

A

A-Dome Studio Bed & Breakfast, 266–67
A. R. Bowman Memorial Museum, 314
Abert Rim, 357
Abigail Scott Duniway Home, 180
Abruzzo, 173
A.C. Gilbert's Discovery Village, 177
Adams Cottage Bed & Breakfast, 266
Adam's Place, 224
Adler House Museum, 412
Adrian, 450
Affiliated Tribes of Northwest Indians, 19–20
Agate Desert, 260–61
agate hunting, 94
Agency Lake Resort, 350
agriculture, 13
Ainsworth State Park, 167
air service, 13
Albany, 179, 180, 183, 198
Albany Regional Museum, 179
Albert Powers Memorial State Park, 106
Alder Dune, 79
Alessandro's 120, 206
Alexis, 150
Alfred A. Loeb State Park, 106, 115
Alkali Springs, 447
Almeda Park, 247
Aloha Junction Inn and Gardens, 143–44
Alpenglow Café, 334
Alton Baker Park, 217
Alvord Desert, 475
Ambrosia, 225
Ambrosia Gardens, 84–85
American Advertising Museum, 131
AMTRAK, 13
amusement parks, 136, 185
Anchor Tavern, 64
Anderson House Complex, 283
Andrews, 472
Angeline's Bakery and Café, 335
Ankeny National Wildlife Refuge, 197
Anne Hathaway's Cottage, 267
antelope, 361, 382, 437
Antelope Creek, 258
Antelope Reservoir, 456
Anthony Lakes, 425, 425–26
Antique Powerland Museum, 177
antiques, 13
Antlers Guard Station, 419
Apple Inn, 219–20
Applegate River, 261–62
Applegate River Lodge, 273
Applegate Trail, 255–56
Applegate Trail Interpretive Center, 242
Applegate Valley. *See* Medford–Ashland–Applegate Valley area
Applegate Valley Historical Society Museum, 255
April's at Nye Beach, 75–76
aquariums, 41–42, 67
Arbor Café, The, 208
Arbors Bed & Breakfast, The, 62
Arch Cape, 56, 60–61
Arden Forest Inn, 267
area codes, 13–14
Arizona Ranch Beach, 109
Arlington, 299
Armitage State Park, 218
Arock, 454
Arthur Johnson Farm and Stage House, 234
Ashland. *See* Medford–Ashland–Applegate Valley area
Ashland Creek Inn, 264–65
Ashland's Tudor House, 267
Ashwood, 314
Aspen Lakes, 325
Aspen Ridge Resort, 362, 364
Astor Haus, 45
Astoria Column, 40
Astoria Inn, 45–46
Astoria Loops, 42–43
Astoria Riverwalk, 40–41
Astoria–Warrenton–Seaside area, 35–49; events, 49; information/emergency, 35; lodging, 45–48; parks/nature areas, 44–45; restaurants, 48–49; sights/activities, 35–44
Atavista Farm, 199
Atiyeh Deschutes River Trail, 288
Auburn, 415–16, 420
Audubon Society of Portland, 142
Aufderheide Memorial National Scenic Byway, 213, 216
Aurora, 135, 176–77, 198–99
Austin House, 432
Australian Outback Country Lodge, 333
Auto Camp Cabin, 258
Avalon Bed & Breakfast, 170
Avellan Inn, 203
Avenue of the Boulders, 261
Avery Park, 194
Azalea, 247–48
Azalea General Store, 235

B

Back Porch, 275
back roads, 14
Badger Creek, 306–7
Baer House Bed & Breakfast, 427
Bailey's Place, 291
Baker Beach, 79
Baker Cabin, 134
Baker City, 415, 427
Baker City Café Pizza a Fetta, 429
Baker City Golf Course, 425
Baker Ranger District, 424
Baker Street Inn, 201

bald eagles, 349–50
Bald Hill Park, 194
Bald Mountain Loop, 305–6
Bald Peak State Park, 191
Baldwin Hotel, 341
Baldwin Saloon, 291
Bandon Dunes, 106
Bandon Marsh National Wildlife Refuge, 109
Bandon Old Town, 104
Bandon–Port Orford area, 102–11; events, 111; information/emergency, 102; lodging, 109–10; parks/nature areas, 106–9; restaurants, 110–11; sights/activities, 102–6
Bandon State Park, 107–8
Banks–Vernonia Linear State Park, 126
Barlow Road, 165–66, 296–97
Barnhouse, 305
barns, historic, 234
Barton County Park, 167
Barview County Park, 54–55
Basin and Range, 17
Baskett Slough National Wildlife Refuge, 196–97
Basta's Trattoria and Bar, 150
Bastendorff Beach County Park, 97–98
Bates Motel, 450
Battle Mountain State Park, 417–18
Battle Rock, 104, 109
Battle Rock City Park, 108, 110
Bay City, 61
Bay House, 75
Bayberry Inn, 267–68
Bayocean, 52–53
Beach Street Bed & Breakfast, 109–10
beaches, 32, 56, 69, 71, 89, 115, 167, 289
Beacon Rock, 157
Bear and Rattlesnake Feed, 409–10
Bear Springs, 304
Bear Valley Meadows Golf Course, 435
Bear Valley National Wildlife Refuge, 349–50
Bearcamp, 245
Beaverton, 143–44
Bed & Breakfast on the Green, A, 199
bed & breakfasts. *See* lodging
Beekman Bank, 257
Beekman House, 255
Beggars-Tick Wildlife Refuge, 142–43
Bella Union, 275
Bella Vista Bed & Breakfast, 170
Bellfountain Park, 194–95
Ben and Kay Dorris State Park, 218
Bend–Sisters–La Pine area, 319–35; information/emergency, 319; lodging, 329–33; parks/nature areas, 327–29; restaurants, 333–35; sights/activities, 321–27; towns of, 319–21
Benham Falls, 326
Benjamin Young Inn, 46
Bennett County Park, 105–6
Benny's International Café, 86
Benson State Recreation Area, 166
Benton County Courthouse, 184
Benton County Historical Museum, 179
Beppe and Gianni's, 225
Bernie's Southern Bistro, 150
Berry Botanic Garden, 137
Beryl House, 170
Bethell Lodging, 204
Beulah Reservoir, 459
Beverly Beach State Park, 69
bicycling, 14; Astoria–Warrenton–Seaside area, 42–43; Bend–Sisters–La Pine area, 323–24; Burns area, 464; Columbia Plateau, 303–4; John Day River area, 433; Klamath Basin–Crater Lake area, 345; La Grande–Union–Elgin area, 389; Lakeview–Paisley–Bly area, 358; Lower Columbia River area, 126; Malheur Refuge–Steens Mountain area, 476; Mid-Columbia River, 288; Mount Hood–Columbia Gorge area, 162; North Willamette Valley, 189; Pendleton–Hermiston–Milton–Freewater area, 380; Portland area, 139; Powder River–Sumpter Valley–Ukiah area, 423; Redmond–Prineville–Madras area, 316; South Willamette Valley, 214
Big Easy Cajun Barbeque, The, 173–74
Big Eddy, 126
Big Jim's Drive In, 291
Big Obsidian Flow, 323
Big Red Barn Bed and Breakfast, 331
Big River, 207
Birch Leaf Farm Bed & Breakfast, 427–28
Bird Track Springs Wildlife Area, 392
bird-watching, 14, 44, 45, 59, 98, 109, 127, 143, 197, 219, 289, 290, 358, 381, 392
Birdhouse Restaurant, 208
Birnie Park, 391–92
Bishop's Close, 137
Bistro, Le, 205–6
Bistro, The, 63
Black Butte, 326
Black Butte Ranch, 325
Black Canyon, 437
Blackberry, 79
Blackfish Café, 75
Blaylock Rest Area, 142
Blitzen, 471
Blitzen River, 474
Blue Basin, 306
Blue Bucket Inn, 459–60
Blue Hen, The, 86
Blue Heron Bistro, 101
Blue Heron Hideaway, 332
Blue Heron Inn, 83
Blue Lake Regional Park, 140
Blue Moon Bed & Breakfast, 268
Blue Mountain Crossing, 385–86
Blue Mountain Hot Springs, 436
Blue Mountains, 17, 389, 422–23
Blue Mountains Scenic Byway, 300, 420
Blue Nile Café, 150
Blue River, 219, 224–25
Blue Sky Café, 63–64
Blue Spruce Bed & Breakfast, 331
Bluehour, 150
Bly. *See* Lakeview–Paisley–Bly area
Bly Ranger District, 358–59
Bly Ranger Station, 356
Boardman, 281–82, 291
Boardman Marina Park, 289
BoatEscape.com, 15
boating/boat excursions, 14–15, 78, 113, 131, 160, 185, 244, 343, 399
Bob Straub State Park, 58
Bombs Away Café, 207
Bonesteele Park, 192–93
Bonneville Dam, 156
Bonneville Fish Hatchery, 168
Bonney Crossing, 304
Bonnie Lure State Park, 167
Boon's Treasury, 181
Borax Lake, 471
Boulder Creek, 240
Bourne, 420
Brand Dinner House, 318
Brandy Bar, 92
Bread and Ink Café, 150
Breitenbush River Area, 189
Brew Pub at Mount Hood Brewing Company, The, 173
breweries, 21, 173, 241, 334
Brey House Bed &Breakfast, 72
Brickrose Cottage, 144–45
Bridal Veil, 169, 173
Bridal Veil Falls, 161, 166
Bridal Veil Lodge, 169
Bridge Creek, 307
Bridge Creek Flora Inn B&B, 308–9
Bridge Creek Wildlife Area, 426
Bridge of the Gods, 156
Bridgewater, 86
Brier Rose Inn, 198

Brightridge Farm, 201
Brightwood, 169
Brightwood Guest House, 172
Britt Gardens, 263
Britt Sequoia, 261
Broken Top, 322, 325
Broken Top Restaurant, 333
Bronco Billy's, 334
Bronze Antler Bed & Breakfast, 407–8
Brookings. *See* Gold Beach–Brookings area
Brookings South Coast Inn, 115–16
Brooklane Cottage, 205
Brooks, 177
Brookside Bed & Breakfast, 171–72
Brown's Bed & Breakfast, 170
Brownsville, 179, 180, 199
Brunk House, 182
Buchanan, 462
Buchanan Site, 462–63
Buck Springs, 465
Buckhead Wildlife Area, 219
Buckhorn Springs, 402
Buffalo Peak Golf Course, 391
buffalo viewing, 405
Bugatti's Ristorante, 149
Bull of the Woods, 167–68
Bull Prairie, 305
Bullards Beach State Park, 107
Bully Creek State Park, 449
Buncom, 257, 276
Bureau of Land Management (BLM), 15
Burns area, 461–67; events, 467; information/emergency, 461; lodging, 465–66; restaurants, 466–67; sights/activities, 462–65; towns of, 461–62
Burnt Mountain, 106
Burnt River Canyon, 414
Burnt River Road, 422
bus service, 15
Bush House, 181–82
Bush's Pasture Park, 192
Butte Creek Mill, 256
Butte Falls, 261
Butterfield Cottage, 37–38
Butteville General Store, 136
Bybee Lake, 139, 143
Byways Café, 150

C

Cabins, Creekside at Welches, The, 172–73
Café Azul, 149
Café Bisbo, 207
Café Castagna, 150
Café Des Amis, 149
Café Rosemary, 333–34
Café Soriah, 225
Caffé Mingo, 150
Caledonian Games, 383
California Gulch, 386
Camassia Nature Preserve, 143
Camp 18 Logging Museum, 36
Camp Harney Site, 463
Camp Polk Site, 321
Camp Wilkerson, 127
Campbell House, 220
Campbell Lake, 359
camping, 15; Astoria–Warrenton–Seaside area, 43; Bandon–Port Orford area, 106; Bend–Sisters–La Pine area, 324–25; Burns area, 464–65; Cannon Beach–Tillamook–Pacific County City area, 54–55; Columbia Plateau, 304–5; Gold Beach–Brookings area, 114; Grants Pass–Rogue River area, 245–46; Harper–Juntura–Drewsey area, 459; Illinois Valley area, 251–52; John Day River area, 434–35; Jordan Valley area, 456; Klamath Basin–Crater Lake area, 345–46; La Grande–Union–Elgin area, 389–90; Lakeview–Paisley–Bly area, 358–59; Lincoln City–Depoe Bay–Newport area, 68; Lower Columbia River area, 126; Malheur Refuge–Steens Mountain area, 476; Medford–Ashland–Applegate Valley area, 261–62; Mid-Columbia River, 288; Mount Hood–Columbia Gorge area, 162–64; North Willamette Valley, 189–90; Oakland–Roseburg–Myrtle Creek area, 238–39; Ontario–Nyssa–Vale area, 449; Pendleton–Hermiston–Milton–Freewater area, 380; Portland area, 139; Powder River–Sumpter Valley–Ukiah area, 423–25; Redmond–Prineville–Madras area, 316; Reedsport–Coos Bay area, 96; Silver Lake–Christmas Valley–Fort Rock area, 368–69; South Willamette Valley, 214–16; Waldport–Yachats–Florence area, 79; Wallowa Valley–Snake River area, 403–4; yurt, 244
Canby, 177, 185, 207
Canby Depot Museum, 177
Cannery Café, 48
Cannon Beach Hotel, 59–60
Cannon Beach–Tillamook–Pacific County City area, 50–64; events, 64; information/emergency, 50; lodging, 59–63; restaurants, 63–64; sights/activities, 50–59
canoeing, 15, 96, 126, 139, 164, 190, 216–17, 239, 262, 305, 325, 346–47, 359, 380, 390–91, 425, 449
Cantrall-Buckley Park, 263–64
Canyon City, 431
canyon overlooks, 165
Canyon Way Bookstore and Restaurant, 75
Cape Arago Lighthouse, 93
Cape Arago State Park, 98, 99
Cape Blanco, 109
Cape Blanco Lighthouse, 104
Cape Blanco State Park, 108, 109
Cape Falcon, 57
Cape Kiwanda State Park, 58, 59
Cape Lookout State Park, 53, 56, 58, 59
Cape Meares, 59
Cape Meares Lighthouse, 53
Cape Meares State Park, 58
Cape Meares State Scenic Viewpoint, 53
Cape Perpetua, 79, 80, 82
Cape Sebastian State Park, 114–15
Cape Sebastian State Scenic Corridor, 113
Capitol Park, 186
Caples House, 124
Captain Ainsworth House, 144
Captain Jack's Stronghold, 342
Captain's Table, The, 117
Carl G. Washburne State Park, 81
Carlton, 199, 207
Carter Dunes, 80
Carver, 134
Casa Jaramillo, 450
Cascade Dining Room, 173
Cascade Head, 57
Cascade Lakes, 190, 216–17, 324–25, 325
Cascade Lakes Highway, 322
Cascade Locks, 162
Cascade Locks Historical Museum, 154–55
Cascade Mountains, 17, 279–80
Cascade Peaks, 322
Cascade–Siskiyou National Monument, 261
Cascades, The, 157
Cascadia State Park, 195
Casey State Park, 264
Cassandra's, 64
Cathedral Tree, 43
Catherine Creek, 391
Catherine Creek State Park, 392
Catlow and Roaring Springs Caves, 471
Cave Junction, 251
caves, 22–23, 82–83, 251, 366, 475
Cedar Grill, 101
Cedar Grove National Scenic Trail, 435
Cedarplace Inn, 172

Cedarwood Lodge, 224
Celilo Falls, 284
Century Garden Bed & Breakfast, 145
Chambers House, 220–21
Chameleon Café, 75
Champoeg State Park, 191
Channel House, 71
Chanticleer Inn, 268
Chapman House, 199
Charbonneau Golf Club, 139
Charbonneau Grave Site, 453–54
Charleston, 100–1
Chateau Le Bear Bed & Breakfast, 248
Chateaulin, 274
Chemult, 352–53
Chemult Ranger District, 345
Cherry Creek County Park, 105
Chetco River Inn, 116
Chetco Valley Historical Museum, 112–13
Cheyenne Social Club, 451
Chez Jeanette, 75
Chickahominy Reservoir, 465
Chief Joseph Cemetery Historical Monument, 397
Children's Museum, 255
Chiloquin, 345
China Ditch, 234–35
Chinese Cemetery, 415
Chinese Massacre Site, 398–99
Chinese Walls, 417
Chip Ross Park, 194
Chitwood, 67
Chives, 117
Chowder Bowl Newport, 76
Christmas Valley, 365–69
Christmas Valley Desert Inn, 369
Christmas Valley National Back Country Byway, 366
Chukar Park, 459
cities, 15
City of Prineville Railway, 314
Civil War Encampment and Reenactment, 49
Clackamas, 133
Clackamas Lake Ranger Station, 160
Clackamas River, 164
Clarno Palisades, 301–2
Clatskanie City Park, 127
Clatsop County Courthouse, 40
Clear Lake, 216, 217
Clemens Park, 81
Clementine's Bed & Breakfast, 46
Cliff House, 84
climate, 15–16, 26–27
Cline Falls State Park, 317
Clinkerbrick House, 145
Cloud 9 Bakery, 408
Cloverdale, 61
Clyde Holliday State Park, 437
Coast Inn, 72
Coast Range, 17
Coe, Urling C., 279–80
Cold Springs National Wildlife Refuge, 381
Colliding Rivers, 238
Collier Memorial State Park, 348
Collier Memorial State Park Logging Museum, 341
Colonel Silsby's Bed & Breakfast, 268
Columbia, 167
Columbia County Courthouse, 125–26
Columbia Gorge: *see also* Mount Hood–Columbia Gorge area; parks, 166–67; waterfalls, 164–65
Columbia Gorge Hotel, 155, 160–61, 168, 173
Columbia House, The, 290
Columbia Plateau, 17, 292–311; events, 311; information/emergency, 292; lodging, 307–11; parks/nature areas, 306–7; restaurants, 311; sights/activities, 294–306; towns of, 292–94
Columbia River, 38, 167; *see also* Lower Columbia River area; Mid-Columbia River; Campsite, 284; Gorge, 162, 286–87; Mouth of, 38, 42
Columbia River Gorge Discovery Center–Wasco County Museum, 283
Columbia River Highway, 160, 162
Columbia River Inn, 46
Columbia River Maritime Museum, 35–36
Columbian Café, 48
Column Trail, 43
Condon, 293, 300, 311
Condon Motel, 310
Conklin's Guest House, 331
Connie Hansen Garden, 67
conservation groups, 16
Cookie Tree Bakery and Café, 383
Cooley's Gardens, 186
Coolidge House Bed & Breakfast, 268
Coos Bay. *See* Reedsport–Coos Bay area
Coos Bay Manor, 100
Coos Bay Wagon Road, 94, 236
Coos County Historical Museum, 92
Coos County Logging Museum, 103
Coquille Point, 109
Coquille River, 106, 109
Coquille River Drive, 105
Coquille River Lighthouse, 103–4, 110
Coquille River Museum, 102
Cornucopia, 416
Corral Springs, 378
Corvallis, 199–200, 205–6, 207
Corvallis City parks, 194
Cottage Grove, 212, 215, 219–20
Cottage Grove Historical Museum, 211
cottages. *See* lodging
Cottonwood Meadow Lake, 359
Cottonwood Meadows Trail System, 360
Cottonwood Reservoir, 359
counties, 16
Country Cottage Café and Bakery, 275
Country Inn Bed & Breakfast, 221
Country Oaks Farm, 198
Country Willows B&B Inn, 268–69
Courthouse Elm, 237
Courtyard Inn, The, 199
Cove Hot Springs Pool, 391
Cove Palisades State Park, 317
covered bridges, 16, 67, 78, 184, 212, 235–36, 244, 258
Cow Creek, 237
Cow Lakes, 456
Cowboy Dinner Tree, 369
Cowslip's Belle Bed & Breakfast, 269
Crack in the Ground, 368
Craft Cabin Trail, 464
Crane, 458–59, 462
Crane Mountain National Recreation Trail, 360
Crane Prairie Reservoir, 329
Crater Lake. *See* Klamath Basin–Crater Lake area
Crater Lake Highway, 262–63
Crater Lake Lodge, 353
Crater Lake National Park, 22, 344, 346, 347, 348, 353
Crater Lake Resort, 350–51
Crater Lake Rim Road, 344
Crater Lake Tours, 343
Crawfish Lake, 426
Crazy Norwegians, 111
Creek House, The, 450
Creekside Inn, the Marquee House, 203–4
Crescent Beach, 56
Crescent Lake, 345
Creswell Historical Museum, 211
Cricketwood Country, 329
Crook County Courthouse, 314
Crooked River Gorge, 315
Crooked River National Grasslands, 318
Crooked River Railroad Company, 315
Crossroads Grill, 225
Crowley Road, 459
Crown Point, 166
Crystal Crane Hot Springs, 466
Crystal Springs Rhododendron Garden, 137

Crystalwood Lodge, 352
Cucina Biazzi, 274
Cummins Creek Wilderness Area, 81, 82
Curry County Historical Museum, 112
Cutsforth County Park, 306

D

D River, 68
Dabney State Recreation Area, 166
Dallas, 183, 186
Dallas City Park, 194
Dalles Dam Tour Train, 286
Dalles, The, 282, 284–86, 290–91
David Hurst Barn, 234
Dawn Redwood, 136
Dawson House, 352–53
Dayton, 182–83, 200, 206
Dayville, 438
Dead Indian Memorial Road, 260, 262
Deadhorse Lake, 359
Deadline Falls, 239, 240
Dean Creek, 98
Deepwood Estate, 182
Deer Flat National Wildlife Refuge, 449–50
Delbert Hunter Arboretum and Botanic Garden, 186
Delintment Creek Trail, 465
Delintment Lake, 465
Delta Café, 150–51
DeMoss Springs, 306
Denman Wildlife Area, 264
Depoe Bay. *See* Lincoln City–Depoe Bay–Newport area
Depot Deli, 335
Deschutes Brewery, 334
Deschutes County Historical Center, 321
Deschutes Motel, 310
Deschutes National Forest, 323–24
Deschutes River, 284, 304
Deschutes River Crossing, 296
Deschutes River State Recreation Area, 288
Deschutes River Trail, 326
Detroit, 200, 207
Detroit Lake State Park, 189
Devils Elbow State Park, 81
Devils Flat, 239
Devils Lake State Park, 68–69
Devils Punch Bowl State Park, 69, 70
Devine Summit Trail, 465
Dewitt Museum, 430
Diamond, 468, 478
Diamond Crater, 474
Diamond Hotel, 478
Diamond Lake, 238–39
Diamond Lake Resort, 351
Diamond Loop Back Country Byway, 472–73
Diamond Peak, 349
Diamond Stone Guest Lodge and Gallery, 333
Dibble House, 179–80
Dielschneider Carriage House, 201
Doerner Fir, 105
Dog Lake, 359
Dogs for the Deaf, 258–59
Doris Café, 151
Dorris Ranch, 212
Dory Festival, 64
Douglas County Museum of History and Natural History, 232
Drain House, 232
Drake Park, 327
Drewsey, 457–60
Drewsey Café, 460
Drift Creek, 67, 82
Drift Creek Falls, 68
Drift Inn Bed & Breakfast, 219
drive-in movie theaters, 184–85, 379, 388
Dufur, 308
Dufur Pastime Saloon, 311
Dufur Threshing Bee, 311
Dufur Valley Bed & Breakfast, 308
Dug Bar, 398
Dundee, 191, 206
Dundee Bistro, 206
Dunshee House at Face Rock, 110
Durkee, 416
Durkee Steak Feed, 429

E

E. E. Wilson Wildlife Area, 197
E. H. Carruthers Park, 44
E. R. Corbett State Park, 328
Eagle Cap Wilderness, 392, 405–6
Eagle Cap Wilderness campgrounds, 390
Eagle Creek, 167
Eagle Creek Campground, 156
Eagle Creek Golf Course, 164
Eagle Crest Resort, 316
Eagle Point Golf Course, 262
Eagle Ridge Park, 348
Eagle Rock Lodge, 223
eagles, 349–50
Eagle's View Bed & Breakfast, 62–63
East Lake Resort, 332–33
East View Country Inn, 204
Eastern Oregon Guide Association, 18
Eastern Oregon Museum, 412
Eastmoreland, 139
Echo, 378
Echo Historical Museum, 376
Echo Library, 381
Echo Meadows, 378
Ecola Creek, 39
Ecola Point, 55
Ecola State Park, 53, 59
Edison's Village, 343
Edwin K Bed & Breakfast, 83
Eel Lake, 97
Egg Cup Inn, 204
El Charrito, 208
El Toreo, 466
El Torero, 149
Eldorado Ditch, 431–32
Elgin. *See* La Grande–Union–Elgin area
Elgin Opera House, 387
Elijah Bistow State Park, 218
Elk City, 68
elk feeding, 418
Elk River, 106, 109
Elkhorn Drive Scenic Byway, 420–21
Elkhorn Valley Golf Course, 190
Elkhorn Wildlife Management Area, 418, 426–27
Elkqua Lodge, 241
Elks Temple, 311
Elliot House, The, 318
Elliot State Forest, 88
Ellmaker State Park, 70
Elmira, 220
Elowah Falls, 166
Elsinore Theatre, 181
Elusive Trout Pub, The, 174
Emigrant Creek, 465
Emigrant Hill, 377–78
Emigrant Hill Road, 379, 388
Emigrant Lake, 262
Emigrant Springs State Park, 386, 392
Empire Lakes Park, 96
Enchanted Country Inn, 221
Enchanted Forest, 185
End of the Oregon Trail Interpretive Center, 132
English Rose, The, 84
Enterprise, 397, 408
Enterprise Wildlife Area, 406
Entheos Estate, 203
Erin Lodge, 253
Ermatinger House, 133
Erratic Rock State Park, 188–89
Esparza's Tex-Mex Café, 151
Estacada, 167
estuaries, 98–99, 109, 115
Eugene, 211–14, 218–22, 224–25
Eugene Riverfront Trail, 214
Eugene Saturday Market, 212
Eureka Bar, 398
events, 16; *see also* under specific places
Evergreen Aviation Museum, 178
Ewing Young Oak, 188
Excelsior Inn, 219

Excelsior Inn Ristorante Italiano, 224
Exceptional Place to Bed & Breakfast Inn, An, 71–72

F

Face Rock, 107
Falcon's Crest Inn, 168
Fall Creek State Recreation area, 215
Falls Camp, 464
family activities: Astoria–Warrenton–Seaside area, 41–42; Bandon–Port Orford area, 104–5; Bend–Sisters–La Pine area, 321; Cannon Beach–Tillamook–Pacific County City area, 53; Columbia Plateau, 299; Gold Beach–Brookings area, 113; Grants Pass–Rogue River area, 244; Illinois Valley area, 250–51; Klamath Basin–Crater Lake area, 343; La Grande–Union–Elgin area, 388; Lakeview–Paisley–Bly area, 357; Lincoln City–Depoe Bay–Newport area, 67; Medford–Ashland–Applegate Valley area, 258–59; Mid-Columbia River, 286; Mount Hood–Columbia Gorge area, 160; North Willamette Valley, 185; Oakland–Roseburg–Myrtle Creek area, 236; Ontario–Nyssa–Vale area, 448; Pendleton–Hermiston–Milton–Freewater area, 379; Portland area, 136; Powder River–Sumpter Valley–Ukiah area, 418–19; Reedsport–Coos Bay area, 93–94; Silver Lake–Christmas Valley–Fort Rock area, 366; Waldport–Yachats–Florence area, 78–79
Farewell Bend, 447
Farewell Bend State Park, 426
farmer's markets, 16, 138, 160
Farrell Homestead, 314
Fat Albert's Breakfast Café, 151
Favell Museum of Western Art and Indian Artifacts, 341
Fern Falls, 239
Fern Ridge Wildlife Area, 219
Fernhill Park, 140
ferry boat rides, 185
field stations, 479
Fields, 469, 473
Fields Café, 479
Fiesta Guadalajara, 451
Fiorella's, 353
fire lookout rentals, 113, 244, 250–51, 357, 366
Fischer House Cottage, 205
Fish House Inn, 438
Fish Lake, 261, 476
Fishermen's Bend, 194
fishing, 16–17, 426
Five-Mile Point, 99
Flagstaff Hill, 414
Flavel House, 37, 46
flea markets, 429
Flery Manor, 248
Fleur de Sel, 208
Flippin Castle, 124
Floed-Lane House, 233
Floras Lake House by the Sea, 110
Floras State Park, 108
Florence. *See* Waldport–Yachats–Florence area
Fogarty Creek State Park, 69
Foley Station, 395
Forest Grove, 144, 149
Forest Hills Golf Course, 139
Forest Park, 140
Fork, The, 296
Fort Astoria, 40
Fort Clatsop, 38
Fort Clatsop Loop, 42–43
Fort Dalles Museum, 282–83
Fort Henrietta, 378–79
Fort Henrietta Days, 383
Fort Hoskins, 183
Fort Klamath, 342, 351–52, 353
Fort Rock, 23, 365–69, 368
Fort Rock Camp, 285
Fort Rock Cave, 366
Fort Rock Valley Homestead Days, 369
Fort Smith Bed & Breakfast, 221
Fort Stevens Historic Area and Military Museum, 36
Fort Stevens State Park, 43, 44–45
Fort Yamhill Blockhouse, 182–83
Fossil, 293–94, 298, 303–4, 308–10, 311
fossil beds, 299, 301–3
Fossil Café, 311
Fossil Lake, 367
Fossil Lodge, 309
Fossil Motel and RV Park, 310
Fossil Museum, 295
Foster Farm, 159
Foster Lilac, 162
Four County Point Trail, 127
Four Rivers Cultural Center, 446
Fourmile Canyon, 296
Franklin Street Station, 46
Fratelli, 151
Frazier Farmstead Museum, 376–77
Freewater. *See* Pendleton–Hermiston–Milton–Freewater area
Fremont National Forest, 358, 368
Fremont National Recreation Trail, 359–60
Frenchglen, 468, 473, 476
Frenchglen Hotel, 478–79
Frona County Park, 106
Frontier Country Restaurant, 206

G

Gables, The, 205
Gahr Farm, 205
Galena, 420
Gallery, The, 335
Gangloff Park, 391
gardens, 17, 22, 67, 136–38, 185–87, 212–13
Gardiner, 92
Garibaldi, 62
Gates, 206
Gearhart, 48–49, 360
Gedney Gardens, 145
General Hooker's Bed & Breakfast, 145
Genoa, 149
George Rogers Park, 142
Georgian House, 145–46
Georgie's Beachside Grill, 76
Geppetto's, 274–75
Gerber Reservoir, 362
Ghost Creek Golf Course, 139–40
ghost towns, 292–93, 411, 415–16, 419–20
Gilliam County Museum, 294–95
Gin Lin Trail, 257–58
Gleneden Beach, 75
Gogi's, 274
Gold Beach–Brookings area, 112–17; events, 117; information/emergency, 112; lodging, 115–16; parks/nature areas, 114–15; restaurants, 117; sights/activities, 112–14
Gold Hill, 272
gold panning, 236, 419
gold rush, 228, 257–58
Golden, 243
Golden and Silver Falls State Park, 97
golf courses, 17–18; Bandon–Port Orford area, 106; Bend–Sisters–La Pine area, 325–26; Columbia Plateau, 305; Gold Beach–Brookings area, 114; John Day River area, 435; La Grande–Union–Elgin area, 391; Lincoln City–Depoe Bay–Newport area, 68; Medford–Ashland–Applegate Valley area, 262; Mount Hood–Columbia Gorge area, 164; North Willamette Valley, 190; Oakland–Roseburg–Myrtle Creek area, 239; Pendleton–Hermiston–Milton–Freewater area, 380; Portland area,

139–40; Powder River–Sumpter Valley–Ukiah area, 425; Redmond–Prineville–Madras area, 316; South Willamette Valley, 217
Goose Lake State Park, 360
Gordon Ridge Road, 299
Gorge View Bed & Breakfast, 170
Government Camp, 168, 169, 173
Governor Patterson State Park, 81
Gracie's Landing, 71
Grand Ronde, 200–1
Grande Ronde River Campgrounds, 389–90
Grande Ronde Valley, 385, 388–89
Grandview, 46
Granite, 416–17
Granny Franny's Farm, 200–1
Grant County Historical Museum, 431
Grant House Bed & Breakfast, 427
Grants Pass–Rogue River area, 242–49; events, 249; information/emergency, 242; lodging, 247–49; parks/nature areas, 246–47; restaurants, 249; sights/activities, 242–46
Grape Vine Inn, 269
Grassy Knob, 108
Grateful Bread, 64
Grave Creek, 244
Green Gables Bed & Breakfast, 72–73
Green Springs Inn, 273
Greenhorn, 420
Greenlea Golf Course, 139
Griffin Gulch, 419–20
Grizzly Peak, 262
Grotto, The, 141
Grove of the States, 142
Guest House at Stone House Farm, 290–91
Guest House, The, 47–48
guides, 18
Gulch, 456
Gustav's Bier Stube, 151
Guy W. Talbot State Park, 166

H

Hager Grove Pear Tree, 188
Hager Mountain, 366
Haines, 415
Haines Steak House, 429
Halfway, 411, 427–28
Hallquist Hollow Bed & Breakfast, 84
Hamilton River House, 249
Hammond, 47
Hanan Trail, 360
Hanley Farm, 256
Hans, 334
Hardman, 298–99
Harlow House, 157
Harney City Site, 463
Harney County Historical Museum, 462
Harney Lake, 474
Harney Lake Sand Reef, 469
Harper, 457–60
Harp's, 110–11
Harris Beach State Park, 113, 115
Harrison House, 199–200
Hart Mountain National Antelope Refuge, 361
Hat Point Scenic Drive, 401
Hat Rock, 377
Hat Rock State Park, 381
Hatfield Marine Science Center, 67
Havenshire Bed & Breakfast, 247–48
Haystack Reservoir, 316
Haystack Rocks, 54, 58, 59
Headwaters of the Metolius River, 323
Heathman, The, 149
Hebo, 55, 56–57
Hebo Lake, 55, 56–57
Heceta Head Lighthouse, 78
Hellgate Boat Excursions, 244
Hells Canyon, 23, 398–99, 402, 406
Hells Canyon Bison Ranch, 419
Hells Canyon Scenic Byway, 389, 400–1, 421
Helvetia Tavern, 150
Hemlock Lake, 239
Henderson Grave, 446–47
Hendricks Park Rhododendron Garden, 212–13
Heppner, 303, 304–5, 310
Heritage Museum, 36, 178
Heritage Trees, 188, 214, 237, 261
Hermiston. *See* Pendleton–Hermiston–Milton–Freewater area
Heron Haus, 146
Heron Lakes, 139
Hersey House and Bungalow, 269
Heryford Inn Bed & Breakfast, 363
Higgins, 149
High Desert Golf and Learning Center, 325
High Desert Museum, 321
Highway 99, 187, 213, 259
highways, 18
hiking, 18; Astoria–Warrenton–Seaside area, 43–44; Bandon–Port Orford area, 106; Bend–Sisters–La Pine area, 326; Burns area, 465; Cannon Beach–Tillamook–Pacific County City area, 55–57; Columbia Plateau, 305–6; Gold Beach–Brookings area, 114; Grants Pass–Rogue River area, 246; Illinois Valley area, 252; John Day River area, 435–36; Klamath Basin–Crater Lake area, 347; La Grande–Union–Elgin area, 391; Lakeview–Paisley–Bly area, 359–60; Lincoln City–Depoe Bay–Newport area, 68; Lower Columbia River area, 126–27; Malheur Refuge–Steens Mountain area, 476–77; Medford–Ashland–Applegate Valley area, 262–63; Mid-Columbia River, 288–89; Mount Hood–Columbia Gorge area, 164–66; North Willamette Valley, 190; Oakland–Roseburg–Myrtle Creek area, 239; Pendleton–Hermiston–Milton–Freewater area, 380–81; Powder River–Sumpter Valley–Ukiah area, 425–26; Redmond–Prineville–Madras area, 316–17; Reedsport–Coos Bay area, 96–97; South Willamette Valley, 217; Waldport–Yachats–Florence area, 80–81; Wallowa Valley–Snake River area, 404
Hillsboro, 135, 150, 180–81
Hinds Walnut Tree, 237
Hines, 461–62, 466–67
Historic Broetje House, 144
Historic Columbia River Highway Scenic Byway, 22, 286, 288
Historic Orth House, 272
Historic Union Hotel, 394
historical markers, 18
historical museums, 18; *see also* museums
H.J. Andrews Experimental Forest, 214
Hole in the Ground, 368
Hole in the Wall Landslide, 423
Holiday Farm Restaurant, 224–25
Holmes River Ranch Inn, 438
Home by the Sea Bed & Breakfast, 110
Home Run Pizza Parlor, 353
Home Spirit Bakery Café, 48
Homestead Bed & Breakfast, The, 71
Homestead Village Museum, 366
Honker Inn Lodge, 363
Hood River, 154, 168–69, 170–71, 173–74
Hood River County Museum, 155
Hood River Hotel, 168–69
Hoover Creek, 304
Hoover-Minthorn House, 179

horse and buggy tours, 448
Horse Creek, 82
horse-drawn trolleys, 418
horseback riding, 404–5
Horseshoe Ranch, 353
Horsetail Falls, 161, 165
hospitals, 35, 65, 77, 91, 102, 112, 123, 130, 153–54, 176, 211, 242, 250, 254, 281, 292, 312–13, 354, 365, 384, 396, 430, 457, 468
Hostess House, 146
Hot Lake Resort, 387
hot springs, 19, 436, 463–64
Hotel Condon, 308
Hotel Oregon, 201–2
hotels. *See* lodging
House of Hunter, 240
House of Rogue, 71
Howard J. Morton State Park, 218
Howard Prairie, 262
Howell House, 202
Howell Territorial Park, 125
Hoyt Arboretum, 138
Hudson House Bed & Breakfast, 61
Hudson-Parcher Campground, 126
Hug Point State Park, 45, 57
Hughes House, 108
Hull-Oakes Lumber Co., 183–84
Humbug Mountain State Park, 108
Hutson Museum, 155
Hyatt Reservoir, 262

I

I and C Hotsprings, 463–64
Idanha, 207
Idlewild Campground, 464
Idlewild Loop Trail, 465
Illinois River, 251–52
Illinois River State Park, 252
Illinois Valley area, 250–53
Imnaha, 407
Imnaha Motel, 408
Imnaha River campgrounds, 403
Imnaha River Canyon, 401
Imnaha River Inn Bed & Breakfast, 407
Imnaha River Loop, 400
Imnaha River Trail, 404
Imperial River Company, 307, 311
Independence, 178
Indian Creek Golf Course, 164
Indian Lake, 380
Indian Point, 55–56
Indian reservations, 19–20
information, 26
Inn at Arch Rock, 70
Inn at Haystack Rock, 60
Inn at Nesika Beach, 116
Inn at the Gorge, 170
inns. *See* lodging
Inskip Station, 453
International Rose Test Garden, 22
Ione, 293, 303, 310
Iris Inn, The, 269
Iron Gate Estate Bed & Breakfast, 352
Irrigon Wildlife Area, 290
Irvington Inn, 146
Ivy House, The, 248

J

J. J. Collins Marine Park, 127
Jack Morgan Park, 69
Jackman Park, 476
Jackson Bottom, 143
Jackson F. Kimball State Park, 347, 347–48
Jacksonville, 256–57, 265–66, 272, 274, 275–76
Jacksonville Inn, 265–66, 274
Jacksonville Museum of Southern Oregon History, 255
James F. Bybee House, 125
James Wimer Barn, 234
Japanese American Historical Plaza, 134
Japanese gardens, 138
Jarboe's, 63
Jarboe's Grill, 207
Jason Lee Campsite, 66
Jefferson County Museum, 313
Jefferson Street Depot, 395
Jensen Artic Museum, 178
Jerry's Jet Boats, 113
Jessie M. Honeyman State Park, 81–82
jet boat rides, 113, 399
Jewell Meadows Wildlife Refuge, 45, 128
Joaquin Miller Cabin, 431
Joel Palmer House, 206
John B. Yeon State Scenic Corridor, 166
John Day Fossil Beds National Monument, 23, 301–3, 306
John Day River area, 284, 430–39; information/emergency, 430; lodging, 438–39; parks/nature areas, 436–38; sights/activities, 430–36
John Day River Crossing, 296
John Neal Memorial Park, 193
John St. Café, 151
Jones Beach, 167
Jordan Craters, 455
Jordan Valley area, 452–56
Joseph, 407–8
Joseph Canyon, 402–3
Joseph Canyon Viewpoint, 397
Joseph H. Stewart State Park, 264
Journey Through Time Scenic Byway, 301, 421
JP's on the Green, 383
Jubilee Lake, 391
Jubilee Lake National Recreation Trail, 391
Juniper Acres Bed & Breakfast, 329–30
Juntura, 457–60
Justa Pasta, 151

K

Kah-Nee-Ta Resort, 316
Kalmiopsis, 252
Kalypso, 63
Kam Wah Chung and Co., 432
Keefer's Old Town Café, 111
Keeney Pass, 446
Kelty Estate Bed & Breakfast, 201
Ken's Artisan Bakery, 151
Kerbyville Inn, 253
Kerbyville Museum, 250
Kiger Mustang Overlook, 473
Kilchis River Park, 55
Kimberly, 435, 438–39
Kingston Prairie Preserve, 196
Kinzua, 303–4
Kinzua Hills Golf Course, 305
Kinzua Site, 297
Kirkwood Historic Ranch, 399
Kittiwake Bed & Breakfast, 85
Kjaer's House in the Woods, 221
Klamath Basin–Crater Lake area, 340–53; events, 353; information/emergency, 340; lodging, 350–53; parks/nature areas, 347–50; restaurants, 353; sights/activities, 340–47
Klamath County Museum, 340–41
Klamath Falls, 345, 352, 353
Klamath Lake, 23
Klamath Marsh National Wildlife Refuge, 350
Klamath Mountains, 17, 245, 260
Klamath Ranger District, 345
Klamath Wildlife Complex, 349
Klootchy Creek Spruce, 42
Knott Street Inn, 146
Koberg Beach State Recreation Site, 289
Kokanee Café, 334
Koontz Grave, 378
Kornblatt's, 151
Korner Post Restaurant, 207
Kum-Yon's, 101
Kuraya's, 225

L

La Casita, 383
La Fiesta, 275
La Grande Country Club, 391
La Grande Drive-In, 388
La Grande–Union–Elgin area, 384–95; events, 395; information/emergency, 384; lodging,

393–95; parks/nature areas, 391–93; restaurants, 395; sights/activities, 385–91
La Pine. *See* Bend–Sisters–La Pine area
La Pine State Park, 328
La Serre Restaurant, 86
Ladd Marsh, 393
Lafayette, 180, 201
Lafayette Schoolhouse Antique Mall, 190
Lake Abert, 361
Lake County Museum, 355
Lake Dorena, 220
Lake Ewauna, 346, 349
Lake Ewauna Wildlife Refuge, 346
Lake House Bed & Breakfast, 74
Lake in the Woods, 239
Lake Marie, 97
Lake of the Woods, 113, 345–46, 347
Lake of the Woods Resort, 351
Lake Oswego Golf Course, 139
Lake Owyhee State Park, 449
Lake Wallula River, 380
Lake Wallula River Trail, 382
Lakecliff Estates, 170
Lakes Loop, 360
Lakes Trail System, 360
Lakeside Terrace Motel, 369
Lakeview–Paisley–Bly area, 354–64; events, 364; information/emergency, 354; lodging, 362–64; parks/nature areas, 360–62; restaurants, 364; sights/activities, 355–60; towns of, 354–55
Lakeview Ranger District, 358
Lakeview to Steens Back Country Byway, 357
Land's Inn Bed & Breakfast, 438–39
Lane County Historical Museum, 211
Langlois, 110
Lanham, 80
Lara House, 330
Laslow's Northwest, 149
Last Tollgate, 159
Latourell Falls, 161, 164–65, 166
Laurel Beach, 167
Laurel Hill, 158–59
Laurelhurst Park, 140
Laurelwood Manor, 272
Lava Butte, 326
Lava Cast Forest, 323
Lava Lands Visitor Center, 326
Lava River Cave, 323
Laverne County Park, 105, 106–7
Lawen Store, 463
Lazy Rockin' B 'n' C Ranch, 331–32
Leaburg, 222
Leach Botanical Garden, 138
Lehman Hot Springs, 419, 428
Lela's Bakery Café, 275
Lemolo Lake, 238
Leslie Gulch, 23, 455
Lewis and Clark Heritage Canoe Trail, 126
Lewis and Clark National Wildlife Refuge, 126
Lewis and Clark State Recreation Site, 166
Lewis and Clark Trail, 20, 38, 43, 124–25, 157, 283–85, 377
libraries, 20
Lighthouse Bed & Breakfast, 110
Lighthouse Park, 44
lighthouses, 51–52, 53, 66, 69, 78, 93, 97, 103–4, 108, 110
Lily of the Field Bed & Breakfast, 220
Limpy Botanical Interpretive Trail, 246
Lincoln Beach, 71
Lincoln City–Depoe Bay–Newport area, 65–76; events, 76; information/emergency, 65; lodging, 70–74; parks/nature areas, 68–70; restaurants, 75–76
Lindgren Cabin, 37
Link Creek Basin, 325
Link River Trail, 347
Linn County Historical Museum, 179
Lion and the Rose Victorian, The, 146–47
Lithia Park, 264
Lithia Springs Inn, 269–70
Littell's Bed & Breakfast, 61
Little Log Church and Museum, 78
Little North Fork parks, 193
Little Zigzag Falls, 165
Lobenhaus Bed & Breakfast, 199
Locomotive, The, 225
Lodge at Granite, The, 428–29
Lodge at Summer Lake, The, 363–64
lodging, 20–21; Astoria–Warrenton–Seaside area, 45–48; Bandon–Port Orford area, 109–10; Bend–Sisters–La Pine area, 329–33; Burns area, 465–66; Cannon Beach–Tillamook–Pacific County City area, 59–63; Columbia Plateau, 307–11; Gold Beach–Brookings area, 115–16; Grants Pass–Rogue River area, 247–49; Harper–Juntura–Drewsey area, 459–60; Illinois Valley area, 252–53; John Day River area, 438–39; Jordan Valley area, 456; Klamath Basin–Crater Lake area, 350–53; La Grande–Union–Elgin area, 393–95; Lakeview–Paisley–Bly area, 362–64; Lincoln City–Depoe Bay–Newport area, 70–74; Lower Columbia River area, 128; Malheur Refuge–Steens Mountain area, 478–79; Medford–Ashland–Applegate Valley area, 264–74; Mid-Columbia River, 290–91; Mount Hood–Columbia Gorge area, 168–73; North Willamette Valley, 198–205; Oakland–Roseburg–Myrtle Creek area, 240–41; Ontario–Nyssa–Vale area, 450; Pendleton–Hermiston–Milton–Freewater area, 382; Portland area, 143–49; Powder River–Sumpter Valley–Ukiah area, 427–29; rates, 7; Redmond–Prineville–Madras area, 318; Reedsport–Coos Bay area, 100; Silver Lake–Christmas Valley–Fort Rock area, 369; South Willamette Valley, 219–24; Waldport–Yachats–Florence area, 83–86; Wallowa Valley–Snake River area, 407–8
Log Cabin Inn, 223
Logan Valley, 437
London, 217–18
Lone Pine Guest Ranch, 465–66
Lonerock, 300
Lonesome Hickory, 261
Loon Lake, 96
Lord Bennett's, 111
Lost Creek, 258
Lost Creek Lake, 264
Lost Creek State Park, 70
Lost Forest, 367–68
Lost Lake, 96
Lostine, 396, 409
Lostine Guard Station, 405
Lostine River campgrounds, 403
Lostine Tavern, 409
Lovejoy's, 86
Lowell, 212
Lower Columbia River area, 123–28; information/emergency, 123; lodging, 128; parks/nature areas, 127–28; sights/activities, 124–27
Lower Crooked River Back Country Byway, 315
Lower Deschutes Fish and Wildlife Area, 289
Lower Deschutes River Back Country Byway, 315
Lower Owyhee River Canyon, 450
Luscher Farm Dog Park, 140
Lynrd's Spud Cellar, 291

M

M. Crow & Co., 396
M&F Drive-In, 379
MacDonald-Dunn Research Forest, 187, 189, 194
Macleay Village, 178
Macmaster House, 147
Madras. *See* Redmond–Prineville–Madras area
Magenta, 207
Magone Lake, 434
Mail Boat Hydro Jets, 113
Malheur Cave, 475
Malheur City, 417
Malheur Crossing, 447
Malheur Field Station, 479
Malheur Lake, 474
Malheur National Forest, 434–35
Malheur National Wildlife Refuge, 23, 473, 476, 477–78
Malheur Refuge Headquarters, 469
Malheur Refuge–Steens Mountain area, 468–79; information/emergency, 468; lodging, 478–79; parks/nature areas, 477–78; restaurants, 479; sights/activities, 469–77; towns of, 468–69
Mamacita's, 395
Mann Lake, 476
Manzanita, 62, 63–64
Maple River Bed & Breakfast, 169
Mapleton, 215
Mapleton Hill Pioneer Trail, 80
maps, 21; North Central, 278; North Coast, 32; Northeast, 372; Northwest, 120; Oregon, 6, 8; South Central, 338; South Coast, 88; Southeast, 442; Southwest, 228
Marche, 224
Maria C. Jackson State Park, 106
Marial, 243–44
Marion County Historical Society Museum, 177
Marion Forks Restaurant, 207
Marjon Bed & Breakfast Inn, 222
markets, 212
Marshfield Sun Printing Museum, 93
Mary S. Young State Park, 141
Mary's Peak, 189, 190
Matsukaze, 249
Mattey House, 202
Maud Williamson State Park, 192
Maupin, 307–8, 310, 311, 313
MAX, 130
Maxwell Point, 59
Maxwell Siding Railroad Museum, 377
Mayer State Park, 289
McBee Motel Cottages, 63
McCall House Bed & Breakfast, 270
McCormick and Schmick's Seafood Restaurant, 149
McCoy Creek Inn, 478
McCully House, 276
McDowell Creek Falls, 189, 190
McGarry House, 221
McGillivray's Log Home, 220
McKay Creek National Wildlife Refuge, 381
McKee, 258
McKenzie Bridge, 223
McKenzie Pass–Santiam Pass Scenic Byway, 321
McKenzie Pass Scenic Highway, 321–22
McKenzie River, 214, 217, 218
McKenzie River Guides Association, 18
McKenzie River Highway, 214–15
McKenzie River Inn, 223–24
McKenzie River Trout House, 222
McKenzie River Valley, 22
McKenzie View, 222–23
McLoughlin House, 133
McMinnville, 178, 183, 201–2, 205, 206
McNary Wildlife Area, 381
Meacham, 387
Meadow Lakes, 316
Medford–Ashland–Applegate Valley area, 254–76; events, 276; information/emergency, 254; lodging, 264–74; parks/nature areas, 263–64; restaurants, 274–76; sights/activities, 255–63
Memaloose Island, 285
Memaloose State Park, 289
Memorial Lumberman's Park, 57–58
Menagerie, 195–96
Merenda Restaurant and Wine Bar, 334
Merlin, 249
Metolius Fish Overlook, 329
Metolius River, 323, 326
Metzler County Park, 167
Miami River Inn, 61
microbreweries, 21, 173, 241, 334
Mid-Columbia River, 281–91; events, 291; information/emergency, 281; lodging, 290–91; parks/nature areas, 289–90; restaurants, 291; sights/activities, 282–89; towns of, 281–82
Middle Santiam River, 196
Midsummer's Dream B&B, A, 267
Midtown Café, 63
mileage, 21–22
Mill Creek, 317–18
Mill Creek Gardens Bed & Breakfast, 204
Mill Inn Bed & Breakfast, 330
Miller Island, 349
Millicoma Marsh, 96
Mills End Park, 140–41
Milo McIver State Park, 167
Milo's City Café, 151
Milton. *See* Pendleton–Hermiston–Milton–Freewater area
Milwaukie, 144
Minam State Park, 392
Mingus Park, 97
Minto-Brown Park, 192
Minto County Park, 194
Mirage, 450
Mirror Lake, 165
Mission Mill Village, 177–78
Mitchell, 294, 310
Mitchell Monument, 356
Molalla, 179, 208
Molalla River State Park, 191
Mom's Pies, 225
Monet, 274
Monmouth, 178, 202
Monteith House, 180
Monteith Riverpark, 195
Monument Rock, 437
Mookie's Place, 225
Moonshine County Park, 69
Morgan Lake, 390, 392
Morical House Garden Inn, 270
Morning Star, 52
Moro, 293, 311
Morrow County Courthouse, 298
Morrow County Museum, 295
Morton's Bistro Northwest, 206
Mo's, 76
Mosier, 282, 310
Mosier House, The, 310
Mosier Twin Tunnels, 288
Moss Springs Guard Station, 388
motels. *See* lodging
Motor Vu Drive-In, 184
MotorVu Drive Drive-In, 185
Mount Ashland, 260
Mount Bachelor, 23, 322–23
Mount Hebo, 53–54, 55, 57
Mount Hood, 22, 154, 162–64, 171, 304, 322, 329
Mount Hood Bed & Breakfast, 171
Mount Hood–Columbia Gorge area, 153–74; events, 174; information/emergency, 153–54; lodging, 168–73; parks/nature areas, 166–68; restaurants, 173–74; sights/activities, 154–66; towns of, 154
Mount Hood Loop, 161–62
Mount Hood National Forest, 168
Mount Hood Railroad, 160
Mount Howard Tramway, 400

Mount Jefferson, 322, 328
Mount Pisgah, 217
Mount Pisgah Arboretum, 213
Mount Tabor Park, 141
Mount Thielsen, 348–49
Mount Washington, 328
Mountain Lakes, 348
movie theatres, 184–85, 379, 388
Moyer House, 180
Mt. Ashland Inn, 273–74
Mt. Hood Hamlet, 171
Mt. Hood Manor, 169
Mt. Scott Hideaway, 147
Muddy Frogwater Festival, 383
Mulino, 203, 207–8
Mulino Airport Café, 207–8
Mulino House, 203
Multnomah Falls, 161
Multnomah Falls Lodge, 157, 173
Munson Creek Falls State Park, 58
Museum at Warm Springs, 313
Museum of the Oregon Territory, 132
museums: Astoria–Warrenton–Seaside area, 35–36; Bend–Sisters–La Pine area, 321; Burns area, 462; Cannon Beach–Tillamook–Pacific County City area, 50–51; Columbia Plateau, 294–95; Gold Beach–Brookings area, 112–13; Grants Pass–Rogue River area, 242; historical, 18; Illinois Valley area, 250; John Day River area, 430–31; Klamath Basin–Crater Lake area, 340–41; La Grande–Union–Elgin area, 385; Lakeview–Paisley–Bly area, 355–56; Lincoln City–Depoe Bay–Newport area, 65–66; Malheur Refuge–Steens Mountain area, 469; Medford–Ashland–Applegate Valley area, 255; Mid-Columbia River, 282–83; Mount Hood–Columbia Gorge area, 154–55; North Willamette Valley, 176–79; Oakland–Roseburg–Myrtle Creek area, 231–32; Ontario–Nyssa–Vale area, 446; Pendleton–Hermiston–Milton–Freewater area, 375–77; Portland area, 131–33; Powder River–Sumpter Valley–Ukiah area, 412–13; Redmond–Prineville–Madras area, 313–14; Reedsport–Coos Bay area, 92; Silver Lake–Christmas Valley–Fort Rock area, 366; South Willamette Valley, 211; Waldport–Yachats–Florence area, 77–78; Wallowa Valley–Snake River area, 396
music, 22
Must-See Sights, 22–23
Myrtle Creek. *See* Oakland–Roseburg–Myrtle Creek area
Myrtle Creek–Canyonville Scenic Historic Tour, 237
Myrtle Creek Golf Course, 239
Myrtle Creek Trail, 464
Myrtle Grove Park, 95
myrtlewood groves, 95, 105, 107, 237–38

N

Narrows, The, 469
national forests, 23
National Historic Oregon Trail Interpretive Center, 413
Native Americans, 19–20, 373, 396–99
Natural Café, 275
Naucke House, 250
Neahkahnie Mountain, 53, 56, 57
Neawanna Creek, 45
Necanicum Estuary Park, 44
Nee Mee Poo National Recreation Trail, 404
Nehalem Bay State Park, 57
Nehalem Falls, 54
Neil Creek House, 270–71
Neptune State Park, 81, 82
Nestucca River, 55
Nestucca River Back Country Byway, 54
Netarts Spit, 56
New England House, 85
New River, 106, 109
Newberg, 179, 203
Newberry Crater, 323
Newberry Crater Trail, 324
Newberry National Volcanic Monument, 325, 326, 332–33
Newell House Museum, 179
Newport. *See* Lincoln City–Depoe Bay–Newport area
Newport Belle Bed & Breakfast, 73
Newport Waterfront, 66
Nez Perce Crossing, 398
Nez Perce Indians, 396–99
Nez Perce National Historic Park, 397–98
Nez Perce War, 373
Niagara County Park, 194
Niagara Falls, 56
Nick's Italian Café, 206
99W Drive-In, 184–85
North Bend, 101
North Chetco River, 114
North Fork John Day Wilderness, 426
North Fork Siuslaw, 79
North Fork Umatilla, 392
North Lincoln County Historical Museum, 65
North Santiam River, 194
North Santiam State Park, 194
North Umpqua River, 238, 239
North Willamette Valley, 175–209; events, 208–9; information/emergency, 175–76; lodging, 198–205; parks/nature areas, 191–97; restaurants, 205–8; sights/activities, 176–91
Northwestern Motel, 310
Nor'Wester, 117
Nutcracker Sweet Bed & Breakfast, 200
Nyssa. *See* Ontario–Nyssa–Vale area

O

Oak Hill Country Bed & Breakfast, 271
Oak Hills Golf Club, 239
Oak Island, 126
Oak Springs Fish Hatchery, 307
Oak Street Hotel, 169
Oak Tree Bed & Breakfast, 144
Oakland Museum, 231–32
Oakland–Roseburg–Myrtle Creek area, 231–41; events, 241; information/emergency, 231; lodging, 240–41; parks/nature areas, 240; restaurants, 241; sights/activities, 231–40
Oakridge, 216
Oaks Amusement Park, 136
Oar House, 73
Oasis Café and Motel, 460
Oasis Resort, The, 307–8
Oatman Flat Deer Viewing area, 369
OC&E Woods Line, 345
Ocean Haven, 83
Ocean House, 73
Oceanside, 62, 63, 64
Ochoco Lake State Park, 317
Octopus Tree, 58
Odell Lake, 346
Officer's Inn, 47
Olallie Lake Scenic Area, 164
Old Aurora Colony Museum, 176–77
Old Chief Joseph's Grave, 398
Old Highway 30, 421
Old Parkdale Inn, The, 171
Old Perpetual Geyser, 357
Old Time Fiddlers Contest, 409
Old Tower House, The, 100
Old Town, 41
Old Town Café, 408
Old Welches Inn Bed & Breakfast, 172
Old Wheeler Hotel, 60
Omar's, 275
Ona Beach State Park, 70
Oneonta Falls, 161

Oneonta Gorge, 161, 165
Ontario–Nyssa–Vale area, 445–51; events, 451; information/emergency, 445; lodging, 450; parks/nature areas, 449–50; restaurants, 450–51; sights/activities, 446–49
Ontario State Park, 449
Opal Creek, 195
Opal Lake, 217
Orchard View Inn, 202
Oregon Bed and Beach, 74
Oregon Brewers Guild, 21
Oregon Caves National Monument, 22–23, 251, 252
Oregon City, 133, 135–36, 144
Oregon City Golf Club, 140
Oregon City Trolley, 131
Oregon Coast Aquarium, 67
Oregon Coast History Center, 66
Oregon Coast Music Festival, 101
Oregon Coast Trail, 81
Oregon Conservation Network, 16
Oregon Country Fair, 226
Oregon Department of Fish and Wildlife, 16–17, 19, 27
Oregon Dunes National Recreation Area, 88, 95, 96
Oregon Farmer's Market Association, 16
Oregon Garden, 186
Oregon Guides and Packers Association, 18
Oregon History Center, 132
Oregon Islands National Wildlife Refuge, 59, 70, 109, 115
Oregon Military Museum, 133
Oregon Mountain Cruise Car Show, 409
Oregon Museum of Science and Industry, 132
Oregon Parks and Recreation Department, 25
Oregon Shakespeare Festival, 276
Oregon Slope, 449
Oregon State Marine Board, 15
Oregon Tourism Commission, 15, 25
Oregon Trail, 11, 19, 23, 158–59, 165–66, 295–97, 377–78, 385–86, 413–15, 446–48
Oregon Trail Agricultural Museum, 446
Oregon Trail Regional Museum, 412–13
Oregon Travel Commission, 18, 21, 26
Oregon Vortex, 258
Oregon Zoo, 29, 136
Orient Café, 291
Original Pancake House, The, 151
Oswald West State Park, 57
Otis, 74
Otter Rock, 70
Our Lady of Guadalupe Trappist Abbey, 190
Our Place in the Country, 204
Out 'n' About Treesort, 252
Outback National Scenic Byway, 343–44
outfitters, 18
Oval Door, The, 221–22
Overlook Beach Trail, 80
Owen Cherry Tree, 214
Owen Rose Garden, 213
owls, 168, 389, 393
Owyhee Dam, 448
Ox Bow Trade Co., 431
Oxbow Ranch, 439
Oxbow Regional Park, 140

P

P Ranch, 470
Pacific City. *See* Cannon Beach–Tillamook–Pacific City area
Pacific Coast Scenic Byway, 67–68, 79, 94, 105, 113
Pacific Crest National Scenic Trail, 347
Pacific Northwest Truck Museum, 177
Pacific Rest Bed & Breakfast, 72
Pacific View Bed & Breakfast, 116
Pacific Way Bakery and Café, 48–49
Pack Trail, 96
Packsaddle, 194
Page Springs, 476
Painted Hills, 302
Paisley. *See* Lakeview–Paisley–Bly area
Paisley Ranger District, 358
Palmerton Park Arboretum, 247
Pana-Sea-Ah, 71
Pancake Mill, 101
Pangea, 275
Panorama Lodge, 170–71
Panorama Point, 166
Papandreas, 335
Paradise Café, 111
Park View Bed & Breakfast, 223
Parkdale, 154, 171
Parker House Bed & Breakfast, 382
parks: Astoria–Warrenton–Seaside area, 44–45; Bandon–Port Orford area, 106–8; Bend–Sisters–La Pine area, 327–29; Cannon Beach–Tillamook–Pacific County City Area, 57–58; Columbia Plateau, 306; Gold Beach–Brookings area, 114–15; Grants Pass–Rogue River area, 246–47; Illinois Valley area, 252; John Day River area, 436–37; Jordan Valley area, 456; Klamath Basin–Crater Lake area, 347–48; La Grande–Union–Elgin area, 391–92; Lakeview–Paisley–Bly area, 360; Lincoln City–Depoe Bay–Newport area, 68–70; Lower Columbia River area, 127; Medford–Ashland–Applegate Valley area, 263–64; Mid-Columbia River, 289; Mount Hood–Columbia Gorge area, 166–67; North Willamette Valley, 191–95; Oakland–Roseburg–Myrtle Creek area, 240; Ontario–Nyssa–Vale area, 449; Pendleton–Hermiston–Milton–Freewater area, 381; Portland area, 140–42; Powder River–Sumpter Valley–Ukiah area, 426; Redmond–Prineville–Madras area, 317; Reedsport–Coos Bay area, 97–98; South Willamette Valley, 218; Waldport–Yachats–Florence area, 81–82; Wallowa Valley–Snake River area, 405
Pasquale's Ristorante, 168–69
Paula's Bistro, 111
Pawn Old Growth, 80
Pearl Bakery, 151–52
Peavy Arboretum, 186–87
Peavy Cabin, 419
Pedigrift House, 271
Peerless Hotel and Restaurant, 265
Pelican Pub, 64
Pelican's Perch Lodge, 62
Pelota Fronton, 452–53
Pelton, 316
Pendleton–Hermiston–Milton–F reewater area, 375–83; events, 383; information/emergency, 375; lodging, 382; parks/nature areas, 381–82; restaurants, 383; sights/activities, 375–81
Pendleton River Parkway, 380–81
Penland Lake, 305
Pete French Round Barn, 470
Peter Iredale Loop, 43
Peter Iredale Shipwreck, 41
Peter Weaver Barn, 234
Pheasant Falls, 56
Pheasant Valley Orchards B&B, 171
Phillip W. Schneider Wildlife Area, 437–38
Phillips Lake, 423–24
Philomath, 179
Pho Van Bistro, 152
Picture Gorge, 303
Pilaf, 275
Pilot Butte Drive In, 334–35

Pilot Butte State Park, 328
Pine Meadow Inn, 249
Pine Mountain Observatory, 321
Pine Ranger District, 424
Pine Room, 466
Pine Tavern, 335
Pine Valley Community Museum, 413
Pinehurst Inn at Jenny Creek, 265
Pinewood Bed & Breakfast, 394
Pioneer Cemetery, 413–14
Pioneer-Indian Museum, 232
Pioneer Indian Trail, 57
Pioneer Park, 327, 412
Pioneer Woman's Grave, 159
Pistol River State Park, 115
Pittock Mansion, 133
Place Apart Bed & Breakfast, A, 382
Plantation Trail, 56
Polk County Courthouse, 183
Polk County Museum, 178
Ponderosa Pine Inn, 248
Pookie's Bed 'n' Breakfast on College Hill, 222
population, 26
Port Hole Café, 117
Port Orford. *See* Bandon–Port Orford area
Portland area, 129–52; events, 152; information/emergency, 129–30; lodging, 143–49; parks/nature areas, 140–43; restaurants, 149–52; sights/activities, 131–40
Portland Classical Chinese Garden, 137
Portland Guest House, 147
Portland International Airport, 13
Portland Saturday Market, 138–39
Portland's White House, 147
Portside, 100–1
Powder River Accessible Fishing Facility, 426
Powder River Bed & Breakfast, 427
Powder River–Sumpter Valley–Ukiah area, 411–29; events, 429; information/emergency, 411; lodging, 427–29; parks/nature areas, 426–27; restaurants, 429; sights/activities, 412–26; towns of, 411
Powder River Valley, 414–15
Powder River Valley reservoirs, 423
Powell's City of Books, 139
Power City, 381–82
Power of the Past Museum, 413
Prairie City, 430, 433, 439
Precott Beach, 125, 167
prices, 7
Prineville. *See* Redmond–Prineville–Madras area
Prospect, 266
Prospect Hotel, 256, 266
Pueblo Mountains, 475–76
Puget Island, 125
Pulpit Rock, 286
Pumpkin Ridge Golf Course, 139–40
Punchbowl Falls, 165

Q

Quail Point Golf Course, 262
Quail Prairie, 113
Quail Run Golf Course, 325
Quail Valley Golf Course, 140
Queen of Sheba, 152
Quilter's Inn at Aurora, 198
Quinz Mediterranean, 275

R

R & R Drive In, 408
Rags to Walkers Guest Ranch, 332
railroads, 26, 53, 160, 286, 314–15, 400, 418
Rainie Falls, 246
Raphael's, 383
Red Buttes, 264
Red Hills, 206
Red Tail, 140
Redmond–Prineville–Madras area, 312–18; information/emergency, 312–13; lodging, 318; parks/nature areas, 317–18; restaurants, 318; sights/activities, 313–17; towns of, 313
Redwood Grove Nature Trail, 114
Redwood Highway, 251
Reedsport–Coos Bay area, 91–101; events, 101; information/emergency, 91; lodging, 100; parks/nature areas, 97–99; restaurants, 100–1; sights/activities, 92–97
Rendezvous Grill and Tap Room, The, 174
Repose and Repast, 200
Reptile Man's Living Museum, 155
Reserve Vineyards and Golf Club, 140
Resort at the Mountain, The, 164
rest areas, 23–24
restaurants, 24; Astoria–Warrenton–Seaside area, 48–49; Bandon–Port Orford area, 110–11; Bend–Sisters–La Pine area, 333–35; Burns area, 466–67; Cannon Beach–Tillamook–Pacific County City area, 63–64; Columbia Plateau, 311; Gold Beach–Brookings area, 117; Grants Pass–Rogue River area, 249; Harper–Juntura–Drewsey area, 460; Klamath Basin–Crater Lake area, 353; La Grande–Union–Elgin area, 395; Lakeview–Paisley–Bly area, 364; Lincoln City–Depoe Bay–Newport area, 75–76; Malheur Refuge–Steens Mountain area, 479; Medford–Ashland–Applegate Valley area, 274–76; Mid-Columbia River, 291; Mount Hood–Columbia Gorge area, 173–74; North Willamette Valley, 205–8; Oakland–Roseburg–Myrtle Creek area, 241; Ontario–Nyssa–Vale area, 450–51; Pendleton–Hermiston–Milton–Freewater area, 383; Portland area, 149–52; Powder River–Sumpter Valley–Ukiah area, 429; Redmond–Prineville–Madras area, 318; Reedsport–Coos Bay area, 100–1; Silver Lake–Christmas Valley–Fort Rock area, 369; South Willamette Valley, 224–26; Waldport–Yachats–Florence area, 86; Wallowa Valley–Snake River area, 408–9
Rhea Creek, 303
Rhododendron Festival, 86
Richardson Park, 218
Richmond, 299
Rickreall, 178
Ricky D's Pizza and Ice Cream Parlor, 208
Ridgeview Bed & Breakfast, 456
Riley, 464
Rimrock Springs Wildlife Area, 318
Rinehart Stone House, 448
Ring of Fire, 224
Rio Café, 48
Ritter Hot Springs, 436
River House, The, 110
River Walk Inn, 222
Riverfront Park, 192, 194
Riverhouse, 64
Riverhouse, River's Edge Golf Course, 325
Riveridge Golf Course, 217
River's Edge Inn, 219
Riverside Fish and Wildlife Area, 459
Riverside Park, 240, 246, 391
Riverside School House Bed & Breakfast, 439
Riverview Bed & Breakfast, 240–41
Riverview Guesthouse, 147–48
road reports, 24
Roaring River Park, 195

Rock Creek, 80, 82, 238
Rock Creek Reservoir, 305
rockhounding, 24–25
Rocky Point Resort, 351
rodeos, 25
Rogue Ales Public House, 76
Rogue Reef Inn, 116
Rogue River, 113, 114, 115; *see also* Grants Pass–Rogue River area
Rogue River Guest House, 272
Rogue River Guides Association, 18
Rogue River Loop, 244–45
Rogue River National Recreation Trail, 246
Rogue River Ranch, 243–44
Rogue River Trail, 264
Rogue–Umpqua Divide, 240
Rogue–Umpqua National Scenic Byway, 236–37, 259
Romeo Inn, 271
Roosevelt elk, 98, 128, 197
Rooster Rock State Park, 157, 166
Rorick House, 283
Rose City, 140
Rose Cottage, 148–49
Rose Farm, 133
Rose River Inn, 47
Roseanna's Café, 63
Rosebriar Hotel, 46–47
Roseburg. *See* Oakland–Roseburg–Myrtle Creek area
Roseburg Station Pub and Brewery, 241
Rose's Deli and Bakery, 152
Round Butte Dam, 317
Row River Trail, 214
Rowena Crest, 287, 289

S

Saddle Mountain, 43
Saddle Mountain State Park, 45
Sage Country Inn, 466
Sagehen Hill Nature Trail, 465
Sahalie Falls, 165
Salem: lodging, 203–4; parks/nature areas, 192; restaurants, 206, 208; sights/activities, 177–78, 181, 182, 185–86
Salishan Golf Links, 68
Salmon-Huckleberry, 167
Salmon River, 168
Salmon River Retreat, 169
Salmon River Trail, 165
Salmon Run Golf Course, 114
Salmonberry County Park, 79
Salmonberry Inn, 72
Salsa Rita's, 111
Salt Creek Waterfall Loop, 217
Samuel H. Boardman State Park, 115
Sand Island Park, 127–28
Sandcastle Contest, 49
Sandelie Golf Course, 140
Sandlake Country Inn, 61
Sandpines Golf Links, 68
Sandy, 171–72, 174
Sandy Pioneer Museum, 155
Sandy River, 158
Santiam River Resort, 204–5
Sarah Helmick Park, 194
Sather House, The, 330
Sauvie Island, 125, 126, 128
Sauvie Island Bed & Breakfast, 128
Sauvie Island Wildlife Area, 127
Sawyer Park, 327
Scandinavian Midsummer Festival, 49
Scaponia Park, 127
scenic byways, 14; *see also* scenic drives
scenic drives: Astoria–Warrenton–Seaside area, 42; Bandon–Port Orford area, 105; Bend–Sisters–La Pine area, 321–22; Burns area, 464; Cannon Beach–Tillamook–Pacific County City Area, 53–54; Columbia Plateau, 299–301; Gold Beach–Brookings area, 113–14; Grants Pass–Rogue River area, 244–45; Harper–Juntura–Drewsey area, 458–59; Illinois Valley area, 251; John Day River area, 432–33; Jordan Valley area, 454–55; Klamath Basin–Crater Lake area, 343–44; La Grande–Union–Elgin area, 388–89; Lakeview–Paisley–Bly area, 357; Lincoln City–Depoe Bay–Newport area, 67–68; Malheur Refuge–Steens Mountain area, 472–74; Medford–Ashland–Applegate Valley area, 259–60; Mid-Columbia River, 286; Mount Hood–Columbia Gorge area, 160–62; North Willamette Valley, 187–88; Oakland–Roseburg–Myrtle Creek area, 236–37; Ontario–Nyssa–Vale area, 449; Pendleton–Hermiston–Milton-Freewater area, 379; Powder River–Sumpter Valley–Ukiah area, 419–22; Redmond–Prineville–Madras area, 315; Reedsport–Coos Bay area, 94; Silver Lake–Christmas Valley–Fort Rock area, 366; South Willamette Valley, 213; Waldport–Yachats–Florence area, 79; Wallowa Valley–Snake River area, 400–1
Schminck Memorial Museum, 356
Schreiner's Iris Gardens, 185–86
Schroeder Park, 247
Scio Depot Museum, 178–79
Scottsburg, 233
Scottsburg–Drain Historic Tour, 236
Sea Cliff Bed & Breakfast, 73
Sea Dreamer Inn, 116
sea lions, 82–83
Sea Quest, 85
Seal Rock State Recreation Site, 82
SeaRose Bed & Breakfast, 62
Seaside. *See* Astoria–Warrenton–Seaside area
Seaside Aquarium, 41–42
Seaside Museum, 36
Seaside Promenade, 41
Seaside Saltworks, 38–39
Seasons, 335
Secret Garden, The, 222
Seeder's Desert Rose Bed & Breakfast, 318
Seneca, 464
sequoias, 135
Serenity Bed & Breakfast, 85
Service Creek, 305
Service Creek Stage Stop Bed & Breakfast, 309
Settlemier House, 180
Shaniko, 292–93, 297
Sharps Creek, 80
Shaw's Oceanfront Bed & Breakfast, 60–61
Sheep Rock, 302–3
Shelton-McMurphy-Johnson House, 211
Shepherd's Dell Falls, 161
Sherars Falls, 303
Sheridan, 204
Sherman County Courthouse, 297–98
Sherman County Museum, 294
Shevlin Park, 327
Shilo Oasis, 408
shipwrecks, 41, 45
Shirley's at Agate Beach, 76
Shively Park, 44
Shore Acres, 98
Shrader Old Growth Trail, 114
Shrew's House, 265
Side Door Café, 75
Siletz River Parks, 69
Siltcoos Beach, 80
Siltcoos Lake, 79, 80
Silver Creek Canyon, 190
Silver Falls State Park, 22, 187–88, 193
Silver Grill Café, 206–7
Silver Lake, 365–69
Silver Lake Mercantile and Motel, 369
Silver Spur Motel, 466
Silverton, 181, 186, 204, 206–7, 208
Simpson Reef, 99

Siskiyou coast, 114
Siskiyou Mountains, 245, 260
Siskiyou National Forest, 88, 108, 113
Sisters. *See* Bend–Sisters–La Pine area
Sisters Bakery, 335
Siuslaw Harbor, 79
Siuslaw Pioneer Museum, 78
Siuslaw River Drainage, 80
Sixes River, 109, 114
Sixth Street Bistro and Loft, 174
Sky Lakes, 348
Skyhook Motel, 310
Slide Mountain, 357
Slocum Creek, 456
Smith Lake, 139, 143
Smith River, 96
Smith River Country Fair, 101
Smith Rock State Park, 23, 315, 316, 317
Smock Prairie Schoolhouse, 297
Snake River. *See* Wallowa Valley–Snake River area
Snake River Crossing, 446
Snake River–Mormon Basin Back Country Byway, 422
Snow Camp, 113
snow sports, 25
Sod House, 469–70
Sod House Ranch, 470
Soda Mountain, 261
Sonshine Bed & Breakfast, 438
South Beach, 74
South Beach State Park, 69
South Coyote Butte, 476
South Fork Alsea River Back Country Byway, 213
South Fork John Day River Back Country Byway, 432–33
South Park Blocks, 141
South Slough, 95, 96–97
South Steens, 476
South Umpqua River, 239
South Willamette Valley, 210–26; events, 226; information/emergency, 210–11; lodging, 219–24; parks/nature areas, 218–19; restaurants, 224–26; sights/activities, 211–18
Southern Oregon History Center, 255
Southern Pacific Railroad Depot, 256
Southpark, 152
Sparta, 416
Spinners, 117
Spirit Mountain Casino, 201
Spouting Horns, 68, 79
Spray, 294, 311
Spray Asher Motel, 311
Spring Branch Wildlife Area, 406
Spring Creek, 346, 389, 393
Spring Kite Festival, 64
Springbrook Hazelnut Farm, 203
Springfield, 211, 222–23, 225
Springfield Depot, 211
Springfield Museum, 211
Springwater Corridor, 139, 143
Spruce Goose, 178
Spruce Run Park, 43
Squaw Creek Ranch, 332
Squaw Lakes, 262
St. Bernards, a Bed & Breakfast, 60
St. Patrick's Day Celebration, 311
St. Paul, 179
Stage Stop Road Interpretive Center, 155
Stallard Stage Stop, 458
Stang Manor Bed & Breakfast, 394
Stangel Buffalo Ranch, 405
Stanton County Park, 240
Starkey Elk Project, 393
Starvation Creek State Park, 166
state forests, 25
State Line Road, 344
state parks, 25; *see also* parks
state symbols, 25–26
statistics, 26
Stayton, 204
Steam Donkey, 92
Steelhead Run Bed & Breakfast, 241
Steens Mountain, 23, 474–77; *see also* Malheur Refuge–Steens Mountain area
Steens Mountain Back Country Byway, 474
Steiger Haus, 202
Stein's Pillar, 315, 316–17
Stephens, 233
stern-wheeler cruises, 78, 160
Sterne, Laurence, 12
Stevens-Crawford House, 133
Stewart Park, 240
Stockman's Motel and General Store, 450
Stonehedge Gardens, 173
Strawberry Hill, 82
Strawberry Mountain Trails, 433–34
Strawberry Mountains, 432, 433, 435, 437
Succor Creek Road, 454–55
Succor Creek State Park, 456
Sullivan's Gulch Bed & Breakfast, 148
Summer Jo's, 249
Summer Lake, 355, 361
Summer Lake Hot Springs, 364
Summer Lake Inn, 362–63
Summer Lake Wildlife Area, 358
Summit Trail, 435
Sumpter, 428
Sumpter Bed & Breakfast, 428
Sumpter Museum, 413
Sumpter Valley. *See* Powder River–Sumpter Valley–Ukiah area
Sumpter Valley Dredge, 417
Sumpter Valley Railroad, 418
Sumpter Valley Railway Route, 421–22
Sumpter Valley Wildlife Area, 427
Sun Pass Ranch, 351–52
Sunriver, 320, 332
Sunriver Getaway, 332
Sunriver Nature Center, 329
Sunriver Resort, 325–26
Sunset Bay, 96, 98
Sunset Bay State Park, 99
Sunstone Gem Collection area, 357
Susan Creek Falls, 239
Susanville, 420
Suttle Lake Resort, the Boat House Restaurant, 334
Sutton Creek, 80
Swallow Ridge Bed & Breakfast, 330–31
Swan Island Dahlias, 185
Sweek House, 133–34
Sweet Home, 189, 204–5
Sweetwater Inn, 70
Swick Creek Old Growth Trail, 435
Sylvia Beach Hotel, 73–74

T

Table Rock, 260, 262
Table Rock Trail, 435–36
Table Rock Wilderness, 195
Tad's Chicken 'n' Dumplins, 174
Taft Waterfront Park, 69
Tahkenitch Creek, 80
Tall Winds Motel, 311
Tamarack Inn Bed & Breakfast, 394–95
Tamastslikt Cultural Institute, 375–76
Tamawanas Falls, 165
TamKaLiks Celebration, 409
Taylor Creek, 245
Taylor Dunes Trail, 80
Ten Depot Street, 395
Ten-mile Creek, 80
10th Avenue Inn, 48
Tern Inn Bed & Breakfast, 61
Terwilliger Vista Bed & Breakfast, 148
This Olde House, 100
Thompson's Bed & Breakfast, 352
Three Arch Rocks, 59
Three Capes Scenic Loop, 54, 62
3 Doors Down Café, 150
Three Sisters, 322, 328–29
Threemile Lake, 80
Tidal Raves, 75
tide pools, 58–59, 70, 82, 99, 109, 115
Tigard, 148
Tillamook. *See* Cannon Beach–Tillamook–Pacific City area

Tillamook Air Museum, 50–51
Tillamook County Pioneer Museum, 51
Tillamook Guides Association, 18
Tillamook Head, 39, 43
Tillamook Rock Lighthouse, 51–52
Tillicum Beach, 79
Timberline Lodge, 159
Timpanogas Lake, 217
Tina's, 206
Todd Lake, 326
Toketee Falls, 239
Toledo History Museum, 66
Tom McCall Point/Preserve, 288–89
Tom McCall Waterfront Park, 141
Tom Pearce Park, 247
Tou Velle State Park, 263
Touvelle House, The, 272
Trail of Ten Falls, 190
train excursions, 26, 53, 160, 286, 314–15, 400, 418
train service, 13
transportation, 13, 15, 130
Trask River Park, 55
Travel Information Council, 18
Tres Café, 207
Trout Creek Mountains, 475–76
Trout Creek Trail, 316
Troutdale, 172, 174
Troutdale Rail Museum, 154
Tryon Creek State Park, 141–42
Tualatin, 133–34
Tualatin Hill Nature Park, 143
Tualatin Plains Presbyterian Church, 180–81
Tub Mountain, 447
Tudor House, 148
Tumalo Feed Co., 335
Tumalo State Park, 327–28
Twilight Creek Eagle Sanctuary, 45
Twin Bridges Memorial Park, 69
Twin Springs, 449
Two Color Guard Station, 388
Tyee, 80, 239
Tyee Lodge Oceanfront Bed & Breakfast, 74

U

Ukiah. *See* Powder River–Sumpter Valley–Ukiah area
Ukiah–Dale Forest State Park, 426
Umatilla Chemical Depot, 382
Umatilla County Historical Society Museum, 376
Umatilla Marine Park, 381
Umatilla National Forest, 390, 424–25
Umatilla National Wildlife Refuge, 289–90
Umatilla Rapids, 377
Umatilla River Road, 379
Umbrella Falls, 165
Umpqua Discovery Center, 93
Umpqua Dunes Trail, 97
Umpqua Lighthouse, 97
Umpqua Lighthouse State Park, 97
Umpqua River, 97
Umpqua River Lighthouse, 93
Under the Greenwood Tree Bed & Breakfast, 272–73
Underground Tours, 379
Union. *See* La Grande-Union–Elgin area
Union County Museum, 385
Union Pacific Train Depot, 448
Unity Lake State Park, 436–37
universities, 26, 186
Upper Klamath Lake, 346
Upper Klamath Lake Jetboat Tours, 343, 344
Upper Klamath Lake Loop, 344
Upper Klamath Lake National Wildlife Refuge, 346, 350
Upper McCord Creek Falls, 166
Upper Metolius River campgrounds, 324
Upper North Santiam Area, 189
Upper Table Rock, 262
Uppertown Firefighters Museum, 36
U.S. Forest Service cabin rentals, 388, 405, 419, 436
Utilla Agency, 378–79

V

Vale. *See* Ontario–Nyssa–Vale area
Valley/China Creek Trail, 80
Valley of the Giants, 68
Valley of the Rogue State Park, 244, 246–47
Van Patten Lake, 426
Vernonia Lake, 127
Vida, 223–24, 225–26
Vida Café, 225–26
Viento State Park, 166
Village Bistro and Bakery, 241
Virginia Lake, 126
Vista House, 156
Volcanic Legacy Scenic Byway, 343

W

Wagner House, 103
Wagontire, 462, 464
Wahclella Falls, 165
Wahkeena Falls, 161
Waldo Lake, 214, 218
Waldo Park Sequoia, 188
Waldo Tree, 261
Waldport Heritage Museum, 77
Waldport–Yachats–Florence area, 77–86; events, 86; information/emergency, 77; lodging, 83–86; parks/nature areas, 81–83; restaurants, 86; sights/activities, 77–81
walking tours: Fossil, 298; La Grande–Union–Elgin area, 386–87; Lakeview–Paisley–Bly area, 356; Medford–Ashland–Applegate Valley area, 256–57; North Willamette Valley, 181, 182, 183; Oakland–Roseburg–Myrtle Creek area, 233–34; Ontario–Nyssa–Vale area, 448; Pendleton–Hermiston–Milton–Freewater area, 378; Portland area, 134–36; Powder River–Sumpter Valley–Ukiah area, 415
Wallace Dement Myrtlewood Grove, 105
Waller Hall, 181
Wallowa County Courthouse, 397
Wallowa County Museum, 396
Wallowa Lake, 401–2
Wallowa Lake Lodge, 408
Wallowa Lake State Park, 405
Wallowa Mountain Loop Road, 400–1
Wallowa Mountains, 401
Wallowa Valley Barn Tour, 409
Wallowa Valley–Snake River area, 23, 396–410; events, 409–10; information/emergency, 396; lodging, 407–8; parks/nature areas, 405–7; restaurants, 408–9; sights/activities, 396–405
Wallowa-Whitman National Forest, 403–4, 424, 434
Walls of Rome, 455–56
Walluski Loop, 43
Walnut Park, 194
Walton Beach, 167
Walton Ranch, 197
Wanaket Wildlife Mitigation Area, 382
Warner Lakes, 360
Warrenton. *See* Astoria–Warrenton–Seaside area
Warrenton Waterfront Trail, 43, 44
Wasco County Courthouse, 286
Washington County Museum, 132
Washington Park, 141
Water Street Inn, 204
Waterloo, 218
Watson Falls, 239
Waverly Lake, 195
Wayfarer Resort, 224
Wayside Lodge, 85–86
Weasku Inn, 249
weather, 15–16, 26–27
Welches, 172, 174
Well Spring, 295
Wells Ranch House, The, 273

Wenaha-Tucannon, 406
Wenaha Wildlife Area, 406–7
West Coast Game Park, 29, 104–5
West Linn, 148–49, 149
West Myrtle Creek, 465
Westfall, 458
Westlund's River's Edge Bed & Breakfast, 128
whale-watching, 53, 67, 79, 94, 105, 113
Whale's Tale, 76
Wheeler, 60
Wheeler County Courthouse, 298
Whiskey Creek Cabin, 243, 246
Whiskey Run Beach, 94
White River Canyon Overlook, 165
White River State Park, 306
White River Wildlife Area, 307
Whitehorse Park, 247
Whitehorse Ranch, 472
Whitman Overlook, 387
Whitman, Walt, 11
Whitney, 417
Wilbur, 233
Wild and Scenic Rivers, 28
Wild Rogue Wilderness, 247
wilderness areas, 28; Bandon–Port Orford area, 108; Bend–Sisters–La Pine area, 328; Columbia Plateau, 306–7; Grants Pass–Rogue River area, 247; Illinois Valley area, 252; John Day River area, 437; Klamath Basin–Crater Lake area, 348–49; La Grande–Union–Elgin area, 392; Lakeview–|Paisley–Bly area, 360; Malheur Refuge–Steens Mountain area, 477–78; Medford–Ashland–Applegate Valley area, 264; Mount Hood–Columbia Gorge area, 167–68; North Willamette Valley, 195–96; Oakland–Roseburg–Myrtle Creek area, 240; Powder River–Sumpter Valley–Ukiah area, 426; Redmond–Prineville–Madras area, 317–18; South Willamette Valley, 218; Waldport–Yachats–Florence area, 82; Wallowa Valley–Snake River area, 405–6
Wildflour Bakery, 408–9
Wildflower Grill, 75
Wildhorse Casino and Resort, 383
Wildhorse Resort Golf, 380
Wildlife Images Rehabilitation and Education Center, 244
wildlife refuges, 27–28; Astoria–Warrenton–Seaside area, 45; Bandon–Port Orford area, 109; Bend–Sisters–La Pine area, 329; Cannon Beach–Tillamook–Pacific County City Area, 58–59; Columbia Plateau, 307; Gold Beach–Brookings area, 115; Harper–Juntura–Drewsey area, 459; John Day River area, 437–38; Klamath Basin–Crater Lake area, 349–50; La Grande–Union–Elgin area, 392–93; Lakeview–Paisley–Bly area, 360–62; Lincoln City–Depoe Bay–Newport area, 70; Lower Columbia River area, 126, 127; Malheur National Wildlife Refuge, 23; Malheur Refuge–Steens Mountain area, 477–78;Medford–Ashland–Applegate Valley area, 264; Mid-Columbia River, 289–90; Mount Hood–Columbia Gorge area, 168; North Willamette Valley, 196–97; Oakland–Roseburg–Myrtle Creek area, 240; Ontario–Nyssa–Vale area, 449–50; Pendleton–Hermiston–Milton–Freewater area, 381–82; Portland area, 142–43; Powder River–Sumpter Valley–Ukiah area, 426–27; Redmond–Prineville–Madras area, 318; Reedsport–Coos Bay area, 98–99; Silver Lake–Christmas Valley–Fort Rock area, 369; South Willamette Valley, 219; Waldport–Yachats–Florence area, 82; Wallowa Valley–Snake River area, 406–7
Wildlife Safari, 29, 236
Wildwood Recreation Site, 168, 305
Wiley's World of Pasta, 275
Willamette Falls, 136
Willamette Falls Locks, 135
Willamette Gables Bed & Breakfast, 198–99
Willamette Mission Cottonwood, 188
Willamette Mission State Park, 191–92
Willamette River Jetboat Tours, 131
Willamette Shore Trolley, 131
Willamette Stone, 135
Willamette University, 186
Willamette Valley, 17; *see also* North Willamette Valley; South Willamette Valley
William L. Finley National Wildlife Refuge, 197
William M. Tugman State Park, 97
Williamson River, 346
Willow Creek, 295–96
Willow Creek Valley, 303
Willow Creek Wildlife Area, 289
Willson Park, 186
Wilson Cottages and Camp, 353
Wilson Ranches Retreat B&B, 309–10
Winchester Bay House, 100
Winchester Country Inn, 265, 274
Winchuck Beach, 115
Winchuck River, 114
Wine Country Farm, 200
Winema National Forest, 345
wineries, 28, 190–91, 200, 203, 239–40, 252, 263
Winston, 234
Winter Ridge, 361–62
Wolf Creek Inn, 243, 247
Wolfe Manor Inn, 271
Woodburn, 180
Wooden Shoe Bulb Company, 185
Woods House, The, 271–72
Woolery House Bed & Breakfast, 310
World Forestry Center, 132
Worst Food in Oregon, The, 466–67
Woven Glass Inn, The, 148
Wright's Point, 464

Y

Yachats. *See* Waldport–Yachats–Florence area
Yachats State Park, 81, 82
Yankee Tinker Bed & Breakfast, The, 144
Yaquina Bay Lighthouse, 66, 69
Yaquina Bay State Park, 69
Yaquina Head Lighthouse, 66, 69
Yaquina Head Natural Area, 70
Yaquina Pacific Railroad Society, 66
Ye Olde Castle, 466
Yellowjacket Campground, 464–65
Youngberg Hill Vineyard Inn, 202
Youngs River Falls, 39–40
Youngs River Loop, 43
Yummy Garden, The, 152
yurt camping, 244

Z

Zeller's Resort, 407
Zell's: An American Café, 152
Zenon Café, 225
Zigzag, 162
Zigzag Canyon Overlook, 165
zoos, 29, 136